Beware the Evil Eye

BEWARE
THE EVIL EYE

The Evil Eye in the Bible and the Ancient World

—Volume 2—

Greece and Rome

JOHN H. ELLIOTT

 CASCADE *Books* · Eugene, Oregon

BEWARE THE EVIL EYE
The Evil Eye in the Bible and the Ancient World
Volume 2: Greece and Rome

Cascade Books
An Imprint of Wipf and Stock Publishers
199 W. 8th Ave., Suite 3
Eugene, OR 97401

www.wipfandstock.com

PAPERBACK ISBN: 978-1-49820-499-6
HARDOVER ISBN 13: 978-1-4982-8577-3

Cataloging-in-Publication data:

Elliott, John Hall.

Beware the evil eye : the evil eye in the Bible and the ancient world / John H.
Elliiott.

xxxvi + 334 p. ; 23 cm. Includes bibliographical references and indexes.

ISBN: 978-1-49820-499-6

Vol. 2: Greece and Rome.

1. Evil eye. 2. Evil eye—Greece. 3. Evil eye—Rome. 4. Envy. I. Title.

GN475.6 E45 2016 v. 2

Manufactured in the U.S.A.   03/28/2016

Frederick William Danker *in memoriam*
lexicographer supreme, expert in Hellenistic Greek
and biblical exegesis,
demanding teacher, intrepid colleague, dear friend,
and energetic partner in projects of justice and mercy

"If I tell not the whole truth,
let white turds of crows disgrace my head,
and let Ulius and frail Pediatia and that thief Voranus come
to piss and shit on me!"

(HORACE, *SATIRES* 1.8, PRIAPUS SPEAKING)

CONTENTS

ILLUSTRATIONS

PREFACE

This four volume study traces evidence of Evil Eye belief and practice in the ancient world from Mesopotamia (c. 3000 BCE) to Late Roman Antiquity (c. 600 CE), with particular attention to the Bible and post-biblical traditions of Israel and early Christianity.

Belief in the Evil Eye is a long-standing and widespread folk concept that some persons are enabled by nature to injure others, cause illness and loss, and destroy any person, animal or thing through a powerful noxious glance emanating from the eye. Also known as "fascination" (Greek: *baskania*; Latin: *fascinatio*), this belief holds that the eye is an active organ that emits destructive emanations charged by negative dispositions (especially malevolence, envy, miserliness, and withheld generosity). These emanations arise in the heart or soul, and are projected outward against both animate and inanimate objects. The full constellation of notions comprising the Evil Eye complex includes the expectation that various prophylactic words, gestures, images, and amulets have the power to counter and avert the damaging power of the Evil Eye.

From its likely origin in ancient Sumer (3000 BCE) and its early spread to Egypt and the Circum-Mediterranean region, to its later movement eastward to India and westward and northward to Europe, the belief eventually made its way from "old worlds" to "new." It now constitutes a cultural phenomenon with personal, social implication, and moral implications that has spanned the centuries and encircled the globe.

Beware the Evil Eye concentrates on the Evil Eye phenomenon in the ancient world, with new and extensive attention to mention of it in the Bible and the biblical communities of Israel and early Christianity. Volume One opens with an introductory overview of references to, and research on, the Evil Eye from the ancient past to the modern present (Chapter One). Chapter Two of Volume One examines Evil Eye belief and practice in ancient Mesopotamia and Egypt. Volume Two is devoted to evidence on the subject in ancient Greece and Rome. The analysis of Evil Eye belief and practice in Mesopotamia, Egypt, Greece and Rome summarizes a century of research since the milestone two-volume study of Siegfried Seligmann, *Der böse Blick und Verwandtes* (1910), and describes the ecological, historical, social, and cultural contexts within which the biblical texts are best understood. Within the geographical and cultural matrix detailed in these first two volumes, the evidence of Evil Eye belief and practice in the Bible is then examined in Volume Three. A final volume considers post-biblical evidence of Evil Eye belief and practice in Rabbinic Israel (Chapter One) and early Christianity (Chapter Two) through Late Antiquity (c. 600 CE). Concluding reflections on the import and implications of our study (Chapter Three) close this final volume. Throughout this study we are treating the Evil Eye in antiquity not as an instance of vulgar superstition or deluded magic, but as a physiological, psychological and moral phenomenon whose operation was deemed explicable on rational grounds; for discussion see Vol. 1, pp. 26-27.

ACKNOWLEDGMENTS

As with Volume One, I am most grateful to the host of friends and informants in North America and abroad who have so generously supplied me with first- and second-hand accounts of Evil Eye incidents, Evil Eye amulets, and Evil Eye research. My special thanks, once again, to Dick Rohrbaugh for his critical reading and feedback on the content and shape of Volume 2.

Thanks too to editor in chief K. C. Hanson as well as Ian Creeger, patient and expert typesetter, for advice on this second volume and getting it into final shape.

ABBREVIATIONS

ANCIENT TEXTS/SOURCES

Josephus

Ant.   *Antiquities of the Jews*

Life   *The Life*

War   *Jewish War*

Philo of Alexandria

Drunkenness   *On Drunkenness/De Ebrietate*

Flaccus   *Against Flaccus/In Flaccum*

Post.   *On the Posterity of Cain/De Posteritate Caini*

Pseudepigrapha of the Old Testament

Test. Sol.   *Testament of Solomon*

Testaments of the Twelve Patriarchs

T. Benj.   *Testament of Benjamin*

T. Dan   *Testament of Dan*

T. Gad   *Testament of Gad*

T. Sim.   *Testament of Simeon*

RABBINIC WRITINGS

b.	Babylonian Talmud (*Babli*)
m.	Mishnah

GREEK AND ROMAN WRITINGS

Adesp.   *Adespota* [fragments of unknown authors]
Comicorum Atticorum Fragmenta. 3 vols. Edited by T. Kock. Leipzig: Teubner, Vol. 1, 1880; Vol. 2, 1884
Comicorum Graecorum Fragmenta. Edited by G. Kaibel. Vol. 1.1. Berlin: Weidmann, 1899

Aelian

Nat. An.	*De natura animalium. On Animals*
Var. hist.	*Varia Historia. Historical Miscellany*

Aeschylus

Agam.	*Agamemnon*

Choephori/Libation-bearers
Prometheus Bound
Persians

Aesop

Vita Aes.	*Vita Aesopi*

Agathon

Frag.	Fragment

Alciphron

Ep.	*Epistles*

Alexander (Pseudo-) of Aphrodisias

Probl. phys.	*Problemata physica*

Antisthenes

Frag.	Fragment

Apuleius

Met.   *Metamorphoses*

Aristophanes

Ach.   *Acharnenses*

Frag.   Fragment

Knights/Equites

Peace/Pax

Wealth /Plutus

Aristotle

De anima

De cael.   *De caelo*

De sens.   *De sensu et sensibilibus*

Gen. An.   *De generatione animalium*

Insomn.   *De Insomniis*

Meteor.   *Meteorologica*

Politics

Aristotle (Pseudo-)

Problemata inedita

Probl. phys.   *Problemata physica*

Athenaeus

Deipn.   *Deipnosophistae*

Auct. Priap.   *Auctor Priapeorum = Carmina Priapeia/Corpus
                    Priapeorum*

CAF   *Comicorum Atticorum Fragmenta*. Edited by Theodor
                    Kock. 3 vols. Leipzig: Teubner, 1880–1888

Carmina Priap.   *Carmina Priapeia*. Cf. *Auctor Priapeorum/Corpus
                    Priapeorum*

CGF   *Comicorum Graecorum Fragmenta*. Edited by G. Kaibel.
                    Berlin: Weidmann, 1899

CGL	*Corpus Grammaticorum Latinorum*

Cicero

Ac.	*Academicae Quaestiones*
Ad Atticum	*Epistulae ad Atticum*/Letters of Atticus
Admiranda, Frag. 4 (lost)	
Agr.	*Orationes de lege agraria contra Rullum*
Brutus	
De fato	
De legibus	*De legibus*
De nat. deor.	*De natura deorum*
De orat.	*De oratore*
De univ.	*De universo*
Ep. Luc.	*Epistle to Lucillius*
Orator ad M. Brutum	
Tusc. Disp.	*Tusculan Disputations*
Verr.	*Actio in Verrum*/The Verrine Orations

Comica adesp.	see above, *Adespota*

Corrina

Frag. 10	Fragment 10

Democritus

Frag.	Fragment

Demosthenes

Orat.	*The Orations of Demosthenes*

Diels-Kranz, *FVS*	*Die Fragmente der Vorsokratiker.* Edited by Hermann Diels and Walter Kranz. 3 vols. 6th ed. Berlin: Weidmann, 1951–1952 *Testimonia* 1–170 (siglum A); *Fragmenta* 1–298a (siglum B)

Dio Chrysostom

Orat.   *Orationes*

Diogenes Laertius

Lives   *De vitis philosophorum* (*Lives and Opinions of Eminent Philosophers*)

Dioscorides

De med. mater.   *De materia medica*

Epictetus

Disc.   *Discources*

Epig. Gr.   See Kaibel, *Epig. Gr.*

Euripides

Alcestis
Iphigenia in Aulis
Orestes
Suppliant Women

Frag.   Fragment

FGrHist   *Die Fragmente der griechischen Historiker.* Edited by F. Jacoby. Berlin: Weidmann, 1923–

Grattius

Cynegetica

GVI   *Griechische Vers-inschriften.* I: *Die Grabepigramma.* Edited by W. Peek. Berlin: Akademie Verlag, 1955

Heliodorus

Aeth.   *Aethiopica*

Herodotus
Hist.   *Histories*

Homer
Iliad
Odyssey

Horace
Epist.   *Epistles*

Justinus
Hist. Phil.   *Historiae Philippicae/Philippic History of Pom-*
                       peius Trogus

Juvenal
Sat.   *Satires*

Kaibel, *Epigr. Gr.*   *Epigrammata Graeca ex lapidibus conlecta.*
                       Edited by Georg Kaibel. Berlin: Reimer, 1878;
                       reprinted 1965

Kassel-Austin, *PCG*   *Poetae Comici Graeci.* 8 vols. Edited by R. von
                       Kassel and C. Austin. Berlin: de Gruyter, 1983–
                       2001

Lewis and Short, *Latin Dictionary*   *A Latin Dictionary* by Charlton T.
                       Lewis and Charles Short. Oxford: Clar-
                       endon, 1879; reprinted, 1991

Libanius
Ep.   *Epistles*

LIMC   *Lexicon Iconographicum Mythologiae Classicae.*
                       1981–

Livy
Ab urbe condita libri (in 45 books)

Menander
Sent.   *Sentences*

Nonius Marcellus
De Comp.   *De Compendiosa Doctrina* (20 books). Edited by Wallace
                   M. Lindsay. Leipzig: Teubner, 1903

Pausanius
Descr.   *Description of Greece*

PCG   see Kassel-Austin, *PCG*

Persius
Sat.   *Satires*

Petronius
Sat.   *Satyricon*

Philostratus
Imagines

Philostratus, Flavius of Athens
Life   *Life of Apollonius of Tyana*

Pindar
Frag.   Fragment
Isthmian Odes
Nemian Odes
Olympian Odes
Pythian Odes

Pliny the Elder
NH   *Natural History*

Pliny the Younger
Ep.   *Epistles*

Plutarch

Adv. Col.	*Adversus Colotem/Against Colotes*
An seni	*An seni respublica gerenda sit*
De amore prolis	
De cap.	*De capienda ex inimicis utilitate*
De curios.	*De curiositate*
De frat.	*De fraterno amore*
De invidia	*De invidia et odio*
Demetrius	
De recta	*De recta ratione audiendi*
De tranq.	*De tranquillitate animi*
De tuenda	*De tuenda sanitate praecepta*
Dio	
Mul. virt.	*Mulierum virtutes*
Mor.	*Moralia*
Non posse	*Non posse suaviter vivi secundum Epicurum*
Quaest. Conv.	*Quaestiones Convivales (Convivial Questions/Symposium/ Table Talk)*
Quaest. Rom.	*Quaestiones Romanae et Graece*

Pollux

Onom.	*Onomastikon*

Quintilian

Inst. orat.	*Institutio oratoria*

SB	*Sammelbuch griechischer Urkunden aus Ägypten*, 1915–

Seneca

Ep.	*Epistle*
Ep. Luc.	*Epistle to Lucillius*
Nat.	*Quaestiones naturales (Natural Questions)*

Sophocles

Electra
Philoctetes

Stobaeus, Johannes

Stobaeus, *Anth./Ecl.*   Johannes Stobaeus, *Anthologium/Eclogues*

Suetonius

Lives of the Caesars
  Augustus
  Gaius Caligula
  Julius Caesar
  Nero
  Vespasian
  Vitellius

SVF   *Stoicorum Veterum Fragmenta*. Edited by J. von Arnim. (1903–24). 3 vols; vol. 4 (indexes by M. Adler). Leipzig: Teubner, 1903–1924; reprinted, Stuttgart 1978

Symmachus

Ep.   *Epistles*

TGF2 ed. Nauck   *Tragicorum Graecorum Fragmenta*. Edited by August Nauck. 2nd ed. Leipzig: Teubner, 1889

TGF ed. Snell   *Tragicorum Graecorum Fragmenta*. 5 vols. Edited by Bruno Snell. Göttingen: Vandenhoeck & Ruprecht, 1971

Theophrastus

Char.   *Characteres*
Hist. plant. *Historia plantarum/History of Plants*
Sens.   *De Sensu et sensibilibus*

Thucydides

Hist.   *History of the Peloponnesian War*

TLG   *Thesaurus Linguae Graecae*

TLL   *Thesaurus Linguae Latinae*. 11 vols. Leipzig: Teubner, 1900–1999; Saur, 2000–2006; Berlin: de Gruyter, 2007–

Varro

Ling. Lat.	*De Lingua Latina*

Vegetius

Mulomedicina	*P. Vegeti Renati. Digestorum artis mulom-edicinae Libri.* Edited by Ernest Lommatzsch. Leipzig: Teubner, 1903

Virgil

Aen.	*Aeneid*
Ecl.	*Eclogues*

EARLY CHRISTIAN WRITINGS

CCL/CCSL	*Corpus Christianorum, Series Latina.* Turnhout: Brepols, 1953–
CSEL	Corpus Scriptorum Ecclesiasticorum Latinorum. Vienna: Verlag der Österreichischen Akademie der Wissenschaften; Hoelder-Pichler-Tempsky, 1866–1957

Gregory of Nyssa

De Beat.	*De Beatitudinibus*
Orat. Cat.	*Oratio catechetica magna/The Catechetical Oration*

Jerome

Vulgata	*Biblia Sacra: Iuxta Vulgatam versionem.* 2 vols. Edited by R. Weber. Stuttgart: Württembergische Bibelanstalt, 1969

John Chrysostom

Hom. 1 Cor. 12:13	*Homiliae in primum epistulam ad Corinthios* 12.13 (on 1 Cor 4:10)

Lactantius

Inst.	*Divinarum institutionum libri septem*

PG   Patrologia Graeca. Patrologiae Cursus Completus, Series
            Graeca. Edited by J. P. Migne. 161 vols. Paris: Garnier Freres,
            1857–1866

PL   Patrologia Latina. Patrologiae cursus Completus: Series Lati-
            na. Edited by J. P. Migne. 221 vols. Paris: Garnier, 1844–1880

Tertullian of Carthage

De carne	*De carne Christi*
Scorp.	*Scorpicae*
Virg. vel.	*De virginibus velandis*

Vulg.	*Vulgata*, see Jerome

INSCRIPTIONS, EPIGRAPHA, OSTRACA, ICONOGRAPHY

BGU   *Ägyptische Urkunden aus den staatlichen Museen zu Ber-
            lin* Griechische Urkunden. 15 vols. Berlin: Weidmann,
            1895–1983

BM   Siglum for objects in the British Museum

CIG   Corpus inscriptionum graecarum. Edited by A. Boeckh. 4
            vols. Berlin, 1825–1877

CGL   Corpus Grammaticorum Latinorum

CIL   Corpus inscriptionum latinarum. Begun by T. Mommsen. 17
            vols. Berlin: Reimer, 1862

CLE   *Carmina Latina Epigraphica.* Edited by F. Büchler and E.
            Lommatzsch. Leipzig: 1930

Diels-Kranz, FVS *Die Fragmente der Vorsokratiker.* Edited by Hermann
            Diels and Walter Kranz. 3 vols. 6th ed. Berlin: Weidmann,
            1951–1952 (originally, 1903). Vol. 2. *Testimonia* 1–170 (si-
            glum A); *Fragmenta* 1–298a (siglum B)

Epigr. Gr. See Kaibel, *Epigr. Gr.*

FGrHist   *Die Fragmente der griechischen Historiker.* Edited by F. Jacoby.
            Berlin: Weidmann, 1923–

GVI   *Griechische Vers-inschriften. I. Die Grabepigramma.* Edited by
            W. Peek. Berlin: Akademie-Verlag, 1955

GMPT   *The Greek Magical Papyri in Translation, Including the Demotic Texts.* Edited by Hans Dieter Betz et al. Chicago: University of Chicago Press, 1986. See PGM

Hunt and Edgar, *Select Papyri* 1, 2   Hunt, A. S. and C. C. Edgar, translators and editors

        Select Papyri. Vol. 1. *Non-Literary Papyri, Private Affairs.* LCL. Cambridge: Harvard University Press, 1932

        Select Papyri. Vol. 2: *Non-Literary Papyri; Public Documents.* LCL. Cambridge: Harvard University Press, 1934

IG   *Inscriptiones Graecae.* Berlin, 1873–

IG2   *Inscriptiones Graecae, editio minor.* Berlin, 1913–

IGLS   *Inscriptions grecques et latines de la Syrie.* Edited by L. Jalabert, R. Mouterde, et al. Paris: Geuthner, 1929–

ILS   Inscriptiones Latinae Selectae. Edited by H. Dessau. 3 vols. In 5 parts. Berlin: Weidmann, 1892–1916

IGRRP   *Inscriptiones Graecae ad res romanas pertinentes.* Edited by René Cagnat. Vol. 1. Paris: Leroux, 1901

Kaibel, *Epigr. Gr. Epigrammata Graeca ex lapidibus conlecta.* Edited by G. Kaibel. Berlin: Reimer, 1878

Kassel-Austin   *Poetae Comici Graeci.* Edited by R. von Kassel and C. Austin Macleod. 8 vols. LCL. Cambridge: Harvard University Press, 1913–1967

LIMC   *Lexicon Iconographicum Mythologiae Classicae*, 1981–

O.Amst.   *Ostraka in Amsterdam Collections.* Edited by R. S. Bagnall, P. J. Sijpestein et al. Studia Amstelodamensia ad epigraphicam, ius antiquum et papyrologicam pertinentia, 9. Zutphen, 1976

O.Flor.   *The Florida Ostraka: Documents from the Roman Army in Upper Egypt.* Edited by R.S. Bagnall. Greek, Roman and Byzantine Monographs 7, Nos. 1–31. Durham: Duke University, 1976

OGIS   *Orientis Graeci Inscriptiones Selectae.* Edited by W. Dittenberger, 2 vols. Leipzig: Hirzel, 1903–1905

PAES   Première Année des Etudes de Santé

PDM   *Papyri Demoticae Magicae.* Translated in *The Greek Magical Papyri in Translation Including the Demotic Spells,* edited by H. D. Betz. Chicago: University of Chicago Press, 1986

PGM   *Papyri Graece Magicae. Die griechischen Zauberpapyri.* Edited by K. Preisendanz. 2 vols. Berlin: Teubner, 1929, 1931. 2nd ed. by A. Heinrichs. 2 vols. Stuttgart: Teubner, 1973–74. See ET: *Greek Magical Papyri in Translation,* edited by H. D. Betz

P.Brem. Die Bremer Papyri. Edited by Ulrich Wilcken. Berlin: de Gruyter, 1936

P.Leid. *Papyri Graeci Musei Antiquarii Publici Lugduni-Batavi.* 2 vols. Edited by C. Leemans. Leiden: Brill, 1843, 1885

P.Lond. *Greek Papyri in the British Museum.* 7 vols. Edited by F. G. Kenyon et al. Vols. 1 and 2 edited by F. G. Kenyon; Vol. 3 edited by F. G. Kenyon and H. I. Bell; Vols. 4 and 5 edited by H. I. Bell. London: British Museum, 1893–1974. Also P.Mag. Lond

P.Mag. = PGM

P.Mag.Leid.W. *Leiden Magical Papyrus W.* Edited by A. Dieterich, *Abraxas: Studien zur Religionsgeschichte des spätern Altertums.* Festschrift für Hermann Usener. Leipzig: Teubner, 1891

P.Mag.Lond. = P.London 1

P.Mag.Par. = C. Wessely, ed. *Griechische Zauberpapyrus von Paris und London.* Denkschrift der kaiserlichen Akademie der Wissenschaft, Philosophische.-historische Klasse 36.2. Vienna: Tempensky, 1888, 27–108; *Die Pariser Papyri des Fundes von El-Faijûm.* In Denkschrift der kaiserlichen Akademie der Wissenschaft, Philosoph.-Historische Klasse 37.2. Vienna: Tempsky, 1889: 97–256. *Wiener Denkschrift* 36/2 (1888) 44–126; 42/2 (1888) 139–48

P.Mich University of Michigan Papyri. Various editors. 1931–

P.Oxy. *The Oxyrhynchus Papyri.* Edited by B. P. Grenfell and A. S. Hunt et al. 72 vols. London: Egypt Exploration Society, 1898–1972

P.Petr. *The Flinders Petrie Papyri.* 3 vols. Edited by J. Mahaffy and J. Smyly. Dublin: Academy House, 1891–1905

PPM *Pompei: pitture e mosaici.* Edited by I. Baldassare and G. Pugliose Carratelli. 10 vols. Rome: Istituto della enciclopedia italiana, 1990–2003

P.Rein I *Papyrus grecs et démotiques recueilles en Égypte.* Edited by T. Rienach, W. Spiegelberg, and S. de Ricci. París: Leroux, 1905 [Milán 1972] = PapRein

PSI   *Papiri greci e latini*. Pubblicazioni della Società italiana per la ricerca dei papyri greci e latini in Egítto. Florence: Arini, 1912–

P.Thead.   *Papyrus de Théadelphie.* Edited by P. Jourget. Paris: Fontemoing, 1911

P.Turner   *Papyri Greek and Egyptian: Edited by Various Hands in Honour of Eric Gardner Turner on the Occasion of His Seventieth Birthday.* London: British Academy by the Egypt Exploration Society, 1981

Rev.Ég.   *Revue égyptologique.* Paris, 1880–

SB   *Sammelbuch griechischer Urkunden aus Aegypten.* Begun by F. Preisigke in 1915, continued by F. Bilabel, E. Kiessling, and H.-A. Rupprecht. 26 vols. and in progress. Strassburg: Trübner

SEG   *Supplementum Epigraphicum Graecum.* Leiden: Brill, 1923–1971. Edited by H. W. Pleket and R. S. Stroud et al. Amsterdam: Gieben, 1972–

SVF   *Stoicorum Veterum Fragmenta.* 3 vols. Edited by H. von Arnim (1903–24). Vol. 4 (indexes by M. Adler). Leipzig: Teubner, 1903–1924. Reprinted Stuttgart: Teubner, 1978

van Haelst, *Catalogue*   J. van Haelst, *Catalogue des papyrus littéraires-juifs et chrétiens.*Université de Paris IV. Série Papyrologie 1. Paris: Publications de la Sorbonne, 1976

ENCYCLOPEDIAS, LEXICA, PERIODICALS, SERIES

AA   *Archäologischer Anzeiger*

ANRW   *Aufstieg und Niedergang der römischen Welt.* Edited by Hildegard Temporini and Wolfgang Haase. Berlin: de Gruyter, 1972–

AnzWien   *Anzeiger:* Österreichische Akademie der Wissenschaften, Vienna, Philologisch-historische Klasse

ArOr   *Archiv Orientalni*

AO   Louvre Museum, Antiquites Oriental

AOS   American Oriental Series. New Haven 1925–

APF   *Archiv für Papyrusforschung und verwandte Gebiete*

ARYS   *Antigüedad, Religiones y Sociedades* (periodical)

BAH	Bibliothèque archéologique et historique, Institut Francais d'Archéologie de Beyrouth. Paris 1921–
BAR	*Biblical Archaeological Review*
BDAG	*A Greek-English Lexicon of the New Testament and other Early Christian Literature.* 3rd ed., revised and edited by Frederick William Danker. Based on Walter Bauer's *Griechisch-deutsches Wörterbuch zu den Schriften des Neuen Testaments und der frühchristlichen Literatur.* 6th ed., edited by Kurt Aland und Barbara Aland, with Viktor Reichmann and on previous English editions by W. F. Arndt, F. W. Gingrich, and F. W. Danker. Chicago: University of Chicago Press, 2000
BCH	*Bulletin de correspondance hellénique.* Paris, 1877–
BE	*Bulletin épigraphique* (in *Revue des études grecques*) 1888–, replacing *Bull. Épigr.*
BIFAO	Bulletin de l'Institut Francais d'Archéologie Orientale au Caire, Le Caire
BM	British Museum
BTB	*Biblical Theology Bulletin*
CBQ	*Catholic Biblical Quarterly*
CGL/ GL	Corpus Grammaticorum Latinorum
CRAIBL	Comptes rendus des séances de l'Académie des Inscriptions et Belles-Lettres. Paris, 1857–
DACL	*Dictionnaire d'archéologie chrétienne et de liturgie.* Edited by F. Cabrol and H. Leclercq. 15 vols. Paris: Letouzey et Ané, 1907–1953
Daremberg-Saglio	Charles Daremberg and Edmond Saglio, editors. *Dictionnaire des antiquités grecques et romaines.* 10 vols (5 double volumes). Paris: Hachette, 1877–1919
EPRO	Études préliminaires aux religions orientales dans l'Empire romain
GRBS	*Greek, Roman and Byzantine Studies*
HDA	*Handwörterbuch des deutschen Aberglaubens.* 10 vols. Edited by H. Bächtold-Stäubli and E. Hoffmann-Krayer. Berlin: de Gruyter, 1927–1942; Reprinted, 1987
HERE	*Encyclopaedia of Religion and Ethics.* 13 vols. Edited by James Hasting et al. Edinburgh: T. & T. Clark, 1908–1927. 4th ed. reprinted, 1958
JAC	*Jahrbuch fürAntike und Christentum,* 1958–

JHS   *Journal of Hellenic Studies*

JRA   *Journal of Roman Archaeology*

ISBE   *The International Standard Bible Encyclopaedia.*4 vols. edited
             by James Orr, et al. Revised edition by Melvin G. Kyle. Chi-
             cago: Howard-Severance, 1929; revised and reedited by G. W.
             Bromiley. Grand Rapids: Eerdmans, 1979–88

LCL   Loeb Classical Library

LIMC   *Lexicon Iconographicum Mythologiae Classicae.* Vols. 1–9.
             Zurich and Munich: Artemis and Winkler, 1981–1999;
             Supplementum vol. Düsseldorf: Artemis, 2009

Moulton-Milligan   James Hope Moulton and George Milligan. *The
             Vocabulary of the Greek Testament Illustrated from the Papyri
             and Other Non-Literary Sources.* London: Hodder & Stough-
             ton, 1930

OCD   *Oxford Classical Dictionary*

ÖAW   Die Österreichische Akademie der Wissenschaften

PW   *Paulys Realencyclopädie der classischen Altertumswissenschaft.*
             Edited by A. F. Pauly. Vols. 1–6 (1839–1852). New edition
             begun by G. Wissowa (1890) et al. 70+ vols. Stuttgart:
             Metzler, 1892-1980

RAC   *Reallexikon für Antike und Christentum.* Edited by Franz
             Joseph Dölger and Hans Lietzmann. Stuttgart: Hiersemann,
             1950–

REG   *Revue des études grecques*

RGG³   *Die Religion in Geschichte und Gegenwart.* 3rd ed. 6 vols. and
             index. Edited by Kurt Galling et al. Tübingen: Mohr Siebeck,
             1957–65

RhM   *Rheinisches Museum für Philologie*

TRE   *Theologische Realenzyklopädie.* Edited by Gerhard Krause and
             Gerhard Müller. Berlin: de Gruyter, 1977–

TDNT   *Theological Dictionary of the New Testament.* 10 vols. Edited
             by Gerhard Kittel and Gerhard Friedrich. Translated by Geof-
             frey W. Bromiley. Grand Rapids: Eerdmans, 1964–76

ZPE   *Zeitschrift für Papyrologie und Epigraphik*

OTHER ABBREVIATIONS AND SIGLA

adj.	adjective
adv.	adverb
a.k.a.	also known as, alias
act.	active
anon.	anonymous
aor.	aorist
BCE, CE	Before the Common Era; Common Era (replacing BC/AD)
c.	*circa* (about)
cent.	century
cf.	confer, see
chap(s).	chapter(s)
codd.	codices
col.	column
cp.	compare, contrast
ET	English translation
fl.	*floruit* (flourished, was active at a certain time)
fig.	figure
FS	Festschrift
gen.	genitive
HT	Hebrew Text, a.k.a. MT (Hebrew Massoretic Text)
ill(s).	illustration(s)
inv. no.	inventory number
JHE	John H. Elliott (as translator)
l(l)	line(s)
lit.	literally
MT	Massoretic Text a.k.a HT (Hebrew Text)
n.f.	neue Folge
no(s)	number(s)
n.r.	neue Reihe
P.	Papyrus
part.	participle
pass.	passive
per.	person
Pl.	Plate

pl.	plural
p(p).	page(s)
Prol.	*Prologus* (prologue)
Ps.-	Pseudo- (inaccurately ascribed to)
Q	Qumran
RP	Raccolta Pornografica ("Pornographic Collection" of the Naples National Archaeological Museum)
SBL	Society of Biblical Literature
s.v.	*sub voce* ("under the [listed] word")
v.l.	*varia lectio* (variant reading)
[ ]	Square brackets identify textual material supplied by the translator of the original source or by the present author (JHE)

I

INTRODUCTION

The earliest evidence of Evil Eye belief and practice in the ancient world comes from Mesopotamia and Egypt. We have examined that material, most prominently Evil Eye incantations and amuletic Eyes of Horus in chapter 2 of Volume 1. In the present volume we turn now to the most extensive sources of this belief in antiquity—the cultures of Greece and Rome, from Homer through Late Antiquity (800 BCE—600 CE). In this period, features of the belief found in Mesopotamian and Egyptan sources, such as the existence of an Evil Eye demon, are expanded to the point where an "Evil Eye belief complex" becomes apparent. This complex of features associated with the Evil Eye—human eye as key organ of information, eye as active not passive, eye as channel of emotions (especially envy) and dispositions, especially of envy, arising in the heart, possessors, victims, defensive strategies and amulets—generally is assumed rather than stated explicitly or at length, yet is essential to an understanding of the literary references to the Evil Eye, whether brief or extended, and the abundant amuletic evidence. This current volume, along with chapter 2 of Volume 1, set and illuminate the context for examining Evil Eye belief and practice in the Bible and the biblical communities, the focus of Volume 3.

In the Greek-speaking Hellenistic world, it was customary in personal letters to include the wish that the recipient and/or members of the family "remain unharmed by the Evil Eye," or "be kept safe from the Evil Eye," using a a form of the adjective *abaskantos* or the related adverb *abaskantôs*. This is illustrated by various personal letters over several centuries and all from Egypt.

1

In a first-century papyrus letter (c. 25 CE), a certain Theôn recommends his brother Herakleides to an official named Tyrannos. He concludes his letter with the wish:

> Before all else, I pray that you have health and the best of success, *unharmed by the Evil Eye* (abaskantôs). (P.Oxy. 2.292, c. 25 CE)[1]

A late first-century letter of Indike "to her lady Thaisous" concludes:

> Salute my lord Theon and Nikoboulos and Dioskopos and Theon and Hermokles—may they be *unharmed by the Evil Eye* (tous abaskantous). (P.Oxy. 2.300)[2]

A papyrus letter from Egypt (98–103 CE) opens with the statement:

> First of all, it is imperative through this letter to greet you and your children—may they be *unharmed by the Evil Eye*" (se apasesthai kai ta abaskanta [s]ou [p]aidia). (BGU 3.811)[3]

A second-century personal letter from Sempronius to Saturnila, his mother, opens with the wish:

> Before everything, I pray for your health and that of my brothers, *unharmed by the Evil Eye* (abaskantôn) . . . (Selected Papyri 1 §121=Rev. Ég. [1919], p. 204)[4]

At the close of a personal letter of Apollonius of Lykopolis to the strategos Apollonius in Heptakomia on business matters (Hermopolis, Egypt, c. 116–120 CE), the writer concludes with a conventional wish concerning the Evil Eye:

> I wish you good health, Lord Apollonius, along with your children kept safe from the Evil Eye (ton abaskanton paidion). (P.Brem. 20.18).[5]

A second-century private letter ends:

---

1. Hunt and Edgar, *Select Papyri* 1 (1932) 296–97, §106; White, *Ancient Letters* 1986:188–89, no. 79. On this epistolary convention and on the use of *abaskantos* as a personal name see also *Beware the Evil Eye*, Vol. 1, chap. 2 (Egypt) and below, p. 39. On the Papyri discovered in Oxyrynchus, Egypt, see Patterson 2011:60–68, esp. 66 on P.Oxy 2.292. On the site of Oxyrynchus and daily life there see Parsons 2007.

2. See White 1986:93, no. 94.

3. Moulton-Milligan 1930:106.

4. Hunt and Edgar, *Select Papyri* 1 (1932) 318–19, §121; White 1986:180–81, no. 113; Deissmann 1923:160–61.

5. Wilcken 1936:57.

> [Greet] . . . his children—may they be *unharmed by the Evil Eye*
> (*ta abaskanta autou tekna*). (P.Oxy. 46.3312)[6]

A second-century personal letter regarding the marriage of a certain Sara-
pion concludes with the wish:

> Greet most noble Alexandros and his Sarapion and Theon and
> Aristobleia—may they be *unharmed by the Evil Eye* (*tous abas-
> kantous*)—and Aristobleia's children." (P.Oxy. 46.3313)[7]

A second-third-century CE personal letter to a schoolboy from his mother
ends with the greeting:

> Many salutations from your sisters and the children of Theo-
> nis— may they be *unharmed by the Evil Eye* (*ta abaskanta paidia
> Theônidos*)—and from all our friends by name. (P.Oxy. 6.930)[8]

An early third century CE personal letter from a schoolboy to his father
concludes with the wish:

> Goodbye, my lord and father, and may you prosper, as I pray, for
> many years along with my brothers—may they be *unharmed by
> the Evil Eye* (*abaskantois*). (Rev. Ég., 1919, p. 201)[9]

Another third century personal letter from Pausanius to his brother Hera-
clides concludes with the greeting:

> Many salutations to my lady mother and my sister and our
> children—may they be *unharmed by the Evil Eye* (*ta abaskanta
> hêmôn paidia*). (P.Oxy. 14.1666)[10]

Christian papyri letters reveal this same practice. Several examples
dating from the third and fourth centuries CE are cited and discussed in
Volume 4, chapter 2. These letters show that Christians and non-Christians
took the Evil Eye threat quite seriously and used the same letter-writing
convention for safeguarding loved ones from the harmful Evil Eye.

Three personal letters even contained the wish that the recipient's favorite horse be kept safe from the Evil Eye. In one letter (O.Flor. 15, Egypt,
end of the second century CE), the writer, Publius, hopes that his son Atre-
ides is in good health "with your horse kept safe from the Evil Eye" (*meta*

---

6. Horsley, *New Docs* 3 (1983) 7–9, §1.

7. Ibid., 10–15, §2.

8. Hunt and Edgar, *Select Papyri* 1 (1932) 334–35, §130.

9. Ibid., 338–39, §133.

10. Ibid., 360–61, §149.

tou abaskantou sou hippou, lines 2–3 and repeated in lines 8–9).[11] A second letter (*O.Flor.* 18, Egypt, end of the second century CE), similarly wishes its addressee, a certain Theon, good health, "with your horse kept safe from the Evil Eye" (*meta tou abaskantou sou hippou*, lines 3–4).[12] The phrase (partly restored) also occurs in a third letter (*O.Amst.* 18, Egypt, end of second century CE).[13]

This wish for safety from the Evil Eye, which is presumed to cause illness, misfortune, and death, is not only a feature appearing in ancient personal Greek correspondence, pagan and Christian. This epistolary custom is rooted in a prominent Circum-Mediterranean and Near Eastern belief with a wide dissemination and a long history. The Greek adjective *abaskantos* ("unharmed by, safe from, the Evil Eye"; lit. "not Evil-Eyed") and its related adverb *abaskantôs,* found in these and other ancient Greek texts, belong to a broad family of terms of the Greek root *bask-*. Most of these terms concern the Evil Eye and malice that is thought to be projected from the eye and conveyed by ocular glance.[14] The numerous occurrences of terms of this word family in literature, personal letters, and amulets that protect against the Evil Eye are a significant part of an array of evidence of Evil Eye belief and practice in the Greek and Roman worlds. While the earliest evidence of this belief in antiquity comes from Mesopotamia and Egypt, as examined previously in chapter 2 of Volume 1, it is the worlds of Greece and Rome where a relative trickle of earlier evidence becomes a torrent.

Dread of the Evil Eye, extensive evidence shows, pervaded the Greek and Roman worlds from the time of Homer (eighth century BCE) to Late Antiquity (sixth–seventh centuries CE) and beyond. "Naturalists, physicians, historians, philosophers, and poets," Siegfried Seligmann notes, all "believed in the power of the (Evil-Eyeing) glance."[15] As was also the case in Mesopotamia and Egypt, when Greeks and Romans were not explicitly speaking of the Evil Eye in hushed tones, they were engaging in a diversity of strategems devised for anti-Evil Eye protection. Extensive commerce and trade of the Greeks with Egyptian and Mesopotamian empires provided the conduit for exchange of cultures, worldviews, and beliefs, including that of the Evil Eye. The belief appears to have made its way to Greece from Mesopotamia at an early point. Walter Burkert, describing Near Eastern influence

11. See Youtie 1979; Horsley, *New Docs* 1 (1981) 70.

12. Youtie 1979; Horsley, *New Docs* 1 (1981) 70.

13. Youtie 1979; Horsley, *New Docs* 1 (1981) 70. Youtie translates, "your horse, which I pray may be preserved from the evil eye."

14. On this terminology, including the word *abaskantos* used as both an adjective and a proper names see below, pp. 37–39.

15. Seligmann 1910 1:31.

on Greek culture in the early Archaic age, has proposed that figurines, curses, and healing rituals were introduced to Greece from Mesopotamia during or prior to the Archaic period (800–480 BCE).[16] The Evil Eye belief also may have been among the many beliefs and customs that the Greeks, according to Herodotos,[17] adopted from the Egyptians. From Alexander the Great (336–323 BCE) onward, a Greek and then subsequent Roman expansion eastward and westward, northward and southward across the Mediterranean Sea brought about an intersection and cross-fertilization of cultures in which Evil Eye belief and practice flourished as never before. Sustained contact with Egypt, especially from the period of the Ptolemies onward, assured the influence of Egypt upon Greece and Rome and, in turn, Greek influence in Egypt via the Macedonian dynasty of the Ptolemies. Rome, already influenced by Etruskan Evil Eye belief, then absorbed, and geographically extended, this cultural mix. Evil Eye belief and practice among Greeks and Romans exemplifies the syncretism of the Hellenistic Age and its amalgamation of cultural traditions.

The continuity of features of Evil Eye belief from Mesopotamia and Egypt to Greece and Rome is striking: the concept of an Evil Eye demon; the understanding of the eye as an active, rather than passive, organ; the certainty that an Evil Eye was capable of inflicting great harm, illness, and even death;[18] the assumed vulnerability of all persons, but especially of children and birthing mothers; the use of anti-Evil Eye apotropaics (gestures, words, and devices that "turn away" [Greek *apotrepein*] evil forces),[19] such as incantations, the plethora of Eyes of Horus (*udjat* eyes) and other amuletic eyes, and the protective colors of blue and red. Greek and Roman traditions expand the body of ancient Evil Eye lore. These traditions supply the richest source of information in the ancient world on the Evil Eye, its victims and possessors, descriptions of how it works, the damages it causes, and the myriad means for protecting against it and warding it off. The consistency of essential features of Evil Eye belief and practice throughout the regions and across the centuries of the ancient world is one of its most remarkable characteristics.

16. Burkert 1992:67–68, with concurrence by Stratton 2007:41 and 195 n10.

17. Herodotus, *Hist.* 2.51, 48–90, 123, 177.

18. The ancients believed that "evilly-disposed persons might harm their victims in one of three ways, namely, by look, voice, or touch; but the most to be feared was the look." (Callisen 1937:453).

19. The term *apotropaic* derives from the Greek verb *apotropein* ("drive away," ("ward off") and denotes any object, word or gesture employed to *avert or ward off* evil of any kind.

The evidence of Evil Eye belief and practice in the Circum-Mediterranean region takes various forms: literary texts (poetry, tragedy, comedy, philosophic writings, table talks, geographical-cultural accounts), pottery, military shields and breastplates, papyri, inscriptions, mosaics, plaques affixed to the door frames of houses, statues, figurines, art, and thousands upon thousands of amulets for personal and public display. This evidence is of crucial importance for detecting and illuminating instances of Evil Eye belief and practice in the biblical writings and their implied social dynamics. In the following survey of evidence of Evil Eye belief and practice from the Greco-Roman world, we exclude in this volume references to the Evil Eye in the Greek biblical writings and the parabiblical literature (e.g., the Old Testament Pseudepigrapha, Qumran, Philo, and Josephus) and post-biblical Jewish and Christian sources. This material will be treated in Volumes 3 and 4. Our survey here ranges from the pioneering study of Otto Jahn in 1855[20] to Thomas Rakoczy's more extensive analysis of the Greek literature (1996). It treats all relevant literary, inscriptional, and epigraphic sources along with the abundant material evidence from Greece and Rome. We will also take into account all the relevant secondary literature now on hand.[21]

This volume on the Evil Eye in Greek and Roman sources joins chapter 2 of Volume 1 on the Evil Eye in Mesopotamian and Egyptian cultures to provide the historical, social, and cultural matrix within which the biblical references to the Evil Eye—our primary focus of attention—are best understood and interpreted.

20. Jahn (1813–1869), German archaeologist, philologist, and historian, has given us the first modern critical study on the Evil Eye in Greco-Roman antiquity, with abundant citation of ancient sources. His assumption of an early existence of the belief recently has been challenged by Schlesier (1991). In his contribution to a retrospective volume on Jahn's work and influence, Schlesier claims that cogent evidence of the belief stems only from the Roman imperial period. Rakoczy (1996:4 and n8 and *passim*) and the present study present evidence proving this claim to be in error.

21. On the Evil Eye in Greek and Roman antiquity see Jahn 1855; Story 1877; portions of Elworthy 1895/1958; Seligmann 1910, 1922, 1927; "Malus oculus" in *Harper's Dictionary of Classical Literature and Antiquities* 1896, *s.v*; Perdrizet 1922; Budge 1930/1978:354–65; Geffcken 1930; Meisen 1950; Kötting 1954:476–79; Marcadé 1961; Engemann 1975; Moreau 1976/1977; Walcot 1978:77–90; Potts 1982; J. B. Russell 1982; Siebers 1983; Luck 1985:61–131, 176–225; Tupet 1986:2606–2610; Dickie 1987, 1990, 1991, 1993; Bernidaki-Aldous 1988; DeForest 1993; McCartney 1992; Rakoczy 1996; Ogden 2002:222–26; Greenfield 2006; Alvar Nuño 2006–2008, 2009–2010, 2012a, 2012b; Faraone 2013; Lovatt 2013:328–36 (Evil Eye as instance of the "assaultive gaze"). On the Evil Eye and witchcraft in the Zoroastrian literature see Frachtenberg 1918:419–24. On the penetrating gaze see also Barton 2002:216–235 and Bartsch 2006 (penetrating phallus against penetrating gaze). Also relevant are studies and theories on the eye and vision, on the linkage of the Evil Eye with envy and praise, on apotropaic images of male and female genitalia and apotropaic manual gestures, and analyses of anti-Evil Eye amulets. Studies on the Evil Eye in Israel and Christianity are listed in Volumes 3 and 4.

2

EVIL EYE BELIEF AND PRACTICE IN GREECE AND ROME

FROM HOMER TO LATE ROMAN ANTIQUITY (800 BCE-600 CE)—AN OVERVIEW

Evidence of Evil Eye belief among the Greeks likely reaches as far back as the Homeric era (eighth century BCE). The earliest appearance in literature of the conventional expressions for "Evil Eye," namely *baskainein* and its family of terms, are from the fifth century BCE. Pherecrates, a Greek poet of Athenian Old Comedy (fifth century BCE), provides the earliest literary attestation of the verb *baskainein*. Referring to the Evil Eyeing by a dead animal, a hunter complains,

> The dead hare casts an Evil Eye upon me (*ho lagôs me baskainei tethnikôs*). (Pherecrates, Frag. 189)[1]

The comic poet Aristophanes (c. 445–385 BCE) offers the earliest literary attestation of the adjective/substantive *baskanos* (*Knights* 103; *Wealth* 571).[2]

1. For the verb in this century, see also the orator Isocrates, *Antidosis*, 62.3; *To Philip*, 11.4; *Panathenaicus*, 135.10.

2. Rakoczy 1996:121 and n373. Rakoczy notes that Sophocles (496–406 BCE) in Frag. 1034 R, according to a gloss of Hesychius, used *baskanos* as an adjective with the sense of "thankless" and that this may be the earliest literary trace of this word family. On *baskanos* in Aristophanes see Dickie 1995.

A fragment of an astrological work attributed to Pythagoras (sixth century BCE), contains a list of features of persons born under the astrological sign of Cancer and includes Evil-Eyeing persons (*baskanoi*).[3] However, this attribution and its date are uncertain. Plato (c. 429–347 BCE), in his dialogue *Phaedo* (95b) has the first attested literary use of the noun *baskania*.

The relatively infrequent mention of Evil Eye in the early period, it has been speculated,[4] was due to the prevalent fear that the *mere utterance* of the word "Evil Eye" would bring it into action (as in the adage, "speak of the Devil and he will appear"). Mention was made instead only of "eye" or "envy" (*phthonos*), the emotion with which the Evil Eye was most closely associated.[5] This "Sprachtabu" has continued down through the centuries and is still alive in places like Naples, Italy, where the mere utterance of the word *malucch* [for *malocchio*] or *jettatura*, or *fascino* is ominous and dangerous. F. T. Elworthy recounts instances of this from his personal experience in Italy.[6] However, the belief itself has left earlier traces in Greek culture. This is evident in numerous older texts where, as we shall see, envy, consistently associated with the Evil Eye, is said to have a damaging effect through intent looking, ocular glare, or oblique glance.[7]

Early intimations of belief in an Evil Eye may be seen in the *Iliad* of Homer and in Hesiod, where use is made of verbs of seeing with a causative force, thereby presuming an active, rather than a passive, eye. More on this active eye theory follows below. On this reading, in *Iliad* 1.105 Agammenon in his fury casts harmful glances at a certain Calchas with his Evil Eye.[8] Evidence of the belief is also found in the repeated mention of features conventionally associated with Evil Eye belief and practice in later texts: the eye understood as an active fiery force, the destructive power of an angry glance, and the eye's connection with the emotion of envy. These eventually formed elements of what became the Evil Eye complex in later time. Our text of the *Iliad* also illustrates the assumed connection of the heart as locus of emotion and the eyes as conveyer of emotion. Robert Fagles's translation captures it well:

3. Pythagorus, Frag. 11.2.136 (ed. Zuretti 1934).

4. Rakoczy 1996:41, 61–62, 83 n204.

5. On the substitution of *phthonos* for the dangerous term *baskania,* as amulets illustrate, see also Matantseva 1994.

6. Elworthy 1895/1958:17–19.

7. See also Rakoczy 1996:42–120.

8. *Kalchanta prôtista kak' ossomenos proseeipe.*

Agamemnon—furious, his dark heart filled to the brim, blazing
with anger now, his eyes like searing fire. With a sudden, killing
look he wheeled on Calchas first. (Homer, *Iliad* 1.102–105)

Thus already Homer (eighth century BCE) spoke of the angry glance,
the threatening power of the ocular stare, and "fiery blasts" emitted from
the eye.[9] Centuries later, Persius, Roman poet and satirist (first century CE),
speaks of "burning eyes" (*urentis oculos, Satires* 2.34), another formulation
presuming the eye to be an active rather than passive organ and producing heated rays. A related notion was that of the *oblique glance* or *looking
askance* (sidelong look) as an expression of malicious intentions and an Evil
Eye. Solon (sixth century BCE) describes opponents of his reform "looking
at me obliquely (*loxon*) with their eyes, as at an enemy."[10]

Hesiod, Greek oral poet and contemporary of Homer (eighth century
BCE) tells of certain demons, which with their Evil Eye (*kakên opin*) punish
the offenses of humans and gods (*Theogony* 220–222). In commenting on a
personified Envy as humanity's constant companion, the poet is the first to
speak of ever-present envy (*zêlos*) linked with fearsome eyes (*stugerôpês*),[11]
thereby making the explicit connection of envy and ocular glance, i.e. the
"envious glance" (*Neidblick*):

Envy (*Zêlos*), foul-mouthed, delighting in evil, with fearsome
eyes, will go along with wretched men one and all. (Hesiod,
Works 195–196)

Rakoczy considers this passage of Hesiod the first time in world literature
that explicit reference is made to an "envious glance."[12]

Pindar (c. 522–448 BCE), Greece's greatest lyric poet, writing of victory and defeat in athletic and literary contests, refers more to envy than
any other Greek author. His *Odes* illustrate how the association of envy
and glance continued into the classical period and was attributed to humans as well as deities. His *Fourth Nemian Ode* (473–465 BCE) describes a

---

9. Homer, *Iliad* 1.103–105; 1.200; *Odyssey* 4.150; 19.446; Rakoczy 1996:42–55.

10. Solon, Frag. 34.4–5. For Evil Eye as "oblique eye" see Herodas, *Mimiambi* 4.71
("stare at obliquely," *epiloxoô*); Rakoczy 1996:61, 106. For the Roman notion see Horace,
Epist. 1.14.37 (*obliquo oculo*). Ovid (*Met.* 2.787) describes a personified Envy/*Invidia*
looking at the fleeing goddess Minerva obliquely; cf. also Apollonius of Rhodes, *Argon.*
4.475–476; Rakoczy 1996:56–62, 155–69.

11. Noted by Rakoczy 1996:53 and 64 n118.

12. So Rakoczy 1996:64 n118. On Homer and Hesiod regarding the "angry look,"
see Rakoczy 1996:42–55.

contestant looking enviously and maliciously (*phthonera . . . blepôn*), at his rival.[13] Another Ode declares that

> the evil workings of envy are warded off, if a man who attains the summit and dwells in peace escapes dread arrogance. (Pindar, *Pythian Ode* 11.55–56)[14]

Aeschylus (525–456 BCE) and Euripides (c. 485–c. 406 BCE), likewise knew of the Evil Eye and its association with envy. They gave it prominence in their writings and assumed a familiarity with the Evil Eye on the part of their audiences.[15] Aeschylus's famous tragedy, *Agamemnon* (458 BCE), depicts the great Greek conquerer of Troy, Agamemnon, as a classic target of envy and the Evil Eye of the gods.[16] Excelling all humans in glory by virtue of his victories on the battlefield, he naturally attracts the greatest amount of envy.[17] Upon his triumphant return from Troy to Argos, Clytemnestra, his wife, prepares his way to the palace by spreading purple tapestries for him to walk on. In revenge for his earlier sacrificing their own daughter Iphigenia to gain victory at Troy, Clytemnestra seeks to have Agamemnon fall victim to divine envy by urging him to walk upon cloths reserved for honoring the gods. Although aware of his exposure to this divine envy (v. 904), Agamemnon removes his sandals and reluctantly treads upon the purple tapestries, but with the wish, "may no envious eye strike me from afar" (*mê tis prosôthen ommatos baloi phthonos*).[18] The drama illustrates several basic notions of ancient psychology relevant to Evil Eye belief and practice. For one thing, envy was thought to be conveyed by the eye while originating in the heart:

> [I]t's not in every man's nature to admire another man's good luck without envying him at the same time. When the poison of envy attacks the heart of the envious it doubles his pain and he

13. Pindar, *Nemian Ode* 4.39–41. Rakoczy (1996:64 n118) considers this the first attested association of *human* envy (and not the abstract personification of envy as in Hesiod) and ocular glance in all of literature.

14. The gods, on the other hand, have an "envyless eye" (*aphthonon opis*), Pindar, *Pythian Ode* 8.70–71; 10.20–21). On envy in Pindar see Garcia Lopez and Morales Otal 1984; Bulman 1995.

15. Rakoczy 1996:9–10, 104; on Aeschylus, 73–96; on Euripides, 97–104.

16. See Moreau 1976/1977, named by Rakoczy (1996:4 n7) "the first study of the Evil Eye in [Greek] literature." Moreau saw the Evil Eye implied in references to a fixed stare, *derkesthai*.

17. Rakoczy 1996:7–11, 73–93.

18. Aeschylus, *Agam.* 946–947. Another possible reading, preferred by Rakoczy (1996:82–83), is "may no divine eye of envy strike me from afar."

himself is weighed down by his own misfortune when he sees another man's good fortune. (Aeschylus, *Agam.* 832–839)[19]

As in Hesiod and Pindar, moreover, the envious (Evil) Eye, is depicted here also as emitting rays comparable to arrows, which had deadly effect on the victims they struck: from the eyes of Zeus is cast the thunder-bolt.[20] Envy is conveyed through an active (evil) eye. Divine envy, furthermore, is deemed to strike those who excel in success, glory and praise. Safer is the lot, therefore, of the mediocre who do not excel, who do not stick out so as to attract the ocular lightning bolts of the gods:

> Great glory hath such jeopardy. Zeus's eye-glance scathes, his lightning scars the soaring peaks that touch the stars. Give me the ease of an unenvied lot; to be hailed 'Conquerer' delights me not. (*Agam.* 468–71)[21]

Thus ambition, glory, and excessive praise excited the envious eye of the gods. The conventional term for Evil Eye, *baskania*, does not yet appear here; but basic features of the belief are in place. The Evil Eye is present here, Rakoczy observes, in all but name.[22] In the Archaic Period, envy of the gods is not always linked with punishment of the unjust. It is, however, seen as the cause of the misfortune experienced by all humans, just and unjust alike. Croesus, the wealthiest of mortals, was a victim of divine envy.[23]

Prior to the fifth century, envy, while frequently a concern, was regarded simply as a feature of human nature, with no attempt at analysis. Euripides shows how in time envy and the Evil Eye became a topic of reflection, including attempts at definition.[24] A fragment of Euripides's drama *Ion* (c. 425 BCE) is typical.[25] It comments on the immensity of envy's harm and wonders about its precise location in the human body (hands? bowels? eye?). Both the eye and the hand were employed in later time as means for protecting against an Evil Eye.[26] Euripides (*Suppliant Women* 240–242)

---

19. Translation by G. Theodorus 2005. For envy connected with eye and heart see, e.g. *Anth. Pal.* 11.193; 16.355; Pindar, *Pythian Ode* 2.90–91, and often thereafter, including the Bible; cf. Rakoczy 1996:8–9; and volumes 3–4 of the present work.

20. See also Aeschylus, *Persians* 81–82, for the metaphor.

21. Translation by Cookson 1952:57; cf. also v. 241.

22. Rakoczy 1996:7–11.

23. Ibid., 93. On the envy of the gods see Walcot 1978:22–37, 38–51; Rakoczy 1996:247–70; and below, pp. 98–102

24. Rakoczy 1996:97–104, also on the Evil Eye as illness and on the evil hand.

25. Euripides, *Ion*, Frag. 403 (*TGF²* ed. A. Nauck); also in Stobaeus, *Anth./Ecl* 3.38.8, and Aelian, *Nat. an.* 3.17.

26. On the *mano cornuta, mano fica*, hand of Miriam (*hamesh*), hand of Fatima

states: Of the three groups of citizens, the wealthy, the poor, and those in
between, "the have-nots, those who lack the essentials of life, are motivated
by envy and they release 'evil stings' on those who have." These are most
likely thought of as stings conveying envy and released from the eye. Euripides (*Iphigenia in Taurus* 1217–1218) also attests the covering of the head as
protection against an Evil Eye.[27]

In his history of the Greek-Persian wars, Herodotus (c. 484–c. 424
BCE) recounts Solon's warning to enormously wealthy Croesus of Lydia:
"the power above is full of envy and fond of troubling our lot" (Herodotus, *Hist.* 1.32). Hence the need for moderation in all things. He depicts a
dreadful vengeance sent from the gods to punish Croessus for considering
himself the happiest of men (*Hist.* 1.34). Polycrates, "the most famous victim of divine envy," did not deserve the death he died. He was an innocent
victim of the gods' envious Evil Eye. King Amasis of Egypt in a letter to
Polycrates of Samos laments: "your great prosperity does not cause me joy,
since I know the gods are envious (*to theion . . . phthoneron*)" (Herodotus,
Hist. 3.40).[28] Since divine envy attacks human prosperity, his advice is that
Polycrates take his most valued possession and throw it away (*Hist.* 3.40).
"Envy," he further indicates,

> so natural to humankind, arises in those given much power,
> especially kings who can be envious of the most virtuous among
> their subjects and wish their death. (Herodotus, *Hist.* 3.80)

Envy and the Evil Eye strike that which excels and sticks out (*hyperechein*):

> Do you see how god with his lightning always strikes the larger
> animals, and will not allow them to grow insolent, while those
> of a smaller size do not aggravate him? How likewise his bolts
> always fall on the highest houses and the tallest trees? So he
> plainly enjoys bringing down everything that exalts itself (*ta
> hyperechonta*). Thus a mighty army is often vanguished by a few,
> when god in his envy (*phthonêsas*) sends fear or storm from
> heaven, and they perish in a way unworthy of them. For God
> allows no one to have high thoughts but himself. (Herodotus,
> *Hist.* 7.10)

(*hamsa*), Eye of Horus (*udjat*), apotropaic (Evil) eye under attack and other eye amulets
see below, pp. 181–94, 210–46.

27. See similarly, Virgil, *Aen.* 3.405–407 on the veiled head as protection against
the Evil Eye of the stranger (*hostilis facies*), and, in the Christian post-biblical period,
Tertullian, *Virg. vel.*15.1–3.

28. On Herodotus and the envy of the gods see Schuler 1869.

Thus divine envy is thought to reduce in size those who stand out among the rest and "grow too big for their britches." Centuries later Horace repeats the thought: "It is the mountaintop that the lightning strikes" (Horace, *Odes* 2.10).

It is writings of the fifth and fourth centuries that first attest use of what has become the standard conventional terms for Evil Eye, namely *baskanos, baskainein, baskania* and paronyms.

The dramas of Aristophanes (c. 445–c. 385 BCE) contain the earliest literary occurrences of the adjective/substantive *baskanos* (*Knights* 103; *Wealth* 571). In his comedy *Wealth* (*Plutus*), the character Poverty is called "you spiteful Evil Eye possessor (*baskanos*)! But still you shall squall for contending that all had better be poor than be rich!" (Aristophanes, *Wealth* 571).[29]

In this context, *baskanos* can also imply a slanderous quality: Poverty does not lie though she is slanderous.[30] Aristophanes also employs the substantive *ho baskanos* as a term of reproach for a slanderous slave (*Knights* 103–104). Demosthenes (384–322 BCE) uses *baskanos* as a substantive to denote a malignant Evil-Eyed person (*Orat.*18.132.3; 18.139.6).[31] *Baskanos* can also serve as an abusive label to defame opponents as particularly nasty and vulgar.[32] The verb *baskainein* can have the related sense of "denounce."[33] *Baskanos* in later time appears in the fulsome phrase for Evil Eye, *baskanos ophthalmos.*[34]

Thus *baskanos* can denote "someone who possesses or casts an Evil Eye."[35] It can also denote a "slanderous person" or "slanderous speech." In this latter case, its malice is connected with the act of speaking and the tongue, thus illustrating the connection of Evil Eye, evil mouth and evil tongue. Ancient Akkadian texts connect Evil Eye and evil mouth,[36] as do later Latin writers relating Evil Eye (*malus oculus/fascinatio/fascinare*) and evil tongue (*mala lingua*). Catullus (*Poems/Carmina* 7.12) refers to his

29. This is a modified version of Benjamin Bickley Rogers's translation, substituting "Evil-Eye possessor" for Rogers's "malevolent witch" and regretably spoiling Rogers's rhyme of "witch" and "rich."

30. So Rakockzy 1996:127.

31. Chantraine 1968:167, s. v., renders *baskanos* as "someone who casts a spell" (*jette un sort*).

32. Demosthenes *Orat.* 18. 108, 119, 242; 21.209; cf. Rakoczy 1996:127 n399.

33. Demosthenes *Orat.* 18.189; 18.307; see Rakoczy 1996:126–27.

34. Plutarch, *Quaest. Conv.* 5.7.1 [Mor. 680C; 682A]; cf. Alciphron, *Ep.* 1.15. For the superlative *baskantikos*, see Plutarch, *Quaest. Conv.* 5.7.5 [*Mor.* 682D].

35. So also Rakoczy 1996:126.

36. Thomsen 1991/1992:21; see Vol. 1, chap. 2.

kisses that the curious cannot count or "fascinate with an evil tongue" (*mala fascinare lingua*). Virgil links an evil tongue with praise and envy. He tells of a singing match between Thyrsis, a shepherd, and Corydon, a goat herder. The latter wishes to sing as sweetly as his idol Codrus, and Thyrsis responds,

> Shepherds of Arcady, crown with ivy your rising bard, that Codrus' sides may burst with *envy* (*invidia rumpantur*); or, should he praise me unduly, wreathe my brow with foxglove, lest his *evil tongue harm* (*noceat mala lingua*) the bard that is to be. (Virgil, *Ecl.* 7. 21, 25; LCL trans.)

The text illustrates the fear of praise coming from the envious and resulting in injury, and the link of envy with an evil tongue, identical to the association of Evil Eye and evil tongue.

The term *baskanos* also appears as a modifier of *daimôn* and denotes the "Evil-Eyeing demon" (*ho baskanos daimôn*). This demon eventually was identified with the "envious demon" (*ho phthoneros daimôn*), as envy and the Evil Eye became associated and eventually equated.[37] Evil demons in general were regarded as a major cause of misfortune, injury and death. Philosophers such as Democritus, Empedocles, Plato, Xenocrates, and Chrysippus took the existence of such *phaula daimones* most seriously.[38] According to Aeschylus, evil demons caused the demise of the Greek army at Salamis (*Persians* 1005–1007).[39] Such demons were seen as personifications of punishing powers such as the *Ate* ("Ruin"), *Erinnyes* (the Furies), or even *Dikê* ("Justice").[40] Various potencies were named *baskanos* (e.g., Daimon, Moira, Ares); others were named *phthoneros* (e.g., Daimon, Hades, Thanatos, Moira, Tyche, Nemesis). Hades, deemed "envious" and seen as a prominent cause of death (*Anthologia Palatina* 7.712), was later called *baskanos* as well.[41] Centuries later, Plutarch wrote of the athlete Polycrites of Naxos having fallen victim to an Evil Eye and envy,[42] with her grave accordingly named, "grave of the Evil Eye (*baskanou taphos*).[43]

---

37. See Geffcken 1930.

38. Rakoczy 1996:113 n337. On *daimôn* see Andres 1918 and on its semantic history see Nowack 1960.

39. For "evil demon" (*kakos daimôn*) see also Aeschylus, *Persians* 354; for "evil and envious *daimon*" see Plutarch, *Alcibiades* 33; Xenophon, *Cyropedia* 5.1.28.

40. Rakoczy 1996:94 n254; 118 n361.

41. Rakoczy 1996:118 and n361. An undated funery epigram from Stratonikeia portrays the Evil Eye of Hades as being consumed with envy over the beauty of the deceased (Kallinikos).

42. Plutarch, *Mul. virt., Mor* 254F.

43. See Rakoczy 1996:118.

An early reference to the "envious demon" appears in a fragment of a fifth century BCE poetess, Corrina of Tanagra, who speaks of *ho phthoneros daimôn* which threatens children.[44] The tragedy of Sophocles (c. 496–406 BCE), *Electra* (1466–1467), attributes the death of Orestes to "the envious demon."

The Evil Eye demon and the envious demon gradually were equated and merged, with both, in all likelihood, developing from the concept of the envy and destructive eye of the gods.[45] Rakoczy traces this development to the fourth and latter centuries when the nouns *phthonos* and *baskania* also were being used synonymously.[46] The adjectives *baskanos* and *phthoneros* were used alike to identify this daimon as a spirit possessing an Evil Eye full of envy that is directed at youthful beauty in particular.[47] The association and frequent synonymous use of *baskanos* and *phthoneros* and their respective word families remained constant in the ancient world, the Middle Ages and beyond; it is a feature of biblical writings as well.

The related neuter term and diminuative *baskanion* appears as early as Aristophanes to designate an "anti-Evil Eye device" that protects the shops of bronzeworkers from the Evil Eye.[48] *Probaskanion* as an anti-Evil Eye apotropaic appears in Plutarch's *Table Talk* concerning the Evil Eye (*Quaest. Conv.* 5.7.3 [*Mor.* 681F]).[49] The biblical writing, *Epistle of Jeremiah* (v. 69/70), mentions a *probaskanion* erected in a cucumber field to ward off the Evil Eye; see Volume 3, chap. 1.

The previously mentioned fragment of Pherecrates (Frag. 189: "The dead hare casts an Evil Eye upon me") is instructive on several counts. First, it shows that *animals* as well as gods and humans were thought to possess and cast an Evil Eye. Other examples will be presented below. Second, the fact that the animal is *dead* shows that there is no connection of the Evil Eye with magic, which would require the intention of some living agent. Third, the Evil Eye is assumed to work automatically, with no involvement of intentionality. When the Evil Eye is linked with envy, on the other hand, intention and moral disposition are usually involved. Later centuries show

44. Corrina of Tanagra, Frag. 10 (ed. Page); Rakockzy 1996:117.

45. W. G. Sumner, in his classic study, *Folkways* (1960/1906:428–38), saw the notion of an Evil Eye linked with the concept of uncleanness and both as "products of demonism."

46. Rakoczy 1996:117.

47. So Geffcken 1930:38; Herter 1950:27; Rakoczy 1996:118.

48. See Aristophanes, *Frag.* 592.2 (ed. Edmonds). Chantraine 1968:167, under *baskanos*, translates *baskanion* as "an object that protects against charms, an amulet."

49. See also *Vita Aes.*, recension G 16 for ugly hunchbacked Aesop mocked as a *probaskanion* for his owner.

that the Evil Eye eventually was thought to operate both inadvertently and intentionally. The Evil Eye's operating automatically even in the case of the dead may explain the custom of covering the eyes of the dead so they cannot injure the living, or hooding the heads of those to be executed so that their eyes cannot wreck revenge on those present at the execution.[50] The head of the Gorgon/Medusa and its death-dealing eye, we shall see below, lost nothing of its power even when separated from Medusa's body.[51]

Often hereafter terms of the *bask-* family are joined to verbs of seeing and glancing, which explicate the act of looking and staring implied in these *bask*-terms. One early example is a Comic fragment which asks:

> Why are you looking so sharply at the alien evil, you most Evil-Eyeing person, while you look past your own affairs? (*Comica adesp.* 359)[52]

The sentiment resembles a question posed by Jesus in the Gospel of Matthew about removing the log in one's own eye before concerning oneself with the speck in another's eye (Matt 7:3–5): "Why do you see the speck that is in your brother's eye, but do not notice the log that is in your own eye?"

Earliest literary attestation of the noun *baskania* occurs in a dialogue of Plato (c. 429–347 BCE), the *Phaedo*.[53] Countering the praise received for his skillful argumentation, Socrates, Plato's teacher, is quite cautious:

> "My friend," he says, "do not speak loudly, lest some Evil Eye (*baskania*) put to rout the argument that is to come." (Plato, *Phaedo* 95b)[54]

The notion that public praise evoked envy and the Evil Eye is, of course, an old one, as the *Agamemnon* of Aeschylus has shown. Using loud words to praise is all the more dangerous and suspicious. Words of praise evoke envy and the Evil Eye, just as does the sight of a victorious king treading on purple tapestries. The connection of seeing and speaking (Evil Eye and evil tongue) again is evident.

From this point onward, it is *baskania* and its paronyms[55] that serve as the technical and standard terms for "Evil Eye," "injure with the Evil Eye,"

---

50. So Sartori 1899:221–22; Rakoczy 1996:126 n392.

51. On Medusa/Gorgo see below, pp. 134–38.

52. *ti tallotrion, anthrope baskanôtate/ kakon oxyderkeis; to d' idion parablepei* (*Comica adespota* 359, *CAF* [ed. Kock 1888], vol. 3:476).

53. Rakoczy 1996:121.

54. Chantraine 1968:167 translates *baskania* as "evil spell."

55. "Paronyms" are words of the *same* language related to each other by virtue of deriving from the same root; e.g. Greek *baskanos* and *baskania* deriving from the Greek

and protection against the Evil Eye.[56] *Baskania* also now becomes personified and identifies the goddess of fascination or Evil Eye malice (e.g. Callimachus of Cyrene [c. 305–c. 240 BCE]). *Frag.* 1.17 of his poem, *Aetia*).[57] Terms for Evil Eye and envy will be juxtaposed, or used synonymously, or substituted for each other. The practice illustrates the close association long been made between Evil Eye and envy, even when terms of the *bask-* family were not yet used in the literature.[58] Rakoczy notes that Demosthenes (*Orat.* 18.305) used *phthonos*/envy as a substitute for *baskania*. This substitution, he plausibly speculates, may be due to a pervasive *Sprachtabu* against the more dangerous term *baskania*.[59] Explicit juxtapositions are more numerous.[60] A fourth century CE incantation recorded in Aristaenetus (*Epistle* 1.4) aims at protecting simultaneously against the dynamic duo of Envy and the Evil Eye: "Envy, leave beauty alone! Evil Eye Malice, leave comeliness alone!" (*apitô phthonos tou kallous, apitô baskania tês charitos*). It also illustrates the vulnerability of beauty to envy and the Evil Eye.

Many such combinations could have been intended as hendiadyses. A hendiadus is a figure of speech stating two qualitities for the same phenomenon, usually by two nouns joined by "and." The combination makes explicit what was implicit in early centuries: the intimate association of Evil Eye and envy. At the same time, *baskania* and *phthonos* technically are distinguishable, with *phthonos*/envy denoting a disposition, and *baskania*/Evil Eye, the physical conduit and external projection of this emotion.[61] Thus envy would be the disposition or emotion turned into a harmful weapon against others

root *bask-*. "Cognates," on the other hand, are words of *different* languages related to each other by virtue of deriving from the same root of some initial term; e.g. *envy* (English), *envidia* (Spanish) deriving from *invidia* (Latin). The terms often are used inaccurately as synonyms.

56. See Rakoczy 1996:124 and n383. On *baskania* and *baskanos* see also Giangrande 1969; Dickie 1993a.

57. See also PGM/PMag. 4.1451; for Callimachus on *baskania* see Meillier 1979:135, 137–39.

58. Rakoczy 1996:123 n381; see also Matantseva 1994:115 n38 (as illustrated on amulets).

59. So Rakoczy 1996:128 n403; also 41, 61–62, and 83 n204; see similarily Matantseva 1994.

60. See, in later time, Dio Chrysostom, *Orat.* 45.53 (*phthonos kai baskania*); *Orat.* 77/78.15.6 (*phthonos kai to baskainein*); also *phthonos kai zêlotypia* (*Orat.* 44.8.6; 61.13.1; 61.15.6; 77/78.2.9;77/78.14.4); *zêlotypeô kai phthoneô* (*Orat.*74.8.6); *zêloô* and *baskainô* (*Orat.* 77/78.37.7). Philo of Alexandria has many such juxtapositions (see Vol. 3, chap. 1) as does Plutarch, *De recta* [*Mor.* 39C]; *Non posse* [*Mor.* 1090C]; *Quaest.Conv.* 5.7 [*Mor.* 682D].

61. Rakoczy 1996:120. See also the scholium on Plato, *Alcibiades* 2.147c regarding the differences of *phthoneros, epiphthonos,* and *ho baskanos* (Rakoczy 1996:127 n400).

by an active Evil Eye. Common usage, however, did not regularly adhere to this distinction.

In connection with Plato, it is appropriate to say a further word about *envy and Evil Eye of the gods*, since it is Plato who weighs in against the notion of divine envy and is instrumental in bringing about its demise. This divine envy (*phthonos theôn*), it was believed, was provoked by humans who attempted to rise above their allotted station in life and sought more than their fair share of the goods at hand. The envy of the gods, sometimes also named *nemesis*, a concept that was then personified as the goddess Nemesis, consisted in their intense displeasure, indignation at, and intolerance of human *hybris* (unlimited ambition), immodesty, bragging, or ostentatious piety. Such behavior aroused divine envy, which would then, through a divine Evil Eye, strike down such arrogant persons "on the make," destroy their success, and reduce them to their "proper place." This unsettling notion of divine envy—to which mention is made from Homer onward[62]—cast a long shadow over the Greek world for four centuries or more until Plato, divesting the gods of all passions altogether, declared that "envy is outside the circle of the gods" (*Phaedrus* 247a) and that "God is "free from envy" (*Timaeus* 29e). Plato's view prevailed and thereafter the notion of the envy of gods waned to insignificance.[63]

Plato, finally, is important also for representing what was becoming the prevailing theory concerning the eye and vision in the ancient world, namely that of an active eye and an "extramission theory" of vision. Prior to Plato, the eye, as previously mentioned, was spoken of by poets and dramatists in terms that indicated its presumed active nature. The poets and tragedians were eventually joined by the philosophers and scientists who theorized on the eye as active organ sending forth emanations (Plato, Euclid, Ptolemy, Galen). This so-called "extramission theory of vision" was not without rival in the ancient world, as Epicurus, Lucretius, and Aristole attest. It did prevail, however, as the dominant view through antiquity and the Middle Ages until the advent of modern science. It represented a direct contrast to modern scientific theory and research initiated by Al-Kindi (c.

62. See, e.g., Homer, *Iliad* 11.543 (*nemesaô*); .*Odyssey* 4.118; 5.120; Pindar, *Pythian Odes* 10.20; *Isthmian Odes* 6.39; Aeschylus, *Agam.* 461–474; Sophocles, *Philoctetes* 776 (*nemesis*); *Electra* 1466–67; Euripides, *Orestes* 1362; *Iphigenia in Aulis* 1090; Euripides, *Alcestis* 1036; Herodotus, *Hist.* 1.34; 3.40–47; Aristophanes, *Wealth* 87–91.

63. For studies on envy, envy of the gods, and the association of envy and Evil Eye in antiquity, see below, p. 85, n148. On *aphthonia*, the lack of envy, as a divine attribute see van Unnik 1971, 1973. In connection with Plato, Rakoczy (1996:121–34) also comments on the close connection of nemesis, envy, envy of the gods, and the Evil Eye. On *nemesis* and relevant texts see also Walz 1852; Hornum 1993 (with an appendix of *nemesis* texts); and Kaster 2003, 2005. On nemesis see also below, pp. 99–101, 139.

801–873 CE), Avicenna (c. 980–1037), and Al-Hazen (965–1039) in the Middle Ages. This theory holds that the eye is a passive, receptive organ, processing stimuli entering the eye from without.[64] The dominance of the extramission theory of the eye as active, rather than passive, organ is necessary to grasp in order to understand thinking about the Evil Eye. It provides plausibility to the notion of an active Evil Eye and thus helps account for the wide dissemination of the belief. Our consideration below of salient features of Evil Eye belief and practice will review the history of ancient and modern scientific theory of the eye and vision.[65]

Aristotle (384–322 BCE) had much to say about the specific nature of envy and of its relation to *nemesis*, which we shall consider below in our discussion of envy. In regard to the eye and vision, he and the Peripatetic school seem to have entertained both active and passive eye theories on different occasions. On the one hand, regarding the eye as passive rather than active, he can reject the explanations of the atomists, Plato, and the Stoics and focus instead on the *medium* such as air, which intervenes as an active agent between a passive eye and a passive object.[66] On the other hand, he can view the eye as active, adopting an extramission theory of vision.[67] This is illustrated by his observation in his treatise *On Dreams* concerning the effect of menstruating women's glances on mirrors:

> When menstruating women look into very clean mirrors, the surface of the mirror becomes as a blood-red cloud; and when the mirror is new, it is not easy to remove this dirt; but when it is old, it is easier. (Aristotle, *Insomn.* 459b 27–32)

A further illustration likewise implies the notion of an active, injurious Evil Eye. Aristotle refers to the practice of the pigeon to spit (*emptuei*) on its young three times

> so that they are not injured by an Evil Eye (*hôs mê baskanthôsi*). (Aristotle, Frag. 347)[68]

---

64. The prevailing modern "intromission theory of vision" that the eye is a passive rather than active organ was anticipated centuries earlier by the pioneering research of the Arabian polymath Abu Ali al-Hassan ibn al-Haytham (965–1039 CE; Latin name: Alhazen). In his seven-volume *Book of Optics* (1011–1021 CE) he proved through scientific experimentation the inaccuracy of earlier extramission theory and the correctness of the intromission theory of vision.

65. See below, pp. 57–60, 75–80.

66. Aristotle, *de Sensu* 2.438 a25–a27; *de Anima* 2.7 418 a26–419 b3.

67. Aristotle, *Insomn.* 460a 1–2; 460a 24–25, Rakoczy 1996:134–55, and below, pp. 58–59.

68. Aristotle, *Frag.* 347 = *Fragmenta varia* 7 [ed. Rose]) = *Zoica.* 7.39.347.17). See

Such spitting was a conventional mode of anti-Evil Eye protection.[69] The spitting to which the apostle Paul refers in his letter to the Galatians (4:14) refers to this very practice.[70]

Two passages attributed to Aristotle (=Pseudo-Aristotle) and representing Peripatetic tradition include specific mention of the Evil Eye and provide additional details of Evil Eye belief and practice. The first affirms the actuality of the Evil Eye (*ou pseudos esti to katabaskainesthai*) and continues,

> For vision, because it is strongly moved, spreads a remarkable force, since they [those seeing] send it forth with the help of fire-like breath (*pneuma*). (Pseudo-Aristotle, *Problemata inedita* 3.52)[71]

Looking with an Evil Eye (*katabaskainein*) is explicitly identified here as an act of vision involving blasts of fire-like breath projected from the eye. This concept becomes standard in ancient Greek, Roman, Israelite and Christian thinking about the Evil Eye.[72] The notion of an active eye underlies the later Italian term *jetttore* for "a person *casting* (*jettare*, "to cast, throw, project") the Evil Eye."

A second important passage occurs in the *Problemata physica* (c. 250 BCE), a redactional stage of the Hippocratic tradition and part of the *Corpus Aristotelicum*. Attributed posthumously to Aristotle, it is a text of major importance for features of Evil Eye belief and practice and for a nuanced, scientific explanation of its effect at meals.[73] Book 20 of the *Problemata physica* deals with the practical use of plants and herbs. The question presented in the passage (*Prob. phys.* 20.34, 926b 20–31) is "why is rue [the herb] said to be a means of protection against the Evil Eye (*dia ti to pêganon baskanias phasi pharmakon einai*, 926b 20).[74] Both *baskania* and the verb *baskainein* appear in this comment.

> Why is rue (*to pêganon*) supposed to be a protection/cure (*pharmakon*) for the Evil Eye (*baskania*)? Is it because people expect to be struck by the Evil Eye (*baskainesthai*) when they have eaten

also Athenaeus (*Deipn.* 9.394B) and Aelian (*Var.hist.* 1.15) referring to this same practice and adage: *tôn neottôn genomenôn, ho arrên emptuei autois, apelaunôn autôn ton phthonon, hôs phasin, hina mê baskanthôsi.*

69. See also Theocritus, *Idyls* 6.39; Pliny, *NH* 28.35, 39, and below pp. 176–80.

70. On this Pauline text see Vol. 3, chap. 2.

71. *Aristotelis opera omnia*, ed. Bussemaker 4:332.

72. See C. G. Gross on "the fire that comes from the eye" (1999).

73. See Rakoczy 1996:141–55 (text on 1996:141 n467), who finds here an enlightened attitude toward Evil Eye "singular in the ancient world" (1996:142).

74. *Pharmakon* in this context means "protection" or "means of healing."

greedily? Or when they are anticipating food not agreeing with them and are suspiciously inclined to what is brought to them? For instance, when they take anything from the same table for themselves, they offer a share to another with the words "so that you do not Evil-Eye me (*hina mê baskanêis me*)." All diners partake nervously in the drink and food presented. The result [of this unease] is that these [i.e. the food and drink] are either forcibly retained [in the body] or are spit out as the food rises and is vomited out and gas develops from the liquids, which cause complaints and stomach-aches. Now when one ingests rue beforehand, which has a natural warming effect, this loosens the organ that receives the food as well as the remaining body. Thus the enclosed air can then escape. (Pseudo-Aristotle, *Prob. phys.* 20.34, 926b 20–31)

The text is noteworthy on several counts. First, it is one of the earliest appearances in literature of the verb *baskainein*. Second, it illustrates the dread of the Evil Eye in the simple affairs of everyday life, and meals in particular. Third, it shows that the Evil Eye was thought to cause illness of various kinds, including vomiting, upset stomach, and gas while dining. This has a bearing on the biblical texts that concern the Evil Eye at meals. dining, and eating (Prov 23:6; Sir 14:10; Deut 28:54–57; Mark 7:1–23).[75] Fourth, it indicates that the herb rue (*to pêganon*), like garlic, was one of the means employed for warding off the Evil Eye at table and preventing negative effects. Fifth, it describes how and when the herb was used. Rue was ingested before a meal because it was thought to protect against the ill effects of an Evil Eye (*baskania*) that was active at meals and endangered the diners. In later time, silver metal replicas of sprigs of rue, known as the *cimaruta*, were worn as amulets under the assumption that even an image of the herb alone sufficed to stifle the Evil Eye.[76] Sixth, this text, however, goes on to present a scientific physiological explanation of how rue actually works. It is an account that considers the physical malady of upset stomach, vomiting, and the physical properties of rue for settling an upset stomach. Ingested rue neutralizes the effects of eating too quickly, which was done in order to avoid being struck by the Evil Eye of a fellow diner. Hasty eating results in inadequate digestion, which in turn leads to the accumulation of gas causing pain. Rue has a warming effect that relaxes the stomach and allows accumulated gas to escape. On the medicinal properties of rue, see Pliny, *NH* 20.51.131–143.

75. See Racoczy 1996:141–55; also Seligmann 1910:1:234–40; 1922:379–81; Gifford 1958:48–50.

76. For an illustration see Seligmann 1:296–97, figs. 50a, 50b.

This explanation, as Rakoczy stresses,[77] is remarkable in that it does not treat rue simply as an apotropaic protective against the Evil Eye (as was supposed in later as well as earlier time). Rue rather is explained as a natural remedy for an upset stomach. The diners ascribe the upset to the Evil Eye. The explanation indicates the direct physical cause of the vomiting to be hasty eating, and states the medicinal effect of rue for alleviating the vomiting resulting from this hurried consumption. The Evil Eye is not entirely ignored or denied as a cause, but is treated as a remote, rather than direct, cause of upset stomachs. The direct cause of the malady (hasty eating) is distinguished here from the remote fear of an Evil Eye active at meal settings, which prompted gobbling down food in the first place. The ill effect that the diners wanted to avoid—namely harm from an Evil Eye—they ironically brought about by eating too rapidly. This diagnosis of an Evil Eye case, according to Rakoczy, is unique among ancient references to the Evil Eye.[78] It shows how the belief remained in vogue, even in the presence of scientific explanations.

A final point of interest is that the text records the custom of diners offering a portion of food to others lest these dining companions cast an Evil Eye which either spoils the food or strikes the diners with upset stomachs. The custom either involves assuring that all diners get the *same amount* of food to forestall envy directed against some eating more than others. Or the practice assures that all diners eat of *the same food* so that if any have spoiled it with their Evil Eye, all, including the Evil Eye casters, will be poisoned. Either concern could have been operative.[79] In any case, this practice could well lie behind the latter custom of *tipping* those serving meals. This mode of sharing food or, more precisely, money for food, forestalls the servers from envying and Evil-Eyeing the food and the diners they serve. "Tip" and "tippling" (drinking) are cognates in English. The German for "tip" is *Trinkgeld* (literally, "money for a drink") and likewise appears to presuppose the custom.[80] Anthropologist George Foster (1972) has cogently traced this custom of tipping to fear of envy and the Evil Eye.

This juxtaposition of Evil Eye belief and practice with a rational explanation of the soothing effects of a medicinal herb appears to be unique in the ancient world. Not only does it involve a remarkably enlightened understanding of rue and and the cause of stomach ache; it also shows how Evil Eye belief and scientific reasoning can coexist cheek by jowl.

77. Rakoczy 1996:141–55.
78. Ibid., 143–44, 275.
79. See ibid., 142 n470.
80. So also the French for "tip," *pourboire* (lit." for a drink").

Elsewhere Aristotle, in explaining types of distress or grief, juxtaposes *phthonos* and *baskania* and defines them as "grief at the good fortune of others" (*Divis* 52–53). We will return to this point when we look more closely at the association of the Evil Eye and envy.[81]

The Hellenistic Age (beginning 332 CE) and the broader Greco-Roman period (332 BCE–sixth century CE) saw a marked increase in literary references to the Evil Eye and the *baskanos daimôn*, a proliferation of anti-Evil Eye amulets and apotropaics, and a waning of mention of the envy of the gods. Important texts, apart from the biblical writings which we shall be examining separately, include the *Quaestiones Convivales/Table Talk* of Plutarch, the *Aethiopica* of Heliodorus, the *Argonautica* of Apollonius of Rhodes, and the discussion on physical maladies by Alexander of Aphrodisias—all to be discussed below. These texts, like the ones already discussed, show how over centuries educated persons as well as commoners took seriously the envy of the gods, the existence of envious and Evil-Eyed demons, and the projecting of envy and malice through Evil-Eyeing humans. These are not beliefs restricted to the unenlightened masses but were held across the social spectrum. Evil Eye belief and practice attested in the Greek sources is mirrored in the Roman sources down through Late Antiquity.

EVIL EYE TERMINOLOGY

The conventional, most frequently employed, Greek terms for "Evil Eye," "injure with the Evil Eye, "Evil Eye malice," "protection against the Evil Eye" etc. were words of the *bask-* root: *baskanos* (adjective and substantive), *baskainein* (verb), *baskania* (noun) and their numerous paronyms. This *bask-* word group is a large one. Its size and wide semantic field indicate the importance and breadth of the concept involved. This family of terms does not appear in Homer or Hesiod or in literature prior to the fifth century BCE. However, it has been suspected that references to the Evil Eye were implied when mention was made of the eye casting a destructive or injurious glance.[82] Terms of the *bask-* family appear more frequently only in later Greek texts (e.g. Demosthenes, Plato, Aristotle, Strabo, and the Hellenistic poets), but the concept of the Evil Eye itself is very ancient.[83] The long and constant association of the Evil Eye and envy (more on this below) has also

81. As to Aristotle's mention of *baskanos*, see also *Fragmenta varia* 8 (ed. Rose) (= *Historica* 8.44.559.22) regarding a tomb called "tomb of the Evil Eye" (*baskanou taphos*).

82. See Rakoczy 1996:39–96.

83. Bernand 1991:97–98

led scholars to suspect that references to *phthonos* (envy) also implied, or perhaps even substituted for, explicit mention of *baskania, baskainein,* or *baskanos* etc. under the pressure of a *Sprachtabu* against the use of dangerous terms. Beginning in the fifth century, the terms initially appear more frequently—in comedy and invective discourse more than than in tragedy or poetry, perhaps because *bask-* terms were regarded as vulgar and unfit for poetry and literature.[84] In this case, the term *envy (phthonos)*, which was so consistently associated with the Evil Eye, would have substituted for *bask-* terms. Modern Greek offers a similar case where the less dangerous terms *to mati* ("eye") or *matiasma* ("Evil Eye") are considered less dangerous and offensive than *vaskania* ("Evil Eye") and are used in place of *vaskania*. As for the practice of avoidance of use altogether, many contemporary Neopolitans are still reluctant to even utter their term for Evil Eye namely *jettatura* or *malucch.*

   Baskanos and *baskainein*, as already indicated, are attested in Greek literature since the fifth century BCE[85] and *baskania* since Plato.[86] The etymology of *baskainô* and its family of terms is uncertain.[87] Thomas Rakoczy (1996:124 n384, 124–25) lists three possibilities: (1) derivation from *baskein* ("to speak, speak evil of") and *baxis* ("expression") thus leading to *baskainein* ("to hex with words"; German: *beschreien*); (2) origin as a loanword from the Thracian-Illyrian region, based on the Indogermanic root *bha-* ("speak") and parallel to *phêmi, phaskô* (cf. Latin *fascinare, fascinus, fascinatio*); (3) *baskanos* could be a kind of magical *binding* similar to *fascinus* derived from *fascis* ("bundle") or *fascia* ("band"); cf. Greek *phaskides*. The first two theories have in common the idea that the root is fundamentally linked with the act of speaking and have the greater weight than no. 3. This idea accords with the later connection of injurious looking and injurious speaking.[88]

   The more cogent theory combines elements of (1) and (2). *Baskainô*, related to the verbs *bazô, baskô, phaskô* ("speak, say") and traceable to Thracia-Illyria (Hofmann 1966 *s.v.*), is likely based on an Indo-germanic root *bha-* (rendered with *beta* or *phi*) meaning "to speak." This root is identical

84. So Rakoczy 1996:256 n19.

85. *baskanos*: Aristophanes, *Knights* 103, *Wealth* 571; *baskainein*: Pherecrates, Frag. 189 (Kassel-Austin, *PCG*) (=Frag 174 in LSJ). For *baskanos* in the sixth century BCE see possibly Pythagorus, Frag. 11.2 136 (ed. Zuretti 1934).

86. Plato, *Phaedo* 95b.

87. See Hoffmann 1966; Frisk 1973; Chantraine 1968:167; see also Seligmann 1910 1:4–5, 31; Delling 1964.

88. Seligmann (1910 1:31), representing a minority opinion that found no following, takes *baskainein* to derive from *phaesi kainein*, "to slay with the eyes."

with the root *bha-* meaning "to appear" (compare *phêmi* and *phainô*, respectively; Hofmann 1966:396–397). In Greek, the initial *bh* was rendered by *beta* (thus *baskainô*, *bazô* ["speak, say"], *baskô* [akin to *bainô*, "go"]) or by *ph* (thus *phaskô* ["say, assert"], *phêmi* ["say, assert"], *phainô* ["cause to appear, make known"]). In Latin, the initial *bh* was rendered by *f* (thus *farior*, "speak" and *fascino* for *baskainô*, *fascinus* for *baskanos* etc.). No aspect of the *bask-* terms themselves concerns the eye or seeing. Eventually however, words of this root denoted evil speaking (of evil and slanderous words) as well as evil harmful looking, evil tongue as well as Evil Eye, slanderous speech as well as malicious glance. *Baskainô* clearly means "to slander" in Plutarch, *Life of Pericles* 12.1, as well as "to Evil Eye" (*Quaest. Conv.* 5.7); in Aristophanes and Demosthenes, as noted above, terms of the *bask-* word family denote slanderous speaking as well as malicious looking. A similar combination of evil looking and evil speaking appeared centuries earlier in the Akkadian incantation cited in Volume 1, chapter 2, which spoke of "the Evil Eye, the Evil Mouth, and the Evil Tongue."[89] In Latin texts, *mala lingua* ("evil tongue") also appears occasionally in connection with *malus oculus* ("Evil Eye").[90] Literary contexts in which *bask-* terms appear, however, as well as iconography of the Evil Eye (and envy) and accompanying inscriptions as on amulets, demonstrate the common connection of *bask-* terms with the eye, glance, and seeing.

The verb *baskainein* is a denominative construction from *baskanos*. The adjective *baskanos*, has the sense of "evil-eyeing," "possessing an Evil Eye," or "malicious" (looking at)" or "slanderous, defamatory" (speaking). It is thus used in connection with malicious looking or speaking.[91] *Baskanos* as substantive can have the meaning *slanderer*.[92] *Baskanos* as adjective meaning "Evil-Eyed" modifies *ophthalmos* in the expression *baskanos ophthalmos*, "Evil Eye."[93] It also appears frequently in the phrase *baskanos*

---

89. Vol. 1, chap. 2.

90. Catullus, *Poems* 7.11–12 (*mala fascinare lingua*); Virgil, *Ecl.*7.28. On the etymology of *bask-* see Rakoczy 1996:124–25 who views the word family as originally more associated with speaking and an evil tongue than with looking and an evil eye; see also Seligmann 1910 1:4–5; Delling 1964. A connection of *fascinus* to *fascia* ("band"; cf. Greek *phaskides*) or *fascis, fasces* ("bundles") with the sense of something "attached" has also been suspected.

91. For "malicious, slanderous, defamatory" (speaking), see Aristophenes, *Knights* 103–104, *Wealth* 571; Demosthenes *Orat.* 18.242, 317; cf. Strabo, *Geog.* 14.1.22. For malevolent looking see Plutarch, *Fabius Maximus* 26.3. *Demetrius* 50.5; *Dio* 47.3; *De laude* [*Mor.* 540B]; *An seni* [Mor 796A]; *De frat.* [*Mor.* 479B].

92. See Demosthenes *Orat.* 18.132; Vettius Valens, *Anth.* 358.5).

93. Plutarch, *Quaest. Conv.* 5.7 [*Mor.* 680C; 682A]; cf. Alciphron, *Ep.* 1.15; also *Anth. Pal.* 5.22.5–6. For *baskanos* modifying *omma* (eye), *baskanon omma*, see Nonnus,

daimôn, the "Evil Eye demon." Plutarch, in his *Life of Dio* (2.6), writes of "evil demons with the Evil Eye, who send envy (*prosphthonounta*) against virtuous men" (*ta phaula daimonia kai baskana prosphthonounta*), linking the Evil Eye explicitly with demons and envy. These demons seek to impede the good deeds of the virtuous and to incite in them feelings of terror and distraction to make them shake and totter in their virtue, lest they obtain a happier condition than these demons after death.[94] A novel by Chariton, *Chaereas and Challirhoe* (first–second centuries CE) refers often to a *baskanos daimôn* that turns good events to ruin (1.1.16; 3.2.17; 6.2.11). *Baskanos* and *phthoneô*, Evil Eye and envying, are linked here as well.[95] A stirring novel of the next century, the *Aethiopica* by Heliodorus, has a main character, Theagenes, complaining about the noxious effect of the Evil-Eyeing demon (*daimon baskanias*, a synonym of *baskanos daimôn*, 2.1.3). A detailed theory concerning the demon, its link with envy, and the destruction it causes is also presented.[96] The Christian apocryphal *Acts of Thomas* (mid-third century CE) likewise speaks of a *baskanos daimôn* (§§43–44) and in §100 an Evil Eye (*baskanos ophthalmos*, mss. U, P) is identified as an "evil demon" (*ponêros daimôn*, Ms. P).[97] *ActsThom.* 2 tells of a certain Charisius, minister to an Indian king, who complains this *baskanos ophthalmos* (Evil Eye) has alienated the affection of his beautiful wife. The variant to this reading of *baskanos ophthalmos* (ms U) is *phthoneros daimon* (ms H), showing the equivalency of both expressions and the association of Evil Eye and envy.

Many references to the *baskanos daimôn* occur in funerary epitaphs of the imperial period.[98] The *baskanos daimôn*,[99] alias the *phthoneros daimôn* (Envy demon)[100] is identified with Hades and often in funerary inscriptions and tomb epitaphs is said to be responsible for the deaths of those remembered in the epitaphs.[101] A funerary inscription at Aezanis in Phrygia likewise

---

Dionysiaca 31.74.

94. For the *casting* of envy (*prosphthonoun*) see also Plutarch, *Alexander* 33; *Camillus* 36.

95. Chariton *Chaereas and Challirhoe* 4.1.12; 5.1.4–5. For *baskanos* (substantive) linked with *phthonos* see also Galen, *De libris propriis liber* 19.21.

96. See *Aeth.* 3.7; 4.1.12; 5.1.4–5; see also Pausanius, *Descr.* 3.9.7; 7.14.5–6.

97. Bonnet 1959:212.

98. So Peek 1960:31 and Rakoczy 1996:102 n296

99. See, e.g., CIG 2.3715, *baskanos hêrpase daimôn*; Kaibel, *Epigr. Gr.* no. 345, line 1.

100. See, e.g., CIG 4.6858, *tôi phthonerôi daimoni;* cf. also IG 14.1362; *ActsThom* 100 etc.

101. See e.g. Kaibel, *Epigr. Gr.*, no. 496, line 6: *baskainei tois agathoi[s Aidês]*; cf. also no. 381, line 3: *Aideô baskaniois* (case of a four year old girl's death). See also no. 734,

mentions *baskanos ê phthonos*, "Evil Eye or envy," as causing death.[102] This *baskanos daimôn*, a Greek equivalent or version of the Mesopotamian Evil-eyed demon, is most likely the personification of *baskania* and *baskosynê* (as also the figures of Lilith, Gulla/Goula). There is no mention of this *baskanos daimôn/phthoneros daimôn* in the Bible, however—a remarkable and note-worthy difference. Post biblical Christians, on the other hand, eventually equated this *baskanos daimôn* with the Devil/Satan.[103]

Baskanos used as a substantive can denote "a person or creature with an Evil Eye," "an Evil-Eyeing person or creature," "fascinator," *jettatore* (Ital.), "one who has and casts an Evil Eye."[104] It is part of Demosthenes's arsenal of rhetorical put-down terms: "you Evil-Eyeing nobody" (*Orat.* 21.209); "this Evil-Eyeing fraud" (*Orat.* 25.80); "this Evil-Eyed wretch" (*Orat.* 25.83). Strabo (*Geog.* 14.2.7) records that the legendary Telchines of Rhodes were considered by some as "*baskanoi* and *goêtai* ("deceivers"). The superlative, 'most-evil-eyed envier' (*baskanôtatos*) appears in a fragment of a Greek poet (*Comica adespota* 359) cited above on p. 17. A gravestone inscription (third century CE) found at Rome (CIG 4.9669) has an instance of the substantive *baskanos* with the meaning "Evil Eye." A grieving father laments that though he never did anything evil, "falling foul of evil fate and a bitter Evil Eye (*baskanô pikrô*), I suffered such things as no one has (suffered)"—the loss of his dear wife and children.[105] It could, however, also be rendered, "bitter Evil-Eyeing person."

Baskanos as a substantive also can denote "one who *speaks* maliciously, slanderer, defamer."[106] Usage of *baskanos* thus points to the association of

line 2: *baskanôi pikrôi*, "bitter *baskanos*" [causing death] (in the cemetary of Priscilla in Rome).

102. For *baskanos daimôn* in the inscriptions and its association with envy as cause of death see also Kaibel, *Epigr. Gr.* nos. 345, 1; 379, 1; 1140, 4 (a Christian inscription: "Flee Beliar, dragon . . . *baskanos*. . . "); see also CIG 2.2059. 2.3715, 3.6200; 2.1935; 2.2062; 3.3846i, 3847i, 4095; 4.6860. CIG 4. 9688 is a Christian inscription in iambic verse from a cemetery in Rome concerning a Christian who died having suffered an evil fate and from the Evil Eye (*baskanôi*). For *baskanos daimôn* see further Pausanius, *Descr.* 3.9.7; 7.14.5–6; Lucian, *Amores* 25; *Asinus* 19; Chariton, *Chaereas and Challirhoe* 1.1.16; 3.2.17; 6.2.11; Heliodorus, *Aethiopica* 2.1.3; 3.7; 4.1.12; 5.1.4–5.

103. See Kaibel, *Epigr. Gr.*, no. 1140, 4. See also Rakoczy 1996:118; Geffcken 1930:39–40; Meisen 1950:157–58; and Vol. 4, chap. 2.

104. Demosthenes *Orat.* 21.209; Menander, *Perikeiromenê* 279; Strabo. 14.2.7; Plutarch, *Dio* 47.3; *Quomodo adulator* [*Mor.* 60E]; *De cap.* [*Mor.* 92B]; *Mul. virt.* [*Mor.* 254E]; *De tranq.* [*Mor.* 471A]; *De laude* [*Mor.* 543A]; *De frat.* [*Mor.* 485E]; *Praecepta* [*Mor.* 821C]; *Comp. Arist.* [*Mor.* 854D].

105. Horsley 1987:30–31 renders the phrase "bitter malevolence." On *baskanos* in funerary epitaphs see Lattimore 1942.

106. See Demosthenes *Orat.* 18.132; Vettius Valens, *Anth.* 358.5; Strabo, *Geog.*

the Evil Eye with the actions of both looking and speaking (*mala lingua*, "evil tongue").[107]

Baskanos, in sum, appears frequently in the phrase *baskanos daimôn* ("Evil Eye demon"), occasionally in the phrase *baskanos ophthalmos* ("Evil Eye") making explicit the connection of *baskanos* and eye, and is regularly joined with, or equivalent to, the adjective "envious" (*phthoneros*). It denotes malicious activity of looking or speaking with harmful intent, with the former more frequent than the latter. Used as a substantive, it denotes "one who possesses or casts an Evil Eye," an "Evil-Eyed person," and on fewer occasions, "slanderer, defamer" (i.e. one who works evil through speech). *Baskanos* in the Bible is discussed in Volume 3.

The verb *baskainein* ("to look harmfully at; to injure with a glance; to cast an Evil Eye upon; to Evil-Eye someone or thing") is attested since the fifth century BCE. A fragment of the comic author Pherecrates[108] contains the report of a hunter: "The dead hare casts an Evil Eye upon me." Aristotle observed that it is the custom of pigeons to spit on their young chicks to prevent their being injured by the Evil Eye (*hôs mê baskanthôsi*).[109] Later Aristotelian tradition, as noted above, indicated that dining guests share food with others at the table "So that you do not Evil-Eye me (*hina mê baskanêis me*)."[110] Demosthenes, the Greek Athenian orator (384–322 BCE), comments concerning a loyal citizen's appropriate response to Demosthenes' discharge of his responsibilities:

> It was not his duty to look with an Evil Eye (*baskainein*) upon a man who had made it his business to support or propose measures worthy of our traditions. (*Orat.* 18 [*On the Crown*] 307.)

The sixth idyl of Theocritus (third century BCE), the father of Greek pastoral poetry, describes a rustic, Damoetas, seeking to arouse the love of the beautiful Galatea. He imagines himself to be the monster Polyphemus/Cyclops (cf. *Odyssey*, book 9), and tries to win Galatea's affection by claiming to love another. Upon hearing this, she becomes envious and wastes away (verses 25–27), struck by his Evil Eye. Damoetas/Polyphemus, after seeing his image reflected in the water and wanting to avoid Evil-Eying himself, states,

14.2.7, and above, pp. 25–26.
107. On this see further below, pp. 82–83, 176, 273–74.
108. Pherecrates, Frag. 189 (Kassel-Austin, *PCG*) (Frag 174 in LSJ).
109. Aristotle, *Fragmenta varia* 7 (ed. Rose) (= *Zoica* 7.39.347.17) (=LSJ: *Frag.* 347).
110. Pseudo-Aristotle, *Prob. phys.* 20.34, 926b 24.

> I spat three times onto my chest that I might not be struck by (my
> own) Evil Eye (*hôs mê baskanthô de tris emon eptusa kolpon*), for
> this the hag Cotyttaris taught me. (Theocritus, *Idyl* 6.39)

Spitting as a defensive measure against the Evil Eye, we shall see, was common in the ancient world.[111] The apostle Paul mentions the custom of spitting as protective against the Evil Eye in his letter to the Galatians (4:14).[112] Theocritus's *Idyl* 6.39 further illustrates the notion that Evil-Eyed persons were thought capable of auto-fascination, injuring themselves with their own Evil Eye.[113]

Strabo (64 BCE—21 CE), in his Geography (*Geog.* 14.2.7), observes that the tribe of the Telchines was said to be Evil-Eye possessors (*baskanoi*). Also excelling in metal workmanship, they, in turn, were Evil-Eyed (*baskanthênai*) by their envious fellow iron workers.

Like the adjective and substantive, the verb *baskainô* (with the accusative) can also denote maliciously maligning someone ("slander," "disparage," "defame").[114] Here again is evidence of the close association of an Evil Eye and an evil tongue. As with *baskanos* and *baskania*, the verb *baskainô* also is closely linked with envying[115] and is often used (with the dative) as equivalent to "to envy" (*phthonein*) or with the sense of "grudge, begrudge."[116] Another Idyl of Theocritus portrays a quarrel between a pair of rustics involving an Evil Eye accusation. The goat-herd Comatas accuses a shepherd named Lacon of maliciously stealing his goatskin coat with his envious Evil Eye:

> the goat-skin Crocylus gave me . . . and you, villain, even then
> were enviously Evil-Eyeing (*baskainôn*), and now in the end you
> have stripped me naked. (*Idyl* 5.13)[117]

---

111. See also Theocritus, *Idyls* 7.126–127; 20.11; Theophrastus, *Char.* 16.15; Tibullus, *Elegies* 1.2.98; Athenaeus, *Deipn.* 9.50; Herodianus, *Ab excessu* 2.4.5; Aelian, *Var. hist.* 1.15.

112. On this spitting, see Vol. 3, chap. 2; on the apotropaic custom in general see below, pp. 176–80.

113. See also Plutarch, *Quaest. Conv. 5.7* [*Mor.* 682B], regarding a certain Eutelides, who like Narcissis, saw his reflection in the water and in fact did Evil Eye himself (*auton baskainein*) resulting in a deadly illness (*nousos*).

114. Pherecrates, Frag. 189 (Kassel-Austin, *PCG*) (=Frag 174 in LSJ). Demosthenes *Orat.* 8.19; 18.189; cf. Plutarch, *Demosthenes* 16.4.

115. See, e.g. Plutarch, *De recta* 39d; *De cap.* 92c; *De curios.* 518c; *De invidia et odio* [*Mor.* 538D]; Lucian, *Charidemus* 23.

116. See Demosthenes *Orat.* 20.24; Dio Chrysostom, *Orat.* 78.25, 37; Flavius Philostratus, *Life* 6.12; Lucian, *Navigium* 17; Aelian, *Var. hist.* 14.20.

117. For *baskainein* see also Plutarch, *Agesilaus* 22.4; *Pompeius* 21.4. 29.1; *Caesar*

In funeral inscriptions, Hades personified is said to Evil-Eye to death good persons.[118] Alexander of Aphrodisias (third century CE) explains why and how children are injured by persons casting an Evil Eye (*baskainousi*; *Problemata physica* 2.53).

On rare occasion *baskainen* can also have the sense of "being miserly." Lucian of Samosata (second century CE) tells of a certain Eucrates reporting about an Egyptian holy man named Pancrates whose mysterious powers included making a broom perform menial household chores. Eucrates states,

> I was was eager to acquire this power, but I had no way of learning this from him, for he was miserly (*ebaskaine*) with this power, although openly generous with everything else. (Lucian, *Philopseudes* 35)

The association of the Evil Eye with miserliness and stinginess, on the other hand, is a notable feature of the biblical references to ther Evil Eye, as we shall see in Volume 3.

A strengthened form of *baskainein* is the composite verb *katabaskainein* ("injure with the Evil Eye"), which is synonymous with *baskainein* and occasionally joined with *katablepein* ("look intently at").[119] Of Theagenes, one of the main characters of Heliodorus's novel *Aethiopica*, it is said,

> he has an envious gaze and injured you with his Evil Eye by looking (at you). (*Aeth.* 4.5)[120]

The composite verb appears also in *Aeth* 3.8. as well as earlier in Pseudo-Aristotle, *Problemata inedita* 3.52, which insists on the actual existence of the Evil Eye (*ou pseudos esti to katabaskainesthai*).

Another composite of the simple *baskainein* is the verb *probaskainein*, which, the standard Greek dictionary LSJ claims, can also mean "envy before" or "envy because of" something.[121] The compound verbs *katabaskainein* and *probaskainein*,[122] like *baskainein*, primarily denote "injure with an Evil Eye" and illustrate the association of hostile glance and looking with

---

59.6. *Demosthenes* 16.4; *De cap.* [*Mor.* 91B–C]; *De invidia et odio* [*Mor.* 538D]; *Quaest. Conv.* 5.7 [*Mor.* 682B; 683A]; *Praecepta* 806A; Herodianus [3rd CE] *Ab excessu* 2.4.5.

118. See IG 7; cf. Kaibel, *Epigr. Gr.*, no. 581). At Tanagrae of Boetia, near the village of Skimatari and near the church of St. Taxiarchis, is a large stone with an address to death: *[b]askainei tois agathois [Aidês]*, "Hades Evil-Eyes to death good persons" (Kaibel, *Epigr. Gr.*, no. 496, 6, funerary epigram, Greece, second century CE).

119. Plutarch, *Quaest. Conv.* 5.7 [*Mor.* 680C, 682E], joined with *katablepein* (680D).

120. *Aeth.* 4.5: *epiphthonon echôn to blemma kai se têi theai katabaskênas.*

121. LSJ 1471, under *probaskainô*. See also Dickie 1993a.

122. Libanius, *Decl.* 29.2.

envy at someone. In the Greek Bible, the verb *baskainein* occurs in Deut 28:54, 56; Sir 14:6, 8; and Gal 3:1.

An alternative expression for *baskainein/*"to Evil-Eye (someone)" is *kakôs eidenai*, and *ophthênai* (lit. "to look maliciously at," to look intensely at"). Philostratus (second–third century CE) states that a youth imprisoned by the emperor Domitian complained to Apollonius that "the emperor Evil-Eyed me" (*ho basileus kakôs eiden*). Following a search for physical features that could have prompted this on Domitian's part, he is told,

> the emperor must be mistaking all these traits for others, or you would not tell me that you were Evil-Eyed by him" (*kakôs hyp' autou legeis ophthênai*). (Philostratus, *Life of Apollonius of Tyana* 7.42)

The verb *derkesthai* ("to stare," "to flash [with the eye]"), which also appears in connection with the Evil Eye, when used absolutely may also imply casting the Evil Eye.[123]

The noun *hê baskania* means "the Evil Eye," "malign influence of an Evil Eye," or "Evil Eye malice." It also is regularly joined with, or equivalent to, "envy" (*phthonos, zêlos*).[124] In the first attested use of *hê baskania* (Plato, *Phaedo* 95b), Socrates, when praised (*mega legein*) by a companion for his skill in argumentation, warns "do not boast loudly [in your praise], lest some Evil Eying malice (*baskania*) overturn the subsequent argument."[125] Here *baskania* denotes an evil force that is aroused by praise and that then elicits envy. This notion that praise, compliments and admiration arouse the Evil Eye already appeared in Aeschylus's *Agammenon* with Agammenon fearing that his being praised would arouse the envy of the gods (*Agam.* 947) and remains a feature of Evil Eye belief down to the present day. Just as sight of someone's success arouses envy, so also does hearing about it, even indirectly when encountering spoken praise.[126] This association is considered below in the discussion of the Evil Eye complex.[127] *Baskania* is also mentioned, identified with Hades, on funerary epitaphs, as a cause of

---

123. See, e.g., Homer, *Iliad* 11.36–37; *Odyssey* 19.446.

124. This form is to be distinguished from a similar appearing *ta baskánia*, which is the nominative plural of the diminutive, *to baskánion* ("anti-Evil Eye protective").

125. On *baskania* and Plato see Rakoczy 1996:121–34.

126. On the Evil Eye and praise, compliments, and admiration see Maloney 1976: 102–48 and *passim*; McCartney 1924, 1943.

127. For the noun *baskania* see also Hippocrates, *Epistulae* 17, 204, 295; Demosthenes, *Orat.* 19.24; Aristotle, *Prob. phys.* 20.34, 926b; Theophrastus, *Char.* 28.7; *Cyranides* 1.7; 1.21; 4.26; 4.67; 4.72 (in Kaimakis, ed., *Die Kyraniden*, 14–310). On *baskania*, see Dickie 1993a.

death.[128] *Baskania*, the act of malevolent looking, also was associated with slander, the act of malicious speaking. Both were also associated with the third finger of the right hand which was said to be "full of Evil Eye malice (*baskanias*) and slander (*loidorias*)."[129] *Baskania* was personified, like *Phthonos*, as the "Evil Eye goddess" or equated with the goddess *Nemesis*, also regarded as the goddess of the the Evil Eye.[130] Callimachus (third century BCE) asserts that his song was "stronger than the Evil Eye (*baskania*)."[131] The geographer Strabo (*Geog.* 16.4.17) reports that women wore necklaces of cowrie shells as protection "against occurrences of the Evil Eye (*anti baskaniôn*)." The composite noun *probaskanía* also denotes "Evil Eye" (BGU 3.954. 9, sixth century CE).

The association or synonymous use of *baskania* (Evil Eye) and envy (*phthonos, zêlos*) is frequent.[132] "The busybody," Plutach observes (*De curios.* [*Mor.* 518C]),

> is possessed by the affliction called "malignancy" (*epicheirekakia*), a relative of envy and the Evil Eye (*phthonou kai baskanias*).

"Envy," he goes on to clarify, "is pain at another's gain, while malignancy is joy at another's loss." This latter emotion is now known as *Schadenfreude*. Dio Cassius (second–third century CE) reports (*Roman History* 59.17.4) that Caligula, before crossing a pontoon bridge from Bauli to Puteoli, sacrificed to Poseidon, other gods, and the deity *Phthonos*, "lest some *baskania* overtake him." *Baskania* appears nine times in Heliodorus's *Aethiopica* and is explicitly identified as an alias of envy in *Aeth.* 3.7.3.[133] It has been conjectured that the term *phthonos* gradually took on the sense of the more dangerous word *baskania* (Evil Eye), so that the latter term was then less frequently used.[134] Modern Greek use of two terms for Evil Eye, *matiasma* and *vaskania,* seems to involve a similar distinction between less harmful and more harmful terms. *Matiasma* tends to denote the unintentional (and less

128. Bonnard 1991:99–102.

129. *Peri palmôn mantikê* 92, a third-century BCE work attributed to the legendary soothsayer and healer, Melampus.

130. See Callimachus, Frag. 1.17; Seligmann 1910 1:295; Rakoczy 1996:130 n411.

131. Callimachus, *Epigrams* 21.4; . cf. PGM (PMag.) 4.1451.

132. See, e.g., Democritus, Frag. 77 (Diels-Kranz, *FVS* 68 A 77.23–24); Demosthenes *Orat.*18.305; Aristotle, *Divis* 52–53; Teles, *Peri apatheias* 56; Plutarch, *De recta* 39C, 39D; *De curios.* [*Mor.* 518C]; *Quaest. conv.* 5.7.6 [*Mor.* 683A]; *Non posse* [*Mor.* 1090C]; for *baskania* cf. also *De Alexandri* [*Mor.* 344A].

133. Heliodorus, *Aeth.* 2.1.3 (*daimôn baskania*); 2.33.2 (*daimonos baskania*); 3.7.2; 3.7.3; 3.9.1; 3.18.3; 3.19.2; 4.5.4; 4.5.6.

134. So Mantantseva 1994:115 n38 and Rakoczy 1996:41, 61–62, 83 and n204.

harmful) everyday look of envy, whereas v*askania* denotes the intentional malicious use of the evil glance.[135]

A poetical form of *baskania* is *baskosynê,* which appears only infrequently[136] and occasionally on amulets.[137] *Baskosynê* was one of numerous names by which the infant-threatening demon Gyllou was known.[138] *Gyllou* is not a native Greek term, but is rather of Mesopotamian derivation (Babylonian *gallou,* "demon"?), and identified a female demon whose *modus operandi* was similar to that of Lilith, another female demon of oriental origin who operated at night and attacked newly-born babies. A fragment of the Greek poet Sappho (Frag. 44), contains the phrase *Gellous paidophilôtera.* A gloss by the lexicographer Hesychius explains *Gellou,* a non-Greek term, as "ghoul" that steals newly-born infants (*daimôn hên gynaikes ta neogna paidia phasin harpazein*).[139]

The personification of *baskania, baskosynê, phthonos,* and *fascinus* as divinities, and the concept of a *baskanos daimôn,* graphically demonstrate the interpenetration of religion, psychology, and religion, in antiquity and the impossibility of their separation. This is a further reason militating against the prejudicial classification of the Evil Eye as an instance of irrational "magic" and "superstition."[140]

The neuter singular noun *to baskánion* denotes a *protective amulet against the Evil Eye.* The diminuative neuter singular to *baskánion* (plural, *ta baskánia*) is to be distinguished from the feminine singular *hé baskanía.*[141] The first such textual occurrence of *to baskánion* with this meaning is a fragment of Aristophanes [fifth century BCE][142] that is later cited by Julius Pollux (second century CE), as he explains its form, purpose and apotropaic use by metalworkers:

135. Dionispoulis-Mass 1976:42. In the Greek Bible, *baskania* occurs in Wis 4:12 and 4 Macc 1:26; 2:15.

136. Poeta, *De herbis* 51.31; P. Mag. Lond. 122.34; P. Mag. Par. 1.1400.

137. See, e.g., SEG 9.2, no. 818; P.Mag.Lond. 122.34; P. Mag.Par. 1.1400.

138. See Perdrizet 1922:24–25 on Gyllo, including reference to Gyllo as *Baskosyne* in *A Prayer of Saint Michael.*

139. Cf. also Sophocles, *Greek Lexicon,* under *gellô, gelô, gilô.*

140. On this point, see below, pp. 64–65, 69–71, 120–21.

141. For the plural, LSJ gives the meaning "malign influences" (Kaibel, *Epigr. Gr.* no. 381). But this meaning would better fit the plural of *hê baskanía* than the plural of *to baskánion,* i.e. *ta baskánia,* which refers to plural anti-Eye amulets. On the other hand, Bernand (1991:98) indicates that *to baskánion* can designate "an evil spell" as well as "protection against an evil spell" similar to the double meaning of *to pharmakon* ("poison" as well as "poison's remedy.")

142. Aristophanes, Frag. 607 (Kassel-Austin, *PCG*).

> The metalworkers had the custom of making grotesque [probably deformed] objects and hanging them in front of the ovens to ward off (apotropêi) envy (phthonos). These were called "baskánia," as Aristophanes also says: "except when one buys it, needing it as an Evil Eye protective (baskánion) for the oven of a metalworker. (Onom.7.108)[143]

The explanation is another illustration of the connection of the Evil Eye and envy, of amulets as "apotropaics," and of the principle of "like influences like" (a baskánion warding off baskania and envy).

This equivalent term for baskánion, namely the compound probaskánion ("anti-Evil Eye protective device") occurs in the Bible (LXX Ep. Jer. 69/70) denoting a "scarecrow against the Evil Eye" set up in a cucumber patch as mentioned above (p. 16).[144] Probaskanion likewise appears in Plutarch's Table Talk concerning the Evil Eye, where reference is made to "the kind of anti-Evil Eye amulets (to tôn legomenôn probaskaniôn genos)" that are thought to protect against being struck by another's envy (phthonon) or Evil Eye:

> Their strange look attracts the attention of the [Evil] Eye (tês opseôs) so that it exerts less force upon its victims. (Plutarch, Quaest. Conv. 5.7.3 [Mor. 681F])

Here again Evil Eye and envy are linked, while a rational explanation is given of how the amulet works. Phrynichus (second century CE) in his Praeparatio sophistica echoes this description while pointing out the equivalency of baskánion and the less cultured probaskánion:

> "Baskánion," or as the uneducated say, "probaskánion," is a human-like object (but varying a bit from human form), that artisans hang it in their workshop so that their products are not damaged by the Evil Eye (baskainesthai).[145]

Strabo (Geog. 16.4.17) recounts that such anti-Evil Eye amulets were worn by the women of the Troglodytes of Libya. We will have occasion below

143. The verb apotropein ("ward off") also occurs here, the term that gives us the adjective/substantive "apotropaic," meaning something that averts, wards off (evil).

144. LSJ defines probaskánion as a "safeguard against witchcraft, amulet, or scarecrow hung up before workshops or in fields," but the definition inadvisably omits reference to the Evil Eye, which the term actually does imply.

145. Phrynichus, Praeparatio sophistica 53.6 (ed. von Borries 1911); cf. also 68. For probaskánia (plural) see BGU 954, 9 [PGM 2. 9, p. 217]; van Haelst 1976 Catalogue, no. 720; Bonneau 1982:24. On probaskania, prosbaskania see Dickie 1993a.

to comment further on how the Evil Eye was thought to operate and to consider numerous other types of anti-Evil Eye devices and stratagems.[146]

Hunchbacks (as deformed figures) were regarded as having apotropaic power and serving as *baskánia/probaskánia* against the Evil Eye. Aesop, the famed teller of fables, was described as small, dark-skinned, squint-eyed, having knit eyebrows, hunchbacked and considered so ugly that his fellow slaves quipped that he was bought by his owner only to serve as a *probaskánion* for his shop.[147] A hunchback appears as an apotropaic in the famous Evil Eye mosaic in Antioch and elsewhere.[148] The terms *baskánion* and *probaskánion* thus denote amulets and figures of any shape and kind employed as protection against envy/theEvil Eye.

Other terms of the *bask*-root include *baskantikos* ("Evil-Eyeing," "malicious," combined with "envious);[149] *baskanôs* (adverb, "with an Evil-Eye"),[150] *ho baskantêr/baskantêros* ("Evil-Eyeing person, Evil Eye possessor" and synonymous with *ho baskanos*, and *hypobaskanos*.[151]

Terms of the *bask*- root beginning with the alpha privative (*abask*-), by contrast with the last mentioned terms, are in greater abundance. *Abáskanos* (adj.) means "free from the Evil Eye," "safe from the Evil Eye," "unharmed by the Evil Eye").[152] The Cynic philosopher Teles of Megara (third century BCE) in his discourse *On Freedom from Passion* (*Peri apatheias* 55–56) juxtaposes *aphthonos* and *abaskanos*, "free from envy and the Evil Eye."[153] The substantive *to abaskanos*, "something free from the Evil Eye/envy," appears in Philo (*Post.* 138) and the adverb *abáskanôs*, "without the Evil Eye/envy,"

---

146. A Christian amulet (sixth century CE) reads, "that you may drive from me, your servant, the Evil Eye demon (*daimona probaskanias*)." Here *probaskania* is a feminine singular noun equivalent to the simplex feminine singular *baskania*, meaning *Evil Eye*; rather than a plural of the neuter *probaskanion*, meaning *anti-Evil Eye amulet*; see Mouton-Milligan 1930:106.

147. *Vita Aes.*, recension G 16 (ed. Perry 1952); cf. also *Vita Aes.*, recension W 16. See Trentin 2009:134–139.

148. On this mosaic see Levi 1941, 1947; Norris 1991:257–58, and below. On the hunchback as apotropaic see below, pp. 126–27, 251–52.

149. Plutarch, *Quaest. Conv.* 5.7 [*Mor.* 682D] ("envious and Evil-Eyed state of mind, habit," *phthontikê kai baskantikê hexis*).

150. Josephus, *Ant.* 11.4.9; Porphyry of Tyre (third century CE) *Life of Pythagoras* 53.

151. Rendered by LSJ, *s.v.*, assuming the equivalency of *baskanos* and *phthonos*, as "somewhat envious"; see Pseudo-Manetho, *Apotelesmatica* 5.45 codd.

152. LSJ, assuming the equivalency of *baskanos* and *phthonos*, Evil Eye and envy, renders "free from envy."

153. In Stobaeus, *Anth.* (ed. Wachsmuth and Hense, vol. 4:56); see also Josephus, *War* 1.9.4 (LSJ: "free from prejudice").

in Marcus Antoninus (second century CE) 1.16. *Abáskantos* (adj., "safe from, secure against, unharmed by the Evil Eye") occurs frequently.[154] The standard Greek-English lexicon of LSJ renders *abáskantos* "*secure against enchantments, free from harm*," without explicit reference to the Evil Eye.[155] In an active sense, according to LSJ, again omitting reference to the Evil Eye, *abáskantos* can mean "*acting as a charm* or *protection against witchcraft*."[156] The Latin grammarian Charisius (c. 400 CE) comments that the Latin expression *praefascine*, which is spoken to assure that no Evil Eye is intended when giving compliments, means

> *sine fascino* [lit. "without the Evil Eye"], which the Greeks call *abaskanta* (*quod Graeci abaskanta dicunt*). (Charisius, *Ars Grammatica* 2.15, CGL 306)

The adjective *abaskánistos* means "safe from, unharmed by, the Evil Eye."[157] The adverb *abaskántôs* means "free from Evil Eye injury," "without being Evil-Eyed."[158] A saying included in the Greek epigram collection, *Anthologia Graeca* (contained in the *Anthologia Palatina*), reads:

> may your long nose be kept safe from the Evil Eye![159]

The use and significance of the adjective *abaskantos* in the papyri is quite interesting. Appearing more than seventy times in the papyri, far exceeding other terms of the *bask-* root, it often was used as a *proper name*.[160] At the outset of this volume we have already seen that the term appears in numerous personal papyri letters containing the wish that X "be safe from,

---

154. CIG 3.5053, 5119 (Nubia); *Cat. Cod. Astr.* 7.234; especially of children, BGU 8.11, al.; *P.Oxy.* 2. 276 (late third century CE); *P.Oxy.* 2.292 (c. 25 CE); *P.Oxy.* 2.300 (first century BCE); *Rev .Ég.* 1919:204 (second century CE); *Rev. Ég.* 1919:201 (early third century CE); *P.Oxy.* 6.930 (second–third centuries CE); *P.Oxy.* 14.1666 (third century CE); *Cyranides* 1.4 (ed. D. Kaimakis 1976) regarding children kept healthy and safe from the Evil Eye; cf. also 2.2.

155. LSJ, *sub abaskantos.*

156. LSJ *sub abaskantos*; see, e.g., *abaskantos anthrôpois kai zôois* (variant reading in Dioscorides, *De materia medica* 3.91. For the meaning, "not harming," again omitting reference to the Evil Eye, LSJ cites P. Mag. Leid.W. 18.7; see also *Vita Aes.* recension W 30.

157. Plutarch, *Amatorius* [*Mor.* 755D]; LSJ renders "free from malice."

158. *P.Oxy.* 2.292.12 (c. 25 CE); SB 7660.13 (c. 100 CE); cf. *Anth. Pal.* 11.267 (= *Anthologia Graeca* 4. 136).

159. *kai gar abaskántôs rina tripêchyn echeis, Anthologia Graeca* 4.136 = *Anthologia Palatina* 11.267.

160. Bonneau 1982:24.

unharmed by, the Evil Eye."[161] An equivalent for *abaskantos* in such expressions is *anepiphthonos* ("unharmed by envy," "safe from envy"). Epicurus, for example, wishes that the young Pythocles, with his outstanding qualities, remains "safe from envy (*anepiphthona*; Plutarch, *Adversus Colotem* [*Mor.* 1124C]).

The term *abáskantos* also was popular as a *proper name.*[162] A papyrus document, P.Oxy. 44.3197 (dated Oct 20, 111 CE), refers to a slave named *Abaskantos* and another named *Abaskantion*. This document records a private agreement among heirs of a wealthy Roman family in Alexandria regarding the slaves allotted to the three heirs.[163] The twice occurring name *Abaskantos*, Horsley notes, "is closely akin to 'Abaskantion the Ethiopian' (line 13)."[164] *Abaskantos* also was the name of a secretary of emperor Domitian and was a name most commonly used of children.[165] Horsley cites four letters, all containing formalized requests that children be kept unharmed by the Evil Eye (*ta abaskanta paidia*), and all but PSI 825 are probably Christian.[166] The letters are are discussed in Volume 4, chapter 2 on the post-biblical Christian evidence. A second century CE letter of Sabinianus "to his brother and lord, Apollinarius" concludes with "I greet the most worthy Abaskantos (*Abáskantos*) and all your household" (P.Mich VIII 499).[167] A third century papyrus, P.Oxy. 40.2937 ii.8, mentions a certain "Abáskantos, surnamed *Kalotychos.*"[168] His surname, meaning "good luck," states in the

161. See above, pp. 2–4.

162. For *abáskantos* as a proper name see CIG 1. 192, 263, 270, 271, 272; see also CIG 2.2457; 2.3006, 3.3865, 4192, 4366, 4418, 4718, 5063, 6278; 4. 6821, 7060; IGRRP 1.347 (funerary inscription, Rome, containing the name of *Satorinôi Abaskantou Klaudianôi Smyrnaiôi,* "Saturninus, son of Abaskantos . . ."). See also *abasskantos* (CIG 1. 1306). Trismegistos, an interdisciplinary portal of papyrological and epigraphical resources (online: http://www.trismegistos.org/index.html) reports a total of 51 occurrences of the name *Abaskantos*. For a Latin instance see Pliny the Younger, *Ep.* 10.11, regarding a Lucius Satrius Abascantus for whom Pliny requests of Trajan the grant of full Roman citizenship. On *abaskantos* as a proper name in Roman Egypt and on its apotropaic function in general see especially Bonneau 1982, whose study on *abaskantos* is the most complete to date.

163. Described in Horsley, *New Docs* 1 (1981) 69–70, no. 24.

164. Ibid., 70.

165. Ibid.

166. P.Oxy 20 (1952) 2276.28 (third century CE); PSI 7 (1925) 825.21–22 (fourth century CE, provenance unknown); PSI 8 (1927) 972.4 (*ta abaskanta sou tekna.* Oxyrhynchos? fourth century CE); and P.Mich. 8 (1951) 519.3–7 (*kai [t]ou (sic) ab[ask] antan sou oikou* . . . , Karanis, fourth century CE).

167. White 1986:182–84, no. 115, esp. letter B, 183–84.

168. Bonneau 1982:26.

positive what his name, *Abáskantos,* expresses negatively.[169] It is quite likely that the name was purposely given to afford permanent protection against injury from the Evil Eye.[170] A Latin text from Nomentum in Italy, *AE* 119, referring to an ". . . Ab]ascantus," possibly a child,[171] illustrates the assumption into Latin of the Greek use of *Abaskantos* as personal name. Tertullian (*Scorp.* 10) speaks of "the Teleti (the perfect ones), the *Abascanti* (those unharmed by the Evil Eye) and the Acineti ("the steadfast ones") as good persons in contrast to the Valentinians.[172]

The problem with translating *baskania* and paronyms with abstractions such as "evil" or "malignancy" (as do some lexicons and various translations of ancient texts) is that such renditions obscure the reality that *baskania* and paronyms always point to the Evil Eye.[173]

Other Ancient Greek Expressions for "Evil Eye"

Beyond the *baskania* family of terms, there are also other, less explicit, expressions for Evil Eye. Terms of the *bask-* family are regularly combined with mention of the eye (*omma, ops, ophthalmos*) and the act of looking at, staring at etc. This association is even more pronounced in one of the expressions for Evil Eye, namely *baskanos ophthalmos.*[174] A related related phrase is the explicit expression *ophthalmos ponêros* (lit. "Evil Eye"),[175] the Latin equivalents for which are *oculus malus* (Sir 14:10) *oculus nequam* (Matt 6:23; 20:15; Luke 11:34), *oculus obliquus* (Horace, *Epist.* 1.14.37), and *oculus malignus* (Grattius [c. second century BCE] *Cynegetica* 399–407). Given this association of *bask-* terms and references to the eye and looking, it is possible that various verbs of seeing, looking askance, staring and the like may also imply reference to the Evil Eye (and envy) where the context makes this likely. This includes such verbs as *ophthalmizein, epophthalimize-*

---

169. So Bernand 1991:103.

170. For the Christian naming of children Abaskantos as a prophylactic measure see Robert 1944, 1951:146, no. 55. Bernand (1991:103) sees the custom of assigning an apotropaic name to neutralize the Evil Eye as originating in Egypt and then adopted in Greece; so also Sauneron 1966:51, 63 and nn77–78.

171. So Horsley, *New Docs* 1 (1981) 70.

172. For the vocative, *abaskante,* see *Vita Aes.,* recension W 30. On *abáskantos* see R. S. Bagnell's note to *O.Flor.* 15.2–3 in Bagnell 1976:54–55; see also Gibson 1975:153–54.

173. Rakoczy 1996 makes the same point.

174. Plutarch, *Quaest. Conv.* [*Mor.* 680C; 682A]; Alciphron, *Ep.* 1.15; *Acts of Thomas* 100.

175. For *ophthalmos ponêros* see Maximus of Tyre, *Philosophumena* 20.7b; and in the Bible, Sir 14:8, 10; 31:13; Matt 6:23, 20:15; Mark 7:22; Luke 11:34.

in; *ophthalmiaô, epophthalmiaô; epophthalmizô;* blepein, epiblepein, katablepein; parablepein, prosblepein.[176] Biblical examples include *epiblepein* (LXX:
1 Sam 2:29, 32, lit. "to look" [*blepein*] "over" [*epi*], and *hypoblepesthai* (LXX:
1 Sam 18:8–9 regarding Saul "looking askance" and envying David with an
Evil Eye, and Sir 37:10, with *hypoblepesthai* [v. 10a] associated with "those
who envy" [v. 10b] and "Evil-Eyed person" [*baskanou*, v. 11]).

Other expressions for Evil Eye are "oblique eye," and "looking askance."
A fragment of Callimachus[177] speaks of the Muses looking at someone as at
a child, but "not with an oblique eye (*othmati paidas mê loxôi*)" and remaining friendly for life.[178] This association of the oblique eye and looking
askance (with an Evil Eye) is also evident in Latin where *oculus nequam* in
the Vulgate translates *ponêros ho baskainôn ophthalmôi* (Sir. 14:8) and *ophthalmos ponêros* (Sir 31:13; Matt 6:23; Mark 7:22; cf. Luke 11:34. In Latin,
as we shall note below, the connection of Evil Eye and looking is even more
evident in the use of *invidere* ("to look over") and its paronyms to translate
on occasion *baskainein* and its paronyms. Thus mention of looking, staring, and menacing use of the eye, or reference to the noxious or poisonous
rays of the eye, may all imply reference to the Evil Eye, with context being
determinative.

"Envy" Paired with, Synonym of, or Replacement for "Evil Eye"

The ancient notion that envy was discharged through the (evil) eye[179] is just
one piece of evidence illustrating the long association of envy with the act of
intense staring and envious looking with an Evil Eye. The consistent linking
of the Evil Eye (*baskania*) and envy (*phthonos, zêlos*) shows that the combination functioned as a hendiadys (two terms for one entity), or that the
two terms functioned as synonyms, or that *baskania* etc. assumed the sense
"envy," (as indicated in LSJ, BDAG), or that *phthonos* etc. on occasion could

176. See Hesychius, Photius, Suidas; eg. *epophthalmiaô*: P.Oxy 14.1630.6 ("envious
eyeing," ep]ophthalm[iôn]tes) in an application for a lease of land at an increased rent
in Greco-Roman Egypt). The verb also apperars in the minutes of a legal proceeding
against a certain Syrion who is charged with "casting an envious eye" (*epopthalmiasas*)
on animals left to to sons by their deceased father (P. Thead. 15 [280–281 CE], Hunt
and Edgar, *Select Papyri* 2 (1934):208–11, §261. See also P.Lond. 5.1674 and Moulton-
Milligan 1930:469 sub *ophthalmos*. On Greek terms in general for seeing and eye see
Prévot 1935.

177. Callimachus, Frag. 1.37–38 (from the *Aitia*)

178. See Rakoczy 1996:58, 230–31. For "oblique eye" or "looking askance" see also
Horace, *Epist.* 1.14.37 (*obliquo oculo*); Apuleius, *Metam.*4.14; Symmachus, *Ep.* 1.48;
Anthol. Pal. 5.22.5; see also above, p. 10.

179. See, e.g., Aeschylus, *Agam.* 947: *mê tis prosôthen ommatos baloi phthonos.*

have the sense of "Evil Eye."[180] Substitution of *phthonos* (the more innocuous and acceptable term) for *baskania* (the more dangerous and avoided term) also appears to have occurred.[181]. Since terms of the *zêlos* word family also could denote envy, specimens of this word family likewise could imply reference to the Evil Eye, with the context again being determinative. Plutarch's *Table Talk,* as indicated above, provides an extensive example of the juxtaposition and association of terms for Evil Eye, looking, and envy.[182] Discoursing elsewhere on the topic of "envy and hate,"[183] Plutarch states:

> for they [those who envy] Evil Eye (*baskainousi*) those who are thought to be good, thinking that they possess the greatest good, namely virtue. And even if they [those who envy] receive some benefit from the fortunate, they are tormented and envy (*phthonountes*) them for both the intention and the power.[184]

The associations and usage found in Plutarch are representative of Greek (and Latin) literature in general. This is not to suggest that *bask-* and *phthon-* families of terms were not distinquishable in meaning. For in general *phthonos* and its family of terms (and *zêlos* and its family of terms) denoted a disposition and feeling that was then transmitted and discharged through

180. For example, for the equation of "envious glance" (*epiphthonon echôn to blemma*) and "look at with an Evil Eye" (*katabaskênas*) see Heliodorus, *Aethiopica* 4. 5: *alla kai toioutos ôn pathoi drimytera hôn dedraken, epiphthonon echôn to blemma kai se têi theai katabaskênas.*

181. It is possible that *phthonos* etc. either took on the sense of *baskania* etc. or that the former was substituted for the latter because in amulets, *phthonos* often replaces *baskania* (the more dangerous word), so Mantanseva 1994:115 n38. The case is similar in modern Greek with its two main expressions for Evil Eye: *matiasma* (and related terms) and *vaskania*. Terms of the first word family for "Evil Eye" (*kako mati* [i.e. *kakon ommation*], *matiazô* [i.e. *ommatiazô*], *matiasma*) are used more frequently than *vaskania* (the more negative and less frequently spoken term). In Naples, Italy, and environs, *jettatura*, the Neopolitan term for Evil Eye, has tended to be avoided altogether. These are modern instances of the the continuing *Sprachtabu*: see above, pp. 9, 18, 25.

182. Plutarch, *Quaest. Conv.* 5.7: *baskainein* (*Mor.* 681D; 683A), *baskania* (*Mor.* 683A), *baskanos* (*Mor.* 680C); *baskantikos* (*Mor.* 682D), *katabaskainein* (*Mor.* 680C, 682B; 682D, 682E); *ophthalmos baskanos* (*Mor.* 680C; 682A), *probaskanion* (*Mor.* 681F); *katablepein* (*Mor.* 682A; 682D); *phthonos* (*Mor.* 682B), *phthonein* (*Mor.* 683A), *phthontikos* (*Mor.* 682D); *kataskopein* (*Mor.* 682E). See also Plutarch, *Dio* 2.6.1; *Demetrius* 50.5; *De recta* [*Mor.* 39D]; *De cap.* [*Mor.* 91B, 92B–C]; *Mul. virt.* [*Mor.* 254E]; *De curios.* [*Mor.* 518C]; *De invidia et odio* [*Mor.* 538D]; *An seni* [*Mor.* 796A]; *Non posse* [*Mor.* 1090C]. For *parablepein* and *bask-*, see Plutarch, *De tranq.* [*Mor.* 496B]; *De curios.* [*Mor.* 515F].

183. Plutarch, *De invidia* [*Mor.* 536E–538E].

184. Plutarch *De invidia* [*Mor.* 538D]. LCL with modification by John H. Elliott.

the conduit of the (Evil) Eye (*baskanos, baskania*) of the envier.[185] This relation of disposition/emotion (envy) and physical mechanism of conveyance (the [Evil] Eye), however, was not always distinguished in everyday usage, with the result that the terms "envy" and "Evil Eye" often were used as synonyms.[186] This association suggests that the Evil Eye may be suspected as potentially present and implied wherever mention is made of envy and looking with envy, with context being the chief arbiter.

This set of terms and concepts pertaining to the Evil Eye remained constant from the Hellenistic period through the end of Late Antiquity, the final period of our study.

EVIL EYE TERMS FROM GREEK TO LATIN

Latin speaking people took over the standard Greek family of terms for Evil Eye (*baskanos* etc.) by transliterating them into Latin equivalents.[187] According to the system of sound changes of letters in Indo-European languages as articulated in Grimm's Law, one shift involves: *bh→ b→ p→ phi*. In Greek, an initial sound *bh of the Thracian or Illyrian (Indo-European) term from which *bask-* was borrowed, was rendered by the letter *beta* (thus *baskainô, bazô, baskô*) or the letter *phi* (thus *phaskô, phêmi, phainô*). In Latin, the bi-labial fricative *f* represents the Greek bi-labial fricative *phi*, thus *farior* ("speak") corresponds to Greek *phêmi* ("speak"; Greek *phi* → Latin *f*). Latin letters *s, c, n, s* of *fascinus* are the counterparts of Greek *s, k, n, s* of *baskanos*. Thus Latin *fascinus* most probably derives from, and transliterates, Greek *baskanos*. Similarly, *baskainô* was transliterated as *fascino, baskania* as *fascinatio* etc. This development is supported by the comment of Aulus Gellius

185. Concerning Plato, *Alcibiades* 2.147c, for instance, the scholiast explains the relation of *phthoneros* and *baskanos* (Rakoczy 1996:127 n400).

186. A similar pair of terms that are related but distinguishable, are "envy" and "jealousy." Their use as synonyms, however, is typical of modern parlence, but not ancient custom which regarded envy and jealousy as involving distinctly different emotions and social dynamics. On this see below, pp. 86–93.

187. The relation of the Greek and Latin terms is debated. Seligmann (1910 1:31) gave four theories regarding the derivation of *fascinare*: (1) from *fari*, "speak, call"; (2) from *fascis* or *fascia*, "bundle, binding" used in the magical arts; (3) from *phaskein*, "to affirm, boast"; or (4) from *baskainein*, meaning *phaesi kainein*, "to slay with the eyes." He regards *fascinare* as derived from *baskainein*: "The Latin *fascinare*, as stated, is supposed to have derived from *baskainen*, to slay with a glance" (Seligmann 1910 1:31) On the etymology of *fascinare* etc., a more recent theory connects *fascin-* to Latin *farior*, "speak"; cf. Greek, *phêmi*, "speak." Chantraine (1968:167) rejects the derivation of *fascinus* from *baskanos*, though admits that we cannot advance beyond conjecture with this family of terms. I find the transliteration theory, however, most probable.

(second century CE) that the lexicographer and grammarian Cloatius Verus (first century BCE—first century CE)

> derived [Latin] *fascinum* from [Greek] *bascanum* and [Latin] *fascinare* from [Greek] *bascinare* (*fascinum appellatum quasi bascanum et fascinare esse quasi bascinare*). (Aulus Gellius, *Attic Nights* 16.12.4)[188]

In regard to the transliteration of the Greek terms into Latin, the Greek verb *baskainô* became Latin *fascino, effascino* ("casting an Evil Eye" or "wagging a malicious tongue"); the Greek substantive *baskanos* became Latin *fascinator* (the person who injures or "fascinates" with an Evil Eye or evil tongue); the Greek noun *baskania* became the Latin noun *fascinatio, effascinatio* ("Evil Eye injury"),[189] and the Greek neuter noun *baskanon* became the Latin noun *fascinum* (neut.) or *fascinus* (masc.).

Baskanos (Greek) and its Latin equivalent *fascinum/fascinus* designate an apotropaic means for warding off the Evil Eye, and, in a transferred sense, identifies the image of a phallus (and testicles), which was one of the chief amulets for warding off the Evil Eye in the Roman world. A *fascinus/**fascinum* consisting of an image of the phallus (and testicles), often enclosed in a leather pouch or metal capsule (*bulla*), was hung by Roman parents around the necks of their children until adulthood to safeguard them against the Evil Eye.[190] *Fascina* (plural of *fascinum*) also were engraved or in bas-relief on stones of public thoroughfares or affixed to doorposts of private houses—both at Pompeii—for protection against the Evil Eye.[191] *Fascinus* also could designate the phallus as personified deity representing virility and fertility.[192] This Latin transliterating of Greek Evil Eye terms is illustrative of the close

Illus. 1
Bronze *fascinum*
amulet with loop for
wearing
(from Seligmann 1910
2:241, fig. 185)

188. On this relation of the Greek and Latin terms see also Wünsch 1910:462; Rakoczy 1996:124, Moulton-Milligan 1930:106 (sub *baskainô*) and Hofmann 1966:33.

189. *Fascinato* is Jerome's rendition of *baskania* in Wis 2:24, which is both a transliteration and translation.

190. Plautus, *Miles* 5.1.6 (lines 1398-1399): Macrobius, *Sat.* 1.6.9; Marquardt 1886 1:84.

191. For *fascinum* see Aulus Gellius, *Attic Nights* 16.12.4 (citing Cloatius Verus); Pliny, *NH* 28.39; Horace, *Epodes* 8.18 (*fascinum* identifying a flaccid penis); Petronius, *Sat.* 138; Arnobius Afer, *Adversus Nationes* 5.176; Macrobius, *Sat.* 1.6.9. See also Hofmann 1966:33; Moulton-Milligan 1930:106. On the apotropaic function of the *fascinum* at Pompeii see M. Arditi 1825.

192. See Pliny, *NH* 28.39. For further discussion of these apotropaic *fascina* see below, pp. 195–209.

proximity and remarkable similarity of Greek and Roman Evil Eye beliefs and practices. The further Latin rendition of *baskania, baskainein*, etc. on occasion as *invidia, invidere*, etc. makes explicit in Latin what was always implicit in Greek—namely the close association and often synonymity of "Evil Eye" and "envy," and of Evil Eye malice and looking.

Other terms of the Latin *fascino* word group likewise bear related meanings.[193] *Praefiscine* (variants: *praefiscini/ praefascine/praefascini*), an adverbial form from *prae-fascinum* and meaning "no Evil Eye intended," or the expression *praefiscine dixerim*, were uttered when admiring or praising an object and wishing to assure those present that the praise was not motivated by an envious Evil Eye.[194] Thus, the English terms "to fascinate," "fascination," are rooted in the ancient concept of "casting a harmful Evil Eye," "overlooking and injuring with an Evil Eye."

Latin, in the noun *invidia*, its related verb *invidere*, and its adjective *invidus*, has linguistically enshrined the association of the Evil Eye with envy, as well as the relation of envying to looking. The assocation of the eye (Greek: *opthalmos/os/omma* and Latin: *oculus*) and the injurious glance (Greek: *baskainô*; Latin: *fascino*) with envy (Greek: *phthonos, zêlos*) is preserved and conveyed explicitly in Latin. The Latin verb *invidere* (*in* + *videre*, lit. "look" (*videre*) "upon" (*in-* [second meaning]) has the negative sense of "look askance at" or "look maliciously or spitefully at," "cast an evil eye upon"[195] or in a transferred sense, "to envy or grudge one anything."[196] This sense is preserved in the older English translation "to overlook" which

---

193. See *fascinatio, effascinatio* ("injury by Evil Eye or tongue"), *fascinator* ("one who casts an Evil Eye"), *fascinatorius* ("of or belonging to the Evil Eye"), *fascinosus* ("with a large *fascinum* [phallus]"); *infascinabilis* ("that cannot be Evil-Eyed"), and *infascinate* (adverb: "without being Evil-Eyed"). The translations offered by Lewis-Short, *A Latin Dictionary, sub vocibus*, such as "enchantment, enchanter" etc. for terms of the *fasc-* root, misleadingly suggest the use of a song or charm and fail to indicate to the general reader that these terms refer to the Evil Eye and (envious) looking.

194. For *praefiscini* see Plautus, *Asinaria* 2.4.84, lines 491–493 (*praefiscini hoc nunc dixerim*); *Casina* 5.2.51; Nonius, *De comp.* 153.12; Petronius, *Sat.* 73.6 (*homo praefiscini frugi*); Titinius in Charisius, *Ars Grammatica* 2.13, GL 274. For the alternate spelling *praefascine*, see Plautus, *Rudens* 2.5.4 (lines 459–461); Aulus Gellius, *Attic Nights* 10.24.8; for *praefascine dixerum*, Apuleius, *Florida* 3.16. The grammarian Charisius (*Ars Grammatica* 2.15, GL 306) explains *praefiscini/praefiscine: praefiscine, id est sine fascino, quod Graeci abaskanta dicunt.* ("*praefiscine*, that is, 'without fascination/the Evil Eye,' what the Greeks call *abaskanta*"). Could the Latin *praefiscini* have been derived from the Greek *probaskain-* just as *fascinus* derives from *baskanos*? On the expression see also Frommann 1675:60–63; Jahn 1855:62; Elworthy 1895/1958:16–17; Wieland 1986.

195. Lewis-Short *sub invideo*, 995, I.A. See, e.g., Cicero, *Tusc. Disp.* 3.9.20; Catullus, *Poems* 5.12 (*ne quis malus invidere possit*).

196. Lewis-Short *sub invideo*, 995 II.A. See, e.g. Plautus, *Truculentus* 4.2.30; Cicero, *De orat.* 2.52.209; *Ac.* 2.2.7; *De univ.* 3.

once had the meaning of "to look over (and harm) with an Evil Eye."[197] The noun *invidia* ("envy") thus entails an act of "looking "upon" something with malicious intent, i.e. that it be destroyed. The Latin terminology of *invidia, invidere* etc. makes it clear that envy and envying is an action of *vision* (*videre, invidere*)—the action of looking followed by an ocular glance, gaze, or stare that conveys the evil disposition of envy and the malice of an Evil Eye. This connection that is enshrined in the Latin is important to note, for it makes explicit what is often only implicit in other languages such as Greek and Hebrew. Thus where there is the Evil Eye, envy may well be lurking as well; where there is envy, there is the shadow of the Evil Eye. This association of Evil Eye and envy is also implied in the Hebrew and Greek writings of the Bible and is explicit in Jerome's Latin translation, the Vulgate, where *invidere* translates *baskainein* and *invidus* renders *baskanos*, as we shall see in Volume 3. This association is further discussed below as a key element of the Evil Eye belief complex.

The Latin equivalent for Greek *ophthalmos ponêros* (Evil Eye) is *oculus malus* (Vulgate Sir 14:10) or *oculus nequam* (Vulgate Sir 14:8; 31:14; Matt 6:23; 20:15; Luke 11:34) and such synonyms as *oculus invidus* ("envious eye"), *oculus lividus* (lit. "blue eye" and in a transferred sense, "spiteful, envious eye"), *oculus malignus* ("malicious, stingy eye"),[198] *oculus urens* ("burning, envious eye")[199] or *oculus obliquus* ("eye looking askance),"[200] the Greek equivalent of which is *ophthalmos loxos*.[201] The Latin *oculus malus* is preserved in various Romance languages; for instance, Spanish (*mal de ojo/ mal ojo*), Italian (*malocchio;* cf. *occhio cativo*), and French (*mauvais oeil*). Italian expressions vary geographically in terminology and dialect. In Naples, *malocchio* becomes *maluuch* or is known by the terms *jettatura* (*casting the evil eye* [from *gettare*, "to cast, throw"), *jettatore* ("Evil Eye caster," "fascinator").[202]

Among synonymous expressions for Evil Eye were references to "harmful" or "malevolent looking" and "poisonous glance." Thus, with the expression, *veneficos aspectus* (lit, "poisonous glance") Pliny (*NH* 28.30) may be speaking of the Evil Eye. This was the plausible conclusion of W. H.

---

197. MacLagan 1902 *passim;* see also the synonymous expression, "to blink" (MacLagan 1902:17).

198. Grattius, *Cynegetica* 406.

199. For the verb *uro* meaning *envy* see Horace, *Epist.* 2.1.13.

200. Horace, *Epist.* 1.14.37.

201. Rakoczy 1996:272. See also the scholium to Aristophanes, *Plut.* 571.

202. Valetta (1794/1814) wrote about *"fascino volgaramente detto jettatura"* ("the Evil Eye called in the vernacular, *jettatura"*). He himself was considered a *gran jettatore* (Jahn 1855:31).

S. Jones, who translates *hominum monstrificas naturas et veneficos aspectus* with "persons possessed of powers of witchcraft and of the evil eye."[203] Pliny says that he mentioned them previously, probably referring to persons who harm and kill with their Evil Eye glances (*NH* 7.16–18, *effascinantium . . . visu effascinent*).

In sum, always conveying a sense of malice and malignity, terms of the *baskanos* word group and their Latin cognates denote a malicious or slanderous person or personage who injures objects by word or glance (*baskanos, baskanter; fascinus, fascinator*), the act of casting and harming with an Evil Eye or evil tongue (*baskainein, katabaskainein, probaskainein; fascinare; effascinare*), the Evil Eye and its malign influence (*baskania, baskosynê, probaskania; fascinatio; effascinationes*), or an expression (*praefascine*), amulet (*baskanion, probaskanion; fascinus/fascinum*) or identification/personal name (*abaskanos, abaskantos, abaskanistos*—often synonymous with *aphthonêtos, aphthonos, aphthonia*, "unenvied," "without envy/Evil Eye") for warding off and protecting against the Evil Eye.

Baskania (*fascinatio*) is sometimes personified as a deity or demon, while *baskanos daimôn* identifies the Evil Eye demon specifically. Terms of the *bask-* word family are regularly combined with terms for envy (*phthonos* etc.), and often the terms for Evil Eye and envy are employed interchangeably. This close connection of Evil Eye and envy continues among the Romans and is made explicit in the Latin terminology for Evil Eye and envy. The Romans took over into Latin both the terms and the concepts associated with the Evil Eye in Greek. The Latin language absorbed terms of the Greek *bask-* family and did not translate but rather transliterated *bask-* terms into *fasc-* equivalents, so that *fascinatio* renders *baskania* and so forth.

Other Greek expressions for Evil Eye such as *ophthalmos ponêros* were translated into Latin: *oculus malus, oculus nequam* etc. The Latin terminology for *envy* (*invida, invidere, invidus* word family), since it involves the act of looking (*vid-*) makes explicit the association of envy and *looking* (askance, obliquely, sidelong and malevolently) that is usually present but often only implied in Greek discourse. Terms of this *invidia* family often are used synonymously with words for Evil Eye, or to translate Greek terms for Evil Eye, so that *invida* etc. substitutes for *fascinatio* etc. In Latin, as in Greek, terms for looking, staring, gazing intently can also imply reference to the Evil Eye.[204] This linguistic proximity of Greek and Latin concerning the Evil Eye is matched by a similar proximity in the concepts associated

203. Pliny, *Natural History*, LCL, vol. 8, 1963:23.

204. On the Greek optical vocabulary in general, see Mugler 1964; and Moreau 1976/77.

with the Evil Eye (i.e. the Evil Eye complex) and the apotropaic strategies and means for warding off and protecting against the Evil Eye. As Greek Evil Eye belief and practice extended, and expanded upon, Mesopotamian and Egyptian practice, so Roman language and practice absorbed and extended Greek terminology, beliefs, and practices. This becomes clear as we next consider key elements of the Evil Eye belief complex appearing in both Greek and Latin texts.

Translations of *baskania* etc. or *fascinatio* etc. with terms such as "envy" or "malice" or "spell" or "witchcraft" and the like are common but problematic. Such renditions of ancient texts according to *presumed sense* of the original Greek and Latin terms fail to communicate the role of the eye and looking, the eye as active organ, and its function as a transmitter of destructive energy. The translations of the verb as "to charm" or "bewitch," "to cast a spell, put a curse/spell on, hex, jinx," are inaccurate and misleading for similar reasons. First, they fail to indicate that it is the eye that is under discussion, with all its associated traits. Second, each of these terms has its own specific meaning or realm of reference which may have nothing to do with the Evil Eye. Any connection of the Evil Eye with curse, jinx, hex or bewitch may be more in the mind of the translator than in that of the ancient author.

In this study, for the sake of accuracy and clarity about ancient word usage, I shall translate Greek and Latin terms consisistently with "Evil Eye," "to Evil-Eye," "injure with an Evil Eye," etc. This does not imply that the original Greek and Latin did not have further connotations such as envy, miserliness, or malice in general. My intention is only to provide English transations that consistently render terms of the Greek (*bask-*) and Latin (*fascin-*) word families with some form of "Evil Eye." This is to give modern readers some sense of the frequency of the appearance of these terms in ancient discourse and artifacts.

3

SALIENT FEATURES OF EVIL EYE BELIEF AND PRACTICE

AN ANTHROPOLOGICAL LIST OF KEY FEATURES

In his important anthology of anthropological studies on the Evil Eye from past to present, anthropologist Clarence Maloney (1976) lists seven aspects of Evil Eye belief and practice that are conventionally found in Evil Eye cultures around the world, i.e. cultures where Evil Eye belief flourishes:

(1) power emanates from the eye (or mouth) and strikes some object or person;

(2) the stricken object is of value, and its destruction or injury is sudden;

(3) the one casting the evil eye may not know he has the power;

(4) the one affected may not be able to identify the source of power;

(5) the evil eye can be deflected or its effects modified or cured by particular devices, rituals, and symbols;

(6) the belief helps to explain or rationalize sickness, misfortune, or loss of possessions such as animals or crops;

(7) in at least some functioning of the belief everywhere, envy is a factor.[1]

The list is a useful summary of key and consistently attested aspects of Evil Eye belief and practice in modern time and across cultures. It also

1. Maloney 1976:vii–viii.

47

is remarkable in its consistency with features of ancient Evil Eye belief and practice as described in the most extensive trestise of the ancient world on the Evil Eye, namely the *Symposium* or *Table Talk* of the influential philosopher and biographer, Mestrius Plutarch of Chaeronea, Greece (50–120 CE), the *Quaestiones Convivales* (5.7.1–6; *Mor.* 680C–683B).

PLUTARCH

In the seventh dialogue/question of the fifth book of his *Quaestiones Convivales (Convivial Questions)*, Plutarch presents a dinner discussion, a Symposium or Table Talk, devoted to the topic "concerning those who are said to cast an Evil Eye" (*peri tôn katabaskainein legomenôn*, *Quaest. Conv.* 5.7.1 [*Mor.* 680C]). Such discussions normally accompanied banquets. This one included the host Mestrius Florus and his four guests, Plutarch, Patrocleas, Soclarus, and Gaius, the son-in-law of Florus. This is the fullest emic or native informant discussion from antiquity on the Evil Eye, its salient features, how it works, and measures taken to avert it.[2]

Representing the general state of knowledge of educated elites on the subject, the text opens with doubts concerning the Evil Eye that are quickly countered by the host and close friend of Plutarch, Mestrius Florus, who seeks to establish a serious, educated explanation of the phenomenon based on actual physical data. The ensuing discussion among the five speakers recounts various ideas concerning the eye and vision in general as well as notable features of the Evil Eye in particular.[3] The conversation demonstrates what at that time was accepted as rational and credible—not just by common folk but by educated, upper-class elites as well. For Plutarch and his companions the Evil Eye was no matter of vulgar superstition, but an actual physical reality whose operation could be explained on rationale grounds.[4]

What follows is a summarization of the discussion showing the flow of the conversation, with paraphrase or direct quotation where appropriate.[5]

2. On Plutarch's discussion see Hauschild 1979:16–23; Dickie 1991; Rakoczy 1996:186–205.

3. Matthew Dickie (1995:18) sees Plutarch (*Quaest. Conv.* 5.7.2–3 [*Mor.* 680F–681F, 682F]) particularly reliant on the presocratic philosopher Democritus (c. 460–370 BCE) who used his theory of atomic particles to account for the capacity of the eyes of the envious to cause bodily and psychic upset (Diels-Kranz, *FVS* 68 A 77). Plutarch's discussion represents, in Dickie's view (1991), an amalgam of Democritus's particle theory of vision, peripatetic pneuma theory, and notions presented in the Aristotelian *Problemata*. On this text and theories of vision see also Rakoczy 1996:186–205.

4. As Rakoczy (1996:187 and *passim*) repeatedly and rightly has emphasized.

5. I follow the Loeb Classical Library translation by Clement and Hoffleit (1969)

An initial unit sets the stage and presents the thinking of the host, Mestrius Florus (*Quaest. Conv.* 5.7.1 [*Mor.* 680C–F]). "Once at dinner a discussion arose about people who are said to cast an Evil Eye (*katabaskainein*) and to have an Evil Eye (*baskanon . . . ophthalmon*)" (*Mor.* 680C).[6] "While everybody else pronounced the matter completely silly and scoffed at it, Mestrius Florus, our host, declared that actual facts lend astonishing support to the common belief" (680C).[7] It is not warranted, Florus went on, to reject these facts for want of an explanation (680C). The correct method of procedure is rather to first establish the facts and then by means of logic determine their explanation (680D). Among the many unexplained phenomena that are on record is the fact that there are some persons "who seriously hurt children by looking at them (*katablepein ta paidia*), impairing their susceptible, vulnerable constitutions," but who are less able to similarly harm the stable health of adults (680D).[8] However, Mestrius Florus continued, the so-called Thibaeans living near Pontus in Asia Minor, according to Phylarchus, a historian of the third century BCE, were deadly not only to children but to adults as well as (680E).[9] Victims who were subjected to the glance (*to blemma*), breath (*tên anapnoên*), or speech (*tên dialekton*) of the Thibaeans "wasted away and fell ill (*têkesthai kai nosein*)," as attested by the half-Greeks who bought slaves for sale from there (680D-E). An Evil Eye, in other words, was thought to work in tandem with an evil tongue or mouth (breath, speech; cf. *mala lingua*, and see also 680F). All three—looking, breathing, speaking—involved emanations from the body. In this regard, Mestius Florus continues, illness can be due to contact and infection (680E). But it also does happen sometimes, as previously mentioned, that persons are also injured by a harmful glance (*prosblephthentes*; 680F).[10] This is not to be disbelieved just because the reason is hard to provide (680F).

At this point, Plutarch joins in and responds that Mestius Florus has pointed the way to an explanation in his referring to "effluences (*tas*

---

6. The LCL renders *katabaskainein* here and 682E and *baskainen* in 681D with "cast a spell." But the expression "Evil Eye" (*baskanon ophthalmon*) and the standard Evil Eye terminology throughout the dialogue argue that the verb is best rendered "cast an Evil Eye" here and hereafter. LCL "bewitch" in 682B is misleading for the same reason.

7. Heliodorus's novel, *Aethiopica*, presents another instance where the Evil Eye as a cause of illness is doubted by one character but defended by another. On this text, see below, pp. 65–71.

8. Here is the conventional view that the Evil Eye is a cause of illness, especially of vulnerable children.

9. For the Phylarchus reference see the fragment in FGrHist 81 F 79a.

10. Note that terms of the *blep*- root join *bask*- words as terminology for the Evil Eye.

aporroias) from the body" (*Quaest. Conv.* 5.7.2; *Mor.* 680F; cf. 681A). "For odor, voice, and breathing are all various emanations (*apophorai*) from living bodies that produce sensation [in other bodies] whenever the sense organs of sense are stimulated by their impact . . . In all probability, the most active stream of such emanations is that which passes out through the eyes (*dia tôn ophthalmôn*). For vision (*hê opsis*), being very swift and borne by a substance (*pneuma*) that gives off a flame-like brilliance, radiates a wonderous power (*dynamin*)" (680F–681A).[11] Consequently one both "experiences and produces" (*paschein kai poiein*) many effects through one's eyes. Whether one is governed by pleasure or displeasure is determined by what one sees (*tôn horatôn*; 681A). As persons are harmed through their eyes/vision (*dia tês opseis*), so they also influence others and inflict harm on others through these same eyes (681B).[12]

One example of this power of the eye/vision/looking (*opsis, emblepein*) involves the chemistry of love where lovers melt each other with their amorous glances (681A–B) "The answering glances (*hai antiblepseis*) of the young and beautiful[13] and the efflux from their eyes (*to dia tôn ommatôn ekpipton*), whether it be light (*phôs*) or a current of particles (*rheuma*), melts the lovers and destroys them in bittersweet pleasure" (681B) . . . "The glances of the beautiful kindle fire, even when returned from a great distance, in the souls of the amorous" (681C).[14] So it is entirely reasonable to believe that it is through their eyes that persons are passively influenced and experience harm, on the one hand, and influence others and inflict injury, on the other hand (681B). Seeing (*prosblepein*) and being seen (*prosblepesthai*) wound more deeply than do touching or hearing, and kindle fire even over great distance (681C).[15] A second instance of the eye's power is how people are

11. These ideas concerning emanations from the body, including the eye, firmly echo the particle theory of Democritus as mentioned above, p. 49. Eventually Democritus and his theory of *eidola* are explicitly mentioned (*Mor.* 682F–683A; cf. Democritus, Frag. 77 (Diels-Kranz, *FVS* 68 A 77).

12. Plutarch thus allows that the eye can function both passively (*paschein*) and actively (*poiein*), though the latter trait seems to prevail.

13. The young and beautiful were deemed typical victims of the Evil Eye and envy; see also Plutarch, *Non posse* [*Mor.* 1090C].

14. The notion of particles or beams of light flowing from the eye echoes peripatetic notions found in the Aristotelian corpus; cf. Ps-Aristotle, *Problemata inedita* 3.52 cited above, p. 28. Rakockzy (1996:193) suspects a common source. When the emanation is thought of as a beam of light, the eye is then comparable to a lamp that casts forth light, as in Jesus's word about a good and an Evil Eye (Matt 6:22–23).

15. The melting and fire-kindling nature of the eye recalls comparison of the eye to the sun sending forth the fiery rays or to a lamp emitting beams of light. Cf. also ocular aggression through hostile staring and intense gazing as typical of Mediterranean cultures (Gilmore, *Aggression*, 1987a).

cured of the illness of jaundice by looking at a yellow-colored plover (*charadrios*, 681C).[16] The bird sucks out the illness of the viewer, which passes like a stream through the viewer's eye (*dia tês opseôs*), and takes it into itself (681C). These birds themselves cannot directly look at (*prosblepousin*) at those with jaundice, but turn away and keep their eyes (*ta ommata*) closed (681D). This is not because the birds begrudge (*ou phthonountes*) the effect of their healing power, as some think, but to avoid being wounded themselves (681D).[17] Third, the power of the eye is evident in the fact that illnesses (*ta nosêmata*) of the eye are more contagious and instant that other illnesses, showing how "penetrating and swift the power of the eye to take in illness (*pathous*) or direct it (*prosbalein*) against another" (681D).[18]

A third guest, Patrocleas, joins the discussion (*Quaest. Conv.* 5.7.3 [*Mor.* 681D]). Moving beyond the physiological effects, he inquires about the psychical aspect (*ta de tês psychês*) of casting an Evil Eye (*to baskainein*; 681D):[19] how can a glance of the eye (*tês opseôs*) spread harm to the persons who are looked at (*tous horômenous*)? (681D). Plutarch answers that the body is affected when the mind and emotions are aroused, as when amorous thoughts arouse the genitals or when pain, greed, or jealousy (*zêlotypiai*) cause one to change color and lose health (681D–E).

> Envy (*ho phthonos*), ensconced by nature in the mind more than any other passion also fills the body with evil . . . When, therefore, individuals under envy's sway direct their glance at others, their eyes, which are close to the mind and draw from it envy's evil, then attack these other persons as if with poisoned arrows (*pepharagmena belê*). (681E)[20]

16. The plover is a yellowish bird, the sight of which was thought to cure the yellow illness of jaundice, according to the principle of *similia similibus*, "like influences like," "like against or curing like." Yellow color attracts and heals yellow illness. Pliny (*NH* 30.94) also mentions this cure: "There is a bird called 'jaundice' (*icterus*) from its color. If one with jaundice looks at it, he is cured, we are told, and the bird dies."

17. The belief is that the eyes of both the victims and those of the birds of healing are conduits of energy so that harm can come from looking directly into another's eye. This is consistent with the idea that humans too should always avoid looking into the eye of Evil Eye possesors. Note also that the verb *phthonein*, generally meaning "to envy" in this context is best rendered "begrudge."

18. The active agency of the eye is clear here, as well as its expelling or casting forth (*prosbalein*), a concept basic to casting an Evil Eye, as expressed by the Italian terms *jettatura, jettatore* (from *jettare*, "to cast, throw").

19. The LCL translation of *to baskainein* as "the casting spells" is misleading. It obscures the fact that the focus of this entire dialogue is on the power of the (Evil) Eye, ocular glance and vision, and not the casting of spells.

20. Consideration of envy is natural to the discussion of the eye and the Evil Eye because it is assumed to operate through the eye. Patrocleas ranks envy as the passion

Artists attempt to render this morbid condition, when painting the face of a personified version of envy (*tou phthonou*).[21] Envy attacks victims through a noxious glance of the eye. Envy and Evil Eye work in tandem, as Plutarch's observation above indicates (*Mor.* 681E).[22]

This comment also illustrates the understanding of the eye as channel of the disposition of envy. Patrocleas concludes that it is thus neither paradoxical nor incredible that those who look with envy at others should impact the objects of their gaze (*tous prosorômenous*; 681E–F). "In general, the emotions of the mind increase the violence and energy of the body's powers" (681F). This explains, he adds, how so-called anti-Evil Eye amulets (*probaskaniôn*) are considered a protection against envy (*phthonos*): they attract the eye (*opsis*) of the envier by their unusual appearance (*tên atopian*) so that the eye's glance is diverted to the amulet and exerts less impact on the victims (682A).[23]

A fourth guest, Soclarus, objects that there is a problem with linking the Evil Eye with envy (*Quaest. Conv.* 5.7.4 [*Mor.* 682A]). Allowing as true what some say about the victims of the Evil Eye (*hoi baskainomenoi*), the dinner guests know full well, he states, that "some people believe that friends and relatives, and in some cases even fathers, have the Evil Eye (*ophthalmon baskanon*)," so that their wives will not show them their children nor allow the children to be looked upon (*katablepesthai*) for very long (682A–B).[24]

---

most deeply engrained in the mind and corruptive of the body as well. For envy as worst of the passions and harmful to the body see also Basil, Homily 11, "On Envy" (PG 31. 372–385) discussed in Vol. 4, chap. 2. Compare Sir 31:13: "Remember that an Evil Eye (*ophthalmos ponêros*) is a wicked thing; what has been created more evil than an Evil Eye."

21. On the iconography of envy see Dunbabin and Dickie 1983; Slane and Dickie 1993.

22. Patrocleas's comparison of the emissions from an envious Evil Eye with poisoned arrows graphically illustrates the assumed active, aggressive and harmful power of the envious Evil Eye. For this analogy see also Aeschylus, *Agam.* 241, 468; *Persians* 81–82.

23. This is one of several theories on how anti-Evil Eye amulets work. It claims that the amulet's strange or grotesque appearance attracts the Evil Eye of the envier and diverts its attention, thereby weakening the force directed at the intended victim.

24. Children are universally regarded as potential victims of the Evil Eye (and envy). For more on this point see below under "Victims of the Evil Eye" including one's own family, pp. 61–62, 121, 146–53. Plutarch elsewhere (*De frat.* [*Mor.* 485]) urges that brothers make every effort to avoid envying one another. If they find it impossible to envy, then they should at least direct their Evil Eye at persons outside the family (*trepein exô pros heautous apocheteuein to baskanon*), like politicians who divert internal sedition by promoting foreign wars (*De frat.* [*Mor.* 485E]). As to the protection of infants and family members, the strategy is concealment—hiding the children from view, or restricting the length of time they can be looked at.

How, in this close circle of family, he asks, can the emotion be that of envy?[25] And, he further asks, what will you say about those who are reputed to Evil-Eye themselves (*heautous katabaskainein*)? (682B).[26] You must have heard of that, or at any rate read these lines:

> Fair once were, fair indeed, the tresses of Eutelidas;
> But he Evil-Eyed himself (*auton baskainein*), that baneful man,
> Beholding (him)self in river's eddy; and straight the deadly sickness (*nousos*) . . . (682B)[27]

The legend, Soclarus explains, is that Eutelidas, handsome in his own estimation, and being affected by what he saw with his eye (*opsis*) [i.e. the reflected image of himself in the water], fell ill (*nosênai*) and lost his beauty with his health. How are these extraordinary phenomena to be accounted for, he asks (682B).

Soclarus's contribution to the conversation mentions several important details. (1) Friends, relatives and parents can have the Evil Eye and harm one another within the close family circle. (2) A strategy of protection is mentioned: to protect vulnerable children in this circle, mothers hide them from the sight of fathers who have the Evil Eye or limit the time fathers can look at the children. (3) It is also believed that people can Evil-Eye themselves (autofascination), with Eutelidas being a classic example. (4) This Evil-Eyeing of one's own family members or of oneself illustrates that the Evil Eye can operate involuntarily. (5) These notions call for an explanation of the relation of the Evil Eye and envy, which is previously postulated in 681E–F. (6) All this is presumed to be common knowledge, however difficult the cases are to understand.

Plutarch (*Quaest. Conv.* 5.7.5) next takes up Soclarus's question about persons Evil-Eyeing their own relatives and even themselves. He points out how the emotions, long engrained in the mind, often work contrary to a person's will (682C). Thus it is no surprise that habit causes those who have brought themselves into an envious and Evil-Eyed state (*tên phthontikên kai baskantikên hexin*) are moved against their own relatives and friends

25. The objection presumably rests on the assumed unliklihood that fathers would intentionally envy *their own children*.

26. Once again the LCL translation "bewitch" for *katabaskainein* fails to communicate an explicit reference to casting of an Evil Eye, despite the explicit mention here of looking (*katablepesthai*).

27. Plutarch citing Euphorion (third century BCE, Frag. 175. in *Collectanea Alexandrina*, ed. Powell). Note the similarity to the Narcissus myth (admiring his reflection in the water and thereby Evil-Eyeing himself) and the danger of beholding one's reflection in a mirror, as well as the myth of Medusa and later the myth of Cyclops in Theocritus, *Idyls* 6.39. On self-fascination see below, 29–30, 55–56, 119, 151.

(*ta oikeia*) consistent with their pathological condition (682D).[28] In these circumstances they are acting in accord with their nature rather than their will, and thus an envious disposition (*hê diathesis*) moves an envious person (*phthonon*) to act enviously (*phthonikôs*) in all things (682D). It is thus natural for one to cast an Evil Eye (*katablepein*) more often on one's own relatives and friends and to hurt them more than others (682D).[29] Plutarch also finds it "not unreasonable" that Eutelidas and all others said to have Evil-Eyed themselves (*katabaskainein heautous*) suffered this misfortune (682E). Good health is precarious and health can wax and wane. When persons experience their health improving, they look carefully at themselves (*heautous epiblepôsin*), looking intently (*kataskopein*) at their bodies with wonder. When their physical condition suddenly worsens, this decline is attributed to their having Evil-Eyed themselves (*heautous katabaskainein*) by looking at themselves (682E).[30] While the looking was intentional, the ill effect clearly was not, thus illustrating the belief that the Evil Eye operates unintentionally as well as volitionally. Plutarch then returns to the case of Eutelidas and similar others in explaining how autofascination (Evil-Eyeing of oneself) most frequently happens (682E–F). He quotes the legend of handsome Eutelidas gazing into the water and inadvertently Evil-Eyeing himself, falling ill and losing his beauty.

Thus, when Evil-Eyed persons behold their reflection in the water, it is thought, autofascination occurs

> by streams of particles (*rheumatôn*) [flowing from the eyes of the beholders on to the water] being reflected from sheets of water or other mirror-like surfaces, rising like vapor, and returning to the beholders (*tous horôntous*), so that they themselves are injured by the same means by which they harm others [namely noxious emissions from the eye]. Perhaps when this [attack by the Evil Eye] happens in the case of children, the blame is often

---

28. Here Plutarch invokes the Aristotelian concept of habit shaping character traits like that of envy.

29. Presumably because a person is more frequently in the presence of family and friends than of others. Plutarch's explanation implies the assumption that the Evil Eye and envy, in being traits of nature rather than choices of will, can operate involuntarily rather than intentionally, as he explains a few lines later.

30. This explanation turns from envy as the cause of injury to looking at oneself as a cause. When persons, who have visually examined themselves (*heautous epiblepôsin*, *kataskopein*) in pleasure at their good health, suddenly experience a decline in health, it is thought that this decline was caused by their having looked at themselves and hence having Evil-Eyed themselves (*heautous katabaskainein*).

wrongly assigned to those who gaze at (*tôn enorôntôn*) them
(682E–F).[31]

These cases of self-fascination illustrate how the Evil Eye was thought to
be governed by nature rather than by will and to operate automatically and
unintentionally.

Gaius, son-in-law of the host Mestius Florus, now joins the conversation (*Quaest. Conv.* 5.7.6 [*Mor.* 682F–683A]) to remind everyone not to
ignore Democritus's venerable theory of vision and its concept of images
(*eidola*)[32] that are projected from the eye (*Mor.* 682F). Democritus, Gaius
recalls, says that envious persons (*tous phthonountas*) emit these images (*ei-
dôlôn*) "not altogether unconsciously or unintentionally" and that these images are infected with the envious persons's wickedness (*mochthêrias*) and
Evil Eye malice (*baskanias*; *Mor.* 683A, referring to Democritus).[33] These
images and their malice (when projected) adhere to and permanently reside
in persons who are struck by the Evil-Eye (*tois baskainomenois*), disturbing
and harming them in both body and mind (683A). Plutarch agrees, asserting
that "the only things that I denied to the emanations (*tôn rheumatôn*) were
life and free will" (683A)—without getting into any spooky notions of sen-
tient, purposeful shapes and apparitions, which can be discussed tomorrow
(683A–B). Plutarch appears to be rejecting any notion that the emanations
had an existence of their own apart from the humans from whom they ema-
nated. Whereas Gaius cites Democritus to affirm some role of intentionality
and consciousness in the process, Plutarch himself (682C–F) allows little
place for the will, especially in the light of the possibility of self-fascination.
Plutarch's familiarity with Democritus' atomistic theory of vision and his
supposed presumption of an active eye is evident here, however Plutarch's
reliance on Democritus may be judged.

More detailed review of this debate would take us too far afield.[34]
It is sufficient for our purpose to note the points on which Plutarch and

31. With this final comment, Plutarch seems to be suggesting that it is is not others,
who with their Evil Eye harm children, but rather that children Evil-Eye themselves—a
rather singular notion.

32. LCL: *simulacra.* Plutarch's reliance on Democritus, the fifth century BCE philosopher and atomist scientist, and his presumed extramission theory of vision and
emission of particles/images is now expressly stated; cf. also *Quaest. Conv.* 5.7.2 [*Mor.*
681A].

33. Democritus, Frag. A 77 (Diels-Kranz, *FVS* 68 A 77).

34. For varying positions see Dickie (1991; 1995:16–17) and Rakoczy (1996:191–92
n708, 204–5). In contrast to Dickie (Plutarch gives a variant of Democritus's theory),
Rakoczy finds a substantive difference while at the same time agreement on the eye
as active organ and looking as a means of causing harm. On Democritus's theory see
Baldes 1975.

Democritus agree: vision as involving the flow of particles, atoms, tiny images conveyed through the air, with an Evil Eye projecting particles/images ladened with malice, often connected with envy, and injurious to children and others.

Dickie notes that this extramission theory also "found its way into two collections of physical and medical conundrums, one ascribed to Aristotle[35] and the other to Alexander of Aphrodisias."[36] This positive reception of the theory, as demonstrated also by the comments of Pliny the Elder and Aelian, shows the extent and strength of this extramission theory among the *hoi polloi* and educated alike.

It is highly instructive to compare the data of Plutarch's dialogue with the seven aspects listed by Maloney and cited above as typical of Evil Eye belief and practice across the globe. The comparison shows that basic features of the belief complex have a two thousand year history going back to the first century CE and beyond.

ANCIENT AND MODERN VERSIONS COMPARED

In regard to Maloney's first point, the notion of power emanating from the eye presumes the concept of an *active eye* that is basic to the so-called *extramission theory of vision*. This is the most prevalent of varying ocular theories in the ancient world.[37] Four differing theories of vision have been delineated.[38] I present them here in modified form. One school of thought attributed visual sensation to "effulgences" (*aidola*), thin layers of atoms thought to stream from the surface of *objects* of sight via the air into the eye of the beholder. This is the so-called *intromission theory of vision*, proponents of which included the atomists Leucippus (fifth century BCE), Democritus (c. 460–370 BCE) and Epicurus of Samos (341–270 BCE).[39] "They believed that isomorphic images (or *eidola*) streamed off objects and entered the eye, where they were sensed."[40] The Epicurean poet Lucretius (94–55 BCE) held a similar view. Versions of a second theory, favored by Alcmaeon of Croton

---

35. Dickie 1995:17; Pseudo-Aristotle, *Problemata inedita* 3.52 (*Aristotelis opera omnia*, ed. Bussemaker 4:332)

36. Alexander of Aphrodisias, *Probl. phys.*2.53 (in *Physici et Medici Graeci minores*. ed. Ideler, 1841, 1:67–68).

37. See Seligmann 1910 2:454–62; Rakoczy 1996:19–37.

38. See Allison 1987:62–66.

39. Plutarch, however, whose speaker Gaius cites Democritus (Plutarch, *Quaest. Conv.* 5.7.6 [*Mor.* 682F–683A]), appears to regard Democritus as considering the eye to be an *active* agent emitting noxious particles.

40. C. G. Gross 1999:58.

(early fifth century BCE), Parmenides (fifth century BCE), Empedocles, Pythagorians, Stoics, and the majority of ancient voices (Euclid, Ptolemy, Galen et al.), held that the eye is an *active* agent producing or transmitting particles of ray-like energy. "The eye," Alcmaeon stated," obviously has fire within it, for when one is struck this fire flashes out. Vision is due to gleaming . . ."[41] Empedocles (fifth century BCE),[42] for example, compared the eye to a lamp, as did Jesus centuries later (Matt 6:22–23/Luke 11:33–36), explaining that the eye contains an "elemental" or "primal" fire (*ôgygion pyr*) whose energy is conveyed outward from the body to the object of vision. This is the so-called *extramission theory of vision*. Plutarch (*Quaest. Conv.* 5.7) gives the fullest expression of this view, along with a description of how the Evil Eye works. Plutarch (*Quaest. Conv.* 5.7.6 [*Mor.* 682F–683A]) regards Democritus as representing an extramission theory of vision: "Democritus says that these *eidola* are emanations emitted not altogether unconsciously or unintentionally by the envious (*tous phthonountas*), and are charged with their wickedness and Evil Eye malice (*baskanias*)." (In actuality, however, Democritus conceived of atoms emitted *not by the eye of the viewer but by the object viewed*.) Plato also held the extramission theory of vision. Describing the human body, he expressed the notion of the eyes containing and emitting fire ("light-bearing eyes," *phôsphora ommata*): "When the eye is functioning well, this fire within us is pure (*eilikrinê*) and flows through the eyes out into the world" (*Timaeus* 45b–46a).[43] He added that vision resulted from the light projected from the eyes coalescing with effluences streaming from the objects seen. Fourth, Aristotle [384–322 BCE], and his Peripatetic school seem to have entertained both active and passive eye theories on different occasions,[44] and spoke of the eye as both passive and active.[45] While criticizing the theory of an active eye and conceiving of the eye as passive and receptive (in *de Sensu* [in *Parva Naturalia*] 437a b25–27), Aristotle could on other occasions speak of the eye as an active agent. Writing about the marring effect that the look of menstruating women has on

41. Alcmaeon (Frag. A 5), cited by Theophrastus, *Sens.* 7; cf. C. G. Gross 1999:58.

42. Empedocles, Frag. 31 B84 (Diels-Kranz, *FVS* 31 B 84, vol. 1:342.4–9), and cited in Theophrastus, *Sens.* 7.

43. For Plutarch's version of Plato's theory of vision (in *Timaeus*) see *Quaest. Conv.* 1 [*Mor.* 626C].

44. Rakoczy 1996:134–55; Allison 1987:81 n11 distinguishes between Aristotle's "mature opinion" (*de Sensu* and *de Anima*) and earlier accounts (*Meteor.* 3.2.372a 19–21; 3.372b34–373a19; 4.373a35–b13; b32–33; 374b11, 12; cf. *De cael.* 2.8.290a17–24; *Gen. An.* 5.1.781a3–13.

45. Aristotle, *Insomn.* 459b 27 (*paschei . . . poiei*); cf. also Plutarch, *Quaest. Conv.* 5.7 [*Mor.* 682] (*paschein kai poiein*).

mirrors, he explains that the polluting power of the menstrual blood exits through the eyes and then damages the mirror on which the look falls:

> When menstruating women look into very clean mirrors, the surface of the mirror becomes as a blood-red cloud; and when the mirror is new, it is not easy to remove this dirt; but when it is old, it is easier. (Aristotle, *Insomn.* 459b 27–32)[46]

This theory of the eye emitting a damaging power is consistent with the notion of an Evil Eye emitting noxious rays on hapless victims.[47] His theory concerning menstrual blood and ocular emission is cited frequently thereafter in connection with references to the Evil Eye and its operation.[48]

Among these schools of thought, the extramission theory of vision was predominant in the ancient Mediterrean world, was known also in India and China, and continued in the West throughout the Middle Ages. Its proponents formed a vast array of intellectual luminaries including Alcmaeon, Empedocles, Parmenides, Plato, Euclid (*fl.* fourth–third century BCE), Theophrastus (c. 371–c. 287 BCE), Pythagoreans, Perpatetics, Stoics, Philo (c. 30 BCE–40 CE), Seneca (c. 4 BCE—65 CE), Pliny the Elder (23/24–79 CE), Plutarch (c. 50–120 CE), Galen (129–199 CE), Heliodorus (*fl.* 220–250), Augustine (354–430), al-Kindi (ninth century) Thomas Aquinas (c.1225–1274), Roger Bacon (thirteenth century), Leonardo da Vinci (1452–1519), Martin Luther (1483–1546), Galileo (1565–1642), Thomas Willis (1621–1675), and J. W. von Goethe (1749–1842).[49]

Presuming this theory of the eye and vision, Plutarch has one of the speakers, Gaius, explicitly mention Democritus's theory of images (*aidôla*) emitted from bodies[50] as authoritative explanation of how an active Evil Eye operates (*Quaest. Conv.* 5.7.6 [*Mor.* 682F–683A]). Democritus's theory, as presented by Plutarch, of the lasting deleterious effect of the emanations from an envious Evil eye when they strike a victim also explains how the Evil Eye can be thought to cause illness and the slow wasting away of humans and animals. It is the power of the *eidola*, negative energy-laden atoms sent forth from the eye, that strike, wound, and wither victims of an envious

---

46. For an active Evil Eye see also See also Aristotle, *Fragmenta varia* (ed. Rose) 7 = *Zoica* 7.39.347.17, and in the Aristotelian Peripatetic tradition, Pseudo-Aristotle, *Problemata inedita* 3.52 and *Probl. phys.* 20.34, cited above pp. 21–22.

47. See Rakocsy 1996:134–40; Seligmann 1910 1:93–94.

48. See, e.g., Thomas Aquinas, *Summa Theol.* I, *Quaest.* 117, Art. 3; also Marcillio Ficino (*De fascino*, 1583, 1589), Roger Bacon (*Opus maius* 4.7), Paracelsus, among others.

49. On the history of the extramission theory of vision, see also Vol. 3, chap. 2.

50. Democritus, Frag. A 77 (Diels-Kranz, *FVS*, 68 A 77).

Evil Eye. "The harm that *baskania* does, notes M. Dickie, occurs, according to Plutarch, because the eyes, which are positioned close to the soul, draw into themselves the evil with which *phthonos* has filled the soul. As a result, when men rest their eyes in envy on something, their glances fall like poisoned darts on that object."[51] Plutarch states that just as odor, speaking, and breathing produce emanations that can injure susceptible objects, so can the eye, which emits fiery rays. The eye emits a "flame-like brilliance" (*Mor.* 681A), light or particles that strike and wound victims (*Mor.* 681B, E). The ocular glance or eye "kindles passion/fire" (*Mor.* 681C). Seeing and being seen have more power than even touching or hearing (*Mor.* 681C), and are potent even over long distances (*Mor.* 681C). It is the eye that primarily determines one's pleasure or displeasure (*Mor.* 681A). The eye is the organ through which humans harm and are harmed (*Mor.* 681B, 683A). Illnesses of the eye are more contagious and instantaneous than other illnesses, allowing rapid admission to, and emission from, the body (*Mor.* 681D). The harmful emissions of envy from the Evil Eye are comparable to "poisoned arrows" (*Mor.* 681E) or a physical blow (*Mor.* 681D).

Concerning Maloney's second point: The *stricken victims* specifically mentioned by Plutarch are indeed valued; namely one's own children, other family members, and friends (*Mor.* 680D, 682A, 682F), and one's own life and health (*Mor.* 682B, 682E, 682F). In the history of Evil Eye belief and practice, children, on whom the perpetuation of the family rests, are the most frequently mentioned victims. Plutarch adds a reason for their particular vulnerability: their weak and susceptible physical constitutions that have not yet stabilized and grown firm like those of adults (*Mor.* 680D). The "young and beautiful" are likewise mentioned as typical victims (*Mor.* 681B) and for the same reason.[52] Lovers, too, bring pain to each other with their powerful glances (*Mor.* 681A–C), as described also later in Heliodorus's novel, *Aethiopica* (4.5.4–6).[53]

3. Whether or not *Evil Eye possessors* are aware of their power is not addressed directly by Plutarch. Lovers may or may not be aware (*Mor.* 681A–C, D), as is also the case with fathers (*Mor.* 682A), children (*Mor.* 682F), and alien tribes such as the Thibaeans (*Mor.* 680D). Fascinators who Evil-Eye themselves (*Mor.* 682B, E, F) are either unaware or woefully

51. Dickie 1991:26. Rakoczy (1996:108) clarifies a minor difference in the explanations of Plutarch and Democritus. In contrast to Plutarch's exposition, Democritus' atomist theory postulated that emissions proceeded not only from the eye but from a person's entire physical body. On the active agency of the eye and its projection of particles, however they are in full agreement.

52. See also Plutarch, *Non posse* [*Mor.* 1090C].

53. On victims of the Evil Eye see below under "Victims of the Evil Eye."

negligent in taking proper precaution. The consciousness of the possessor, however, is a question that overlaps the issue of whether the Evil Eye operates intentionally or unintentionally. Plutarch, as well as other sources ancient and modern, allow for both possibilities.

Unintentional operation of an Evil Eye is indicated where exotic tribes like the Thibaeans are thought to have the Evil Eye *by nature* (*Mor.* 680D), when family members and friends harm those who are near and dear (*Mor.* 682A, D), when lovers share erotic glances (*Mor.* 681A–D), or in the case of autofascination (*Mor.* 682B, E–F). These are instances when damage is thought to be caused by persons looking intently and admiringly at their own bodies (*Mor.* 682E), or at one another as lovers, or where envy and the Evil Eye are thought to be driven by nature and habit rather than by will (*Mor.* 681E, 681B–D, 682D ["even against the person's will"). *Intentional use of the Evil Eye* occurs when Evil Eye possessors feel and purposely direct envy and malice against others with the intent to injure and harm, as when fascinators direct illness toward others (*Mor.* 681D). Uncertainty about who has an Evil Eye and where it might strike calls for constant vigilance and complete proctection (681F, 682A).

Maloney's list does not include an item about persons conventionally suspected of possessing and casting an Evil Eye. But this is an important point and one on which there seems to be some degree of cross-cultural agreement: any living entities, and even dead animals, may have an Evil Eye, but persons with unusual ocular features or impairments and those who are physically deformed, or social or economically deprived, or who have cause to be highly envious, are generally deemed to be likely fascinators.[54]

4. Uncertainty about the Evil Eye as the specific source of harm and illness is always a factor. Plutarch mentions this uncertainty at the outset (*Mor.* 680C), before he marshals the evidence to prove that the Evil Eye is a cause of illness and loss. The uncertainty would involve: (1) whether or not it was an Evil Eye that caused the damage (*Mor.* 680D–F); (2) if by someone's Evil Eye, then by whose (lover? family member? one's own Evil Eye?); and (3) how it might be cured (*Mor.* 681C–D).

5. The Evil Eye can be deflected or diverted by amulets. Anti Evil Eye amulets (*probaskania*) with a strange or grotesque appearance are said to divert the gaze of the fascinator from victim to the amulet, thereby weakening or eliminating its noxious effect on the victim (*Mor.* 681F–682A). Cure of yellow jaundice can be accomplished by looking at a plover, a yellow bird thought to absorb the illness of yellow jaundice possibly caused by the Evil

54. On possessors and casters of the Evil Eye (fascinators) see below under Fascinators.

Eye. The underlying rationale is that "like works against like" (*similia simili-bus*). Other amulets or apotropaic gestures such as the image of an eye (eye of Horus, eye under attack) or use of the color blue against a blue Evil Eye were thought to be effective on the basis of the same principle. The *probas-kania* (anti-Evil Eye amulets, *Mor.* 681F–682A), as mentioned above (pp. 16, 35), are mentioned in a biblical source as providing protection against crop loss (*Epistle of Jeremiah* 69/70)[55] Other ancient texts indicate devices, rituals, and symbols deployed for modifying or curing harm wrought by an Evil Eye, from Mesopotamian incantations onward.

6. The Evil Eye belief *explains or rationalizes sickness, misfortune, loss, and illness*, as the dialogue illustrates. Plutarch indicates that the Evil Eye (and envy) are considered causes of illness and injury and even explains how the damage is wrought[56] and causes a wasting away.[57]

7. *Envy* is regularly associated with the Evil Eye.[58] Envy, the passion most deeply rooted in the mind, contaminates the entire body with evil (*Mor.* 681E), so that all emanations of the body are poisoned by envy. This explains the connection of an Evil Eye and an evil tongue (*Mor.* 680D–E)— both are conduits of evil emanations. The poisonous emanations of envy are automatically activated and are transmitted through the (evil) eye (*Mor.* 681E–F, 682F), apart from the consciousness and intention of the fascinator (*Mor.* 681E–F). Anti-Evil Eye amulets (*probaskania*) are employed against envy (*Mor.* 681F).[59] As the linguistic evidence discussed above indicates, this association of Evil Eye and envy was ubiquitous and one of the most constant features of Evil Eye belief from antiquity down to the present.

To these seven points listed by Maloney we may add a few more basic features or aspects of Evil Eye belief and practice mentioned by Plutarch.

8. Plutarch shows that *Greek terms for "eye," "vision," "looking" etc. are polyvalent. Ops, omma* (lit. "eye") can also have the extended sense of vision, gaze, glance, looking, beholding, depending on the context. All can be synonyms for "Evil Eye" or "looking with an Evil or envious Eye," with the context being determinative. Plutarch's use of various verbs for seeing, beholding, looking at (*katablepein, prosblepein, emblepein, antiblepein,*

55. On amulets and protective strategies and devices see below, pp. 155–266.

56. *Mor.* 680D, E, F; 681B, D–E; 682A–B, D–F; 683A.

57. *Mor.* 680E; cf. also Theocritus, *Idyl* 6.39 (a girl, Galateia, becomes envious and wastes away).

58. *Mor.* 681E–F; 682A, C–D, F–683A.

59. For Plutarch's justaposing Evil Eye and envy elsewhere see also *Dio* 2.6.1; *Demetrius* 50.5; *De recta* [*Mor.* 39D]; *De curios.* [*Mor* 518C]; *De cap.* [*Mor.* 91B–C]; *Mul. Virt.* [*Mor.* 254E; *De frat.* [*Mor* 485E]; *De invidia* [*Mor.* 538D]; *Quaest. Conv.* 5.7 [*Mor.* 680B; 681F; 682A, D; 683A]; *An seni* [*Mor.* 796a]; *Non posse* [*Mor.* 1090C].

antiblepseis; horan, prosoran) in this context are all related to looking with
an (envious) Evil Eye (*baskainein, katabaskainein*).[60] This is the case in other
sources as well.

9. The Evil Eye encompasses *both seeing and speaking*, both an Evil Eye
and an evil tongue or breath (as with the Thibaeans, *Mor.* 680D–E).

10. Evil Eye belief includes belief in the existence and threat of deities
and demons,[61] among which are the deity *Baskania* (the personification of
the Evil Eye) and the *baskanos daimôn* (Evil Eye demon).

11. Plutarch attests the belief that Evil-Eyed persons/fascinators can
Evil-Eye themselves (682B–F), a notion of autofascination also attested elsewhere. A funery inscription from Arsameia[62] speaks of any person "who
tries to conceal cowardly hatred that springs from jealousy/envy[63] even
while his hostility tries to deny (the fact), and *melts his own eye over someone
else's good fortune*" (line 216)—that person will be punished by the gods.[64]
Beside portraying one's envying as *melting one's own eye* (cf. Sir 18:18), it
also names a "base heart" as the locus of evil disposition (line 229), as do
numerous biblical texts. Not only can praise and admiration of another
arouse an Evil Eye, but also admiration of oneself, as in the case of Narcissus
and Eutelidas (*Mor.* 682B, D); see also Theocritus (*Idylls* 6.39) concerning
a certain Dametas, who admired his own image reflected in the water and
to protect himself from self-fascination, spit three times on his own chest.

12. Regarding the Evil Eye as a cause of illness is a consequence of the
belief that success or misfortune do not just happen (impersonal causation
as assumed in modern Western thought). Such failure, illness, misfortune
and even death, it is believed, rather is caused by some *personal* agency either human or superhuman (divine or demonic). At instances of such suc-
cesss or misfortune the question asked is not "*why did this happen?*" (as
modern Westerners ask) but rather "*who/what caused this? Who made this
happen? Who has it in for me? "Did I do this to myself?*"

---

60. *Baskainein: Mor.* 681D; 683A; *katabaskainein: Mor.* 680C; 682B, D, E. See also
other works of Plutarch including *Non posse* [*Mor.* 1090C] (*hypo de baskanias kai
phthonou prosorasthai*); *Mul. virt.* [*Mor.* 254E] (*katablepein*); *parablepein:* (and *bask-*):
De amore prolis [*Mor.* 496B]; *De curios.* [*Mor.* 515D].

61. Plutarch speaks of "the evil and Evil-Eyeing demons" (*ta phaula daimonia kai
baskana, Dio* 2.5–6.1).

62. I. Arsameia, *Antiochus I,* lines 210–220; text and translation in Danker
1982:251.

63. Danker renders "jealousy," but "envy" is preferable.

64. The entire inscription, a "Declaration by Antiochus I of Kommagene Providing
for the Eternal Memory of his Beloved Father Mithradates Kallinikos," (c. 50 BCE) is
given in Danker 1982:247–52, §42.

13. The ideas of Plutarch's speakers echo the theory of an active eye and an extramission theory of vision that was current for centuries, thus pointing to the constancy of the notions.

14. Plutarch and his spokesmen do not simply recount phenomena concerning the Evil Eye and envy, but offer *educated explanations* of how the (evil) eye works by emitting particles, how the ocular glance strikes its victims like poisoned arrows, why children are notable victims, how the Evil Eye serves as a conduit of particles poisoned with envy, how amulets divert the Evil Eye's glance, how being struck by an envious Evil Eye can be cured, how possessors of the Evil Eye can Evil-Eye themselves. The comments reflect an interest in logical assessment of the data and rationale understanding.

15. This conception of the Evil Eye is presented not as an instance of vulgar superstition typical of the uneducated masses. Nor is there any mention of magic or sorcery. This is rather the "scientific" knowledge of upper class, educated elites, explaining as best they can on the basis of current knowledge. The conversation demonstrates how in educated circles, as well as among the *hoi polloi* of the ancient world, the Evil Eye was regarded not as superstition (though so alleged by some) but as a natural phenomenon explainable in the conventional scientific terms of that time. This is a point stressed repeatedly by Rakoczy[65]—and with justification. Plutarch makes no reference to the Evil Eye in his treatise on superstition (*De superstitione* [*Mor.* 164E–171F]) and in this *Table Talk* on the Evil Eye raises the issue of superstition only to deny it. If ancient science, like modern science, is characterized by close observation, careful logic, and stringent deduction, then explanations concerning the active functioning of the eye and the operation of an Evil Eye must be seen as examples of ancient science and not of ignorant or superstitious popular musing. Ancient scientific minds, it is essential to keep in mind, regarded the Evil Eye and its operation as a physical reality working in accord with natural properties and potencies as then understood. The plausibility of this belief rested on the prevalent notion that the eye was a active agent whose emissions were comparable to the sun projecting rays of light or to a lamp emitting beams of light or to an archer shooting arrows from his mighty bow. This notion of vision pervaded the ancient world and was held by the biblical characters and authors as well. Jesus's comparison of the eye to a lamp (Matt 6/Luke 11) is plausible only on the basis of this idea of the eye as an active entity.

65. Rakoczy 1996:5, 112, 256 and *passim.*

Pseudo-Aristotle's discussion of avoidance of an Evil Eye when dining (*Prob. phys.* 20.34, 926b 20–31) reflects a similar attempt at rational explanation.[66] Heliodorus of Syria in his *Aethiopica* offers another.

Two centuries after Plutarch, Heliodorus of Syria published a popular novel that entailed an episode involving injury from an Evil Eye. An extended comment on how this occurs shows both similarities with, and differences from, Plutarch's earlier account. The text is Heliodorus's romance, *Aethiopica* (third–fourth century CE), the longest and best constructed of the extant ancient Greek novels.[67] A healing procedure is also mentioned (*Aeth.* 4.65)—a rarity in the Greco-Roman literature on the Evil Eye.

Set in Egypt where Evil Eye belief and practice had long thrived, the *Aethiopica* is a fantastic romance concerning the adventures of a pair of lovers, Chariclea and Theagenes. Chariclea is the daughter of the king and queen of Ethiopia, and adopted daughter of an Egyptian priest, Charicles, her frequent traveling companion. Theagenes is a Thessalian warrior, whom Chariclea met after she was sent to Greece under the tutelage of Charicles. Their initial meeting and its consequences is recounted in book three, where the Evil Eye (*baskania*) figures prominently (*Aeth.* 3.7—4.5).

The pair had participated in a procession at Delphi led by Chariclea. Theagenes was victor in a race and Chariclea crowned him with the victor's crown. Their eyes met and they gazed intently at one another. Chariclea thereupon falls ill with running eyes and claims a headache (3.7.1). Her adoptive father and tutor Charicles, unaware of the real cause of her distress, namely being smitten by love, turns to his friend, Calasiris the priest, about his daughter's illness. Calasiris advises that it is not surprising that in such a procession before a huge crowd a beautiful young girl like Chariclea should have attracted an Evil Eye (*ophthalmon . . . baskanon*, 3.7.2). This assumption that public exposure of women makes them vulnerable to the Evil Eye, we should note, continues down to the present, It explains, in addition to other reasons, why females from past to present have been sequestered and have covered themselves with veils and robes from head to foot.[68] It was also for this reason that Chariclea was wearing an amulet (bearing a figure

66. See above, pp. 21–23.

67. Sandy (1982) offers an analysis of *Aethiopica*'s literary construction and subsequent history of reception. Yatromanalakis (1988:194–204) examines "Baskanos, Love and the Evil-Eye in Heliodorus' *Aethiopica*"; Dickie (1991) compares the positions of Heliodorus and Plutarch on the Evil Eye. Democritus's theory, according to Dickie (1990), underlies the account of Heliodorus as it did that of Apollonius's *Argonautica*. Rakoczy (1996:205–13) discusses the novel's attention to the Evil Eye and assesses the analysis of Dickie.

68. For antiquity see Tertullian, *Virg. vel.* 15:1–3 (discussed in Vol. 4, chap. 2); for the modern period see Brögger 1968.

of Athena with a Gorgo replica on her shield) as protection against the Evil Eye.[69] Her father then asks Calasiris whether he is among the many that believe in the Evil Eye (3.7.2). Calasiris assures him that he is indeed, and provides an erudite explanation (3.7.3) of how it works:

> [I]t happens in this way: The air flowing about us all, and pen-
> etrating the eyes, nose, and breath, and all the passages to the in-
> ner parts, and carrying with it the exterior qualities and humors
> with which it is imbued, carries an infection with it into those
> who draw it in. Whenever anyone looks with envy (*phthonou*)
> upon beautiful objects, the ambient air becomes charged with a
> malignant quality, and that person's breath (*pneuma*), laden with
> bitterness, blows hard upon the person near him. This breath,
> made up of the finest particles, penetrates to the very bones and
> marrow, and engenders in many cases the illness (*nosos*) of envy
> (*phthonos*), which has received the appropriate name (*onoma*)
> of the influence of the Evil Eye (*baskania*).[70]

Scepticism is registered, as in Plutarch's *Table Talk*, but is also overcome in the end. The mention of doubt may serve not so much to question
the reality of the Evil Eye as to set the stage for this learned explanation of
how it occurs.[71] Here in the *Aethiopica* an affirmation of the existence and
functioning of the Evil Eye (*to katabaskainesthai*) is followed by the comment, "for vision, because it is strongly moved, spreads a remarkable force,
since they (those seeing) send it forth with the help of fire-like breath (*pneuma*)." The explanation is similar to, but also variant from, that of Plutarch
some centuries earlier. In place of effluxes from the eye (Plutarch) or from
the entire body (Democritus), here it is the surrounding and penetrating *air*
that is said to be the medium by which envy, alias the Evil Eye, is conveyed
from fascinator to victim to cause illness. Focus on the *air* as the key element between the fascinator and the victim recalls Aristotle's attention to
breath's condensing on a mirror and his air-borne theory of contagion.[72]
Thus Heliodorus appears to present a pastiche of several theories, as Dickie
and Rakoczy have argued.[73] The notion of the eye as active organ, however,

69. So Yatromanolakis 1988.

70. Following, with minor modifications, the translations of Story 1877:158 and Lamb, *Ethiopian Story,* 1961:75–76.

71. So Rakoczy 1996:208.

72. Aristotle, *Insomn.* 459b 27–32; see also Pseudo-Aristotle, *Problemata inedita* 3.52 (*Aristotelis opera omnia,* ed. Bussemaker 4:332). On Aristotle, see also above, pp. 20–24, 29, 58–59, and Rakoczy 1996:134–40.

73. Dickie (1991) reviews various possibilities of literary relationship, concluding that Plutarch was Heliodorus's main source. "Heliodorus gets from Plutarch the idea

the association of Evil Eye and envy, and the looking at another with envy
as a cause of illness and injury are basic elements of the Evil Eye complex
known to both Heliodorus and Plutarch.

In support of this explanation, Calasiris mentions the illness of ophthalmia, how plague is affected by atmosphere, and how intense looking
affects lovers (3.7.4–5), the last of which echoes words of Plutarch on the
same subject:[74]

> The origin of love is also an argument to the same effect, which
> owes its first beginning to sight, which strikes its passion into
> the soul. And for this very good reason: the eyes, being of all
> the passages and openings of the body the most susceptible, the
> most fervent, the most readily receptive of surrounding affec-
> tions, and drawing to itself, by its warm spirit the influence of
> love . . . And if some strike with an Evil Eye (*katabaskainousin*)
> those whom they love and are well disposed to, one must not be
> surprised if those who are by nature envious (*physei gar phthon-
> erôs echontes*) do not what they wish but what nature compels
> them to do. (*Aeth.* 3.7.5, 3.8.2)[75]

Love starts with looking, and looking conveys passion to another's soul.
The eyes are the most receptive of bodily openings and draw in this passion. Both the Evil Eye and envy can strike their victims "by nature," i.e.
involuntarily.

The explanation advances a breath-borne theory of contagion not
mentioned by Plutarch but found in such theorists as Aristotle and Galen. Support for the theory includes not only the role that sight plays in
lovemaking and wooing, but the effect of the bird called the *Charadrios* or
plover, which can draw jaundice from the bodies of those who suffer from
this illness.[76]

---

of offering a scientific explanation of *baskania*" but his explanation differs radically
from that of Plutarch. It builds rather on "an air-borne theory of contagion such as
Galen expounds" (Dickie 1991:18, 24). Rakoczy (1996:205–13) presents a differently
nuanced view.

74. Plutarch, *Quaest. Conv.* 5.7.2 [*Mor.* 681A–C].

75. Heliodorus's statement appears to be a reconstruction of ideas from Plutarch,
Quaest. Conv. 5.7 [*Mor.* 681A–E; 682C–D]. A further point in common is the cure
of jaundice by the plover (*charadrios*; 3.8.1); cf. Plutarch, *Quaest. Conv.* 5.7.2 [*Mor.*
681C–D]).

76. Compare Plutarch, *Quaest. Conv.* 5.7.2 [*Mor.* 681C–D] on the *Charadrios*/plo-
ver with notions concerning the basilisk (not in Plutarch), a mythical beast whose gaze
and breath, it was thought, could wither and destroy whatever they strike (Pliny *NH*
8.33.78; 29.66. On the "jaundice bird" see also Pliny, *NH* 30.94.

Other references to the Evil Eye are also made throughout the novel.[77] Previously in the story, worry was expressed that the *baskania* of a *daimôn* might deprive a man of a substitute daughter (2.33). Mention also was made of the eye of Chronos striking a family and bringing misfortune (2.24), and of a woman with irresistable charm who captured persons by the net that she dragged behind her and that was hurled "from her eyes" (2.25).

After the explanation of how the Evil Eye works, Theagenes falls ill, showing the same symptoms as his beloved Chariclea, and he yawns (3.11), suggesting that he too had been struck by an Evil Eye (*baskania*).[78] Next to Chariclea, he was the most prominent and hence most vulnerable person in the crowd. (The Evil Eye, we recall, was thought to attack those who most excelled and stood out.) Charicles, convinced that the Evil Eye is the cause of his adopted daughter's illness, approaches Calasiris as a healer of the Evil Eye (3.19) with the confidence that it can be healed. Still later, the possibility is entertained that her illness was caused unintentionally by the Evil Eye (*baskania*) of Theagenes, her admirer (4.5). His feeling toward her was not that of a malevolent enemy but of an adoring lover, who could nevertheless do his beloved unintentional but actual harm by Evil-Eying her (*katabaskênas*) with his "envy-inflected glance" (*epiphthonon blemma*, 4.5). Four notable elements of the Evil Eye belief complex appear here: (1) the connection of the Evil Eye with envy, (2) its activation by admiration, (3) its unintentional operation; and (4) its causing illness. All this is quite serious and plausible and in no way connected with vulgar magic which Calasiris rejects (3.16.3–4).

Toward the end of this episode (4.5), Calasiris the priest treats the afflicted Chariclea with a healing ritual for relief from the Evil Eye. Calasiris uses laural, a tripod, fire and incense. He speaks a prayer, waves laurel over the body of the ill girl from head to foot, whispers secret words, yawns, and names Theagenes as the one responsible. These steps are perhaps a parody of an Apollonian oracle and ritual meant to amuse. They are also similar, nonetheless, to actual procedures used for healing then and in modern Circum-Mediterranean settings.[79] This ritual for healing a victim of the Evil

---

77. For terms of the *bask-* family in the *Aethiopica* see *baskania*: 2.1. (*daimôn baskanias*); 2.33. (*daimonos baskania*); 3.7 (*phthonos*= *baskania*); 3.9; 3.18; 3.19; 4.5 (twice); *baskainein* (4.5); *katabaskainein* (3.8; 4.5); also *ophthalmos baskanos* (3.7; 3.11).

78. Yawning also occurs later in the healing of the affliction caused by the Evil Eye (4.5.2–3). Calasiris yawns as part of his healing ritual, simulating the yawn of an old woman traditionally engaged to cure Evil Eye attacks (Dickie 2000:246–47).

79. See Schmidt 1913:603–5; Campbell 1964:339; Brögger 1968:15–17; Yatromanolakis 1988:202–3; and Rakoczy 1996:211–12.

Eye is the only such description in ancient Greek and Roman literature, but parallels procedures indicated in much earlier Sumerian texts.[80]

Further mention of envy (*phthonos*) on the part of various characters illustrate the conventional connection of the themes of the Evil Eye and envy.[81] Eventually after numerous harrowing adventures of the lovers and Calasiris, Chariclea's actual identity as daughter of the Egyptian queen is revealed, she is reunited with her parents, the lovers marry, and her illness disappears.

To summarize, salient aspects of Evil Eye belief and practice as mentioned by Plutarch appear here in Heliodorus's *Aethiopica* as well: the eye conceived as an active organ, whose power can cause injury and illness; the high value of its victims—in this case beautiful youths in love; lovers as admiring and possibly Evil-Eyeing one another; uncertainty of both Evil Eye possessors and victims as to whether the Evil Eye was the cause of illness and if so, whose Evil Eye it was; unintentional as well as intentional operation of the Evil Eye; cure of the Evil Eye as possible—in this case through a healing ritual; the Evil Eye (and envy) as explanation of illness's origin; the Evil Eye as linked with envy (which is also known as *baskania*); envy as transmitted by looking and hence via an Evil Eye; polyvalent terms for eye, vision etc.; personal causation of evil (in contrast to mere happenstance); echo of earlier scientific theories of the eye and vision; an informed explanation of Evil Eye operation, with no accusations of magic or sorcery but only an amalgam and modification of earlier educated theory. Writing for upper-class literate popular consumption, Heliodorus and Plutarch both present not vulgar but educated explanations of how the Evil Eye and envy bring about their damage and why the belief is plausible and to be taken seriously.[82]

Rejecting the notion that Calasiris was a perpetrator of fake hocus-pocus, G. N. Sandy observes in his literary analysis of the novel that:

80. See Langdon 1913:11–12, Plate 3; Ebeling 1949:209; Thomsen 1992:29 and Vol. 1, chap. 2.

81. These include a younger brother's envy of his elder brother's elevation as priest (7.2); the envy of a royal woman, Arsace, of the love of Theagenes and Chariclea (7.7, 10, 26; 8.7); Theagenes' concern that even his beloved Chariclea might feel envious (7.21); and Achaemenes' envy of Theagenes who is favored and honored as Arsace's cupbearer (7.27) and as the beloved of Chariclea (7.29).

82. Dickie (1991:21–23, 28) maintains that Calasiris's discussion of the Evil Eye (3.7–9) was not meant to be taken seriously but is rather a "tongue in cheek" pseudo-explanation "having fun at Charicles' expense." This is convincingly rejected by Rakoczy (1996:210 n776) who contests each of Dickie's three main points. The dissimilarities among the similar passages of Heliodorus and Plutarch, and Heliodorus's "lack of internal coherence" (Dickie 1991:29), even if granted, are insufficient to prove an intent on Heliodorus' part to mock and make fun.

Heliodorus's portrayal of Calasiris is that of a true-to-life Egyptian holy man of his age. There is a tendency in this age to view him and his kind through the cynical eyes of a Lucian, to dismiss his religious practices as fake hocus-pocus. This is to overlook the reputation of Egypt and the character of ancient religion, of the Neoplatonism contemporary with the composition of the Aethiopica, of such a *Wundermann* as Peregrinus and, most important, the summary of Calasiris's words as he and Chariclea are unwilling witness to a scene of necromancy:

For it is not right for a prophet either to attempt or to take part in these practices. For prophets, communication with the divine derives from proper sacrifices and holy prayers, but I come to the uninitiated by actually crawling along the ground among corpses, just as this unfortunate encounter has provided the opportunity to see this Egyptian woman doing. (*Aethiopica* 6.14.7)

The passage simultaneously distinguishes between religious mystery and magic and unites them in the person of Calasiris. While expressing high-minded aversion to popular magic, he nonetheless applies the information obtained from its application to the advancements of the divinely ordained goal of the story.[83]

In the texts of both Plutarch and Heliodorus, the most extensive discussions of the Evil eye in antiquity, the Evil Eye is regarded not as a case of vulgar superstition of the ignorant mases, but as firmly accepted by educated upper-class elites as an actual physical phenomenon of nature.[84] Scepticism on the part of some is registered in both sources, but then is met and countered with explanations of how the eye, the Evil Eye, and envy work. These explanations are based on what were then regarded as physical realities and natural properties. No one labels or classifies it as an instance of magic or sorcery. Injury from the Evil Eye is brought about, not by the application of esoteric knowledge, the use of incantations, or manipulation of certain powerful substances, but only by the physical properies of the eye itself and the corrosive power of envy that the eye releases. These properties are regarded as noxious but also as bequeathed by nature.

83. Sandy 1982:74.

84. So also Rakoczy 1996:211–12, calling for necessary attention to the shifting boundaries between theoretical knowledge and magical praxis. The boundary shifts as substantiated knowedge increases and unsubstantiated belief diminishes over time. With this fluidity of boundaries, "magic" and "superstition" have no utility as descriptive or analytical concepts.

THE ANCIENT EVIL EYE BELIEF COMPLEX IN DETAIL

Extended texts on the Evil Eye such as those of Plutarch and Heliodorus, coupled with an array of brief references to the Evil Eye in literary texts, personal letters, inscriptions, amulets and the like, reveal a regularly appearing cluster of features that we can identify as an Evil Eye belief complex. I am using "complex" to denote a constellation of interrelated experiences, sensations, thoughts, beliefs, feelings, and actions situated within, and influenced by, a still larger cultural system of knowledge, perceptions, values, expectations and norms. This constellation of factors centers on the eye and the act of looking/gazing/staring—for good or evil. It is this constellation of factors that gives the belief its plausibility and power. Let us then first consider the basic compenents of this complex and then additional salient features of Evil Eye belief and practice in Greco-Roman antiquity. By identifying most of the recurrent features of this belief and practice, we gain a basis for anticipating and detecting the presence of this belief and associated behavior in literary texts, art, and artifacts, even when not explictly mentioned.

The credibility of the Evil Eye notion rests on a foundation of interrelated beliefs and premises including the conception of the eye as an active rather than passive organ and a related extramission theory of vision; a presumed relation of eye and mouth (looking and speaking, an evil eye and an evil tongue) and of eye and mind/spirit/heart; the connection of the (evil) eye and looking with envy, which itself is fueled by a notion of the limited nature of all goods, rivalry and struggle to attain these goods, and a notion that one person's gain automatically means another person's loss. To this complex also belongs the notion that the emotional malice conveyed by the Evil Eye and the harm it causes can be thwarted, warded off or repelled by certain apotropaic devices and strategies.

The Eye as Vital and Preeminent Organ

"The eyes," Desmond Morris writes, "are the dominant sense organs of the body," supplying an estimated 80 percent of our information about the outside world. Over the centuries this opinion seems to have prevailed.[85] The ancients valued the eye as one of the most important organs of the human body and chief source of information. Eye-witness accounts of events were deemed the most trustworthy. Use of the eye and vision provided knowledge of, and influence over, objects over great distance. Varro observed that

---

85. Morris 1985:49; on the eyes, see Morris 1985:45–64, including 57–60 on the Evil Eye and its aversion; for Evil Eye aversion also 105 (spitting) and 200 (baring buttocks).

> *Video* ["I see"] is from *visus* ["sight"], which is from *vis* ["strength"]; for the greatest of the five senses is in the eyes. For while no one of the senses can feel that which is a mile away, the strength of the sense of the eyes reaches even to the stars. (Varro, *Ling. lat.* 6.80)

Since the eyes are the chief means of apprehending reality, Plato and the Church Fathers spoke of the apprehension of God as the "beatific *vision* of God.[86]

In the ancient physiognomic tradition, which held that moral character was indicated by somatic signs, eyes were deemed a paramount indicator of one's nature and character.[87] Pseudo-Aristotle frequently remarks how eyes are distinguishing markers of various character types.[88] Polemon (*Physiognomonica* 1.20) devotes almost one-third of his work to the topic of the eye. Cicero recalls that the physiognomist Zopyrus claimed to discern men's character from scrutinizing their bodies, eyes, faces and brows (*De fato* 5.10). The eyes in particular, he noted elsewhere, reveal the stirrings of the heart:

> Nature has so formed his human features as to portray therein the character that lies hidden deep within him; for not only do the eyes declare with exceeding clarity the innermost feelings of our hearts, but also the countenance, as we Romans call it, which can be found in no other living being, save man, reveals the character. (Cicero, *De legibus* 1.9.26)

In successful oratory, he explains,

> everything depends on the countenance, while the countenance itself is dominated by the eyes . . . For delivery is wholly the concern of the feelings, and these are mirrored by the face and expressed by the eyes. (Cicero, *De orat.* 3.221–223)

"The eyes," Pliny the Elder asserted (*NH* 11.52.139), "are the most precious part of the body (*pars corporis pretiosissima*) and the part that distinguishes life from death by the use it makes of daylight." He then proceeds to give information on how the eye, its physiology, double pupils, eyebrows, and

---

86. See the magisterial study of W. Deonna 1965 on the primacy of the eye in antiquity (and beyond) and the eye as window of the body (1965:1–52); see also Wilpert and Zenker 1950.

87. Pseudo-Aristotle, *Physiognomonica* 811b15–28; 812a38–812b13 and Polemon, *Physiognomonica* 1.107–170.

88. Pseudo-Aristotle, *Physiognomonica* 807b1, 7, 19, 23, 29, 35; 808a1, 3, 8, 9, 12, 16, 28, 30, 34; 808b6; 812b8; 813a21.

eyelids were regarded in his day. The eyes, he observes, are windows to the mind and soul:

> No other part of the body supplies greater indications of the mind/soul (*animi*)—this is so with all animals alike, but especially with man—that is, indications of self-restraint, mercy, pity, hatred, love, sorrow, joy . . . in fact, the eyes are the abode of the mind (*in oculis anima habitat*). (Pliny, *NH* 11.54.145)[89]

Philostratus, commenting on physical features revealing character, mentions a person's eyes, eyebrows and cheeks, and states similarly:

> For in many cases a man's eyes reveal the secrets of his character, and in many cases there is material for forming a judgment and appraising his value in his eyebrows and cheeks, for from these features the dispositions of people can be detected by wise and scientific men, as images are seen in a looking-glass. (Philostratus, *Life of Apollonius of Tyana* 2.30, LCL trans.)

The eye, across cultures, could represent the entire body or the entire person.[90] Representations of eyes were inscribed or painted on Neolithic Chinese and Bronze Age Celtic funerary pottery, presumably to ward off humans and hostile spirits. Eyes adorned and protected bowls and drinking vessels and their users, homes and their residents, ships and their contents. The eye served as potent image of various deities. Symbols of the eye included items with a similar shape, such as circles, concentric circles, ovals, the *kteis* (term for the female genitals which, when open, had an eye-like shape), the "eye" of the penis, and the fish, among other things.[91] The eye in antiquity and beyond has been associated with life, fecundity, perception, intelligence, thought, understanding, faith, vigilance, surveillance, security, light, fire, sun, moon and stars, and deity.[92] All such eye shapes or features were potentially associated with an Evil Eye—either as qualities threatened by an Evil Eye or items capable of countering an Evil Eye.

The Eye as Active Organ and Ancient Theories of Vision

The prevalent view of the eye in antiquity, as already noted, held that it was an active organ projecting particles of energy, a view that remained

89. See, similarly, Quintilian, *Inst. Orat.* 11.3.75; Lactantius, *De Opificio Dei* 8.12.
90. Deonna 1965:14, 115.
91. See Deonna 1965:25–26, 68; Gravel 1995:56–60, 91–100, 121–24.
92. See Deonna 1965:48 and *passim* for a full discussion.

dominant through Late Antiquity and the Middle Ages.[93] Prior to any attempt at scientific explanation of the eye and the process of vision, the eye was universally considered an active organ that cast forth light (Mesopotamia, Egypt, Homer, Hesiod and thereafter). The Greek poets and tragedians, as noted above, spoke in terms that implied a view of the eye as active organ.[94] Pindar (*Frag.* 123) cannot imagine desire failing to ignite the heart of anyone who "has seen the rays flashing from the eyes of Theoxenos." Straton of Sardis (second century CE), a homoerotic poet included in the *Palatine Anthology/Anthologia Graeca*, says of a boy: "Your eyes are sparks, Lycinus, divinely fair; or rather, master mine, they are rays that shoot forth flame."[95] Plutarch, as we saw above, also shares this concept: The eye, he states, emits a "flame-like brilliance" (*Quaest. Conv.* 5.7 [*Mor.* 681A]), light or particles from the eye strike and wound victims (*Mor.* 681B, E). The ocular glance or eye "kindles passion/fire" (*Mor.* 681C).[96] Pliny (*NH* 11.55.151) tells of the eyes of night-roaming animals like cats that "shine and flash" (*fulgent radiantque*) in the dark," of the wild goat and the wolf whose eyes "gleam and shoot out light" (*splendent lucemque iaculantur*) and of fish that "shine out (*refulgent*) even in the dark."

Alcmaeon of Croton, a natural philosopher of the early fifth century BCE, was the first Greek to comment directly on the nature of vision.[97] He spoke of an inner fire of the eye which had active potency.[98] With the development of specific *theories* of vision, one of the earliest scientific discussions advanced an emanation theory of apperception. This was first formulated by the scientist, philosopher and poet Empedocles (c. 493–c. 433 BCE), as indicated by Plato (*Meno* 76cd) and Plutarch (*Quaest. Nat.* 19 [*Mor.* 916D]). Empedocles, like Alcmaeon, presumed the eye to be an active organ and therefore comparable to a lamp projecting light.[99] Vision, he maintained, involved particles emanating from the eyes and meeting particles emitted by the object viewed. Though the evidence is only fragmentary in the case of both Alcmaeon and Empedocles, it suffices to demonstrate an understanding of the eye as active and projecting fire-like rays of light. This became

93. Elliott 1988, 1990, 1991, 1992, 1994, 2005a, 2005b, 2007a, 2007b, 2008, 2011, 2014, 2015, 2016B; Rakoczy 1996:19–37, 186–216; and above, p. 60.

94. See above, pp. 9–24.

95. Straton, "The Boyish Muse" in *Anthologia Graeca*, Book 12 (ed. F. Jacobs, 1817).

96. See also Heliodorus (*Aethiopica*), Alexander of Aphrodisas (*Problemata physica*), and Athenaeus (*Deipn.* 13.564bc).

97. So Rakoczy 1996:21.

98. Alcmaeon Frag. A 5 (Diels-Kranz, *FVS* 24 A5).

99. Empedocles, Frag. 31 B84 (Diels-Kranz, *FVS* 31 B 84, vol. 1:342.4–9), cited by Aristotle, *De sens.* 2.437 b23–25. On Empedocles' theory of vision see O'Brien 1970.

the basis for the later atomic theory of the *eidola* ("images") formulated by Democritus of Abdara.[100] Vision, he postulated, occurs through the impact of *eidola* (lit. "images," films) shed from the surfaces of sensible objects (perceiver and perceived) upon the soul-atoms through the sense organs.[101] Epicurus held a similar view.

Plato provides the first, more than fragmentary, exposition of this theory of vision and an active eye. When the gods fashioned the human body and the eyes, he observes, they designed the eyes to give light, involving a pure and gentile fire flowing through the eyes coalesing with daylight and forming together a stream of vision (*Timaeus* 45). In the *Theatetus*, Plato transmits approvingly anonymous tradition concerning the senses (156–157), which also presumes an active eye. The eye emits a glance (*opsis*) that merges with energy emitted by an object to create color (i.e. white) and an observed white object (156).

This view of the eye as active and the "extramission (or 'emission') theory" of vision were dominant among the differing theories of vision in the ancient world and through the Middle Ages, and in fact until modern time. It was held, in various versions, by the majority of ancient authorities including Alcaemon, Empedocles, Parmenides (fifth century BCE), the Pythagoreans, Plato, Theophrastus (c. 371–c. 287 BCE, though pupil of Aristotle), the Stoics, Euclid (fourth–third century BCE), Lucretius (94–55 BCE), Ptolemy (100–175 BCE), and the famous and influential anatomist and physician Galen of Pergamum (125–c. 199 CE). It is the theory assumed by Plutarch (c. 50–120 CE), Heliodorus (*fl.* 220–250 CE), and Alexander of Aphrodisias (*fl.* third century CE) to explain the working of an eye and an Evil Eye. Aristotle, who considered, and vascillated between, both extramission and intromission views, was an early but lone advocate of the latter.[102] Later stages of the Aristotelian tradition show a preference for and return to the extramission theory.[103] This extramission view was held by leading

100. Rakoczy 1996:191 n706; see also above, pp. 57–60.

101. On Democritus's theory of vision see Baldes 1975; Burkert 1977; Dickie 1991; Rudolf 2011.

102. For Aristotle on the eye as active see Aristotle, *Insomn.* 459b 27–32 and Aristotle, Frag. 347 (ed. Rose). For his contesting of Empedocles see Aristotle, *De Sens.* 2.437b14; see also 2. 437b23–438a5. On his vascillation, see Rakoczy 1996:134–40.

103. Pseudo-Aristotle, *Probl. phys.* 20.34, 926b 24 and *Problema inedita* 3.52; see Rakoczy 1996:144–55. On active or passive eyes and ancient theories of vision see Deonna 1965:143–96 (143–47 on alternative theories); O'Brien 1970; Hahm 1975; Lindberg 1976; Betz 1979, 1995:442–49; Allison 1987:62–66; Beare 1996:14–23; Rakoczy 1996:19–37, 186–216. Park 1998:34–35, 39–41 (with diagrams of theories from Aristotle to Newton); Markus 1999; The subject is discussed below in greater detail in connection with components of the Evil Eye belief complex.

intellectuals as well as the common people. Roman authors wrote less on the subject of vision, but where they did it is clear that they too presumed both an active eye and the reality of an Evil Eye.[104] Old Indian texts of the Veda, Egyptian tradition, and Chinese texts likewise presumed an active eye along with a menacing Evil Eye.[105] This holds true also, as we shall see in Volume 3 for the biblical communities of both the Old and New Testaments.

Although contending theories of vision postulating a passive eye were occasionally proposed (e.g. by Aristotle), the theory of an active eye was dominant throughout antiquity. Its continuation in the West through the Middle Ages and beyond is illustrated by philosophers and theologians Thomas Aquinas (1225–1274) and Marsilio Ficino (1433–1499) in his commentary on Plato's *Symposium* and Ficino's treatise on the Evil Eye, artist Leonardo da Vinci (1452–1519), and theologian and reformer Martin Luther (1483–1546).[106]

Scientific and popular conversion to another theory of vision was slow in coming and sporadic in occurrence.[107] In the tenth century, the scientific experiments of the brilliant Arabian physicist, Abu Ali Al-Hasan Ibn al-Haytham (965–1039 CE), whose Latin name was *Alhazen*, dealt a major blow to the extramission theory. His pioneering study on light and vision, the seven-volume *Book of Optics* (*De Aspectibus*, 1021 CE), proved the inaccuracy of the extramission theory and the superiority of intromission theory, even though it took centuries for the recognition of this in the West. Light, he maintained, consisted of rays originating not in the eye but in association with the object seen. Light enters the eye; it does not exit from the eye. With a series of arguments he showed that the extramission theory of vision was untenable. In its place he introduced a new introversion theory combining the positions of Euclid (*Optics*) on rays and the visual cone of Ptolemy's extramission theory (*Optics*) stressing the impact of rays falling perpendicularly on the lens of the eye.[108] Although his wide-ranging research earned him the title of "father of modern optics," his conclusions regarding the eye and vision were not adopted in the West for several centuries after his death.[109] It was not until the seventeenth century and even

104. See Seneca, *Nat.* 1.3.7; Pliny, *NH* 11.55.151; Varro, *Ling. lat.* 6.80; Augustine, *On the Trinity* 11.2.4; Rakoczy 1996:37 and n97.

105. Allison 1987:65–66; Rakoczy 1996:37.

106. See Rakoczy 1996:107–8; for other authors holding this active eye theory see also Story 1877:162–64, 181–82, 183–205; Dundes 1992:260–61.

107. For a brief summary of the contending views of extramission and intromission theories of vision and their representatives, see C. G. Gross 1999.

108. On Alhazen's achievement see ibid., 59–60.

109. On this monumental figure of Arabic science see al-Kahalili 2011.

later that the extramission theory was challenged and then slowly replaced. In 1612 the learned Francis Bacon (1561–1626), philosopher, lawyer and one time tutor to King Edward VI, in his famous essay on Envy (*Essays of Counsels, Civil and Moral*, ninth essay), still conceived of envy and the Evil Eye as involving "an ejaculation or irradiation of the eye." The envious gaze "emitteth some malign and poisonous spirit, which taketh hold of the spirit of another, and is likewise the greatest force when the cast of the eye is oblique" (*On Envy*, 56, 64).[110]

The tide turned in the West with the research on vision and optics of such figures as Franciscus Maurolycus (1494–1575), Johannes Kepler (1571–1630), Thomas Harriott (1560–1621), Rene Descartes (1596–1650) and with the scientists working with a wave theory of light (Johannes Marcus Marci de Kronland [1595–1667], Francesco Maria Grimaldi [1618–1663], Robert Hooke [1635–1703], and Christiaan Huygens [1629–1695]). As a result, modern science has now established definitively that the eye is a receptive not a projective organ. Light enters the eye, passes through the cornea to the retina and its receptor cells, forming chemicals creating electrical impulses that the optic nerve transmits to the brain. Vision involves a complex system of photoreceptors, an adjustable ocular lens that focuses incoming light on these photoreceptor cells, and a neural program in the brain to interpret the signals they send. These signals encode information about the position, shape, brightness, distance and movement of visual stimuli and the brain transforms them into images.

The extramission notion of vision was still strong enough in the popular mind in the mid-seventeenth century that "Thomas Browne felt it necessary to set the record right in his *Pseudodoxia Epidemica* [1646])."[111]

Abandonment by the scientific community of the earlier extramission theory of vision and of the eye as an active organ removed the scientific basis on which the plausibility of an Evil Eye projecting injurious rays had rested. This fatal scientific blow to the rationality of the Evil Eye concept seems not to have registered with vast segments of modern populations. Interestingly, both an extramission theory of vision and Evil Eye belief and practice persist in post-Enlightenment societies today, not only among "less developed" nations or ethnic groups, but also in the popular culture of American comic books (Superman and his X-ray vision) and comic strips (Evil Eye Fleegle in Al Capp's comic strip, "Li'l Abner"; the cartoon of Hagar the Horrible)"[112] and even among educated college students. Even though

---

110. See Rakoczy 1996:107 n312.

111. Potts 1982:5.

112. See Vol. 1, chap. 1, "Overview."

the intromission theory of vision is now scientific orthodoxy, a startling 2002 study of American college students found that 50% of them still hold the obsolete extramission theory of vision and the notion of an active eye.[113] Where Evil Eye belief flourishes, there the eye will still be thought of—consciously or unconsciously—as an active organ emitting rays or particles of energy or light.

In contrast to the modern science of the eye and optics and the prevailing intromission theory of vision, the ancient texts on the Evil Eye that we are examining in this study all reflect the presumption of an active eye and an extramission theory of vision. It is this presumption, informed by the educated knowledge of that era that gave belief in the Evil Eye its plausibility and power.[114] "It was indeed the contagiousness of certain evil diseases that probably most influenced the educated as well as the most ignorant among the Greeks and Romans to believe in the dangers of effluvia and exhalations."[115] These bodily emissions, in turn, provided a material and scientific basis for postulating emissions also from the eye and conveyed via the ocular glance. Intense staring, moreover, was considered an intimidating form of aggression, as is the case in the animal kingdom generally, and as remains so in modern Evil Eye cultures.[116] Loss of eyesight or blindness, on the other hand, was a disastrous disability and often viewed as punishment from the gods for gross malignity and hybris.

Like the "eyes" of the celestial sphere, the sun and the moon, the human eye was thought to project rays or beams of light. Thus it was comparable to a lamp, which like the sun, cast forth beams of light. Just as rays of the sun burn and destroy objects on earth, so, it was believed, rays or emissions from the eye (both human and animal) could strike victims and cause injury, illness, or even death by burning. Pliny, the Roman naturalist, citing reports of alien tribes who injure with the Evil Eye (*effascinantium*), mentions the Triballians and the Illyrians, who are reported to "injure by the Evil Eye (*effascinent*) and who kill those at whom they stare for a longer time, especially with furious eyes (*iratis oculis; NH* 7.2.16–18). In Athenaeus's *Deipnosophistae* (13.564bc), Hippodameia says of Pelops that he had "a kind of lightning-flash in his eyes. . .with it he scorches me with the flame." A hieroglyph of an eye emitting rays appears in the Demotic Magical

---

113. Winer 2002; for European-American college students registering belief in the Evil Eye see also Jones 1992.

114. This is stressed also by Rakoczy (1996) throughout his study.

115. McDaniel 1918:341.

116. See, e.g., Gilmore 1987a on ocular aggression in Andalucia, Spain, and Gilmore 1987b on the Circum-Mediterranean more generally; also Meerloo 1971; Coss 1974.

Papyri in connection with a ritual for healing a person of ophthalmia.[117] Israel's literature also compares the eye with the sun and lightning. *1 Enoch* 106:5, 10 states that "His [infant Noah's] eyes are like rays of the sun"; v. 10 continues: "And he opened his eyes and made the whole house bright" (implying that his eyes emitted rays of light). Dan 10:6 describes a human figure whose face was "like the appearance of lightning" and whose eyes were "like flaming torches." The New Testament book of Revelation (1:14) speaks of a human figure whose "eyes were like a flame of fire." Jewish Talmudic tradition tells of two rabbis (Eleazar ben Hyrcanus and Simeon ben Yohai) who with their Evil Eyes *scorched* their victims to ashes.[118] This belief, of course, is presumed in all metaphors of the eye as a lamp, as in Jesus's words in Matthew 6:22, "The eye is the lamp of the body" or in its Lukan version, "No one after lighting a lamp puts it in a cellar or under a bushel, but on a stand, that those who enter [the residence] may see the light. Your eye is the lamp of your body" (Luke 11:33–34a). Plutarch (*Quaest. Conv.* 5.7 [*Mor.* 681A–E]) spoke of the eye emitting particles "as something fiery" (681A), of the glances of the eye "kindling fire" (681C), and of an ocular aggression "as with poisoned arrows" (681E).

The eye, in other words, was thought of as an organ casting forth powerful projectiles analogous to solar rays, fiery darts, or poisoned arrows. The pupil in particular, is the changing part of the eye, the door, it was thought, through which light passed outward while the iris remained stable. "The iris is thus pierced," according to the renown physician Galen, "in order to let out the light that comes from the brain."[119] "The pupil," McDaniel notes, "was the entrance as well as the point of departure for evil."[120] A "darkened eye" (*opthalmos skoteinos*), in contrast to a eye full of, and projecting, light, is like a "dimmed" or "melted" eye, one whose fire has been extinguished, whose power has been lost, and which casts no light—a darkened and non-functioning lighthouse. The metaphor of light as positive and darkness as negative, in other words, also belongs to the conceptual complex of vision and the Evil Eye.

There are numerous terms for "eye" and "vision" in Greek; they are generally polysemous in Greek and Latin, with meanings varying according

---

117. PDM 14.1097–1103. The ritual prescribes oil to which salt and nasturtium seed has been added. With the oil, "anoint the man who has ophthalmia with it, write this on a new papyrus, and make it into a papyrus roll on his body: 'You are the eye of heaven,' in the writings . . . [eye with rays is located here]" (*The Demotic Magical Papyrus of London and Leiden,* col. 20).

118. *b. Bava Metzi'a* 59b, 84a; *b. Shabbat* 33b, 34a; cf. *b. Nedarim* 7b.

119. Galen, *De usu partium corporis humani* 10.6.

120. McDaniel 1918:341 n2.

to context. Thus Greek *ops* (from the root *op-*) can mean "voice" or "word" as well as "eye" or "face" (*ops* equivalent to *opsis*).[121] The related noun *opsis* can have the senses of "aspect," "appearance" or "countenance," "face" or "visual impression." It also can designate (2) the thing seen; or (3) vision, appearance; or the power of sight or seeing. The plural *opseis* can denote the organs of sight—the "eyes," or the iris or pupil of the eye. It can also designate "visual rays" thought to proceed from the eyes.[122] The noun *opôpa* can mean "sight," "seeing" or "outward appearance"; or "eyeball" or "eyes." The related verb *opsomai*, serving as a future of the verb *horaô*, means "see." The related noun *ophrys* means "eye brow." Further related Greek terms for eye and seeing include *ophthalmos* ("eye" [of a human or of heaven]; or, by extension, "dearest, best" [since the eye was considered the most precious part of the body]), *omma* ("eye" [of human or of heaven]; "light," "that which brings light"; " face"; "eye-hole" [of a helmet]), *ommatoô* ("furnish with eyes"); *osse* (neuter plural, [the two] "eyes"); the related verb *ossomai* ("see," " look"; " see with the mind's eye"). The verb *horaô* likewise has multiple senses: "see," "look," "have sight," "see to," "look to"; "behold," "perceive," "observe"; "discern"; see "visions,"; "interview" (LSJ). Terms of the same root include *horasis* ("seeing," "act of sight"; "eyes"); *horma* ("that which is seen," "visible object," "sight"); *horatês* ("beholder"). Synonyms for seeing, looking, beholding include *blepô* (and compounds *hypoblepô, katablepô*), and, as we have now seen, also verbs of the *bask-* root meaning, "to look maliciously and injure with an Evil Eye (*baskainô, katabaskainô* etc.). The verb *derkesthai* means "to stare" and, like other verbs for seeing/looking, is used in conjunction with *bask-* terms with the meaning, "to stare with an Evil Eye."[123] All these terms presume use of the eye as an active organ sending forth emissions from the eye directed at some object, with the possibility of either postive or negative effect.

The Latin terms for "eye," "see," " look," "behold," etc. likewise are polysemous. *Oculus* ("eye"), related to Greek *omma, osse, ossomai*, is kindred with Sanskrit *akshi, aksha*, Indo-Germanic *ok-je*,[124] and can mean "the power of seeing," "sight"; a human "eye"; or, figuratively, an "eye" of the

---

121. See Chantraine 1968 3–4:811–13 on *opôpa, opsomai, omma, osse, ophthalmos*. This parallels the polysemous nature of *bask-* terms, which denote either evil eye or evil tongue. On Greek terms for eye in Greek tragedy see also Hanson 1987.

122. Plato, *Timaeus.* 45c, 46b; Aristotle, *Meteor.* 1.6.343a; 2.9.370a 19; Athenaeus, *Deipn.* 13.564bc. On these terms and their meanings see LSJ, *sub vocibus*.

123. On terms for eye in Greek tragedy see Hanson 1987.

124. Lewis and Short, *Latin Dictionary, sub oculus.* See also the cognates *agaid* (Old Irish), *augo* (Gothic), *Auge* (German); *occhio* (Italian); *ojo* (Spanish); cf. English: *oculist; monocle; ogle*.

heavens, a luminary projecting light such as sun, moon and stars;[125] a "spot" resembling an eye, as on a panther's hide or on a peacock's tail;[126] or, a principal adornment of states (such as their major cities or attractive sites).[127] *Oculus* occurs in expressions such as "to cast one's eye upon," "glance at,"[128] "to covet" (with one's eyes),[129] "apple of my eye, my darling" (as a term of endearment).[130] As already noted, *oculus* also appears in various expressions for "Evil Eye": *oculus invidus, oculus lividus, oculus malus, oculus malignus, oculus nequam, oculus obliquus*. The *oculus* word family includes a broad range of terms.[131] In their standard *Latin Dictionary*, Lewis and Short list these terms and their meanings and note as well that "the ancients swore by their eyes" (as by something very precious).[132]

These Greek and Latin terms and their usage make clear the wide range of associations and analogies and the great importance attached to the eye, vision, the act of looking, and the intense gaze. The metaphor of light as positive and darkness as negative also belongs to the conceptual complex of vision. The eye was thought of as "full of" the entities of light or darkness. To be blind was to have a "dark(ened) eye" (*skoteinon omma*).[133] An envious Evil Eye was also considered a "dark" or "darkened eye" (*skoteinos ophthalmos*).[134]

125. See *mundi oculus* ("*eye of the world*"), of the sun (Ovid, *Met.* 4.228); *stellarum oculi* ("*eyes of the stars*"; Pliny, *NH.* 2.5.4).

126. Pliny, *NH.* 8.17.23; 13.15.30.

127. See Cicero, *De nat. deor.* 3.38.91 (*hi duo illos oculos orae maritimae effoderunt* [Corinth and Carthage]). He refers also to certain villas as "the eyes of Italy" (*ocellos Italiae*; *Ad Atticum* 16.6.2); See, similarly, Justinus, *Hist. Phil.* 5.8.4 referring to Athens and Sparta as the "two eyes of Greece" (*ex duobus Graeciae oculis*).

128. Plautus, *Asinaria* 4.1.24.

129. Cicero, *Verr.* 2.2.15: *adicere ad rem aliquam*; also Cicero, *Agr.* 2.10.25.

130. Plautus, *Pseudolus* 1.2.46: *bene vale, ocule mi!*

131. The verb *oculare* ("furnish with eyes," "make to see," "make visible," "enlighten"); *oculariarius* (*of* or *belonging to the eyes*), *ocularis* (of or belonging to the eyes); *oculare* (a neuter sing. substantive denoting "*medicament for the eyes*," "*eye-salve*"), *ocularis, ocularius* (*of* or *belonging to the eyes*; an "*occulist*"); *oculariter* (adverb, "*with the eyes*"); *oculatus* (an adjective meaning,literaraly, "*furnished with or having eyes*," "*seeing*"; in a transferred sense, "*eye-shaped*," "*ornamented with stars*," "*starred*"; "*that which strikes the eye*," *exposed to view*," "*visible*," "*conspicuous*"); *oculeus* (adjective, "*full of eyes*"; transferred sense, "*sharp-eyed, sharp-sighted*"); *oculissimus* (adjective, "*dearest*," again because the eye was still viewed as the most precious or dear part of the body); *ocultius* ("*as one's own eyes*," i.e. most dearly).

132. Lewis and Short, *Latin Dictionary*, sub *oculus*; see Plautus, *Menaechmi* 5.9.1: *si voltis per oculos jurare, nihilo magis facietis*.

133. Euripides, *Alcestis* 385; cf. Ps 68:24 LXX.

134. *T. Benj.* 4:2; see also Vol. 3.

Given the fact that the eye was considered such a powerful and preeminent organ, it is no surprise that representations of the eye and Evil Eye under attack should figure prominently in the arsenal of amulets constructed to ward off the Evil Eye. Thought to operate according to the principle of *similia similibus* ("like influences like"), images of an eye were deemed to afford protection against an Evil Eye. Apotropac eyes included the Egyptian Eye of Horus, eyes painted on the outside and inside of drinking bowls, eyes on the prows of ships, and depictions of an Evil Eye attacked by an assortment of hostile creatures. The various uses of representations of eyes to repel the Evil Eye are discussed below in more detail.[135]

The Association of an Evil Eye and an Evil Tongue

A further ancillary element of the Evil Eye belief complex was a presumed connection between an Evil Eye and an evil tongue, looking maliciously and speaking maliciously (*oculus malus* and *lingua mala*).[136] Plutarch quoted Phylarchus (FGrHist 81F 79a) concerning the Thibians near Pontus on the Black Sea, who were deemed "deadly not only to children but to adults" through "the glance (*to blemma*) and the breath (*tên anapnoên*) and the speech (*tên dialekton*) of these people."[137] The Roman poet Catullus [84–54 BCE] rhapsodizing on the avalanche of kisses shared between himself and his beloved Lesbia, wishes for a multitude of "kisses, which neither curious *eyes* shall count nor an evil *tongue* fascinate" (*Poems* 7.11–12).[138] Eyes and tongue here are associated and it is the tongue rather than the eye that is said to "fascinate" (*fascinare*, i.e. harm with an Evil Eye).[139] "Evil Eye," "Evil Mouth," and "Evil Tongue" were already associated centuries earlier in the Mesopotamian Akkadian incantation cited in Volume One, chapter 2.[140] We might also recall that *baskainô* and its family of terms is suspected to derive from a root, *bask-/phask-*, that can mean "*speak* (evil words)" as well as "*look* (with ill will and harmful intent).[141]

---

135. See below, pp. 230–45.

136. Compare the relation or equation of the Greek roots *bask-* (looking) and *phask-* (speaking) and the combination of looking and speaking in old Akkadian texts (Thomsen 1991:21–22); see Vol. 1, chap. 2.

137. Plutarch, *Quaest. Conv.* 5.7.1 [*Mor.* 680E].

138. *nec pernumerare curiosi possint nec mala fascinare lingua.*

139. See also Virgil, *Ecl.* 3.103 (*oculus . . . fascinate*), 7.28 and Rakoczy 1996:121–28 on the association of evil looking and evil speaking.

140. See Vol. 1, chap. 2.

141. See above, this Volume, pp. 25–26, 29.

The Association of Eye and Heart

The eye, furthermore, was regarded as a window to the soul or mind or heart, and as a channel outward of the emotions, including love, hate, jealousy, envy and the full range of the passions, as Plutarch shows.[142] Cicero, commenting on the importance of the face and eyes in the communication process, states that,

> everything depends on the countenance, while the countenance itself is dominated by the eyes . . . For delivery is wholly the concern of the feelings, and these are mirrored by the face and expressed by the eyes. (Cicero, *De orat.* 3.221–223)

The eye is window to, and manifestation of, the soul and feelings of the heart.

> The eyes declare with exceeding clarity the innermost feelings of our hearts. Likewise the countenance, as we Romans call it, which can be found in no other living being, save man, also reveals the character. (Cicero, *De legibus* 1.9.26, LCL)[143]

Elsewhere he stated, "For as the face is the image of the soul, so are the eyes its interpreters" (Cicero, *Orator ad M. Brutum* 17.59–60). The connection of the eye with the heart, as the seat of thought, desire, disposition, and emotion, is also assumed by the biblical authors, as we shall see, and is illustrated in Christian statements as found in *P.Oxy* 1.28: "they are blind in their hearts and do [not] have sight [. . .]"; cf. also *Gos. Thom.* 28.[144]

The Association of the Evil Eye with Envy

Among the dispositions thought to arise in the soul or heart, envy (Greek: *phthonos, zêlos;* Latin: *invidia*) was among the most feared, despised, and condemned.[145] Envy, in turn, is inseparably linked with, and often equated

142. See Plutarch, *Quaest. Conv.* 5.7.2 [*Mor.* 681A–C] (regarding love and amorous glances); 681D (the frenzy of hounds dims their sight); 681E–F; 682C–D (envy, along with other passions, is rooted in the soul [*psychê*]).

143. Lucretius thought the mind, the ruling organ of entire body, to be near the heart (*On the Nature of Things* 3.94–322). See also the Arsameia inscription cited above, p. 63.

144. On the association of eye and heart see also Deonna 1965:4–52, 66 and nn4–5. See also Volume 3 for this association in Israel and the Jesus movement.

145. On *phthonos,* paronyms, and etymology see Chantraine 1968 3–4:1202; *zêlos* and paronyms, Chantraine 1968, 1–2:400

with, the Evil Eye. Thus one of the classic studies on envy in antiquity contains a chapter devoted to the Evil Eye.[146] The Latin language, as we have already seen, has lexically encoded this connection of looking (with an Evil Eye) and envy in the terms *invidere* ("to envy," lit. "to look [*videre*] over [*in-*] with ill will"), *invidia* ("envy" arising from looking) and paronyms—all of which have the root *vid-* ("look") as their base. Other evidence, as we have also already noticed, includes the regular juxtaposition of terms for eye, looking, envy, and the Evil Eye. The person held to be an Evil-Eyed person who casts a harmful Evil Eye (a *baskanos* or *fascinator*) is someone who, by virtue of his/her powerful eye, is perceived as dangerous or injurious or morally evil, or anti-social and a threat to the common good. Envy (*phthonos*), which is thought to be discharged from an Evil Eye, is attributed the same negative qualities. In Greek literature, envy was associated with the Evil Eye since Demosthenes, Plato, Aristotle, Strabo, and the Hellenistic poets. Terms of the *bask* family appear more frequently in combination with envy only in later Greek texts, but the concept itself and its association with envy is very ancient.[147] The basis of this association becomes clear when we consider the nature and processs of envy and then compare the similar traits of envy and the Evil Eye.

EXCURSUS ON ENVY

Envy was a much-discussed and much-deplored emotion in the ancient world—by Greek, Roman, and Christian authors alike.[148]

146. Walcot 1978, with ch. 7 (pp. 77–90) on the Evil Eye.

147. Bernand 1991:97–98; Sanders 2014.

148. See Plutarch, *On Envy and Hate* (*De invidia et odio*); Dio Chrysostom, *Orat.* 67, 68; Stobaeus, *Anth./Ecl.* 3.38. Christian: *1 Clement* 4; Gregory of Nyssa, *Life of Moses* 2.256–259 (SC 1.282–284); *Orat. Cat.* 6 (PG 45, 28–29); *De beat.* 7 (PG 44.1285–1288); Cyprian, *De zelo et livore* (CSEL 3.1); Basil of Caesarea, Homily 11 on Envy (*Peri phthonês/De invida*; PG 31.372–385).

On the nature of envy, its salient features, and its association with the Evil Eye in the ancient world, see Davidson 1923; Ranulf 1933–34; Seyrig 1934; Merlin 1940; Steinlein 1944; Wifstrand 1946; Stevens 1948; Odelstierna 1949 (commenting on Wifstrand 1946); Bernet 1950; Eitem 1953; Schaupp 1962; Milobenski 1964; Nusser 1964; Nikolaou 1969; Walton 1970; ; van Unnik 1972; Walcot 1978; Dunbabin and Dickie 1983; de la Mora 1987:3–27; Dickie 1987; Schoeck 1955, 1970:141–61; Bernand 1991:85–105; Dunbabin 1991; Limberis 1991; Slane and Dickie 1993; Brillante 1993; Elliott 1994; 2007a, 2007b, 2008, 2016a; Rakoczy 1996:104–20, 247–70 and *passim*; Hagedorn and Neyrey 1998; M. Nicholson 1999; Horst 2000; Malina 2001:108–33; Kastor 2003, 2005:84–103, 180–87; Konstan 2003, 2006; Konstan and Rutter 2003; Kaster 2005; Gershman 2011a, 2011b; Hinterberger 2013. De la Mora 1987 traces historically the use and shifting nuances of *phthonos* and *zêlos* from Homer through the Greco-Roman age.

Envy—A Complex of Thoughts, Emotions, and Behaviors

The disposition of envy involves a *complex* of thoughts, emotions and be-haviors. It commences with an awareness (by viewing) of the good fortune or happiness of another person perceived as a rival, distress over this good fortune or prized possession of the other, and the desire that the person be deprived of it.[149] It comprises a system of social relations between the envier and the envied and a social dynamic, both of which are situated within a larger system of meanings, values, and normative expectations.[150]

This brief definition of envy can be further elaborated as to its *key elements* (cognitive and emotional) and *psychological and social dynamics*. Envy is (1) a *mix of emotions* (distress, resentment, and malice) that is kindled in (2) a *person or group* (3) upon their *learning* of, mostly by *viewing*—"envy is emphatically an act of perception"[151]—some *success* or form of *prosperity* (4) enjoyed by *another person or group* (5) of relatively *equal social status and perceived as a rival.* (6) The envying agent, *comparing* his/her own situation with the improvement of the situation of the other (7) and presuming a *limitation of all goods* (i.e. reckoning with a notion of "lim-ited good") (9) experiences a *feeling of distress* over the thought that the gain of one's rival has occurred only through one's own personal loss (with gain and loss determined as a zero-sum game). (10) The envier, concluding that she/he thereby has become *inferior to her/his advancing successful rival,* (11) *feels resentment* over this perceived inferiority and reduction in status, and (12) consequently *maliciously wants* the successful person to be *deprived* of the thing that has caused the enviers's distress, loss and inferiority. The ancients also believed that this feeling of envy (13) arose in the *mind/soul/ heart* and (14) *was conveyed to and through the eye,* (15) from which it was *ejected* and then *directed at the object arousing the envy.* Ancient definitions and discussions of envy (and of the Evil Eye) mention one or more of these aspects but not the full ensemble.

149. "Complex," as used here and also when we speak of the Evil Eye belief *com-plex,* refers to a constellation of interrelated factors, a pattern of connected components stable over time. This generalized definition of envy is indebted to the work of Gregory White and Paul Mullen (1989) on jealousy (and envy).

150. On the phenomenon of envy see the classic studies of sociologist Helmut Schoeck (1987), of anthropologist George Foster (1972), of political philosopher Gon-zalo Fernández de la Mora (1987), and of psychologist Melainie Klein (1957, 1975). On envy (and jealousy) generally see also Raiga 1932; Ranulf 1933–34; Stein 1974; W. Evans 1975; Silver and Sabini 1978a, 1978b; Ghosh 1983; A. and B. Ulanov 1983 (esp. pp. 177–179, "A Note on the Psychological Literature on Envy"); Berke 1988; White and Mullen 1989; Parrott 1991; Parrott and Smith 1993; Nicholson 1999.

151. Schoeck 1970:19.

Envy, Jealousy and Zeal

This foregoing description concerns envy, not jealousy with which it is often confused in modern parlence.[152] The ancients related, but distinguished, envy and jealousy and ascribed them different moral valences. In modern speech, on the other hand, envy and jealousy are regularly used as synonyms, supposedly with little, if any, difference in meaning. At least one contemporary dictionary, *Webster's New Collegiate Dictionary* (1977), however, points out under its entry for "envious," that jealousy and envy, while having something in common, "are not close synonyms and can rarely be interchanged without loss of precision or alternation of emphasis" (1977:382). The etymology of the English term "envy" is traced to the thirteenth century and ultimately to Latin via the Old French: "About 1280 envie, feeling of ill will of another's good fortune, borrowed from Old French *envie*, from Latin *invidia*, from *invidus*, envious, from *invidere*, look with ill will upon, envy (*in-* upon) and *videre* to see."[153] Envy is a disposition involving looking (which sets the envy process in motion). In due course this initial looking degenerates into looking with ill will and malevolent intent.

It is important, then, that we be clear on the comparative and distinctive features of envy and jealousy, and of the related emotion of *zeal*. These three terms refer to emotions having certain characteristics in common but also substantive differences. That which relates these three emotions is an *intensity* or *high degree of feeling* marking all three. The modern terms "zeal" and "jealousy" are also related linguistically since "jealous, jealousy" as well as "zealous, zeal" are both cognates of the Latin *zelus, zelotypia* which in turn are cognates of the Greek *zêlos, zêlotypia*. This is the case not only for English but also for Italian (*zelo, gelosia*), Spanish (*celoso, celo*), and French (*jaloux, jalousie*), from which the English *jealous, jealousy* more immediately derive.[154] From a sociolinguistic point of view, however, zeal, jealousy and envy entail different social relations and dynamics.[155]

---

152. Schoeck and Foster discuss at length the differences between envy and jealousy. For the contemporary psychological distinction of jealousy and envy see also Salovey and Rodin 1988, 1989; White and Mullen 1989; Salovey 1991; Salovey and Rothman 1991; Parrott 1991; Parrott and Smith 1993; Purshouse 2004.

153. *Chambers Dictionary of Etymology* 2001:335, *sub* envy.

154. The French term *jalousie*, taken over into English, can also denote a *blind or shutter* of a house having horizontal slats sloping over louver boards to adjust air and light. Excluding sun and rain, the jalousie also blocks others outside the home from looking in and having their envy aroused.

155. I employ here material from my 2007b and 2008a articles on envy, jealousy, and zeal in the Bible.

Zeal marks the intensity of feeling one person or group has in regard to something or someone, some other group, or some deity. It can have either positive or negative promptings and consequences, expressing a high degree of devotion and loyalty on the one hand, or blind fanaticism on the other. It can also shade into feelings of ardor and positive affection, or negative anger, fury or wrath. Being zealous is being enthusiastic about something, showing earnest concern, setting one's heart on something. Zeal is not about possessing, or necessarily about rivalry; by contrast, jealousy and envy are.

Jealousy is intense feeling concerning one's possessions and one's rivalry with others. Jealousy arises in a *social situation* of perceived rivalry between two persons or groups, with the jealous person or group fearing the loss of something possessed due to the machinations of a rival. *Jealousy is intense concern for protecting one's possessions from the encroachments of perceived rivals.* One biblical dictionary correctly defines it as "the intense emotion aroused by the infringement of one's right (or presumed right) to exclusive possession or loyalty."[156] In regard to the *interpersonal relations* involved, jealousy involves threesomes or triads—the jealous agent, the object presumed to be possessed, and a rival third party.[157] *Envy*, by contrast. is *an interaction of only two parties*, the envier and the envied.

Jealousy, like zeal, can be *either positive or negative*, depending on circumstances and social-cultural context. On the one hand, it can be perceived *negatively* as a feeling of insecurity and vulnerability to attack and loss. In biblical times, it could also be viewed positively as an expression of emotional attachment and responsibility toward those under one's control so as to protect lives and to secure group well-being. In this sense, husbands are laudably jealous concerning their wives, and parents and patrons are appropriately jealous concerning their children and clients. The biblical book of Numbers (5:11–31) describes a ritual to be performed by a husband overcome by a "spirit of jealousy" concerning the fidelity of his wife, with his jealousy viewed positively.

A feeling often confused with jealousy but better categorized as "competitiveness" or "friendly rivalry" is the desire to possess what rivals and neighbors possess, but with no interest in harm to the rivals. *Aemulatio* is the term used by Latin authors for this disposition. Its Greek equivalent was one aspect of *zêlos* and paronyms.[158]

---

156. Opperwall and Wyatt 1982:972. Unfortunately, despite the apt definition of jealousy, the entry repeatedly treats jealousy and envy as synonyms.

157. Schoeck 1970:88.

158. See Aristotle, *Rhetoric* 2.11.1–4. Malina (2001:126–28) appropriately distinguishes envy from jealousy, and translates the *zêlos* of which Aristotle speaks, not as "emulation" (its conventional rendition) but as "competitivenes." "Competitiveness" is

Envy is an *intense feeling* like zeal and jealousy, and, like jealousy, concerns the *possession* of someone or something, but has *no positive quality*, since its desire is for loss and destruction. While zeal and jealousy can be either positive or negative, depending on the situation, envy is always evil and never virtuous. The *jealous* person is anxious about some valued good that he or she possesses and wants to keep. The *envious* person is grieved at the valued good that someone else has, with the wish that the rival lose it. *Jealousy* fears damage to *self; envy* intends damage to *others*. *Jealousy* involves wanting to keep what one has. *Envy* involves wanting others to lose what they have. *Jealousy* is more *defensive* in its orientation and concerns intense interest in *retaining* what one possesses. *Envy* is more *offensive* in orientation and concerns malice directed against the success of others.

Arising in a social situation where one person or group sees perceived rivals gaining something of value, envy is the grief or pain experienced at the sight of this success/happiness and the wish that the rival be dispossessed of it. Contributing toward a sense of inferiority deriving from a comparison of self with the fortunate other is a notion of "limited good," a belief that in this "zero-sum game of life" all the good things of life are in limited and scarce supply so that whenever anyone gains, another must lose.[159] The price for your rise in status and honor is my demotion and shame. Improvement in your situation makes us look bad and inferior by comparison. So our interest is in keeping you and all ambitious persons "in their place." "The peg that sticks up will be struck down." Even if an envier gives food or alms to others—an ostensibly positive act—the envier can begrudge the gift as constituting a loss to the envious giver. Accordingly, envy and the Evil Eye (by which envy is directed at targets) can entail or imply miserliness, stinginess, tightfistedness and begrudging. Since envy involves malice and harmful intent toward others, it is obviously inimical to social harmony and group cohesion and often is condemned together with the vices of strife and dissension. On the other hand, to *be* envied, while dangerous, can also be a feather in one's cap since this shows that the envied person is deemed to possess something that is highly valued and in limited supply.[160] Finally, whereas envy is frequently linked with the Evil Eye; zeal and jealousy are

---

preferable to "assertive jealousy," which Malina uses as a synonym for competitiveness. The dynamic is not that of jealous protection but of competitive imitation.

159. Foster 1972.

160. On envy linked with the notion of limited good see Foster 1965; 1972; Malina 1979, 2001:81–107, 108–33; Pilch and Malina 1998:59–63, 122–27; Hagedorn and Neyrey 1998:20–22; Neyrey and Rohrbaugh 2001; on Evil Eye, envy, and limited good see Elliott 1988, 1990, 1991, 1992, 1994, 2005a, 2005b, 2007a, 2011, 2014, 2015, 2016a.

not. In the world and language of Shakespearean drama, Othello is the tragic exemplar of jealousy, and Iago, the despicable agent of envy.

Greek and Roman Distinctions of Envy, Jealousy, and Zeal

The proximity of these emotions (envy, jealousy, and zeal) was apparent to both the Greeks and the Romans.[161] Ancient Greek had two main words for envy, *phthonos* and *zêlos*. *Phthonos* and its family of terms[162] always meant *envy*. *Zêlos* and its family of terms,[163] on the other hand, could denote *envy* or *jealousy* or *zeal*, depending on the social or literary context.[164] *Zêlos* often was paired with *phthonos*[165] or was used interchangeably with *phthonos* in the same context.[166] Thus their pairing often functioned as a hendiadys. This overlap in usage led to various efforts at sorting out meanings and usage, especially of jealousy, competitiveness (emulation), and envy.[167]

Aristotle related and then distinguished *phthonos* and *zêlos* (*Rhetoric* 2.10–11, 1387b–1388b), indicating in the process some of the chief features of envy. *Phthonos*, he explained, is "pain/distress/grief (*lypê*) at the good fortune of others" (*Rhet.* 2.9, 1386b).[168]

161. See the texts and their discussion in Hagedorn and Neyrey 1998; Malina 2001:108–33, and Elliott 1992:53; 1994:55; 2007b; 2008; 2016a.

162. The family of *phthonos* terms is a large one including *phthonos* (envy), *phthonein* (to envy), *phthoneros* (envious); *epiphthonein* (to envy, bear a grudge), *epiphthonos* (adj., liable to envy, arousing envy, envious), *epiphthonôs* (adv., with envy); *diaphthonein* (to envy); *aphthonos* (adj., without envy, ungrudging, generous, plentiful); *aphthonêtos* (adj., "unenvied, bearing no grudge, bounteous"), *aphthonia* (freedom from envy, liberality; of things: plenty, abundance); *aphthonôs* (adv., "without envy," "sufficiently").

163. The terms include *zêleuô, zêlos, zêlotypeô, zêlotypia, zêloô, zêlôma, zêlôsis, zêlôteos, zêlôtês, zêlôtikos, zêlôtos; homozêlia; parazêleô, parazêloô, parazêlôsis; antizêlos.*

164. On *zêlos* and paronyms see Chantraine 1968: vols. 3–4:400; Stumpf 1964.

165. See, e.g., Democritus, Frag. B 191 (Diels-Kranz, *FVS* 68 B 191); Lysias, *Funeral Oration* 48; Plato, *Philebus* 47e, 50c; *Laws* 3.679c (*zêloi te kai phthonoi*); 1 Macc 8:16; *T. Sim.* 4:5; 1 Clement 3:2; 4:7, 13; 5:2.

166. Plato, *Symposium* 213c; *Laws* 679c; Epictetus, *Disc.* 3.22.61; Plutarch, *De frat.* [*Mor.* 485D–E]; *De cap.* [*Mor.* 86C; 91B]; *De tranq.* [*Mor.* 470C; 471A]. The Old Testament parabiblical writing, the *Testament of Simeon,* is an especially good example; for *zêl-* terms see 2:6, 7; 4:5, 9; for *phthon-* terms see 2:13, 14; 3:1, 2, 3, 4, 6; 4:5, 7; 6:2. Among the other *Testaments of the Twelve Patriarchs* see *T. Dan* 1:6 and 2:5; *T. Gad* 4:5; 5:3; 7:4; *T. Benj.* 4:4. See also the Christian writing, 1 Clement 3:1—6:4.

167. On the distinction of envy and jealousy (and emulation) in the ancient world see Davidson 1923; Elliott 2007a, 2007b, 2008, 2016a; Malina 2001:108–33.

168. See also Plutarch, *De curios.* 6 [*Mor.* 518C]. In addition to the distress felt by envy, Plato (*Philebus* 48–49) had also described as envy the pleasure that one finds in the misfortune of others, a feeling also identified as *epichairekakia* and today labeled as

Envy (*phthonos*), Aristotle states, is

> a certain kind of distress at apparent success on the part of one's peers in attaining the good things that have been mentioned, not that a person may get anything for himself but because of those who have it. (Aristotle, *Rhet.* 2.10.1, 1387b)[169]

Envy is a feeling of distress, grief, displeasure (*lypê*). It is directed at one's peers and what they possess. It involves a desire not to obtain for oneself what these others possess (i.e. it is not emulation), but that these others be deprived of what they have that gives them pleasure. It is a not a desire to gain for oneself but that others lose.

> We envy those whose possession of, or success in, something is a reproach to us [and consider it] our own fault that we have missed the good thing in question; this annoys us and excites envy in us. (Aristotle, *Rhet.* 2.10, 1388a)

Envy, Aristotle observes, starts with my looking at, and comparing myself to, peers and their good fortune. This comparing leads to the thought that another's success constitutes a reproach to me for having not gained the good thing in question. This in turn promotes in me a feeling of inferiority and deprivation that arouses envy, namely a feeling of distress over what others possess (and that I do not) and the desire that they lose it.[170] *Zêlos* can have the negative sense of envy or of jealousy, but can also denote something positive that spurs to laudable action. Whereas *phthonos* always focuses on intended harm to *others*, *zêlos* focuses on the *self*.[171] This sense of *zêlos*, Aristotle went on to note, is "pain/distress due not to the fact that another possesses [valued goods] but to the fact that we do not" (*Rhet.* 2.11, 1388a). Here *zêlos* is best rendered "emulation" (Latin, *aemulatio*) or "competitiveness." Emulation

> is a species of competition, and, therefore, presupposes antagonists or opponents . . . Egoistic, indeed, emulation is, and has to be classed under the natural desire of superiority or power, but it is not selfish; it is compatible with generosity of character and good-will, which neither envy nor jealousy is.[172]

Schadenfreude. Aristotle is more consistent in his use of terms. On Plato and envy see Milobenski 1964:21–48, and on this point, 49–53.

169. Translation by G. A. Kennedy 1991.

170. On Aristotle's discussion of envy see Milobenski 1964:59–96; and on his definition and delineation of envy in Aristotle's *Rhetoric*, pp. 59–74.

171. See Milobenski (1964:69–70) on Aristotle's comparison of *phthonos* and *zêlos*.

172. Davidson 1923:322–23, esp. 322.

Emulation differs from envy. "To emulate is to wish to be like someone, to identify with that someone out of admiration. Emulation is not spiteful, self-seeking, begrudging, or malicious, as is envy. Emulation does not seek to hurt the rival, just to equal or surpass."[173] "Competitiveness" is the rendition of Aristotle's *zêlos* favored by Bruce Malina.[174] This laudable quality, like emulation, involves striving for excellence and the valued goods of life and expresses the competition so omnipresent in Greek agonistic society. Thus the polysemic term *zêlos,* when not having the sense of malicious envy or bitter jealousy, can mean competition for something esteemed and emulation of someone virtuous and can be judged noble and praiseworthy.

Whereas Aristotle stressed a positive aspect of *zêlos* in its spurring of wholesome and productive competition to better oneself, the Stoic philosopher Chrysippus noted the negative aspect of grief or pain (*lypê*) involved in *phthonos, zêlos,* and *zêlotypia.* His succinct, nuanced definition is representative of the Stoic view and was often quoted; see, e.g., Diogenes Laertius, *Lives of Eminent Philosophers* 7.111:

> *phthonos* is distress at the good things befalling others;
>
> *zêlos* is distress at the good things befalling another, which good things one had wished for oneself;
>
> *zêlotypia* is distress at the good things befalling another, that one himself already has.[175]

This distinction of the related terms *phthonos, zêlos,* and *zêlotypia* is virtually identical to the distinctions made by the Stoic orator Cicero in his *Tusculan Disputations* between envy (*invidia, invidentia*), rivalry (*aemulatio,* identifying one aspect of *zêlos*), and jealousy (*obtrectatio,* equivalent to *zêlotypia*):

> Envy is distress incurred by reason of a neighbor's prosperity; rivalry (*aemulatio*) is for its part used in a twofold way, so that it has both a good and a bad sense. For one thing, rivalry is used of the imitation of virtue (but this sense we make no use of here, for it is praiseworthy); and rivalry is distress, should another be in possession of the object desired and one has to go without it oneself. Jealousy (*obtrectatio*), on the other hand, is what I understand to be the meaning of *zêlotypia,* distress arising from

---

173. Berke 1988:294 n58.

174. Malina 2001:127–28.

175. *phthonon de, lypên ep' allotriois agathois*
zêlon de, lypên epi tôi allôi pareinai hôn autos epithymei
zêlotypian de, epi tôi allôi pareinai ha kai auto echei.
(Diogenes Laertius, *Lives* 7.111 = SVF 3.412 [ed. H. von Arnim]).

the fact that the thing one has coveted oneself is in the possession of the other man as well as one's own. (Cicero, *Tusc. Disp.*
4.7.16–4.8.17)

The threefold senses of *zêlos* (in addition to that *of "zeal")* are aptly
summarized by Anselm Hagedorn and Jerome Neyrey in their 1998 study
on the anatomy of envy: "*zêlos* can mean both [*sic*] attacking envy, good [i.e.
positive] emulation, and defensive jealousy."[176] While jealousy, like envy, can
have negative force (e.g.excessive possessiveness) and consequences, it can
also, like emulation, be valued positively and regarded as honorable when,
for instance, this feeling moves one to guard and protect one's family and
homestead. *Zêlos, zêlotypia*, and paronyms often have the sense of jealousy
rather than envy when joined with *phthonos* and paronyms. In these cases,
they are not part of an hendyadis composed of *phthonos* and *zêlos/zêlotypia*
and indicating one negative emotion of envy; they rather join envy in lists of
different emotions. Criteria for determining which sense of *zêlos* is intended
(envy, emulation, jealousy, zeal) include the immediate literary context, the
adjacent or conjoined terms, and the nature of the social dynamic described.

Envy, itself, Aristotle observes, is "a kind of pain at the sight of [an-
other's] good fortune" (*Rhet.* 2.10.1 LCL). It is a distress not at lacking some
good oneself but at another's mere possession of it. Cicero echoes this centuries later. "Envy is distress incurred by reason of a neighbour's prosperity"
(*Tusc. Disp.* 4.8.17, LCL). Plutarch agrees: "Envy is pain at another's good"
(*On Being a Busybody* 6 [*Mor.* 518C], LCL). The feeling of envy could be
similar to, or overlap with, other emotions (other than jealousy, competitiveness, and zeal) such as hatred,[177] resentment, anger; bearing a grudge;
bearing malice toward another; feeling malevolent or vengeful toward another; feeling enmity, ill intent, spite, gall, poison toward someone; feeling
embittered over something; feeling miserly and ungenerous, unbenevolent,
unkind, merciless, hostile, murderous toward another; feeling inferior; feeling reduced in status; resenting another's superiority or perceived superiority; feeling unwilling admiration; grudging praise; being "green with envy";
longing to change places with another; wanting another's possessions damaged, harmed, broken, destroyed; intending another's injury, illness, loss, or
death. Among the vices and affects, envy is always negative, never neutral
or positive.[178]

The emotion of envy, prompted by looking and seeing the good fortune
of others, was thought, then, to be communicated outward through the eye.

176. Hagedorn and Neyrey 1998:19.

177. See, e.g., Plutarch, *De invidia* [*Mor.* 536E–538E].

178. Aristotle, *Nic. Eth.* 1105 b22.

This organ conveyed, projected and directed the envy and malice against its victims. As already noted, the Latin terms for envy reflect the association of looking with ill will (*invidere*) and the emotion of envy (*invidia*). The eye and looking play a double role: first in *seeing* something distressful that arouses the feeling of envy, and secondly, in projecting and conveying the malice outward through a damaging ocular glance.

Envy and the Evil Eye

We are now in a position to summarize the salient features of envy and its relation to the Evil Eye.[179] Hagedorn and Neyrey (1998), guided by the classic study of anthropologist George Foster and his "anatomy of envy" (Foster 1972), lists several important aspects of envy in the ancient world.[180] To a summary of their features we can add a few further comments and illustrative texts.

After defining envy and distinguishing it from jealousy, as we have done above, Hagedorn and Neyrey describe the socioeconomic and psychological conditions that breed envy.[181] These include (a) the agonistic nature of ancient Greek society with its love of competition, fighting, feuding, and rivalries of all kind; (b) a prevailing notion of "limited good" that held that all goods and resources of life were in limited and scarce supply so that in the constant competition for these resources, any person's gain implied another's loss; and (c) an endless quest for honor, fame, and prestige (*philotimia*) as one of the most important of the "limited goods."[182] "All were socialized to compete for honor as well as to envy those who in fact succeed."[183]

The notion of limited good is fundamental to the thought process, emotions, and action of envy (and the Evil Eye), as anthropologist George Foster (1965, 1972) has shown, and deserves an additional comment. In his influential study, "The Anatomy of Envy" (1972), Foster has shown that an essential ingredient of the envy process was the widely held notion of

---

179. Ancient classical and Christian discussions of envy also include, beside Plutarch, Dio Chrysostom, *Orat.* 77/78; Stobaeus, *Anth./Ecl.* 3.38; Gregory of Nyssa, *Life of Moses* 2.256–259 (SC 1, 282–284); *Or. Cat.* 6 (PG 45.28–29); and *De beat.* 7 (PG 44.1285–88); *De zelo et livore*; and Basil, Homily 11, "On Envy," (PG 31, 372–85).

180. Hagedorn and Neyrey 1998:15–38.

181. Ibid., 17–20, 20–25.

182. See Gouldner 1965:41–77; Walcot 1978:52–76; Vernant 1988:29–56.

183. Hagedorn and Neyrey 1998:25.

"limited good." His earlier study on "Peasant Society and the Image of Limited Good" (1965), defined this concept:

> By "Image of Limited Good" I mean that broad areas of peasant behavior are patterned in such a fashion as to suggest that peasants view their social, economic, and natural universes—their total environment—as one in which all of the desired things in life such as land, wealth, health, friendship and love, manliness and honor, respect and status, power and influence, security and sagety, exist in finite quantity and are always in short supply, as far as the peasant is concerned. Not only do these and all other "good things" exist in finite and limited quantities, but in addition there is no way directly within peasant power to increase the available quantities."[184]

This presumption of limitation (beginning with the limit on arable land) feeds the urge to compete rather than cooperate with one's neighbors and to regard them as rivals. In the struggle over these limited resources, gain by one's rival automatically entails loss on one's own part, since distribution of these goods is a zero-sum game. If one family moves up the economic and social ladder, another is moved down. Promotion of one always occurs at the cost of demotion of another. This prompts a constant comparison of one's own situation with that of one's neighbors and vigilance toward any change. Beholding any positive change in the condition or well being of my neighbor, I reckon that this could only have happened at my expense, with his gain making me feel inferior by comparision. Resenting his gain at my perceived loss and loathing this feeling of inferiority, I feel envious malice toward the neighbor and desire his/her loss of the thing prompting my distress, resentment, and sense of loss and inferiority. Anyone "who is seen or known to acquire more becomes much more vulnerable to the envy of his neighbors."[185]

The notion was clearly popular in antiquity, in respect to both a sense of limitation and a notion of a zero-sum game. "Can the sun add to his size?" Seneca asks rhetorically,

> Can the moon advance beyond her usual fullness? The seas do not increase in bulk. The universe keeps the same character, the

---

184. G. Foster 1965:296. This notion is found to be prevalent in peasant societies living on the edge of subsistence, faced with unpredictable harvests, and constant competition over goods and services necessary for bare survival but also for the maintenance and enhancement of a family's social position, reputation, and honor.

185. G. Foster 1972:169.

same limits. Things which have reached their full stature cannot grow higher. (*Ep.* 2.79.8–9)

"People do not find it pleasant to give honor to someone else," Iamblichus states, "for they suppose that they themselves are being deprived of something."[186] This reluctance to give for fear of losing is echoed in Plutarch's observation concerning holding back praise when hearing a good speech out of fear of self-deprivation: "As though commendation were money, he feels that he is robbing himself of every bit that he bestows on others" (*On Listening to Lectures* [*Mor.* 44B]).[187] Dio Chrysostom comments on Hesiod's *Works and Days* (§2) where Hesiod speaks of potters and craftsmen who are envious of one another. Plutarch explains that this is

> because each would make less profit from his occupation, whatever that occupation may be, if there were many of a similar occupation. (*Orat.* 77/78.3; cf. 77/78.11, 14)

Neyrey and Rohrbaugh (2001) show how this notion of limited good lies behind and explains numerous biblical passages and related texts.[188] There is a Serbian saying that illustrates the notion of limited good: "The sun has to set for someone so that it can rise for someone else." Or as Gore Vidal once put it: "It is not enough to succeed; others must fail."[189]

On the macro-social level, the notion of limited good contributes to the level of competition already rampant throughout ancient societies, exerting a drag on any efforts at economic or social change. On the psychological and micro-social level, this image of limited good is a major presumption, mostly unreflected, that fuels the envier's distress at, and resentment of, another's good fortune and the malicious wish for its destruction. It is also this association of ideas and feelings concerning envy and its action that animates belief in envy's sibling, the Evil Eye.[190]

The *objects envied* include any signs of success, prosperity, or cause of happiness: good health, many male children, abundant harvests, fertile flocks, victory on the battlefield or at the athletic stadium or on the stage or

186. *Anonymus Iamblichi*, Frag. 1.237 (Diels-Kranz, *FVS*, vol. 2:400).

187. See also Plutarch, *An seni* [*Mor.* 787D].

188. For example, Josephus, *Life* 25.122–123; *War* 1.459; *Ant.* 2.255; 4.32; Philo, *Drunkenness* 28.110; Gen 27:30–40; Judg 7:2; 1 Sam 18:6–9 [and Saul's envy of David]; Mark 6:1–5; 9:38–41; 10:35–45; and especially John 3:22–30; cf. also Fronto, *Letters* 4.1.

189. Quoted by Gerard Irvine, "Antipanegyric for Tom Driberg," memorial service for Driberg (8 December 1976).

190. On envy and limited good see above, p. 88 n160.

in the law court[191]—in short, all manifestations of good fortune that improve one's life, enhance one's standing on the social ladder, and cause others to feel inferior by comparison. "The higher the fortune, the more it excites envy," according to Pindar (*Pythian Odes* 11). The *targets of envy*, Seneca states, are riches (*Epistle to Lucillius* 11.87) and those who are successful: "the less the success, the less the envy" (*Ep. Luc.* 5.42). "Envy is a pernicious dart directed at the best" (*Ep. Luc.* 8.74). Children, who represent the delight and future of the family, are particular objects of envy.

Enviers and the envied, like fascinators and the fascinated with whom they are often identical, come from all walks of life, though envy transpires most frequently not vertically on the social ladder but horizontally among those on the same level and who complete as rivals. It occurs most frequently, Aristotle indicates, between peers and those who are near to one another in time, place, age, possessions, reputation and the like (*Rhet.* 2.10.1, 1386b). Cicero concurs: "People are especially envious of their equals, or of those once beneathy them when they feel themselves left behind and fret at the other's upward flight" (*De orat.* 2.52.209). Sibling envy is commonplace, along with envy among family members, friends, and those of the same occupation.[192] This is a prominent theme in the Bible as well, with such rivalries as Cain and Abel, Sarah and Hagar, Joseph and his brothers, Saul and David and those mentioned in *1 Clement* 4–6—as discussed in Volume 3, chapter 2 and Volume 4, chapter 2. Those are unusually envied whose possessions and position are within the envier's grasp.[193] The brilliant Socrates, however, also was an innocent victim of human envy.[194]

Envy of the Gods

Envy was typical not only of all mortals, but also of the gods (*opis theôn* [lit. "eye of the gods"]; *phthonos theôn* ["envy of the gods"]).[195] "Man is naturally

---

191. See Aristotle, *Rhet.* 2.10.1, 1387b; Pindar, *Pythian Odes* 10.20, *Isthmian Odes* 6.39; Sophocles, *Ajax* 157; Xenophon, *Cyropedia* 7.5.77; Isocrates, *Antidosis* 141–142; *On the Team of Horses* 16.32–34; Herodotus, *Hist.* 6.16.2–3; Thucydides, *Hist.* 6.16.2–3; Sallust, *War with Catiline* 6.3.

192. See Hesiod, *Works and Days* 25–26; Xenophon, *Memorabilia* 3.9.8; Cicero, *De. Orat.* 2.52.209; Plutarch, *De frat.* [*Mor.* 486B].

193. Walcot 1978:30.

194. Plato, *Apology* 18d.

195. For envy of the gods (*phthonos theôn*), see Homer, *Iliad* 11.543 (*nemesaô*); *Odyssey* 4.118; 5.120; Pindar, *Pythian Odes* 8.71–72; 10.20; 11.54; *Nemian Odes* 8.21–22; *Isthmian Odes* 2.43, 6.30 and Frag. 83.4–5 (ed. Bowra); Aeschylus, *Persians* 362, 454–455, 709–711; *Agam.* 826 ff., 946–947; Sophocles, *Philoctetes* 776 (*nemesis*); *Electra*

envious, however powerful, and so the gods, fashioned in man's image, are also envious."[196]

From Homer onward, the gods are portrayed as envious and resentful of human achievement. On the one hand, envy is a feature of their capricious nature: "You gods are cruel and more inclined to envy than the rest" says Homer speaking through the nymph Calypso (*Odyssey* 4.118; 5.120). Divine envy can strike successful athletes and poets alike. A victorious athlete at the 69th Olympiad is met with the wish that "the envy of the gods does not destroy his happiness" (Pindar, *Pythian Odes* 10.20). A winning poet declares: "Let no envious god disturb the sweet rest I wish to live in" (Pindar, *Isthmian Odes* 6.39). Divine envy is viewed as directed against powerful humans perceived as approaching the gods in power and glory.[197] This notion became prominent in the political fortunes of fifth-century Greece, according to Peter Walcot,[198] when Greeks encountered the enormous wealth and power of eastern potentates like Croesus of Lydia or Cyrus and the kings of Persia. The envy of the gods, however, could also strike homegrown Greek tyrants usurping the power of the state.[199] The adjectives *polyzêlos* and *polyzêlotos* (*much-envied*) were used as epithets for tyrants and kings.[200]

In Homer's writings, envy of the gods (*phthonos theôn*) represented an unnamed, indeterminate, but malevolent divine force causing misfortune. In the later stage of the classical age (c. 500 BCE), as Greek society opened up socially, economically, and politically, *phthonos theôn* took on the sense of a specific hatred and retribution of the gods towards mortals who challenged their prerogatives and power[201] as illustrated in the works of Pindar (518–438 BCE), Aeschylus (525/4–456 BCE), and Herodotus (484–c. 420 BCE). Herodotus speaks more often of the envy of gods than other

---

1466–67; Euripides, *Alcestis* 1036, 1135; *Orestes* 971–974; 1362; *Iphigenia in Aulis* 1090, 1093–1097; *Suppliant Women* 348; Aristophanes, *Wealth* 87–91. Herodotus, *Hist.* 1.32.1; 3.40–47; 4.205; 7.10; 7.46.4; 8.109.3. Thucydides (*Hist.* 7.77.3–4) tells of divine envy directed against the state. On the envy of the gods see Schuler 1869 (Herodotus); Ranulf 1933–34 ("jealousy of the gods"); Milobenski 1964; Walcot 1978:22–51; de la Mora 1987:7–8; Rakoczy 1996:247–70 and *passim*.

196. Walcot 1978:38.

197. See Eitrem 1953.

198. Walcot 1978:31–37.

199. Ibid., 38–51.

200. Ibid., 40–41; cf. also *arizêlos* and *epizêlos*. This is similar to the use of *abaskantos* ("unharmed by the Evil Eye") as a proper name, though with apotropaic, not declarative, function.

201. Ibid., 31.

authors,[202] introducing the view that deity is *always* envious and reaching into every human life, whether princes or paupers. "I know for certain," Herodotus insisted, "that the gods are envious [*phthoneros*]" (*Hist.* 3.40–47). Solon, Herodotus observes, announces to Croessus: "the power above us is full of envy and fond of troubling our lot" (Herodotus, *Hist.* 1.32). Divine envy reduces in size those humans who get too big for their britches (*Hist.* 7.10.5). Military undertakings were always vulnerable to envy of gods and the divine Evil Eye.[203] It is mentioned only once in Greek comedy (Aristophanes, *Wealth* 90–92 [388 BCE]), apparently being too deadly and earnest a danger for comedy.[204] Excessive praise attracted the envy of the gods, and this envy produced "evil stings" and poisonous arrows."

Rakoczy sees the envy of gods (*phthonos theôn/theou; theion phthoneron*) not as a primitive element of prehistoric folklore, as generally assumed. It was rather a construction of the Greek poets of the fifth century BCE, prompted by the human everyday experience of envy already related to belief in the Evil Eye, a potency attributed to the gods as well.[205] "Where the Evil Eye is feared, there the envy of the gods also is feared."[206] The Evil Eye demon could also be the agent of justified envy.[207]

Divine envy eventually was imagined as directed against all human achievers "on the make," those who stand out from the crowd and excel, those who attempt to rise above their allotted station in life and seek more than their fair share of the goods at hand, those whose ambition breeds hybris and arrogance.

> God, when he envys (*ho theos phthonêsas*), destroys with his lightning (*keraunoi*) all that stands out. He directs his missles (*ta belea*) into large houses and trees, for he sets right all that stands out. (Herodotus, *Hist.* 7.10)

Aristotle (*Rhet.* 2.9, 1386 b17) notes the the proximity of *nemesis* and *phthonos*, while also indicating their difference: *nemesis* is the justified displeasure over the good fortune of evil persons; *phthonos* is the unjustified

---

202. Rakoczy 1996:264–65.

203. Herodotus, *Hist* 7.10.5; 7.46, 8.109.3; *Th.* 7.77.3–4; Rakoczy 1996:261.

204. So Rakoczy 1996:264.

205. Ibid., 247–70, although already established as a concept in the pre-fifth-century literature (257).

206. Ibid., 256–57.

207. See Lucian, *Amores* 25 ("*ho baskanos daimôn enemesêse*"); Chariton, *Chaereas and Challirhoe* 3.2.17 (". . . *enemesêse . . . ho baskanos daimôn*); cf. also 1.1.16; 6.2.21. For the association of divine *nemesis* and human envy (*phthonos*) see Gorgias, Frag. B 6 (Diels-Kranz, *FVS* 82 B 6); also Diodorus Siculus, *Library* 31.9.4.

resentment over the well being of good persons. Personified as a goddess, Nemesis was the divine agent of justice and vengeance who punished human transgression of the natural, proper order of things and the arrogance that caused it.[208] She represented the strict supervision of the gods over humanity, moving humans to practice moderation not excess, not succumbing to hybris and efforts to exceed their human limits, but respecting their allotted station in life. Representing divine "displeasure at undeserved happiness,"[209] Nemesis punished wealthy Croesus "for deeming himself the happiest of men" (Herodotus, *Hist.* 1.34.1). Nemesis abhors ostentatious human bragging about accomplishment and success and is the just avenger of hybris and immoderation. Praise of self and others also provokes envy and the Evil Eye and so attracts Nemesis to the scene. "The conception of hybris and nemesis, Martin Nilsson has observed in his study on Greek folk religion, "had a popular backgkround in what the Greeks called *baskania*, the belief, still common in southern Europe, that excessive praise is dangerous and a cause of misfortune."[210] Nemesis later appears as synonymous with envy in general.[211] Illustrating the proximity of nemesis and envy, the related Greek verb *nemesan* in later literature takes on the sense of *phthonein* or denotes the action of the *baskanos daimôn*,[212] thus linking nemesis to both envy and the Evil Eye.[213] Romans spoke of the deity Nemesis only by her Greek name, Pliny informs us, and had the practice of calling on her aid for protection against the Evil Eye (*effascinationibus*).[214]

This unsettling notion of divine envy ready to strike at any moment, mentioned from Homer onward, cast a long shadow over the Greek world for four centuries or more until Plato. Aristophanes had begun to treat the notion with irony. Zeus is depicted as a "vulgar being, sad at the prosperity of others and aiming at canceling it."[215] Aristophanes's character, blind Wealth/Plutus declares, "Zeus has done this to me out of his envy (*phtho-*

208. On *nemesis* see Herter 1935, Hornum 1993 (Appendix 1: collection of *nemesis* texts), Konstan 2003, and above, p. 33; below, pp. 139, 166, 168, 198.

209. Milobenski 1964:79, 82, 83, 85.

210. Nilsson 1961:109.

211. See Gorgias, Frag. B 6 (Diels-Kranz, FVS 82 B 6): "divine nemesis. . . and human envy"; Plutarch, *Adv. Col.* 1124 = Epicurus, Frag. 161 (ed. Usener); cf. also Ovid, *Met.* 5. 69; Straton, *Anthologia Graeca/Anth.Pal.* 12.229.

212. Lucian, *Amores* 25, *ho baskanos daimôn*; also Chariton, *Chaereas and Challirhoe* 3.2.17; Nonnus, *Dionysiaca* 39.292.

213. Rakoczy (1996:131) underlines the relation of nemesis, envy, and the Evil Eye, which all appear in similar social situations.

214. Pliny, *NH* 28.22.

215. De la Mora 1987:7.

nos) toward humans . . . he is particularly envious these days of those with property."[216] Eventually, Plato, divesting the gods of all passions altogether, declared that "envy (*phthonos*) is outside the circle of the gods" (*Phaedrus* 247a) and that God is free from envy:

> The [creating demiurge] is good, and in him that is good no envy (*phthonos*) ever arises concerning anything. And being devoid of envy, He desired that all should be like Himself, so far as possible. (Plato, *Timaeus* 29e)

Aristotle (*Metaphysica* 1.983a) agreed: "But it is impossible for the Deity to be envious *(phthoneron)*." This enlightened view prevailed, and thereafter the notion of the envy of gods waned to insignificance. Aristotle regarded the notion of divine envy as a creation of the poets, not a feature of folk belief but as an intellectual explanation for the reversal of great happiness.[217] In the Hellenistic period, Polybius (second century BCE) writes at the conclusion of his history that he hopes to remain safe from the "envy of *Tychê* ['Fortune']," envy now being associated with an abstract concept of fate.[218]

The early association of both envy and the Evil Eye with the eye and the act of looking makes it possible, if not likely, that the Evil Eye of mortals and gods was implied when only envy and eye were explicitly mentioned. In respect to the Evil Eye of the gods, this would be the case in the early literary sources (prior to the fifth century BCE), where envy and eye are mentioned but no explicit reference to Evil Eye occurs. From the Hellenistic period onward, attention focuses on human envy and human Evil Eyes, together with dread of the envious Evil-Eyed demon, the *baskanos daimôn*.

Envy, the Deplorable Human Vice

"Envy, "Herodotus notes (*Hist.* 3.80.3), "is natural to humanity and has been so from the beginning."[219] Envy that groans over another's prosperity was thought to arise in the heart (Aeschylus, *Agam.* 832–837). "Envy," declares Socrates, "is a festering wound of the soul."[220] The ancients reckoned the

216. Aristophanes, *Wealth* 87–91 (translation by de la Mora 1987:7).

217. Rakoczy 1996:268; Dickie 1987:120.

218. Polybius, *Hist.* 39.8.2. On envy of the gods, in addition to sources listed in note 195 above, see Rakoczy 1996:104–20 and 247–70. On *aphthonia*, the absence of envy, as a divine attribute see van Unnik 1971, 1973.

219. See also Demosthenes, *Orat.* 18.315.

220. A saying of Socrates preserved in Stobaeus, *Anth./Ecl.* 3.38.48

heart, as also the mind or the soul, as the cognitive and affective center of human personality. "Heart," "mind," or "soul" were varying terms for "the inner person" in contrast to what is external and visible to others. God alone can read the heart.

Bruce Malina, building on the work of Bernard de Géradon,[221] has observed that biblical authors, and perhaps also Greeks and Romans, spoke of human activity and thought in terms of metaphors, using "heart" for thinking or feeling, "mouth" for speaking, "hands" and "feet" for acting and the like. These different organs were thought to represent different actions associated with three interpenetrating yet distinguishable zones of the human body: "the zone of emotion-fused thought, the zone of self-expressive speech [mouth/speech, ears/hearing]and the zone of purposeful action [hands, feet, arms, fingers, legs and doing, touching, coming, going, giving, making and so on]."[222] The eyes and the heart belong to the zone of "emotion-fused thought" and the activities of these organs, such as seeing, looking at, knowing, thinking, understanding, remembering, choosing, and feeling. The expression "emotion-fused thought" highlights the overlap of thinking and feeling. The linkage of eye with heart (or mind or spirit) and the actions of looking, thinking, and feeling appear to underlay descriptions of the process of envy and the Evil Eye.[223] Plutarch illustrates the association of envy with both eye and soul, the cognitive-emotional command center: The eyes (*tas opseis*) of the envious, he notes, are "close to the mind/soul (*psychê*) and draw from it the evil influence of the passion [envy] and then asail that person as if with poisoned arrows" (*Quaest. Conv.* 5.7.3 [*Mor.* 681E] LCL). The Latin language encodes this association of envy and eye in its terms for envy: *invidia, invidere* [lit. to "look over"] and paronyms. Envy, Horace (65–8 BCE) states, is expressed through the eyes (*ex oculis invidere, Odes* 3.24.32). In this respect as well, envy and the Evil Eye are related. Because it was conveyed through the eye, envy's reach was enormous—as far as the eye could see. "Let no eye's envy strike me from afar," mutters the victorious but anxious Agamemnon returning home from Troy (Aeschylus, *Agam.* 947).

The anthologist John Stobaeus (fifth century CE), in his collection of thirty-nine sayings on envy (*Anthologium/Eclogues* 3.38), records an early attempt by Hippias of Elis (c. 485–415 BCE) to distinguish two types of envy (*phthonos*); (a) one that is just (when one envies an evil man being honored)

---

221. Malina 2001:68–75; de Géradon 1958.
222. Malina 2001:68.
223. On heart and body metaphors see also Leeb 2008 and below, pp. 84–85.

and (b) one that is unjust (envy directed at good persons).[224] This notion, however, was not adopted; envy subsequently was viewed as always evil and malicious.

Early on, Isocrates (436–338 BCE) had underscored the pervertedness of envy:

> Some have been so brutalized by envy (*hypo tou phthonou*) and are so hostile that they wage war, not on depravity, but on prosperity; they hate not only the best men but the noblest pursuits; and, in addition, they destroy, whenever they have the power, those whom they have cause to envy (*phthonêsôsin*). (Isocrates, *Antidosis* 141–142)

Plato lists envy (*phthonos*) among the "tyrannical cravings" (*epithymiai tyrannida, Laws* 9.863e). He states that it harms not only individuals but also the people as a whole: "When our city reached its glory, it suffered the destiny that men inflict on whatever is well achieved, first emulation (*zêlos*) and then envy" (Plato, *Meno* 242a).[225] Envy was reckoned as a underlying cause of actual military wars.[226] Envy, according to Plato, was the motive behind the tragic death of the great Socrates. In his *Apology*, Plato presents Socrates attributing his condemnation and death to the envy, slander, and malice of his enemies (*Apology* 2, 54). Eventually envy was considered by most moralists as the worst of the vices, and the opposite of generosity and liberality. "Envy is the worst of all evils," Menander declares.[227] "Young man . . . it is envy, worst of all vices, that's made you waste away, and does so now and will do so again, the godless failing of an evil soul."[228] Because of its danger to both envier and envied, it was warned against in no uncertain terms. "Envy no one (*phthonei mêdeni*)" the Delphic Canon (sixth century BCE) urged,[229] just as it insisted, "Control your eye" (*o[ph]thalmou krat[ei]*).[230]

Plutarch, in his *Table Talk* on the Evil Eye, tells of artists who painted the face of Envy (*Phthonos*) and how they tried to render the evil (*ponêria*)

224. Hippias, Frag. B 16 (Diels-Kranz, *FVS* 86 B 16 = Stobaeus, *Anth./Ecl.* 3.38.32).

225. His comment also shows how emulation, a positive action, could under circumstances morph into negative envy.

226. Aristotle, *Nic. Eth.* 1131a; Plutarch, *De tranq.* [*Mor.* 473B]; *De frat.* [*Mor.* 487F]; Epictetus, *Disc.* 3.22.61; 3.29.26; Dio Chrysostom, *Orat,* 77/78.17–29; cf. Milobenski 1964:3, 15–16, 103.

227. Unidentified minor fragment, Allison 1921:487.

228. Unnamed play attributed to Menander, quoted by Stobaeus, *Eclogue* 3.33.29 in Balme 2001:487.

229. Number 60 of the 147 injunctions of the Delphic Canon (one version: Ai-Khanum Stele, Afghanistan, third century BCE), Judge 1993:6.

230. *The Delphic Canon*, No. 102, Judge 1993:7.

with which envy fills the body; but he gives no further details of who or how or under what circumstances.[231] The Roman poet Ovid (43 BCE—17 CE) provides a graphic description of personified envy in his *Metamorphoses* (2.760–832) which describes Envy (*Invidia*) visited by the goddess Minerva. This portrait, de la Mora has observed,[232] "is the most repulsive figure of Greco-Latin mythology, and his [Ovid's] verses are the most damning poetic sentence on any passion." It captures many of the features conventionally associated with envy and looking with an Evil Eye:

> Pallor spreads over her [Envy's] face, her whole body appears emaciated, her gaze is always indirect [= oblique] (*nusquam recta acies*), her teeth are discolored/livid (*livent*) with decay, her breast is green (*virent*) with bile, and her tongue drips with poison. She smiles only at the sight of pain. She never sleeps, but lies awake with multiple cares. She beholds (*videt*) with regret the successes of men, and pines away at the sight (*videndo*). She gnaws, and being gnawed herself is her own punishment. (Ovid, *Met.* 2.775–782)

Requested by Minerva to poison a certain maiden named Aglauros, Envy agrees and prepares to leave. The scene provides further detail of Envy's destructive power:

> Envy, looking obliquely (*obliquo*) at Minerva as she [Envy] flees [and sets out to poison Aglauros], utters a few murmurs, and grieves at Minerva's coming success. She takes her staff, wound with strands of briar, and sets out, shrouded in dark clouds. Wherever she passes, she tramples the flower-filled fields, withers the grass, blasts the highest treetops, and poisons homes, cities and peoples with her breath. (Ovid, *Met.* 2.787–794)[233]

Eventually Envy poisons Aglauros and causes her to waste away; finally Mercury turns her to stone (*Met.* 2.812–832).

This lurid portrait encapsulates several aspects of envy: the connection of envy (*invidia*) and seeing (*acies, videre,* looking *obliquo*) and thus a connection with an Evil Eye,[234] palor and green as envy's color, an emaciated visage and pining away, an oblique glance, pleasure only at the pain of others, displeasure at the success of others, infliction of self-injury, a burn-

231. Plutarch, *Quaest. Conv.* 5.7.3 [*Mor.* 681E].

232. Mora 1987:16.

233. Translation by John H. Elliott, modifying the translation of A. S. Kline. On envy in Ovid, see Shiaele 2010.

234. *Acies* for "eye" and the verbs for seeing (*videt, videndo*) are apt for the action of *invidia* (envy aroused by seeing).

ing of the eye that causes withering, drying up and destruction of crops and humans, damage to what excels (the highest treetops), and harm to all through emanations of eye and mouth.[235] These are features associated with Evil-Eyed figures as well. This similarity provides yet another instance of the close association and often virtual equation of envy and the Evil Eye among the ancients. The notion that both the envious and the Evil-Eyed can injure themselves with their power, as noted below, also belongs to this constellation of common features.

Envy/*invidia* is called *infelix* ("unhappy") by Virgil (*Georgics* 3. 37) since sight of the prosperity of others always prompts unhappiness in the envier.[236] Pictorial representations illustrate this sense of *Invidia*. Lucian of Samosata (*De calumnia* 5) suggests that in Apelles' famous painting of Calumny (fourth century BCE) the figure that led Calumny was *Phthonos* depicted as "a pale and ugly male figure, with a sharp look to his eyes and the appearance of one who has become emaciated as the result of a long disease."[237]

The iconography of Envy (*phthonos/invidia*) in Greco-Roman art is the topic of an excellent study by Katherine Dunbabin and Matthew W. Dickie (1983) with extensive discussion, documentation, and eight plates. The literary and iconographic traditions attest the regular association of envy and the Evil Eye, with depictions of the envious emaciated Evil-Eyer denigrating and slandering fortunate rivals, maliciously willing their harm and loss, and experiencing internal torment leading to self-choking and suicide.[238]

A third century mosaic from the entrance corridor of a Roman villa at Skala on the island of Kephallenia in the Ionian Sea, Dunbabin and Dickie note, shows a figure of a naked young man torn and bleeding from beasts attacking his upper and lower torso from right (lion, leopard) and left (tigress, leopardess). His right eye is narrowed and his left, damaged. His arms are crossed over his chest and with both his hands he is choking himself. The inscription below the image explains its meaning: the figure is a likeness of envy rendered in stone by Krateros and the words announce its demise.

> O Envy (*Phthonos*), for you also the painter has drawn this likeness of your baneful spirit, which Krateros has made in stone, not because you are honoured amongst men, but because with

235. Compare the similar and earlier description of envy (*zêlos*) in Hesiod, *Works and Days* 195–201.

236. Dickie 1983:66.

237. Ibid., 68.

238. As illustrated by the several figures presented on Plates 1–7 of Dunbabin and Dickie 1983.

an Evil Eye you grudge (*baskainôn*) mortals their prosperity you
have put on this form. Stand, then, before the eyes of all; stand,
wretch, bearing the hideous sign of that wasting that affects the
envious (*phthoneroi*).[239]

"The hands clasping the throat," Dickie notes in a related study,[240] represent
either the *phthoneros* [the envious person] in his unhappiness trying to do
away with himself by strangulation, or his choking with pent-up emotion
over the good fortune of others, or a combination of both of these notions."[241]

The special merit of this Kephallenia mosaic is its combination of
image and inscription. The mosaic, similar to numerous other artistic and
literary representations of Envy and the Evil Eye, presents the acute suffering of the envious Evil-Eyed person, here by self-choking and elsewhere
from attacking beasts or both.[242] The envier, the inscription explains, inflicts
injury on him/herself as well as on others.

The motif appears also in a gold pendant (c. 100–200 CE) found on
Cyprus and now in the British Museum. The pendant depicts a naked male
figure with his hands clutching his throat, probably representing *Phthonos*
(Envy).[243] The British Museum collection also includes a hollow terracotta
upper-body fragment of *Phthonos* as a male figure with grotesque features,
bald, with his head thrown back, and strangling himself with both hands.[244]

The idea of enviers harming themselves with their envying[245] is consis-
tant with the parallel theme of Evil-Eyed persons harming themselves with

239. Text and translation from Dunbabin and Dickie 1983:8, with John H. Elliott
addition of "with an Evil Eye" before "grudge" in order to fully render *baskainôn*. On
the mosaic see also Kallipolitis 1958; Dunbabin and Dickie 1983:8–10, 33–37, Plate 1a,
b and Plate 2a; Dickie 1983:68 and Bernand 1991:105. For similar inscriptions from
East and West against *Phthonos/Invidia* mostly in floor mosaics or affixed to lintels and
doorframes, similar to those against the Evil Eye, see the collections of inscriptions
listed in Dunbabin and Dickie 1983:36–37, notes 190–192. For similar images of self-
choking see Dunbabin and Dickie 1983, Plates 2–6; on the motif see also the evidence
listed in Dickie 1983:69.

240. Dickie 1983:68.

241. For choaking and self-strangulation as an envy motif see also the evidence
listed in ibid., 69.

242. Dunbabin and Dickie 1983:9.

243. BM Inv. no. 1895, 1025.4.

244. British Museum inv. no. EA37604. For other terracotta representations of
Phthonos from Egypt see the Ashmolean Museum, Oxford, no. 1982.901, from 'Man-
sheer,' the Greek city of Ptolemais; Bonacasa 1997:100, fig. 5, with an Evil Eye on its
head; Breccia 1930: no. 402 and Pl. xxxi:2 and 5; Dunbabin and Dickie 1983: pl. 3b;
Vogt 1924: pl. cv: 6.

245. See also Hippias, Frag. B 16 (Diels-Kranz, *FVS* 86 B 16); Democritus, Frag.
B 88 (Diels-Kranz, *FVS* 68 B 88); Isocrates, *Antidosis* 9.6; Horace, *Epist.* 1.2.57–58;

their own Evil Eye.[246] In fact, *Phthonos* here has been taken as equivalent to, or inclusive of, "Evil Eye:

> Through the image and the inscription together at the entrance, the *phthoneroi* [enviers] receive the strongest of warnings against indulging their evil inclinations. The potential bearers of the Evil Eye, those whose grudges against the splendour and prosperity of the house or its occupants might threaten to blight them, are turned back on the threshold compelled by both word and image to suffer themselves the ill effects of their own *baskania* [Evil Eye]."[247]

The purpose of this and similar mosaics was apotropaic, safeguarding the home and its inhabitants "against the malice and evil eye of *phthonos*."[248] The iconographic images of Envy provide us a sense of how Envy and enviers were envisioned, how they were thought to bring harm to themselves, and how these images were used to ward off envy itself. Dunbabin and Dickie speculate that over time "the notion of the *phthoneros* causing his *own* wounds weakens to a more simple wish that he may burst, choke or suffer some similarly undesireable fate" and that external causes of harm eventually are added to the image, such as strangling snakes and other attacking beasts.[249] Amulets against the Evil Eye display the same characteristics, thus further illustrating the close association and frequent indentification of envy and the Evil Eye.

Other conventional features of envious (and Evil-Eyed) persons are their pallor, fierce and bitter gaze, grinding teeth, frowning brow with eyebrows pulled down around the eyes, hunched back, bent or deformed body, and their similarity to venomous creatures such as snakes and scorpions.[250]

Prominent among the ancient characters associated with envy and the Evil Eye was Megaera, mythical daughter of Uranus and one of the furies. Persephone, the epic poet Nonnus (fifth century CE) writes, gave to the goddess Hera the fury (Greek; *Erinys*) *Megaera*, so that Megaera with her Evil Eye (*baskanon omma*) would help fulfill the desire of Hera's envious (*zêlê-monos*) heart.[251] According to Claudian, she had "envious eyes" (*oculisque*

Curtius Rufus, *Historiae Alexandri Magni* 8.12.8.

246. See above, pp. 29–30, 55–56, 63, 119, 151.

247. Dunbabin and Dickie 1983:37.

248. Ibid., 9.

249. Ibid., 37.

250. Ibid., 16–19.

251. Nonnus, *Dionysiaca* 31.74–75.

. . . *liventibus*).[252] Eventually she came to be regarded as a personification of envy.[253] Roman authors stressed her horrible external appearance.[254] According to the *Orphica Lithica* (220–221), the stone *galactite* was hung around the necks of children to counteract the eyes of Megaera bearing evil intent (*kakomêtios osse Megairês*, 226). In Pergamum, Asia Minor, a small altar of the third century CE was discovered, dedicated to Megaira and having an apotropaic function.[255] She is one of the several figures that envy and the Evil Eye have in common; on Megaera see also below, 133, 264.

The *color* traditionally associated with envy was some pale shade of blue, blue-green, or pale green (Latin: *livor, lividus*), the color of lead, paleness, and lifelessness. Nowadays the expression in the West is to be "green with envy"; but in the Middle East and Circum-Mediterrean these colors shade into one another so that green, blue and turquoise (*lapis lapzuli*) were the colors associated with both envy and the Evil Eye.[256] The Latin term *livor* and its paronyms in the post-Augustan period assume the extended meaning of *envy, spite, malice, ill will*, and serve as synonyms of *invidia* and its family of terms.[257] *Livor* and its adjective *lividus*, "livid," denoted a *pale blue, green or leaden color*. It described something as ashen, pallid, pale, anemic, bloodless, lacking color and life, in contrast to something flush and full of life. Envy personified, in turn, is said to be pallid in the face.[258] The verb *liveo*, "to be of bluish or greenish color—of the color of lead," meant, figuratively, *to be envious, to envy*.[259] *Livor*, envy, and the Evil Eye are thus related and at times interchangeable. An amulet for warding off the illness of a reddish eruption of the skin (*ignis sacer*) reads, "*sacred fire, father Livor pursues you*" (*Ignis sacer, Livor pater te sequitur*). "*Livor pater* can only be 'the evil eye.'"[260] Envy's color, *livor*, as the color of pallor, paleness and lifelessness, was consistent with the belief that envy caused dessication and withering leading to weakness and death. Protection against pale envy was afforded by

252. Claudian, *Against Rufinus* 1.79, 147 (concerning Megaera).

253. Nonnus, *Dionysiaca* 10.35; 12.217–218; 21.108; 31. 79–80; 32.100–111, 119–121.

254. Virgil, *Aen.* 12.845–848; cf. also Lucan, *Civil War* 1.577; 6.730.

255. Radt 1983:453.

256. On the color blue see Ball 2001:231–49; Pastoureau 2001; Brown 2009; Deutscher 2010, chapters 1 and 9 and appendix. On the overapping of blue and green see Mourad 1939:64, 240.

257. See Lewis and Short, *Latin Dictionary*, 1073, *sub liveo, lividus, livor.*

258. Ovid, *Met.* 2.775–782; cf. also Cyprian, *De zelo et livore* 8.

259. See Tacitus, *Ann.* 13.42; Martial, *Epigrams* 6.86.6; 11.94.1. Also related are *lividinans* ("envious") and *lividulus* ("envious," Juvenal, *Sat.* 11.110).

260. So Versnel 2002:118, citing the text in Önnerfors 1988, no. 14.

the strong colors of blue and red, as described below under apotropaic colors. Blue, for example, was regularly employed as a color for clothing, cultic vestments and paraments in Israel's cult,[261] for houses, animal coverings and prized possessions to protect against both envy and the Evil Eye. Like red, the color blue has been employed for millennia to ward off the Evil Eye. The practice is still current in modern Circum-Mediterranean countries where blue is a favored color of houses, articles of clothing, and of the omnipresent blue glass amulets, some shaped as blue eyes, that protect cars, buses, shops, and offices and the like from the Evil Eye.[262]

Despite the negative verdict on envy, a prevalent sentiment nevertheless held that "it is better to be envied than to be pitied (Herodotus 3.52.5). Being envied was a public acknowledgement of one's good fortune and prestige. Epicharmus, a fifth century BCE Sicilian comic, observes:

> Who would wish not to become envied, friends?
> It is clear that the man who is not envied is nothing.
> When you see a blind man, you pity him; but not a single person
> envies him.[263] (Epicharmus, Frag. 285)

Yet the dilemma is obvious: good fortune is a boon, but it attracts envy, and envy can bring about damage, loss and death.

Plutarch, in his essay *On Envy and Hate*,[264] along with Dio Chrysostom (*Orations* 77/78), summarizes ancient thought about envy. He mentions the irrational nature of envy (*Mor.* 536–537)[265] and the possibility only of weakening envy but not eliminating it entirely (*Mor.* 537A). Prosperity, he states, is a chief target of envy, whether actual or merely perceived so by the envier (*Mor.* 537A); enviers do not admit their envy (*Mor.* 537D–E). He also distinguishes envy from another related passion that we today call "Schadenfreude," joy over another's misfortune:

> Since, then, it is the searching out of troubles that the busybody desires, he is possessed by an affliction called "malignancy" (*epichairekakia*), a brother to envy and spite. For envy is pain at

261. See Vol. 3, chap. 1.

262. See, e.g., Vol. 1, Illus. 1.10. On the assumed apotropaic power of blue and red see below, pp. 255–60.

263. Epicharmus, Frag. 285 (ed. Kaibel, *Epigr.Gr.*)= Stobaeus, *Anth./Ecl.* 3.38.21. Cf. similarly Pindar, *Pythian Odes* 1.85; Plutarch, *De invidia et odio* [*Mor.* 538B].

264. Plutarch, *De invidia* [*Mor.* 536E–538E].

265. Cicero (*Tusc. Disp.* 3.9) likewise stresses that envying (*invidere*) is inconsistent with wisdom and not to be found in a wise man.

> another's good, while malignancy (*i.e.* Schadenfreude) is joy at
> another's sorrow. (*De curios.* 6 [*Mor.* 518C])[266]

Envy, Plutarch held, aims not at harming human beings themselves (as does hate), but only at destroying their fame and glory, "the part that cast them [the enviers] in the shade" (*De invidia et odio* [*Mor.* 538E]).

Envious persons, like Evil Eye possessors, can injure themselves. Antisthenes (446–366 BCE), founder of the Cynic school at Athens, pupil and friend of Socrates, makes an observation that often is cited thereafter: "As iron is eaten away by rust, so is the envious devoured by this passion."[267]

There are numerous Greek and Roman artistic depictions of envy and the Evil Eye as personified figures in emasciated condition, choking or strangling themselves.[268] As illustration, a small cigar-shaped vase, apparently an unguent container, was found at Corinth (in a drain to the east of the Odeon) dating to the second half of the second century CE. It resembles a similar vase discovered in Cracow, Poland.[269] A moldmade vessel of Knidian fabric, it is long and narrow, with an oval mouth and a rounded end in the form of a phallus. The relief decoration consists of a human head and torso below the mouth of the vessel; the bottom shows a phallus and wings. The face is grotesque, with half-open mouth, fleshy lips, bushy eyebrows and bulging eyes. The left arm and hand of the figure stretch up to clutch at the throat.[270] Slane and Dickie, in their close study of the vase, conclude that the figure represents a personified version of either Envy (*Phthonos*) or the Evil Eye (*Baskania*) since its features (strangling gesture of left hand at the throat, sharply bent head, grimacing mouth and knit eyebrows) "are characteristic elements of the iconography."[271] An epigram from the Hellenistic period (*Anth. Pal.* 11.193) states that "envy, though an evil, has something good about it: it causes the eyes of the envious and their hearts to waste away."[272] This self-injury includes the melting of the envier's own eyes, i.e. the loss of sight. A funerary inscription from Arsameia in Asia Minor (mid first century BCE) of Antiochus I of Kommagene concerns provisions to

---

266. Previously Plato (*Philebus* 50a) had considered this another form of envy: "envy (*phthonos*) is pleasure (*hēdonē*) at the misfortune of others."

267. Antisthenes, Frag. 13 (ed. Jacoby, FGrHist 508 F 13); Diogenes Laertius, *Lives*, 6.1.5 (ed. Hicks 1925 2:7).

268. See Dunbabin and Dickie 1983 and Plates 1–6; Slane and Dickie 1993:494–96, Plate 85 and nn80–88.

269. See Slane and Dickie 1993 and plates 85 and 86 for photographs of both.

270. Description in ibid., 484–85, with further detail.

271. Ibid., 486; cf. Dunbabbin and Dickie 1983, esp. 30–31.

272. Cited by Slane and Dickie 1993:497.

preserve the memory of his deceased father Mithradates Kallinikos. It contains a warning that any person approaching the tomb who tries to conceal cowardly hatred that springs from envy [Danker: jealousy] . . . and *melts his own eye* (lines 215–216) over someone else's good fortune" and wishes ill against these sacred statutes is consigned to the "implacable wrath of all the gods."[273] The disposition referred to is clearly envy, not jealousy; the motif of envy "melting" or "dimming" the eyes appears in biblical and related texts as well.[274]

Anselm Hagedorn and Jerome Neyrey include the Evil Eye in a list of mechanisms of envy; the list calls for furthter comment.[275] For Hagedorn and Neyrey, the love of honor (*philotimia*) is the primary motive behind envy, "a highly prized commodity from Homer to Augustine" (1998:35).[276] They indicate four acts intended to thwart being envied; namely, (1) concealing one's prized possession from the view of potential enviers; see the advice of Seneca to Lucillius: "You will avoid envy if you avoid being seen, do not boast of your riches, and are happy in private" (*Ep.* 18.105); (2) denying the existence of these possessions; (3) symbolic sharing (i.e. offering a "sop") or (4) actual sharing of goods and resources with potential enviers, along with the practice of moderation aimed at not attracting envy.[277] On the whole, their study ably situates the disposition of envy, its features and social dynamic, within the larger cultural system of values, expectations and norms of the Greco-Roman world. To their observations can be added a few further features of envy that locate it in the orbit of Evil Eye belief and practice.[278]

The behavior in which enviers engage to reduce the status of the envied or cause them harm can take various forms. Hagedorn and Neyrey (1998:32–34) list and discuss: (1) ostracism or banishment from the group of anyone who is becoming too prominent; (2) gossip and slander directed against the envied to diminish their social standing and honor; (3) the violent feuding of families and tribes, with (4) litigation as another form of feuding; (5) inflicting physical damage on the envied one through an Evil

---

273. *I Arsameia*, Antiochus I, lines 210–220, translation by Danker 1982:251, italics added.

274. See Vol. 3, chap. 1.

275. Provided by Elliott 2007a and summarized here.

276. Aristotle, *Rhet.* 2.10.2–3; Xenophon, *Memorabilia* 3.3.13; Plutarch, *De invidia et odio. Mor.* 537B; Augustine, *City of God* 5.12. On honor and shame as ancient Mediterranean core values see Malina 2001:27–57.

277. Hagedorn and Neyrey 1998:36–38.

278. See Elliott 2007a.

Eye; and (6) resorting to homicide (envious Cain's murder of Abel, Saul's attempts to kill David).

Even praise and admiration of other persons or things were regarded as likely expressions of envy and an Evil Eye having an injurious effect. The Latin aphorism *"laudet qui invidet"* can be translated either "one who envies, praises"[279] or "one who praises, envies."[280] The first rendition expresses the thought that the seemingly positive action of praise masks actual malicious envy (and an Evil Eye). The second expresses the notion that praise is (always) an outright expression (not a mask) of envy (and an Evil Eye). The point in either case is that where there is praise, there is the possibility, if not likelihood, of envy and the Evil Eye. Praise can mask envy and envy can prompt hypocritical praise. This then led to the minimizing or avoidance of praise altogether lest one be suspected of harboring envy and an Evil Eye. "Because I love him, I would not overload him with praise" Pliny the Younger writes in one of his letters.[281] Or, if admiration and praise were deemed unavoidable, then the practice in ancient time was to add the disarming expression *praefiscini dixerim,* which asserts that with the praise "no Evil Eye is intended"[282] The equivalent assurance in modern time is the Yiddish expression, *kein einhoreh,* "no Evil Eye intended." Other expressions accompanying praise, "Grazia a Dio" ("thanks be to God") or "Mashallah" ("as God wills") render thanks to God for the object praised, hereby disavowing any envious design of the admirer's part. In this way the admonition is taken seriously, "Don't Say 'Pretty Baby' lest you zap it with your Eye."[283]

Although envy is a feature of the human condition, it can be contained or minimized. The institution of ostracism was one such means. Ostracism, the banishment of a citizen from the city (Athens) for ten years, removed from sight not only unpopular persons but also those whose virtue was so pre-eminent as to far outstrip that of their fellow citizens, thereby arousing envy. Ostracism was "not a punishment but a way of relieving the tension produced by envy," Walcot (1978:58) has noted. Prompted by a desire for social parity and equality in the state, Aristotle observes (*Pol.* 3.13, 1284a), ostracism banned those who predominated too much in wealth, social connections, or political influence. It functioned similar to the division of inheritances into equivalent shares and to the performance of liturgies

279. Elworthy 1912:611.

280. Gravel 1995:8.

281. Pliny the Younger, *Ep.* 1.14.10; see also Pliny the Elder, *NH* 7.16, 19.50.

282. See above, pp. 44–45 and n195, and below, pp. 154–55.

283. Maloney 1976:102–48 and *passim*; see also E. S. McCartney 1992:9–38 on "praise and disparise in folklore."

(services on behalf of the public) by wealthy citizens and even to the institution of democracy in general.[284] Agathon, a contemporary of Euripides,
declares:

> There would not have been envy in life for man,
> if we were all begotten on equal terms.[285]

Generosity, too, was a major counter-force to envy, and in fact was its
opposite. Terms of the *aphthon-* family (lit., "without envy") had the sense
not just of *freedom from envy* [not exposed to envy or not arousing envy]
but also *not withholding, generosity, liberality, abundance.*[286] Acts of generosity were a further symbolic, though limited, way of leveling disparity, and
thereby minimizing occasion for the feeling of envy to arise. Among the
biblical communities, as we shall see, generosity was also regarded as the
antithesis of having an Evil Eye.[287]

Living modest and moderate lives was another way to minimize envy.
Dio Chrysostom (*Orat.* 77/78.26) advised following the Cynic sage in divesting oneself of all the possessions that attract envy and developing an
indifference to wealth, prestige and praise. This indifference would also aid
oneself in avoiding the temptation to Evil Eye (*baskainein*) those with possessions, prestige, and skill (*Orat.* 17, 25).

As early as Homer, envying was connected with the act of looking.[288]
Eventually it was associated explicitly with an Evil Eye. Of the range of
emotions associated with the Evil Eye, envy is chief. The Greek and Latin
terms for envy and Evil Eye, as noted above, are often mentioned in tandem,
sometimes with this combination serving as a hendiadys (two terms for one
entity). On occasion, the terms envy and Evil Eye also are used synonymously. On still other occasions, terms for "envy" (*phthonos* etc.) may have
been substituted for terms for "Evil Eye" (*baskania* etc.), an action perhaps
reflecting a tabu against the utterance of a dangerous term such as "Evil
Eye."[289] This is in accord with the custom of substituting less harmful or

284. Walcot 1978:58–59.

285. Agathon, Frag. 24 N= Stobaeus, *Anth./Ecl.* 3.38.12; cf. similarly Plato, *Laws*
679B-C

286. See *aphthonêtos*, adj. ("unenvied, beyond the reach of envy; bearing no grudge
against; bountiful"); *aphthonia*, noun: ("absence of envy, freedom from envy or grudging; liberality, plenty, abundance"); *aphthonos*, adj. ("without envy, free from envy;
ungrudging, bounteous"); *aphthonôs*, adv. ("enough"); *aphthontôs*, adv. ("sufficiently");
see LSJ *sub vocibus* and Milobenski 1964:28 n22.

287. See Vol. 3, chaps. 1 and 2.

288. Rakoczy 1996:42–55, 63–72.

289. Ibid., 41, 61–62, 83 n204.

offensive terms with words considered safer and more socially acceptable, i.e. the practice of euphemism.

It was envy, not jealousy or zeal, that was associated with the Evil Eye, both explicitly and implicitly. Censure of envy regularly went hand in hand with dread of the Evil Eye.

Of the the several dispositions associated with the Evil Eye such as miserliness, stinginess, begrudging, or ungenerosity, envy is the one most frequently mentioned. In their respective qualities, in fact, these dispositions and envy overlap.

Envy and the Evil Eye in Sum

The preceding Excursus on envy, its features and interpersonal process, mentions several characteristics that envy and the Evil Eye have in common. These include their operation through the physical eye, looking, and the deadly glance; their negative valuation and worst ranking among the vices; their omnipresent danger to valuable possessions; their arousal by admiration and praise; their antipathy toward what excels and stands out; their causing injury to self as well as others; their common association with figures like Megaera; their link with the color blue-green; their danger to communities as well as individuals; the harm done to self by both envy and the Evil Eye; and the similar strategies and apotropaic devices used to avoid, counteract or repel envy and the Evil Eye. It is thus no surprise that the Evil Eye and envy were regularly were mentioned together, combined in such labels as *baskanos phthoneros* ("envious Evil-Eyer") and *ophthalmos phthoneros* ("envious [evil] eye"), or even considered as virtually identical phenomena. Indeed, Heliodorus (*Aethiopica* 3.7.3) voices one common opinion in his day that "*baskania* is the proper name of *phthonos*." Similarly, in *Aethiopica* 4. 5 "envious glance" (*to blemma epiphthonos*) is equated with "look with an Evil Eye" (*katabaskênas*).

This connection and often identification of the Evil Eye and envy also is attested by the amuletic evidence. Amulets for repelling the Evil Evil are so similar in design and inscriptional terminology to those for repelling envy, that the terms *phthonos* (envy) and *baskania* (Evil Eye) on numerous amulets appear to have been used interchangeably.[290] Consequently, where the Evil Eye is mentioned, envy is often suspected, and where a charge of envy is levelled, an Evil Eye is often thought to be at work.[291]

290. So Merlin 1940:489 and n4; Mantantseva 1994:115 n38 and Rakoczy 1996:41, 61–62, 83 and n204.

291. On the Evil Eye and envy see Schoeck 1955/1992, 1970; Stein 1974; Walcot

Although closely associated, however, they were not the same thing, as we have already indicated. Envy is the passion, the feeling, the venom that rotted the soul and resented the prospering and well-being of others. The Evil Eye is the physical mechanism, and malicious looking the means, by which envy and other forms of malice were thought to flow from perpetrator to victim.[292]

The Working of an Evil Eye—Ancient Emic Theories

A final element of the Evil Eye belief complex involves how the ancients understood the Evil Eye to actually work.[293] Here we focus on so-called "emic" data and explanations presented by the ancient authors themselves. We distinguish this from "etic" theories constructed by modern scholars to explain the Evil Eye belief in terms of modern science. Our interest at this point is in ancient theories and explanations. Unfortunately, ancient explanations of the phenomenon are few and far between, despite the ubiquity of traces of the phenomenon itself. For the most part, references to the Evil Eye generally amount to a word or phrase here and an occasional sentence there. The extended discussion in Plutarch's *Table Talk*, and the briefer, though extended, comments of Heliodorus and Alexander of Aphrodisias are rare and welcomed exceptions.

Having already considered the explanations of Plutarch and Heliodorus,[294] we can now consider briefly the observations ascribed to Alexander of Aphrodisias (c. 198–211 CE). His explanation of how the Evil Eye causes illness reflects a vein of medical thinking about the imbalance of bodily fluids.[295]

> Why do certain persons cast an Evil Eye (*baskainousi*) and especially against children? Because their [the children's] nature is sensitive and variable. What transpires is as follows. There are certain persons who, due to the wickedness (*kakias*) of their souls, have a nature that is bitten by what is beautiful. When their

---

1978; Pocock 1981; Elliott 1988, 1990, 1992, 1994, 2005a, 2007a, 2007b, 2008; 2016a, 2016b; Dundes 1992:263–264; McCartney 1992:31–32; Gravel 1995:7–8, 42–44; Malina 2001:108–33.

292. Rakoczy 1996:120 aptly notes that *phthonos* is envy as a personal characteristic; *baskainein* is the *exercise* of envy via an Evil Eye.

293. On ancient theories see Deonna 1965:143–96; Rakoczy 1996:186–216; and Volume 3, chap. 2.

294. For Plutarch and Heliodorus, see above, pp. 49–71.

295. On (Pseudo-)Alexander of Aphrodisias, *Problemata physica* 2.53, see also Rakoczy 1996:213–16.

wickedness is awakened by limitless envy (*tôi ametrôi phthonôi*), it [this wickedness] shoots forth from the pupils [of the eyes] like a poisonous destructive beam (*aktis*). When it [wickedness] penetrates the envied person through the eyes, it changes soul and nature into an insalubrious mixture, decomposes the bodily fluids, and leads the bodies of these persons to illness (*noson*). (Pseudo-Alexander of Aphrodisias, *Problemata physica* 2.53)

The statement mentions several familiar aspects of the Evil Eye while also adding something new to the picture. The Evil Eye attacks children in particular; it is aroused by what is beautiful, especially in persons with wickedness in their souls; this wickedness is awakend by limitless envy and shoots from the eyes' pupils like poisonous beams and causes illness. The new element is how illness specifically is caused; namely by the noxious glance of the envious Evil Eye disrupting the normal balance of bodily fluids of the victim.[296] The theory is based on Hippocrates' notion of balance and imbalance (of heat/cold; dry/wet) underlying health or illness.

Thus Alexander too speaks of optic beams projected from an active eye. Evil-Eyed persons, he explains, have their wickedness awakened by limitless envy and then shot from the pupils of the eyes like "a poisonous destructive beam (*aktis*)" which then penetrates the envied person through the eyes. "For this reason," he continues, "people who wish to remain pure protect themselves from, and avoid looking at (*blepein*), corpses. For the optic beams (*optikai aktines*) that strike the dead bodies bear, by way of a back-reflection (*antanaklasin*), a certain uncleanness (*molysmos*) to the soul [of the viewer] through the eyes."[297] The illness brought about by the glance of the Evil Eye is due to the imbalance of bodily fluids it created. Pseudo-Alexander represents yet another brief effort at providing a rational, scientific explanation of the Evil Eye, how it works, and how it causes illness.

Combining information we have gathered from our preceding examination of Plutarch and Heliodorus, along with briefer comments from Aristotle,[298] later Aristolean tradition[299] and from Pseudo-Alexander of Aphrodisias, we can piece together a composite picture of how the Evil Eye was thought to work.

---

296. See also Pseudo-Alexander of Aphrodisias, *Probl. phys.* 1.35, on the disruption of equilibrium.

297. Pseudo-Alexander of Aphrodisias, *Probl. phys.* 2.53. Compare the similar comment of Plutarch on how the plover avoids looking at persons afflicted with jaundice so as to avoid being wounded by the sight of them (*Quaest. Conv.* 5.7 [*Mor.* 681C]).

298. Aristotle, *Insomn.* 459b 27–32 and *Frag.* 347 (ed. Rose).

299. Pseudo-Aristotle, *Prob. phys.* 20.34; *Problema inedita* 3.52.

(1) The eye was conceived as an active organ. In the process of vision, it emits rays, or streams of particles, or exhalations of infected air, that are directed at objects with harmful effect. Variations of this extramission theory of vision differed as to what was thought to be emitted and by whom. (1) Democritus of Abdara had posited an atomic theory of *eidola*, atoms or material images emitted from objects that are seen.[300] This theory concerns emissions produced by the *objects seen*, rather than ocular emissions of the viewers. But it supplies the theory of *eidola* that is then taken over by proponents of an extramission theory of vision. (2) A far greater number of authors conceived of the *eye of the viewer emitting particles or ocular rays* similar to the rays of the sun or to poisoned arrows or the glance and squirting of poisonous serpents.[301] Thus the eye was thought comparable to a lamp casting forth light (Empedocles [c. 490–430 BCE] *Peri physeôs*, Frag. 31 B 84).[302] Pseudo-Alexander of Aphrodisias (*Probl. phys.* 2.52–53) imagined the ocular glance to *disrupt the balance of bodily fluids* and thereby cause illness. Heliodorus, on the other hand, proposed that it was the *ocular exhalation of air* infected with envy that was the damaging agent (*Aeth.* 3.7.3; 4.5.6), reflecting an amalgam of, and variation on, earlier theories, including Plutarch and Aristotle.[303]

(2) These ocular emissions, it was believed, have the power to *cause injury and damage* when they strike their targets. Illness caused by either a human Evil Eye[304] or a *baskanos daimôn*[305] is one such common injury. Occasionally the illness is described as a "wasting away," a "drying up," or "withering"[306]

---

300. See above, pp. 49, 51, 56–60, 75 and Rakoczy 1996:104–20, 208–9 n771.

301. For example, Aeschylus, *Persians* 81–82; Plutarch, *Quaest. Conv.* 5.7; *Mor.* 680F-681C; Pseudo-Alexander of Aphrodisias *Probl. phys.* 2.52–53.

302. Diels-Kranz, *FVS*, Frag. 31 B 84 (vol. 1:342).

303. See Aristotle, *Insomn.* 459b 27–32; and Plutarch, *Quaest. Conv.* 5.7; *Mor.* 680F-681C; Dickie 1991; Rakoczy 1996:134–40. On contending theories in general see also Rakoczy 1996:107 n312, 134–40 n463, 208–9.

304. For the human Evil Eye causing injury and illness see Pseudo-Aristotle, *Prob. phys.* 20:34; Plutarch, *Quaest. Conv.* 5.7 [*Mor.* 680D–F; 681B, D; 682B, D–F]; Heliodorus, *Aeth.* 3.7, 4.5; (Pseudo-) Alexander of Aphrodisias *Probl. phys* 2.52–53.

305. For the *baskanos daimôn* causing illness, see below on amulets; for a Christian text referring to the *baskanos daimôn* see the *Address to the Greeks* 38 discussed in Vol. 3, Chap. 2.

306. Theocritus (*Idyls* 6.39) tells of a girl, Galateia, becoming envious and bringing a wasting away upon herself. Plutarch (*Quaest. Conv.* 5.7 [*Mor.* 680D–E]) mentions the Thibaeans of Pontus causing victims to fall ill and waste away by their Evil-Eye glance, breath and speech.

Uncertainty can exist in particular situations as to whether or not an Evil Eye was the cause of a particular injury, illness or loss, and if a cause, whose Evil Eye it was. Looking into the eye of a sick person (for instance, of someone with jaundice), it was believed, also could transmit the illness from the sick to a healthy person via the illness streaming from the sick person's eye.[307] This belief is consistent with the ancients's understanding of the working of an Evil Eye.[308]

The notion that the Evil Eye and envy cause illness continues in modern time. Writing on *Everyday Life in the Middle East*, Donna Lee Bowen and Evelyn A. Early (1993) note that when Middle Easterners consider causes of illness, "[w]hile exploring all possible paths, one suspects that children become ill, pregnancies fail, and healthy mothers wither because of others' maliciousness or because one has flaunted one's good luck in others' faces. But one only believes it *a posteriori*."[309] One woman of Cairo, an informant named Zainab, reflected on the recent death of her daughter during emergency abdominal surgery while still a young bride. Zainab the mother admires modern medicine but still stated,

> You know, I think my daughter actually died from envy when she was a bride. I haven't told you before. She had an easy life because her mother-in-law lived with her, and the woman next door envied her that and her youth. This woman came in when my daughter was sleeping and told her to get up. My daughter said she was tired. The woman said, 'Why? You have become pretty; your stomach is round; you must be pregnant.' She put her hand on my daughter's stomach and from that moment my daughter started having pains. A week later she was dead. (Bowen and Early 1993:107)

"Such concepts as envy, fate, and mushahara [being stricken with inability to bear children or breast-feed]," they explain (1993:108), "are more than folk beliefs; they are part of a social and cultural system which helps a woman to control her life." "She has not substituted religion or 'folk medicine for medical solutions'"; rather she has mobilized a repertoire of beliefs shared by her society to deal with the vagaries and the harshness of everyday life.[310]

---

307. (Pseudo-)Alexander of Aphrodisias *Probl. phys.* 2.42. See also Plutarch's comment on those who suffer from jaundice being healed by looking at the yellow plover (*Quaest. Conviv* 5.7.2 [*Mor.* 681C–D].

308. So Rakoczy 1996:184–85; cf. also Gifford 1958:10, 37.

309. Bowen and Early 1993:106.

310. Ibid., 107.

(3) An Evil Eye can operate either *voluntarily or involuntarily*; it may fascinate intentionally or inadvertently, consciously or unconsciously. A malicious glance is cast *intentionally* when the envious fascinator feels displeasure at the good fortune of another and wishes that the person lose what gives him pleasure and the envier displeasure. Divine envy of humans involved *intentional* punishment by the gods of human arrogance, hybris, and impiety. An Evil Eye that is exerted consciously and intentionally can be controlled by an act of will and becomes a moral matter. This is not the case when the Evil Eye is set in motion unconsciously and unintentionally.

An Evil Eye, like envy, we have seen, can also be activated *unconsciously* and *unintentionally*. Lovers, for example, can unintentionally Evil-Eye one another.[311] parents can unwillingly Evil-Eye their own children.[312] friends and relatives can Evil-Eye each other.[313] Social pressure, as John Winkler had observed, can also activate an unwitting Evil Eye: "The social force of prescribed enmity, manifested in competition, gossip, and envy, is so strong that its deleterious effects can even be executed unconsciously and unwittingly, as in the case of the evil eye."[314] Certain exotic tribes, we have seen, were thought to possess an Evil Eye by nature and to injure objects unintentionally.[315] Those who are envious by nature do not do what they want to do, but what it is their nature to do, according to Plutarch and Heliodorus.[316]

There are moral implications of an Evil Eye conceived as inherited and operating involuntarily. Where this is the case, those possessing an Evil Eye are not held morally responsible for any misfortune thought to result from their glance. The damage is naturally caused but unintentional. Nor is any misfortune that occurs thought to be deserved on the part of the victims. Accidents, illness and death may be deemed as caused by an Evil Eye, but through no fault of either the viewer or the viewed. The possessor of such an Evil Eye is publically known and no move is made to punish. The injury caused is judged to be not a result of malicious intent but the consequence of an involuntarily operating Evil Eye and glance. The strategy of those in the vicinity of such an Evil Eye possessor is to avoid being looked at, avoid direct eye contact, or to withdraw from sight altogether. Potential victims such as family members, children, and and prized possessions (animals, goods, good health) are concealed or denied existence. When the Evil Eye

---

311. See Plutarch, *Quaest. Conv.* 5.7 [*Mor.* 680C–683B]; Heliodorus, *Aeth.* 4.5.6.

312. Plutarch, *Quaest. Conv.* 5.7.1 [*Mor.* 682A].

313. Plutarch, *Quaest. Conv.* 5.7.1 [*Mor.* 682A, 682D].

314. Winkler 1991:216.

315. Pliny the Elder, *NH* 7.2.16–18; Plutarch, *Quaest. Conv.* 5.7 [*Mor.* 680D].

316. Heliodorus, *Aeth.* 3.8.2; see also Plutarch, *Quaest. Conv.* 5.7 [*Mor.* 682A–F]).

activates beyond the intention and control of the possessor, then attention focuses not on the morality of the act or of the actor, but on the prudence and self-protection of the potential victims. In this case, the onus is on everyone within reach of the fascinator to engage with this person only with great caution—to avoid direct eye-contact, to evade being overlooked, and to protect oneself as best one can, without casting blame.

(4) The most dramatic instance of involuntary Evil-Eying is the *Evil-Eying of oneself, autofascination*,[317] equivalent to the envier, who also was thought to harm and choke him/herself. The conclusion to a funery inscription (second-third centuries CE) referring to envy found in the excavation of the church of St. Irenaeus, France, reads:

> Envy (*Phthonos*) is a great evil. Nevertheless there is something good in it: it consumes the eyes and the heart of the envious (*phthonerôn*).[318]

(5) The *Evil Eye* can convey *the feeling of* envy and they are regularly mentioned together. Envy, like other dispositions, arises in the heart/mind/spirit, is conveyed to, and expressed through, the eye by looking/staring/glaring. This malevolent envious look causes the damage or destruction of the good fortune or success of the targeted person or object.

(6) The *victims* of an Evil Eye are persons, animals and objects of high value and can include family members, infants, children, friends and lovers, domestic animals, fields and crops, and even oneself.

(7) *Harm* from both the Evil Eye and envy can be *avoided or thwarted* or cured through various rituals, strategies and protective devices.

(8) Having an Evil Eye and feeling envious, according to the ancients, were *natural features of human physiology* and could be understood and explained through knowledge of nature and natural processes. Educated explanations of Evil Eye operation appealed to a diversity of learned theory, with no reference to, or accusations of, magic or sorcery. They presented a rationale case for the plausibility of the Evil Eye as a phenomenon of nature, based on the available scientific information of the time. This point deserves a further word of comment.

---

317. Plutarch, *Quaest. Conv.* 5.7.4 [*Mor.* 682B, E–F]; *Anth. Pal.* 11.192. See also Seligmann 1910 1:104–5; 1922:141–43.

318. de Boissieu 1854:490 and fig. 19. On the literary and iconographic sources see Dunbabin and Dickie 1983; Dunbabin 1991.

The Evil Eye—A Phenomenon of Nature, Not a Vulgar Superstition

The Evil Eye was a firm and pervasive item of ancient folk belief, but was not regarded as a form of ignorant, vulgar superstition. This point is rightly and repeatedly emphasized by Thomas Rakoczy[319] and more recently by Antón Alvar Nuño.[320] Rakoczy correctly insists that there was "an established physiological doctrine," as illustrated by the questions treated in the Corpus Aristotelicum, Plutarch, and the later Alexandrian medical school, and transmitted by generations of educated elites. This tradition reckoned with the actuality of the Evil Eye and expressed specific ideas of how it worked.[321] "The Evil Eye thus shows itself to be a perduring phenomenon pervading the entire ancient world, deriving its power from the conceptualizations of vision with which it was related."[322] Alvar Nuño similarly and cogently insists that "El mal de ojo no es una actividad mágica." Its chief features were not consistent with those of magic; it was not proscribed as magical or superstitious in the ancient world; but in fact was included under the umbrella of Roman state religion (see the god Fascinus).[323] The explanations given in the Corpus Aristotelicum and by Plutarch, Heliodorus and Pseudo-Alexander of Aphrodisias, show that the Evil Eye was regarded as a phenomenon of nature that could be explained in a rational, scientific manner based on the available knowledge of the day. Sceptics are acknowledged, but as Plutarch illustrates in his *Table Talk*, it is a philosopher who provides the explanation of the Evil Eye that convinces everyone. What is said in Heliodorus's *Aethiopica* about the Evil Eye is serious deliberation and is in no way connected with the vulgar magic which the knowledgable Calasiris rejects (3.16.3–4). The scepticism of which Plutarch and Heliodorus speak involves lack of knowledge of the facts concerning the Evil Eye, they insist, not doubt about its existence. That lack of knowledge is met and overcome with explanations of how the eye, the Evil Eye, and envy work. Both Plutarch and Heliodorus proceed on the assumption that presentation of the facts is sufficient to convince. These explanations are based on what were then regarded as physical realities and natural properties. In the texts available to us, the Evil Eye was not dismissed as an item of unenlightened thinking or

319. Rakoczy 1996.

320. Alvar Nuño 2006–2008; also 2009–2010, 2012a, 2012b.

321. Rakoczy 1996:5, 112, 212, 256, 271.

322. "Der böse Blick erweist sich daher als eine die gesamte Antike durchdringendes kulturelles Langzeitphänomen, das seine Kraft aus den mit ihm verwandenten Vorstellungen vom Sehen zieht" (Rakokzy 1996:196).

323. Alvar Nuño 2006–2008:107–12.

labeled as an ignorant and obsolescent idea. These most extensive discussions of the Evil Eye in antiquity do not treat the Evil Eye as an instance of magic or sorcery. This same acceptance of an Evil Eye as a natural (though problematic) aspect of human nature underlies biblical references to the Evil Eye. For readers today, understanding the Evil Eye phenomenon and the ancient texts that discuss it requires that we avoid erroneously classifying it as an ancient instance of ignorant superstion and magic. Accordingly, in this study we examine it contextually, focusing on how the ancients understood and described it on their own terms.[324]

As canons of rationality, perceived regularities of nature, plausibility structures, and boundaries between demonstrable fact and postulated belief shift from historical period to historical period, and as they vary from culture to culture, so shifts the plausibility of concepts such as the Evil Eye.[325] Concepts once deemed demonstrated by nature (such as an active eye) in a later time are found unsupported by empirical fact. The concept or belief is then either abandoned or lives on as an atavistic relic. This is the case with Evil Eye belief and practice in the industrial world of the twenty-first century. How and why this belief and practice endures in a world of Iphones and neutron bombs is a fascinating question that begs for scrutiny from a variety of disciplines.

This completes our consideration of the Evil Eye complex as it is found in antiquity—a constellation of ideas, notions, feelings and behaviors associated with the belief and that gave it its plausibility and power. Components of this complex include ideas concerning the eye as active organ emitting particles, the power of the ocular glance and its deleterious effect, the connection of eye and mouth (looking and speaking) as well as eye and heart/mind/spirit (as locus of thought, dispositions, and intention), the Evil Eye as connected with and conduit of the feeling of envy and its set of characteristics, along with the similarity and often interchangeability of Evil Eye and envy and the negative valence of both, envy and Evil Eye both as a cause of illness, damage or loss of possessions; and the belief that the malignant effects of both the Evil Eye and envy could be avoided or repelled by virtually identical devices and behaviors.

With this fundamental complex of beliefs concerning theEvil Eye in view, we can now consider further salient features of Evil Eye belief and practice. Among these features are the persons conventionally suspected

324. On our preferred method of examining Evil Eye belief and practice as distinct from the categories of superstition and magic see also previously, Vol. 1, chap. 1, pp. 26–27 and the literature cited there, with the addition of Phillips 1986, 1991 (preferring "unsanctioned religious activity" to "magic").

325. Rakoczy 1996:212.

and/or accused of having and casting an Evil Eye (fascinators), those regarded as typical victims of an Evil Eye (the fascinated), typical dangerous occasions of Evil Eye attack, and the array of means employed for protecting against or warding off (apotropaics, amulets), or in some few cases curing attacks of the Evil Eye (fascination).[326]

Possessors and Wielders of the Evil Eye

Fascinators (Greek: *baskanos*; Latin: *fascinator*), those thought to possess and cast an Evil Eye, could come from all walks of life: rich and poor, princes and paupers, educated and ignorant, female and male, children and adults, ingroups and outgroups, neighbors and strangers, humans and animals. They include personages from both the natural and supernatural realms: Evil-Eyed humans as well as gods, demons such as the *baskanos daimôn*, the Furies, monsters, mythological figures, and animals, both actual and imaginary. Ancient figures suspected or accused of fascination included Medusa/Gorgo, Medea, Polyphemus the one-eyed Cyclops, the Furies, the mythical basilisk, specific ethnic and exotic groups (such as the Telchines, the Thebians, Egyptians, Triballi and Illyrians), Aesop the fabulist, Domitian the Roman emperor, and Lucius Apuleius, the Latin prose writer and author of *Metamorphoses/The Golden Ass*.[327] Thomas Rakoczy's study on the Evil Eye opens with a discussion of the "Wolfsblick" ("wolf's-stare") as symbol of the widespread fear of the threatening power of the eye.[328] Ovid knew of certain persons whose eyes "harm everything by their very glance" (*Met.* 7.366). Cicero mentions a certain Titinius in Rome, who by his Evil-Eyed fascination deprived the famed orator Curio of his speech when Curio was denouncing against him.[329]

In regard to some fascinators, it is their *eyes and unusual ocular features* that give them away.[330] *Blind persons*, whose deprivation of sight prompts their envy of sighted persons, of course, could be fascinators. Their blindness, moreover, could be seen as divine punishment for having had and casted an Evil Eye. In the Sophoclean tragedies (*Oedipus Tyrannus* 1306 and

326. Ogden 2002:224 lists fifteen features associated with the Evil Eye and its aversion, most of them similar to features mentioned in this study.

327. On Evil-Eyed fascinators see Elworthy 1958/1895:17–36; Seligmann 1910 1:65–168 (listing humans, animals, monsters and legendary creatures, supernatural, and inanimate entities); Rakoczy 1996:155–69.

328. Rakoczy 1996:13–17.

329. Cicero, *Brutus* 60; Story 1877:185.

330. See Seligmann 1910 1:66–84.

Oedipus at Colonus 149–156), E. Bernidaki-Aldous has argued, Oedipus as a blind beggar was thought by the choruses to have been punished by the gods for his Evil Eye.[331] Blindness was viewed as punishment for some trait or transgression and was counted among the worst of sufferings. King Theseus comforts blind Oedipus (*Oedipus at Colonus* 567–568) and, because of his compassion and humanity, is protected from Oedipus's Evil Eye since he, Theseus, does not fear it. In Egyptian mythology, we recall,[332] Horus, god of the bright sky, was blinded by the storm-god Seth. Horus, however, took back his eye (in form of a cornelian stone) from Seth[333] so that the restored "Eye of Horus" was seen as a powerful symbol and effective amulet for warding off the Evil Eye.[334] Beside blindness, *other ocular impairments* (strabismus, wandering eye) or *ocular features* (red eyes, eyes with double-pupils, single eye, knit eyebrows) were considered fascinators because their eyes and eyebrows gave them away.[335] This association of notable ocular features, ocular impairment, and blindness with having an Evil Eye is relevant to the argument over the Evil Eye in Paul's letter to the Galatians to be discussed in Volume 3. Paul, once blinded (Acts 9:1–19) and perhaps marked by a striking ocular feature (knit eyebrows) was accused of having an Evil Eye and then turned the charge back on his accusers.[336]

Behind this association lay the notion that a human's external appearance was evidence of his/her internal character and qualities. You could tell a book by its cover, so to speak. This view, emerging in influence with the *Physiognomonica* of the Aristotelian school (third and later centuries BCE),[337] maintained that a person's physical appearance revealed mental and moral states. This opinion, as Antón Alvar Nuño points out, was consistent with, and likely influenced, the notion of that Evil-Eyed persons and their malicious disposition were detectable by certain noteworthy ocular features.[338] The sophist Marcus Antonius Polemon of Laodicea (c. 88–144 CE), for example, "developed an extremely elaborate semiology of the eye" and maintained "that a small pupil is a sign of an evil character,[339] while

---

331. Bernidaki-Aldous 1988.

332. See Vol. 1, chap. 2.

333. Scene 23 of the Ramesseum papyrus; cf. A. C. Bouquet 1954:58.

334. See Vol. 1, chap. 2; Griffiths 1960; Helk 1979.

335. See Seligmann 1910 1:66–78.

336. See Vol. 3, chap. 2.

337. See R. Foerster, *Scriptores physiognomonici Graeci et Latini*, 1893.

338. Alvar Nuño 2012:304–5.

339. Polemon, *Physiognomonica* 1.5v (ed. R. Foerster 1893). *Ubi pupillam cum oculo comparatam nimia invenis pro oculi ambitu magnitudine eiusque nigrum inaequale reperis, eius possessori in agendo malitiam adiudicato;* Nuño 2012:305 and n42.

small, 'concave' eyes indicate insidiousness and envy."[340] Reddish or dry eyes, according to Polemon, betray malice and injustice, while glistening, humid eyes reveal a praiseworthy character."[341] Pliny the Elder (*NH* 7.16–18), reporting on foreign ethnic groups said to possess double pupils and the Evil Eye and Ovid (*Amores* 1.8) describing the old woman Dipsas and her double-pupiled eyes illustrate the spread and influence of this physiognomic view. The "science" of physiognomy attempted to detect character, qualities, virtues and vices of a person through attention to such indices as size, stature, cranial shape, countenance, facial features and the like.[342] Cicero, to take another example, mentions "the 'physiognomist' Zopyrus, who professed to discover men's entire characters from their body, eyes, face and brow" (*De fato* 5.10). Cicero himself, commenting on the importance of the face and eyes in the communication process, states that,

> everything depends on the countenance, while the countenance itself is dominated by the eyes . . . For delivery is wholly the concern of the feelings, and these are mirrored by the face and expressed by the eyes. (Cicero, *De orat.* 3.221–223)

The eye, in other words, is window to, and manifestation of, the soul and dispositions and feelings of the heart. "Nature," he writes, has so formed human features

> as to portray therein the character that lies hidden deep within [a person], for not only do the eyes declare with exceeding clarity the innermost feelings of our hearts, but also the countenance, as we Romans call it, which can be found in no other living being, save man, reveals the character. (Cicero, *De legibus* 1.9.26)

Pliny the Elder (*NH* 11.54.141–145) agrees, stating that the eye, more than any other part of the body, supplies greater indications of the mind—this is so with all animals alike, but especially with man—that is, indications of self-restraint, mercy, pity, hatred, love, sorrow, joy . . . "in fact, the eyes are the abode of the mind."

Consequently, *persons with unusual ocular features or impairments*[343] are judged to be likely fascinators with malice in their hearts since their eyes and ocular zones give them away. This includes the one-eyed, the cross-

---

340. Polemon, *Physiognomonica* 1.12r (ed. R. Foerster 1893): *Si oculum parvum et cavum vides, possessori eius dolum et insidias, invidiam et emulationem tribuito*; cf. Alvar Nuño 2012a:305–6 and n43.

341. Polemon, *Physiognomonica* 1.7v, 1.16r; cf. Nuño 2012a:306 and n44.

342. See Malina and Neyrey 1996.

343. Seligmann 1910 1:66–80.

eyed, those with an oblique eye,[344] with deeply-set eyes or red eyes,[345] or eyes with double pupils.[346] Common wisdom took the pupil of the eye to be the soul resident in the eye as a manikin or "little girl."[347] The Greek noun *korê* ("young girl") is rendered in Latin as *pupa, pupula, pupilla* ("girl," "little girl," "mannikin," "pupil"). Pliny states (*NH* 28.64) concerning a person suffering from ophthalmia that "as long as the pupils of his eyes (*oculorum pupillae*) reflect an image (*imaginem, i.e.* a mannikin), his death need not be feared." A *dikoros* was someone having eyes of different colors or two pupils ("little girls") in one eye. Double pupils

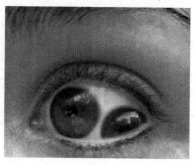

Illus. 2

A human eye with two pupils (*pupula duplex*), regarded as an indicator of someone possessing an Evil Eye

(*pupula duplex*) could have symbolized doubled visionary and destructive power.[348] Ovid describes an old woman named Dipsas, confidante of his girlfriend and adept in the ways of the Magi, as having eyes with double pupils (*pupula duplex*) that shot out lightning-like rays (*Amores* 1.8). Double-pupilled eyes signaling Evil Eyes were attributed also to foreign tribes (Pliny, *NH* 7.2.16–18), such as the Thibii in Pontus and the mythical Telchines of Rhodes and others, as we shall see momentarily.

Eyebrows too were an indicator of fascinators.[349] Eyebrows lying low on the face, according to Pliny (*NH* 11.114, 274–275), like *eyebrows knit together*, "denote malevolence and envy (*malivolos et invidos*). The eyebrows "are our chief means of displaying contempt" and pride, which "is born in the heart, but it rises to the eyebrows and hangs suspended there."[350] Suetonius (*Aug. 79*) made a point of noting that Augustus's "eyebrows met [above the nose]" (*supercilia coniuncta*). Zoologist Desmond Morris (1985:46) comments on the association of knit eyebrows with malicious intentions.

344. Latin: *oculus obliquus* (Horace, *Epist.* 1.14.37); German: *Scheelsucht*.

345. Persius, *Sat.* 2.34.

346. Cicero, *Admiranda*, Fragment 4; Pliny, *NH* 7.2.16–18; 11.54.142; cf. Seligmann 1913:106–7; McDaniel 1918:335–46. Rakoczy 1996:164–69. On the Evil Eye, ocular pathologies and double pupils see, most recently, Alvar Nuño 2012a.

347. See Smith 1902.

348. So McDaniel 1918, against Smith (1902), who speculated that the first and normal pupil was the seat of the soul and that a second pupil was seat of a demon possessing the owner and motivating his malice.

349. Seligmann 1910 1:73, 75.

350. Pliny, *NH* 11.50.138, LCL translation.

He explains that heavy eyebrows link the owner to hairy negative fantasy figures and that knit eyebrows "gives the owner a sinister darkened brow the whole time and makes him seem permanently threatening and hostile." The feature of knit eyebrows is relevant to the apostle Paul, who also was described as having knit eyebrows (*Acts of Paul and Thecla* 3) and who was accused of injuring the Galatians with an Evil Eye.[351] A one-eyed Cyclops as a fascinator is the subject of a story by Theocritus (*Idyl* 6.39).[352]

Other physical abnormalities also are regarded as telltale signs of fascinators.[353] This includes those who are physically deformed (such as hunchbacks),[354] menstruating women losing their blood,[355] barren wives and infertile husbands, widows lacking protecting males, the sickly plagued with poor health, hags, crones and aged males lacking the vitality of youth. Epileptics, suffering from what Hippocrates, the father of medicine (469–399 BCE), called "the sacred disease," also were suspected of fascination.[356] Later writers do not utter the word "epilepsy" itself, perhaps because it was considered ill-omened. The preferred periphrasis for epilepsy among Romans was *comitialis morbus* (the "conciliar illness")—(the *comitia* or council was adjourned if anyone succumbed to it, since it was regarded as of divine origin). Theophrastus (*Char.* 16.15) states that a superstitious person viewing a mad man or an epileptic spits on his own chest, that is, employs the standard anti-Evil Eye gesture for self-protection. Pliny (*NH* 28.35) commenting on the healing and protective potency of spitting and saliva, states, "We spit on epileptics in a fit (*comitialis morbos*), that is, we repel contagion." "In a similar way [i.e. by spitting], we ward off Evil Eye fascinations (*fascinationes*) that follow meeting a person lame in the right leg" (ibid.). Common to such persons is their lack of some natural quality or ability, a lack that would arouse in them an envy of others who are physically whole and in good health. On the homeopathic principle of *similia similibus* ("like influ-

351. See Vol. 3, chap. 2, and on knit eyebrows, Seligmann 1910 1:75.

352. See above, pp. 29–30.

353. See Seligmann 1910 1:78–80.

354. On deformity and disability in Greece and Rome see Kelley 2007; Trentin 2011. On the hunchback, see also Trentin 2009.

355. On menstruating women, see Aristotle, *Insomn.* 459b 27–32; though not using standard Evil Eye terminology, he nevertheless notes the active agency of eye and the act of looking.

356. For epilepsy as the "divine illness" or the "sacred sickness" see also Herodotus, *Hist.* 3.3 concerning the Persian king, Cambyses. The treatise on epilepsy traditionally ascribed to Hippocrates actually dates from the end of the fifth century or beginning of the fourth century BCE. It also is the first pamphlet-length attack on magic as a fraudulent enterprise (Bremmer 1999:3). On epilepsy see Lesky and Waszink 1965; Tempkin 1971; Leven 1995.

ences like"), replicas of some potential fascinators (e.g. hunchbacks) were also used to repel and counteract the Evil Eye, as is the case with the "gobbo" (hunchback) in modern Italy.[357] Aesop (620–560 BCE), composer of fables, had physical features that qualified him as a likely fascinator. He was a dark-skinned foreignor, squint-eyed, with knit eyebrows and a hunched back.[358] At the same time, his being an ugly hunchback prompted his fellow slaves to quip that his master bought him to serve only as a *probaskanion* to keep the master safe from an Evil Eye (*Vita Aes.* 3).[359]

Given the association of the Evil Eye with envy, as we saw in Plutarch's *Table Talk* on the Evil Eye (*Quaest. Conv.* 5.7 [*Mor.* 681E]), *envious persons* are automatically suspected of possessing and casting an Evil Eye. Recall that envy resents and seeks the destruction of the goods of others; it, is fueled by the supposition that all the good things of life are limited and in short supply, so that any benefit accruing to others constitutes a loss to oneself. Euripides (*Suppliant Women,* 240–242) states that, of the three groups of the citizenry, the wealthy, the poor, and those in between, "the have-nots, those who lack the essentials of life, are motivated by envy, and they release 'evil stings' [from an Evil Eye] on those who have."

Beside envy, the disposition of miserliness once was linked with the Evil Eye by Lucian of Samosata (*Philopseudes* 35, cited above, p. 31). This, however, was rare in the Hellenistic literature. In the bibiical writings, by contrast, being miserly, stingy, withholding, ungenerous, tight-fisted, and giving only grudgingly or with resentment, are repeatedly depicted as manifestations of an Evil Eye.[360]

Even *family and friends, parents, siblings, and adoring lovers* can wield a harmful Evil Eye.[361] Plutarch urged brothers to avoid envying (and Evil-Eyeing) one another at all costs. If they find it impossible not to envy, then they should at least direct their Evil Eye (*baskanon*) at persons outside the family (*trepein exô pros heautous apocheteuein to baskanon*), like politicians who divert internal sedition by promoting foreign wars (*De frat.* 485E). Both Plutarch and Heliodorus, as we have seen above, relate how *young lovers* also were thought to be both casters and victims of the Evil Eye. *People of the same occupation* aso could Evil-Eye one another.[362]

---

357. On the hunchback/gobbo, see below, pp. 251–53.

358. On the various descriptions of Aesop's features see Trentin 2009:134–39. On Aesop see also below, pp. 144, 251.

359. Jahn 1855:67.

360. See Vol. 3, chaps. 1 and 2.

361. See Plutarch, *Quaest. Conv.* 5.7 [*Mor.* 681B; 682A]; and Heliodorus, *Aeth.* 4.5.

362. See Theocritus, *Idyls* 5.13, concerning a goatherd and a shepherd. This is the case in the parable of Jesus concerning the laborers in the vineyard, Matt 20:1–15.

Strangers, foreigners, outsiders, barbarians, exotic and alien "others" — these were especially suspect of having the Evil Eye. Certain foreign tribes were singled out for repeated mention. In the Hellenistic era, Greeks considered the Egyptians as *baskanoi* and envious by nature (Philo, *Flaccus* 29). Pliny Elder the historian (23–79 CE) in his *Natural History* reports on the basis of information from Isigonus and Nymphodorus that in Africa

> there are certain families with the power of the Evil Eye (*effasci-nantium*) who, by means of their praise (*laudatione*), can cause meadows to dry up, trees to wither and infants to perish. (Pliny, *NH* 7.2.16, LCL)

Isigonus added, Pliny continues, that

> there are people of the same kind among the Triballians and the Illyrians, who also with a glance (*visu*) injure by the Evil Eye (*effascinent*) and who kill those at whom they stare (*intueantur*) for a longer time, especially with furious eyes (*iratis oculis*), and that their Evil Eye (*malum*) is most felt by adults; and that what is more remarkable is that they have two pupils in each eye (*pupillas binas in oculis singulis*). (*Natural History* 7.2.16)

The phenomenon of the noxious double-pupilled eye, Pliny adds, is further attested by Apollonides regarding tribes in Scythia and Pontus and is known also to Cicero.

> Apollonides also reports that there are certain females of this description in Scythia, who are known as Bythiæ. Phylarchus states that a tribe of the Thibii in Pontus, and many other persons as well, have a double pupil (*geminam pupillam*) in one eye and the figure of a horse in the other . . . Cicero also, one of our own writers, remarks that the glance (*visu*) of all women who have double pupils (*duplices pupillasis*) is injurious everywhere. (*NH* 7.2.17–18)[363]

Plutarch also mentioned the Thibii of Pontus, whose looking (*blemma*) and speaking (*dialektos*), according to Phylarchus,[364] "were deadly not only to children but also adults" (Plutarch, *Quaest. Conv.* 5.7.1 [*Mor.* 680D–E]). Pliny sees this as nature's doing:

---

363. This remark is not contained in any of Cicero's extant writings, but the reference may be to his *Admiranda*.

364. Phylarchus, Frag. 79a (FGrHist 81 F 79a).

she thought fit to implant poisons throughout the body, and with some persons in the eyes as well, so that there should be no evil anywhere that was not present in humans. (*NH* 7.2.18)

This passage of Pliny is rich in information about the Evil Eye. It indicates not only the Roman ascription of the Evil Eye to exotic foreign tribes, but also the ocular features of fascinators ("double pupils" and "furious eyes"). The Evil Eye, further, injures through staring and is aroused by lavish praising.[365] The lethal effect of Evil-Eying praise is the withering of meadows and trees, as well as the killing of infants and adults. It is found in various tribes and with women in particular. Last but not least, it is "implanted by nature" and hereditary, and therefore active apart from consciousness and intent. It is a remarkable constellation of beliefs that Pliny attests and expected his audience to find plausible. Moreover, he describes it not as an instance of magic but as a phenomenon of nature.

Pliny's view is consistent with, and likely influenced by, the Greek physiognomic tradition. Pliny's account illustrates how double pupilled eyes and an Evil Eye were attributed to peoples on the margins of the civilized Mediterranean world: the North-African desert and the most remote part of the Black Sea area; familes from unknown tribes of the Libyan desert and from the untamed Balkan mountain peoples of Illyria and Thrace. They represented the alien, the "other," of undomesticated realms, as underscored by Anton Alvar Nuño.[366] "In a similar way," Alvar Nuño notes, Pliny includes the Bitiae, a special group of women among the Scythians, and the Thibii, located in the most remote part of the Black Sea."[367] For Greeks they represented uncivilized barbarism, and for Romans they were peoples resistant to Roman control and domestication. His inclusion of Roman women with pupilla duplex in his list of Evil Eye fascinators, Alvar Nuño further suggests, adopts an existent Hellenistic tradition and expands on Cicero's writing (probably the *Admiranda*, now lost). Pliny "updated the tradition regarding the double pupil by emphasizing 'wild places' resonant at Rome in his own day, and taking over Cicero's material locating the phenomenon in Italy itself."[368] The Evil Eye appears both in peoples on the margins of civilized society as well as with Roman women at the very heart of the empire.

A century later, Aulus Gellius (c. 130–c. 180 CE) in his *Attic Nights*, recalls the reports of Pliny and others concerning Evil-Eyed peoples of Africa:

365. On the traditional association of praise, envy and the Evil Eye in classical antiquity see McCarthy 1992.

366. Alvar Nuño 2012:314–15.

367. Ibid., 314.

368. Ibid.

[I]n the land of Africa there are families of persons who possess the voice and tongue of fascinators (*voce atque lingua effascinantium*), and who have the power, by vehemently praising (*forte laudaverint*) beautiful trees, plentiful crops, charming children, excellent horses, and strong, well-fed cattle, to bring about the sudden death of all without any other cause. That with the eyes too a fatal Evil Eye is cast (*oculis quoque exitialem fascinationem fieri*) is written in those same books, and it is said that there are persons among the Illyrians who kill by their gaze (*qui interimant videndo*), those at whom they have looked for some time in anger; and that those persons themselves, both men and women, who possess this power of harmful gaze (*qui visu tam nocenti sunt*), have two pupils in each eye (*pupillas in singulis oculis binas habere*). (Aulus Gellius, *Attic Nights* 9.4.7–8)[369]

This comment illustrates several of the features associated with an Evil Eye: the association of the Evil Eye with an evil voice and evil tongue (*mala lingua*) and with the act of praising; fascinators as including both men and women; the fatal damage done by the Evil Eye and gazing; the variety of victims; ocular irregularity (double pupils) as a mark of fascinators; and the inherited nature of the Evil Eye.

The Telchines, legendary metal craftsmen of Rhodes, were especially notorious as fascinators with the Evil Eye and were repeatedly mentioned. Callimachus (*Aetia* 1, verse 17) denounces his critics as "Telchines" and "you deadly race of *Baskania*."[370] Strabo (*Geog.* 14.2.7) states that the Telchines were considered by some as *baskanoi* (fascinators) and *goêtai* (vulgar magicians), while others thought them to have been Evil-Eyed (*baskanthênai*) by rival craftmen because of their outstanding skill, and that this was the source of their negative reputation. Diodorus Siculus (*Library* 5.55.3) asserts that the Telchines were envious (*phthoneroi*) in teaching their crafts. Ovid (*Met.* 7.366–367) insists that they destroyed everything with their eyes and glance. Alciphron (*Ep.* 1.15.5) regarded an envious fellow traveler that had an Evil Eye (*baskainôn*) "worse than a Telchine's."[371] They were considered to be the first to work with bronze and

---

369. John H. Elliott translation modifying that of LCL; see also Story 1877:149–50.

370. Callimachus, Frag. 1.17 (ed. Pfeiffer). The Telchines were thought to be descendents of *Nemesis*, personified goddess of *Baskania*; cf. Rakoczy 1996:130 n411.

371. The lexicographer Hesychius identifies the Telchines as *baskanoi, goêtes, phthoneroi*. On the Telchines see also Herter 1934 5.A.1., cols 197–224; Ogden 2002:25–26.

with iron, that metal with mysterious magnetic power that was used as an apotropaic against the Evil Eye.[372]

Conceiving of an Evil Eye as a *physical and inheritable trait* of foreign tribes or exotic peoples, or of certain persons in one's community, puts its operation in the category of inadvertent behavior. Deeming it a characteristic that is conferred by nature, inherited, and passed on across generations, removes it from the realm of personal volition and hostile intent. When so conceived, those thought to possess an Evil Eye are not held morally responsible for any misfortune resulting from their glance as noted above (pp. 120–21).

As for *human strangers who are not total aliens,* Pliny (*NH* 28.39) indicates that, at the appearance of *strangers* (presumably from another part of the neighborhood or village), nurses took defensive measures, spitting thrice to safeguard infants against fascination. Virgil, when recounting the practice of having one's head covered when confronting a stranger, may also have had in mind protection against the stranger's Evil Eye.[373]

The custom of fearing the stranger as potential fascinator continues in modern time. Writing on hospitality in the Muslim Middle East, A. Kanafani discusses rites of hospitality and the status of the stranger or guest. She observes that

> [t]he stranger is more dangerous than powerful . . . The guest is (also) a powerful agent of evil eye, which can be defined as a force emanating from a person's envy which can cause harm with varying degress of intensity.[374]

Evil Eye accusations are often employed to label and "expose" purported-ed fascinators. Suspecting, hinting at, or claiming directly that someone or some group has an Evil Eye is a first step toward making a public Evil Eye accusation. An outright accusation involves a charge that so-and-so has an Evil Eye and in a particular instance has used this eye to damage or harm another person or group or object. The intent of the accusation is to mark and stigmatize the accused (perceived as a dangerous rival) as a deviant who violates, or is ignorant of, social values and norms of one's group. The result of a successful accusation is the demeaning, degrading, disgracing and discrediting of the accused in the court of public opinion. Such formal Evil Eye accusations were no doubt customary among ancient Greeks and

---

372. On the apotropaic use of iron objects against the Evil Eye, see below, pp. 265–66. On the association of the Evil Eye with iron working in modern Ethiopia see Finneran 2003.

373. Virgil, *Aen.* 3.405–407, *hostilis facies.*

374. Kanafani 1993:134.

Romans, since the features and classes of fascinators were well-known. Few recorded accusations, however, are extant.

The Greek pastoral poet Theocritus (c. 300—c. 260 BCE) tells of a quarrel between a goatherd named Comatas and a shepherd named Lacon. Comatas directs an Evil Eye accusation against the latter, charging Lacon with stealing his goat skin and striking him with his Evil Eye (*baskainôn*; Theocritus, *Idyl* 5.13). An accusation of employing "poisonous arts" to steal one's neighbors' crops is reported by Pliny the Elder (*NH* 18.41–43). He recounts the story of a liberated slave, Gaius Furius Chresimus, who, having successfully cultivated his small farm, became an object of envy (*invidia*) because his little plot had larger yields than his neighbors' bigger estates. He was publicly accused of enticing away their crops by the "poisonous arts" (*veneficiis*). In his self-defense he brought into the Forum his daughter, and his ploughs, tools, and oxen. Pointing to them, he said: "Fellow citizens, these are all my [so-called] poisonous arts (*veneficia mea*). I cannot show you [my real tools]: my midnight labors, early risings, sweat and toil." He was acquitted by unanimous verdict.[375] In Volume 3, chap. 2 we shall examine the apostle Paul's letter to the Galatians in which Paul responds to an Evil Eye accusation leveled against him.

The *starring eyes of the dead* were thought to be full of Evil-Eyed envy for the living and hence channels of the Evil Eye. To protect the living who were required to deal with the corpse, the custom arose of putting coins on the eyes of the corpse to impede its Evil Eye.[376]

Mythological figures and deities also reckoned among those deemed to be fascinators with an Evil Eye. These too were thought to have the power to harm and kill with their active Evil Eyes.[377] It was therefore imperative to avoid looking directly at such creatures so as to avoid being injured, killed, or turned to stone.

The *Erinnyes* or *Furies* were furious avenging goddesses whose heads were wreathed in serpents and whose eyes were bloodshot. One of the three Furies, *Megaera*, reputed daughter of Uranus (Pseudo-Apollodorus, *Library* 1.3), was regarded in late antiquity as the personification of envy and as having an envious Evil Eye.[378] She is described as "bearing the Evil Eye" (*baskanon omma pherousa*)[379] and as having "envious eyes" (*oculis*

375. For a case of accusation of the use of charms and witchcraft, see the charges leveled against the writer Apuleius, c. 158 CE and his defense (Apuleius, *Apology* 42–43).

376. So Sartori 1899:221–22.

377. See Seligmann 1910 1:138–48.

378. See the Egyptian poet Nonnus of Panopolis, *Dionysiaca* 10.35; 12.217–218; 21.108; 31.73–75, 79–80; 32.100–111, 119–121.

379. Nonnus, *Dionysiaca* 31.74.

liventibus).[380] Her name means "begrudging" in Greek (*megairein*), and Apollonius of Rhodes (*Argon.* 4.1670), portraying Medea's Evil-Eyeing of the monster Talos, uses the verb *megairein* (*emegêren*) as equivalent to *baskainein*, the standard verb for "to Evil Eye." Roman authors stressed her horrible external appearance[381] Around the necks of chidren were hung amulets of the stone galactite to protect them from the malicious eyes of Megaera.[382] Paulus Silentarius, in the *Ecphrasis of Hagia Sophia*, attributes responsibility for the collapse of part of a building to *phthonos* (160–163), the *Telchines* (193–195), *baskaniê* and *Megaira* (220–221), which suggests that at this later time (sixth century CE), all four were different names for the same personification of envy and the Evil Eye.

Another mythical powerful female was *Medea*, minor goddess, priestess of Hecate, whose oblique glance was fatal.[383] The Hellenistic epic of Apollonius of Rhodes (third century BCE), *The Argonauts*, tells of the voyage of Jason and his shipmates on the Argo to retrieve the Golden Fleece from remote Colchis. In one key episode (4.1638–1693), Medea, with her

Illus. 3

Sketch of a Spartan gorgoneion with hideous features (from Seligmann; 1910, 2:377, fig. 217).

Evil Eye, delivers Jason and the Argonauts from Talos, the bronze monster guarding the island of Crete.[384] As Talos attacks the Argonauts' ship by hurling missles, Medea, chanting thrice then praying thrice, with her "inimical eyes" (*echthodopoisin ommasi*) Evil-Eyed (*emegêren*) the Evil Eye (*opôpas*) of bronze Talos, dispatching sparks of light (4.1665–1673). Weakened by Medea's oblique glance/Evil Eye glance (*omma loxon, oculus obliquus*), Talos stumbled, fell, and bled to death from an injured heel (4.1679–90). The scene, reflecting an

---

380. Claudian, another Egyptian poet, *in Rufinium* 1.138.

381. Virgil, *Aen.* 12.845–848; Lucan, *Civil War* 1.577; 6.730.

382. *kakomêtios osse Megairês* (*Orphica Lithica* 222–226, esp. 226); Johnston 1995:384–85.

383. On Medea as fascinatrix, see Luck 1985:14–15, 66–67; Dickie 2001:35–36, 93–94, 134–35.

384. Apollonius, *Argon.* 4.1669, 1635–1690. On this Evil Eye episode see Rakoczy 1996:155–69; Luck 1985:66–67; Dickie 1990; Schaaf 2014.

old tradition,[385] is depicted on the well-known Ruvo krater (latter fifth century BCE), which presents Medea, placed between the Argo and the Dioscuri-Talos group, with her head inclined and wounding the bronze monster Talos with her oblique glance.[386] Her oblique eye/glance (*omma loxon, oculus obliquus*) is one of several forms of Evil Eye attack. The story also shows how the Evil Eye was visualized as a potent weapon that could be wielded intentionally. According to Rakoczy. this is "the sole extant description of an intentional use of the Evil Eye" in antiquity and "the sole description of an Evil Eye in action."[387] It also shows how the Evil Eye was thought to injure at a distance, and how one Evil Eye possessor fought the Evil Eye of another.

Medusa, alias the *Gorgo*, was yet another notorious Evil Eye possessor. The Gorgones in Greek mythology were one of several female trinities along with Harpies, the Keres, the Erinnyes, and the Graiae. *Medusa* (possibly originally an earth goddess), was daughter of the marine deities Phorcys and Ceto, and a Gorgo along with her sisters Sthenno and Euryale.[388] "The gorgo" is "the grim one," "the ghastly, terrible one,"

"grim face," who, according to Homer (*Iliad* 11.36–37), "looks horribly (*derkesthai*) with fearsome eyes."[389] The Greek adjective *gorgos, gorgê, gorgon* means "grim, fierce, terrible." Having vied in beauty with Athena/Minerva, according one mythological tradition, Medusa was transformed into a monster with a round, ugly face, a scowling visage with glaring, bulging, bloodshot eyes, bared teeth, protruding tongue, snakes for hair and a deadly visage and glance that turned victims to stone. According to Ovid (*Met.* 4.794–803), Medusa's beautiful hair at-

Illus. 4
Sketch of Perseus decapitating Medusa/ Gorgo, Metope of Temple C, Selinus (modern Selinunte), Sicily, sixth century BCE (from Seligmann 1910, 1:76. fig. 2)

385. See Rakoczy 1996:160–64.

386. Rakoczy 1996:160–64 with plates. He stresses the antiquity of the motif of Evil Eye attack through an oblique glance and its history prior to Apollonius.

387. Rakoczy 1996:156, 275.

388. Hesiod, *Theogony*, 276; Apollodorus, *Library* 1.157–159; Ovid, *Met.* 4.753–803.

389. See also Homer, *Iliad* 8.348–349 (Hector's eyes "glaring like those of Gorgo or murderous Mars"; see also *Odyssey* 11.633 ("that awful monster Gorgo" in Hades).

tracted Poseidon, who raped her and left her to be punished by her rival, Athena, Jove's daughter. Athena then transformed her beautiful locks into serpents. She was hateful toward humans and furious; no mortal could look on her and survive her lethal visage and gaze.[390] In Greek literature, according to Rabun Taylor, "the gorgon's power of petrifaction first appears in the early fifth century BCE, when Pindar writes of the 'stony death' she visited upon the men of Seriphus (*lithinon thanaton, Pythian Odes* 10.48)."[391] Some versions of the Medusa/Gorgo myth[392] describe how the monster was hunted down and slain by the hero Perseus through cunning and with the aid of Athena/Minerva and her shield. Avoiding looking at the monster directly and glimpsing instead her reflection in the mirror surface of his upraised shield, Perseus approached and decapitated the sleeping monster with his sword and then used her severed head (*gorgoneion*) to petrify other victims (Atlas, Phineus, Polydectes). He eventually delivered the head to Athena who affixed its

image to her shield. The first Greek literary mention of the *gorgoneion*, the severed head of Medusa, occurs in two passages of Homer's *Iliad* (5.741; 11.36–37); but these may have been secondary interpolations. Another strand of the Medusa/Gorgo myth told of Medusa beholding her frightful visage in the mirror surface of Perseus's shield and petrifying herself through her own lethal gaze. She thus died of self-

Illus. 5

Sketch of a Gorgoneion on Athena's shield, fragment of a vase decorated by the Amasis Painter (sixth century BCE) (from Seligmann 1910, 1:95, fig. 6)

390. Aeschylus, *Prometheus Bound* 799; *Choephori* 1049. On Medusa's petrifying look see Jahn 1855:59–60; Mack 2002; and Taylor 2008:169–96 ("The Mirrowing Shield of Perseus") which includes "The Reflexive Evil Eye: Was Medusa a Victim of Her Own Gaze?"(2008:182–88), with a following appendix on "Medusa and the Evil Eye" (2008:203–5).

391. Taylor 2008:171.

392. Like most myths, this one too was an agglomeration of sources and reworkings, akin to the Egyptian Horus myth. In the process of accretion, the figures of Medusa and the Gorgo eventually were merged. On Perseus and the Gorgo(ns), see Hartland 1894–96; Phinney 1971.

fascination.[393] Another and yet older tradition (reflected in Euripides' *Ion*) tells of Athena, the "beaming-eyed" daughter of Zeus, slaying Gorgo, a chthonic daughter of *Gê*, in the battle of the giants, thereby reducing the destructive power of Gorgo's Evil Eye, Athena thereby gained for herself, as *gorgôpis* ("gorgo-eyed," (Sophocles, *Ajax* 450), some of the Gorgo's ocular power. Athena then carved an image of the Gorgon on her breastplate. The modern artist Gustav Klimt recalls this version of the myth in his painting, *Pallas Athena*. The versions of the myth thus account for representations of the head of the Gorgo/Medusa, i.e. a *gorgoneion*, on the shields of Athena and Agammemnon[394] and subsequently on the shields and breastplates of Greek warriors. Depictions of her severed head and fearsome

Illus. 6

Gorgoneion on Greek drinking cup (*kylix*), Stattliche Antikensammlung, Berlin. (Photo by John H. Elliott)

---

393. On Medusa/Gorgo see Homer, *Iliad* 8.349 (implied "glaring eyes"); Euripides, *Hercules Furens* 990; Ovid, *Met.* 5.240–241 ("fierce gaze of the snake-haired monster"); Lucan, *Civil War* 9.683–699. Taylor (2008:169–96, 203–5) disputes the self-petrification interpretation as lacking ancient support and favors the first version (2008:170). For fragments and versions of the myth see Homer, *Iliad* 8.349, 11.36–37 (Gorgon's head on shield); Hesiod, *Theog.* 270–283; Strabo, *Geog.* 10.5.10; Lucian, *Dialogi deorum* 14; Pausanius, *Descr.* 2.16.3, 2.21; Apollodorus, *Library* 1:157–159, 2.4.3; Ovid, *Met.* 4.604–803, 5.240–241; Lucan, *Civil War* 9.659–699 (describing the head of the Gorgo and pointing to both eye and mouth, 9.679–680); see also Garber and Vickers 2003 for a collection of sources in translation. On Medusa/Gorgo see also Roscher 1879; Six 1885; Furtwängler 1886–1890 1:1701–28 (the Gorgo in art); Hartland 1894–96; Leclercq 1933; Roheim 1940; Howe 1954; Croon 1955; Frazer 1967; Phinney 1971; von Geisau 1979a, 1979b; Siebers 1983:1–26 and *passim*; Vernant 1985; Krauskopf and Dahlinger 1988; Potts 1982:26–37 and Appendix A (the Gorgo on coins); Krauskopf and Dahlinger 1988 (illustrations); Ribichini 1999 (3 illustrations); Wilk 2000; Stern 2002 (illustrations); Garber and Vicjers 2003; Taylor 2008:169–96, 203–5. On contributions of Greek art to the Medusa myth see Wilson 1920.

394. Homer, *Iliad* 5.741; 11.36–37. For depictions of the gorgoneion on Athena's shield see Seligmann 1910 1:92, fig. 5; 95, fig. 6; Taylor 2008:174, fig. 91 (scene on an Apulian bell crater, early fourth century B.C.E) and 2008:194, fig. 103 (scene on another Apulian bell crater, fourth century BCE). see Elworthy 1895/1958:178. For the gorgoneion on Athena's breastplate, see Seligmann 1910 1:98, fig. 7; 102, fig. 8.

visage were deemed replete with apotropaic power[395] in accord with the principle of *similia similibus*, "like is influenced by like."[396] In archaic art, depiction of the *gorgoneion* appears first in the seventh century BCE under Asiatic influence (from Northern Syria via Asia Minor). The frightful image appears not only on military shields and breastplates,[397] but also on gems, cameos, lamps, candelabra, drinking vessels, vases, doors, mosaics, wall frescos, gates, and funery art. It guarded ships, residences, horses, tombs, thoroughfares and public spaces.[398] The apotropaic use of the Gorgo/Medusa head illustrates the prevailing notion that objects possessing Evil Eye potency, such as Evil Eyes, serpents, hunchbacks, and Medusa/Gorgo, also provide effective protection *against* the Evil Eye. On this apotropaic function of Medusa and the gorgoneion on amulets see below, pp. 246–50.

Since Medusa/Gorgo was moved not by envy but by fury, she illustrates how the Evil Eye was not exclusively synonymous with, or a vehicle of, envy. Rabun Taylor presents seven arguments for dissociating Medusa's petrifying her victims with her visage from the phenomenon of the Evil Eye altogether.[399] Against Toby Siebers (1983), who represents the traditional self-petrification view, Taylor insists that in contrast to features of the Evil Eye, Medusa's head has no effect unless the victims look at her, it cannot be counteracted with an amulet, it petrifies even as a decapitated head, it is not powered by envy or malice, its effect is not attended with praise but is overtly automatic, and it concerns not an entity belonging to the ingroup but the threat of an alien outsider. The Medusa head constituted an apotropaic against an Evil Eye, he allows, but was not an agent of the Evil Eye itself. Variant strands of the tradition, however, show how the Medusa/Gorgo myth expressed both the notions that (a) whoever looked at Medusa's horrifying visage, or (b) whoever was struck by her flashing eye, immediately would be turned to stone. In any case, it can be said that the Gorgo figure is "the consequence of human fear of the glance [and the antagonistic visage] increased to monstrous proportion."[400]

Another famous mythological ocular phenomenon is the one-eyed giant *Polyphemus, the Cyclops* (lit. "round-eyed one"). In the tradition he

395. See Lucian, *Philopatris* 8.

396. On the Gorgo/gorgoneion as an anti-Evil Eye apotropaic, including illustrations, see Elworthy 1895/1958:158–66 and figs. 47–55; Seligmann 1910 1:138–40, 2:305–8 and figs. 217–21, 227.

397. Dio Chrysostom (*Orat.* 77/78.26) refers to cowardly hireling soldiers "who affect plumes and crests and Gorgons on their shields."

398. On phylacteries protecting public spaces see Faraone 1987.

399. Taylor 2008:169–96, 203–5.

400. Rakoczy 1996:92.

morphed from a savage but pastoral figure in Homer to a monster in later
time whose one eye was a potent Evil Eye. Homer tells of Odysseus on his
return home from Troy entering the land of the Cyclops and encountering
Polyphemus, the One-Eyed One, who attempts to hinder Odysseus's further
travels. Odysseus escapes by driving a fiery stake into the giant's single eye
(*Odyssey* 9.106–565). The depiction of the scene on an amphora is likely
intended to repel the Evil Eye.[401] Centuries later, Polyphemus is depicted in
the sixth Idyl of Theocritus (third century BCE) as an amorous figure whose
single eye functions as an Evil Eye so that the monster has to take steps to
avoid Evil-Eyeing himself (Theocritus, *Idyl* 6.39).[402]

Illus. 7
**Sketch on a Greek amphora portraying the blinding of
Polyphemus (from Seligmann 1910, 2:155, fig. 143)**

As to the *gods*, their envy was communicated through their Evil Eyes,
as noted above.[403] According to Plutarch, the goddess Isis killed a child, son
of the king of Byblos, with her noxious glance (*De Iside et Osiride* 17 [*Mor.*
357D]). Not only did the goddess *Athena* bear an image of the Gorgo on
her shield; she even was identified as Gorgo by the residents of Cercina.
Because of her annihilating glance, she was named *Gorgopis* ("Gorgo-eyed")
and *Glaukopis* ("Blue-eyed").[404] *Nemesis*, conceived of as an avenging goddess, was the personification of divine indignation. With her Evil Eye she
punished mortals who were arrogant, insolent, and impious. This goddess
was said to envy and Evil-Eye the beauty of a certain Alexis.[405] A Greek spell
protecting a horse against the Evil Eye appears to associate Nemesis and the
Evil Eye:

401. So Seligmann 1910 2:163.
402. On the Polyphemus myth see Glenn 1978.
403. See above, pp. 97–101.
404. Seligmann 1910 1:150–51.
405. Straton, in *Anth. Pal.* 12.229.

> Go, *nemesôth*/Nemesis, go out, stay off from the amulet-protect-
> ed horse, who was born from his own mother, O you Evil Eye, as
> far as the earth is separated from heaven.[406]

H. S. Versnel takes the strange word *nemesôth* as a corruption of Nemesis
and maintains convincingly that in this spell "Nemesis is an *alias* of the Evil
Eye."[407] This makes sense, given the parallelism of the terms here and the
conventional linkage of Nemesis and Evil Eye.[408]

Baskania likewise was personified as the goddess of fascination and
the Evil Eye. Callimachus, in the Prologue to the *Aetia* (1.1.17), addresses
and dismisses his critics as "Telchines" (a notorious Evil-Eyed people)
whom he characterizes as "*Baskania's* entire race."[409] The Greeks personified
envy (*phthonos*), cousin of the Evil Eye, as well.[410] and on amulets invoked
the god Serapis to vanguish Envy.[411] Even the *planets and stars* were thought
to possess and exercise an Evil Eye.[412]

In the realm of the *demons*, it is the *baskanos daimôn* ("Evil-Eyeing
demon") and the *phthoneros daimôn* ("envy demon") that are the notorious
fascinators and wielders of the Evil Eye. Their particular targets are infants
and children, similar to the Mesopotamian demoness Lamashtu. This appears to be a cross-cultural concept which we met also in the Mesopotamian
records and which recurs in other cultures down through the centuries.[413]
The envy demon who threatens youth is mentioned as early as the fifth
century BCE.[414] It is taken conventionally as the equivalent of the Evil-Eye
demon. Just as Evil Eye and envy were often equated, so were their respective demons. Plutarch (*Life of Dio* 2.5) also tells of "evil demons with the

406. Text and translation by Versnel 2002:135–136 of a text given in Heim 1892, no. 45.

407. Versnel 2002:136.

408. On the Evil Eye of Nemesis and other gods see Seligmann 1910 1:150–54; see also above, pp. 15, 19, 33, 100–101.

409. PGM 4.1451.

410. Callimachus has *Phthonos* (Envy) whispering into Apollo's ear, "I do not like a poet who does not sing as much as the sea." See also Callimachus' *Hymn to Apollo* (106–113). On Envy as personified, see also above, pp. 53, 103, 108–10.

411. Seligmann 1910 2:317–18; Bonner 1950:96–97, 277. For the parallel Roman personification of *Invidia* (Envy) see, e.g., Ovid, *Met.* 2.708–835.

412. See Manetho, *Apotelesmatica* 5.44–45 (*baskanôi ommati*); Seligmann 1910 1:166–68; Rakoczy 1996:236.

413. See examples in Kaibel, *Epigr. Gr.,* nos. 345, 348, 379, 381, 569, 579; also Geffcken 1930:37–38. On Lamashtu, infants, and the Evil Eye, see Vol. 1, chap. 2. On demons in general in the Greco-Roman period see Andres 1918; Colpe et al. 1976; Brenk 1986.

414. Corrina of Tanagra, Frag. 10 (ed. Page).

Evil Eye, who send envy (*prosphthonounta*) against virtuous men" aiming to destroy their virtue and honor.[415] The *baskanos daimôn* figures prominently in the novels of Chariton (*Chaereas and Challirhoe* [first–second cents. CE], 1.1.6; 3.2.17; 6.2.11) and Heliodorus (*Aeth.* 2.1, 33 and 3.7) as a force turning good to ill and as an attacker of youth. Inscriptions, funery and apotropaic, are replete with mention of the *baskanos daimôn* and formulas designed to ward it off.[416]

The *baskanos daimôn*, often combined with *phthonos*, was also seen as a cause of death.[417] When Hades, the realm of the dead, was personified, Hades too was regarded as an Evil-Eyed fascinator.[418] Related to the *baskanos daimôn* as afflicter of infants was *Gylou/Gulla*, the child-stealing demon, who was similar to Lilith, feared in Israel as a demon attacking and killing mothers and newborns, similar to the Mesopotamian demoness, Lamashtu.

Animals and creatures, real and fabulous, also were reckoned among the fascinators.[419] The earliest attestation of the verb *baskainein* in literature appears in a statement concerning a *dead hare* casting an Evil Eye. It is a fragment of the comic poet Pherecrates (fifth century BCE), Frag. 189, which tells of a hunter fearing that "The dead hare casts an Evil Eye upon me." In this case, not only was an *animal* thought to have an Evil Eye, but a *dead one* in the bargain. This text shows that the Evil Eye has no possible connection here with magic, since a dead animal and not a human magician is the agent. It also illustrates how the Evil Eye was thought to work automatically with no intentionality involved. This may have some connection to the customs of covering the eyes of corpses and covering the heads of those to be executed, in order to protect the executioner from revenge and

415. On the equation see also Rakoczy 1996:118.

416. For example, CIG 1.2059 (*baskainou daimonos aphêirethê*); CIG 2.3715 (*mê baskanos hêr[p]a[se] daimôn*, funerary inscription, Apamea); CIG 3.6200 (*baskane daimôn*, funerary inscription, Rome; possibly also 3.6313 (*baska[ne daimôn]*); CIG 2.1935 (epigram above door of church, village of Melinado, Zacyntho-Aegean Islands: *ho phthonos autos eauton eois beleessi damazei*); CIG 2.2062 (*baskanos daimôn*); CIG 4.6858 (*tôi phthonerôi daimoni memphometha*).

417. See Kaibel, *Epigr. Gr.*, no. 345, 1 (*baskanos daimôn*, Apamea in Bithynia, funerary); no. 379,1 (*baskanos ê phthonos*, Aezanis); no. 379, 1 (*baskanos ê phthonos*, Aezanis); no. 734, 2 (*baskanôi pikrôi*, Rome, cemetary of Priscilla); CIG 3.3846i (*baskanois = baskanos daimon* as cause of death); CIG 3.3847i (*baskanos ê phthonos*); CIG 3.4095 (*baskanos*, funerary, Galatia); CIG 4. 6860 (*Moireôn baskanos . . . phthonos*). On *baskanos daimôn* see also above, pp. 19, 31–38, 63, 86.

418. Kaibel, *Epigr. Gr.*, no. 381, 3 records a metrical funery epitaph regarding a four year old girl who was caused to die by the Evil-Eye malevolence of Hades (*Aidôi baskanois*; Epigr. Gr. 381); see Bernand 1991:99 for the complete text.

419. Seligmann 1910 1:120–48; Rakoczy 1996:169–86, and on the "wolf's eye," 13–17.

from being harmed by the Evil Eye of the executed.[420] The decapitated head
of the gorgon grasped by the hand of Perseus, it was thought, lost nothing of
its noxious power. One of Aesop's fables, "The Snail and the Statue," tells of
a *snail* with an Evil Eye. It had attached itself to the molding of the pedestal
of a staute of the Medician Venus. Seeing the admiration aroused by the
statue's beauty, the snail tried to obliterate it with its Evil Eye.[421]

Wolves were renown for their sharp vision as well as their danger to
humans; because of the rays supposedly emitted by their eyes, they too were
feared as fascinators.[422]

Birds of prey also were deemed fascinators. Callimachus, in a fragment
from the second book of the *Aitia* (Frag. 43.61–65) mentions the *harpasus*,
a bird of prey, hated by the founding fathers of the city for damaging with
its Evil Eye (*baska[i]nei*) a tower under construction along with the land
surveyeors. *Owls* too were thought to fascinate. The Latin poet Ausonius
(fourth century CE) in his *Mosella* (308–310), tells of an owl made by Ik-
tinos, the chief builder of the Athenian Parthenon. It was bedecked with
magical colors and attracted birds of all kinds, which it killed with its glance,
while at the same time warding off fascination.[423] It was perhaps the sharp
vision and ocular power of these birds of prey, like that of wolves, that led to
their association with the Evil-Eyed glance.

Snakes, serpents also were thought to cast an Evil Eye.[424] Aeschylus
(*Persians* 81–82) speaks of the "arrow-shooting glance" of a serpent, which
Rakoczy (1996:169) regards as "the earliest reference to the Evil Eye of an
animal." Serpents with the Evil Eye appear frequently in ancient Egyptian
texts. The serpent Apophis with its Evil Eye opposed the Sun-god Re.[425] The
death-dealing Gorgo/Medusa, as we saw above, had serpentine hair. The
common belief was that serpents had a sinister stare and sprayed venom
from their eyes (Euripides, *Orestes* 479–80). The Evil Eye as active organ
projecting harmful rays was compared to serpents that spit their venom
against their victims.

Three creatures sharing common lethal anti-Evil Eye qualities are described by Pliny the Elder in the eighth book of his *Natural History*: the

420. See Rakoczy 1996:126 n392.

421. Dodsley 1897:234.

422. Virgil, *Ecl.* 9.53–54; Pliny, *NH* 8.80; Theocritus, *Idyls* 14.22. On wolves see
Seligmann 1910 1:121; 2:134 and on the Wolf-stare (*Wolfsblick*), Rakoczy 1996:11–17,
170–71, and above, p. 124.

423. See Seligmann 1910 1:124; 2:117; on owls see also Meisen 1950:146, 153; Rakoczy 1996:172–73 n621. See below, pp. 261–62.

424. See Seligmann 1910 1:126–32.

425. *Book of the Dead* 108.13; cf. also 149.105; Bourghouts 1973:114ff, 140ff.

catoblepas, the basilisk, and the wolf. The first (*catoblepas*) is a fabulous creature of western Ethiopia. Always looking down at the ground—*Katoblepas*
(Greek) means, literally, "downward-looker"—it nevertheless is "deadly to
the human race, as all who see its eyes expire immediately."[426] The lethal
power of this figure is similar to that attributed to Medusa/Gorgo: sight of
it causes immediate death.[427] The second is the mythological serpent-like
basilisk of Cyrenica, North Africa.[428] Depicted as a snake or lizard or dragon, it was called "*regulus*, the king of serpents" (Isidore of Seville, *Origines*
12.4.6) and was associated with the cockatrice (Heliodorus, *Aeth.* 3.8.2). Its
glance, breath, smell, and touch were considered fatal, as was the sight of
this creature. It routs snakes with its hiss and even

> kills bushes not only by its touch but also by its breath; it scorch-
> es grass and bursts rocks. Its effect on other animals is disas-
> trous: it is believed that once one was killed with a spear by a
> man on horseback and the infection rising through the spear
> killed not only the rider but also the horse. (Pliny *NH* 8.33.78,
> LCL with modification by John H. Elliott)

Illus. 8
Sketch of a mythological basilisk, African style (from Seligmann 1910, 1:113,
fig. 10)

This description of the basilisk is strkingly similar to the iconography of amulets displaying a cavalier spearing a prostrate demoness, which on occasion
is explicitly identified as *Baskosynê* (Evil-Eyeing Malice). Its noxious emanations likewise are akin to those attributed to an Evil Eye. Subsequently it
was associated by Christians with the devil (influenced by Rev 12:9–10) and
was often pictured in churches and book illustrations.[429] The third creature

426. Pliny, *NH* 8.32.77 LCL; see also Aelian *Nat. an.* 7.5.
427. Seligmann (1910 1:140–41) in fact identifies the Gorgo with the Catoblepas.
428. Pliny, *NH* 8.33.78–79; 29.19.66; cf. Galen, *De theriaca ad Pisonem* 6–7 (ed.
Kühn, vol. 14:233).
429. On the basilisk see Seligmann 1910 1:141–47 and figures 9–13; 2:470–71 on its

is the wolf, the sight of which was also deemed harmful. If the wolves "look at a man before he sees them, this temporarily deprives him of utterance."[430] All three creatures, by Pliny's account, have a harmful effect on other living beings by exuding injurious emanations (ocular rays, breath, smell). In the case of the *catoblepas* and wolf, beholding them has dire consequences. It is thus not surprising that all three beasts have been associated with the Evil Eye, its emanations, and its noxious power.[431] Moreover, with animals, as with humans, the eye is understood as an active, not passive, organ.

Among insects, the *locust* or *grasshopper* (*mantis*) was deemed capable of fascinating.[432] In ancient Rome, when persons fell ill without clear cause, the people cried, *Mantis te vidit*, "some Mantis/grasshopper/fascinator has overlooked you."[433] The mantis, alias *graus seriphos*, was called *baskania*.[434] Since withering and drying up of persons and crops was damage attributed to the Evil Eye, the association of locust with drought and withering likely led to their identification as fascinators.

In antiquity, evidence of *historical human beings* being stigmatized as fascinators is sparcer than in later time. Aesop, composer of fables, was a slave who was said to possess several physical features that qualified him as a likely fascinator: he was a small, dark-skinned foreignor, ugly, squint-eyed, with knit eyebrows, and a hunched back.[435] At the same time, as we have already seen (above pp. 36, 127, 144), his fellow slaves quipped that it was these features that led his master to acquire and use him as an apotropaic for protection against an Evil Eye (*Vita Aes.* 3). Like the Gorgo, he was thought to both wield and defend against an Evil Eye. In his *Lives of the Twelve Emperors*, Suetonius indicates that Gaius Caligula (*Gaius* 35) was notorious for his envy of persons low and high. He also ranks envy among Nero's dominant characteristics (*Nero* 33, 53). The emperor Domitian was explicitly accused of casting an Evil Eye. Philostratus (170–c. 247 CE) in his *Life of Apollonius of Tyana*, tells of Apollonius (c. 40–c. 120 CE) once meeting a youth in prison. Having come to Rome to study law, the handsome youth first was admired by Domitian, and then became the victim of the emperor's Evil Eye (*ho basileus kakôs eiden*). After considering what fea-

mention in the Old Testament see Vol.3, chap. 1.

430. Pliny, *NH* 8.34.80. LCL.

431. See also Rakoczy 1996:178.

432. Elworthy 1895/1958:15, 144; Seligmann 1910 1:135; 2:469–70.

433. Frommann 1675:19; Seligmann 1910 1:135.

434. Scholion on Theocritus, *Idyls* 10.18; see also Seligmann 1910 1:135; 2:469–70; Rakoczy 1996:173–74.

435. On the various descriptions of Aesop's features see Trentin 2009:134–39.

tures of the youth might have caused Domitian to do this (blue eyes? nose? hair? mouth?), Apollonius states, "Surely the emperor must be mistaking all these features for other persons, or you would not tell me he has Evil-Eyed you."[436] Details of the account suggest that Domitian's Evil-Eyeing resulted from his unguarded *praise* of the boy. Domitian, according to the youth, "failed to spare what he had praised." Praise, as we have seen, masked an Evil Eye as well as prompted an Evil Eye. Lucius Apuleius (c. 125–c. 180 CE) was suspected of being an Evil-Eyeing fascinator and was accused of having injured a boy through witchcraft and incantation—a charge against which he defended himself in his *Apology* (chs. 42–43).

Suspected *fascinators,* in sum, included humans, deities, demons, animals, insects, mythological figures and fabulous beasts. With some categories of human fascinators, their having an Evil Eye was thought to be a permanent and hereditary condition conferred by nature. In some cases, the fascinator might be unaware of having an Evil Eye and might not intend its damage. This is similar to envy, which could be aroused and directed either consciously or unconsciously. Also similar to envy, the fascinator, was thought capable of harming him/herself. In other cases, both the Evil Eye and envy could be set in motion with malice aforethought. The *baskanos demon* and the envy demon, were, in all cases, malignant and malevolent. Less attention was devoted to the moral implications of Evil Eye fascination, in comparison with the enormous energy expended on identifying fascinators as sources of danger and on efforts to protect against them.

Since intense and extended staring was taken as the activation of aggression, an Evil Eye, and envy, such staring and glaring naturally was discouraged. This disapproval of staring continues in modern time, whether or not it is known to have anything to do with the Evil Eye.

Victims and Targets of the Evil Eye

Who and what attracts an Evil Eye and envy? The general answer is anyone and anything of value in the culture: healthy, handsome, successful humans; beautiful children; happy newlyweds; victorious competitors; thriving crops and abundant harvests—anything that could evoke praise and admiration and the envy and displeasure of one's peers.[437] The potential *victims* of Evil-Eye attack are, like the fascinators, all-inclusive—birthing mothers, newborn babies, infants of both sexes, beautiful males and females in the bloom of youth, male and female lovers, victorious athletes, conquering warriors,

436. *kakôs hyp' autou legeis ophthênai, Life of Apollonius of Tyana* 7.42.
437. On vulnerable animate and inanimate objects see Seligmann 1910 1:189–244.

any persons enjoying success, happiness, and public acclaim. However, it is the newly-born, infants and children in their minority that are repeatedly mentioned as vulnerable to Evil Eye malice. Their fragile physical condition, it was believed, as well as the beauty and vitality of their youth that attracted the Evil Eye. *Dangerous occasions* included critical and transitional moments of personal life (birth, puberity, marriage, death); publically-held contests where persons complete with rivals for literary or athletic prizes; public celebrations of military victories; gatherings of crowds or mobs; and the appearance of strangers or entering the presence of strangers. Since the Evil Eye lurked everywhere, constant vigilance was called for and powerful protection.

We find many more references to the fascinators than we do to the fascinated, with the exception of constant comment on birthing mothers, endangered babies, infants and youth. In addition to texts mentioning specifc victims of the Evil Eye, the myriad amulets and protective devices against the Evil Eye often reveal who were considered potentional victims of the Evil Eye.

Infants, children, and those in the bloom and beauty of youth are foremost among the potential victims of the Evil Eye. This is the case from Mesopotamian incantations[438] down through modern time. In the Greco-Roman period the Roman satirist Persius Flaccus (34–62 CE) writes:

> Behold, how the grandmother or older aunt/
> removes the boy from the crib, and his forehead and moist lips/
> first purifies with the infamous finger and atoning spittle/
> knowledgable thereby about warding off burning eyes.
> (Persius, *Satires* 2.31–34)[439]

In addition to indicating the vulnerability of the child, these lines illustrate further features of the Evil Eye: protective aid is afforded by knowledgable older female relatives; it is a "burning" or "withering" (*urentis*) glance of the Evil Eye that causes drying up, hence the counteracting use of spittle (*saliva*). To ward off the Evil Eye, the extended rigid middle finger (*digitus infamis*) also is displayed.[440]

---

438. On infants as victims in Mespotomian incantations see previously, Vol. 1, chap. 2.

439. *Ecce avia aut metuens divum matertera cunis/*
exemit puerum frontemque atque uda labella/
infami digito et lustralibus ante salivis/
expiate, urentis oculos inhibere perita. Cf. Jahn 1855:45.

440. On spitting to protect against an Evil Eye, see below, pp. 176–80; on the *digitus infamis* (extended middle finger) see below, pp. 189–91.

As evidence of the parents' fertility and guarantors of the family's continuity, children were precious to the family and the source of great joy, pride and honor. They were essential to the perpetuation of the family and in their mature years, to its defense. Being barren and bereft of children was a familial disaster and cause of personal and familial shame. The rate of infant mortality was high in the ancient world, however, and many did not survive childbirth and the early years. "In preindustrial society . . . a third of the live births were dead before they reached the age of six. By sixteen something like 60% of these live births would have died."[441] Death, it was believed, was caused by any of a host of deadly agents (Megara, Mormo, Strix, Gello alias Gyllou alias *Baskosynê* ["Evil Eye malice"])[442] and especially by an Evil Eye of demons or humans. The vulnerability of children to all kinds of illness and epidemics, coupled with the fragility of their physical constitutions, lent plausibility to this aspect of Evil Eye belief. Plutarch explained that it was the "susceptible, fragile constitutions" of infants and youth that made them so vulnerable to the Evil Eye (*Quaest. Conv.* 5.7.1 [*Mor.* 680D]), a thought echoed by Alexander of Aphrodisias, stating that their "nature is sensitive and variable" (*Probl. phys.* 2.53).[443]

Therefore cautious steps were taken to afford protection to the young. Among the Greeks, Euripides (*Ion* 1421) indicates that a gorgo image was woven into children's apparel as an apotropaion.[444] Among the Romans, children, from infancy on, wore anti-Evil Eye amulets (*fascina, crepundia, bulla*) until reaching their majority.[445] In his study of the Roman family, Keith Bradley remarks that

> [t]he widespread resort to amulets is a sign of the widespread awareness in Roman society of the frailty of childhood, and

441. Carney 1975:88.

442. Perdrizet 1922:24–25; Johnston 1995.

443. On children as victims of the Evil Eye see also Pliny, *NH* 7.16; Plutarch, *Quaest. Conv.* 5.7 [*Mor.* 682A, F]; *Isis et Osiris* 17 [*Mor.* 357D–E]; *Non posse* [*Mor.* 1090C]; Alex. Aphr., *Prob. phys.* 2.53; Pliny, *NH* 7.2.16, 28.39; Varro, *Ling. lat.* 7; Quintillian, *Inst. Orat.* 6, proem. In Jewish tradition, e.g., *b.Bava Batra* 141a; see also Vol. 4, chap. 1. In Christian literature: Gal 4:19; Tertullian, *De carne* 2; Lactantius, *Div. inst.* 1.20.36 and Vol. 4, chap. 2. See Jahn 1855:40, 45; Geffcken 1930:36–40; Dunbabin 1991:32; Elliott 1988, 1990 1991, 1992, 1994, 2005a, 2005b, 2007a, 2011, 2014, 2015, 2016b; Rakoczy 1996:152–53; and in modern time, deMartino 1959 40 ff; Maloney 1976:64, 166 and passim; Dundes 1992 passim.

444. Jahn 1855:60 n120.

445. Plautus, *Miles* 5.1.6, line 1399; *Rudens* 4.4.10, lines 1154–71 (for a list of a girl's apotropaic *crepundia* [rattles]); 4.4.127 (gold *bulla*); Varro, *Ling. lat.* 7; Macrobius, *Sat.* 1.6.9. On the donning of protection until the attainment of majority see also Dolansky1999. On these amulets see below, pp. 253–55.

perhaps also of the well-recognized inadequacies of doctors in solving medical problems. It was easier to trust the protective powers of the superhuman than the restorative capacities of mortals: '*medicus enim nihil aliud est quam animi consolatio*' ['a doctor is nothing other than the soul's consolation']. (Petronius, *Satyricon* 42.5)[446]

Two favored amulets for children among the Romans were the phallic amulet (*fascinum*) and the *bulla* (metal or leather container or pouch) with anti-Evil Eye content, both usually worn as pendants around the neck. "Children sometimes wore the former in the form of finger rings but other amulets were worn around the neck. They brought the protection of the god of the divinized penis Fascinus, who fended off the influence of the sometimes strikingly visible Evil Eye."[447] Horace (*Epodes* 8.8) notes that women touch infants with their wet tongues to protect them against the Evil Eye.[448] Other strategies included hiding infants from the view of others, even of their own parents,[449] spitting on them when strangers appeared,[450] and not allowing them to be praised or admired. Romans also entrusted these vulnerable infants and birthing mothers to the protection of deities such as Fascinus (personification of an anti-Evil Eye apotropaic) and Cunina, goddess of the cradle.[451]

The beauty of youth and the fresh vitality of young lovers also attracted the envious Evil Eye.[452] Plutarch attributes to the Evil Eye and envy (*baskanias kai phthonou*) also to the fragility and instability of youth and beauty:

People believe that beautiful persons (*kalous*), when they are looked at (*prosorômenos*), suffer injury through the Evil Eye and envy (*hypo de baskanias kai phthonou blaptesthai*) because it is precisely physical beauty [of youth] that most quickly suffers a reversal because of the instability of the [youthful] body." (Plutarch, *Non posse* [*Mor.* 1090C])

---

446. See Bradley 2005:89.

447. Ibid., 89–90.

448. See also Pliny, *NH* 28.39.

449. Plutarch, *Quaest. Conv.* 5.7.4 [*Mor.* 682A].

450. Pliny, *NH* 28.39.

451. Pliny, *NH* 28.39; Lactantius, *Div. Inst.* 1.20.36; Augustine, *City of God* 4.11.4; cf. also Tertullian, *De carne* 2.

452. Catullus, *Poems* 5.9–12; cf. also 7.11–12; Plutarch, *Quaest. Conv.* 5.7.2 [*Mor.* 681B]; Heliodorus, *Aeth.* 3.7.4–5 (the beautiful girl Chariclea); Alexander of Aphrodisias, *Probl. phys.* 2.53.

The handsome Eutelidas beheld his good-looking reflection in the water and Evil-Eyed himself, losing both his beauty with his health.[453]

The vulnerability of the young to the Evil Eye extended even to *young animals*. Aristotle[454] mentions young pigeons, stating that the pigeon spits thrice on its young to protect them from the Evil Eye.[455] The poet Virgil has a shepherd complain,

> I do not know what (Evil) Eye (*oculus*) is Evil-Eyeing [and injuring] (*fascinat*) my tender lambs. (Virgil, *Ecl.* 3.103)

The danger extended to *adult animals* as well. Hunting dogs were potential targets and so were protected by amulets against the Evil Eye (*oculi maligni*).[456] This assumed vulnerability of prized domestic animals has continued down through modern time and includes the cattle in the Scottish highlands, cows in Ireland (protected by St. Brigit's cross), pigs in rural England, horses and camels (of Turks, Arabs), and sheep in Greece, India, and China.[457]

Virtuous persons can also attract the Evil Eye. Plutarch (*Life of Dio* 2.5) tells of "evil demons with the Evil Eye, who send envy (*prosphthonounta*) against virtuous men." These demons seek "to impede their good deeds, try to incite in them feelings of terror and distraction to make them shake and totter in their virtue, lest by a steady and unbiased perseverenace they should obtain a happier condition than these beings after death." The friendship or concord existing between two persons or parties was considered vulnerable to Evil Eye attack and therefore not publicly acknolwledged.[458]

Persons enjoying *unexpected or sudden success and prosperity*—perceived though the lens of limited good as obtained at the cost of others—were possible targets of the Evil Eye. This included victors in military campaigns or in athletic contests. Agammenon, royal conquerer of Troy, since so successful, was the classic target of the Evil Eye (both of humans and of the gods).[459] The victorious female athlete Polycrites of Naxos fell

---

453. Plutarch, *Quaest. Conv.* 5.7 [*Mor.* 682B, E]. In the Christian *Acts of Thomas* (100), a certain Charisius complains that someone's Evil Eye (*baskanos ophthalmos* [ms U]) alienated the affection of his young wife.

454. Aristotle, Frag. 347, ed. Rose; see Athenaeus, *Deipn.* 9.394B.

455. See also Athenaeus, *Deipn.* 9.50; Aelian, *Nat. an.* 1.35. See Aelian, *Var. hist.* 1.15 for young pigeons.

456. Grattius, *Cynegetica* 399–407; cf. Vegetius, *Mulomedicina* 5.73.

457. See MacLagan 1902; Campbell 1964:338; Maloney 1976 *passim*; Dundes 1992 *passim*.

458. Dickie 2001:109.

459. Aeschylus, *Agam.* 468–471, 946–947; *Persians* 362; Rakoczy 1996:73–96.

victim to a *baskanos daimôn* or a *baskanos Phthonos* (an envy demon with an Evil Eye).[460] She died at the moment of victory without enjoying her honors, with the result that her grave is called *baskanou taphos* ("grave of the Evil Eye").[461] The conquering Roman general was protected by a *fascinum* (image of a phallus and testicles) attached to his triumphant chariot (Pliny, *NH*.28.39).

The *wealthy* were regarded as the likely targets of the envious Evil Eye of the "have-nots."[462] *Lovers* too were vulnerable to the envious Evil Eye—a key theme in Heliodorus's romance, *Aethiopica*.[463] Catullus sings of lovers who take precautions:

> Then, when we have made many thousands [of kisses], we will [intentionally] confuse our counting, so that we may not know the reckoning, nor any malicious person enviously Evil-Eye us (*nequis malus invidere possit*) when he knows the [precise] number of our kisses." (Catullus, *Poems/Carmina* 5.9)

A further song (7.11–12), continuing the thought of 5.9, speaks of "kisses, which neither curious eyes shall count nor an evil tongue fascinate (*quae nec pernumerare curiosi possint nec mala fascinare lingua*), illustrating the linkage of envy, an Evil Eye and an evil tongue.

Persons enjoying *robust health* were potential targets of the Evil Eye (Plutarch, *Quaest. Conv.* 5.7 [*Mor.* 682E]). The *ill and the blind* were thought to have been made so by an Evil Eye.[464] The words on some amulets explicitly indicate that the Evil Eye was considered one of several possible causes of illness (against which the amulet afforded protection). A silver amulet made for a certain Syntyche addresses a variety of illnesses. After summoning the "great and holy name of the living God Dammamanaios and Adonaios, and Iao and Sabaoth," it conjures "all spirits, every falling sickness, every hydrophobia, the Evil Eye (*ton baskanon ophthalmon*)" and every violent demonic attack.[465]

Was *impotence* caused by an Evil Eye? Encolpius, the protagonist of Petronius' story, *Satyricon,* is treated by an old woman for his impotence or, as formulated today, erectile disfunction (131.4–5). The ritual involves

---

460. Rakoczy 1996:132 n420.

461. Plutarch, *Mul. virt.* [*Mor.* 254E].

462. Euripides, *Suppliant Women* 240–242.

463. See also Plutarch, *Quaest. conviv.* 5.7 [*Mor.* 681B].

464. See Alexander of Aphrodisias, *Probl. phys.* 2.42; 2.52–53; on the blind, such as Oedipus, see Bernidaki-Aldous 1988.

465. See Pelliccioni 1880. On this amulet see also below, p. 225. On epilepsy as the "falling sickness" caused by the gods see Tempkin 1971.

procedures that suggest that the impotence was seen as caused by an Evil Eye. These include the aid of an *old crony*, her use of *spittle* mixed with dirt, marking his forehead with the her *middle finger* (*medio . . . digito*), the infamous *digitus infamis* directed against an Evil Eye, *reciting a spell*, then ordering Encolpius to *spit three times* on his chest and to *toss pebbles* wrapped in *red cloth* inside his garment *three times in a row* while uttering a *spell*. The spittle, middle finger, red cloth, and spitting three times are all well-known and well-documented anti-Evil Eye measures. If this is an illness caused by an Evil Eye, this episode also would be an instance of an Evil Eye curing ritual. Centuries later, the Christian Church father, John Chrysostom of Antioch, Syria, inveighs against a similar practice of nurses in baths attempting to protect their infant charges from the Evil Eye with colored threads, spittle, mud, and the middle finger.[466]

The Evil Eye can afflict not just the wealthy and beautiful but also simple, ordinary people. Dio Chysostom (*Orat.* 43.2) fears that he and other residents of Prusa are the targets of others' Evil Eyes, reflecting the worry of common folk everywhere. Ordinary women, according to Strabo (*Geog.* 16.4.17), fearing fascination, wore necklaces of musselshells (cowrie shells) "against the Evil Eyes" (*anti baskaniôn*). Consequently, everyone has to be on guard and adequately protected.

Autofascination, persons inadvertently striking *themselves* with their own Evil Eye, was also thought possible.[467] Such was the case with the handsome Eutelidas, who, admiring his own attractive reflection in the water, Evil-Eyed himself and lost his beauty with his health,[468] similar to the handsome Narcissus.[469] Plutarch speculates that this also may be the case with children, who actually Evil-Eye themselves though others are blamed—a quite singular theory.[470] The single-eyed, Evil-Eyeing giant Polyphemus, who admired himself, spit thrice onto his own chest to avoid the Evil Eyeing himself (Theocritus, *Idylls* 6.39–40). In these instances of autofascination, the act is obviously unintentional.[471]

---

466. See Vol. 4, chap. 2.

467. See Plutarch, *Quaest. Conv.* 5.7.4 [*Mor.* 682B] (*tôn heautous katabaskainein*); 682E (*katabaskainein heautous . . . heautous epiblepôsin . . . heautous dokousi katabaskainen*).

468. Plutarch, *Quaest. Conv.* 5.7.4 [*Mor.* 682D–E].

469. On the myth of Narcissus, who beheld his reflection in the pool of water, fell in love with what he saw, and destroyed himself with his own Evil-Eyed gaze see Ovid, *Met.* 3.339–510, and on its artistic depictions and implications see Taylor 2008:56–89.

470. Plutarch, *Quaest. Conv.* 5.7.4 [*Mor.* 682F].

471. For suspected self-fascinators see above on Medea and Medusa.

Objects, activities, and situations also can attract or be vulnerable to an Evil Eye. "Growing crops in the field, beautiful children, excellent horses, strong, well-fed cattle"—all died suddenly from no other cause than the Evil Eye (Aulus Gellius, *Attic Nights* 9.4.7–8). According to Pliny the Elder,[472] gardens had a quasi-sacred nature and so, like the Roman forum, were protected by apotropaics (images of satyrs or of *fascina*) against "the Evil-Eyeing of the envious (*invidentium effascinationes*)." Farms and fields too were deemed susceptible to envy and the Evil Eye. Pliny also tells of a certain Caius Furius Chresimus who was more successful at farming than his neighbors and fell victim to their envy. They accused him of having used spells (*veneficiis*) to entice away their crops to his own property, a practice forbidden in the Twelve Tables, Rome's first code of laws. He was indicted but acquitted because of his eloquent defense of his innocence.[473] A writing of the Greek Bible, the *Epistle of Jeremiah* 69/70, speaks of a cucumber field that was thought vulnerable and so was protected by an anti-Evil Eye apotropaic (*probaskanion*; see also above, pp. 16, 35, 62). The public baths were another location where Romans were especially exposed to the Evil Eye.[474]

Animals as victims of the Evil Eye were mentioned above (young animals).[475] Fear of the loss of prized animals to Evil Eye attack continues in modern time. These have included cattle in the Scottish highlands; horses and camels among the Turks and Arabs, pigs in rural England, and cows and goats in India. In rural areas of contemporary Greece, children and sheep are deemed the two most indicators of social prestige and so the most prone to Evil Eye attack.[476]

Products made in workshops were deemed vulnerable. Metalworkers suspended amulets (*baskania*) in their foundaries to protect their metal wares and their ovens against damage from the envious Evil Eye.[477] For similar reasons, ship and boat owners painted eyes on the prows of their vessels to protect them and their cargo from the Evil Eye.[478]

472. Pliny, *NH* 19.19.50; cf. 37.54.145.

473. Pliny, *NH* 18.41–43. For crops and fields as vulnerable to fascination and for laws against fascination see also Pliny, *NH* 28.2; Seneca, *Nat.* 4.7 and of the Roman Twelve Tables (450 BCE), Table 7, Law 3 and Table 8, Law 8a (against crop incantation).

474. Dunbabin 1989.

475. See also Jahn 1855:40; Seligmann 1910 1:210–20.

476. See MacLagan, 1902; Campbell 1964:338; Maloney 1976:107 and *passim*; Dundes 1992 *passim*.

477. Aristophanes, Frag 607 (Kassel-Austin, *PCG*); Pollux, *Onom.* 7.108. For modern practice see Maloney 1976:102–48 (India); Teitelebaum 1976:63–75 (Tunisia).

478. See below under amulets and protection.

In general, all objects and possessions of value, including one's health, personal reputation and social standing, family members and especially children, prized domestic animals important to the livelihood of the family and indicative of the high status of the owners (camels, horses, cows, pigs, lambs, goats, hunting dogs)—all could attract the envy and malice of the Evil Eye.

Among the *actions* arousing or masking an Evil Eye and *envy, praise, admiration* and *boasting* (i.e. self-praise) were high on the list.[479] Countering the praise received for his skillful argumention, Socrates is quite cautious: "My friend," he says, "do not speak loudly [in boasting], lest some Evil Eye (*baskania*) put to rout the argument that is to come" (Plato, *Phaedo* 95b).[480] Agammenon was well aware that his being praised could attract a thunderbolt cast by the envious Evil Eye of Zeus (Aeschylus, *Agam.* 468–470). With boasting and self-praise one could unintentionally Evil Eye oneself. The giant Evil-Eyeing Cyclops, Polyphemos, had admired himself and so had to spit on himself to avoid his own Evil Eye (Theocritus, *Idyl* 6.39–40). Admiration of others could also unleash an inadvertent Evil Eye. The character Theagenes in Heliodorus's novel *Aethiopica* was thought to have inadvertently Evil-Eyed the beautiful Chariclea through his admiring her (*Aeth.* 3.7; 4.5). The church father Tertullian reported that the non-Christians of his day (second century CE) also regarded an Evil Eye activated by "unbounded praise and glory" (*Virg. vel.* 15, PL 2:959).[481] The association of praising and the Evil Eye is another example of the assumed relation of speaking (praise) and looking (Evil Eye), mouth and eye.

Praise and admiration, therefore, were expressed only cautiously and with accompanying assurances, so as to avoid being suspected of Evil-Eyeing envy. A slave in Plautus's comedy *Rudens* (third to second centuries BCE), after flattering himself for his skill at drawing water realizes his jeopardy and exclaims *Praefiscine!* ("no Evil Eye intended!") to protect himself from his own flattery.[482] A slave in another of Plautus's plays, *Asinaria*, when about to brag, likewise blurts out *Praefiscine!* in self-protection.[483] The Latin grammarian Charisius cites in his *Ars Grammatica* (book 2.13) a passage of Titinius[484] in the lost Roman play, *Setina*. When a suitor was declaring his

479. See Aeschylus, *Agam.* 947; Plato, *Phaedo* 95b; Virgil, *Ecl.* 7.21, 25; McCartney 1992, Maloney 1976:102–48 and Maloney 1976 *passim*, and above, pp. 33, 112–13, 145–46, 149.

480. See Story 1877:159. On boasting that attracts an Evil Eye see McCartney 1924.

481. On praise arousing the Evil Eye see also McCartney 1992:9–39.

482. Plautus, *Rudens* 2.5.4, lines 458–461,

483. Plautus, *Asinaria* 2.4.84, lines 491–493.

484. A Latin poet in the Plautine style, c. 160 CE.

love and praise for a certain Paula, a friend who was present, cried out, "By Pollux! you had better add, '*Praefiscini*,' lest you fascinate her!"[485] *Praefiscini* has the meaning, "no Evil Eye intended." Charisius, commenting on the preposition *prae*, notes that the composite term *praefiscine* means "free of an Evil Eye," equivalent to the Greek *abaskanta* ("*praefiscine, id est sine fascino, quod Graeci abaskanta dicunt*").[486] In certain parts of modern Italy, in similar precarious situations, the protective expression employed is "si mal occhio non ci fosse." ("May the Evil Eye not strike it"). Equivalent modern expressions include the Yiddish "kein einhoreh" ("no Evil Eye [intended]"), or Arabic *Mashallah* ("As God wills") or Italian "Grazia a Dio" ("thanks be to God")—expressions disavowing any interest to possess, harm, envy or Evil-Eye an object and putting it under the blessing of God.

Even counting one's blessings can attract an Evil Eye. Deeming himself "the happiest of mortals" drew down upon wealthy Croesus the envious Evil Eye of the gods (Herodotus, *Hist.* 1.32–34). The concern that praise, compliments, and admiration expose one to an Evil eye continues through modern time.[487]

Dangerous Situations Where an Evil Eye May Lurk

Liminal life situations were in general dangerous; i.e. moments of transition in one's personal life. At *birth and nursing*, mothers and neonates were deemed vulnerable to the Evil Eye, as already indicated. At *weddings*, where young, beautiful and happy couples were the center of attention, envious Evil Eyes were also thought to lurk. *Public processions, large gatherings and crowds* (Heliodorus, *Aeth.* 3.7.2), *athletic and poetry contests* (Pindar), *military expeditions* and *victory celebrations*—these too were situations where an Evil Eye could strike.[488] *Dining and meals* were opportunities of social interaction, of comparison of reputation and status, of envy among peers, and hence likely occasions for an Evil Eye to strike. For this reason consumption

485. *Pol! tu ad laudem additio 'Praefiscini,' ne puella fascinator,* Charisius, *Ars Grammatica* 2.13, CGL 274.

486. Charisius, *Ars Grammatica* 2.13 (ed. Barwick 1964/1925), CGL 274. On use of the expression and its variants see above, pp. 37, 44, 111.

487. See Dionisopoulos-Mass 1976:44–45; Flores-Meiser 1976:160. For contemporary customs concerning praising and means for averting harm from praise see Maloney 1976:102–48.

488. Military expeditions attracting the envy of the gods: Aeschylus, *Persians* 362; Herodotus *Hist* 7.10.5; 7.46, 8.109.3; Thucydides, *Hist.* 7.77.3–4; and military triumphs: Pliny, *NH* 28.39; Rakoczy 1996:261. Entering a strange town also posed a danger according to the rabbis; see Vol. 4, chap. 1.

of the herb rue was prescribed prior to meals to ward off an Evil Eye.[489] Plutarch, in fact, set his extensive discussion of the Evil Eye (*Table Talk*) in the context of a meal.[490] Servers at meals also are protected. A Roman mosaic from Dougga, Tunisia (second century CE), portrays two slaves carrying wine jars for a banquet and wearing typical slave clothing and necklaces bearing anti-Evil Eye amulets.[491] Concern over the Evil Eye at eating and dining is mentioned also in the Bible (Deut 28:54–57; Prov 23:6; Sir 14:10; Mark 7:1–23).[492] Avoiding the Evil Eye at meals may have been the stimulus for the practices of concealing what one is eating or even *that* one is eating.[493] In addition to the intentional sharing of one's food, the *symbolic* acts of sharing—the sop and the tip in contemporary cultures—also are traced to the desire to avoid the Evil Eye.[494] Romans held that the public baths too were a place where a naked body exposed to view was vulnerable to the Evil Eye.[495]

Even the mere utterance of the word "Evil Eye" was perilous, probably along the lines of the adage, "speak of the Devil and he will appear." According to this *Sprachtabu*, the expression "Evil Eye" was avoided or replaced with terms for envy, its frequent, but less dangerous, partner (i.e. *phthonos* for *baskania*).[496] The custom has persisted for millennia so that in modern Naples, Italy, merely speaking the words *jettatura* or *malluch* (*malocchio*) is deemed dangerous and therefore avoided.

Precautions and Protection against the Evil Eye and Envy— Strategies and Means (Words, Actions, Amulets)

Where the Evil Eye is thought to lurk everywhere, constant vigilance and effective protection is the prescribed order of the day. Precautions headed

---

489. Pseudo-Aristotle, *Prob. phys.* 20.34, 926b 20–31.

490. Plutarch, *Quaest.Conv.* 5.7 [*Mor.* 680C–683B].

491. Described by Rostovtzeff 1957 1:288.

492. On the Evil Eye, social meals and eating see Rakoczy 1996:141–55; also Seligmann 1910:1:234–40; 1922:379–81; Gifford 1958:48–50; Elliott 1988, 2005a.

493. For a contemporary example of the latter see the picture of an Abessinian eating at the side of the road and covering himself completely (in Knuf and Knuf, 1984:154); see also the comment of Rakoczy 1996:143.

494. Foster 1972; Hagedorn and Neyrey 1988; see below pp. 160–61.

495. See John Chrysostom, *Hom. 1 Cor. 12:13* (PG 61.105–106). Dickie 1995:31–32; see also Dunbabin 1989.

496. So Rakoczy 1996:41, 61–62, 83 n204.

off the arousal of an Evil Eye and envy, and an arsenal of protective measures were employed for countering and neutralizing their damaging effect.

Precautions against Damage from the Evil Eye (and Envy)

Anti-Evil Eye *precautions* were steps taken to avoid being a target of the Evil Eye and envy in everyday activities. included engaging in acts of avoidance, concealment, denial, self-deprecation and self-diminution, moderation, and real or symbolic sharing of goods and resources.[497]

1) *Avoidance* took various forms. One entailed avoiding, or practicing caution in, places and situations where an Evil Eye might be present. Places of competition and celebration, cemetaries and latrines (gathering-place of foul spirits and demons), gardens, fields of crops, athletic stadia, public forums, and thoroughfares were among the sites where an Evil Eye could be expected to strike. Where not explicitly mentioned, these locations can sometimes be deduced from the apotropaics found there.[498] In regard to person-to-person interactions, one avoided looking directly into the eyes of any suspected fascinator.

Praising, complimenting, or admiring other things or persons, especially children, was avoided to escape any suspicion that these actions conveyed or masked an envious Evil Eye.[499] Tobin Siebers observes that praise is ambivalent, involving a positive compliment but also possible embarrassment or malicious intent, thereby requiring a questioning of the motives of the praiser. The Evil Eye concept "provides a frame within which the disruptive and ambilvalent nature of praise is rendered more stable."[500] Pliny the Elder (*NH* 7.16) cited Isigonus and Nymphodorus who told of families in Africa with the Evil Eye (*effascinantium*) "whose praising (*laudatione*) causes meadows to dry up, trees to wither, and infants to perish." See also the similar comment on praise by Aulus Gellius (*Attic Nights* 9.4.8) cited above, p. 130.

The Roman military general celebrating his triumph required protection against praise and adulation, hence the *fascinus* affixed to his chariot.[501] "Because I love him, I would not overload him with praise," Pliny

497. See G. Foster 1972:175–82; Berke 1988:48–56; Hagedorn and Neyrey 1998: 36–38.

498. See below under amulets, pp. 219–66.

499. See E. S. McCartney 1992 for ancient examples, and Malony 1976:102–48 for modern cases.

500. Siebers 1983:43.

501. Pliny, *NH* 28.39; cf. Versnel 1970:70 n2.

the Younger wrote in one of his letters.[502] Where a sense of limited good prevails, compliments are regarded as an expression of envy or aggression, and so must be accompanied with a verbal assurance that the praise veils no envious Evil Eye. So when praise, compliments, or admiration could not be avoided altogether, they were accompanied with equivalents of the expression "no Evil Eye intended." To a word of praise the Greeks added *abaskantos* ("[may X be kept] safe from an Evil Eye")[503] and the Romans, *praefiscini [dixerim]* ("no Evil Eye intended").[504] The custom of avoiding praise and admiration or accompanying it with words of disavowal of malevolent intent continues in modern time.[505] In Italian, one adds to a word of admiration or praise, *"si malocchio non ci fosse"* ("may the Evil Eye not strike it"); in Greek, *'s ta matia* ("no [Evil] eye");[506] in German, *"unberufen"* ("no summoning of the Evil Eye"); or in Yiddish, *kein einhoreh* ("no Evil Eye [intended]"). Arabic *Mashallah* ("as God wills") or Italian "Grazia a Dio" ("thanks be to God") are added to disavow any envy or intent to harm with an Evil Eye by putting the object under the blessing of God. "God bless it" is uttered in Ireland when looking at a child, to acknowledge God as protector and source of blessing.

Spitting when praising in order to block and disaver the Evil Eye was also practiced.[507] In some regions of Greece today, an old Greek woman, when she has praised something, will immediately spit three times and say *"ptou, ptou ptou, sto kako phthiarmo, i.e. phthou, phthou phthou (ei)s to(n) kako(n) phthiarmo(n) (= baskanon)"* ("spit, spit, spit against the malignant Evil Eye").[508] This accords with the general practice of spitting in order to defend against an Evil Eye.[509]

2) A second precaution entailed *concealing* vulnerable persons (especially children), valued things, indications of one's bountry, or evidence of good fortune, success and prosperity. Personal names were concealed, with children instead labelled "number one" (*Primus*), "number two" (*Secundus*)

502. Pliny the Younger, *Ep.* 1.14.10; see also Pliny the Elder, *NH* 7.16, 19.50.

503. This was similar to the precautionary wish expressed in personal letters, which we have examined above, that "So-and-so be kept safe from the Evil Eye"; see above, pp. 2–4.

504. Plautus, *Asinaria* 2.4.84, lines 491–493.; *Rudens* 2.5.4; Aulus Gellius, *Attic Nights* 10.24.8 (uttering either *praefiscine* or *praefiscini*).

505. For Palestine see Jaussen 1924:398–399, for India and South Asia, Maloney 1976:102–48.

506. Jahn 1855:57 n112, 61.

507. Libanius, *Ep.* 714.

508. Seligmann 1910 2:214.

509. On spitting as defense against an Evil Eye see below, pp. 176–80.

etc. Keeping children dirty concealed their vitality and beauty from the Evil-Eyeing fascinators. Obscuring or confusing numbers was a related way of avoiding an Evil Eye. So Catullus writes in his fifth song to Lesbia:

> When we have enjoyed our many thousands [of kisses],
> then confuse their numbers [so as] not to know them,
> lest some Evil Eye in envy strike us,
> then 'tis known how many we have." (*Poems/Carmina* 5.9–12)

His seventh poem contains the same idea, but with reference to fascinating with an *evil tongue*:

> May the curious be unable to count them, so that no evil tongue
> may fascinate us. (Catallus, *Poems/Carmina* 7.11–12)[510]

3) *Dispraise* is akin to concealment. Speaking in disparaging, belittling, or derogatory fashion about one's children ("Nasty, ugly little thing")[511] or calling them demeaning names ("Stupid") was intended to confuse and so repel an Evil Eye.[512] The assumption was that the envious and Evil-Eyeing fascinators have no interest in what is ugly, filthy and base. The rationale is similar to that underlying the Greek farmer's practice of cursing and abusing the seed while sowing it,[513] and the Romans sowing rue in the same fashion[514] or praying that the prolific basil seed never produce fruit.[515]

4) *Denial* is likewise akin to concealment: denying any experience of success, good fortune, vibrant heath, or state of happiness and contentment so as not to be a target. According to the notion of "limited good," such well-being could only come at the expense of others and consequently would arouse an envious Evil Eye. In the contemporary Arab world, it has been noted, "Successful people greatly fear the vicious eye and often rich people denounce the reality of their fortune to keep away the bad influence of envious eyes."[516] A related practice is found in the contemporary Western world where, when one is asked about the condition of one's health, "how are you?" responds "not too bad," or "it could be worse."

---

510. "*Quae nec pernumerare curiosi/ Possint, nec mala fascinare lingua.*" Cf. similarly Virgil, *Ecl.* 7. 21, 25.

511. See E. S. McCartney 1992:12, 27.

512. For modern examples see Siebers 1983:41–43.

513. Theophrastus, *Hist. plant.* 7.3.3; 9.8.8; Plutarch, *Quaest. Conv.* 3 [*Mor.* 700F–710A].

514. Pliny, *NH* 19.120; Palladius, *On Agriculture* 4.9.13–14.

515. Pliny, *NH* 19.120. On the tactic of concealing see also Story 1877:230–31.

516. Hamady 1960:172, cited by Foster 1972:176–77.

5) *Self-deprecation or self-effacement* is yet another mode of conceal-ment and denial. This entails rejecting compliments with a show of humil-ity: "I do not deserve your praise, " "I am not worthy of your admiration." It is one form of modesty and moderation.[517]

6) *Practicing moderation* in all things enables one to avoid excelling or exceeding measures of propriety and thereby escaping an envious Evil Eye. It was common wisdom that "Fortune has a knack, when men vaunt themelves too highly, of laying them unexpectedly low and so teaching them to hope for 'nothing in excess' (*mêden agan*)."[518] "A person avoids provoking others to envy by moderating desires and behavior that manifest ambition and attract attention. It was part of ancient lore that lightning strikes the tallest tree or highest mountain. Moderation cautions against striving to be that tall tree or high mountain."[519] "A low profile is essential for avoiding the Evil Eye and the envy of one's peers or the gods.[520]

7) *Sharing* one's possessions (food, clothing, shelter, valued goods) with others was thought to keep one safe from envy and the Evil Eye. It is a form of appeasement to placate those who could cast an Evil Eye. This can involve either the *actual sharing* of goods and services (as in hospital-ity or material response to requests for aid or for public benefactions) or the *symbolical sharing* of a portion of the thing valued (a figurative "sop"). "Sop behavior" offers a small present or token of good will in the hope of "sopping up" and placating the possible envy and Evil Eye of others.[521] A sop is akin to a bribe that buys off resentment and forestalls an envious Evil Eye.[522] In contemporary societies this includes tips to waiters serving meals, offering small prizes to losers of games, sending postcards from expensive vacations to friends stuck at home: "Having a wonderful time, wish you were here" (and please do not harm me with an envious Evil Eye). Better tip the waiter than have one's food spoiled by his/her Evil Eye.[523] Sop behavior

517. On disallowing excessive praise of oneself see Plutarch, *Sept. sap. conv.* [*Mor.* 164C]. On modesty counteracting envy and an Evil Eye in modern life see Schoeck 1970:54–55; Foster 1972:177.

518. Diodorus Siculus, *Library* 15.33.3.

519. Hagedorn and Neyrey 1998:38. For this commonplace see Aeschylus, *Agam.* 456–458; Herodotus, *Hist.* 7.10; Horace, *Odes* 2.10.1–12. On the danger of standing out and excelling see above, pp. 13–14, 99.

520. Dundes 1992:296.

521. A sop, literally, is a piece of bread or food dipped or steeped in a liquid.

522. See Foster 1972:175–82; Berke 1988:54–56; Dundes 1992:293.

523. "Tip" derives from "tippling" (drinking alcohol and liquor in small amounts) and is given ostensibly so that the recipient might tipple like the tipper tipples and thereby be dissuaded from envying with an Evil Eye. The German for "tip," *Trinkgeld*, makes linguistically explicit the purpose of the sop: *Trink*= "drink"; *Geld* = "money";

around the events of death and burial (food given to bereaved families; visits to gravesites) has the effect of reducing the possible envy of the bereaved and of the dead themselves and forestalling the Evil Eye. The sharing of one's resources with the needy not only forestalls being struck by the Evil Eye of others. It is also the opposite and alternative to casting an Evil Eye oneself. Biblical texts concerning the Evil Eye, as we shall see, describe it as a display of ungenerosity, stinginess, tight-fistedness, and begrudging help to others in contrast to giving liberally (e.g. Deut 15:7–11; 28:54–57; Prov 23:6; Sir 14:3, 10; Tob 4:7, 16; Matt 6:22–23/Luke 11:34).[524]

Protection: Apotropaic Strategies, Modes and Means of Protection

Apotropaic strategies, and modes and means of protection comprised acts of speaking or writing powerful words, incantations, and prayers; spitting; manual gestures; touching and exposure of the genitals; and reliance on a vast array of anti-Evil Eye amulets.[525] A collective term for various means of protection employed against the Evil Eye is the Latin word *apotropaica* (plural), designating all means employed *to ward off, drive away* evil forces. The term *apotropaion* (singular) derives from the Greek *apotropein*, meaning "to drive away," "ward off" evil in any form and from any source—gods, demons/spirits, humans, animals dead or alive, including envy and the Evil Eye. Anti-Evil Eye protectives were known as *baskánia* or *probaskánia*, whose function was to "ward off" (*apotropêi*) envy, the Evil Eye and various forces of evil.[526] *Apotropaica* (English: "apotropaics") include powerful words, sayings, incantations,[527] curses,[528] manual gestures, and actions such as spitting, affixing plaques and protective devices to houses and shops,

---

thus "money to buy a drink."

524. See Vol. 3.

525. On Greek and Roman apotropaic words, actions, amulets and protection in general see Arditi 1825; Story 1877:206–38; Bellucci 1897; Leclercq 1907 (amulets, and against the Evil Eye, 1907:1843–47; *bulla*, 1910; Evil Eye [*mauvais oeil*], 1934:1936–41); Seligmann 1910; Freire-Marreco et al. 1910; Wünsch 1910:461–65; Lafaye 1926 (*fascinum, fascinus*); Konietzko 1932; Merlin 1940; Cintas 1946; Bonner 1950, 1951; Meisen 1950:147–57; Elworthy 1958/1895:115–449; Budge 1978/1930; Robert 1981 (Greek amulets); Gager 1992:218–42 (on amulets and counterspells). Kotansky 1991, 1994, 1995, 2002; Bailliot 2010 (Ch. 2 on "Beliefs and Iconography: Prophylactic Symbols and Amulets"). For literature on amulets see also below, p. 228, n866. On Israelite, Christian, and Jewish apotropaics, see Vols. 3 and 4.

526. See Julius Pollux, *Onom.* 7.108.

527. Incantations were *sung, intoned,* or *chanted* words or expressions, from the Latin *cantare*, "to sing."

528. On curses see Gager 1990.

placing mosaics at house threshholds, and the wearing and employing of amulets of various kinds and sizes. The presumed power and effectiveness of these apotropaic strategies and devices appears to have rested on a concept of mimesis according to which a representation of an object enjoys the power of, or the power over, that object.[529] Underlying this notion is an assumed "sympathy" between two similar entities such that "like influences like" (*simila similibus*)—more on this below in connection with amulets. Amulets, tokens worn or carried on one's person to protect against evil forces, curses, spells in general, as well as the Evil Eye in particular, are discussed in more detail below.

Basic to thinking regarding protection against the Evil Eye was the ancient concept that "the power to bless and heal is inseparable from that to harm and destroy." The power that harms can itself be employed to protect and avert injury.[530] Thus the terms *baskanon, baskanion, fascinum* denote both the powers that harm and the powers that protect from harm, fascination and protection against it.[531] This duality, Jahn observes, is quite evident in the myth of the Gorgo, one of whose drops of blood kills, the other of which heals (Euripides, *Ion* 1003–1005). The Gorgoneion (severed head of Medusa) likewise was thought to both harm and protect. The concept is consistent with and cousin to the principle of "like influences like" (*similia similibus*).

These anti-Evil Eye protectives came in all forms, shapes and sizes and show the merging of diverse cultural traditions. Thus features of Mesopotamian and Egyptian anti-Evil Eye apotropaics appear in Greek and Roman, Hebrew and Christian apotropaics.[532] The apotropaics (amulets, words, gestures, and actions) manifest a syncretistic character, a merging of Evil Eye traits across cultures, so that it is often difficult, if not impossible, to ascertain original provenance of the amulets or to distinguish among Roman, Greek, Egyptian, or Mesopotamian "types" of apotropaics. The syncretistic nature of the apotropaics makes it equally difficult to distinguish Christian from Jewish or both from Greco-Roman apotropaics.

Many apotropaics, as their form, color and other qualities suggest, seem to owe their design and assumed effectiveness to the related concepts of "sympathy" and similarity. In his account of plants and herbs, Pliny the

---

529. See Taussig's thesis on *Mimesis and Alterity* (1993).

530. Jahn 1855:61–62.

531. Jahn 1855:62; Deubner 1910:435.

532. For illustrations of the appearance of features of Mesopotamian Evil Eye lore in texts centuries later see Ford 2000.

Elder[533] mentions the phenonema of "sympathy and antipathy" (*sympathia et antipathia*): the attraction or aversion existing between natural entities such as plants and other agents or objects.[534] Plutarch, commenting on sicknesses and remedies, mentions the proverbial wisdom upon which many act:

> thinking to expel and dispel wine with wine, and headache with headache. (Plutarch, *de tuenda* 11 [*Mor.* 127])

Or, as another axiom puts it:

> (One drives out) a nail with a nail and a peg with a peg. (Pollux, *Onomastikon* 9.120; Athenaeus, *Deipn.* 44A)

A third-century Christian writing, the *Acts of Thomas*, puts it in terms of drugs and counter-drugs: "Some drugs make other drugs ineffective" (*Acts of Thomas* 10.127).[535]

James Frazer regarded this principle of similarity (*similia similibus*, "like influences like") as one of magic's two basic "laws" of causation: similarity (imitation) and contact (contagion).[536] This principle of similarity, however, is hardly unique to magic, but is basic to ancient learned medicine and modern science as well. This ancient concept as discussed by Pliny the Elder and others[537] was adopted centuries later as the fundamental axiom of homeopathy. "A substance producing symptoms in a healthy individual can alleviate similar symptoms originating from illness."[538] The medieval physician Paracelsus (alias Theophrast von Hohenheim, 1493–1541), considered by many the founder of homeopathy, formulated this as one of the basic principles of homeopathic healing: *similia similibus curantur* ("likes are cured by likes"). Samuel Hahneman, M.D. (1755–1843), also viewed as an alternative founder of homeopathy, was, in any case, indebted to Paracelsus and in 1796 reasserted the principle of "likes are cured by likes." Modern science continues to reckon with this concept. For instance, scientists derive from venomous and deadly serpents, scorpions, lizards, and cone snails

---

533. Pliny *NH* books 20–31.

534. Pliny, *NH* 20 1.1–2; for example, magnetic stone attracting iron, or water dousing fire, among numerous other examples (for plants see *NH* books 20–24). On the concept of sympathy and antipathy among ancient authors see Weidlich 1894.

535. *Pharmaka hetera dialuei hetera pharmaka.*

536. Frazer, *Golden Bough*, 3rd ed., Vol. 1: Part 1, *The Magic Art and the Evolution of Kings in 2 vols.*, vol. 1, Ch. 3, Sympathetic Magic, 52–219, esp. 52.

537. For a later representative see Hieronymus Fracastorius [1478–1553], *De Sympathia et Antipathia Rerum* [On the Sympathy and Antipathy of Things] 1555.

538. Jonas 2005 *sub* "homeopathy."

venom toxins that are then used to create venom-based cures. A 2013 article in the *National Geographic* on the employment of deadly venom as a curative agent from past to present reports that venom-based cures appear "in Sanskrit texts from the second century A.D."[539] The ancient enemy of Rome, Mithridates VI of Pontus (c. 67 BCE), was reported to have been

> saved twice on the battlefield by shamans who administered steppe viper venom to his wounds. (Cystallized venom from the snakes is now a medical export from Azerbaijan). Cobra venom, applied for centuries in traditional Chinese and Indian medicine, was introduced in the West in the 1830s as a homeopathic pain remedy. John Henry Clarke's *Materia Medica*, published around 1900, describes the venom as alleviating many ills, even those caused by venom. "We should always endeavour to use the same drug to cure as produced the symptoms."[540]

Transforming venoms into cures in present medical science moved into high gear in the 1960s when the English clinician, Hugh Alstair Reid, discovered that a protein of the venom of the Malayan pit viper prevented blood-clotting, which in turn led to the production of the clot-busting drug Arvin. The truth of "like against like" underlies modern as well as ancient pharmacology and has been basic to the production of amulets and apotropaics against the Evil Eye.

This rational principle of similarity ("like against like") appears to underlie the development in apotropaics from physical apotropaic object to imitative gesture to abstract concept. Apotropaics could develop over several stages from (1) an *initial natural object or action* (e.g. phallus [and testicles], spittle, ejaculation, horn, red stone) deemed to possess an innate power to (2) a symbolical representation by a *physical gesture* resembling the object in some quality such as form or movement or element (*digitus infamis* imitating a phallus, *a mano fica* imitating a phallus inserted into a vagina, spitting), to (3) *natural objects or artistic representations* resembling the initial object or secondary gesture in one more more qualities (such as phallic-shaped vases or vulva-like cowrie shells; or a mosaic depicting ejaculation. serpents, swords) to (4) *spoken or written words* referring to the initial object or action (*baskanos/fascinus*; *ptui-ptui-ptui* for spitting) whose mere *uttering* was deemed powerful, to (5) the abstract concept of the initial object or action and their various associations (concepts of phallocentricity, ribald or obscene expressions; notions of fertility, aggression, insult, shame, and the like). There are Evil Eye apotropaics that illustrate one of

539. Holland 2013.
540. Ibid., 75.

more of these five stages. Any of these apotropaic stages could be subjected to a taboo prohibiting their display or expression altogether or requiring a euphemistic and approved substitute ("male member" for "phallus;" "female member" for "vulva, cunt"; "envy" for "Evil Eye"; "coming" for ejaculation or orgasm; "expectorate" for "spit" etc.). The *combination* of motifs and qualities (shapes, color, material, media) and of images themselves (*mano fica* with phallus, eye with phallus, hunchback with eye, phallus with bell, Eye of Horus from blue or red stone, *mano cornuta* or *mano fica* colored red or blue) intensified the apotropaic's power.

This basic principle of similarity, sympathy and antipathy, was operative in thinking and practice concerning aversion of the Evil Eye: eye against eye, powerful object against powerful object. This entailed a presumed homology between two objects—either an Evil Eye and a counter eye, an (Evil) eye and a vulva, a phallus and an extended finger, a vulva and a cowrie shell, a yellow stone and jaundice, and so on. Thus, the power that harms is the same that can protect.[541] "They say the urine of eunuchs," Pliny recounted (*NH* 28.18), "is highly beneficial as a promoter of fruitfulness in females"; that is, the substance from an infertile person was used to prevent infertility in others. The principle of "like influences like" is also apparent in the *terminology* for anti-Evil Eye prophylactics. In Greek, a protective against *baskania* and *baskanoi* ("casters of the Evil Eye") is termed a *baskanon, baskanion* or *probaskanon, probaskanion*. Amulets such as necklaces of mussel or cowrie shells, were designated as *anti baskaniôn* ("against the Evil Eye"; Strabo, *Geog.* 16.4.17). We see here that terms of the *bask*-root designated both (a) the Evil Eye and (b) protectives against the Evil Eye. The same holds for Latin. A protective against *fascinatio* and *fascinatores* ("casters of the Evil Eye") was named a *fascinum*. Similarly, entities thought to *inflict* an Evil Eye were used as well to *inhibit* an Evil Eye (the eye itself, Medusa head/ gorgoneion, gobbo/hunchback).[542] In accord with this thinking, representations of an eye in various shapes and designs (a blue eye, an eye of Horus, an eye surrounded by attacking enemies) were used to protect against an Evil Eye. Other apotropaics involved objects and images deemed to be highly powerful, such as depictions of the male genitals (*baskanon, fascinum*) and female genitals (represented by cowrie shells, sheela-na-gigs displaying exposed vulva and spread thighs), simulations of copulation (*mano fica*) or of ejaculation (spitting), or of an outstretched hand, or images of horns, of a "horned hand" (*mano cornuta*), or amulets colored blue and red. Still others

---

541. Jahn 1855:62 and n128, Kuhnert 1909:2009–10; Lafaye 1926:985. On the principle of sympathy and its practical applications see Budge 1958/1895:48–86, 107–9.

542. Pliny, *NH* 28.65.

involved grotesque or ridiculous objects and images intended to frighten or distract the Evil Eye or in some cases attract the Evil Eye to themselves rather than to the user of the apotropaion (such as the Gorgo/Medusa, masks, dwarfs and humpbacks, and the *homo cacans/shitting man*).

Some protectives seem created with the Evil Eye specifically in mind, such as images of an eye under attack. Other general apotropaics used to repel various types of evil and demonic forces were thought effective against the Evil Eye as well; e.g. representations of Priapus and the colors blue and red. On the whole, there seems to have been much overlap in the kinds of apotropaics thought to be effective against various types and sources of harm. For example, Priapus, the god of fertility and virility, was depicted with a huge phallus. The image of the phallus was placed prominently at the entrance to houses, fields, and in public spaces to assure familial fertility as well as the fecundity of crops and herds. Bes, the "weak-sighted" Egyptian dwarf-like divinity with ugly appearance, likewise was portrayed with a monstrous phallus, and gave protection against everything evil, especially Evil Eye threats to infants and birthing mothers.[543] These figures had phalluses that did "double duty," symbolizing fertility and simultaneously warding off the Evil Eye.[544] The image of a phallus and testicles (*baskanon, fascinum*) often was employed as a protective against the Evil Eye in particular. A phallic-like equivalent used as a manual gesture was the *digitus infamus* (an extended middle finger from a clenched hand). Since the phallus was considered to be especially powerful against the Evil Eye, the term *fascinum* eventually came to designate the phallus itself.

Protection through Words and Expressions

Evil Eye apotropaics fall into a wide range of categories. These include words and actions as well as amulets. *Words* entail incantations, spoken or written prayers, invocations, imprecations, and powerful formulas spoken or inscribed on parchment, papyprus, potsherds or inscribed on stones, gems, clay, wood, metals and other media.[545] *Actions* comprise various measures, such as making certain manual gestures, spitting, touching the genitals, and wearing amulets. *Amulets*, in turn, are natural and manufactured objects thought to be endowed with power and generally worn on the body.

543. On Bes in Egypt see also Vol. 1, chap. 2.

544. See Jahn 1855:68–79; Rakoczy 1996:153.

545. On the power of words and words of power in general in antiquity see Röhrich 1962; Versnel 2002; see also Heim 1892. See Drexler 1899 (amulets, gems, texts) and Önnerfors 1988 for ancient conjurations and their survival in European culture.

(1) *Invocations of Divine Power* **(spoken or written)**

Appeals or prayers were made to certain *divinities,* or their names were invoked, for protection against the Evil Eye and envy. Among the divinities, the god *Fascinus* was venerated as the protector of children and also of triumphant generals against envy and the Evil Eye. An image of this god, a *fascinum* (phallus and testicles), was suspended beneath the chariot of generals celebrating military victories (Pliny, *NH* 28.39) Children wore a phallic image, *fascinum,* around their necks until they reached their majority. Pliny indicates (*NH* 28.22) that Romans also invoke the Greek divinity *Nemesis* for protection against the Evil Eye (*effascinationibus*), "for which purpose there is at Rome an image of the goddess on the Capitol, although she has no [indigenous] Latin name." The Roman goddess *Cunina* was the protector of cradles (*cunae*), the newborn and their mothers. "Cunina, who watches over infants in the cradle, drives away the Evil Eye (*fascinum*)," reports Lactantius.[546] The Greek-Egyptian god Serapis likewise was thought to afford protection. On one side of a gem[547] functioning as an amulet, the figure of Zeus Serapis is displayed, with the inscription on the reverse reading *nika ho Serapis ton phthonon* ("Serapis conquers envy/the Evil Eye").[548] Another glass amulet (CIG 4.8515) is inscribed with words, *Me[g] a to onoma Sarapis* ("Great is the name of Serapis"). The inscription, *Eis Zeus Serapis, Baskanos darêsetô* ("Zeus Serapis is unique, let the Evil Eye be flayed") protected a house.[549] A similar inscription affixed to a house read, *Eis Zeus Serapis, Baskanos lakêsetô* ("Zeus Serapis is unique, let the Evil Eye be banished").[550]

The gods provided *charis,* "generous benefaction," which was the opposite of *baskania* and *phthonos.*[551] *Charis* originally meant "emanation from God, human, or animal bearing blessing"[552] which was the antithesis of an Evil Eye and envy. The gods effected good fortune through their blessing glance of *charis.* The eyes of Zeus, Apollo, and the Muses brought light and

546. Lactantius, *Div. Inst.* 1.20.36 (*Cunina, quae infantes in cunis tuetur ac fascinum submovet*); see also Augustine, *City of God* 4.8, 11, 21, 24, 34.

547. Mertens-Schaaffhausen Collection, no. 1631.

548. Meisen 1950:148; Elworthy 1895/1958:303 and on Serapis, 302–304; Seligmann 1910 2:317.

549. Fabretti 1702:468, no. 104; cf. also Weinreich 1919:26; Meisen 1950:148.

550. Seligmann 1910 2:318; for the protection afforded by other gods, see Seligmanm 1910 2:318–22.

551. Dörrie 1981:315–33, especially 322–23 on *charis* vs. *phthonos* (and *baskania*).

552. Dörrie 1981:322, "segenwirkende Ausstrahlung von Gott, Mensch or Tier."

blessing. Minerva in particular, was considered the goddess of the blessing look, which *baskania* could not endure.[553]

Some (foreign) divine names carried particular power. Pliny the Elder (*NH* 28.22) lists among Roman customs the invoking of the Greek goddess *Nemesis* by her proper Greek name for protection against attacks of the Evil Eye (*effascinationibus*). An image of the goddess stood at Rome's capitol, he notes, but she was known only by her powerful Greek name, which had no Roman equivalent.[554] In modern time, a prayer for protection from the Evil Eye was included in the baptismal rite of the Greek Orthodox Church prior to the revision of the liturgy in 1929.[555] In both Jewish and Christian prayer practice, Psalm 91, the "protection prayer," has been recited and cited on amulets as a defense against evil, including an Evil Eye.[556]

(2) *Spoken/Chanted Words and Expressions*

Beside appeals to gods and petitioning them through prayer, pronouncing *certain formulas or incantations*, i.e. singing a charm[557] were deemed effective prophylaxis. We recall the association of eye and mouth/tongue, looking and speaking, *malus oculus* and *mala lingua*, similar to the meanings of the Greek terms *baskein/baskainein* and *phaskein*. Looking and speaking, it was believed, could harm, while speaking could also protect from harm. This notion of sympathy lies at the base of all apotropaic strategies, including words.[558] Consistent with this, even the words *baskanion* or *fascinum* could designate both things that damage and things that protect from damage.

Incantations against the Evil Eye appear as early as Mesopotamian sources.[559] Initially incantations were sung (*carmina*), then recited, and eventually written upon a material object that in some cases was worn as an amulet.

Among the *adjurations* of the Evil Eye and envy, the popular "be gone, (Evil Eye)!" (IG 14.1306; CIG 3.6131c), "Evil Eye, don't touch me!" or "back to you, (Evil Eye)" (Greek: *kai sy*, Latin: *et tibi*) appear on several apotropaics found in public spaces.[560]

553. Ovid, *Met.* 2, 760–785.

554. This Greek goddess was the personification of divine retribution and of divine indignation at undeserved good fortune (LSJ, *sub nemesis* A, B). See also Ammianus Marcellinus *Roman History* 14.

555. For this prayer see Vol. 4, chap. 2.

556. Trachentenberg 1970:158; Schrire 1982:140–43, 147, 157–58, 159, 160, 170.

557. The word *charm* derives from Latin *carmen* ("song"); cf. *carminare*, "to sing."

558. Jahn 1855:61–62.

559. For these Mesopotamian incantations see Vol. 1, chap. 2,

560. See Meisen 1950:156–57 and below, pp. 170–77.

Spoken expressions, we have seen,[561] accompanied compliments and the giving of praise to assure that the praise was not motivated by envy or an Evil Eye. Those who complimented added the words, "No Evil Eye intended" (*praefiscini* or *praefiscine*, *praefascini*, *praefascine*, or *praefiscini dixerim*) to assure no presence of envy or malicious intent. The Greek expression *phthonos d' apestô* ("no envy here") with which Clytemnestra accompanies her praise of her returning husband Agamemnon (Aeschylus, *Agam.* 904) served a similar purpose.[562] A related practice was to speak or write the word *abaskantos* ("safe from the Evil Eye") when mentioning children and family, as the Greek papyri letters cited above indicate.[563] The practice is similar in function to speaking the words *proskynô Adrasteian* ("I honor Adrasteia") before submitting to the dangerous glance of Nemesis (alias "Adrasteia," and personification of divine envy).[564] The Latin expressions *absit omen* ("let there be no evil omen") and *absit invidia* ("let there be no envy") had the same averting intention.

In modern time, accompanying praise and compliments with expressions disavowing any motivation of envy and the Evil Eye ("no Evil eye intended," "thanks be to God," etc.) remains a widespread custom. In rural England it was a custom, when passing a farm-yard where cows were gathered for milking, to say "The blessing of God be on you and all your labor." A Scotsman, on hearing praise, might spit on his finger, moisten his eyelids, and say, "Wet your eye, and do not blight me.'" Or he might moisten his finger on his tongue and and apply the finger to the speaker's eyelids, saying "Wet your eye for fear I may be wounded."[565] These added expressions are thought to deny or cancel any hint of envy and the Evil Eye. Sometimes out of spite they are intentionally omitted.

Ancient Roman marriage ceremonies included the recitation of ribald verses (*fescennina*, possibly from *fascinum*).[566] These verses and bawdy songs were sung to ward off the Evil Eye and invoke good fortune.[567] "Obscenity—crude outright obscenity that made one laugh and look

---

561. See above, p. 113.

562. McCartney 1992:23, 31.

563. See above, pp. 2–4.

564. Alciphron, *Ep.* 1.33; Walz 1852:23.

565. MacLagen 1902; Gifford 1958:65.

566. Alternatively, the term may derive from the village Fescennia in the Italian Campagna where the *fascinum* was connected with the amusements of the Fescennina; see Story 1877:229–30.

567. Horace, *Epist.* 1.145; Catullus, *Poems* 61.120 (his ode on the marriage of Julia); Elworthy 1958/1895:16–17; Adams 1982:4–5, 11.

away—was a powerful defense against the evil eye."[568] This included also "anything concerning sex and copulation, anything representing the male or female sexual organs."[569] In the early period, the bride was compelled to sit on a representation of the phallus of the ithyphallic god Mutunus Tutunus,[570] whom the Greeks called Priapus."[571] J. N. Adams, commenting on Latin sexual terminology, notes that "the rite was no doubt intended to promote fertility as well as ward off evil."[572] These two functions of a practice or apotropaic object—to protect against evil and to confer fertility—are generally impossible to separate. By fulfilling the first, the object assists in the second. Thus the deity Priapus both protected against the Evil Eye[573] and granted fertility.[574] Similarly, Augustine records, at the festival of the phallic Liber Pater, phalluses were placed in baskets and brought to crossroads where they were displayed. This display was accompanied by the uttering of apotropaic obscenities—all to repel the Evil Eye.[575] This practice of ancient Greeks and Romans, Theodore Schrire notes, is still found "in recognizable form," among modern Western peoples.[576]

Protective expressions are also employed when one suspects being under attack from an Evil Eye. In Jewish tradition, one fearing the Evil Eye puts his thumbs in his opposite palms and announces, "I [NN] am of the seed of Joseph over which the Evil Eye has no power" (*b. Berakoth* 55b; cf. *b. Bava Metzia* 84a).[577] Muslims similarly defensively intone: "May God protect us from the Evil Eye when it envies." The Irish take the offensive against the suspected fascinator, declaring, "The curse be upon thine eye"; "Ill on your eye, bird shit on the back of that."[578]

568. Marcadé 1961:26.

569. Ibid. Such verses were composed, for example, by Augustus and used against Pollio, according to Macrobius (*Sat.* 2.4.21).

570. Lactantius, *Inst.* 1.20.36; Augustine, *City of God* 4.11, 6.9; 7.24; cf. Herter 1927:423; 1938:1719–20; 1978:15.

571. Augustine, *City of God* 4.11; 6.9; cf 7.24.

572. Adams 1982:5.

573. Herter 1932:111, nos. 81–82.

574. Ibid., 225.

575. Augustine, *City of God* 7.21, 7.24 (*sic videlicet Liber deus placandus fuerat pro eventibus seminum, sic ab agris fascinatio repellenda*); Adams 1982:5. Seligmann (1910 2:194) on the other hand, regards the intent of the practice as only to assure fertility and not to counter an Evil Eye.

576. Schrire 1982:7.

577. Referring to the biblical Joseph who, with God's aid, survived the envious Evil Eye of his brothers (Genesis 37–50); on this see also Vol. 4, chap. 1.

578. Gifford 1958:62; see Jahn 1855:34, 46–47; DiStasio 1981 for other sayings specifically countering the Evil Eye or envy.

(3) *Written Words and Expressions*

Many of such spoken apotropaic words were also written down on parchment, papyrus, or potsherds or were inscribed on stones, gems, wood, gold and silver lamellae, vases, lamps, and other objects. Such inscribed words are "inscriptions" which can be used as independant apotropaics or combined with other apotropaic designs and images, as on amulets. In Israel and in Christian circles this also involved words or phrases from Sacred Scripture, especially the Pentateuch and the Psalter, the names of God, Jesus Christ, angels; or verses from prayers, worship, and liturgy.[579]

Many ancient Greek and Latin apotropaic expressions adjured the Evil Eye and envy and were intended to repel them. The form and content of the Evil Eye and envy apotropaics are so similar as to suggest the equation of both evils. The following are typical.[580]

(1) The Greek exclamation *ERRE* ("be gone!" "take off!" "beat it!" "scram!"), appearing next to phallic symbols in floor mosiacs (IG 14.1306) addresses the Evil Eye to drive it away. The accompanying phalluses and vulva indicate the expression's apotropaic intent. *Erre,* the opposite of *chaire* ("greetings!" "hello"), was spoken when the presence of an Evil Eye was suspected. Another such expression (CIG 3.6131c, Tor dei Conti, Rome) appears next to a nude female exposing her vulva above a phallus.[581] The exclamation had the same protective purpose as the phrase *kai sy* ("you too") discussed below.

(2) The Greek exclamation *PATAXI BASKANOS* ("Evil Eyer, be smitten!") was written on a phallus displayed in bas-relief on the wall of a house in Beirut, Syria. Apparently it was addressed to passers-by to protect the home and its inhabitants from their potential Evil Eyes.[582]

(3) The Greek directive *PARAGE KAI MÊ PHTHONI* ("Pass by [or "keep going"] and don't envy"), an inscription written on a public edifice and likewise addressed to passers-by, was found in Kanatha and Migdall, Syria.[583]

579. See Vol. 4, chaps. 1 and 2.

580. For most of these see Meisen 1950:156–57; Engemann 1975:34–35 and Plates 8b; 11a, d. By contrast, an unsual gem engraved with an image of an Evil Eye under attack is accompanied by words surmised to have been derived from Homer, *Iliad* 5.290–291 ("So he spoke and hurled; and Athena guided the spear upon his nose beside the eye, and it pierced through his white teeth."); see Mastrocinque, 2003, no. 390, citing Le Blant 1898:104–5; Seyrig 1934:1.

581. See Jahn 1855:48.

582. Waddington 1870: nos. 2360, 2406; Perdrizet 1900:293; Leclercq 1907:1844) regards it as Christian.

583. Pedrizet 1900:293; Leclercq 1907:1844, regarding it as Christian.

(4) The Greek exclamation *KE HO PHTHONÔN RHAGÊTÔ* ("may the one who envies burst asunder!") is part of an inscription found in Brake, Syria. The inscription commemorates the construction of a temple courtyard.[584]

(5) A stone of smokey blue-grey agate (late Imperial period) in the Seyrig amulet collection shows a naked male figure wrapped by a large serpent and attacked by a host of creatures, with words addressed to Envy: *PHTHONE ATYCHI*, "Envy, no luck for you!"[585] This depiction of a personified envy under attack is parallel to those amulets portraying the Evil Eye under attack.

(6) The Latin exclamation *HOC VIDE, VIDE ET VIDE, UT PLURA VIDERE* ("look at this, look, look, so that you might have much to see"; CIL 8.11683) appears on a stone found in Thala southwest of Zama Regia (Tunis). The stone also displays images of two plants (garlic?) and a phallus between which the inscription is located. Similar inscriptions are found on a mosaic in Carthage (CIL 8.24670) and on a floor mosaic in Lambiridi, Algeria (CIL 8.23131). The latter reads: "Evil- Eyed Envy, live and look so that you are able to see many things" (*Invide vive et vide ut possis plura videre*). The inscription puns on the relation of *Invidia* (envy) and *videre* ("look," "see") and illustrates the continued connection of envy, looking and ocular activity. Two door lintel plaques found in Algeria display the commands *INVIDE VIVE VIDE* ("envy, live [and] look") and are accompanied by phalluses.[586] Another door plaque reads *INVIDE* (envy) with the *IN* and *VIDE* separated by representations of a palm and two phalluses.[587]

(7) A Greek mosaic inscription at the threshold of a wealthy residence in Beirut, Syria (395–636 CE) protects the home and its inhabitants from envy and the Evil Eye. It reads in part:

> Envy (*Ho phthonos*) is a great evil (*kaistos*); however; it has some beauty/ it consumes the eyes (*ommata*) and the heart of the envious (*phthonerôn*).[588]

(8) A black stone amulet originally in private possession at Sousse in Tunisia depicts on the obverse side an image of the sun-god Helios drawing a bow. On the reverse a Greek inscription (SEG 9.2, no. 818) appears to

584. See Waddington 1870, no. 2415; also nos. 2360, 2406, 2415; and CIG 3.5819, 6792. For a Christian example see Vol. 3, chap. 2 and Vol. 4, chap. 2.

585. Bonner 1950:97 and 277, no. 148.

586. See Gsell 1922, nos. 113, 864.

587. Gsell 1922, no. 3709.

588. The envy mosaic is now located in the National Museum of Beirut, Lebanon. It frequently is mistakenly referred to as "the jealousy mosaic."

be addressed to an Evil Eye possesser: "Don't touch me, Evil Eye; Helios is pursuing you!" (*MÊ THIGÊS MOU, BASKOSYNÊ, DIÔKEI SE HÊLIOS*).[589]

(9) A plaque affixed to the front wall of a residence at Pompeii with a baking oven contains a *fascinum* accompanied by the Latin declaration *HIC HABITAT FELICITAS* ("here happiness dwells")—because the *fascinum* averts the Evil Eye.[590]

(10) The Greek expression *KAI SY* ("you too"; "[the same to] you")[591] addresses the potential envier or fascinator, warning that any Evil Eye cast will bounce "back to you." This interesting apotropaic calls for further comment.

EXCURSUS: THE APOTROPAIC EXPRESSION KAI SY ("YOU TOO")

The Greek expression *kai sy* ("you too," "[the same to] you too"), which may have been spoken in social interactions, has been found in written form on floors, thresholds, walls, colonnades, over lintels, or on tombs to ward off evil[592] and in particular the Evil Eye (IG 14.233).[593] The related expression *kai soi* ("to you too") is a likely variant, as its Latin equivalent *et tibi, et tibi sit* ("to you too," "may it be to you too") suggests.[594] The intention of the expression was to repel, "bounce back," and inflict on the the Evil-Eyeing sender any harm that might have been sent—"here's back to you," "the same to you!" The appearance of the expression alongside a winged phallus indicates it, like the phallus, a standard Evil Eye apotropaic, also was designed to repel the Evil Eye.[595] It also may have been used on occasion to include the addressee into the protection of the amulet and

589. Bonner (1950:97) comments on the reading's uncertainty (*bksn* as an unusual abbreviation of *baskosynê*).

590. For the inscription see CIL 4.1454. The *fascinum* is in relief on a travertine plaque attached to the bakery oven owned by Modesto, Pompeii (Regio VI, vi, 18, Via delle Terme), first century CE. It is now in the the Naples Archaeological Museum, Raccolta Pornographica, no. 27741. See also Johns 1982:65, illus. 47 (Photo by Fabrizio Parisio); Clark 2003:102, illus. 68 (Photo by Michael Larvey).

591. IG 14.233 = *kai soi* (Herter, "Genitalien" 1978:17); compare the Latin equivalent, *et tibi* (Levi 1941:225–26).

592. See Brenk 1998:38 n16; 1999.

593. Jahn 1855:61.

594. So Herter 1978:17; Levi 1941:225–26; 1947; Norris 1991:257–58; Slane and Dickie 1993:490–92 and n44. See also Mouterde 1959:63–64, no. 6; the examples in Giangrande 1967:20, and Dubuisson 1980.

595. Jahn 1855:61.

to convey a positive wish for good health: "good health and safety *to you too!*"[596] Most experts stress its apotropaic intent, as James Russell (1980) illustrates. He considers the expression *kai sy* a possible apotropaic against the Evil Eye with the intent of turning back the malice of an Evil Eye to its possessor. The words, he writes, have the sense and force of "to hell with you!" A fuller expression, *kai sy erre*, would have the same sense: "to hell with you too!"[597] Dunbabin and Dickie add, as a further equivalent, the phrase *kai sou*. These words appear in the Kephallenia floor mosaic in the inscription addressing the figure of Envy and accompanying an image of Envy choking itself. "This formula is used to express the wish that the malice which *phthoneroi* [enviers] intend may rebound upon them and to turn back the ill will of the *baskanos ophthalmos* [Evil Eye] against itself."[598] On a relief carved on a rock face near Burdur in Pisidia [Asia Minor], they add, "the Eye is attacked by a scorpion, snake, crab, another animal, and a phallus, and pierced by a spear and a dagger" [and] "the inscription *baskane kai sou* ['You too, Evil Eyer!'] is written above."[599] The import is that any fascinators seeing this will suffer the same fate as the Evil Eye being attacked.

Three juxtaposed apotropaic floor mosaics were found in the village of Jekmejeh southeast of Antioch on the Orontes, Syria, in a building designated by its discoverers as the "House of the Evil Eye" (second century CE). Two mosaics have the expression *KAI SY* ("you too!"). One mosaic depicts an Evil Eye attacked by a trident, sword, and circle of figures as well as by the enlarged phallus of a horned dwarf. The phallus extends backward between his legs; he stands to the left of, and facing away from, the eye. Above the dwarf are the Greek words *KAI SY*.[600] A second mosaic in the same location has the expression KAI SY appearing above the figure of a hunchbacked youth holding two sticks in each hand and warding off the Evil Eye.[601] The words in the Antioch mosaics, along with the other

596. As in IG 12.3.1027 (*tois philois*), so Herter 1978:17. For *kai sy* see also Jahn 1855:61 n122; Abd el-Mohsen el-Khachab 1956:118–22, Ill. 2, Plate 1a; Levi 1941, 1947; Russell 1980, 1998; Morris 1991:257.

597. J. Russell 1980:126.

598. Dunbabin and Dickie 1983:35.

599. Ibid., 36, citing Bean 1960:50, no. 98, Plate 12c.

600. Antakya Archeology Museum, Antakya, Turkey, Inventory no. Antakya 1024.

601. Floor mosaic, House of the Evil Eye, Antioch, Syria, second century CE. Antakya Archeology Museum, Antakya, Turkey, Inventory no. Antakya 1026/a. On this Antioch mosaic see Levi 1941, 1947; Dubuisson 1980; Russell 1980; Dunbabin and Dickie 1983:36 and Plate 8a; Norris 1991:257; Slane and Dickie 1993:490; Brenk 1999b:172–173; Cimok 1996; Cousland 2005; also Antioch: The Lost Ancient City. Catalogue (with essays) of an exhibit at Worcester Art Museum, Massachusetts, 10/8/2000.

apotropaic items, likely were intended to protect the residence and its inhabitants. This tallies with the discovery of the expression on portals, lintels, and thresholds. Frederick Norris (1991:257) holds that "the inscription *kai sy* is intended to bring laughter and thus to break the spell of any evil spirits" and is comparable to "the proverbial 'you too, buddy.'" Frederich Brenk stresses the ambiguity of the expression and strongly doubts that the words have any relation to Julius Caesar's last words *et tu, Brute*.[602].

Illus. 9

Floor mosaic, House of the Evil Eye, Antioch, Syria: Evil Eye attacked, dwarf over whose head is the inscription *KAI SY* ("you too"). Second century CE, Antakya Museum, Antakya, Turkey.

Similar words, *kai sy*, "you too," occur above the main inscription on an honorary stele (of Egyptian provenance) once erected in honor of Nero and now housed in the Fitzwilliam Museum, Cambridge, England.[603] Brenk observes that "[t]he formula, then, seems to exercise a power and a 'prophylactic' function equal to that of the ancient Egyptian symbols" (that are also found on the stele).[604] He finds it similar to the *kai sy* inscription of the Antioch mosaic and in this case also disputes any connection with the Evil Eye. The formula, he maintains, could be benevolent rather than malevolent, offering a greeting from the dead when on tombs, or an imprecation. He considers it uncertain that the *kai sy* of the Fitzwilliam stele was meant to ward off the Evil Eye. If inscribed earlier than the following inscription regarding Nero, it may have had the sense of "you too will die."[605] On the other hand, the ambiguity of the *kai sy* expression makes it possible that it could have an apotropaic force here on the Fitzwilliam stele as it does in the Antioch mosaic. For one thing, traces of Evil Eye belief and practice in the Greco-Roman world

602. Suetonius, *Lives of the Twelve Emperors, Life of Julius Caesar* 82.2 reports concerning Caesar's assasination that "some have written that when Marcus Brutus rushed at him, he [Caesar] said in Greek, 'you too, my child (*kai sy, teknon*)?'"

603. See Brenk 1998, text on p. 32, photograph on p. 49; also Brenk 1999b, photograph on p. 169, text on p. 170.

604. Brenk 1999b:170.

605. The writing in the photograph supplied by Brenk seems to indicate that *kai sy* and the inscription below it were from different hands.

are far more recurrent than Brenk allows.[606] Secondly, Slane and Dickie (1993:490–492) provide extensive evidence from across the Mediterranean region of the *kai sy* or *et tibi* formula appearing in tandem with phalluses, with the combination intended to ward off the Evil Eye (and envy). The accumulation of anti-Evil Eye elements, including *kai sy*, phalluses, hunchback and attacked eye, in the Antioch mosaic make certain their anti-Evil Eye function there as elsewhere.[607]

To the eight examples provided by Slane and Dickie could be added the words *kai sy* found centered in the threshold of a mosaic floor discovered in Magdala in the Galilee by Franciscan excavators.[608] Virgilio Corbo (1978), claiming a first century CE dating for the floor, though a later third-century date is also possible, noted the similarity to the Antioch expression, but said little else about the inscription. It likely to have had the same repellent intent against the Evil Eye as the other instances of *kai sy*. The expression *Eis kephalên soi* ("on your [own] head") may have been used with the same intention.[609] Two rectangular marble panels from the island of Delos show in relief two phallic monsters with phalluses as heads confronting one another, with the accompanying expressions *touto emoi* (lit. "this to me") and *kai touto soi*, "and this to you").[610] Slane and Dickie see here the one monster saying to the other: "what I have received in the eye, I will repay to you." The two plaques," they convincingly conclude, "suggest very strongly that when *kai sy* accompanies the representaton of a phallus it means *kai touto soi;*" i.e. "and the same to you," and constitutes an expression intended to repel the Evil Eye.[611]

Such apotropaic inscriptions regularly accompanied other apotropaic designs such as the *fascinum* or gorgoneion, at the portals of residences for protection against the Evil Eye and envy.[612] A similar apotropaic function of the mezzuzas affixed to the portal of Jewish residences and of crosses affixed to portals of Christian homes is discussed in Volume 4, chapters 1 and 2, A related Celtic practice in Ireland centuries later is the affixing of St. Brigid's crosses woven of straw to the walls of barns to protect the animals. The predecessor of St. Bridget was the pagan Gaelic goddess Bri-

606. Brenk 1999b:174, citing the minimalist position of M.-L. Thomsen (1992) concerning the centuries-earlier Mesopotamian evidence.

607. *Pace* Brenk 1998:43; 1999b:174.

608. Corbo 1978 with figs. 71–76

609. Scholion to Aristophanes, *Wealth* 525; Plato, *Euthyphro* 283e; Cicero, *Ad Atticum* 8.5.1.

610. Slane and Dickie 1993:492.

611. Ibid.

612. For additional portal inscriptions see CIL 8.8509; IG 9.1.601; *Anth. Pal.* 10.111.

git, "the female sage."[613] An Irish charm against the Evil Eye, suggesting an association of pagan and Christian heavenly-mother figures, spoke of

> the Spell the great white Mary sent to Bride the lovely fair,
> for sea, for land, for water, and for withering glance . . .
> (E. S. Gifford 1958:60)

PROTECTION AGAINST THE EVIL EYE (AND ENVY) THROUGH THE MOUTH

(1) The Extended Tongue

In addition to enabling speech against the Evil Eye and envy, the mouth also provided the tongue as apotropaic weapon. An *extended tongue* can communicate contempt and insult, but also defiance against an Evil Eye. It has been suggested that the extended tongue, like an extended middle finger, simulates a phallus,[614] one of the most potent of the Evil Eye apotropaics (see below). An extended tongue is one of the features of the anti-Evil Eye images of the hideous Gorgo (Medusa) and of the ugly Egyptian god Bes, as it is of modern adaptations of the Gorgo images.[615] Women touch infants with their wet tongues to protect them against the Evil Eye, Horace noted (*Epodes* 8.8). A link of tongue and eye is also evident in the association of an Evil Eye (*malus oculus*) and an evil tongue (*mala lingua*), malicious looking with malicious speech or slander. The Greek term *baskania* could denote or imply both.[616]

(2) Spitting and Spittle

A further prophylactic gesture involving the mouth is the act of *spitting* and the use of *spittle*.[617] One use of spitting, spittle (*sputum*), and saliva was as a means of *healing and curing*. Pliny commented on the powerful proper-

---

613. MacCulloch 1911.

614. Jahn 1855:83

615. For the Gorgo see Illlustrations 3–6, 28, 53.; for Bes, Illus. 56.

616. See above, pp. 26, 27, 29, 33, 71, 82–83, 130.

617. Greek: *ptuein, ekptuein, emptuein, epiptuein, epiphthuein;*Latin: *spuere, adspuere, conspuere, despuere, expuere, inspuere, respuere; sputare; insputare.* Saliva and spittle in popular thinking, Muth observes (1954:26), embody a "life-force" that effectively thwarts sickness and the lethal Evil Eye. Nicholson 1897 describes the shift in viewing spitting and the production of saliva as, first, actual acts of healing to then symbols and even words of healing and protective power.

ties of saliva and spittle (*NH* 28.36–39). The Roman emperor Vespasian is reported to have used spittle in healing a blind man and a man with an incapacitated hand.[618] The New Testament records that Jesus also healed with spittle and by spitting (Mark 8:23; John 9:6). Saliva mixed with honey also was a lotion for the throat.[619] Spitting could also be a gesture of *insult*[620] or of *defiance*. Already among the Sumerians and Babylonians, spittle and spitting had both positive and negative functions.[621]

Confronting persons deemed dangerous called for protective spitting. A city girl spits on her own breast to protect herself from an undesired rustic suitor (Theocritus, *Idyl* 20.11). Another spits for protection against an old man professing his love (Tibullus, *Elegies* 1.2.98).

As a prophylactic against, or cure of, the Evil Eye, spitting combined aspects of defense, defiance and cure.[622] In discussing the curative power of spittle, Pliny the Elder explained that Romans spit to ward off the Evil Eye:

> We [Romans] *spit* (*despuimus*) on epileptics (*comitiales morbos*), in this way repelling the contagion. Similarly, [by spitting] we ward off Evil Eyeing (*fascinationes*) and the evil that follows from meeting a person who is lame in the right leg. We also ask forgiveness of the gods for a too presumptuous hope by spitting into our own chests. The same reason again accounts for the custom, when using any remedy, of spiting on the ground three times by way of ritual, thereby increasing its efficacy." (*NH* 28.36 LCL with modification by John H. Elliott)

Nurses, Pliny notes, also protect their infant charges from the Evil Eye by spitting on them or in their presence:

---

618. Tacitus, *Hist.* 4.81; cf. Suetonius, *Vespasian* 7. For spittle and spitting to heal see also Plautus, *Captivi* 3.4.18; Pliny, *NH* 27.75; 28.35; 28.48, 61,77; 28.30, 29.12, 32; 32.29); Petronius, *Sat.* 131.4–5; Varro, *De re rustica* 1.2.27; Story 1877:208–214; Nicholson 1897.

619. Suetonius, *Vitellius* 2.

620. Jahn 1855:83.

621. Contenau 1947:140–41. On the powers ascribed to spitting and saliva throughout history see also Bergen 1890; Sittl 1890:120; Crombie 1892; Nicholson 1897; Elbogen 1916; Crooke 1920; Selare 1939; Muth 1954:26–27; Lanczkowski 1962.

622. See Jahn 1855:83–86; Story 1877:208–14; F. W. Nicholson 1897; Seligmann 1910 1:293–98, 2:207–16; Crooke 1920 (on oneself, 100; on another for immunity from sorcery, witchcraft, or the Evil Eye, 100–101; on children against the Evil Eye, 101, 102); Elbogen 1916:100–104; Elworthy 1958/1895:412–13, 416–23; Frazer and Gaster 1959:270–71; Lanczkowski 1962: cols. 229–30; Rakoczy 1996:147–52. On the use of spittle and spitting in modern time against the Evil Eye see Maloney 1976:81, 91, 121, 132–33; Morris 1985:105; Gravel 1995:109–10.

On the arrival of a stranger, or if a sleeping baby is looked at
(*spectetur*) [it is customary] for the nurse to spit three times
(*terna adspui* or *despui*)[623] even though the baby also is under
the divine protection of Fascinus, guardian not only of babies
but of generals, a deity whose worship is entrusted to the Vestal
Virgins. (Pliny, *NH* 28.39)

Theophrastus (*Char.* 16.15) also knows the custom of spitting when spot-
ting a madman or epileptic (regarded as a potential fascinator). An old
woman (grandmother? aunt?), according to Persius (*Satires* 2.31–34), protects an infant removed from the crib by touching the baby's forehead and
lips with her notorious middle finger (*digitus infamus*) and saliva to ward off
"burning eyes" (*urentes oculos*), i. e. the Evil Eye of others. Even male adult
pigeons were said to spit on their newborn to protect them against the Evil
Eye.[624] Spitting also warded off the envious Evil Eye of the goddess Nemesis,
who was attracted by the handsomeness of a certain Alexis.[625]. Spitting on
one's own chest was a means of self-protection against the Evil Eye. Polyphemus, the one-eyed Cylops, spit three times on his chest to avoid Evil-Eyeing
himself (Theocritus, *Idyl* 6.39).[626] One spit in this manner especially when
singing one's own praises,[627] since praise and admiration aroused an envious
Evil Eye. One also spit when praising others to disclaim casting an Evil Eye
and to prevent their being Evil-Eyed.[628] This spitting when praising had the
same protective aim as did the customary accompanying formula, "no Evil
Eye intended."

Generally the protective act involved *spitting three times in succession.*[629] similar to the threefold practice in curing.[630] Spitting thrice often
also accompanied incantations. "Sing thrice," a wife is advised concerning

---

623. The spitting was directed either at the baby (*adspui.* one variant reading) or at
the ground (*despui,* an alternate variant reading).

624. Aristotle, *Frag.* 347; Athenaeus, *Deipn.* 9.394B (*genomenôn tô neottôn ho arrên emptuei autois, hôs mê baskthôsi*). The fuller version of Aelian (*Var. hist.* 1.15, *tôn
neottôn genomenôn, ho arrên emptuei autois, apelaunôn autôn ton phthonon, hôs phasin,
ina mê baskanthôsi*) equates envy and the Evil Eye (*phthonon . . . baskanthôsi*) and the
apotropaic function of spitting is expressed in the verb *apelaunôn* ("*driving away* the
envy").

625. Strato, *Anthologia Graeca/Anth. Pal* 12.229.

626. Strato, *Anthologia Graeca/Anth. Pal* 12.229. See also Callimachus, Frag. 687,
for women spitting on their breasts.

627. Lucian, *Navigium* 15; Juvenal, *Sat.* 7.112.

628. Libanius, *Ep.* 714; McCartney 1992:30.

629. Theocritus, *Idyls* 6.39; Pliny, *NH* 28.39.

630. Petronius, *Sat.* 131; Lucian, *Necyomantia* 7.

an incantation, "and, having sung your incantation, then spit thrice."[631] The repeated spitting increased the power of the act. Moreover, "uneven numbers" [in contrast to even numbers] Virgil observed (*Ecl.* 8.8), are the god's delight."

In regard to the logic behind spitting to repel an Evil Eye, folklorist Alan Dundes plausibly argues that spitting, like phallic ejaculation which it resembles,[632] produces a liquid that counteracts the dryness and withering thought to be caused by an Evil Eye. A liquid symbol of life thus is enlisted to counteract a cause of dessication and death.[633] Since the Evil Eye was deemed to cause dryness, withering, dessication, and eventually death, liquid symbols of fecundity and life such as saliva, semen and breast-milk, were thought to provide effective counter-measures. Dundes stressed not only the symbolic equivalence of the liquids spittle and semen,[634] but also the related equivalences of the "liquid-bearing symbols" of testes and breasts, of eyes and breasts, testicles and eyes, ejaculating phalluses and "ejaculated" rays from the sun and eye, and the singular phallus and singular eye (see also the *phallus oculatus*).[635] Such equivalance extended to the male and female genitals in general and to genital symbols such as the *mano fica* signifying intercourse, the *digitus infamis*/extended middle finger signifying the phallus, the exposed vagina, the image of a parturient women, (i.e. woman in labor), and the *sheela-na-gig* signifying reproduction and birth as symbols of life versus the dessicating and death-dealing force of the Evil Eye. Pierre Gravel, explaining the logic underlying Evil Eye apotropaics, has argued similarly that forces and symbols of fertility, procreation and life (especially the genitals and images thereof) are believed to counteract those of illness, dessication, and death.[636] This practice of spitting to protect against the Evil Eye is especially relevant to our discussion in Vol. 3, chap. 2 of the apostle Paul and his refutation of the charge of injuring his hosts with an Evil Eye—"you did not spit when you first met me" (Galatians 4:14).

Old women in particular, fabled for their knowledge and skill in healing, were deemed adept in warding off, or curing, Evil Eye injury by spitting. "Let there be an old woman to spit and ward off what is unlovely"

631. Tibullus, *Elegies* 1.2.

632. For apotropaic images of an ejaculating phallus at Pompeii see Baldassare and Carratelli 1990: I:399, Pl. 3; II:929, Pl. 1; II:931, Pl. 4. For Roman Tunisia: Foucher 1960, no. 57.011, pp. 4–5, Pl. IV:a. See also below, pp. 201–2, 204.

633. Dundes 1992:265–98.

634. Ibid., 276. The ancient rabbis had made this association of semen and saliva, with the latter used as a metaphor for the former; see *b. Niddah* 16b.

635. Dundes 1992:276–83.

636. Gravel 1994:36, 100–112 and *passim*.

(Theocritus, *Idyl* 7.126–127).[637] The healing role of women and the sense
of their power in confronting the Evil Eye continues in modern time. From
Southern Italy comes the report of a woman spitting thrice on a child, an act
seen as countering the sucking away of the mother's milk which would deprive the child of nourishment.[638] Anthropologist John Campbell describes
Greek shepherds in the North West of Greece, the Sarakatsani, whose honor
code encourages envy and whose customs include numerous stratagems for
warding off the Evil Eye. Regarding the Evil Eye as infected by the Devil,
they consider it the cause of the illness of humans and animals, the failure
of dough to rise, impotence, and a particular threat to children and sheep.
They spit three times on anything that arouses admiration and envy as a
precaution against the Evil Eye.[639] An old Greek woman, when she has
praised something, immediately spits three times and says "*phthou-phthou-
phthou sto kako phthiarmo*"[640] ("spit-spit-spit against the Evil Eye").[641]
Simply *saying the word* "I spit" (*ptuô*) three times in succession, or uttering
the phrase "ptui, ptui, ptui," are related tactics against the Evil Eye. Juvenal,
the Roman satirist (c. 60–140 CE) tells of Roman women of lower rank
who learn of their futures "with much smacking of lips (*poppysma*) against
evil influences" (*Sat.* 6.584).[642] This smacking of the lips, Green notes, was
made "to avert the evil eye or similar maleficent influences."[643] *Poppysma*
(a Greek term retained in Latin) is a noun likely representing the sound of
ptui-ptui-ptui (or *po-po-po*), which resembles the sound made when spitting
three times in succession by persons to ward off the Evil Eye.[644] The later
German expression *toi-toi toi*, (which is equivalent in sense and function to
the English saying "knock on wood" [to ward off evil forces]), has a virtually
identical sound and most likely derives from this threefold Greek term and
apotropaic custom.

637. See also Persius, *Sat.* 2.31–34; Petronius, *Sat.* 131.4–5.

638. De Martino 1959:63–64; Hauschild 1979:186–87.

639. Campbell 1964:337–38.

640. The fuller version: *phthou-phthou-phthou (ei)s to(n) kako(n) phthiarmo(n)* (=
baskanon).

641. Seligmann 1910 2:214.

642. Green, translator of *Juvenal, the Sixteen Satires* 1974:149.

643. Green 1974:160 n41

644. For the Greek paronym *poppysmos* see Xenopon, *De re equestri* 9.10; Plutarch,
Quaest. Conv., 713B. For Latin *poppysmus* as a protective sound also made when seeing
lightning see Pliny, *NH* 25.25 (plural).

Protection against the Evil Eye through the Hand, Fingers, and Manual Gestures

(1) The Hand

The *hand* and *one or more of its fingers* also were frequently engaged to thwart the Evil Eye.[645] The hand symbolized both divine power and protection as well as human threat and injury or resistence thereof.[646] Egyptian amulets of an open hand symbolized liberality and generosity.[647] The hand could represent the entire body, and a *manus mala* ("evil hand")[648] could *project* envy and evil.[649] A funerary epigram (second-third centuries CE) wishes a premature death to any tomb robber who might stretch out his "envy-ladened hand."[650] An inscription, IG 14.2012 (94 CE), mentions the "envious hand of Hades." The hand, however, and manual gestures, were also used to *protect against* evil, envy,[651] and the Evil Eye.[652] The hand held upright with all five fingers extended and palm facing outward is a universal gesture for "stop," "halt," from prehistoric cave paintings to the present. Conveying this meaning, it also was employed to halt the advance of the Evil Eye.[653] Schrire (1982:8) traces this apotropaic use of the hand back to Carthiginian practice and the Hand of Baal "found on Carthaginian inscriptions in upraised and benedictory positions."[654] The Museo Civico Archeologico of

645. Jahn 1855:53–57; Elworthy 1895/1958:235–76, 293–342; Elworthy 1900:145–271; Seligmann 1910 2:164–88 and figs. 83, 145–64. On ancient apotropaic gestures in general against the Evil Eye see Jahn 1855:53–57, 80–86; Sittl 1890:123–24; Elworthy 1958/1895:233–76; Kötting 1954, 1978; Kötzsche 1986; De Jorio 2000. On similar modern anti-Evil Eye gestures see Bauer 1903; Barakat 1973; Morris 1979, 1985; Morris et al. 1979, 1994; Axtell 1991:40, 41, 53–55, 74, 85–87, 100–101, 140, 153 De Jorio 2000:165–73, 214–19 and *passim*. On hand gestures more generally see Niederer 1989 (in relation to praise, shaming, and Schadenfreude).

646. Seligmann 1910 2:164–88; MacCulloch 1913.

647. Budge 1978/1930:173 and 172, fig. 11.

648. Petronius, *Sat.* 3.63.

649. Ovid, *Met..* 2.798–799 (the hand of envy causing illness); Statius, *Silvae* 5.1.137.

650. GVI 1375 (ed. Peek 1955).

651. Bacchylides, *Ode* 5.188–189 ("driving off envy with both hands").

652. On the apotropaic hand (hand amulets and amulets depicting hands) see Jahn 1855:53–58, 101–106, including votive hands and Plate 4, nos. 2a, 2b, 3 (*mano pantea*), 9 and 10 (*mano fica*) and Plate 5, nos. 1 (hand), 2 (*mano fica*) and 3 (hands); Usener 1873:407–9 (commenting on Jahn 1855:101–06); Seligmann 1910 2:164–88 and figures 83, 145–73; Potts 1982:11–14; Kötzsche 1986; Rakoczy 1996:97–104.

653. Jahn 1855:56–57, figs. 150–53; Seligmann 1910 2:168–72, 176–79.

654. Schrire 1982:8. See Cintas 1946, Plate XIX, No. 127, p. 133.

Bologna, Room IX (Roman Collection, Case two), displays five such open hand amulets. In the post-biblical period, this protective hand continued to be employed as an anti-Evil Eye apotropaic by both Jews and Muslims. Jews called it the *Hamesh* (Hebrew for "five") and the "Hand of Miriam," after Miriam, the sister of Aaron and Moses. Muslims dubbed it the *Hamsa* (Arabic for "five") and the "Hand of Fatima," after the honored daughter of the prophet Mohammed.[655]

(2) The *Mano Fica*

The *mano fica* ("fig hand") is a manual gesture used in antiquity and down through the centuries to ward off the Evil Eye. It is a fisted hand (generally the right hand) with the thumb inserted between the index and middle fingers thereby forming a gesture known as the "fig" (*mano fica, mano in fica* in Italian; *mano figa*, Spanish; *mano higa*, Portuguese).[656] Behind the gesture lay the ancient notion of the thumb as representative of the phallus. The insertion of the thumb "between the index and middle finger is meant to represent the penis entering the vagina."[657] It was a gesture symbolizing both sexual intercourse and the female vulva. Ovid took it to represent the clitoris in the vulva (*Fast.* 5.433).

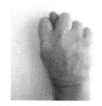

Illus. 10

Mano fica **gesture (Photos by John H. Elliott)**

Sexual gestures like this one, the *mano cornuta*, the *digitus infamis* (replicating an erect penis), the "crotch grab" (hand clutching the genitals), or the spread-legged display of the female vulva all enlisted the awesome power of the genitals to repel the considerable power of the Evil Eye. The same thinking lay behind the figural representations of these gestures and of genitalia on amulets and devices protecting homes, shops, and public spaces. The gesture continues in use in modern time.[658]

655. On these Jewish and Muslim amulets see Vol. 4, chaps. 1 and 2.

656. On the fig and the *mano (in) fica*, and "making the fig" see Jahn 1855:80–81 and plates 4 and 5; Elworthy 1895/1958:255–58; Olck 1909; Seligmann 1910 2:184–88; Vasconcellos 1925 and figs. 23, 33, 39; Rettenbeck 1955; Reichmann 1969; Sittl 1890:123–24; Herter 1978:18; De Jorio 2000/1832:xciii, 214–19, 239–40, 307, 427–30, and Plate VII, 475 and Plate XX, no. 1; Marcadé 1961.

657. Corbeill, *Nature Embodied*, 2004:49.

658. For use and global distribution see Morris et al.1979:147–60 with illustrations and photographs on xxvi, 147, 148, 150, 153; for its use against the Evil Eye, see 149,

The fig tree was sacred to many peoples (Greece, Rome, India, China, Japan). Muslims call it the "tree of heaven" and revere it because Mohammed swore by it. Greeks thought of the fig as a gift from Dionysus, god of agriculture and wine. Along with the phallus, the fig was associated with fertility and used in festivals of Dionysus. According to Roman legend, Rome was built at the site where a fig tree caught Romulus and Remus floating down the Tiber river in a basket. The heart-shaped form of the fig (Latin *ficus*, Italian *fica*, Spanish *figa*, Portuguese *higa*) represented the conventional form of the yoni or vulva. Roman ritual celebrated the fertilization of Juno Caprotina, goddess of the fig tree, by her lustful horned goat god.[659] The fig thus had sexual connotations, symbolizing the genitalia (phallus as fig tree; vulva as fig) and intercourse (merging of phallus and vulva, "harvesting figs").[660] It has been noted that "[in] late popular Latin, *ficus* may have taken on the sense 'female *pudenda*.' Ital. *fica* = '*pudendum muliebre*' is usually taken as a late Latin calque on *sykon* (Greek: "fig") in another of its senses (see Aristophanes, *Pax* 1354)."[661]

The *mano fica* gesture was known already in ancient Egypt.[662] Ovid provides one of the few literary references to the *mano fica* gesture. In connection with his comment on the Roman observation in May of the nocturnal Lemuria festival, Ovid tells of someone who "makes a sign with his thumb thrust in the middle of his closed fingers" (*signaque dat digitis medio cum pollice iunctis*) as a gesture of *self-protection*.[663] A bronze figure of Priapus making the *mano fica* with his upraised right hand was found at Herculaneum.[664] A classic medieval example of a double *mano fica* appears in Dante Alighieri's *Commedia Divina* (*Inferno*, Canto 25, lines 1–3). A thief (Vanno Fucci of Pistoia), extends both arms toward heaven, with both hands making the *mano fica* ("*con amendue le fiche*"), and declares, "Take that, God, I aim them at you!" In this case, the context suggests that the polyvalent gesture most likely communicates defiance rather than providing protection against the Evil Eye. Desiderius Erasmus mentions the *mano*

152, 156.

659. Rose 1959:217.

660. See Aristophanes, *Pax* 1344–1350—wedding song, cf. Buchheit 1960; Reichmann 1969:650–51; on "making the sign of the fig" (*facere ficum*; Italian, *fare la fica*; Spanish, *dar la higa*) see Herter 1978:18. On the fig. see also Condit 1947 (*mano fica* signals "screw you," 1947:5).

661. Adam 1982:113–14.

662. Bonnet 1971:29; K. Gross 1969:925.

663. Ovid, *Fasti* 5.433–434.

664. A copy was reported in *De' Bronzi d' Ercolano* 2:383, plate 94 and is partially reproduced in De Jorio 2000:241, fig. 11, with discussion (239–42).

fica in a sermon from 1524.[665] A cautious young woman displaying a *mano fica* for self-protection while receiving a suitor's visit appears in Gerard Terborch's painting, *The Suitor's Visit*, c. 1658.[666] As she faces a well-dressed young man bowing before her, she unobtrusively makes a *mano fica* with one of her two folded hands at her waist.[667] De Jorio shows how this ancient gesture was still employed by his fellow Neapolitans in nineteenth century Italy.[668] Desmond Morris and his colleagues discuss and illustrate use of the gesture from ancient to modern time.[669]

Illus. 12

Mano higa/fica **wooden amulet from Brazil, Julian Pitt River Museum, Oxford (Photo by John H. Elliott, with permission)**

Illus. 11

Sketch of a bronze composite amulet of *mano fica* **and phallus, Herculaneum, Italy (from Seligmann 1910:2:227, fig. 178)**

Representations of the *mano fica* (in ivory, silver, bronze, wood) have been used as amulets against the Evil Eye, often in combination with other apotropaics such as phalluses.[670] The gesture continues to be used in modern time for protection but also for sexual invitation, comment, and insult.

665. Roodenburg 1991:180 n7.

666. See Roodenburg 1991:154–55.

667. Ibid., 155, fig. 7.1. The painting is now in the National Gallery of Art, Washington, D. C., Andrew W. Mellon Collection.

668. De Jorio 2000/1832:474–75, Plate XX, no. 1 illustrating the *mano in fica*; also 214–19, 241–42 and Figure 11; pp. 427–30 and Plate VII.

669. Morris 1979:147–60.

670. For illustrations see Jahn 1855:81 (sketch of a bronze amulet in the Dresden collection [combination of a *fica* on right, phallus on left, vulva below and ring for amulet above and below]; also Plate 4, nos. 9, 10; Plate 5, no. 2); Elworthy 1958/1895:242, figs. 102, 111, 164; Seligmann 1910 2: figs. 174–77 and for composites: figs. 178–80; Bonner 1950 Plate 20, nos. 371 (Mich. 26171), no. 372; Röhrich 1960:143, fig. 32, 144, fig. 35 (mano fica by A. Dürer); Johns 1982:73, ill. 56 (Roman cylindrical bone amulet with phallus on one end and *mano fica* on the other), 57 (Roman bronze amulet combining phallus, *mano fica*, and crescent); Potts 1982:8–9, figs. 4, 6; Gravel 1995: fig. 8.2 (bas-relief, Roman Libya, winged phallus and *mano fica*); Morris et al. 1979:149, 150, 153; De Jorio 2000/1832:241, figure 11 (detail of an engraving of a small bronze figurine from Herculaneum [Museo Nazionale, Inv. No. 27773] of Priapus with an upraised

(3) The *Mano Cornuta*

The *mano cornuta* ("horned hand") is another manual gesture for countering an Evil Eye.[671] It is a fist (generally the right hand) from which are extended the index finger and little finger making a shape resembling a set of animal horns. This bicornate shape when made by the hand was later known in Italian as the *mano cornuta* or "horned hand."[672] To "make the horns" (*fare la corna*) as a manual gesture is to form and display the *mano cornuta*.[673]

 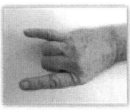

Illus. 13
Mano cornuta **gesture (Photos by John H. Elliott)**

Throughout antiquity, horns (single or a set of two), the sign of the power and vitality of male animals (bulls, goats, stags), were used to symbolize human strength, sexual potency, and fertility.[674] Horns, or replicas of horns, or horned objects such as the "horned moon," and the horseshoe, or objects made of horn, therefore, were used as amulets to protect against dangerous forces, including the Evil Eye.[675] De Jorio mentions fifty instances of horns engraved on the walls at Pompeii.[676] Of these fifty, fifteen were sus-

---

right hand making a *mano fica*). The Archaeological Museum of Cordoba, Spain, displays Roman phallic images that include an amulet composite of a *fascinum* and a *mano fica*. For a large collection discovered at the Roman military colony of Camulodunum in today's Colchester, Essex, England, see Crummy 1979.

671. Röhrich 1967:20–24 comments on the similar historical development of the *mano fica* and the *mano cornuta*; cf. also Corbeill, 2004:49.

672. Italian *cornuta* from *corno*, "horn"; Latin, *corna*; Greek, *keras*.

673. In modern time a distinction is made between the *mano cornuta* held vertically or horizontally. The former ("goat horns") is used to point out a cuckolded husband who is equated with a horned billy goat (Spanish: *cabrón*). The latter is used to ward off an Evil Eye; see Blok 1981; Morris 1979:120–46.

674. See Blok 1981:427–40 on horn symbolism in the Mediterranean region.

675. See Jahn 1855, Plate 4, no. 1, Plate 5, nos. 1, 4, 5; Elworthy 1895/1958:181–220, figs. 76–89; Elworthy 1900:1–144; Seligmann 1910 1, figs. 23, 60–69 and 2:135–38; Gravel 1995:118–19 and figs. 22.1–3.

676. De Jorio 2000/1832:158. These were presented originally in the volume, *Gli ornate delle pareti ed i pavimeni delle stanza del antica Pompeii incise in rame* [Napoli:

pended horns (simple horns or horns accompanied with phalluses).[677]
Horns coupled with phalluses, like horns combined with the *mano fica*,

represented intensified power.[678] Single horns (*corno*) used as amulets have been colored red, likewise to enhance their potency.

The *mano cornuta* could be made as a physical gesture; representations of the gesture are found in ancient art and in the form of amulets.

Illus. 14

Red *corno* amulet (plastic, originally of horn) against the Evil Eye (John H. Elliott collection)

It has been suggested that the earliest evidence of the *mano cornuta* comes from the Tjehun, an ancient Libyan tribe in west Egypt, c. 2500 BCE.[679] Like the *mano fica*, the assumed power of the *mano cornuta* was based on the sympathetic principle of resemblance and the act of imitation (*similia similibus*)—a "horned hand" imitating natural powerful horns. The crescent-moon with its "horns" and the similarly shaped horseshoe each had the same form and apotropaic function as the *mano cornuta*. The manual gesture had more than a single meaning depending on its positioning. Held vertically and and pointing upward it could signal a cuckolded husband;[680] displayed horizontally, as in the Herculaneum fresco (see below) its aim was to ward off the Evil Eye. The god Baal was invoked by Philistines and Phoenicians, according to Schrire (1982:8), for protection against the Evil Eye. A manual gesture imitating the "Horns of Baal" was made (making a fist with extended index and little fingers) to ward off the Evil Eye.

The earliest instance known to me of a *mano cornuta* on Italian soil possibly warding off the Evil Eye involves a wall fresco of an Etruscan tomb

Stamperia reale, 1838] now in the library of the Naples National Archaeological Museum [= earlier Royal Bourban Museum].

677. De Jorio 2000:161–63.

678. De Jorio 2000/1832:163. For an illustration of an amulet of a bull's head with horns, below which are two phalluses end to end see Jahn 1855, Plate 5, no. 4; for amuletic bull heads with horns also Pl. 5, nos 1 and 5; Pl. 4, no. 1 (bas-relief on oil lamp); Seligmann 1910 1: fig. 60.

679. Wainwright 1961. A Tjehun appears on a Fifth Dynasty Egyptian sculpture as a victim slaughtered by Neuserre, sixth king of the fifth dynasty (c. 2416–2392 BCE). On the *mano cornuta* and horns in antiquity and beyond, and their several meanings, see Elworthy 1895/1958:258–76 and figs. 102, 112–18; Seligmann 1910 1, figs. 60–74; 2:135–41, 173; Kötting 1954:473–82; Röhrich 1960:144, figs. 34, 36, 37; K. Gross 1969:925; Lesky 1969; Morris et al. 1979: xxvi, nos. 11, 128, 135, 136, 137, 139, 140, 141; Engemann 1980; Potts 1982:8–10; . De Jorio 2000/1832: xc, xcvi, 35, 138–73 (166, fig. 9 =Herculaneum fresco), 214, 307, 427–430 and Plate VI; 473 and Plate XIX, no.2.

680. The Greek expression *kerata tini poiein* meant "to give someone the horns" (= to cuckold him); see Artemidorus, *Oneirocritica* 2.1).

in Tarquinia, Italy (Tomba delle Leonesse, 520–500 BCE). The fresco portrays a pair of young dancers involved in a banquet energetically advancing toward each other. The figure on the right is a naked blond male youth with rust-colored skin; the figure on the left is a lightly-clothed, dark-haired and light-skinned girl who is holding up a left hand making the vertical gesture of a *mano cornuta*.[681]

Although a vertical horn-sign, it is likely signaling in this dining context not a cuckolded husband but rather an averting of Evil Eyes.[682] Morris and colleagues note appearance of the gesture on early pottery of the Daunian culture (east central Italy, c. 500 BCE), on an Apulian vase (c. 350 BCE), and "several times on the sixth-century A.D. [Christian] mosaics at Ravenna."[683] It is possible that the Roman satirist Persius (34–62 CE) is referring to the gesture when he speaks of making a manual gesture of "donkey ears":

> O happy Janus, who cannot be pecked at from behind by a crane (*ciconia*)
> nor mocked by a hand nimble at mimicking white donkey ears;
> at whom no tongue can be thrust out as far as a thirsty Apulian hound. (Persius, *Sat.* 1.58–60)

The gesture of donkey ears would require a shape similar to that of the two extended fingers of the *mano cornuta*.[684] According to De Jorio and Neapolitan custom millennia later, the *mano cornuta* was waved around in the air to deflect the Evil Eye in general, or directed against the fascinator, or aimed at the victim to be protected, including oneself.[685]

An assured ancient instance of the *mano cornuta* used apotropaically against the Evil Eye is a Herculaneum fresco depicting a comic scene in which a masked male actor aims his left hand making a *mano cornuta* at a

681. Etruscan Tomb of the Lioness, Necropolis of Monterozzi, Tarquinia, Etruria, Italy. De Agostini Picture Library DAE 10256379. The Cleveland Museum of Art. IML no, 506559. http://library.clevelandart.org/assets/128x102xsmall.php,qi=506559. pagespeed.ic.guyflZq4CW.jpg http://www.maravot.com/Etruscan_mural_dancers.gif

682. This is also the verdict of Ducati (1937:5), Morris et al. (1979:128, with illustration); and Hess and Paschinger (1986:234), among many others. It is contested by J. Engemann (1980:488) (see below).

683. Morris et al. 1979:136–37. On this mosaic see below, p. 190 and note 695; and Vol. 4, chap. 2.

684. The traditional combination of "Evil Eye" and "evil tongue" would also support this possibility. *Ciconia* ("stork") may denote here "a derisory blending of the fingers in the form of a stork's bill" (Lewis Short, *Latin Dictionary, s.v.*).

685. De Jorio 2000:147, 165; cf. also xciii and 427–30 on Pl. VII).

young lady who is being urged forward toward him by an older woman.[686] The image is on the cover of the 2000 edition of De Jorio's volume (juxtaposed to a Neapolitan youth making the same gesture centuries later), as

Illus. 15
Herculaneum fresco, comic figure making the *mano cornuta* **with his left hand. (from Bayardi and Carcani, eds.,** *Le pitture antiche d'Ercolano e contorni* **1762 4:159)**

well as on the cover of the Penguin 1974 edition of Juvenal, *Satires*, translated by Peter Green. Other instances of the *mano cornuta* in ancient sources identified by De Jorio include a vase depicting a leaping satyr with a drinking gourd in his right hand and a *mano cornuta* formed by his left, which is directed at the beaker and himself—in De Jorio's view to protect his joy and his wine from others' Evil Eyes.[687] Another is a fragment of a copper sword belt found at Pompeii showing in bas-relief a figure of Silenus resting his right arm on a wine skin and making a *mano cornuta* with his left hand—interpreted by De Jorio as protecting his wine from the envy of others.[688] A *mano cornuta* gesture, according to Hedwig Kenner (1957:181), appears on a tombstone of the Roman imperial period.[689] A relief on a Palmyrene sarcophagus (260 CE) shows a reclining male leaning on his left elbow and with his right hand making a *mano cornuta*.[690] A limestone funerary relief bust of Lady Haliphat of Palmyra, Syria (dated 231 CE), shows her making the gesture of the *mano cornuta* with her left hand.[691] The *mano cornuta* gesture appears

686. Seligmann 1910 2:137; Schmidt 1913:589; Lesky 1969; Cerulli Irelli 1973:170–71 concerning no. 229; De Jorio 2000:166, figure 9; see 165–68 and 427–30 and Plate VII; Engemann 1980, Plate 3a; The fresco is now in the Naples National Archaeological Museum, inv. no. 9037. Seligmann 1910 2:137 mentions a Pompeian wall painting with the gesture (Casa del Centenario in Pompeii, Reg. IX 8, 3+7, Atrium [2]), also in the Naples National Archaeological museum (inv. no. 9257). This Pompeian group as been identified as Amphitryon and Megara opposite Lykos; for illustrations see *PPM* 1 (1990); 374–75, figures 24–26.

687. De Jorio 2000:168.

688. Ibid., 168–71 and Figure 10.

689. Kenner 1957:181. She notes its similarity to the *mano cornuta* gesture of the right hand of the wife of P. Titius Finitus on a tombstone (beginning of second century CE) in the Vienna Kunsthistorisches Museum, see Schober 1923:84, no. 183, fig. 92.

690. Goodenough (1964, vol 11, fig.145) has an illustration and brief discussion (1964, vol 9:151) but with no mention of the gesture.

691. Freer/Sackler Gallery of Art, Smithsonian's Museums of Asian Art (F1908.236).

also on the Christian sarcophagus of Junius Bassus (died 359 CE) and in the ceiling mosaic of San Vitale in Ravena, Italy; see Volume 4, chapter 2.[692]

In nineteenth century Naples, a flashing of the *mano cornuta* was accompanied with the expression, "Benedica! Mal-uocchie non ce pozzano" ("Blessings! May Evil Eyes not be cast here"). Merely saying the word "corno" repeatedly—"corno, corno, corno" ("horn -horn-horn")—was thought to have similar apotropaic effect.[693] These hand gestures and their figural representations in amulets continue to be used in modern time.[694] Italian has numerous *corno* expressions: *corno* or *cornu* ("horn," often colored red when used as an amulet); *corni della luna* ("horns of the moon"); *avere sulle corna qualcuno* ("to dislike someone"); *fiaccar le corna* ("to take [one] down a peg"); *fare le corna* ("to make a horn gesture against the Evil Eye" or "to cuckold/put the horns on [a husband]"); *dir corna di* ("to speak evil of"); *cornuto* ("horned," "cuckold")." Red plastic replicas of the *mano cornuta* continue to be sold in contemporary Italy.

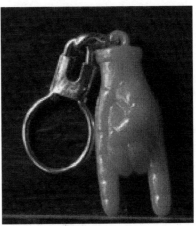

Josef Engemann, in a detailed study of the *mano cornuta* gesture in antiquity (1980), on the other hand, contests it as an ancient apotropaic gesture against the Evil Eye. He argues that (1) none of the pictorial depictions of this gesture, either in their content or context, can be shown to have had the aim of warding off evil or insult;[695] (2) Nor does the gesture appear on ancient amulets

Illus. 16

Modern Italian red *mano cornuta* plastic amulet (John H. Elliott collection)

Engemann (1980:494) indicates that hands with this gesture appear frequently in the imperial art of Palmyra. He claims that this and all other ancient instances of the gesture in pagan and Christian art are "rhetorical gestures" and not for warding off the Evil Eye (1980:493–98, 496).

692. On the Ravenna mosaic see Elworthy 1895/1958:265, fig. 113; Seligmann 1910:2:137, 181 and 1910:1: fig. 71. See also a figure of St. Luke making the *mano cornuta* (Elworthy 1895/1958:266 and fig. 114; Seligmann 1910:2:137).

693. De Jorio 2000:150. It is interesting to note that a connection of horn and eye occurs in the anatomical designations, "keratid artery" in the eye (*keratid* from Greek, *keras*, "horn") and the *cornea* of the the eye.

694. See Morris et al. 1979:120–46 (vertical and horizontal horn-signs) and illustrations on 135–37, 139–41; Barakat 1973 on the *mano cornuta* in Arabic culture.

695. Engemann1980:492, 498.

(in contrast to the frequent occurrences of the *mano fica*).[696] (3) It served rather as an oratorical and pointing gesture and assumed apotropaic import only in the later time of the 1600s.[697] He surveys the opinion of sixteen authors on the ancient evidence; twelve interpret the instances of the *mano cornuta* as apotropaic and four as a gesture of either mockery, contempt, oath taking, or ritual. He then lists numerous examples of the extended index and little finger serving as an oratorical and pointing gesture.[698] His one illustration is of an Etruscan mirror, each of whose sides is engraved with a figure (a male or a female) displaying the gesture.[699] His position involves a self-admitted weak argument from silence that no ancient *mano cornuta* amulet has been discovered. Other figural representations, however, allow, an apotropaic function and deserve more weight than Engemann seems prepared to give them. The detailed study of this scholar deserves a longer response than can be provided here. Experts continue to contest this issue; the last word on the *mano cornuta* in antiquity has not yet been spoken. The vertically held sign and the horizontally held sign, which Morris and colleagues state originated as anti-Evil Eye gestures, continue in use today. The manual horn-sign held *vertically* is used mostly in Portugal, Spain, and Italy.[700] The horn-sign displayed *horizontally* occurs most frequently in France, Italy, and Malta.[701]

(4) The *Mano Pantea*

The *mano pantea*, a hand with the thumb and first two fingers extended (as in priestly blessing), or a hand adorned with a cluster of apotropaic representations, was also employed against the Evil Eye.[702] The clustering of anti-Evil Eye symbols on this hand was thought to enhance its power. Augustine may have been alluding to this gesture in his letter to to Maximus of Madaura (*Epistle* 43) when he mentions the practice

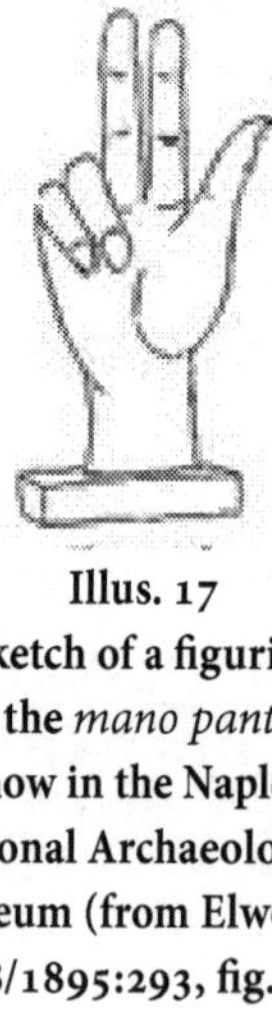

Illus. 17
Sketch of a figurine
of the *mano pantea*,
now in the Naples
National Archaeological
Museum (from Elworthy
1958/1895:293, fig. 136)

696. Ibid., 492.

697. Ibid., 492–98.

698. Ibid., 490–97, following Artelt 1934.

699. Ibid., 493, figs. 1, 2.

700. Morris et al. 1979:129–43.

701. Ibid., 135–46, with illustrations.

702. For illustrations see Jahn 1855, Plate 4 a, b (bronze votive hand); Elworthy 1895/1958:293–342 and figs. 136–48, 156–57; Seligmann 1910 2:181–82 and figs.169–71; on the *mano pantea* see also Elworthy 1900:194–271.

of holding up three fingers (*porrectis tribus digitis*) as gesture of protection against malignant demons.[703]

(5) The *Digitus infamis*

The *digitus infamis,* "notorious finger," the extended middle finger, is another well-known manal gesture for warding off the Evil Eye.[704] This is a manual gesture involving only a middle finger (*digitus medius*)[705] extended vertically from a closed fist—known in North America as "(flipping) the bird," or simply "giving the finger," and signaling a defiant "up yours!" This gesture has a pedigree reaching back to antiquity where it was called the *digitus infamis* ("notorious/disreputable finger"), or *digitus impudicus* ("shameful/wanton finger"), *digitus verpus* ("penis finger"),[706] or *digitus obscaenus* ("obscene finger"). In ancient finger symbolism,[707] the index finger represented the female and mother, the middle finger designated the male and father, and the thumb, the child. The index finger, employed as *digitus salutaris*, was extended to hail and greet. The fourth finger (alias ring finger,

digitus annularis) was the *digitus medicinalus* or *digitus medicus*[708] and was used for touching in cures. The fifth finger, *digitus minimus* (alias "pinkey"), when combined with the index finger with both fingers extended, formed the *mano cornuta.*[709] The middle finger gesture, like the *mano cornuta* and *mano fica*, had multiple meanings and could signal insult, defiance, or contempt as well as defense against the

Illus. 18
Digitus infamis **gesture**
(Photos by John H. Elliott)

703. See Usener 1873:407–9.

704. On the *digitus infamis* see Jahn 1855:81–83; Elworthy 1895/1958:413–15, 422; Morris 1985:157 (photograph).

705. The *digitus medius* ("middle finger")=Greek: *daktulos tritos* ("third finger").

706. *Verpa* denoted *penis/phallus* (Catullus, *Poems* 28.12; Martial, *Epigrams* 11.46.2; *Carmina Priap.* 34; Jahn 1855:81–83) and *verpus* designated a circumcised male (Catullus, *Poems* 47.4; Juvenal, *Sat.* 14.4; Martial, *Epigrams* 7.82.6; 11.94.2).

707. Latin for the specific fingers: *pollex*=thumb; *index digitus,* or *index salutaris*=second/*index finger* (for saluation); *digitus medius,* or *digitus infamis*=third/middle finger; *digitus medicus* or *minima proximus*=fourth finger; *digitus minimus*= fifth finger/pinkey.

708. Pliny, *NH* 30.34.108 (Greek: *daktylos iatrikos*).

709. On ancient finger symbolism see Echtemeier 1835; Budge 1978/1930:126, 304; K. Gross 1969:917–18 for illustrations of finger gestures; Morris 1985:152–60; De Jorio 2000/1832:70, 74, 117, *passim* and plates 19–21.

Evil Eye. Replicating a phallus, an erect penis, it resembles the powerful male sexual organ.[710] "The two bent digits on either side," Morris explains, "symbolize the testicles, and the middle finger is the active phallus."[711] Like the *mano fica* and *mano cornuta*, this notorious middle finger was often enlisted as a potent means for repelling the pernicious Evil Eye.

Ancient use of the extended middle finger as an insulting gesture is mentioned by Diogenes Laertius (*fl.* third century CE) in his *Lives and Opinions of Eminent Philosophers.* Recalling the anecdotes and actions of the Cynic philosopher Diogenes of Sinope (c. 412–323 BCE), Laertius noted that once some strangers to Athens requested to see the great orator Demosthenes. Diogenes of Sinope stretched out his middle finger, pointed to Demosthenes and said, "There goes the demagogue of Athens."[712] "Most people," Diogenes also said, "are so nearly mad that a finger makes all the difference. For, if you go along with your middle finger stretched out, some one will think you mad, but, if it's the little finger, he will not think so."[713] Fingers, in other words, communicated powerful messages, especially the middle finger. Epictetus (*Disc.* 3.11–12) tells of Diogenes once pointing out one of the Sophists not with the customary *digitus salutaris* (extended index finger of right hand) but in an insulting manner—"by extending his middle finger" (*ekteinas ton meson daktylon*). And then, when the targeted man was furious with rage, Diogenes remarked, "That's so-and-so, I've pointed him out to you." Here the gesture could have been used either to insult or to suggest that the sophist had an Evil Eye to be averted. The extended middle finger held horizontally rather than vertically and pointed at a male person could also mock him as effeminate.[714] The Romans also used the gesture to insult and taunt males as effeminates. "Go ahead and laugh, Sextillius, if he calls you a fairy. Let him stick out his middle finger" (Martial, *Epigrams* 2.28).[715] Martial tells of an elderly Cotta extending to three male friends not his index finger (of salutation) but his third "shameless finger" (*ostendit digitum sed impudicum*).[716] The middle finger served as both a sign of defiance

---

710. Jahn 1855:22, 82; Sittl 1890:101–2; Rakoczy 1996:151 n513.

711. Morris 1985:154.

712. Reported by Diogenes Laertius, *Lives* 6.34.

713. Reported by Diogenes Laertius, *Lives* 6.35.

714. See the Greek *skimalizô*, "to jeer at"; scholion on Aristophanes, *Peace* 549: "to hold up the middle finger" as an obscene gesture; see also *skimallos* ("middle finger [?]" LSJ *s.v.*); 1821.308. Greek *katapygôn* was another term for the middle finger used in insulting and obscene gestures (Pollux, *Onom.* 2.184).

715. See also Suetonius, *Augustus* 45, 48; *Gaius Caligula* 56.2.

716. Martial, *Epigrams* 6.70.1–5.

and gesture of protection. Juvenal praises Democritus of long ago for being able to laugh at human foibles and flash the *digitus infamis*:

> If Fortune was threatening, 'Up yours,' he'd say, and give her the *vulgar middle finger* (*mediumque ostenderet unquem*)." (*Sat.* 10.53)[717]

In regard to the finger's association with the Evil Eye, a third century BCE work, *Peri palmôn mantikê* (92.1), comments that the "middle finger" (lit. "third finger," *daktulos tritos*) "is full of *baskania* (Evil Eye malice)." Other sources indicate how it is used to thwart this same malice. "Behold," states Persius Flaccus,

> how the grandmother [or older aunt]/
> removes the boy from the crib, and his forehead and moist lips/
> first purifies with the notorius finger (*infami digito*) and atoning spittle,
> knowledgable thereby about warding off burning eyes (*urentis oculos*).
> (Juvenal, *Sat.* 2.31–34)

The statement indicates several factors associated with the Evil Eye: the vulnerability of infants, the protective role of older women/nurses, the association of middle finger and spittle and the apotropaic function of both, and an understanding of Evil Eyes as "burning eyes." De Jorio has suggested that Persius in his *Satires* (1.58–60) alludes to this same *digitus impudicus* with the term "crane" (*ciconia*), since Neapolitans centuries later also spoke of displaying a *digitus infamis* as *far la cicogna* ("making the crane," often behind one's back).[718] This is the text, we have seen, that also uses "donkey ears" as a likely reference to another anti-Evil Eye gesture, namely the *mano cornuta*.

The "notorious finger" gesture continues in use today, though its use against the Evil Eye is generally overshadowed by its employment as a contemptuous or defiant insult.[719] Thus the *digitus infamis* serves the same purpose as exposing one's backside ("mooning"), males clutching their genitals, or women exposing their genitals to repel an Evil Eye.[720]

(6) The Five Finger Gesture

A final contemporary manual gesture involving all five fingers could also be mentioned. A Greek gesture called the *mounza* involves joining the tips of all five extended fingers to form a point and then directing this toward some

717. Juvenal, *Sat.* 10.53; Green trans., *Juvenal* 1974:206.

718. De Jorio 2000/1832:193–94. For the text, see above, p. 187.

719. Barakat 1973; Morris 1979, 1985:152–60; De Jorio 2000/1832:193–94.

720. Gravel 1995:107–9.

person or suspected source of danger while saying the words, *na ta pente 's ta matia sou!* ("five in your [Evil] Eye") or only *na ta pente!* or *'s ta matia sou!* (cf. the classical Greek: *eis ta ommata sou*, "into your eyes"). To deflect this attack, the person who is addressed displays all ten fingers and cries *na ta deka!* ("ten [into yours]!").[721] Jewish and Islamic hand gestures (Hand of Miriam, Hand of Fatima) to ward off the Evil Eye are discussed in Volume 4, chapters 1 and 2.

PROTECTION THROUGH THE GENITALS

The human genitals and representations of the genitals as manual gestures or on amulets figured prominently among the means for protecting against the Evil Eye.[722] Our preceding discussion of hand and digital gestures has already touched on this. Known as *ta genitalia* (Latin), *ta aidoia* (Greek: "the awesome parts"), *pudenda* (Latin: "the awesome parts"), or *mebushim* (Hebrew: "the shameful parts" or "awesome parts"), or *ta didyma* (Greek: "the twins"—twin testicles or twin ovaries),[723] the genitals of males and females were regarded as the locus of ultimate human power, namely the power of reproduction, the power to produce progeny, extend the bloodline, and ensure the continuation of families, tribes and peoples. Symbolizing fertility and fecundity,[724] male honor and aggression, female vulnerability and sensitivity to shame, the genitals and their representations could have positive significance, as well as both aggressive and defensive implications.[725]

The genitals could be enlisted in the ongoing battle against the Evil Eye in various ways. First, one could *display* one's own genital organs (phallus or vulva) and *expose* them to view. "The exposure of the genitalia was widely believed to thwart and keep at bay pursuing evil forces.[726] The *exposure* of the genitals included the male displaying his phallus (and testicles) and the female spreading her legs and pulling open her vulva. The latter posture is known as the *sheela-na-gig* (figurative carving, generally on stone, of a female exposing her vulva.[727]

721. Story 1877:223.

722. Jahn 1855:48–49, 79–81, 68–81; Sittl 1890:101–2; Seligmann 1910 2:188–207; Fritz 1926:15–18; Herter 1938; 1979:16–22; Dundes 1992:278–89; Slane and Dickie 1993; Gravel 1995:53–61, 81–89 and *passim*.

723. On these terms see Elliott 2005c, 2005d.

724. Gravel 1995:54–61, 81–89 and *passim*.

725. On the genitals generally, see Herter 1938, 1978, 1979; as securing health and wellbeing see Deonna 1938:347–62 (Roman period); Herter 1978:16–22; Gravel 1995.

726. Sheridan and Ross 1975:54. See also Gravel 1995:54–112.

727. On this gesture see Gravel 1995:81–99; Freitag 2004, and below, pp. 210–16.

Second, a person could physically *touch* his or her genitals. The touching of the genitals included the "crotch grab" of the male genitals.[728]

Third, *representations* of the male and female genitalia also served as apotropaics. These images include drawings of genitals (male and female) as well as objects, which like manual gestures, are thought to resemble, or be shaped like, the genitals (phallic like forms; for female genitals, the fig or cowrie shells or sheela-na-gigs). Many genitalic apotropaics involved *combinations* of the phallus or vulva with other forms of protection (e.g. with inscriptions, bells, Evil Eye-attacked designs), thereby constituting composite amulets which increased the protective power.[729]

(1) The Male Genitals (phallus and testicles = *fascinus*)

The Greek term *phallos* and its Latin equivalent, *phallus,* designated the erect male member.[730] The phallus, instrument of penetration, fertilization and reproduction, symbolized strength, power, fecundity, aggression, and honor (male and familial). The frequent exaggeration of its size in artistic and apotropaic depictions was designed to enhance its power. It was the focus of intense and continued cultural fascination. Replicas of phalluses were employed in the fertility cults and their ritual processions. At festivals of the *Dionysia/Bacchanalia,* replicas of the phallus as symbol of fertility were carried through the streets, accompanied by women bearing baskets of figs, a fertility symbol associated with the female vulva. Both symbols were enlisted in Evil Eye protection. At the Roman festival of Liber Pater, the church father Augustine recounts, this god of liquid seed/semen was worshipped with phalluses both to ensure fertility and also to ward off the Evil Eye:

> During the festival of Liber this obscene organ [phallus] was mounted, with great honor, on carts, and exhibited first at the country crossroads, and thereafter conveyed to the city . . . It was obligatory for the most respected mother of a family to place a crown on this disreputable organ in full view of the public. This was how Liber had to be placated to ensure successful germination of seed; this was how the Evil Eye

728. Buonanno (1984:45) comments on the continued custom of touching the genitals for Evil eye protection in Italian-American culture.

729. For reproductions of a phallus with bells attached (among the bronzes of Herculaneum) see Seligmann 1910 2:277, fig. 192; Clarke, 2003:24–25, fig. 7; p. 96, fig. 63; Deschler-Erb 2007. On the phallus and its history as a symbol see Vanggard 1972; Orrells 2005;see also Wagner 1937 and Keuls 1985 with its excellent iconographic illustrations.

730. For other Latin terms (including *mentula, verpa*) and symbols for the male member see Adams 1982:9–79.

(*fascinatio*) had to be repelled from the fields. (Augustine, *City of God* 7.21; cf. 7.24)

As a symbol of fecundity, the phallus could represent not only Dionysus and Liber but also Priapus, the ithyphallic deity of ancient Greece and Rome and god of fertility. Priapus, son of Dionysus and Aphrodite and hailing from the Asiatic coast of the Hellespont, was one of the minor deities but highly regarded in popular imagination. Priapus was thought to bring fertility and

Illus. 19
Wall fresco of Priapus, Casa dei Vettii (region VI.15.1), Pompeii. Priapus depicted as weighing his enormous phallus against a bag of gold and protecting house from the Evil Eye.

blessing for animals, plants and humans and to protect gardens, vineyards, flocks of sheep and goats against thieves, bad weather and illness. "At marriage celebrations," Augustine informs us, "the new bride was invited to sit on the phallus of Priapus" (*City of God* 7.24). He was often depicted with a huge phallus accentuating his potency. The figure of the phallic Priapus was also used apotropaically. At Pompeii, for example, a fresco of the figure of Priapus/Mercury weighing his enormous phallus against a bag of money was positioned at the entrance to the House of the Vetii to ward off the Evil Eye.[731] A parallel statue of Priapus with extended phallus was erected in the garden, and, like the fresco Priapus, was visible from the doorway. Both images, set on a visual axis that magnified their effect, "are apotropaic, that is, they warded off the evil eye, thereby protecting the house."[732]

As the symbol of power, fecundity, and life, the phallus also was associated with Dionysus (Herodotus, *Hist.* 2.48–49), Mercury, Tychon (the deity of luck), Pan, and fertility demons. A figure of Priapus merged with the god Mercury, with caddeucus, moneybag and huge phallus, appears in a Roman fresco from

731. Pompeii location: region VI. 15.1; PPM V 471; see Balch 2008, CD No. 137, for a photograph. See also LIMC VII vol 1:1042, text by W.-R. Megow. On Priapus see Herter 1932; Slane and Dickie 1993 (against the Evil Eye); Megow 1997 and LIMC 8.1 (1997): pp. 1028–44; illustrations in LIMC 8.2 (1997), Plates 680–94, figs. 6–181B; Clarke 2003:20–21, figs. 2, 3; pp. 104–5, figs. 70, 71.

732. Clarke 1991:212 (208–213) and 2003:106, fig. 72, with thanks to colleague David Balch for this reference.

the entrance of a bakery in Pompeii.[733] In Egypt, the phallus was associated with Min (similar to Pan), Bes, and Horus. In the temple of Dea Syria in Hierapolis-Bambyke stood a bronze figure with a large phallus and in the forecourt, two gigantic phalluses.[734] The Egyptian divinity Bes, weak-sighted, deformed, and ugly, like Priapus and Mercury, was also depicted with a huge phallus and was thought to afford protection against everything that disturbed the sleeper and all evil forces, including the Evil Eye.[735] Phalluses embodied the powerful force of vitality and so could also defend against those malignant forces that threatened life and well being, including the Evil Eye.[736] Additionally, the image of the phallus, in the case of some amulets, "represents the threat of anal penetration, that is, buggery" of the envious Evil-Eye possessor.[737] The phallus of Priapus may have been the origin of the use of the phallus as an anti-Evil Eye amulet. If so, this would be one of

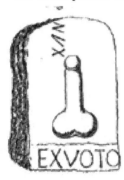

Illus. 20

Sketch of a *fascinum ex voto* on a stone slab, Roman fort, Westerwood, Scotland (from Knight and Wright 1865, Plate 28, fig. 2

many instances of the overlap of similar symbols from different domains and of symbols doing "double duty." It is likely that the variegated symbolism of the phallus (representing fertility, vitality, and both offensive and defensive power) made it such a popular image.[738]

The phallus (and testicles) also was denoted by the term *fascinus* (masculine) or *fascinum* (neuter). The included testicles (evident in numerous representations of the *fascinum*) witnessed to the assured power of the phallus in contrast to the emasculated eunuch's lost reproductive capability.[739] This Latin term *fascinus*, a likely transliteration of the Greek *baskanos*, also designated in general: (a) an Evil Eye or person with an Evil Eye (a fascinator), (b) an object (*fascinus* or *fascinum*) employed to ward off an

---

733. Location: region IX.12.6, date: between 89 BCE and 79 CE, and now in the Naples National Archaeological Museum, inv. no. 8760).

734. Herter 1979:701–7.

735. On Bes, see below, p. 252.

736. See Clarke, 2003:94–113 and illustrations.

737. Slane and Dickie 1993:488–89. Along similar lines, Bartsch 2006:147 proposes that underlying the notion of the phallus as protective against the Evil Eye was the "homeopathic reasoning" that a penetrating phallus defends against a penetrating gaze.

738. On the overlapping symbolism of the phallus see Jahn 1855:68–79 and Rakoczy 1996:153; Friedman 2001.

739. Slane and Dickie 1993:488, referring to a poem in the *Corpus Priapeorum* (15.2–7).

Evil Eye and envy, thus functioning as a *probaskanion*, or (c) the personified divinity *Fascinus* (Pliny, *NH* 28.39). The phallus, when designated *fascinus* or *fascinum*, was identifed as a protective against Evil Eye fascination (*fascinatio, fascinare*). Eventually, *fascinus* and *fascinum* became further Latin terms for phallus (with or without the testicles).[740]

The divinity *Fascinus*, like *Nemesis*, was a personification of a potency, in this case of the phallus (and testicles), similar to the personified divinity *Mutinus Tutinus/Mutunus Tutunus*. The worship of *Fascinus*, according to Pliny the Elder (*NH* 28.39), was entrusted to the Vestal Virgins. He was revered as the divine guardian of tender babies (*infantium*), on the one hand, and of mighty generals/field commanders (*imperatores*), on the other. A *fascinum*, representing the deity Fascinus, Pliny states,

> was suspended under the chariots of military field commanders
> (*imperatorum*) at their triumphal processions, whom it defends
> as a remedy against envy (*medicus invidiae*). A similar remedy of
> the tongue (*medicina linguae*) [of an accompanying slave] urges
> them to look behind themselves, so that *Fortuna*, destroyer of
> fame, may be dissuaded from following. (Pliny, *NH* 28.39)

Success in battle invites envy and an Evil Eye, which a *fascinum* as *medicus invidiae* was meant to thwart. The accompanying "remedy of the tongue" refers to a slave standing next to the commander in the chariot and warning, "look behind you and remember that you are human."[741] Macrobius (fifth century CE) adds that the commanders, on the day of a triumph, also wore around their necks a *bulla* (metal or leather pouch) with apotropaic content for protection against (Evil-Eyed) envy:

> Like the *toga praetexta* worn by magistrates, so the *bulla* was
> donned by generals in the triumph ceremony. They used to display it in the triumph with certain items enclosed inside, which

---

740. See Horace, *Epodes* 8.15. Another designation for an image of a phallus protecting against the Evil Eye was *invidiosis mentula;* see *Eph. Epigr.* III. p. 37, no.111; see also CIL 3.10189.16 ("*Dindari, vivas et invidis mentla*," on a ring [(*mentla* = *mentula=phallus*]). Other terms for phallus included *turpicula res, scaeva, muto, mut[t] onium,* and *satyrica signa.* Hesychius equated Greek *kerambêlon* with Latin *muttonium,* and likewise Greek *probaskanton* with Latin *muttonium.* On *fascinum* see Kuhnert 1909; Seligmann 1910 2:195–202, 318; Wünsch 1910:462; *Thesaurus Linguae Latinae* 6.1 (1912–1926): cols. 299–301. For illustrations see Jahn 1855:81; Seligmann 1910 2, figs. 184–193; Elworthy 1958/1895:154, fig. 42;S 351, fig. 164; M. Grant 1975:30, 31, 105, 108–13, 128–30, 132–34, 138–43, 155; C. Johns 1982 *passim;* Mountfield 1982:5, 6, 66–87; Keuls 1985; Slane et al. 1993:486–94; Clarke, 2003:5, 6, 24–25, 94–113, 152–53; Sáenz Preciado and Lasuén Alegre 2004; Orrells 2005; Moser 2006.

741. *Respice post te, hominem te memento,* cf. Juvenal, *Sat.* 10.41.

they believed to be very potent remedies against envy. (Macrobius, *Saturnalia* 1.6.9)[742]

Illus. 21

Sketch of bronze composite amulets of winged phalluses with bells, Pompeii (from Carcani, ed. 1771 2:399, Plate 97)

Illus. 22

Sketch of a terracotta lamp with fascinum in bas relief (from Seligmann 1910 1:301, fig.51)

Roman children, mostly males, likewise wore a *fascinum*/phallus in a *bulla* around their necks for protection against the Evil Eye and envy until reaching their majority.[743] Varro (*Ling. lat.* 7.97) was most likely referring to the *fascinum* when he describes the pendant suspended from the necks of children as a *turpicula res* ("shameful, unsightly little thing"), and *scaeva* and *scaevola* ("sinister," lit. "things on the left"). Favorite animals too were protected by this means (Ovid, *Met.* 10.114). *Fascina*, often with eyelets at-

742. *Nam sicut praetexta magistratuum, ita bulla gestamen erat triumphantium, quam in triumpho prae se gerebant inclusis intra eam remediis quae crederent adversus invidiam valentissima.*

743. Pliny, *NH* 33.10 (a golden bulla first suspended by Tarquinius Priscus around the neck of his young son); Varro, *Ling. lat.* 7.97, 107; Plautus, *Miles* 5.1.6 (lines 1398-1399); *Rudens* 4.4.127; Livy, *Ab urbe condita* 26.36.5; Suetonius, *Julius Caesar* 84; Plutarch, *Romulus* 25, in imitation of Tuscan kings and Lucumones. Wünsch (1910:462–63) suspects the Roman practice was borrowed from the Etruscans. On the *bulla*/capsule see Saglio 1896; Gerstinger 1954; Schienerl 1984:45–54.

tached, were worn on the body as pendants or broaches, or were carved on gems, finger rings, or on amber, silver, gold or bronze objects of ornamentation. One such amulet displaying a *fascinum* was carved from a section of red-deer antler.[744] A child's gold ring (Roman, date and provenance unknown) has a *fascinum* in bas-relief for protection against the Evil Eye.[745] Equipped with wings and looking like some bizarre flying creature, phalluses or *fascina* also were accompanied by bells (*tintinnabula*) so that sound joined sight in driving off the Evil Eye.[746] *Fascina* adorned oil lamps,[747] accompanied graffiti,[748] and were suspended in homes and workshops as anti-Evil Eye protection.[749] *Fascina* appeared also in wall frescoes. In Pompeii (region VII 9.7.8), a wall fresco in the meat market depicts Io guarded by Argos. On Argos' bent right leg is draped a garment on which a *fascinum* is depicted (perhaps added secondarily?).[750] *Fascina* likewise were affixed to the portals and on the walls of domestic homes.[751] At Pompeii (region VI.6.18), one such plaque at the portal of a house with a bakery displayed a *fascinum* accompanied by the words HIC HABITAT FELICITAS ("Here happiness dwells")—assured by anti-Evil Eye protection.[752] At Pompeii are

744. Johns 1982:64, Ill. 45.

745. Now in the Johns Hopkins University Archaeological Museum, description by Elizabeth Dowdle ("Child's Gold Ring with Phallus). Elworthy (1895/1958:151) mentions a gold *fascinum* serving as a necklace pendant now in the Louvre, Paris; many other examples are in the Museo Archeologico Nazionale di Napoli. On the phallus as apotropaic against the Evil Eye, see Jahn 1855:68–79 and Plate 3.3, 4.1; Elworthy 1895/1958:151, 148–55; Wagner 1937:79–83; Herter 1938:1733–44; Slane and Dickie 1993:486–95.

746. See Jahn 1855, illustrations on pp. 77, 78, 81; Seligmann 1910 2:200 and figs. 189–91; Herzog-Hauser 1937. For phallic tintinnabula at Pompeii and illustrations see Knight and Wright 1865, plates XXV, XXVI, XVII; also M. Grant 1975, 1982; Johns 1982; Gravel 1995, figs. 8.1, 8.2, 8.4, 8.5, 8; Moser 2006.

747. Jahn 1855, plate 4, no. 1; see also plate 5, no. 2 (necklace with assorted amulets including a *mano fica*, a herm on which is a *fascinum*, male and female figures with exposed genitals and beads with "eyes"). For a winged *fascinum* on a Roman oil lamp see Johns 1982:145, ill. 11. For a small oil lamp in the shape of a winged phallus from Pompeii see Mountfiled 1982:67. For a hanging terra-cotta oil lamp from Arles, Gaul, in the shape of a sitting dwarf hugging his own massive phallus see Clarke 2003:152–53.

748. A Pompeian graffito (CIL 4.4498 from Region VI.13.19) by a jealous admirer pleads, "Thyas, don't give your love to Fortunatus. Bye" (*Thyas noli amare Fortunatu[m] . . .Vale*) and includes a crude sketch of a *fascinum* between the final two words.

749. Pollux, *Onom.* 7.108; Hofmann 1966:33; Moulton-Milligan 1930:106.

750. See Balch 2008, CD Plates 181, 181a; also Baldassare, PPM VII, 341, 344, 346.

751. For Pompeii, see Balch 2008, Plate 138 (Region VII 1. 36?) and Plate 139 (Panificio, Region VII 1. 36); see also PPM V 963, VI 721, 896; VIII 866; IX 371; X 179).

752. CIL 4.1454. See above, p. 182,], Illus. 10. See also Cooley and Cooley 2004:90–91, no. E24, now in the *Museo Archeologico Nazionale di Napoli*, Erotic collection

also two images of ejaculating phalluses.[753] In mosaic thresholds *fascina* served the same purpose, as illustrated by the threshold mosaic of a house in Ostia Antica. Rome's ancient habor.[754] Such threshold protection is still found today in contemporary India where wives redesign the threshold area of the home every morning as protection against the Evil Eye.[755] In ancient Beirut, Syria, a bas-relief of a phallus was found inscribed with the legend, *PATAXI BASKANOS* ("Evil Eyer, be smitten!");[756] see above, p. 170.

Illus. 23

Sketch of a scene at Pompeii, *fascinum* plaque on house wall (from Seligmann 1910, 2:249, fig. 187, taken from Carcani, ed. 1771, 2:393, Plate 96

(Raccolta Pornographica [RP]. Inv. no. 27741. Compare CIL 3.5561 (*Felicitas hic habitat, nihil intret mali*, "Here happiness dwells, no evil enters") and CIL 10.8053. Jahn 1855:74–75, esp. 75, speculates unconvincingly that *felicitas* refers to a personified deity; cf. Symmachus, *Ep.* 1.43 (*ne ullo fascino felicitas mordeatur*). On this image at Pompeii see M. Arditi, *Il fascino*, 1825:4; Seligmann 1910 2:198. For illustrations see Mountfield 1982:72; Grant 1985:109; Johns 1992:65, fig. 47; Clarke 2003:102, fig. 68. Plaques with *fascina* did not signal houses as bordellos, as earlier eminent scholars such as Johann Jacob Winckelmann (1717–1768), Paul Hans Brandt (pseudonym: Hans Licht, 1875–1929) and others had proposed. For a photograph of a *fascinum* in a panel set into a wall at a street corner in Pompeii see Johns 1982:63, ill. 12.

753. See *PPM* I:399, pl. 3; II:929, pl. 1; II:931, pl. 4. Also at Tunisia: Foucher 1960, no. 57.011, pp. 4–5, pl. IV:a; Germain 1969, no. 129, p. 94, pl. XLII: 129.

754. Ostia Antica, House of Jupiter Fulminator. See also Clarke 2003:108, ill. 75. Did this *fascinum* double as an image of *Jove fulminator* affording protection against the Evil Eye? On the symbol of lightning or a bundle of lightening used against the Evil Eye see Engemann 1975, esp. 26, 31, 37 and figs. 2, 7, Plate 11c.

755. On this Indian custom of the *Kôlam* see Najarajan 1993.

756. Waddington 1870: nos. 2360, 2406; Perdrizet 1900:293; Leclercq 1907:1844.

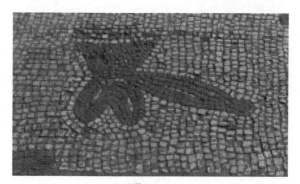

Illus. 24
Threshold mosaic of a *fascinum*, House of Jupiter
Fulminator, Ostia Antica, Italy, first–second century CE
(Photo by John H. Elliott)

One of the three mosaics of the "House of the Evil Eye" located in the village of Jekmejeh southeast of Antioch on the Orontes, Syria and now in the Antioch Museum[757] depicts a hunchbacked dwarf aiming his large exposed phallus against an Evil Eye under attack from a variety of enemies.[758] A Roman black and white threshold mosaic at Sousse,Tunisia, now in the Sousse museum, depicts a phallus and testicles (*fascinum*) pointing downward, flanked by two triangular *kteneis* [representing female vulvae] with the phallus connected directly to the vulva on the left by a stream of ejaculate. An inscription aside the *fascinum* reads: O CHARI. The full wording and meaning of the phrase are uncertain, but the words may be an abbreviation for *charidôtes*, "joy-bringer," an epithet for Hermes and Dionysus.[759]

Fascina also were displayed on gladiatorial helmuts, chariots, tombs, prows of ships (to protect the ship and its cargo), domestic vessels as well as on smaller personal amulets.[760] *Fascina* safeguarded not only homes, but gardens, fields, and work shops. Pliny (*N.H.* 19.19.50) states that in the Roman forum and in gardens *saturica signa* were erected to protect these holy spaces against the Evil-Eying of the envious (*invidentium effascinationes*).

757. Antakya Archaeological Museum, Inv.-no. 1024.

758. See above, Illus. 9, p. 174. See Levi 1941:220–32 (an overview of the various objects attacking the Evil Eye in this and other similar specimens); 1947:29–34; Norris 1991:257–258; on the Antioch mosaics see also *Antioch: The Lost Ancient City*, a catalogue (with essays) of an exhibit at the Worcester Art Museum, Massachusetts. 10/8/2000, http//www.worcesterart.org .

759. Merlin 1915 2:23, no. 181a. Illustration also in Marcadé 1961, fig. 104b; Gravel 1995, fig. 39.1. Sousse Archaeological Museum, inv. no. 10.503.

760. For photographs of *fascina* on Roman gold finger rings and coral jewelry see Johns 1982:66. For a photograph of a fascinum bas-relief on a vase at Pompeii see Mountfield 1982:67.

Saturica signa could designate either satyr masks or phalluses/*fascina*. Augustine (*City of God* 7.21) lamented the Roman custom of erecting *fascina*

in fields to protect the crops against fascination. Julius Pollux (*Onom.* 7.108) tells of *fascina* protecting the metalworkers' forges and products against the Evil Eye. On one of Pompeii's main thoroughfares, the Via dell' Abondanza, a *fascinum* in bas-relief is still visible on one of the street stones, thus protecting the thoroughfare and persons using it from the Evil Eye. At Philippi, Greece, a similar *fascinum* appears in bas-relief on a rock just north of the stadium.[761] Another *fascinum* embossed on a stone is still visible at the Roman ruins of Volubilis, Morocco.[762] *Fascina* also were displayed on city walls. A wall carving

Illus. 25

Fascinum in relief on a paving stone of the Via dell' Abbondanza, Pompeii (Regio VII. 13), first century CE.

(Photo by John H. Elliott)

from Leptis Magna in Libya depicts a *fascinum* accompanied by the words *ET TIBI SIT*, "back to you!" lit. "may it be to you!"[763] This is the Latin equivalent of the Greek expression *KAI SY* (lit. "you too"), as found in the Antioch anti-Evil Eye mosaic (see above, pp. 173–75). Both the Latin and Greek expressions seem to have expressed the wish that any glance from an Evil Eye "bounce off me and return to you." The combination of the saying and the *fascinum* intensified their apotropaic potency. In Rhodes on the island of Delos, remants of huge *fascina* once located at the shrine of Dionysus, line the main thoroughfare; only remains of the testicles and stumps of the phalluses are still visible.[764] The *fascinum*/

761. Photograph in Collart and Ducrey 1975:180, fig. 194, with thanks to Jason Lamoreaux for the reference.

762. Volubilis (Oualili in Arabic) is the largest and best-preserved Roman ruins in Morocco, North Africa. Once a Roman administrative center, the ruins are situated near Moulay Idriss and 30 km north of Meknes, Morocco. The *fascinum*, embossed on the top of a standing stone, is not a sign pointing to a brothel, as stated for tourists, but an apotropaic to ward off the Evil Eye.

763. See also Johns 1982:19, ill. 3 (photograph).

764. Originally they were located at the shrine of Dionysius. See also photograph in Johns 1982:14, ill. 1. For five further samples of phalluses in bas-relief on walls of residences and a sreet-corner of Delos see also Déonna 1938, and P. Bruneau, "Apotropaia déliens" 1964. For free-standing phalluses in Italy see *AA* 69 (1954):203, 207. In regard to monumental apotropaica see Faraone, 1987.

phallus was a symbol of Dionysus and served also as an anti-Evil Eye apotropaic, similar to the representations of Pripaus and his phallus. Representations of phalluses/*fascina* also have been found on an amphitheature in Nimes and a nearby aquaduct.[765] *Fascina* also were inscribed on *ex votos* that were offered in gratitude for successful healings; see, for example, the votive carving of a *fascinus* on a stone from Roman Scotland (see above, Illus. 20).[766]

A threshold mosaic of an Evil Eye attacked by a phallus shaped like a fish (equipped with fish gills and an eye) and two serpents was designed to protect a Roman home in Hadrumetum, North Africa (Moknine, near modern Sousse, Tunisia), third century CE. This mosaic appears to portray a phallus ejaculating into a free-standing eye,[767] a potent combination of phallus and "spitting" (of semen) for warding off the Evil Eye.[768] A phallus of an Ethiopian ejaculating and directing it backward is portrayed in a long fresco in Pompeii in the Casa della Scultore.[769] A floor mosaic from Themetra in Africa Proconsularis (today's Chott Maria, 15 km northeast of Sousse) depicts an Evil Eye attacked from above by a phallus and accompanied by the inscription, "What you see is for the envious; may it go well for the

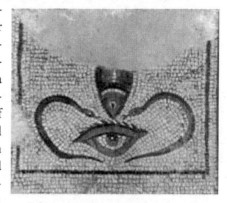

Illus. 26
Roman threshold mosaic of an Evil Eye attacked by an eyed fish-like phallus and two serpents, Hadrumetum, North Africa (modern Sousse, Tunisia), third century CE (from Perdrizet 1922:31, fig.11)

765. Jahn presents a sketch of a winged [double?] phallus (1855:77) and another sketch (1855:78) of a female figure in profile (on left) kneeling before and touching an animal-like figure (on the right) with cloven hoofs and sitting on its haunches; its remaining body is a huge winged phallus and testicles larger than the size of the female. It is an approximately 35 cm high x 47.5 cm wide relief, provenance unknown, in the Bonn Musum (Museum catalogue, nos. 36, 74). It is identified correctly by Jahn as not Leda and the swan but a *fascinus*, whatever else it may also symbolize.

766. See also Johns 1982:5.

767. Bernand 1991:104, illustration on 85; see also Engemann 1969:994; Gravel 1995, fig. 39.2.

768. For an Evil Eye under attack that includes a phallus on/around the eye see also the illustrations in Jahn 1855:96–97; Seligmann 1910 2:95, figs. 117; 99, fig.119; 101, fig. 120.

769. Pompeii, region VIII 7, 24.22; Balch 2008, Plate 284; PPM VIII 719.

good and ill for the evil."[770] A terracotta figure from Greek Egypt of a youth touching an eye, which is attacked from below by a phallus/fascinum, bears the inscription, "I have pierced the eye of the Evil-Eyeing one" (*ophthalmon apetrypêsa ton tou baskanou*).[771] Replicas of phalluses on which eyes have been painted (*phalli oculati*) illustrate the association of eye and phallus in apotropaic symbolism.[772] A sixth century BCE inscription from Itanos on Crete includes a phallus and a spread right hand as protection of the urban quarter.[773] The phallus/ *fascinum* is associated with the fish in some anti-Evil-Eye amulets.[774] The mosaic from the "House of the Evil Eye" in Antioch, Syria, displays a huge phallus of a dwarf directed against an Evil Eye, along with the gills of a fish (see above, Illus. 9, p. 174).[775] André Bernand, writing on envy and the Evil Eye in Greco-Roman culture, lists further examples of phalluses depicted in mosaics and on monuments to ward off the Evil Eye.[776] The studies of Michael Grant on *Eros on Pompeii* (1975), Catherine Johns on erotic images of Greece and Rome (*Sex or Symbol?* 1982), David Mountfield on *Greek and Roman Erotica* (1982) and John R. Clarke on *Roman Sex* (2003) likewise are rich sources

Illus. 27

Sketch of a bronze anti-Evil Eye amulet from Herculaneum: gladiator with monstrous phallus and five bells (from Carcani, ed. 1771, vol. 2: 387 and Plate 95)

770. *Invidiosibus quod videtis B (onis) B (ene) M (alis) M (ale)*. See Foucher 1957:178, fig. 13.

771. W. Weber 1914:100, no. 131 and Plate 12; Bilabel 1926, no. 6295.

772. See Johns 1982:60–61, 66 and ill. 49, 50, 67.

773. Schmidt 1913:587–88; Herter 1938:1734; Rakoczy 153 n521.

774. See Engemann 1969, especially 1969:994 (fish with phallus-like character on an Etruscan bronze lamp with a gorgoneion). Cf. Goodenough 1956 vol 5, illustration 67.

775. Levi 1941; 1947, vol. 2, plate 4c.

776. Bernand 1991:85–105, especially 104–5 (Kôm Trouga in the Egyptian delta; Leptis Magna in Libya, and Zliten in Tripoli). On Evil Eye amulets in Leptis Magna see also Charles Picard (1954:234–43, phalluses on p. 238) and Vergara Caffarelli and Caputo 1966:111. For Zliten see also Aurigemma 1960, vol. 1.1, Plates 71–73 (mosaic of traditional battle of Pygmies and cranes, with a pygmy equiped with a large phallus facing backward and attacking with a club).

for pictorial evidence of Greek and Roman apotropaics against the Evil Eye.[777]

Composite amulets also include the combination of (winged) phalluses and bells, by which sound joined sight in driving off the Evil Eye.[778] In the Naples National Archaeological Museum is a bronze composite apotropaic figure from Herculaneum of a gladiator with a monstrous phallus in the form of a dog or panther and five suspended bells.[779] At Pompeii and Herculaneum were also found winged phalluses with bells.[780] Figures of Priapus showed him with an extended phallus and holding a bell.[781] In sum, the phallus and *fascina*, alone or in combination with other apotropaics, were deemed potent protectives against the Evil Eye and envy.[782]

777. See Grant 1975:9, 30, 31, 50, 53, 84, 85–166 (items from "The Secret Collection" [*Raccolta Pornografica*] of the Naples National Archaeological Museum); Johns 1982:14, ill. 1; 19, ill. 3; 21, ill.5; 50–52, 54–55, 60–75 ("The phallus and the Evil Eye"); 93–95, 61; Mountfield 1982:5, 6, 66–87; Clarke 2003:94–113 (photographs on 94 (Evil Eye attacked); ill. 63 (*tintinnabula*); ill. 64 (*fascinum* at Pompeii, Via della Abondanza); ill. 65 (phallus); ills. 66, 67 (*fascina*); ill. 68 & 69 (*fascinum* and *HIC HABITAT FELICTAS*); ill. 75 (mosaic *fascinum* at Ostia); ill. 76 (Antioch); 110–12 (regarding laughter warding off Evil Eye and figures intended to provoke laughter): also 5 (*tintinnabula*), 6 (*fascinum*), 24–25 (*tintinnabula*); 153 and fig. 105 (dwarf and phallus). On the apotropaic function of lausghter see also Clarke 2007, ch.4.

778. See Jahn 1855:79 and illustrations on pp. 77, 78, 81; phallic tintinnabula at Pompeii in Gravel, figs. 8.1, 8.2, 8.4, 8.5, 8.6; Knight and Wright, plates XXV, XXVI, XVII. See also Espérandieu 1913 5:341–44; cf. 342 (fig. 6994, found in a catacomb in Rome) and Herter 1978:18 (tintinnabulum with phallus attached). See also n747 above.

779. Bayardi and Carcani 1771, vol. 2:387 and Plate 95; see also Espérandieu 1913 5:344. The *Camera Segreta* (rooms 62–63 housing the *Raccolta Pornografica*) of the Naples National Archaeological Museum has been open to the public since 2000; for illustrations of its inventory see Grant, "The Secret Collection," 1975:85–166.

780. Bayardi and Carcani 1771 2:395 (Plate 96), 399 (Plate 97), 403 (Plate 98); 407 (Plate 99). For illustrations see also Grant 1975:138–43; Johns 1982:64, 68; Mountfield 1982:68–69; cf. also Exhibition of the Royal Academy of Art (London 1976), no. 216.

781. Herter 1932:139 no. 44–46; or with a bell on his phallus, Herter 1932:142, no. 68. For the combination of phallus and bells see Jahn 1855:79. For the combination of a *mano fica* (left) with phallus (right) with vulva (below) and ring above see Jahn 1855:81. For the combination of phallus/*fascinus* and animals see Jahn 1855:77, 78, 79 & Plate 5, nos. 4 and 5. For phallic tintinnabula at Pompeii, see Gravel 1995, figs. 8.1, 8.2, 8.4, 8.5, 8.6; Knight and Wright, plates XXV, XXVI, XVII.

782. On the phallus and fascinum as apotropaics, especially against the Evil Eye, see Jahn 1855:68–79; Forlong 1883; Perdrizet 1922:31; Wagner 1937; Herter 1938:1681–748, esp. 1739–40; cf. also 837, 1666–68, 1670–80; 1683–84, 1733–44; Levi 1941; Meisen 1950:144–77; Wright 1957; Koetting 1954:473–82; Elworthy 1958/1895:148–55; Deonna 1965:180–83; Herter 1972, 1978:1–52, esp. 16–22; Budge 1978/1930:15; Bernand 1991:85; Norris 1991:257–58; Dundes 1992:257–312; Gravel 1995:53–74; Johns 1982:60–75 (illustrations); Clarke 2003:94–113 (illustrations). For illustrations of anti-Evil Eye phalluses see also Potts 1982:8, figs. 4, 5; Gravel 1995, figs. 8.1, 8.2, [8.4

Related to the *fascinum* was the inclusion in the ancient Roman marriage ceremony of the singing of jeering, vulgar verses called *Fescennini*
(probably from *fascinum*)[783] to ward off the Evil Eye (*fascinum*).[784] In the
early period a phallic representation was used by the bride. She was compelled to sit on the phallus of the ithyphallic god Mutunus Tutunus[785] "The
rite was no doubt intended to promote fertility as well as ward off evil,"
Adams notes.[786] "These two functions of an object or utterance, as apotropaic and conferring fertility, are often impossible to separate; by fulfilling
the first, the object assists in the second." The ithyphallic deity of ancient
Greece and Rome, Priapus, as noted above, represented and granted fertility and protected against the Evil Eye.[787] The Roman festival of the phallic
Liber pater included replicas of phalluses placed in baskets and brought to
crossroads where they were displayed. This display was accompanied by the
uttering of apotropaic obscenities to ward off the Evil Eye.[788] Respectable
matrons also were forced in public to crown the phallic images. These images were also used to safeguard fields from the Evil Eye (*fascinatio*).[789]

Another term of the *fascin-* root was the expression *praefascine/prae-
fiscini/praefiscine* (adverbial forms from *prae-fascinum*) or *praefiscini*

phallic bird]; 8.5 [polyphallic tintinnabulum]; 8.6?, 9.3 [winged phallus with phallus
and tintinnabula]; 38.1 [copper plate book cover ? with phallic alpha and kteic omega
flanking a Greek cross in the middle,eighth century. France]; 39.1. See also Wolters
1909 and Deschler-Erb 2002 (amulets of phallus and bells, phallus and Gorgo).

The Museo Civico Archeologico di Bologna. Room VI (Greek Collection) and
Room IX (Roman Collection) displays numerous specimens of the apotropaic phallus
or *fascinum*. Room VI (Greek Collection) Case 4B: bronze representation of a pigmy
with huge phallus= "an Alexandria grotesque"; a gold frontal figure of a woman sitting
with her legs spread and exposing her vulva. Room IX (Roman Collection): Case 2: 32
metal "Phallus Amulets against Malocchio," most of which are between 1–2 inches in
size with an eyelet for suspension on a necklace or bracelet, as one amulet on a chain
clearly shows. They include: one mano fica (no. 1679); 5 phalluses combined with a
mano fica; one double phallus; 12 *fascina* (phallus and testicles); and 5 terracotta phallus amulets; also five terracotta phallus amulets, five open hands similar to the open
hand of Fatima, and five terracotta gorgoneia. In Case 6B is a set of Roman earings
including a tiny (1/2 inch) gold fascinum with ring, no. 309.

783. Less likely is the derivation of the name *Fescennini* from the village in the Campagna named Fescennia.

784. Adam 1982:4–5, 11; see Horace, *Epist.* 2. 1.145; Catullus, *Poems* 61.126 (ode
on the marriage of Julia).

785. Lactantius, *Inst.* 1.20.36; Augustine, *City of God* 6.9; 7.24; cf. Herter, "Phallos,"
1938:1719–20; Herter, "De Mutino Titino," 1927:423; Herter, "Genitalien," 1978:15.

786. So also Herter, "De Mutino Titino," 1927:423.

787. Herter, *De Priapo*, 1932:22, 111, nos. 81–82.

788. Adams 1982:5.

789. See Augustine, *City of God* 7.21, 7.24, and above, p. 169, n576, pp. 195–96.

dixerim which stated, "no Evil Eye intended."[790] The Romans added this word to any compliment or expression of admiration or praise to assure that the praise involved no intent to harm with an Evil Eye.[791]

Illus. 28
Sketch of an Etruscan bronze lamp with gorgoneion in center encircled in part by figures of squatting females exposing vulvas (from Elworthy 1958/1895:162, fig. 50)

This is a copy of a museum print in the museum of Cortona, Italy. For the genitals-mouth connection see also *labia* ("lips") for both facial and vaginal lips, the similarity of nose (flanked by two eyes) and penis (accompanied by two testicles), and also the concept of the *vagina dentata* (the menacing vagina outfitted with teeth).

This includes the display of the extended middle finger (*digitus infamis/impudicus*) resembling a phallus, and display of an extended tongue. Objects and gestures *resembling the phallus* also served to counter the Evil Eye. *Lingua* (Latin: "tongue") derives from Sanskrit *lingam* meaning "phallus," thus indicating an association of tongue and phallus, mouth and

---

790. As noted above, pp. 37, 44, 167.

791. See, e.g., Plautus, *Asinaria* 2.4.84, lines 491–493; *Rudens* 2.5.4, lines 458–461; cf. Aulus Gellius, *Attic Nights* 10.24.8 (*praefiscine* and *praefiscini* as equivalent).

genitals.These connections are consistent with the association, mentioned earlier, of *oculus malus* and *mala lingua*, Evil Eye and evil tongue, malicious staring and malicious speaking. Depictions of the head of Medusa/Gorgo, also employed as an anti-Evil Eye apotropaic, include an extended tongue as part of her hideous visage.[792]

(2) The Female Genitals

The female genitalia, the *vulva, cunnus* (Latin) or *kteis* (Greek),[793] also were employed to combat the Evil Eye, though this is attested less frequently than the male phallus.[794] Representations generally entailed an exposed vulva, or a vulva and spread legs—an image, like that of the sheela-na-gig, of which it may be a predecessor, resembling a parturient woman about to give birth.[795] Their function was apotropaic. Cowrie shells, because similar to the vulva in shape, were used as representations of the apotropaic vulva and were worn as amulets.[796] Other objects, because of their similarity in shape to this representation of the vulva and spread legs, were employed for anti-Evil Eye defense. This included sets of bull horns, lunar crescents, horse-shoes, anchors and sheela-na-gigs.[797]

One terracotta figure presents a female sitting on the back of a pig, spreading her legs and exposing her vulva.[798] "Pig" (Greek: *choiros;* Latin,

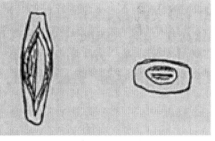

Illus. 29

Sketch of amulets with vulva representations (from Seligmann 1910, 2:285, fig 194) cf. also Jahn 1855, Plate 4, nos. 7 and 8.

792. For Gorgon images, see also in this volume illustrations 3–6, 28, 53.

793. See Gravel 1995:56–59

794. For Latin and Greek designations and symbols of the female genitals see Adams 1982:80–109.

795. Gravel 1995:54–61, 75–89; figs. 15.2–23.4; see also Kirchhoff 1977.

796. Jahn 1855:80; Gravel 1994:110–20. On the symbolism of cowrie shells as apotropaics against the Evil Eye see below, p. 214 and n809, pp. 264–65. On cowrie shells see Murray 1939–1942; Lethbridge 1941. On the cowrie linked with the eye, vulva, fertility and sex-based symbolism see Jeffreys 1942, 1943; Koerper and Whitney-Desautels 1999:86–88. On the sheela-na-gig see Gravel 1995:81–90; Freitag 2004.

797. Gravel 1994:75–89, 118–20 and figs. 16–18.1, 22.1, 22.2, 22.3. Could the replication of this shape in the manual gesture of the *mano cornuta*, along with its reference to "horns" (*cornuta* = "horned"; *corne* = "horns"), suggest that the *mano cornuta* originated as a symbolization of the vulva and spread legs?

798. Seligmann 1910 2:293, fig. 196; cf. also 2:309, fig. 200. The figure is commented on by Jahn 1855:93, who adds, as further illustrations, two small figures of seated naked

porcus) was a vulgarism ("cunt") for the female genitals.[799] The pig (= cunt) in this figure replicates the exposed vulva, and the combination of pig and exposing female does double apotropaic duty. A repeated pose is a representation of a female figure who squats and exposed her vulva.[800] *Cunnus* ("cunt")

Illus. 30
Sketch of a terracotta figure of a woman spreading legs and exposing her vulva while seated on a pig. Figure found in Southern Italy (from Seligmann 2:293, fig. 196. 2:309, fig 200)

Illus. 31
Sketch of an amulet figurine of a woman squatting with spread legs (from Seligmann 1910 2:309, fig. 22)

is related linguistically to Cunina, the name assigned the goddess thought to grant children and to protect infants in their cradle from the Evil Eye/fascination. Figures known as *sheela-na-gigs* (alias *baubo*)[801] also depict females holding open their genital labia in a pose that could symbolize either the female's child-bearing power or the power of her vulva against the Evil Eye and other forces of evil. "Sheela-na-gigs are stone carvings of naked women exposing their genitals . . . with characteristics of both barrenness and fertility," explains Barbara Freitag (2004:3, 8). She argues that "the sheela-na-gig belongs to the realm of folk deities and as such is associated with life-giving powers, birth and death and the renewal of life" (2004:2). The sheela-na-gig

---

women with spread legs (Plate 4, figs. 12, 14) = Seligmann 1910 2:fig. 200.

799. Aristophanes, *Acharnenses* 773–835; cf. *choirothlips*, Aristophanes, *Wasps* 1364; for the Latin see Varro, *De re rustica* 2.4.10; Adam 1982:82.

800. Jahn 1855:47–49 and Plate 4, 12a, b. Jahn (1855:74) thought that this exposure was symbolizing not the fructifying potency of nature but the power of the obscene.

801. On the sheela-na-gig see Gravel 1995:81–90; Freitag 2004. On the baubo see Devereux 1983.

"was regarded as the guarantor of crops, animals and humans. But, in particular, she was the divine assistant at child-birth, who, at the same time, formed a link with the realm of the dead." Freitag knows of research viewing the sheela-na-gig as an anti-Evil Eye apotropaic but does not pursue this point. Gravel explains the sheela-na-gig, "the symbol of a parturient woman" and "fertility effigy" probably originating with the ancient Celts,[802] protected "against the fascination of the Evil Eye."

Illus. 32a
Sketch of a small bronze figurine of woman squatting and exposing her vulva, from Roman Egypt, (from Knight and Wright 1865:137 and Plate XXXI, fig. 4)

Illus. 32b
Sketch of a figurine of a woman exposing her vulva (from Knight and Wright, 1865:137 and Plate XXXI, fig. 5, with no further description)

802. Gravel 1995:81–89 and appendix IV, esp. 81, 88–89.

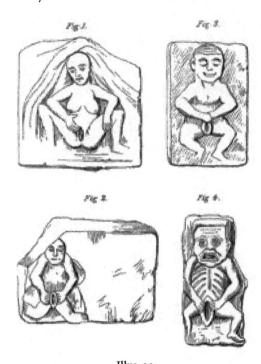

Illus. 33
Four sketches of Sheela-na-gigs from Ireland (from Knight and Wright, 1865, Plate XXIX and p. 133 for indentifications).

Fig. 1: Sheela-na-gig found at Rochestoon church, Tipperery, Ireland, over arch of doorway (from Knight and Wright, 1865, Plate XXIX, fig. 1),

Fig. 2: Sheela-na-gig found at church, County Cavan, Ireland (from Knight and Wright, 1865, Plate XXIX, fig. 2)

Fig. 3: Sheela-na-gig found at Ballinahend Castle. Tipperery, Ireland (from Knight and Wright, 1865, Plate XXIX, fig. 3)

Fig. 4. Sheela-na-gig in Dublin museum, Ireland, origin unknown (from Knight and Wright, 1865, Plate XXIX, fig. 4)

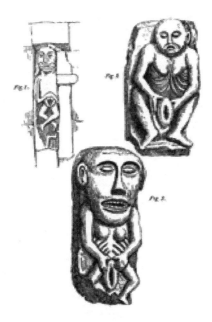

Illus. 34.
Three figures of Sheela-na-gigs gigs from Ireland (from Knight and
Wright 1865, Plate XXX, figs.1–3 and pp. 133–134 for indentifications)

Fig. 1: Sketch of a Sheela-na-gig found in a church on White Island, Lough Erne, County Fermanagh, Ireland (from Knight and Wright 1865, Plate XXX, fig. 1)

Fig. 2. Sketch of a Sheela-na-gig from a razed church, Ireland, and presented to the Dublin museum, Ireland (from Knight and Wright 1865, Plate XXX, fig. 2).

Fig. 3 Sketch of a Sheela-na-gig found 1859 at Chloran, on the estate of Sir. Benjamin Chapman, Killua Castle, Westmeath, Ireland (from Knight and Wright 1865, Plate XXX, fig. 3)

Various representations and symbols of a parturient woman have been associated with sheela-na-gigs and interpreted likewise as protectives against the Evil Eye.[803] An Etruscan depiction of a squatting Gorgo from

803. As stressed by Gravel 1995:75–89. For representations of females spreading their legs (parturient women) see Gravel 1995: figs, 16.1, 16.3, 17.1, 3–7; for analogous images see 18.1, 18. 2; 18.3; 18.4 (ancient Greek anchor amulet), 18.5; 19.6, 8; 38.1; see also Devereux 1983 (on Baubo and the "mythic vulva"). For vulva amulets see also Jahn 1855:79–81, Plate 4, no. 7 (vulva), no. 8 (a coral looking like no. 7); no. 14 (squatting female spreading legs and exposing vulva); Seligmann 1910 2:293 and fig. 196; Winter 1903:197, fig. 6. See also Deonna 1938:93, 94 n8, 100; the Museo Civico Archeologico di Bologna, Room VI (Greek Collection), Case 6B, top: gold frontal figure of woman

Eturia[804] is matched by an Etruscan circular bronze lamp once in the museum of Cortona, Italy, showing a Gorgoneion in the center surrounded on the edge by squatting figures and fish (see above, Illus. 28, p. 208).[805] These appear to be composite apotropaics against the Evil Eye. Objects thought to resemble by their shape the outspread legs of a female included the crescent moon, the horseshoe, the anchor, the bucranium (inverted ox-head), the double-tailed mermaid, and the pentagram.[806] Some amulets combine representations of female and male genitalia to form composite anti-Evil Eye amulets.

Illus. 35

Sketch of an anti-Evil Eye pendant combining depictions of female and male genitalia (from Knight-Wright 1865. Plate XXXIV, fig. 5, identified and described on pp. 146–47)

Stand-in representations of the female genitalia used to avert the Evil Eye also included the fig (*fica*) and cowrie shells, as noted above, and snails,[807] probably because of their similarity in shape to the vulva.[808] The fig (Latin, *fica*, a feminine noun) has heart-shaped leaves thought to resemble the form of the vulva. Roman ritual celebrated the fertilization of Juno Caprotina, goddess of the fig tree, by the lustful, horned goat god (Rose 1959:217). As the phallus was associated with the fig tree, so the vulva was equated with the fig, and sexual intercourse was spoken of delicately as "harvesting figs." Aristophanes's drama *Peace* concludes with a wedding song. As the hero weds his beautiful bride, the chorus sings:

---

sitting with legs spread revealing vulva. Bonner 1950:92–93 describes a red jasper amulet from the Greco-Egyptian period; it appears to be engraved with the figure of a parturient woman seated on a birthing stool.

804. In Gravel 1995, fig. 17.1 (photograph of a bronze plate meant to decorate the front of a chariot). The Etrurian Gorgo is presently in the Pinakothek, Munich.

805. Elworthy 1958/1895:162, fig. 50.

806. See Hidburgh 1942; Gravel 1995:75–79 and figs. 18.1, 18.4, 18.5, 21.1, 22.1, 2, 3 22.3.

807. Jahn 1855, 79–80 and Table 5, no. 6 (shells and an eye of Horus); Seligmann 1910 2, figs. 55, 58.

808. Gravel 1995:119–20 and fig. 15.1; On cowries in Egypt against the Evil Eye, see Vol. 1, chap. 2 on Egypt. On cowries as anti-Evil Eye amulets and as symbols of the eye and the vulva see M. A. Murray 1939. item 165; 1942, item 94, also 1940, items 20, 188, 209; Sheppard 1939; Hornblower 1941, item 81; Lethbridge, 1941, item 37; Meek, 1940, 1941; Walker 1983:182, 294–95, 309, 530; Gravel 1995:119–20.

What shall we do to her?
What shall we do to her?
We shall harvest her;
We shall harvest her.
You shall both live happily,
free from trouble,
picking figs together.
His is large and thick;
Her fig is sweet.[809]
(Aristophanes, *Peace* 1344–1350)

This connection of "fig" and female genitals is apparent in Spanish where *higo* means "fig" and *higa* denotes the female genitalia. In Israel, the rabbis compared a girl's growing sexuality to the ripening of a fig: during childhood she was like an unripe fig; during puberty, like a ripening fig. When she becomes a woman, she is like a fully ripened fig (*m. Niddah* 5:7). This association of genitals and figs likely lies behind the manual gesture of the "fig hand" (*mano fica*) which symbolizes the female vulva as well as the act of sexual intercourse—both warding off the Evil Eye.[810]

Sigmund Freud proposed that the head of Medusa was a monstrous representation of the female genitals, the sight of which causes castration anxiety in the male. Associated in the child's mind with the discovery of maternal sexuality and its denial, it [the Medusa head] has been a powerful amulet providing an image of castration. The snakes on Medusa's head are multiple phalluses; petrifaction represents the comforting erection. "The sight of the Medusa's head makes the spectator stiff with terror, turns him to stone."[811]

(3) Apotropaic Representations of Genitalia

Other images and gestures resembling the male or female genitalia in shape were also employed as apotropaics. A phallus could be symbolized by an extended middle finger (the *digitus infamis/impudicus*), or a vertical pole, or a single verticle drawn line, a single horn (itself a symbol of power), or the nose of the face. For the vulva, there was the similarity of ovular shape

809. See Condit 1947; Buchheit 1960; Reichmann 1969:650–51.

810. For an abstract "ritual symbol" from prehistoric Sicily, which depicts the male phallus (with testicles) penetrating the spread legs and vulva of a standing female, see Gravel 1995, fig. 10.2.

811. Freud, "Das Medusenhaupt" (1922), in *Gesammelte Werke*, ed. A. Freud *et al.* vol. 17:45–48. ET: "Medusa's Head," *Complete psychological works of Sigmund Freud*, ed. J. Strachy. Vol. 18 (1964) 271–74, quotation from p. 273.

linking the vulva with the eye, and the association of vulva and mouth (see the devouring "toothed vagina," the *vagina dentata*).[812] The triad of nose and two eyes, in turn, resembled the phallus and testicles in shape and number; the hair of the eyebrows resembled the pubic hair. Also suggesting a connection of facial parts and genitalia, the liquid from the mouth (spittle) resembled the liquid (semen) of an ejaculating phallus. The manual gestures of hands or fingers symbolized the erect penis ready for penetration, i.e. the phallus (*fascinum, digitus infamis*), the vulva (*fica, mano fica*) or the act of intercourse (*mano fica*).[813]

Amulets having the shape, or bearing representations of, *human genitalia* were also very popular for combating life-threatening forces including the Evil Eye. These genitalic amulets are discussed and illustrated above in relation to manual gestures and the apotropaic use of the genitals.

These apotropaics could provide *defensive protection* in different ways. Primarily they were thought to provide a powerful defense against a powerful attacking Evil Eye by *countering* the Evil Eye's power with power of their own. Or, especially when their size was exaggerated, they could *frighten away* the Evil Eye, as did the hideous head of Medusa (gorgoneion), or frightful masks.[814] Or these amulets could be understood to *arouse ridicule and laughter*, like other apotropaics, and thus *mock and disarm* the Evil Eye and its possessor. Or, if viewed as grotesques, masks might be understood to *attract* the glance of the Evil Eye to themselves, thereby *diverting* it from the human target. Plutarch mentions this theory[815] and Hans Licht incorporates it into his explanation of how phallic amulets worked:

> Of course, the idea was not that 'the eye at once turned way for shame,' but that the 'hostile' eye was so enchanted and fascinated by the sight of the obscene, that it sees only the obscene and for the time being is harmless to everything else. This explains why sexual organs—by preference male—were painted or imitated in plastic art wherever it was thought that the evil eye was especially to be feared. Thus the phallus—often of colossal size—is to be seen almost everywhere; on houses and gates, in public places, on implements in daily use, such as vessels and lamps, on dress and ornaments, on rings, buckles, etc. it was also carried by itself on a handle; it was believed that its effect was sometimes heightened if it was made in the form of an animal, with claws

812. For a Roman lamp handle in vulvate form see John 1982:74, ill. 58.

813. On these associations see also Dundes 1992:276–89.

814. Slane and Dickie (1993:486–94) stress the aggressive significance of the phallus.

815. Plutarch, *Quaest. Conv.* 5.7 [*Mor.* 681F–682A].

and wings, or if lttle bells were attached to it, since the clang of
the metal was considered an effective protection against witchcraft and ghostly beings of every kind. Thus is to be explained
the vogue of the phallic amulet . . .[816]

Another possible explanation is that the *power* of the phallus, as potent
medium of generation, was thought sufficient to counter the power of the
Evil Eye. This included phallus-like objects and gestures such as the *digitus
infamis*. On this principle of "like against like," power against power, the
phallic amulet (as also some other anti-Evil Eye amulets), is deemed not to
attract the glance of the Evil Eye but rather to *repel* it and *drive it off*, as the
term *apotropaic* ("that which drive off") suggests.[817] These understandings
of the working of the Evil Eye were not mutually exclusive but overlapping.
It is fruitless to seek one as "basic."

These genitalic images appear in bas-reliefs or are inscribed on gem-
stones and worn as jewelry; they are employed in plaques affixed to doors
and buildings and in mosaics of door thresholds, as in Pompeii or Ostia Antica or Tunis in North Africa. In Corinth was found a cigar-shaped vase in
the form of a phallus and serving as an unguent container. Its detail shows
it to be an apotropaic against envy and the Evil Eye.[818] A handle of a Roman
terracotta oil lamp (1st century CE) has a vulvate form reresembling the
lips of the vulva and similarly serves to repel the Evil Eye.[819] On the island
of Delos, remains of huge *fascina* line the main thoroughfare of the town.
The genitalic symbols can be employed alone or in combination with one
or more other apotropaic objects or words (e.g. phallus and bells, phallus
against eye, genitalia and accompanying inscriptions).

PROTECTION THROUGH OTHER ACTIONS/GESTURES

As far as *other physical gestures* are concerned, *covering the head* is likely to
have had, as one aim, protection against the Evil Eye.[820] The Christian

---

816. Licht 1932:369–70.

817. Ibid. The discovery of ancient representations of phalluses adorned with eyes
(*phallus oculatus*; Seligmann 1910 2:201 and 281, fig. 193; Perdrizet 1922:31; Deonna
1965:70) has led to a further theory that the eye and the phallus are associated in look
and action. The *singular* Evil Eye (not eyes) was equivalent symbolically to the singular-
ity of the phallus (so Dundes 1992:278–86). Both phallus and eye, moreover, have an
ejaculatory function: phallus ejaculating semen and eye ejaculating ocular rays.

818. Slane and Dickie 1993 on the vase no. C-27-37, Plate 85 (c. second century
CE).

819. Johns 1982:74, illus. 58 (London, British Museum, Greek and Roman, Q1025).

820. See Euripides, *Iphigenia in Taurus* 1217–1218; also Virgil, *Aen.* 3.405–407

church father Tertullian encouraged the veiling of Christian women as protection against the Evil Eye.[821]

The posture of bending over and *displaying the bared buttocks* to a potential Evil Eye possessor (known today as "mooning" someone) or the figure of a squatting *homo cacans* ("shitting man"), as in the Woburn Abbey Marble Evil Eye relief, according to Elworthy (1895/1958:138) also had the purpose of protecting against, or directing defiant insult at, the Evil Eye. In this relief, a figure wearing a Phrygian cap and squatting with his back to the spectator, sits on and exposes his bare buttocks to an Evil Eye attacked by a coterie of creatures.[822] The figure illustrates the comment of Pomponius (*Atellanae fabulae* 129) in Nonius: "Everyone knows that those who shit squatting are numerous" (*Hoc sciunt omnes, quantum est qui cossim cacant*).[823] The connection of defecation and evil is illustrated by a painting at Pompeii next to a latrine. It depicts a squatting man in defecating position between two upright serpents and alongside a figure of the goddess Isis affording protection. The inscription above the man reads: "shitter, beware the

Illus. 36
Homo cacans ("shitting man") wearing a Phrygian cap sitting on an Evil Eye- -a detail of the Woburn Abbey Marble (see below, Illus. 47) (from Elworthy 1958/1895:137, fig. 24)

Evil Eye" (*cacator cave malum*).[824] Could it be that an open anus was feared to be a vulnerable port of entry for forces of evil, hence the protection of the latrine or outhouse with an image of an apotropaic crescent moon? Defecation itself, on the other hand, Dundes argues, was thought to be a means by which the Evil Eye was blinded or repudiated and defiled.[825] Gravel (1995:94), representing a different view, interprets this squatting figure as a woman giving birth in the conventional crouching position and presenting a conventional, but different, anti-Evil Eye apotropaic.

---

where covering the head protects against the Evil Eye [*hostilis facies*] of the stranger.

821. Tertullian, *Virg. vel.* 15, PL 2.959. On this text see Vol. 4, chap. 2.

822. For the complete illustration, see below p. 236 Illus. 47. See also Jahn 1855:30 and Pl. 3, no. 1 (the Woburn Marble); Plate 4, no. 11; Elworthy 1958/1895:137, fig. 24 and 138–41; Deonna 1965:180.

823. Pomponius, *Atellanae* 129 in Nonius, *De Comp.* 1. 191. On the "squatting shitters" (*cossim cacantes*) see also Deonna 1938:361–62.

824. Magaldi 1931:97; cf. Dundes 1992:289; now in the Naples Archaeological Museum (14673176079).

825. Dundes 1992:289–90.

Smearing infants with mud had the aim of safeguarding them from the Evil Eye. The church father John Chrysostom (344–407 CE) inveighed against the custom of midwives, nurses, and female slaves of trying to protect their infants from the Evil Eye at the baths by using mud from the bottom of the bath and smearing it with their middle finger on the foreheads of children: "it [the smearing of mud], they say, drives away the envious Evil Eye."[826] This procedure, Chysostom charges, compromises their having been sealed with the cross by the priest at their baptisms, which alone suffices for protection.[827] This procedure is still practiced in modern time in areas of Greece[828] and Tunisia.[829] On the notion of *simulating a change of sex to confuse* an Evil Eye see Crooke 1913 and Spoer 1926.

PROTECTION THROUGH AMULETS

(1) Definition of Amulet and Terminology

An especially important and popular form of apotropaics are objects known as amulets. Amulets are a subset of apotropaics. An "apotropaic" (Greek: *apotropaion*) means, literally, "that which drives away," from Greek *apotrephein*, "to drive away." As distinguished from apotropaic spoken words, physical gestures, and actions, amulets are material objects made of a wide range of materials considered to have inherent power, and are used to defend against evil of all kinds. An amulet has been defined as "any object which by its contact or close proximity to the person who owns it or to any possession of his, exerts power for his good, either by keeping evil from him and his property or by endowing him with positive advantages."[830] Amulets have been discovered in the ancient world and especially Egypt that date as early as 4000 BCE.[831] Found in all areas of the Circum-Mediterranean and Near East, they number in the hundreds of thousands. They constituted an important and valued item of cultural exchange among Mesopotamians, Egyptians, Greeks and Romans, Israelites and Christians and were used to protect both the living and the dead.

---

826. John Chrysostom, *Hom. 1 Cor.* 12:13 (PG 61.106): *ophthalmon apostrephei, phêsi, kai baskanian kai phthonon.*

827. *Ibid.* See Jahn 1855:82.

828. Jahn 1855:82 n223.

829. Teitelbaum 1976:64.

830. Bonner 1950:2.

831. Pinch 1994:112.

Amulets are objects believed to possess extraordinary power for warding off evil forces, curses, harm of any kind including an Evil Eye and for attracting good fortune for the possessor. Some power (*mana*), quality, virtue, or efficacy enables amulets, so it is believed, to counteract or ward off evil forces. Amulets are employed for both defensive and acquisitive ends. Personal amulets are generally small in size and portable so as to be worn, or attached openly or covertly, on the human body, or attached to the bodies of prized livestock and domestic animals or to any valued object.

Several terms for amulets indicate their use and intended function. "Amulet" itself derives from the Latin *am[m]uletum* (pl. *amuleta*)[832] or possibly *amoletum/amolitum*.[833] Its function, as is indicated by the synonym *phylacterium* transliterating the Greek *phylaktêrion,* is to *guard* or *protect*.[834] "What the Greeks call *phylaktêrion,*" the grammarian Charisius commented, "we call *amuletum* in Latin" (*Ars Grammatica* 1.105.9). If the term derives from *amoletum/amolitum*, it would designate an object designed to *repel* or *avert*, akin to the term *apotropaion* discussed below. Pliny classifies as *amuleta* a brand of wine used as an amulet (*NH* 23.20), spitting on the urine one has voided (*NH* 28.38), and basilisk's blood as a cure for illness and amulet against sorcery" (*NH* 29.66). Suetonius records that Augustus Caesar was frightened by thunder and lightening, "against which he always carried a piece of seal-skin as an amulet" (*Augustus* 90). Most frequently, amulets were objects that were *bound to,* or *tied on* the body, and whose function was to defend against and neutralize evil potencies, including the Evil Eye. This is indicated by the Greek words for amulets: *perierga, periammata, periapta* (from *periaptein,* "to tie on, bind"), or in Latin: *ligaturae, alligaturae* ("things bound" [to the body], from *ligare,* "to bind").[835] The most frequent term in the rabbinic literature for amulet is *kemia,* also meaning "that which is tied on, attached," from the Aramaic *km'* ("to tie on, attach"). "The tall,

---

832. Pliny, *NH* 29.66; 30.138; Charisius, *Ars Grammatica,* 1.105.9; CGL 1.134.3. On the etymology and use of "amulet," "talisman," "charm" etc. see Skemer 2006:1–19.

833. So Luck 1985:19, from *molior,* "repel," "avert."

834. From the verb *phylassein,* "to protect." *Phylaktêria* (plural), small leather cases worn by devout Israelite males on their heads and left arms when praying, contained slips of parchment on which lines of the Torah were written (Matt 23:5). Pliny uses *amuletum* frequently (*NH* 23.20; 25.115; 28.38; 29.66, 83; 30.82, 183; 37. 51, 117) and always in the sense of a protective device. Other synonyms for *amuletum* include *praebia* (Varro, *Ling. lat.* 7.107), *ligatura, alligatura* (Pliny, *NH passim*).

835. See Aelian, *Nat. an.* 12.7 regarding an amulet (*periaptôn*) against being Evil-Eyed (*baskênête*). *Adalligare* also has the sense of "make amulets of" (Pliny, *NH* 30.6.21; 30.30.100) and "bind on as an amulet" (Pliny *NH* 30.6.20; 30.8.26; 30.12.39; 30.20.60, 62; 30.30.101; 30.47.139; 30.47.141 etc.).

indented horns of the scarab beetle," Pliny notes (*NH* 30.47.138), fastened (*adalligata*) to babies serves as an amulet (*amuleti*)."

The Greek word *apotropaion* ("apotropaic"), a general term for anything that "drives away" evil and harm, could also designate an amulet in particular.[836] An apotropaic or amulet designed *for warding off the Evil Eye* was called, more specifically, a *baskanon, baskanion, probaskanon,* or *probaskanion,* or in Latin a *fascinus or fascinum. Talisman,* another generic term for such powerful objects, "could be an Arabic transformation of Greek *telesma,* 'initiation'" (Luck 1985:19).[837] When talismans are distinguished from amulets, the purpose of the *amulet* is to protect while that of the *talisman* is to enhance a quality of the wearer and attract prosperity and good luck (Pinch 1994:105). *Characteres* were amulets with symbols inscribed or written on them. Amulet collections are found in many public museums, as well as in university and private collections.

(2) Production and Materials of Amulets

Amulets were produced and sold by specialists who made them "according to traditional recipes and consecrated them through ritual acts, thereby endowing them with effective power."[838] Amulets consisted of various materials and were given various forms. Folklorist Karl Meisen (1950) lists and discusses minerals, plants, animals, birds, fish, insects, and fabulous creatures, all of which were enlisted to attack and repel the the Evil Eye.[839] The minerals include stones (with or without inscribed designs or expressions) such as amber, bloodstone, hamitite;[840] metals (gold, silver, bronze, iron, copper, lead); and corals (with shapes resembling the female genitalia). Plants included especially those with strong smell, taste, or vivid color such as garlic, rue, and dill.[841] Animals and animal parts (teeth, horn, claws) included especially powerful, dangerous creatures such as the bear, bull, ram, buck, elephant, hippopotamus, wolves, jackels, and snakes/vipers. Birds included the owl, eagle, raven, crow, stork, ibis, swan, and rooster. Other

836. See also the synonym *apôsikakos,* "repelling evil."

837. See classical Greek *tetelesmenon,* perfect past participle of the verb *telein* ("to consecrate").

838. Gager 1992:219. On the the preparation of amulets see Delatte 1961; Wageman 1987.

839. See also the even more extensive lists of Seligmann 1910, 1922.

840. On stones and engraved amulets, see Delatte and Derchain 1964; Halleux and Schamp 1985.

841. See Jahn 1855:106; Seligmann 1910:2:49–112, 1:296–97 (cimaruta amulets); Delatte 1961.

creatures associated with amulets included frogs, fish, scorpions, crabs; insects (ants, bees, flies, circadians, scarabs, locusts); and fabulous creatures (basilisk, *katoblepon*/Gorgo, griffen, sphinx). Images of many of these creatures were depicted on coins, gems, lamps, stones, etc.

Material for amulets also included faience, parchment and papyrus, powerful formulas and verses from sacred texts; leather phylacteries tied to the human body (Israel), pendants, bracelets, rings, arrangements of powerful numbers and symbols; and representations of sacred images (Israel: menorah, shield of David/pentagram; seal of Solomon and Solomon on horseback; Christianity: the cross, saints on horseback). Amulets often were embossed or engraved with apoptropaic images and with inscriptions indicating the owner and intent of the amulet. On amulets were also drawn images or symbols of the gods and of humans; representations of human genitalia and other anatomical parts (eye, teeth, nails, hair, blood); powerful names and words (*carmina, epôidai, logoi dynameôs, Ephesia grammata*); and potent designs (e.g. swastika, Eye attacked, genitalia, cavaliers attacking demons). Amulets worn on the body were of smaller size and often doubled as ornamentation and jewelry, such as engraved or embossed rings,[842] bracelets, pendants, *bullae,* and colored ribbons/threads. Amulets of various sizes were deployed as figures and frescos at strategic locations: entrances to homes (plaques) and at door thresholds (mosaics); in workshops, fields and gardens, public spaces, temples, shrines, tombs, graves and other locales involving valuable property.

Most manufactured amulets had loops or eyelets that allowed them to be hung on necklaces and worn around the neck. Others were enclosed in a container or pouch or capsule made of metal or leather and known as a *bulla,* which was suspended from a necklace. Such *bullae* were worn by Roman youth until they reached their majority. These *bullae* could also contain thin strips of metal (gold, silver, bronze, lead), leather, papyrus or parchment inscribed with powerful words or formulas. *Carmina* (lit. "songs," from which "charms" derives) and *cantationes/praecantiones* ("enchantments," lit. "songs") were intoned forms of protection but could also be written down and likewise worn in *bullae* around the neck.[843] Amulets also were worn on the head or bound on the left arm, or thigh. They included threads of string

Illus. 37
Sketch of a gold *bulla* worn by wealthy Roman youth (from Seligmann 1910 2:313, fig. 202)

842. On rings see W. Jones 1877.

843. On incantations see Kotansky 1991.

colored blue or red tied around the wrist, earrings, pendants with incised stones, engraved rings and bracelets, and all forms of jewelry, whose first function was to protect and then secondarily to adorn. Geraldine Pinch's observation (1994:105) that "[m]ost Egyptian jewelry had amuletic value" applies to ancient jewelry across the cultures. In fact, it is likely that it was from the wearing of amulets that the use of jewelry originated.[844] Protection led to ornamentation. In the Bible, amulets are included in the luxury and jewelry catalogue of Isaiah 3:18–23.[845] The term "amulet" could also be used more generally for protectives (whether worn or not) against any kind of harm.[846]

(3) Taxonomies of Amulets

Various taxonomies of amulets have been proposed. Ernst von Dobschütz, for example, classified "charms" (i.e. apotropaics in general) according to *function*:

A. Defensive charms: (1) prophylactic, (2) counter-charms; (3) curative charms; (4) charms for detecting cause;

B. Productive charms: (5) assuring fertility in family and animals; (6) regulating the weather; (7) assuring safety of birth and continued health of children; (8) love-charms for attracting or harming lovers and ex-lovers.

C. Malevolent Charms (9) tablets for cursing others; charms to injure opponents in horse races; charms causing illness and death.
He also distinguished types of apotropaics: things, actions, and words.[847]

W. M. F. Petrie (1914) divided the 275 types known to him into five large classes for which he coined the terms *homopoeic, dynatic, ktematic, phylactic,* and *theophoric*. Amuletic power, he suggested,was attributed to a *similarity in form,* which linked living creatures to each other (*homopoeic*) or which linked inanimate objects to persons (*dynatic*) or to *possessions* of living persons or to funerary goods for the deceased (*ktematic*). Amuletic power also was attributed to objects affording *protection* (*phylactic*); or to objects in the shape of *deities* or their animal manifestations (*theophoric*).

844. So Daremberg-Saglio 1.1 (1877):252–58, *s.v.* "*amuletum*"; Riess,"Amulett," in Pauly-Wissowa 1:1986; Deubner 1910:438; Hermann 2002:5–6. On ring amulets see Budge 1978/1930:291–305.

845. See Isa 3:20 (*wehallehasim*). On jewelry, see Higgins 1961; Wilkinson 1971.

846. So Deubner 1910:434.

847. Dobschütz 1910:413–30. For a similar classification of Hebrew amulets according to purpose see Schrire 1982:50 (beneficial and benedictory; promotion of health; against the Evil Eye; prevention of miscarriages; promotion of fertility; protection of mother and child at birth).

Many amulets were of the "all purpose" variety and meant to counter an entire range of injuries and illnesses, which could also include those caused by an Evil Eye. Among the more than 2,000 amulets listed by Petrie, for example, are several he specifically identified as anti-Evil Eye amulets.[848]

(4) The Use of Amulets

Such taxonomies register the fact that amulets have served a range of purposes: to provide defense against all forms of harm, injury, and disaster; to drive off evil demons;[849] to protect against the Evil Eye, illness of all sorts and to assure health and prosperity; to protect against storms, lightning, drought, poisonous animals, vermin, and hostile rulers; to effect the elimination of rivals in business and love; to compel the affection of a desired lover; to assure success in labor and business; and to gain victory in athletic contests and the battlefield. Amulets were employed by persons in all levels of society, not only by the "simple" and "uneducated" of the lower class, but by one and all, elites and commoners alike.[850] Reputable physicians like the renowned Galen, in fact, prescribed the use of amulets "even while denying traditional explanations for their success" (Gager 1992:221). Iamblichus in his theurgical treatise *On the Mysteries of the Egyptians* shows how widespread and conventional the use of amulets was. Pliny devotes an entire book (book 28) of his *Natural History* to hundreds of apotropaic strategies and amulets.

Protective amulets in particular were employed and deployed to safeguard all that was deemed valuable and vulnerable to the forces of evil and harm: oneself, one's children and other family members, residences, furniture, domestic animals, gardens, fields, workshops, implements of daily life, clothes, shield and weapons, entire towns, gates, public buildings, sanctuaries, altars, graves and the dead themselves.[851] In general, they were used to control one's fate; assure one's health, success, and prosperity; guard one's children, family, and possessions; and to be successful in love, on the stage,

848. Petrie 1914:11, 16, 27, 28, 29: No. 13 (p. 11) a *mano fica* "a fist, thumb between first and second fingers"; No. 16 (p. 11) a phallus, solely Greco-Roman and not used by Egyptians; No. 104 (p. 26) a horn; No. 106 (p. 27) a coral; No. 107 (p. 27) a Cypraen shell against the Evil Eye and witchcraft; No. 111 (p. 27) a Cardium Edule Shell, "prehistoric to VI dynasty of Egypt" (2190 BCE); No. 114 (p. 27) a Pectunculus Violacesceus shell; No. 124 (p. 28) a bell; No. 128 (p. 28) a Medusa head (but not identified by Petrie as against the Evil Eye); No. 130 (p. 29) a forehead pendant.

849. PGM 4.2625.7; Clement of Alexandria, *Protrepticus* 11, 115.

850. Gager 1992:220–22.

851. Deubner 1910:438.

in athletic competition, and war. Amulets provide us a poignant indication of what possessions people prized, what they thought vulnerable, which forces they deemed powerful, and which forces they feared.

(5) The Potency and Effectiveness of Amulets

The *maladies* against which protection was sought included demon possession, fever, illness of all kinds, wounds, sudden death, fire, drought, and attacks of robbers, in addition to harm from an Evil Eye.[852] A silver amulet safeguarded a certain Syntyche against a host of disorders, including "all spirits," "every falling sickness," "every hydrophobia," violent demonic attack, and the "Evil Eye" (*ton baskanon ophthalmon*).[853] The amulet illustrates how the Evil Eye was considered a cause of illness.[854] Votive amulets are traceable to the Egyptian belief that anything left in a shrine or temple by a grateful patient (e.g. votive replicas of healed body parts) had prophylactic power.[855] The Greek healing cult of Asclepius continued the votive tradition, and it was adopted also in Greek Orthodox Christian tradition.

Increasing the size of the amulet, or the number of amulets, or the number of symbols on a given amulet, increased the amount of protective power.[856] *Composite amulets* combined two or more symbols or potencies in one amulet, such as combining eyes with phalluses, or phalluses with noise-making bells, or a phallus with a *mano fica,* or an Eye of Horus colored red or blue.[857] Necklaces could combine a variety of images. Further aspects of composite amulets include the addition of color (especially blue or red), speaking or writing accompanying words, observing specific rituals,[858] or also touching, licking, or kissing the amulet.[859]

852. Dobschütz 1910:416.

853. Once in the Louvre (Inv. no. Bj 87), this amulet is now lost but described by Kotansky 1991:119.

854. On this amulet see also above, p. 150.

855. Luck 1985:137.

856. Potts 1982:49–59 makes this point in connection with the hundred eyes of legendary Argus, constructor of Jason's ship the Argo (1982:49). The many-eyed beads and multiple pairs of Eyes of Horus or several eyes on vases etc. illustrate the same thought.

857. See the illustrations of Hovorka-Kronfeld 1, 20, Fig. 17; Labatut 1877:252, fig. 310.

858. See Pliny *NH* 26.93; 24.172.

859. Kropatscheck 1907:19.

Illus. 38
Sketch of a necklace *composite* amulet with, *inter
alia*, eye beads, replicas of a *mano fica*, genitalia
images, *homo cacans*, personified envy strangling
itself, and other anti-Evil Eye figures (from
Seligmann 1910 1:305, fig. 52)

The potency and effectiveness of amulets was assessed by their perceived success in warding off evil and misfortune, sustaining health, causing lovers' hearts to melt, and keeping children and loved ones, animals and crops, safe from harm. Amulets were thought to work according to the principles of sympathy and antipathy as expressed in the notion of *similia similibus* ("like influenced by like," "like against like," but also "like cured by like")—power against power, power neutralizing power, power reversing power. The preparation of amulets presumed an association of objects with specific bodily organs, connections of one bodily organ with another, and a belief that illness and injury can be prevented or reversed by powerful words, gestures, herbs, prayer and other actions, and transferred from the body to another object. The notion of sympathy and *similia similibus* is a fundamental principle of homeopathy, a medical practice given scientific expression in the eighteenth century by Dr. Samuel Hahnemann (1755–1843). Homeopathy treats illnesses with remedies consisting of minute doses of substances that produce symptoms similar to the disease or illness. It is based on the natural law of healing: "*similia similibus curantur*," "likes are cured by likes." An illness is cured by those remedies that produce effects resembling the sickness itself. It is the principle also behind the modern medical procedure of inoculation—exposing a body to weakened viruses of a disease that trigger the production of antibodies, which then counter that disease. Pliny the Elder shows how this thinking was current in his time (first century CE). The spleen of sheep or dogs, he observes, is employed to heal human spleens (*NH* 30.51–52). Amulets made from the right foot on a eagle relieve pains on the right side of humans and those from the eagle's left foot relieve pains on the left foot of humans (*NH* 30.54). "The right eye of a frog hung round the neck [of a human] in a piece of untied cloth cures ophthalmia in the right eye; the left eye, similarly tied, cures ophthalmia in the left . . . An amulet of crab's eyes, also worn around the neck, is said to cure ophthalmia" (Pliny, *NH* 32.73). Israelites, reckoning in similar fashion, sought protection against poisonous serpents, the biblical book of Numbers indicates, by fastening a bronze image of a poisonous serpent to a pole and raising it for people to look at and thereby stay safe (Num 21:4–9).[860]

Accordingly, for amulets, and other apotropaics against an Evil Eye in particular, a powerful eye or a representation of a Gorgo/Medusa with frightening eyes and visage, was used to counter a malicious and envious Eye. An Israelite text, the pseudepigraphic *Testament of Solomon*, presumes this same sympathetic principle for neutralizing the Evil Eye in particular. The thirty-fifth of thirty-six astrological decans of the zodiac identifies himself to Solomon with the words,

> I am called Ryx Phtheneoth ("Lord Envy").[861] I Evil-Eye (*bas-kainô*) every human being. My power is annulled by the graven image of the much-suffering eye (*ho polypathês ophthalmos*). (*Testament of Solomon* 18:39)[862]

Eye safeguards against eye. Other amulets presumed the same principle and entailed using the same objects for defense that were thought to cause the harm in the first place. As objects imbued with power, amulets could compel, frighten, distract, avert, counteract, ridicule, demean, defeat, or destroy forces of evil and the menacing Evil Eye.

Amulets, as already noted, are sometimes distinguished from talismans in terms of their different purposes. Amulets protect; talismans enhance a quality of the wearer or promote success and good luck.[863] Over time, articles once designed to protect against the Evil Eye and other forces of evil became ornaments, with their primary function shifting from protection to adornment and the original apotropaic use fading from memory.[864]

860. This apotropaic practice and its report in the Bible lies behind the Christian association of Jesus Christ on the cross with saving power in John 3:14–15: "As Moses lifted up the serpent in the wilderness [cf. Num 21:8–9], so must the Son of Man be lifted up so that whoever trusts in him may have eternal life."

861. *Rhyx* likely reflects *rex* (Latin for "lord"), as *Phtheneoth* reflects *phthonos* (Greek for "envy").

862. On this text see Duling 1993 and Vol. 4, chap. 1. On the principle of sympathy and its continued assumption in Jewish culture of the Middle Ages see Trachtenberg 1970:124–31.

863. Pinch 1994:105.

864. On Greek amulets and various amulet collections around the world see

(6) Anti-Evil Eye Amulets

Anti-Evil Eye *amulets*, as distinguished from anti-Evil Eye physical gestures and actions (uttering words, making manual gestures, spitting, covering the head etc.) that we have previously discussed, are amulets directed against the Evil Eye in particular, while also defending against evil forces more generally.[865] Their purpose was to avert, repel, ward off, defend against, counteract, neutralize, or divert the Evil Eye glance, or incapacitate the Evil Eye possessor. The German ophthalmologist Siegfried Seligmann in his milestone study, *Der böser Blick* (1910), presents the most extensive list of protective strategies and devices (*Schutzmittel*) against the Evil Eye.[866] Our list here is

---

Kropatscheck 1907; Deubner 1910; L. Robert 1981 (responding to Bonner 1950). For amulets from Hellenistic Egypt and Greece see especially Delatte and Derchain 1964 (526 items). This collection includes, beside that of Armand Delatte (up to 193 items), the donated collections of Wilhelm Froehner (1925), of Gustave Schlumberger (1929), and of Adrien Blanchet (1945). On the Frohener collection see Hellmann 2006.

865. On Greek and Roman, Jewish and Christian amulets, including anti-Evil Eye amulets and illustrations, see Jahn 1855 and Plates 3–5; Labatut 1877:252–58 and figs. 300–314, 1910; Tylor 1890, 1891; Rodkinson 1893; Riess 1894; Elworthy 1895/1958 (99 illustrations); Lafaye 1896; Perdrizet 1900, 1903, 1922; Wilken 1900–1901; Winter 1903 vol. 2; Reitzenstein 1904:291–303; Germer-Duran 1906; see also Hildburgh 1906, 1908, 1913, 1942, 1944, 1946, 1951a, 1951b; Kropatschek 1907; Leclercq 1907: esp. cols. 1843–47; Kuhnert 1909 (*fascinum*); Deubner 1910:392–472 ("charms and amulets"); Gaster 1910; Freire-Marreco 1910; von Dobschütz 1910; Kennedy 1910; Naville 1910; Seligmann 1910 (240 illustrations), 1922, 1927; Thompson 1910; Wünsch 1910, 1911; Elworthy 1912:613–614 (lists fifteen Sicilian amulets against *jettatura* exhibited by Pitré at the 1903 Palermo exhibition) among many amulets of other cultures (611–15); Bellucci 1912 (c. 3,000 amulets ancient and modern); Petrie 1914; Laarss 1919; Deiss-mann 1923:160–61; 1927:48, 193, 260, 284, 405; Pfister 1927; Villiers 1927; Budge 1930/1978; Leclercq 1936:1936–41; Row 1938; Marques-Riviere 1938; Merlin 1940; Bonner 1950; Eckstein-Waszink 1950; Meisen 1950:145–77 (Christian: 157–77), Meisen 1952 (Middle Ages); Ratschow 1957; Delatte and Derchain 1964:72–73, 261–264, nos. 369–77; Hansmann and Kriss-Rettenbeck 1966; Engemann 1975, 1980, 1981; Neveron 1978; Robert 1981 (responding to Bonner 1950); Dunbabin and Dickie 1983; Walker 1983:117, 182, 294–95, 309, 530; Schienerl 1984; Faraone 1987, 1991, 2013; Naveh and Shaked 1987; Wagemann 1987:xxxiv–xxxv (eye as fertility symbol and Evil Eye as symbol of fear of unproductivity); Zarzalejos et al. 1988; Bernand 1991:102–103; Dunbabin 1991; Kotansky 1991, 1994, 1995. 2002; Parnell and Olsan 1991 (classification of charms); Gager 1992:218–42; Del Hoyo and Vázquez Hoys 1996; Dickie 2000:304–11; Corti 2001; González-Wippler 2001; Seara 2002; Bailliot 2010. Jude Hill 2007 reports on the amulet collection of British folklorist Edward Lovett. On the many books concerning the preparation of amulets see A. Dellate, *Hebarius*, 3rd ed. 1961; Halleux and Schamp 1985; Wageman 1987. For depictions of amulets see also the *Lexicon Iconographicum Mythologiae Classicae* (15 vols., 1981–1997). On medieval European charms (900–1500) see the research project outlined by Parnell Olsan 1991.

866. Seligmann 1910 2:3–416. He stresses the huge number of amulets found over time, noting that the Italian Joseph Belluci collected more than four thousand

limited to the most prominent of the *ancient* anti-Evil Eye amulets, and cites evidence and scholarly discussions dating beyond Seligmann's publication to the present.

Their Operation

Anti-Evil Eye amulets were thought to operate in the same manner as amulets in general, as described above. Plutarch, in his *Table Talk* concerning the Evil Eye (*Quaest. Conv.* 5.7.3 [*Mor.* 681F]), offered one explanation from a "native's" point of view. He mentions "the kind of anti-Evil Eye amulets (*to tôn legomenôn probaskaniôn genos*)" that are thought to protect against being struck by another's envy (*phthonon*) or Evil Eye: "Their strange look attracts the attention of the [Evil] Eye (*tês opseôs*), so that it exerts less force upon its victims." The glance of the Evil Eye possessor, in other words, is diverted away from the intended human target and is attracted instead to the amulet worn. Elworthy stressed this attraction function of anti-Evil Eye amulets.[867] The amulets designed for diverting and attracting the Evil Eye's glance, he noted, were worn on the outside of one's clothing and were openly exposed to view. Among these he included grotesque figures which aroused curiosity or laughter, the hideous head of the Gorgo/Medusa, engraved masks, images of male and female genitalia, *fascina*, and the *mano fica*. Deformed figures such as the hunchback/gobbo would also fit this intention due to their perceived strangeness.

It is likely, however, that many forms of anti-Evil Eye amulets were designed not to attract but to *drive away, ward off, repel the Evil Eye* through their power which was thought superior to that of the menacing eye—hence their designation as *apotropaic* (i.e. something that *drives away*).[868] Depiction of eyes, of the Gorgo and her bulging orbs, and especially of (Evil) eyes under attack, would fall into this category and would be intended to neutralize and repel an Evil Eye with a power that is similar but superior. This homeopathic principle of similarity, "like influences like," is expressed by Israel's pseudepigraphic writing, the *Testament of Solomon* (18:39), as indicated on p. 227.

Images of genitalia, of hideous Gorgo/Medusa heads, of the Egyptian deity Bes, or of hunchbacks would likewise be understood as exerting a power that frightens off and drives away the Evil-Eyeing glance.

---

anti-Evil eye amulets and displayed them at the 1889 Paris exhibition; see also Elworthy 1895/1958 and its 98 illustrations of amulets.

867. Elworthy 1895/1958:143–57.

868. See Jahn 1855:67, 91–92.

The principle of "like influences like" (and sympathy-antipathy) finds linguistic expression in the terms for Evil Eye and anti-Evil Eye objects. Thus the Greek term *baskanon* functions ambiguously to denote both (a) a malignant Evil-Eyeing person (masculine.accusative singular) and (b) a beneficial anti-Evil Eye apotropaic (neuter nominative singular). This is equally true of the diminuatives *baskanion* and *probaskanion*. This is similar to the ambiguity of the term *pharmakon,* which can designate both (a) a harmful drug or poison (Homer, *Odyssey* 10.210–213), or (b) a healing herb and antidote (Homer, *Odyssey* 10.290–292), depending on context. Similarly a "charm" (*carmen*) is a song that (a) can harm or that (b) can prevent harm (=counter-charm, incantation).

Eyes and Eye-Like Objects

Among the amulets employed against the Evil Eye, representations and *symbols of the eye and of eye-like objects* were among the most prominent. The understanding that the eye was both an organ of power and an instrument of aggression made it a potent weapon against the Evil Eye and ocular malice. Amulets of stone, glass, wood and metal were shaped like eyes or were embossed or engraved with eyes and eye-like images.[869] Images of eyes

Illus. 39
Three Egyptian eye (with blue irises) amulets
(upper left), State Hermitage Museum, Egyptian
Section, St. Petersburg, Russia (Photo by John H.
Elliott)

869. On eye amulets against the Evil Eye and illustrations see Jahn 1855:63–66; Elworthy 1958/1895:126–42; Seligmann 1910 2:144–64 and figures 85–116, 118–25, 127–44, 191, 230–33. Seligmann (1910 2:151–54) adds fourteen new specimens to those presented by Jahn. See also Budge 1978/1930:89 (Plate 6, no.6); 141–42, 174; Koenig 1975; Gravel 1995:91–100 and figs. 8.1, 8.2, 8.3, 8.6, 12.2, 13.1, 13.2, 14.1, 14.2, 14.4, 39.2; Pinch 1994:109 (fig. 56), 111 (fig. 57).

also adorned jewelry, finger rings, shields, helmuts, weapons, and coins. They were drawn on walls of tombs, residences, and public buildings. The oldest examples of apotropaic eyes may go back to the Egyptian Pyramid texts of the Old Kingdom (twenty-fourth to twenty-second centuries BCE).[870] A rare replica of what could be a human eye, free- standing, and blue in color, is displayed in the Egyptian section of the State Hermitage Museum, St. Petersburg, Russia. The popular Egyptian *wedjat/udjat* represented the powerful Eye of Horus (an eye combined with a wing of a falcon, emblem of the falcon god Horus). Eye of Horus amulets made in varying shapes, sizes and colors were highly popular as amulets not only in Egypt but throughout the ancient Mediterranean region and long into the Greco-Roman period.[871] Beads with likely representations of eyes have been found

Illus. 40
Sketches of Eye of Horus amulets from Sardinia
(from Seligmann 1910 2:133, fig. 132)

in Egypt as early as the thirteenth century BCE. Such "eye beads" were combined with other anti-Evil Eye symbols and worn on necklaces for Evil Eye protection.[872] These eye beads may be the predecessors of the seemingly omnipresent blue glass eye replicas that appear everywhere today in Greece, Turkey, Syria, Malta, and Mediterranean regions. They can be seen in shops, offices, on automobiles, trucks, taxis, and buses as well as on boats and ships. The power of the eye is intensified by the apotropaic color blue.

870. Rakoczy 1996:144 n476.

871. On the wedjat/udjat Eye of Horus and the Horus myth see, previously, Vol. 1, chap. 2. For further illustrations of the udjat see Elworthy 1958/1895:126 (fig. 10); Seligmann 1910 2, figs. 127–32; Hermann 2002:48–54, 85–91, 111–12, 115, 150–51.

872. See Potts 1982:22–25 and for illustrations, figs. 35–44; also, earlier, Jahn 1855, Plate 5, no.2.

It was customary also to paint apotropaic eyes on the prows of boats and ships not just so that they can see their way, but also to protect their cargoes from envious Evil Eye attack.[873] The practice is traceable to Egyptian custom,[874] where eyes on boats are attested since the fifteenth century BCE. Several vignettes from the *Book of the Dead* (c. 1420–c. 1100 BCE) show multiple Egyptian vessels with eyes on their prows.[875] At Ostia Antica/Portus, an early seaport of Rome, a bas-relief (second to third century CE) shows a merchant ship entering Ostia, with statues of gods galore and a smaller ship already in the harbor. A large eye appears in the lower right section of the relief, with no relation to the figures of the picture. It was likely added to the scene to protect the ships, their cargos and the commercial undertaking, from any lurking Evil Eyes.[876] Its function paralleled that of the eyes painted on ship prows. This maritime practice continues in modern time.

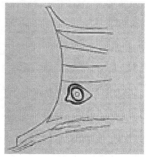

Illus. 41

Sketch of a representation of an eye on the prow of Ulysses' ship (from Seligmann 1910, 2:71, fig. 105)

873. Aeschylus, *Supplices* 716 (*kai prôra prosthen ommasi blepous' hodon*); and Philostratus, *Imagines* 19.3.793 (*blousyroisi de kata prôran ophthalmois hoion blepei*) regarding a pirate ship. See also IG 2².1607.24; Pollux, *Onom.* 1.86; Jahn 1855:63; Torr 1896; Seligmann 1910:2:150–51 and figures 105–116; Hornell 1923, 1924, 1938; Marrion 1968, 1980, 1996; Morrison and Williams 1968; Moreau 1976/77 50–51; Morrison 1980, 1996; Cavendish 1983:891; Johns 1982:80, ill. 62 (black figure cup showing Dionysos in a ship on whose prow is an eye); Rakoczy 1996:144–45 n476 In the Bardo National Museum, Tunis, Tunisia, is a mosaic of a trireme with an eye on its prow. On ancient ships and boats see Cassib 1971; Johnstone 1980; Morrison 1980; Rougé 1981; Morrison and Coates 1996. For apotropaic eyes on ships in the Hellenistic and Roman periods see T. Nowak 2006. For depictions at Pompeii of Roman ships with blue eyes on their prows (first century BCE) see Bragantini and Sampaolo 2009:196–97 (Sala LXIX of the Museo Archeologico Nazionale di Napoli), with thanks to David Balch for this reference. A sixth century BCE Etruscan tomb painting in Tarquinia depicts an eye on the left prow of a boat containing four persons, one of whom apppears to be fishing (photograph in *Archaeology* 63/6 [2010]:41).The Hollywood film "Troy" realistically showed eyes on the prows of the ships transporting the invading Greeks across the Aegean Sea to Troy.

874. Kákosy 1989:209.

875. See *The Book of the Dead, The Papyri of Ani, Hunefer, and Anhaï* (1979:36–37, 52, 67, 84; Papyrus of Ani (c. 1300 BCE) (photograph in *ISBE* 4:663). See previously, Vol. 1, chap. 2 on Egypt. L. Kákosy 1989:209 traces the custom to earlier Egyptian practice.

876. Rostovtzeff 1957 1:152 (description of the "Torlonia Relief") and Plate XXI, fig. 1. Photograph also in Veyne 1987:148.

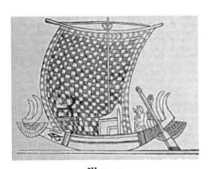

Illus. 42
Sketch of an Egyptian boat with Eye of
Horus on prow, funerary monument of
Ramses III, Thebes (from Seligmann
1910, 2:93, fig. 116)

Illus. 43
Modern Mediterranean boat with set of eyes
on prow

Illus. 44
Greek drinking cup (*kylix*)
with eyes, 540 BCE, Stattliche
Antikensammlung, Munich
Museum (photo by John H. Elliott)

Illus. 45
Sketch of Greek painted drinking
cup (*kylix*) with eyes (from
Seligmann 1910, 2:35, fig 91)

Apotropaic eyes were inscribed or carved in bas-relief on gems, metal, glass, pottery, horn and stone; they were drawn on household vessels, vases, jugs, cups, and bowls. Representations of an eye or eyes appear frequently on Greek black-figured drinking vessels called *kylikes* ("eye cups") from the sixth century BCE.[877] W. Deonna (1957:58–60) discusses an instance of apotropaic eyes on a black-figured bowl (now at Cambridge), which has a Gorgo in place of the pupils of the eyes.[878] Eyes and/or other anti-Evil Eye designs (e.g. *gorgoneia*, phalluses) on both the outside and inside surfaces

877. See also Seligman 1910 2:37–39, figs. 92, 93 and the illustrations in the *Lexicon Iconographicum Mythologiae Classicae* IV, 2 (1988) (eyes on vase); VIII.1 (1997) Plate 287, Hektor 67; Plate 166, fig. 41 (Gorgo accompanied by eyes right and left).

878. Regarding eyes on bowls see also Hildburgh 1946, 1947; Kunisch 1990.

were likely designed to thwart the Evil Eye and other evil spirits from entering the mouth with the wine. Fear of injury from the Evil Eye at meals[879]
may explain the many "eye bowls/eye cups" (drinking bowls, vessels, amphora with open eyes painted on the outside) in use from the sixth century
BCE to the end of the archaic period.[880] The later Jewish Aramaic incantation bowls from Sassanid Babylon (226–636 CE), likely served the same
protective purpose.[881]

Illus. 46
Sketch of set of eyes on a painted amphora from
Vulci, Italy (from Elworthy 1958/1895:141, fig. 25)

Beside the eyes of human or human-like figures, the eyes of *animals*,
real and mythological (serpents, basilisks), and eye-like forms (the "eyes"
on peacock tails) were also ascribed apotropaic power for repelling the Evil
Eye.[882] Pliny (*NH* 28.92–106) records that the Persian magi ascribed great
apotropaic power to the *hyaena*, including the hide of its forehead, for repelling Evil Eyes (*fascinationibus resistere*, 28.101). An amulet of a hyaena's eye
was worn to "avert the evil eye of a god or demon."[883] In contemporary Latin
America, the *ojo de Dios* ("Eye of God") or the *ojo de venado* ("Deer's Eye,"
a large brown seed [*Thevetia nitida*] often combined with red thread) are
worn under outside clothes for anti-Evil Eye protection. It is likely that the
assumed apotropaic power of the *male peacock* was attributed to the *eye-like
shapes* in its tail as well as to its dark blue color.[884]

879. See Pseudo-Aristotle, *Prob. phys.* 20.34, 926 b20–31; Prov 23:6–8; Sir 14:9, 10;
31:12–13; cf. Deut 28:54–57.

880. See Koenig 1975 and Rakoczy 1996:144. For an early sixth-century-BCE
black-figure eye cup with a *fascinum* as a pedestal foot see Johns 1982:93, ill. 76.

881. On the incantation bowls see Isbell 1975; Naveh and Shakad 1987 (for the Evil
Eye, amulets 1 ("eye of . . ."), 2, 13, 14 [from Palestine and Syria] and Bowl 8 [Mesopo-
tamia]); Shaked 1999. See Vol. 4, chap. 1.

882. Siebers 1983:61–63. For illustrations of the basilisk see Seligmann 1910 1:
figures 9–13.

883. Johnston 1995:385.

884. Dio Chrysostom, *Orat.* 12.2–3.

The Evil Eye Attacked—Apotropaic Depictions

A popular elaboration of the apotropaic Eye amulet was the depiction of an *eye (Evil Eye) encircled and attacked by an array of enemies.* Campbell Bonner, in his classic 1950 study of amulets, including Evil Eye amulets, dubbed this image "the much-suffering eye."[885] Bonner took this expression from the *Testament of Solomon*, an Israelite pseudepigraphical writing (first to third centuries CE). *Test. Sol.* 18:39 (cited above on p. 227) declares that the power of Lord Envy "is annulled by the graven image of the much-suffering eye (*ho polypathês ophthalmos*).

The passage, as Bonner indicates (1950:97–98), clearly illustrates the thinking underlying the use of a depiction of an eye under attack to ward off an Evil Eye. Here we have another example of the logic of *similia similibus* and eye-thwarting-eye. The passage also illustrates the complex of eye, Evil Eye and envy. For this type of anti-Evil Eye amulet, however, I prefer the designation "Evil Eye attacked" or "Evil Eye under attack," which highlights the aggressive features of the apotropaic design instead of the eye's suffering. Regarding this form of anti-Evil Eye apotropaic Bonner has observed that

> the commonest of all amulets to ward off the evil eye consists of an apotropaic design which has been found on numeorus monuments, and which, though subject to slight variations, remains the same through several centuries. It represents the eye, wide open, subjected to various inuries and assaled by a variety of animals, birds, and reptiles. (Bonner 1950:97; cf. also 211)

Apotropaic representations of this Evil Eye under attack are widely attested and have been found on lamps, terracotta figures in domiciles, house portals, cultic buildings, graves, and small medallions worn as anti-Evil eye amulets.[886] The *assaults on the (Evil) Eye* include wounding by a spear, a trident, one or more daggers; attacking animals such as dogs, lions, elephants; pecking cranes, ibises, and roosters; and stinging scorpions and snakes. Also included in these attacked-eye amulets are phalluses, fascina, swans, dolphins, owls, stags, fish, turtles, frogs, lizards, crabs, bees, and ants.[887] This image of ferocious attack sought to discourage and turn away an Evil Eye by illustrating the horrible suffering it would be caused to un-

885. Bonner 1950:97–100, 302–3, and for illustrations, Plates 14–15, nos. 292–303, 306; see also Goodenough 1953 2:238–41.

886. Engemann 1975:25–30; Russell 1995:41–42. Jahn's list of amulets depicting the Evil Eye attacked (1855:96–97) is expanded by Seligmann (1910 2:151–56) to thirteen specimens, plus five further Byzantine amulets: see also Elworthy 1895/1958:129–33.

887. Jahn 1855:96–100.

dergo and by pitting power (of attackers) against power (of the Evil Eye). The following are illustrative.[888]

(1) One of the most well-known and discussed representations of such an Evil Eye under attack is a bas-relief on a marble plaque once attached to the portal or a wall of a Roman house and centuries later included in the Woburn Abbey, England, collection of antiquities.[889] It was Otto Jahn's learning of this Woburn relief, once part of the collection of the Duke of Bedford, that prompted Jahn's classic study on the Evil Eye in 1855.[890] Jahn examined the relief and its details in relation to other apotropaics with similar motifs. The marble relief, dated to the early third century C E,[891] measures 1' 6" by 1' 5." It depicts a large human (Evil) Eye surrounded and attacked by an array of enemies. Atop the eyebrow of a left eye squats a *homo cacans* ("shitting man") in Phry-

Illus. 47
Woburn Abbey Marble, Britain: relief of Evil Eye attacked by an array of enemies (from Elworthy 1958/1895:137, fig. 24)

gian dress (identifying the wearer with an Oriental cult) contemptuously exposing his buttocks to the eye. To the right of the *homo cacans* is a gladiator (*retiarius*) standing and attacking the eye with a trident and dagger (or phallus). Below the eye are five creatures also charging the eye: a crow, crane/ibis, scorpion, serpent and lion.[892] Most scholars (including Millin-

888. For illustrations of depictions of the Evil Eye attacked, see, *inter alios*, Jahn 1855, Plate 3, figs. 1–6 and for discussion, pp. 96–11; Elworthy 1895/1958:130–31, figs. 14–17, 19, 24; 137, fig. 24 (Woburn Abbey marble); Picqué 1898:372–74 and figure on p. 372; Seligmann 1910 2:151–56, 312–15 and figures 117–25, 191, 230–34; Perdrizet 1922:27–31, figs. 7–11; Bonner 1950:97–100 and Plates 14–15, nos. 294–304; Goodenough 1953 2:238–40, figs. 1065, 1066; Engemann 1975:25–27, figs 1–5 and Plates 8–14; Dunbabbin and Dickie 1983, Plate 7a, b, c; Maguire et al. 1989:216; Bernand 1991:85; Dunbabin 1991, Plate 5c,d,e; line drawings in Gravel 1995: (8.1 [centaur phallus with phallus attacking an Evil Eye] 8.2 [winged phallus and *mano fica* attacking an Evil Eye]; 8.3 [Woburn marble]; 8.6 [medallions with Evil Eye attacked]; 39.2 [Roman floor mosaic, Moknine, Tunisia, Evil Eye attacked by phallus and serpents]).

889. First described by James Millingen (1818:70–74) and explained as an apotropaic (using *fascinum* in this more general sense) against the Evil Eye. On the marble (also known as the "Bedford slab") and on its Evil Eye details see also Michaelis 1885:313–18; Seligmann 1910 2:115, fig. 123 and 152–56; Elworthy 1895/1958:138–41.

890. According to Jahn 1855:30.

891. Elworthy 1895/1958:139.

892. For further illustrations of the relief see Jahn 1855 Plate 3, no. 1 (discussion: 30–32, 96–100); Seligmann 1910 2:115, fig. 123 (discussion: 152–56); Lafaye 1926:987, fig. 2887; Elworthy 1895/1958:137, fig. 24 (discussion: 138–41); Gravel 1995, fig. 8.3.

gen, Jahn, Michaelis, Elworthy, Seligmann, Perdrizet, Bonner, Dunbabin, Dickie, Gravel) are in agreement that this and similiar apotropaics and amulets are clearly for not merely decoration but for counteracting harm from an Evil Eye. Specimens of "the (Evil) Eye attacked" are numerous; occasionally they include inscriptions identifying them explicitly as directed against the Evil Eye.

(2) An embossed gold medallion (Roman, c. second century CE, provenance unknown), with a loop for wearing, depicts an Evil Eye surrounded and attacked by various creatures including a scorpion, dog, elephant, and bird.[893] A pear-shaped amethyst and two pendant pearls are attached. Its size (length: 3.1 cm, width: 1.8 cm) and design suggest that it was perhaps an earring meant to both adorn and protect.

(3) An amulet medallion for wearing has a representation of an Evil Eye under attack and the words *phthoneros, kakos ophthalmos* ("envier," "Evil Eye").[894]

(4) A Gallo-Roman gold medallion with loop for wearing as a pendent, found in Mainz in 1862, depicts an Evil Eye attacked by a circle of eleven figures including, above the eye, a kneeling man holding a dagger in each hand, two gladiators right and left, a serpent, wolf, and birds. A cornucopia is also depicted.[895]

Illus. 48

Gallo-Roman gold medallion, Evil Eye attacked (from Picqué 1898:372)

(5) A gold medallion from Sicily depicts an Evil Eye attacked by a circle of nine figures (a crocodile, swan, serpent, rooster, dog/wolf, lion, winged fascinum, scorpion and thunderbolt)[896] (Illus. 49a).

(6) A gold medallion with loop (provenance unknown) depicts an Evil Eye attacked by a circle

---

Gravel (1995:94) interprets the squatting figure not as a man defecating on the eye (as Jahn and most others hold), but thinks that "it is more likely to be a woman in the birthing position of the times: squatting."

893. Now in the Johns Hopkins University Archaeological Museum, accession number: FIC.07.225.

894. For the text and description see Bernand 1991:102–103, referring to Delatte and Derchain 1964:72–73 and figure.

895. Picqué 1898, figure of medallion on p. 372. A bequest of the Robiano collection, it is now in the Cabinet des médailles et antiques, Bibliothèque nationale, Paris.

896. Caylus 1764, vol. 6, Plate 38.3; Jahn 1855:96 and Plate 3.2; Seligmann 1910 2:151; 2:95, fig. 117; Elworthy 1895/1958:130, fig. 14; Meisen 1950:153–54.

of eight figures (crocodile or lizard, thunderbolt, elephant, scorpion, fascinum, lion, dog, swan).[897]

(7) A gold medallion from Herculaneum depicts an Evil Eye attacked by a circle of nine figures (thunderbolt, lizard, fascinum, scorpion, star, elephant, swan, fish? serpent).[898]

(8) A gold medallion (provenance uncertain) depicts an Evil Eye encircled by signs of the zodiac and other figures including a *fascinum*.[899]

(9) A bronze medallion with a loop for wearing has on one side the crowned head of emperor Maximianus (286–305 CE) and the inscription "Imp. C. Maximianus P. F. Aug." and on other side, a depiction of an Evil Eye attacked by a hippopotamus, elephant, bees, serpent, lizard, and dog-headed apes.[900]

(10) An amulet medallion from Egypt, with loop for wearing, depicts an Evil Eye whose pupil is pierced by a dagger, with two arrows right and left of the eye.[901]

Illus. 49a   Illus. 49b   Illus. 49c

**Sketches of three medallion amulets depicting an Evil Eye attacked
(from Elworthy 1958/1895:130, figs. 14–16)**

(11) A Byzantine Christian bronze amuletic medallion with a loop for wearing depicts on its reverse side an Evil Eye attacked by a lion, an ibis,

897. Arneth 1850: iv, 96G; Jahn 1855:96 and Plate 3.3; Elworthy 1895/1958:130, fig. 15; Seligmann 1910 2:97, fig. 118.

898. A. C. P. Caylus, 1762, vol. 5, 57, 1.2; Jahn 1855:96 and Plate 3.4; Seligmann 1910 2:99, fig. 119; Elworthy 1895/1958:130, fig. 16; Dölger *Ichthys* 4 (1927), Plate 141.2.

899. Jahn 1855:96 (provenance not indicated). Also mentioned by Jahn is a silver fragment of a similar medallion referred to by Caylus 1752–1764, vol 6:137. Seligmann 1910 2:152 mentions also one round gold plate depicting an Evil Eye surrounded by thunderbolt, fascinum etc. and another round gold plate found in Mainz in 1862 and depicting an Evil Eye attacked by a circle of figues (caterpiller, swan, tortoise, crane or stork, locust (?), dog (?), lizard, and serpent).

900. *Annuaire de la société française de numismatique* 14 (1890):237–39, with illustration.

901. Delatte and Derchain 1964:72–73 with illustration; Bernand 1991:102–3.

a snake, a scorpion, a leopard [?], a trident, and a spear; the accompanying inscription reads: *Iaô Sabaôth Michael, help.* The obverse side shows a cavalier with nimbus, spearing a prostrate female demon, and a lion below; the inscription reads: "One God who conquers evil."[902]

(12) A Byzantine Christian amuletic medallion depicts on the obverse side a cavalier with nimbus piercing with a lance adorned by a cross a prostrate female demon. The encircling inscription reads *pheuge, memidimeni, Solomôn se dioke, Sissinios Sisinnarios* ("flee, Hated One, Solomon drives you away, Sisinnios, Sisinnarios") and identifies the protecting cavalier as Solomon alias St. Sisinnios accompanied by his brother Sisinnarios. The obverse depicts an Evil Eye attacked from above by three daggers, by lions on each side, and from below by a scorpion, serpent and ibis. The word *phthonos* ("envy") appears over the daggers and the whole is encircled by the inscription, *sphragis Solomônis apodioxon pan kakon apo tou phorountos* ("the seal of Solomon keeps away all evil from the bearer").[903] The inclusion of a cross, along with references to Sisinnios, Sisinnarios and Solomon, identify the amulet as intended for Christian use. The name Solomon relates it to Jewish amulets of the same type. This and further cavalier amulets with an Evil Eye attacked are discussed in Volumes 3 and 4.

Illus. 50

Sketch of an engraved gem depicting an Evil Eye attacked (from Elworthy 1958/1895:130, fig. 17)

The Evil Eye Attacked—Depictions on Gems

The motif of the Evil Eye attacked is also found on *gems*.

(13/1) An engraved gem (Florence Museum) depicts an Evil Eye attacked by a circle of eight figures (tortoise, lizard, scorpion, frog, bee, serpent, crab, another bee or ant.[904]

902. Purchased in Syria, the medallion is now in the University of Michigan Kelsey Museum, no. 2611530. See also Bonner 1950, no. 299.

903. Schlumberger 1892:74; Perdrizet 1903:47 and figs. 3–4; Perdrizet 1922:27, figs. 7–8; Dunbabin and Dickie 1983:33 and Plate 8c. See also the Byzantine bronze amulet from Cyzikus, Mysia, Asia Minor, depicting on its obverse an Evil Eye attacked by a lion and on the reverse, Solomon as cavalier lancing a prostrate demoness (Seligmann 1910 2:314–15 and p. 449, fig. 233); on this amulet see Vol. 3, chap. 1 and Vol. 4, chaps. 1 and 2.

904. Elworthy 1958/1895:130, fig. 17.

(14/2) An engraved gem (onyx) cameo depicting an Evil Eye surrounded by a thunderbolt, a head of Jupiter or Serapis, a dolphin and an eagle.[905]

(15/3) An engraved gem (sardonyx) depicting an Evil Eye attacked by a circle of seven figures (owl, serpent, stag, scorpion, dog/wolf, lion and thunderbolt).[906]

The Evil Eye Attacked—Other Materials and Variants

The motif of the Evil Eye attacked is found also on a variety of other materials.

(16/1) The Uhden Collection in Berlin included a brown paste (likely Egyptian provenance) portraying an attacked Evil Eye from which creeps a serpent and which is surrounded by two men (one a gladiator with helmut and shield), a raven, an upupa epops (bird native to Egypt and the Mediterranean region), a bundle of thunder bolts, an elephant and two goats.[907]

(17/2) An interesting variant on the Evil Eye attacked type is a small terracotta figurine from Tarsus, Turkey (first to second centuries CE) and now in the British Museum. It depicts an Evil Eye being *sawn in half* by phallus-headed figures equipped with arms and dressed like men.[908]

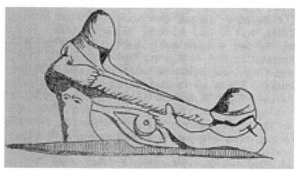

Illus. 51
Sketch of a terracotta figurine of two personified phalluses
sawing in half an Evil Eye with a two-handed saw (first–second
century CE) (from Seligmann 1910, 2:273 fig. 191)

905. Jahn 1855:97 n281 and Pl. 3.7; Elworthy 1895/1958:131 and fig. 18; Seligmann 1910 2:152 and 103, fig. 121.

906. Seligmann 1910 2:152 and 113, fig. 122; Elworthy 1895/1958:131 and fig. 19.

907. Seligmann 1912–1913:99–101.

908. BM (Greek and Roman) 1865.11–18.78; illustrations in Seligmann 1910 2:200, fig. 191; Johns 1982:68, ill. 51.

(18/3) Another variant is a terracotta figure (unknown provenance) of a male youth with his left hand resting on an eye, which in turn, is attacked from below by a phallus. The accompanying inscription reads, "I have bored the eye of the Evil-Eyeing one" (*ophthalmon apetrypêsa ton tou baskanou*).[909]

Other depictions of an Evil Eye under attack protected *homes, gravesites, shops, and public spaces.*

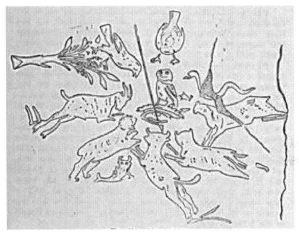

Illus. 52
Sketch of a threashold mosaic pavement, store of pearl
merchants. Basilica Hilariana, Caelian Hill, Rome, depicting
an owl perched on an Evil Eye under attack
(from Seligmann 1910 2:117, fig. 124).

(19/1) A black and white mosaic pavement at the entrance to a sanctuary of Cybele and Attis (Basilica Hilariana vestibule) on the Caelian Hill in Rome (second century CE) and found at the Villa Casali in 1889 depicts an Evil Eye pierced by a lance and attacked by a circle of figures symbolizing deities: a serpent (Saturn), stag (Diana), lion (Cybele), bull (Neptune), scorpion (Mercury), wolf (Mars) male goat (Jupiter), crow/dove (Venus) on a laural branch/pine tree and a raven (symbol of Apollo).[910] An owl perched on the Eye either is an added symbol of an Evil Eye[911] or represents an ally of the Eye.[912] Above this scene stands a tabula ansata with an inscription iden-

909. W. Weber 1914:100, no. 131 and fig. 12.

910. See Bienkowski 1893; Perdrizet 1922:28–29 and fig. 9; Stuart Jones 1926:277, cat. no. 20, Plate 110; Bonner 1950:98.

911. So Perdrizet 1922:29; Meisen 1950:173.

912. So Bienkowski 1983, and as a possibility, Bonner 1950:98.

tifying the location as the Basilica Hilariana: *Intrantibus hic deos propitios et basilica(ae) Hilarianae* ("for those who here approach the propitious gods and those of the Basilica Hilariana").[913]

(20/2) A threshold mosaic at the entrance of a Roman villa in ancient Hadrumetum, Moknine, Tunisia (now in the Sousse Museum) depicts an Evil Eye attacked from above by a phallus (in the form of an eyed fish with gills), and by serpents on right and left (see above, Illus. 26, p. 204);[914] cf. similarly, a terracotta figure of an Evil Eye attacked by phallus.[915]

(21/3) A stele found at Leptis Magna, Libya, depicts a winged two-legged phallus with an additional large genital phallus of its own and a hand making the sign of the *mano fica,* both attacking an Evil Eye.[916]

(22/4) A tabula ansata carved into a stone, also found at Leptis Magna, Libya (third century CE) portrays a kind of centaur with a huge phallus for a nose and an immense genital phallus. The figure attacks an Evil Eye with a lance and its two phallic appendages, assisted by a bird, scorpion and serpent.[917]

(23/5) A sketch in black and red from the Roman-Parthian town of Dura-Europus, Syria, on the Euphrates river (second century CE) depicts an Evil Eye pierced by a dagger and harpoon. Above is a bird of prey flying at the Eye; on each side and from below are attacking serpents.[918]

(25/6) Also at the town of Dura-Europus on the external side of a tower of the city wall is a representation of an Evil Eye attacked by serpents and bored by weapons.[919] On the synagogue at Dura-Europus, Syria (third

913. CIL 6.30973a = ILS 3992. The mosaic is presently located at Rome, Musei Capitolini, Palazzo dei Conservatori, Galleria Superiore I. See *Notitiae degli scavi di antichita* (1889):398–400; (1890):79, 113; *Bulletino di commissione archeologica communale di Roma,* Serie 3, vol. 18 (1890), plates 1–2; Seligmann 1910 2:152–53; and 117, fig. 124; Perdrizet 1922:28–29. Illustrations in Seligmann 1910 2:117, fig. 124; Perdrizet 1922:29, fig. 9; Stuart Jones 1926:277, cat. no. 20, Plate 110; Leclercq 1934:1936–37, fig. 8989.; Dölger *Ichthys* 4 (1927), Plate 290; Nash 1968 1:183–85; Engemann 1975:28–29, Plate 11 a, b; Siebers 1983, plate between pp. 86–87.

914. *Bulletin archéologique du Comité* 1901: clxxxix–clxl and Plate CXC; Gaukler 1910; Perdrizet 1922:31 and fig. 11; Dunbabin and Dickie 1983: Plate 8b; Bernand 1991:104 and fig. on p. 85; Gravel 1995, fig. 39.2.

915. Weber 1914:100, no. 131 and fig. 12.

916. Bandinelli-Caffarelli-Caputo 1964, plate 190; Bernand 1991:105; photograph in Johns 1982:150, ill. 123; line drawing of the same in Gravel 1996, fig. 8.2.

917. Bianchi Bandinelli *et al. Leptis Magna,* 1964, Plate 196; photograph in Johns 1982:94, ill. 77; line drawing of photograph in Gravel 1995, fig. 8.1.

918. Cumont 1926:137–38 and fig. 31.

919. See Engemann 1975:27–28 and fig. 5; Du Mesnil du Buisson 1939:136–137, fig. 97, plate 59.2. On the ceiling tiles of the synagogue at Dura-Europus, Syria (third century CE), are two frescos depicting eyes.

century CE), and its two ceiling tiles depicting apotropaic eyes see Volume 4, chapter 1.

(26/7) A similar sketch in a grave in Palmyra, Syria, depicts an Evil Eye pierced by a dagger and two arrows, surrounded by two birds, two scorpions, a centipede, a rooster, and a serpent.[920]

(27/8) A grave cippus from Aumale (ancient Auzia), Algeria, portrays a father (Geminius Saturninus), a mother, and two children flanking the legs of father and mother. Beneath the feet of the father and mother is an Evil Eye attacked from above by two lions and from below by a circle of creatures (rooster, lizard, snail, scorpion, serpent).[921]

(28/9) Another of the better known depictions of an Evil Eye under attack appears in a colorful floor mosaic of a Roman villa (second century CE) uncovered in the village of Jekmejeh southeast of Antioch on the Orontes, Syria (contemporary Antakya, Turkey). In the entrance to the residence designated as the "House of the Evil Eye," one of the three preserved floor mosaics (Room 2, vestibule, upper floor)[922] designed to ward off the Evil Eye, depicts an Evil Eye pierced by a trident and a sword and attacked by a circle of figures (scorpion, serpent, dog/wolf? centipede, leopard, raven), as well as by the enlarged phallus extending backward between the legs of a hunchbacked dwarf who stands to the left of, and facing away from, the eye. The Greek words *KAI SY* ("you too!") warding off the Evil Eye appear above the dwarf (see above, Illus. 9, p. 174).[923] Doro Levi's 1941 study discusses various objects appearing in this and other depictions of the Evil Eye under attack: swords, tridents, daggers, nails, gladiators, prophylactic animals including serpents, scorpions, dolphins, insects, birds, dogs, panthers, leopards; satyr masks, Medusa heads (alias *gorgoneia*), human phalluses, dwarfs, pymies, hunchbacks, the Greek expression *kai sy* ("you too"), representa-

920. Chabot 1922:101 and plate XVI 3.

921. *Revue archéologique* 7 (1863):293–98 and Plate 8. CIL 8.9057 and CIL Suppl. 3, p. 1960, no. 20738 gives the accompanying inscription. See also Cagnat 1900:38–40 for illustration (38) and description; Seligmann 1910 2:119, fig. 125; Daremberg-Saglio 1877–1919, vol. 2:987; Goodenough 1964 vol. 11, fig. 49 and discussion (1964 vol. 9:55).

922. Now in the Antakya Archaeological Museum, inv. no. 1024. As to the juxtaposition of the three mosaics, Brenk (1999b:172) explains that "before the earthquake of 115, the two original mosaics, the Lucky Hunchback and Baby Herakles Strangling Snakes—apparently also with an apotropaic function—were later covered over by the Evil Eye mosaic."

923. See Levi 1941:220–32 and Plate 56, fig. 121; Levi 1947 1:28–34 and plates, esp. Plate XL; vol. 2, Plate IVa-c, figs. 12–14. Downey 1963:213–14, nos. 61–63; Dunbabin and Dickie 1983:32 and Plate 8a; Norris 1991:257–58; Brenk 1999b:172; Clarke 2003:109, ill. 76.

tions of Heracles, owls, lizards). Levi (1941:229) describes this as "the first actual representation of the "lucky hunchback" in the classical world."

A second mosaic (Room 2 vestibule, under the attacked Evil Eye mosaic), depicts a humpbacked dwarf also accompanied by the apotropaic words KAI SY ("You too").[924] A third mosaic in the same location portrays the figure of a deformed Hercules, strong dispeller of evil *par excellence*, with the head of an adult and body of an infant, strangling two serpents that an envious Hera had sent to kill him in his crib.[925]

(30/10) A marble block from Xanthos, Syria (now in the British Museum) portrays on its frontside figures of Serapis and Isis-Tyche, and on the backside a scene in which various figures (an archer in oriental dress, a dog, jackel, locust, lizard, and snail), are attacking an object that is difficult to decipher. Michaelis (1885 and Plate 58) proposed a phallus but Dunbabin and Dickie (1983:25–27) object that such a depiction would be unique and problematic because the phallus conventionally attacks but is not attacked. Their reasonable suggestion is a figure of envy (*phthonos*). This would be consistent with the figure of Serapis on the front of the marble. And it would accord with Serapis apotropaic inscriptions invoking his protection against envy and and an Evil Eye such as *Eis Zeus Serapis baskanos lakêsetô* ("Zeus Serapis is unique; let the Evil-Eyer burst asunder")[926] and *Nika ho Serapis ton phthonon* ("Serapis conquers envy"). The association of envy and Evil Eye make this likely as does the similarity of the scene to the numerous depictions of an attacked Evil Eye. It thus deserves to be included in our list of apotropaic depictions of an Evil Eye under attack.

(31/11) A relief carved on a rock face near Burdur in Pisidia (Asia Minor) depicts an Evil Eye pierced by a spear and a dagger and attacked by a scorpion, snake, crab, another animal, and a phallus. Written above are the words, *baskane kai sou* ["You too, Evil Eyer!"].[927]

---

924. Levi 1941:228–29 and Plate 56, fig. 120, Panel A. On the apotropaic KAI SY expression see above, pp. 172–75.

925. Levi 1941, Plate 56, fig. 120, Panel B. On the Antioch mosaics see also Levi 1947; Cimok 1996:54, Plate 3 (Hall III, no. 3; Inv. no.1026b [85 x 85 cm]), and 55, Plate 6 (Evil Eye, Hall III, no. 6, Inv. no. 1024 [170 x 150 cm]); Downey 1963:213–14 and Plate, nos. 61–63. Cimok 2000; *Antioch: The Lost Ancient City* Catalogue (with essays) of an exhibit at Worcester Art Museum, Massachusetts. 10/8/2000 and catalogue with essays. http//www.worcesterart.org. See also above, pp. 173–75, 202, 205, 243.

926. Herter 1986: col. 783.

927. Dunbabin and Dickie 1983:36, citing Bean 1960:50, no. 98, Plate 12c.

The Evil Eye Attacked by Cavaliers (and Others)

Numerous amulets and apotropaic art depicting an Evil Evil under attack are accompanied by a representation of a cavalier (rider on horseback) spearing from his horse a supine female figure (demoness) representing the Evil Eye (*Baskania, Baskosynê*); for medallions depicting cavalier figures spearing an Evil Eye, see above, p. 239.[928]. These cavalier amulets have been traced back to Egypt and at least the Ptolemaic period.[929] Egyptian, Syrian,and Palestinian cavalier amulets, generally Jewish and Christian from the third century CE into Byzantine times, adopted the pagan model but identified the cavalier as Solomon or Saint Sissinios. Three such cavalier apotropaics, Christian and Jewish, are discussed in Volume 4, chapters 1 and 2 on the post-biblical Jewish and Christian material.

Envy Attacked

Amuletic depictions of the Evil Eye being attacked are strikingly paralleled by amuletic representations of *envy under attack*. The similarity points to an assumed equivalency of Evil Eye and envy and their defeat by much the same means.

(1) An amulet made of blue agate stone depicts a personification of Envy under attack. A naked male figure is enveloped by the coils of a large snake and besieged by many creatures. To the figure's left is written *phthone*, and to its right, *atychi*: "No luck for you, Envy."[930]

(2) At Ostia Antica, Rome's erstwhile harbor at the mouth of the Tiber, the entrance to a fishmonger's stall (region IV. V. 1) is adorned by a floor mosaic showing a dolphin with a squid in its beak and the inscription, "Envy, I trample you" (INBIDE CALCO TE).[931] Similar to Evil Eye imagery, the motif of envy being trampled or attacked and vanguished, Katherine Dunbabin (1991) has shown, was a common apotropaic motif. The dolphin, regarded as a creature friendly to humans, devours the squid whose black ink represents the "black venomous force of envy." "Taken together, the congruence of word and image and action add up to a powerful protection. The auspicious dolphin crushes the black and greedy squid; the occupants

928. In addition to those listed above on p. 239, see five further medallion amulets, mostly Christian, depicting cavaliers spearing prostrate figures, University of Michigan collection, Kelsey Museum, nos. 26092, 26114, 26119, 26140, 26165. For anti-Evil Eye cavalier amulets see also Peterson 1926:96–109

929. See Perdrizet 1922.

930. Described by Walcot 1978:85.

931. Dunbabin 1991, Plate 4, fig. a. = CIL 14.4757

of the shop trample upon the pavement [mosaic]; by analogy, the reader of the inscription mentally triumphs over the envious enemy" (Dunbabin 1991:35). Dunbabin relates the attack on, and trampling of, envy motif to the image of the trampling of a demoness by a horse and cavalier, which is often combined with an attack on the Evil Eye, as we have seen above. These amulets combining the motifs of a cavalier lancing a demoness and of an Evil Eye under siege are another example of composite amulets. These amulets share the common motif of some evil potency under attack and many illustrate the conception of the Evil Eye and envy as virtually identical evil forces needing to be vanquished.[932]

Medusa/Gorgo/Gorgoneion Images against the Evil Eye

Representations of the severed head of Medusa, alias the Gorgo, appear on amulets to ward off the Evil Eye. This deadly mythological female was considered not just a wielder of the Evil Eye, as noted above, but also a protector against the Evil Eye according to the logic of *similia similibus* ("like influences like"). Her eyes and fearsome visage, it was believed, had the power to petrify the objects that beheld her visage or were struck by her glance. Her

Illus. 53
Sketch of a Gorgo with
extended tongue, as an antefix,
Athens acropolis (from
Seligmann 1910 2:419, fig.
218)

head, according to the myth, even after being severed from her body by Perseus, retained its potency and turned to stone Perseus's enemies when they beheld its horrible countenance. Deployed as an apotropaic and on amulets, the gorgoneion, the severed head of Gorgo/Medusa, with its fierce face, bulging eyes, exposed teeth, extended tongue, and serpentine hair, presented a terrifying aspect to drive off the Evil Eye.[933] Representations of the Gorgon/gorgoneion appear in Greek art as early as the eighth century BCE under Asiatic influence (from Northern Syria via Asia Minor). They are among the oldest figural representations in Western culture. The appearance of the gorgoneion

932. See the medallion amulet of the cavalier Solomon/St. Sisinnios and the inscription *phthonos* ("envy") mentioned above, p. 239. See also the Kephallenia mosaic of *phthonos* attacked, above, pp. 105–6.

933. See also above, Illustrations 3–6, pp. 136–139. On the gorgoneion see Jahn 1855:59–60, 83; Elworthy 1895/1958:158–66 and figs. 47–55; Seligmann 1910 1, figs. 2–8; vol. 2:305–7 and figs. 217–21, 227; Besig 1937; von Geisau 1979b; Potts 1982:26–37 and figs. 45–56, 66–69; Gravel 1995:117–18 and Plate 17.1; Gramiccia and Pagnotta 1989; Stern 2002 (illustrations).

goes back to Hittite prototypes. Potts (1982:30–32) argues for an origin in Babylonia and Assyria because of the cylinder seals and head masks with similar facial features found there, with the apotropaic face extending "far back into prehistory." Gravel holds that the Greeks inherited the image of Gorgo from the Etruscans who had pictured her as a parturient woman, grimacing in the process of giving birth; thus the image is related to the fertility figure of the sheela-na-gig.[934] This shows, he suggests, the intimate link of eye and Evil Eye with fertility and its loss. "The very early Gorgon," he notes, "is best exemplified by the 'Etruscan' Gorgo (ca. 540–530 B.C.) now housed in the Munich Alte Pinakothek. It is a bronze plaque for the front of a war chariot and probably meant to be protection against the Evil Eye in combat."[935] Gravel follows Jane Harrison (1955:191) who identifies the Gorgo as among the apotropaica (*baskania, prosbaskania*) deployed against the Evil Eye and the gorgo mask as one of the most common of such apotropaics.[936] A gorgo image is found in the limestone pediment of the Temple of Artemis, Corfu, c. 600–580 BCE; others are still visible in the Istanbul cistern and at the Apollo temple at Didyma, Turkey. Over the course of centuries, the image of the Gorgo has transformed from horrible to milder expression, from threatening visage with snake-hair (earliest) to neutral image, to beautiful maiden (Medusa Rondanini).[937]

The gorgoneion was depicted on the aegises of Zeus and Athena.[938] Homer also tells of its appearance "fierce and grim" on Agamemnon's shield (*Iliad* 11. 36–37). It decorates and protects warriors' helmets, breastplates, shields, war horses, chariots, and clothing (Euripides, *Ion* 1435–1436). Dio Chrysostom (*Orat.* 77/78.26) speaks of cowardly hireling soldiers "who affect plumes and crests and Gorgons on their shields." Kreusa wrapped the infant Ion in clothing into which was woven a gorgoneion.[939] The gorgoneion appears on coins from the seventh century BCE onward.[940] It also

934. Gravel 1995:12, 81–89, 118 and figs. 17.1, 6–8. For Etruscan gorgoneia (sixth-fifth centuries BCE) see also Hess and Paschinger 1986:272 (and fig. 141), 298, 313, 319, 343, 346, 404.

935. Gravel 1995:118.

936. Ibid.

937. See the Gorgo illustrations in Furtwängler 1886–1890 1:1701–28; Besig 1937; Potts 1982:27–28, 36–37; and Siebers 1983: plate between 86–87. On the history of modification see Wilson 1920, Buschor 1958. See also Camera Cascudo 1949.

938. Homer, *Iliad* 5.741. The myth told of Perseus presenting the deadly head to Athena who placed it on the center of her shield.

939. Jahn 1855:60.

940. Potts 1982:80 gives a list of thirty-six such coins from the seventh century BCE to 244–249 CE.

was put on drinking vessels. Greek drinking cups with low bowls, *kylices*, were used in sixth century BCE Athens with representations of the gorgoneion on the inside of the bowls and on their outsides, depictions of pairs of huge eyes—to safeguard the drinkers from the Evil Eye (see above, Illus. 6, p. 137).[941] The gorgoneion also was drawn on vases, lamps, candelabra, jewelry, gems, cameos, *bullae*, furniture, lamps, juridical tablets, wall frescos, floors. doors, interiors and exteriors of private and public edifices, temples and tombs, shops, construction sites, and ships.[942] A floor mosaic with a gorgoneion is presented in the Archaeological Museum, Cordova, Spain. Greek bakers painted gorgon masks on their ovens to protect the bread. A gold *bulla* (Etruscan or Roman, date and provenance unknown) depicts a Gorgon head in relief.[943]. A gorgoneion appeared, *inter alia,* on a wall of the Athenian acropolis (Pausanius, *Descr.* 1.21.4), at Kephissos by Argos (Pausanius, *Descr* 2.20.5), at the Akkroterion of the Temple of Zeus at Olympia (Pausanius, *Descr* 5.10.2), at a gate at Nikaia, over the entrances of the theatres in Myra, on many houses of Pompei, and at the temple at Didyma, Turkey. Often combined with other symbols, the gorgoneion was associated with Apollo, the apotropaic divinity par excellence. Apollo of Hierapolis carries a gorgoneion and the two were also associated on coins. An amulet against gout, an engraved sardonyx gemstone, discussed by Campbell Bonner in his study of Greco-Egyptian amulets,[944] depicts the association of the Gorgo and Perseus and their role in healing. On a gold lamella amulet the hero Perseus displays the severed Medusa head, with the inscription reading, "Flee, gout, Perseus is chasing you."[945] The gorgoneion image guarded persons, animals, residences, shops, ships, thoroughfares, and public spaces.[946] *Le Collezioni del Museo Nazionale di Napoli* (1989) presents three instances of gorgoneia, one on a statue and two on jewelry.[947]

941. For illustrations see Potts 1982: figs. 65–69.

942. Seligmann 1910 1:138–40, figs. 2–8; 2:147–48, 305–8 and figs. 217–21, 227.

943. Now in the Johns Hopkins University Archaeological Museum, described by Jessica Phippen ("Gold Bulla").

944. Bonner 1950:43, 76.

945. Kotansky 2002:42.

946. On the Gorgo/Medusa and the Evil Eye, including illustrations, see also Jahn 1855:59–60, 83; Elworthy 1895/1958:158–80 (and the gorgoneion on shields as the forerunner of later designs on shields); Ziegler 1910:1650–55; Leclercq 1933:195–99; Besig 1937; Siebers 1983:1–26; Potts 1982:26–37, 80. On the Gorgo/Medusa in in general, see above, pp. 134–38 and p. 138 n393.

947 *Le Collezioni del Museo Nazionale di Napoli* (Gramiccia and Pagnotta, eds., 1989): (1) a statue of Athena Promachos, with image of a *gorgoneion* on her left shoulder, from Herculaneum, Villa dei Papyri (*Collezioni Catalogue* 1989:30 and n185; (2) a finger ring with a *gorgoneion* stamped on a lamina and applied to the disk on the face

The image of the Gorgo/Medusa was similar in grotesqueness to that of the ugly, bug-eyed, dwarf Egyptian divinity Bes. In most representations, the Gorgo, like Bes, sticks out her tongue, probably as a gesture of derision or defiance.[948] From the fifth century BCE onward, however, the appearance of the Gorgo gradually changed from a ferocious to a tranquil visage.[949] The gorgo image as apotropaic continued to be popular in Jewish and Christian circles.[950] In modern art and sculpture, images of the Gorgoneion are still depicted on military shields and breastplates of modern warriors. The General Brock Memorial Monument (dedicated in 1825) located in Queenston Heights, Canada, near the Canadian-United States border depicts a Gorgo on the shield of a warrior as a modern relic of an ancient military custom and still more ancient myth. Brock protected the site against invading U.S. troops coming across the Niagra River during the War of 1812 and preserved it for the British Crown. He was killed in action.[951] Contemporary anti-Evil Eye masks, such as the elaborate wooden models from Sri Lanka, appear to be modern-day variations on the Medusa/Gorgo images of antiquity. Features of the *gorgoneion* are replicated and exaggerated: the menacing eyes as bloodshot and bulging accompanied by bared teeth and an ex-

Illus. 54
Modern Sri Lankan
Gorgoneion-like anti-Evil Eye
mask, with smiling cobras
(John H. Elliott collection)

of the ring, from Cuma, end of the fourth century CE (*Collezioni Catalogue* 1989:209, plate 14 [side view], 14a [top view]); (3) a set of pendant earrings, each with a disk adorned with a *gorgoneion* image, from Taranto, end of the fourth century CE (*Collezioni Catalogue* 1989:211, plate 30).

948. For this gesture of derision, see Persius, *Sat.* 1.58–60 and, in the Bible, Isa 57:4 ("upon whom have you opened your mouth wide and stuck out your tongue?"). Later Christian iconography depicts a lustful devil and gargoyles also leering with protruding tongues.

949. For further iconographic examples of the gorgo/gorgoneion see the *Lexicon Iconographicum Mythologiae Classicae,* vol. 8/1 (1997): IV, 1 (1988):288–345 by Ingrid Krauskopf (321–22 on the Gorgon's apotropaic power); IV, 1 (1988):345–62 by Orazio Paoletti on "Gorgones Romanae"; IV, 2 Plates 163–207, figs 2–350 (Gorgo, gorgones), 163–88; 1288–95, Plates 1–117 (Gorgo in Etruria); pp. 195–207, figs. 2–183 (Gorgo Romanae). NB IV, 2 (Gorgones in Etruria 89; IV, 2, Plate 193 (Gorgo and spread legs, bronze lead, c. 530 BCE); IV, 2, Plate 166, c. 520 BCE The Museo Civico Archeologico di Bologna, Room IX (Roman Collection, Case two), displays five terracotta *gorgoneia.* On an apotropaic gorgo found in Baden, Switzerland see Wolters 1909; and on its combination of gorgo image and phallus, see Deschler-Erb 2007.

950. For Talmudic period Jewish depictions of the Gorgo/gorgoneion/Medusa see Volume 4, chap. 1; for a post-biblical Christian sample see Vol. 4, chap. 2.

951. With thanks for conversations and a field trip with Drs. Gretchen and Dennis Duling living on the now pacific U.S.A–Canadian border in Youngstown, New York.

tended tongue, and cobras, an indigenous Asian serpent, for hair. One of the masks in my personal possession shows the cobras with smiling faces. My informant explained to me that in his Sri Lankan culture, cobras are considered friendly serpents serving not to frighten but to protect. The contemporary TV series "Rome" (BBC/HBO Sept 2005) shows a *gorgoneion* with writhing snakes on a public wall. The popular comic strip of mid-century USA, Al Capp's "Li'l Abner." featured a character named "Evil-Eye Fleegle. His bulging, bloodshot destructive eye, resembling that of the Gorgo, claimed to be so powerful it could challenge the sun.[952] This dreaded denizen of deepest Brooklyn, so the comic strip goes, controlled "nature's most stupefyin' equipment—THE LIMITLESS POWER OF THE HUMAN EYE-BALL." Evil Eye Fleegle was "master of the WHAMMY—TH' MOST POWERFUL FORCE ON OITH!" "His—shudder—single whammy is powerful enough to stop a rampaging elephant dead in its tracks!" "His double whammy kin melt a locomotive in full flight." "His triple whammy kin toin Lake Erie into a mud flat. . . or win the Noo Yawk Mets a pennant." Using only "th' super-natural, trtans-spa-tial power o' [his] INTERPLANE-TARY WHAMMY," he can even stupefy the sun and blast iit from its orbit. His creator, Al Capp, is considered one of America's greatest satirists.[953] Fleegle's moiderous Evil Eye was more than a figment of Capp's fertile imagination; it had a pedigree in the rich European Jewish tradition that was Capp's cultural heritage.

Illus. 55
Evil-Eye Fleegle and his stupifyin' eye
(line drawing by Dietlinde Elliott)

Genitalic Amulets against the Evil Eye

Amulets having the shape, or bearing representations of, *human genitalia* also were very popular for combating life-threatening forces including the Evil Eye. These genitalic amulets were discussed and illustrated above in connection with manual gestures and the apotropaic use of the genitals.[954]

952. Elliott 1988:42; Capp 1953, 1964, 1978.

953. Berger 1978.

954. See above, pp. 195–217.

Grotesques, Hunchbacks, Dwarfs against the Evil Eye

Depictions of *deformed, grotesque, or ugly figures,* or figures in defiant, antisocial acts that border on obscenity, were considered to have apotropaic power against the Evil Eye. Various rationales were entertained. One held that their purpose was to *attract* to themselves the glance from the Evil Eye, thereby diverting it from striking the victim. Another proposed that their horrible, shocking aspect *frightened away* the Evil Eye or to reduced it to a ludicrous laughingstock.[955]

Several anti-Evil Eye designs depict *hunchbacks*.[956] Two representations of hunchbacks were equipped with suspension holes or loops indicating that they were displayed or suspended from the neck as protectives against the Evil Eye.[957] A hunchback appears in the depiction of an Evil Eye under attack in floor mosaics at Antioch on the Orontes, Syria (see above, Illus. 9, p. 174 and pp. 174–75, 202, 243–44).). Here he joins a group of attacking creatures (a scorpion, a raven, a wolf, a sword, a panther, and a dog). Hunchbacks (*gobbo* in Italian)[958] were considered anomalies of nature, and so both bringers of bad luck and protectors against evil, doing double duty similar to the figures of the Evil Eye and the Gorgo. Another Antioch mosaic discussed above (p. 244) depicts a deformed Hercules with the head of an adult and the body of an infant, strangling two serpents that an envious Hera had sent to kill him in his crib. Aesop, writer of fables, we have previously seen,[959] had features—dark-skinned foreignor, squint-eyed, knit eyebrows, and hunched back—that allowed him to be perceived both as a fascinator and a defense against fascination (*probaskanion*), similar to the double function of the Gorgo and the eye itself.[960] Two representations of

955. See Plutarch, *Quaest. Conv.* 5.7,3 [*Mor.* 681F]; Pollux, *Onom.* 7.108. On grotesques averting the Evil Eye see Jahn 1855:66–67, 91; Wace 1903–1904 (list of genre figures [marble statuettes], bronzes of dwarfs, hunchbacks, Africans ["negroes"], miscellenea, and terracotta figures from Asia Minor, Egypt, Italy, Greece, Southern Russia—all from the Hellenistic Roman period and as anti-Evil Eye apotropaics); Engemann 1975:30–34.

956. Wace 1903–1904:105–6.

957. Trentin 2009:148.

958. Italian *gobbo* is a cognate of the Hebrew *gibbēn*. Lev 21:20 refers to a hunchback (*gibbēn*), which is understood by the rabbis as either (a) one having a doubleback or a double spine or (b) "one who has no eyebrows or only one eyebrow" (*m. Bekhoroth* 7:2; *b. Bekhoroth* 43b). The second is derived from the root *gbb*; cf. Lev 14:9. An implication of unusual eyebrows would further relate this figure to the Evil Eye, since joined eyebrows were thought to mark someone with an Evil Eye.

959. See above, pp. 36, 127, 144 on Aesop.

960. *Vita Aes.*, recension G 16; cf. also *Vita Aes.*, recension W 16. On the various descriptions of Aesop's ugly features see Trentin 2009:134–39.

hunchbacks that were equipped with holes or loops were likely used as neck pendant protectives (*baskania*) against the Evil Eye (Trentin 2009:148). In the Museo Civico Archeologico di Bologna (Room VI (Greek Collection): Case 4B) is a bronze representation of a pig-my with huge phallus identified as "an Alex-andrian grotesque."[961]

Illus. 56

Bes, Egyptian deity/demon, Egypt, small ivory plaque, 1550–1070 BCE. (Line drawing by Dietlinde Elliott)

Dwarfs, today more respectfully re-ferred to as "little people," had a reputation of bringing bad luck or, positively, warding off evil spirits and the Evil Eye. The Roman em-peror Augustus, Suetonius reports, "loathed people who were dwarfish or in any way de-formed, regarding them as freaks of nature and bringers of bad luck" (Suetonius, *Augus-tus* 83).[962] On the other hand, the Egyptian divinity Bes was dwarfish, weak-sighted, bug-eyed, and ugly. Like the hideous Gorgo, his statue and images were thought to provide protection against everything evil and what-ever disturbs the sleeper, and in particular, to defend women giving birth and newborn in-fants against the Evil Eye.[963] At Pompeii were found bronze lamps, in the shape of dwarfs riding immense phalluses, designed to ward off the Evil Eye.[964]

A *homo cacans* ("shitting man") appears in the Woburn Abbey relief, joining other figures attacking an Evil Eye (see above, Illus. 36, 47).[965] The image also is found on neck pendants and as statues.[966] The *cacans* figure ap-pears at Pompei in a painting in the so-called House of Sallust.[967] It is defiant

961. On grotesques and the Evil Eye see Wace 1904–1905.

962. On deformed figures, pigmies, dwarfs see *Vita Aes.* 3; Jahn 1855:67, 91, plate 2.1; Seligmann 1910 2:307–8; Dasen 1993; Garland 1995. On Bes, see also Vol. 1, chap. 2.

963. See Erman 1934:147, 395 (with plates); Eitrem 1991:178; *National Geographic* 196/4 (Oct 1999):83.

964. Grant 1975:131–32 and illustrations; the figures are now in the Naples National Archaeological Museum. RP, Inv. nos. 27871, 27872.

965. See also Jahn 1855 Plate 3, no.1.

966. Jahn 1855:86–89, Plate 4, nos. 11a, b, c; Seligmann 1910 2:206–7, 305, fig. 199.

967. Described in the *Giornale degli Scavi di Pompei* ns. 2 (1870):56–59 and in the report *Pompei e la regione sotterata dal Vesuvio nell' anno LXXIX* (1879), II, p. 223, no. 690.

and insulting ("shit on you!") and so could be registering a statement of insult against the Evil Eye. Being pissed and shit on was degrading. Priapus, asserting the truth of what he was saying, declares, if I am lying, "let white turds of crows disgrace my head, and let Ulius and frail Pediatia and that thief Voranus come to piss and shit on me!" (Horace, *Sat.* 1.8.38).[968] Pissing and shitting (*mictum atque cacatum, urina, cacare, mictare*) were forbidden in tombs and shrines, with a plaque usually displaying the prohibition.[969] Exposure of a bare backside ("mooning" in U. S. culture) was and remains a related mode of expressing disrespect, defiance, insult, and of repelling the Evil Eye.[970]

Satyr masks (*satyrica signa*), Pliny notes (*NH* 19.19.50), had a grotesque appearance and were erected in gardens and the Roman forum to ward off the Evil-Eyeing of the envious (*invidentium effascinationes*). They were misshapen figures resembling lustful satyrs that displayed exposed phalluses functioning like *fascina*. The phrase *satyrica signa* may have been applied to *fascina* (phallus and testicles) and *baskánia* as well.[971] These images were placed also at the ovens of smiths "to ward off envy" (Aristophanes, Frag. 540; Pollyx, *Onom.* 7.108).[972] *Theatre masks* could have had a similar intent,[973] such as the one worn by the Herculanean actor displaying the *mano cornuta* in a Pompeian comedy scene.[974]

Bullae and Their Contents against the Evil Eye

Some anti-Evil Eye amulets worn on the body were contained in *bullae* (leather pouches or capsules of metal with loops) which were suspended around the neck (see above, Illus. 37, p. 222). Contents of the *bullae* varied from a *fascinum*, or herbs such as garlic or rue, to fragments of parchment on which potent words were written. Children, so vulnerable to the Evil Eye, wore them until their majority (18 for males) or marriage (Persius Flaccus

---

968. *in me veniat mictum atque cacatum Julius et fragilis Pediatia furque Voranus.* Regarding pissing on someone's effigy as an insult, see Juvenal, *Sat.* 1.131. The emperor Caracalla executed someone for pissing on his statue and effigy (Spartianus, *Caracalla* 5).

969. So Jahn 1855:87–88, with a sketch of a plaque showing Hecate and a prohibiting inscription.

970. Morris 1985:200.

971. So Jahn 1855:67, 91, noting their common apotropaic function.

972. Jahn 1855:67, 91, Plate 2.1. See also Stephani 1863 (St. Petersburg collection): 114; 1866:70–71; 1869:129; 1876:70, 121, no. 24; pp. 144, 146, 157.

973. So Jahn 1855:67; for illustrations see Seligmann 1910 2, figures 223–25.

974. Depictions of this figure (now in the Naples National Archaeological Museum) appear on the covers of *Juvenal, The Sixteen Satires* (Penguin 1974) and De Jorio 2000.

5.31; Pliny *NH* 33.4.25). Triumphant generals did so as well for protection against Evil-Eyed envy.[975] A gold bulla (Etruscan or Roman, date and provenance unknown) is adorned by a Gorgon head in relief.[976] Portraits from the Fayum in Egypt picturing women and children wearing tubular capsules attest their regular use among Egyptians in the Greco-Roman period.[977] Christians continued the practice.[978] *Bullae* also were suspended from the necks of favorite animals (Ovid, *Met.* 10.114). Originally denoting the *container* of amuletic protection, *bulla* eventually took on the meaning of "amulet" itself.

Crescents against the Evil Eye

Like bullae, *crescents*, replicas of the horned moon, or images of bi-cornate bovine heads, and of the spread legs of parturient women, also were worn as apotropaic pendants or were hung about the neck of prized domestic animals (horses, camels).[979] Horsehoes replicating the shape of the crescents and of the spread legs of parturient women (and similar in shape to the *mano cornuta*), served the same apotropaic purpose.[980]

Illus. 57
Sketch of a crescent amulet for wearing, depicting a horned bull's head and a phallus (from Seligmann 1910 1:341, fig. 61)

975. For illustrations see Seligmann 1910 2, figs. 202–204; Labatut 1877, figs. 300, 302. The custom seems to have orginated with the Etruscans (seventh century BCE, Plutarch, *Romulus* 25; Pliny, *NH* 33.4.10); then adopted by the Romans since the monarchial period (Pliny, *NH* 33.1.10 [first hung by Tarquinius Priscus upon the neck of his son]; Plutarch, *Quaest. Rom.* 101; Macrobius, *Sat.* 1.6.9–11; Plautus, *Rudens* 4.4.127; Livy, *Ab urbe condita* 26.36.5; Suetonius, Julius *Caesar* 34). Eventually it was practiced by Christians as well. The BBC television series "Rome" (2005) shows young Octavian wearing a *bulla*.
   On bullae see also Athen. *Deipn.* 12.70; Varro, *Ling. Lat.* 7.108; Cicero, *Verr.* 2.1.58; Juvenal, *Sat.* 5.163; Jahn 1855:42, 44; Marquardt 1886 1:84; Mau 1897; Saglio 1896 1.1:754–55 (and figs. 893, 896, 897 of persons wearing bullae); Deubner 1934; Leclercq 1910:1331–34; Gerstinger 1954; Budge 1978/1930:14–15; Schienerl 1984:45–54; Gager 1992:232–34.

976. Now in the Johns Hopkins University Archaeological Museum, described by Jessica Phippen ("Gold *Bulla*").

977. Parlasca 1966, Plate 50, Nr. 1–2; Plate 17, Nr. 1; pl. 33, Nr. 1; Parlasca 1969–80: vol. 1, nos. 35, 36, 62, 96; vol. 2, nos. 250, 257; vol. 3, nos. 527, 533, 621, 654, 656–57, 659–66, 665, 669–70, 672, 674.

978. Dölger 1932; Gager 1992:232–34.

979. Seligmann 1919 2:138–40 and figs. 150–52. For Israelite use of crescents as amulets see Judg 8:21.

980. See Elworthy 1895/1958:181–232; Gravel 1995:75–89.

Crepundia, *Bells, Noisemakers against the Evil Eye*

Related to *bullae* and crescents were the *crepundia* (clapping objects that made noise), such as *lunulae* that also were hung around necks of children.[981] The noise they made relates them, in turn, to bells (*tintinnabula*), that often were combined with *fascina* and images of the *mano fica* to form composite amulets against the Evil Eye.[982] Their noise, it was thought, drove away the Evil Eye and other baneful forces. In Israel, the bells attached to the robe of Aaron and all high priests (Exod 28:33–34) protected the life of the high priest (Exod 28:35) and drove away maleficent forces, including the Evil Eye.[983] The bells were hung on animals (cf. Zech 14:20) and those suspended in homes and shops undoubtedly had the same apotropaic function. The Christian church father John Chrysostom criticised the practice of his parishioners of using bells and red bracelets to protect infants from the Evil Eye.[984] On Esquiline Hill in Rome was found a gold bell engraved with a Greek anti-Evil Eye inscription (*tois ommasin hypotetagmai*) whose precise meaning is uncertain.[985] It is probable that the modern practice of attaching rattling tin cans to the bumpers of carriages and automobiles transporting newly married couples is a vestige of this ancient practice. Newlyweds were deemed especially vulnerable to the Evil Eye. A twentieth-century account of an Evil Eye incident in a Greek village illustrates the continued use of bells for the protection of animals from the Evil Eye in modern time and provides another conception of how they function:

> An incautious person admired a string of twelve horses he saw one day; at once the bells on the two foremost horses shivered into a thousand pieces, but the horses themselves remained unhurt, the bells having attracted all the evil to themselves. The amulets, in short, are a species of lightning conductor, just as the power of overlooking is thought popularly to be a kind of electricity which resides in the eye. (Hardie 1992/1923:112)

981. Plautus, *Miles* 5.1.6 (line 1399)"; *Rudens* 4.4.110 (lines 1154-71) (list of a girl's crepundia); Jahn 1855:42–43.

982. See Trumpf-Lyritzaki 1981, esp. 172–75 and above, p. 138. On tintinnabulum see also Espérandieu 1913; Herzog-Hauser 1937.

983. Gaster 1969:263–78.

984. John Chrysostom, *Hom. 1 Cor. 12:13* (PG 61.105–106).

985. Trumpf-Lyritzaki 1981: col. 173.

Protective Colors Blue and Red Against the Evil Eye

Certain colors were thought to have apotropaic power, especially blue and red which were employed regularly to ward off the Evil Eye. Color, it was held, revealed an object's essence (Plato, *Timaeus* 67c). Specific colors were associated with, or symbolic of, certain features of terrestrial and celestial life.[986] Blue and red, used to adorn clothing, jewelry, ornamentation, buildings, and myriads of amulets, were the colors deemed most powerful against the Evil Eye.[987] Blue was associated with the sky, the gods, and celestial power.[988] Red was linked with blood and the life force of humans and animals, as well as the burning sun. Both blue and red, and their combination in the color purple, were also the preferred colors of royalty, power, and high status. Egyptian Eye of Horus amulets were of many colors but predominantly of shades of blue and red.[989] Knot amulets also were colored red, blue, green and white.[990] Stones of blue (lapis lazuli, agate, turquoise) and red (ruby, haemalite, jasper, blood-stone) were considered to have apotropaic power and were employed as anti-Evil Eye amulets. These two powerful colors and symbols of life were used to counteract envy and the Evil Eye, whose color was pallor and paleness, symbolizing the dessication, weakness and death they were thought to cause.

Among the predominantly brown-eyed peoples of the Circum-Mediterranean, blue eyes were conventionally associated with aliens, and aliens with the dangerous Evil Eye. The Greek philosopher Xenophanes of Colophon (c. 570–c. 475 BCE) observed that the Thracians associated both these colors with their gods: "The Ethiopians say that their gods are snub-nosed and black; the Thracians, that theirs have light blue eyes and red hair."[991] The nomadic tribe of the Budini among the Sythians, according to Herodotus (*Hist.* 4. 108). also had "deep blue eyes and bright red

---

986. On colors in general see Lamb and Bouriau 1995. On colors in antiquity, including their apotropaic function, see Kranz 1912; Wunderlich 1925; König 1928 (with a comprehensive list of Greek and Latin terms for colors); Hornblower 1932; Kees 1943; André 1949; Cagiano di Azevedo 1954; Dumézil 1954:47–72; Seufert 1955; Schmidt 1962 (on red and blue); Gradwohl 1963 (colors in the Old Testament); Hermann and Cagiano di Azevedo 1969; Marganne 1978. On colors in the Arab world, Mourad 1939 (blending of blue and green).

987. On apotropaic red and blue see Seligmann 1910 1:248; 2:20, 101 and *passim*; on red see also Greenfield 2006; on green (Islam) and yellow (China) as protective against the Evil Eye and evil influences see Seligmann 1910 2:259.

988. Hermann 1969:409 and Dumézil 1954:63–72. On "the language of color" in the Mediterranean world see A. Borg 1999.

989. Hermann 1969:370.

990. Ibid.

991. Xenophanes of Colophon, Frag. 21 (Diels-Kranz, *FVS* Frag. 21 B 16).

hair." He states this without drawing any implications. It is interesting, however, that it is precisely these colors that also were thought to ward off the Evil Eye according to the principle of *similia similibus* ("like influences like"). For Herodotus, of course, the Budini were aliens and thus potentially possessors of the Evil-Eye. In many cultures still today, blue and red threads or bracelets are attached to the wrists of the newlyborn to protect them from the Evil Eye.[992] In apotropaic Gorgon masks from Sri Lanka, blue and red colors are both prominent; see above Illus. 54, 58.

Illus. 58
Sri Lankan wooden Evil Eye mask,
predominantly blue, with feature
of peacock tails
(John H. Elliott collection)

Blue was the color associated with the heavens, the gods, and celestial power. In Mesopotamia and Egypt, blue was a pronounced color of the gods.[993]. It was also the color of mourning[994] as it was in Iran.[995] Among Romans, blue was the color of Jupiter and his attributes, symbolizing heaven.[996] Blue is the prominent celestial color in the several frescos of Mithra slaying the bull (e.g. the fresco of a Mithraeum, second century CE, discovered in Marino, Italy, in 1963).

The color blue, produced by a dye derived from a shellfish (*Murex trunculus*), was costly to make and hence available primarily to the wealthy. In the human realm, blue therefore became associated with wealth, power, and royalty. Blue graced the bodies and the tombs of Egyptian pharaohs. Bluish-purple tapestries adorned the residential palaces of kings, such as the Greek king Agamemnon (Aeschylus. *Agam.* 30) and the Persian king, Ahasuerus (Esther 1:6). Persian royalty wore "a diadem of fine purple linen" (Esther 8:15). In Israel, too, blue, often combined with red, was a prominent color in the house of God and its appointments.[997] Blue amulets and the color blue are prominant in Mesopotamian art, jewelry, ornamentation and monumental structures (such as the façade of ancient Babylon's Ishtar Gate). Assurnasirpal, king of Assyria asserted, "I caused bricks to be baked with blue (enamel) and placed them over the doors." Theodore Schrire, citing this text in connection with his com-

---

992. Maloney 1976:xiv, 7, 8, 120 and *passim*.

993. Herman 1969:373). In Egypt blue was the color of the god Amun (ibid., 367)

994. Ibid., 367

995. Ibid., 375.

996. Ibid., 393.

997. On blue as a prominent color in Israel's tabernacle and temple, see Vol. 3, chap. 1.

ments on blue as an apotropaic color, comments, "This was doubtless done to protect these buildings from the Evil Eye."[998] Blue pearls and bracelets, pendants, necklaces and rings made of blue or indigo cobalt-colored stones such as lapis lazuli, agate, sapphire, amethyst, jasper, blue diamond or turquoise or blue pearls provided anti-Evil Eye protection.[999] as did replicas of blue eyes and the host of amuletic Eyes of Horus.[1000] Free-standing stone replicas of a blue eye are contained in the Egyptian section of the State Hermitage Museum, St. Petersburg, Russia (see above, Illus. 39, p. 230). An apotropaic blue agate stone depicting a personification of envy under attack bears an inscription declaring, "Envy, no luck for you."[1001]

Among animals, it is the blue color of the peacock's tail (along with its eye-like shapes) that made this fowl a protector against the Evil Eye. The fresco of a Pompeii garden scene includes representations of a peacock and a Gorgo, a potent combination of anti-Evil Eye apotropaics (=*probaskania*).[1002] In modern time, in countries of the Circum-Mediterranean, tiny glass blue eyes for averting the Evil Eye are sewn into the diapers of babies or are attached to clothing or to vehicles of transportation. Larger blue glass eyes are sold in profusion in the marketplaces and are worn by the locals. In Greece and Turkey, residences frequently are painted blue.

The color red likewise was employed to protect against the Evil Eye.[1003] Since the color of blood was red and since blood was thought to have apotropaic power[1004] red was ascribed the same potency. In the Ancient Near East, Egypt, Greece and Rome, the color red (or scarlet or crimson) was linked with a variety of things. In general, it was associated with blood, health, life, but also fire, anger, danger, and sickness.[1005] On the one hand, "red counted as the basic color of misfortune."[1006] Unlucky days were written in red in the Egyptian calendar. (Hermann 1969:373). Demons were thought to be red (Homer, *Iliad*. 2.305–306; Pseudo-Callisthenes, *Alexander Romance* 2.33).

998. Schrire 1982:58.

999. On blue as an apotropaic color attested cross-culturally see Seligmann 1910 1:246–47 and *passim*; Patai 1983, ch. 6; Pastoreau 2001.

1000. Hermann 1969:364. See the large collections of Eyes of Horus in the Bologna Museum, the Julian Pitt Rivers Museum, Oxford; the British Museum and other museums.

1001. Described by Walcot 1978:85; see also above, pp. 171, 245.

1002. Now in the Naples National Archaeological Museum, inv. no. 8760.

1003. On the apotropaic power of red across cultures and its uses see Seligmann 1919 2:247–259.

1004. Eckstein-Waszink 1950:413,

1005. Hermann 1969:408–409; Wunderlich 1925.

1006. Hermann 1969:365, 373.

On the other hand, red could also signal or designate power, prestige, and high rank.[1007] Purple (a combination of blue and red) was an intensified marker of preeminent status. In Egypt, red was associated with deities such as Isis and Seth, who murdered his brother Horus.[1008] In Mesopotamia and Israel, red was the color of the East[1009] and the color of the deity Tammuz because of its protective power.[1010] Among Hittites, blue and red were colors of protection and blessing.[1011] In Greece, Athenian assemblies of the people were protected by red cords (Aristophanes, *Ach.* 22; cf. Theocritus, *Idyls* 2.2); in Rome, colored threads were used in a ritual of healing from a possible Evil Eye attack (Petronius, *Sat.* 131.4–5).

Romans associated the color red with the gods (Plutarch, *Quaest. Rom.* 287E); the cult image of Jupiter Capitolinus was painted red each year (Pliny, *NH* 35.157; Plutarch, *Quaest. Rom.* 287D). Red was the color worn also by rulers, military commanders, and priests to advertise their power and high status.[1012] Red/purple was the color donned by Roman youth when they achieved their majority.[1013] At her wedding, the Roman bride donned a red reticulum or veil, a custom also practiced by the Greeks possibly for apotropaic effect.[1014] Red had a role in funeral customs in Sparta and Rome,[1015] possibly to protect against the demons of death and the Evil Eye associated with death.

The color red was thought to have healing power. Epileptics were encouraged to drink gladiators' blood (Pliny, *NH* 28.4). Turtle-blood and pomegranite juice were considered effective against epilepsy, which, in turn, was associated with the Evil Eye (Pliny, *NH* 32.112).[1016] Against earaches red wool was stuffed into the ear (Marcellus Empiricus, *De Medicamentiis* 9.14.37). Rods colored red were thought to protect against human enemies.[1017] Red-colored phalluses, it was believed, warded off thieves, increased the fertility of crops, and secured the safety of the fields.[1018] Red

1007. Ibid.

1008. Ibid., 365, 367, 370.

1009. Ibid., 373, 376.

1010. Ibid., 374.

1011. Ibid.

1012. Ibid., 396–97.

1013. Ibid., 399.

1014. Ibid., 400.

1015. Ibid., 405.

1016. On red as apotropaic see also Pliny *NH* 29.17.64; 30.30.98, 99 etc.

1017. Hermann 1969:405.

1018. See *Carmina Priap.* 1.5; 26.9; 72.2; 83.6; Tibullus, *Elegies* 1.1.17; Ovid, *Fast.* 6.319; Horace, *Sat.* 1.8.5.

clothing protected against lightning; a red milestone defended against hail. Red or purple was used in a curse ritual (Lysias, *Against Andocides* 51). Red had a role in funeral customs in Sparta and Rome[1019] possibly to protect against the demons of death and the Evil Eye associated with death.

Red amulets as well as objects colored red—cloth, clothing, uniforms, shields, jewelry, bridles for animals—were used to protect both humans and animals against the Evil Eye, a practice that has continued into modern time.[1020] This includes red horn amulets (*corni, cornuti*), miniature red hunchback amulets (*gobbos*), red and blue bracelets attached to the wrists of newborns, and red or blue anti-Evil Eye masks from Sri Lanka. In general, red and blue colors enhanced the apotropaic power of objects. Red wax on Roman lead defixion tablets gave them greater potency (Ovid, *Amores* 3.7.29). The red of Israelite warriors' shields and clothing (Nah 2:4; 1 Macc 4:23) had apotropaic power.[1021] In Israel's place of worship and cult as well as in its production of amulets, blue and red were prominent apotropaic colors; see Vol. 3, chap. 1.[1022]

Protective Animals, Living Creatures

Certain animals or animal parts, or depictions thereof, were used to protect against the Evil Eye. The more powerful the animals and the more numerous the cluster of creatures, the greater the protection.[1023] Many anti-Evil Eye amulets, as discussed above, depict an Evil Eye under attack from a circle of powerful creatures that included lions, wolves, dogs, panthers, wild boars, serpents, scorpions, crocodiles, ibises, ravens and more; see above, pp. 235–44. A three dimensional apotropaic figure of a *crocodile* once was suspended above the entrance to the cathedral of Sevilla, Spain.[1024] According to Pliny (*NH* 28.101), the Persian Magi held that among the many remedies supplied by the *hyena* and its parts, the hide from a hyena's forehead averted the Evil Eye, as did an amulet made from a hyena's eye.[1025]

1019. Hermann 1969:405,

1020. Moss and Cappannari 1976:9 and fig. 1.3 and Maloney 1976 *passim*.

1021. Hermann 1969:381.

1022. On the modern use of blue and red against the Evil Eye see Maloney 1976 (blue: 7, 8, 11, 50–51, 58, 310–11 and *passim*; red: 33–35, 126–27 and *passim*).

1023. For extensive lists see Seligmann 1910 2:112–35; 1922; 1927.

1024. Seligmann 1910 2:124 and fig. 56.

1025. Johnston 1995:385.

Representations of *serpents* appear often on amulets and in apotropaic designs for warding off the Evil Eye.[1026] The supposed blue of their eyes[1027] perhaps is related to the idea, based on the principle of "like against like," that serpents not only wielded an Evil Eye but could also protect against the Evil Eye. Brightly painted wooden anti-Evil Eye masks from contemporary Sri Lanka in the author's possession variously depict a face with a fearsome visage with bulging bloodshot eyes, bared teeth, extended tongue, and serpentine hair of cobras understood as protective. The masks are affixed to houses under construction to protect against envious Evil-Eyeing passersby (see above, Illus. 54, 58, pp. 249, 257).

Other living creatures depicted on Evil Eye amulets include *peacocks*. Greek mythology connected eyes with the designs in a peacock's tail. Argus Panoptes, appointed by Hera as guardian of the heifer-nymph Io, was a primordial giant whose epithet *Panoptes*, "all-seeing," led to his being described as having four or more or even one hundred eyes. Ovid states that after Argus, builder of Jason's ship, the Argo, was slain protecting Io, Hera had the hundred eyes of Argus preserved forever in a peacock's tail (Ovid, *Met.* 1.624). The multiplicity of eyes (of Argus and of the peacock's tail) increased the prophylactic power. The peacock's tail also combines these "eyes" with the apotropaic color blue.[1028] The fresco of a Pompeian garden scene features a peacock alongside a Gorgoneion. A contemporary Sri Lankan anti-Evil Eye mask, predominantly blue in color, features peacock tails with "eyes" where other masks display cobras.

Owls, perhaps because of their large staring eyes, were thought to have a deadly glance and thus could represent an Evil Eye or a force counteracting an Evil Eye on the principle of "like against like" (*similia similibus*).[1029] The artificial owl placed at the Athenian Parthenon was intended to attract other birds and slay them with her deadly glance, thereby providing protection to the sacred site.[1030] Owls appear on amulets depicting an Evil Eye or Envy under attack.[1031] A lead amulet from Ammaedara (modern Haidra) shows on one side the image of an owl and on the other an inscription reading, "Envious Envy,

1026. See Seligmann 1910 2:130–31 and figs. 117, 119, 120, 122–25; for serpents on votive hands see figs. 169, 170.

1027. Rakoczy 1996:92, 174 n631.

1028. See also Siebers 1983:61–63. See above p. 258 regarding representations of a peacock and a Gorgo displayed together in a Pompeian garden scene.

1029. Meisen 1950:153. On owls as apotropaics against the Evil Eye, see Seligmann 1910 1:124; 2:117; Merlin 1940; Bonner 1950:98; Meisen 1950:146, 153, 173–74; Opelt 1966; Rakoczy 1996:172–73 n621; Antón Alvar Nuño 2009–2010.

1030. Meisen 1950:153.

1031. Seligmann 1910 vol. 2, figs. 122, 124.

there is nothing for you to do against a soul that is pure and unstained."[1032] The threshold mosaic of the pearl seller's shop on Rome's Caelian Hill depicted an owl as part of a menagerie of creatures attacking an Evil Eye and thereby protecting the shops and its workers.[1033] Owls likewise appear on later Christian anti-Evil Eye amulets; see Volume 4, chapter 2.

Still other protective creatures include *roosters*[1034] *hares,*[1035] *frogs and toads*[1036] *scarabs/beetles,*[1037] *fish,*[1038] *dolphins,*[1039] and *locusts.*[1040]

Among the *mythological creatures*, the *griffen* was thought to afford protection against an Evil Eye.[1041] Bronze griffins found in the excavations of the fifth century BCE temple of Hera and now on display in the museum at Olympia are said to have been designed to protect athletic competitors at Olympia from the Evil Eye.[1042]

Illus. 59
Sketch of an engraved sard gem from the Praun gem collection depicting an owl perched on an Evil Eye under attack (from Elworthy 1958/1895:131, fig. 19)

Protective Plants, Stones, Amber, Shells, and Metals

Plants, herbs, roots, stones, gems, amber, coral, shells, horn, and metals were all enlisted as apotropaics against the Evil Eye.[1043] Plants and herbs include

1032. *Invidia invidiosa n[i]hil tibi ad anima[m] pura[m] et munda[m])]*); see Merlin 1940:486–487.

1033. Illustrated and discussed by Perdrizet 1922:28–29 and fig. 9; see also fig. 10).

1034. Engemann 1975:29.

1035. Siebers 1983:61–63.

1036. Story 1877:217, 218.

1037. Ibid.

1038. Elworthy 1895/1958:354–55 and fig. 50; Eckstein-Waszink 1950:col. 409; for a fish-like phallus combined with a *mano fica* image see Dölger *ICHTHYS* 2 (1922):444, Plate 77, no. 4.

1039. Elworthy 1895/1958:131, fig. 18; Dunbabin 1991 and Plates 4a, 5f.

1040. Elworthy 1895/1958:121–22. Boll 1914:68 n4, citing Fehrle 1912; Rakoczy 1996:173. For more on these and additional protective living creatures see Seligmann 1910 2:112–35.

1041. Seligmann 1910 1:151; 2:310.

1042. My thanks to Richard Rohrbaugh for this information. For further protective beings (human and mythological) see Seligmann 1910 2:304–15; for deities, Seligman 1910 2:316–22; for angels and saints, Seligmann 1910 2:324–28.

1043. On apotropaic plants, herbs, roots, see Story 1877:220–23; Seligmann 1910 1:284–88, 2:49–112; Scarborough 1991:138–74; for coral amulets see Petrie 1914:27; Callisen 1937; Hansen 1981.

the orchid called satyrion (Pliny, *NH* 26.10), dill,[1044] sage, artemisia,[1045] and baccaris.[1046] The herb rue[1047] was considered by Pseudo-Aristotle (*Prob. phys.*20.34) and the Peripetetic school as effective against the Evil Eye when ingested prior to meals. Rue, and, in modern time, metal replicas of sprigs of rue (Italian: *cimaruta*) have been used as anti-Evil Eye apotropaics in Italy, Greece, Persia, India and Guatamala.[1048] The cimaruta amulet (usually silver) is a representation of a sprig of rue together with a composite of numerous symbols each of which independantly guards against the Evil Eye, thereby making it an extremely powerful composite amulet.[1049]

Illus. 60
Sketches of various types of modern cimaruta amulets against the Evil Eye, Naples, Italy
(from Seligmann 1910 1:296, fig. 50a, 50b)

1044. Schnippel 1929.

1045. Story 1877:222.

1046. Ibid.

1047. Greek: *rytê, pêganon*; Latin: *ruta; ruta graveolens*. Cf. Italian, *cim[m]aruta*, an amulet depicting a sprig (*cima*) of rue (*ruta*).

1048. See Elworthy 1895/1958:343–55, figs. 81, 161–62; see also Günther 1905; Seligmann 1910 2:80–83; Maloney 1976:167, 168–71 (as curative); Knuf 1984:169; Rakoczy 1996:145–46. On the "pharmacology of Sacred Plants, Herbs, and Roots," see Scarborough 1991.

1049. Elworthy 1895/1958:343–55 lists thirteen symbols appearing in cimaruta amulets: rue, Diana Triformis, silver, hand, horned crescent, serpent, key, heart, cock, eagle, sword/dart, fish, and lotus; for illustrations of the cimaruta see Seligmann 1910 1:296–97 and figs. 50a, 50b; and Di Stasio 1981:13, 42.

The herb garlic (Greek: *moly*; Latin: *alio*) was considered an especially powerful apotropaic, perhaps because of the strength of its smell and taste. It was thought to possess both curative and prophylactic power. Pliny mentioned it as as a cure for epilepsy (*NH* 20.23.56). Odysseus used moly/garlic as an amulet to keep Circe from turning him into a pig. Pendant capsules worn around the neck contained garlic and other herbs. The greatest of the herbalists, Dioscorides (c. 40–90 CE), states that "[g]arlic, if suspended in a house, brings health to it, and averts all fascination [the Evil Eye] from humans and sheep; hung on the neck in a red cloth it will protect the flock from disease."[1050] Garlic was used throughout the Middle Ages and beyond to drive off witches, demons, and the Evil Eye. In Greek folklore, simply saying the world "garlic" (*skordo*) is deemed effective.

Frankincense was used for fumigating children exposed to the Evil Eye.[1051] Pliny (*NH* 13.9.40) noted that the fruit of fruit-bearing palms, "when polished with the edge of a file, is used in the practice of religion (*religione*) against fascinators (*fascinantes*)."

Stones (and gems) were believed to have an inherent power to ward off evil and the Evil Eye, while also effecting good fortune; figures engraved on such stones and gems (glyptics) enhanced their power.[1052] The stone galacitite was hung around the necks of the newborn to protect them against illness, envy, and the Evil Eye of malevolent Megaera according to the *Orphica Lithica* (24).[1053] Small semiprecious stones set in rings or necklace pendants (*encolpia*) or simply carried in an individual's clothing, were often engraved with *fascina* or potent anti-Evil Eye texts.[1054] Such stones, like finger rings, which already served to bind evil forces (a ring = a "band"), were increased in anti-Evil Eye potency with inscribed or embossed representations of eyes or phalluses.[1055]

1050. Dioscorides, *De materia medica* 3.97, cited by Story 1877:220.

1051. Story 1877:222.

1052. Seligmann 1919 2:24–38. Budge (1978/1930:306–25) describes fifty-five stones and their protective quality, thirty-one of which (especially red, blue or green stones) were used against the Evil Eye.

1053. Seligmann 1919 2:30; Johnston 1995:385.

1054. On apotropaic gems and engraved stones (glyptics) see King 1885; Elworthy 1895/1958:130–33 and figs. 17–19; Seligmann 1910 2:24–38; Bonner 1950; Zazoff 1983; Engemann 1981 has discussed engraved stones and gems [*intaglio*], with illustrations of gem-amulets [col. 287, Ill. 5; col. 288, Ill. 6; col. 292, Ill. 9]; the apotropaic function of stones/gems, cols. 284–94; the role of Solomon [col. 290, Ill. 7; col. 291, Ill. 8]; the label "gnostic" as erroneous [cols. 285–86]; and Christian and Jewish usage). On amber, see Jahn 1855:44; Story 1877:217.

1055. Deubner 1910:437.

Shells, particularly *cowrie shells*, were prized throughout the ancient world for their supposed healing, regenerative, and protective power. Cowrie shell necklaces were worn *anti baskaniôn*, "against the Evil Eye" (Strabo, *Geog.* 14.2.7), most likely because their shape resembled the eye as well as the vulva, themselves powerful organs against the Evil Eye.[1056] Egyptians

wore cowrie-shell necklaces for the same purpose.[1057] The Greek for "cowrie" was *kteis*, which also meant "scallop, comb, or vulva." Romans called the cowrie shell *matriculus* ("little matrix") or *porcella* ("little sow"). Both Greek and Latin terms were used to denote the vulva as generative organ.[1058] "Pig" (Greek: *choiros*; Latin, *porcus*), as noted above, p. 211–212), was a vulgarism ("cunt") for the female genitals. In Northern Arabia around the early 1900s, "almost every woman, every child, every mare and she-camel wears shells around the neck, for the protection from the evil eye."[1059]

Illus. 61

Sketch of a necklace of cowrie shells with an eye (of fowl?) pendant (from Elworthy1958/1895: 128, fig. 13). See also Jahn 1855, Plate 5, no. 6; Seligmann 1910, 1:317, fig. 55.

Among *metals*, amulets of gold and silver (rings, bracelets, pendants etc.) were embossed with apotropaic images and so had prophylactic as well as ornamental value. *Iron*, regarded as a mysterious metal because of its magnetic properties, was considered effective against the Evil Eye.[1060] Iron objects, moreover, when struck, produced loud sounds frightening demons and the Evil Eye.[1061] According to the *Testament of Solomon* (2:6), the demon Ornias feared to touch this metal. Iron could be worn on the person in the form of iron earrings that could be touched when the presence of an Evil Eye possessor was suspected. Horseshoes of iron combined powerful apotropaic properties. Shaped like apotropaic crescents or horned moons, they also made noise when struck and consisted of a metal

1056. Jahn 1855:79–80, Plate 4, no. 8; Seligmann 1910 2:204–6; Gravel 1995:119–20. Potts (1982:45) presents two skulls with cowrie shells for eyes (figs. 79, 80), the latter excavated from ancient Jericho, c. 8,000–7,000 BCE.

1057. Pinch 1994:107; see also Lindsay 1968:132.

1058. Herter 1978:18. See also the 142 small mussel shells known as *choirinai* (Greek: "piglings") and *concha veneris* (Latin: "shell of Venus") also associated with the vulva. (Pinch 1994:107). The cowrie as *porcella* could also represent the great sow goddess, such as Demeter or Ceres (Lindsay 1968:132).

1059. Kennedy 1910:441. On prophylactic cowries in modern times, see also Maloney 1976:80, 117, 122.

1060. Elworthy 1895/1958:220–225; Seligmann 1910 2:6–24; Frazer and Gaster 1959:269–70; Hill and Mundle 1966; Maloney 1976:10, 16, 11, 118; Müller 1976:783–84.

1061. Eckstein-Waszink 1950:403.

with mysterious magnetic properties. They were displayed prominently in homes, animal stalls, and places of work. The legendary Telchines of Rhodes were said to be the first craftmen to work iron and were considered both victims and casters of the Evil Eye.[1062]

Detecting and Curing Injury Caused by the Evil Eye

Far less information exists on procedures followed for detecting and curing injury thought caused by an Evil Eye. Discussing illness remedies (*remedia*) prescribed by the Persian Magi, Pliny the Elder in his *Natural History* (Book 31) repeatedly mentions objects that are *tied* to part of the body (*adalligare*), using a standard term for "amulet." He passes on these remedies as information and without critique, adding only occasionally, "if it is true" (*si verum est*; *NH* 30.143).The curative power of remedies and of medicine, Pliny noted, influenced by a certain school of Greek thought, involved the forces of "sympathy and antipathy" and the equation of "like curing like" (Pliny, *NH* 20.1.1–2). He reports of remedies "recommended by our authorities" who hold that "medicines are produced by that famous sympathy and antipathy between things (*concordia rerum aut repugnantia*; *NH* 29.17.61, LCL). Thus an eye of a crab was used as a medium for healing a human eye; ashes of dogs' teeth mixed with honey were employed for helping children who were slow in teething (*NH* 30.22); a shrew-mouse was used to heal the bite of a shrew-mouse (*NH* 29.89) and so forth.[1063] This logic, as noted above, prompted the use of an eye to avert an Evil Eye, or a powerful object (genitalia, hand gestures, images of Bes or Gorgo and the like) to repeal a powerful Evil Eye.

Procedures for detecting injury caused by the Evil Eye likewise are mentioned only rarely in the ancient sources.[1064] An ancient Mesopotamian ritual preserved in a Sumerian text and listed in Volume one, chapter 2 mentions a procedure involving oil and water.[1065] Matthew Dickie notes that in the Greco-Roman Hellenistic period old women were prominent as healers and purifiers "through the application of amulets and the uttering of incantations, [employed for] forestalling or curing the effects of the Evil

---

1062. Strabo, *Geog.* 14.2.7; Ovid. *Met.* 7. 366–367; Diodorus Siculus, *Library* 5.55.

1063. For an index of illnesses and affections mentioned by Pliny see *Pliny, Natural History* LCL vol. 8 (W. H. S. Jones), 1963:577–83.

1064. This is in contrast to numerous accounts registered in modern medical annals; cf. Maloney 1976 *passim*, Dundes 1992 *passim*.

1065. See Langdon 1913:11–12, Plate 3; Ebeling 1949:209. For the apotropaic use of incense in Mesopotamia see Thomsen 1992:29.

Eye."[1066] Although spittle was employed in cures, as noted above, two texts of Theocritus (*Idyl* 6.39–40 and 7.126–127) referring to spitting thrice in connection with an Evil Eye describe actions for fending off the Evil Eye rather curing its damage. Plutarch records the belief that looking at the yellow bird called *charadrios* (plover) was effective for it drew to itself the poison of the Evil Eye.[1067] This too looks more like diversion than cure. However, Pliny describes a bird, also yellow in color and named *icterus* (Latin: *Galgalus*), which, when looked at, *heals jaundice (NH* 30.94). If Plutarch and Pliny are referring to the same bird and the same belief, then Plutarch's *charadrios/* plover may also have been thought to cure injury from an Evil Eye. In his *Satyricon,* Petronius presents the protagonist Encolpius undergoing a cure for erectile disfunction that perhaps was caused by an Evil Eye. The ritual, carried out by an old woman, involved colored threads, the middle finger and spitting (*Sat.* 131.4–5; see above, pp. 150–51). A procedure involving the use of a hand and three fingers may also be a healing treatment of Evil Eye injury. It is recorded in the *De medicamentis* (15.11) of Marcellus Empiricus:

> To be recited when sober, touching the relevant part of the body with three fingers: thumb, middle finger, and ring finger; the other two are stretched out [= the shape of a *mano cornuta*]. "Go away, no matter whether you originated today or earlier: this disease, this illness, this pain, this swelling, this redness, this goiter, these tonsils, this abscess, this tumor, these glands and the little glands I call forth, I lead forth, I speak forth, through this spell, from these limbs and bones."[1068]

This may suggest that the illness was thought caused by an Evil Eye since the hand is actually making the shape of a *mano cornuta* conventionally employed to repel an Evil Eye. One clear healing ritual is mentioned by Heliodorus in his novel, *Aethiopica.* This is the only such extended description of an Evil Eye healing ritual in ancient Greek and Roman literature, though it parallels details of more ancient Sumerian texts.[1069] The priest Calasiris treats the maiden Charicle, who was struck inadvertently by her lover's Evil Eye (*Aeth.* 4.5). Using laural leaf, a tripod, fire and incense, he speaks a prayer, waves laurel over the body of ill girl from head to foot, whispers secret words, yawns, and names Theagenes as the one responsible.

1066. Dickie 2001:108–9; see also 245–50.

1067. Plutarch, *Quaest. Conv.*5.7 [*Mor.* 681C]; cf. also Heliodorus, *Aeth.* 3.8.1.

1068. Translation by Georg Luck 1985:72–73.

1069. For Mesopotamian texts see Ebeling 1949:209; Thomsen 1992:29; and Vol. 1, chap. 2 of the present work.

This is perhaps a caricature meant to amuse and parody an Apollonian oracle, but is similar to healing rituals still used today in regions of the CircumMediterranean.[1070] Procedures used in modern time also follow a ritual involving oil and a basin of water to detect, counteract, and dispel the effect of the Evil Eye and restore to health. One such procedure encountered in Italy has been described as follows:[1071] (1) Into a glass or basin of water (2) is shaken a drop of oil from a finger tip. (3a) If the oil spreads, this is taken to indicate that the injury was not caused by an Evil Eye. (3b). If oil forms circles or congeals, then the illness is deemed to have been caused by an Evil Eye. (4) In the latter case, certain words are then spoken or chanted three times, and a gesture is made (such as the sign of the cross) over the victim. Illnesses include headaches, melancholy, and loss of strength. Healers are always women (mothers or aunts or other relatives of the victim), or in Naples, state-authorized *fattuchiere* (wise women). Other procedures include use of salt or olive branches blessed in church on Palm Sunday, or imprecations.[1072] George Murdock's 1980 cross-cultural analysis of illness worldwide finds the belief that the Evil Eye causes illness in fifty-four of 139 societies, mainly in the Circum-Mediterrean region. In nine of these societies it is seen as a predominant cause of illness. Eighteen societies regard it an important secondary cause, and twenty-seven societies consider it a minor cause of illness.[1073]

1070. See Schmidt 1913:603–5; Campbell 1964:339; Brögger 1068:15ff.; Yatromanolakis 1988:202–3; and Rakoczy 1996:211–12.

1071. Rush 1974:47–48, cited in Hauschild 1979:188–89.

1072. Hauschild 1979:1900.

1073. Murdock 1980:21, 37–40, 49, 50–51, 58, 61–62, 66. On the Evil Eye as cause of illness see also Cominsky 1976:166–71; Garrison and Arensberg 1976:315–19 (survey of evidence of this aspect of Evil Eye belief in Ethiopia, southern Italy, India, Guatamala, and among Slovak-Americans).

4

THE TRANSCENDENTAL
GOOD EYE

The concept of a "good eye" does not appear coupled with, or contrasted to, that of an Evil Eye in the Greco-Roman literature, as it does in the biblical writings and related traditions. A good eye was a transcendental image for the providence and beneficence of the gods and the celestial powers. The image is mentioned only occasionally and independant of any reference to an Evil Eye.[1] It was not a constituent element of the Evil Eye belief complex.[2] In Egyptian tradition, the good eye was the restored eye of Horus, which was thought imbued with healing and protective power, so that representations of this eye, wedjat eyes, were used as potent amulets against an Evil Eye. Here, too, however, an explicit contrast of good and evil eyes is absent. The explicit contrasts by Jesus and the rabbis of a good eye and an Evil Eye of humans are novel and therefore especially noteworthy.[3]

1. See Seligmann 1910:244–51; 1922:450 ff.; Deonna 1965:96–107, 147–53; Potts 1982:68–78; de la Mora 1987:12.

2. Rakoczy (1996:227–45) proposes that the notion of a "good eye" accompanied that of an "Evil Eye" from Hesiod onward. However, he also acknowledges that "envy and the Evil Eye were facts of everyday life, whereas the notion of a "good eye" ("der gute Blick") "remained a transcendental reality from the beginning" and was ascribed by Greeks and Romans only to deities (1996:277). The images on the Dura Europus synagogue ceiling that he cites as evidence of the pairing of Evil Eye and good eye (1996:228 n6) is late (third century CE), and not Greco-Roman but Jewish. Moreover, both eye images at Dura Europus have been interpreted as Evil Eyes on iconographic grounds; see Engemann (1975:38–39, figs. 8 and 9).

3. See the discussions in Vols. 3 and 4.

The United States of America one dollar bill bears a Masonic symbol of the all-seeing and all-blessing eye of God within the triangular tip of a pyramid. It was called the "Eye of Providence" by its designers, Benjamin Franklin, John Adams, and Thomas Jefferson.[4] It is an interesting modern relic of the ancient notion of a divine protective eye. Apart from the distinctive Egyptian transmogrification of a restored eye of Horus into an anti-Evil

Illus. 62

US dollar bill, with Divine Eye on pyramid apex (Photo by John H. Elliott)

Eye amulet still employed in the Hellenistic period, the concept of a good eye does not appear in Greek and Roman sources in tandem with, or as a counterpart to, an Evil Eye and so is omitted from our analysis of the Greek and Roman Evil Eye texts. In Islamic culture, Seligmann indicates in an appendix on "the beneficial glance,"[5] one calls upon Allah for protection with His eye. One also blesses a child with the words, "the name of Allah be upon you and around you. May the Evil Eye be blinded and never harm my child."[6] For further Islamic Evil Eye tradition, see Volume 4, chapter 2.

4. On the symbol and its history see Potts 1982:68–78.

5. Seligmann 1910 1:244–51.

6. Ibid., 248.

5

SUMMARY AND CONCLUSION

This completes our survey of Evil Eye belief and practice in Greece and Rome through Late Antiquity. The detail of this volume and of the previous one pertaining to Mesopotamia and Egypt now sets the stage and clarifies the social and cultural context for an examination of the appearance of Evil Eye belief and practice in the Bible and the biblical communities.

Over the fourteen centuries from Homer and Hesiod to the end of the ancient world (eighth century BCE to sixth century CE), a wide array of Greek and Roman authors have spoken of the infamous Evil Eye—poets, dramatists, philosophers, historians, naturalists, statesmen, rhetoricians, novalists, and lexicographers. Anti-Evil Eye amulets and other Evil Eye apotropaica of the Greeks and Romans fill our museums.

The ancients understood the Evil Eye to be a natural, albeit dangerous, phenomenon. The types of persons to whom an Evil Eye was attributed (the fascinators), indicate that the Evil Eye was associated with strangers within one's own group and even more so with foreigners and exotics of other lands, with blind persons, one-eyed beings and those with unusual ocular features (such as wandering eye, cross-eyes or knit eyebrows). The Evil Eye was also associated with persons who could be suspected of envy and casting an envious Evil Eye (persons envious of rival peers and their good fortune, widows and widowers of married persons, old persons of the young and beautiful, sick persons of the healthy, mediocre persons of those who stand out and excel etc.). The Evil Eye belief reflects a perception and preoccupation with inequity in daily life, with disparity between the haves and the have nots, the mediocre and the outstanding. The accepted notion of limited good meant that any advance enjoyed by any person or group was perceived as involving a loss to some other person or group—your gain is my loss in the zero-sum game of life. This led to grief over and resentment of the good fortune of others with the wish that it be destroyed. This envy was according to human nature and a process that needed to be kept under control and avoided where possible.

The means employed for protecting against or warding off Evil Eye attack, the words, gestures, and amulets employed, all appear to involve the use of things considered potent, charged with power, in order to counter the harmful and destructive potency of the Evil Eyed glance. This thought of power-against-power, powerful eye or phallus or vulva or spittle against a powerful Evil Eye. Rituals and techniques of protection and healing involved spitting, threefold action, words accompanying actions, and old women.

Fear of the Evil Eye, we have seen, pervaded the cultures of the ancient Near East and circum-Mediterranean from the civilization of the Sumerians of Mesopotamia to late Roman antiquity (2500 BCE—600 CE). The evidence of Evil Eye belief and practice ranges widely and includes literature, personal letters, inscriptions, graffiti, pictorial art, sculpture, engravings, bas-reliefs, monuments, mosaics, incantations, prayers, songs, clothing, jewelry, and multitudes of amulets employed to guard personal, private and public spaces.

The terminology of this belief, in its Greek and Latin expressions, has left its mark on the biblical languages of Greek and Latin as well as on our contemporary languages. Behind the modern term "fascination" is the Greek (*baskania*) and Latin (*fascinatio*) concept of the Evil Eye. The German for "Evil Eye, namely "böser Blick" ("evil glance"), reflects the view of the eye as active and projecting beams of light. "The meaning of the middle high German [*Blick* = *Blitz* = "flash"] was originally "bright beam" (*heller Strahl*); *beam*, used in connection with 'flash,' was eventually used of the eye in a transferred sense; the physical meaning of the stem was retained in 'flash' (*Blitz*)."[1] English "glance," moreover, is a cognate of the German *Glanz* ("brightness, luster, brilliancy, splendor") so that "ocular glance" likewise once implied an active eye projecting light.

The Latin terminology for "envy" (*invidere*, *invidia*) demonstrates the cognitive association of Evil-Eyed *looking* and *envy*. Amulets demonstrate this same association, with those against the Evil Eye similar or identical in form and wording to those against envy. The complex of beliefs associated with the Evil Eye and the strategies used to ward off its noxious effect in fact are still found, in various permutations, in many modern societies and ethnic enclaves over two millennia later. The constancy of these beliefs and

---

1. Kluge, *Etymologisches Wörterbuch* 1963:84, *sub* "Blick."

practices across ancient and later cultures, and their continuation through the centuries are two of the most remarkable features of this phenomenon.

A complex of concepts, we have found, accompany and undergrid Evil Eye belief and practice in antiquity and these are joined by several other salient features.

(1) the eye was viewed as *one of the most important organs* of the body.

(2) The eye was regarded as an *active organ* that projects energy similar to a lamp projecting light, or the sun projecting rays, or a hunter's bow shooting arrows, or a serpent spitting poison, or a god casting ocular thunderbolts. Whether the eye of a demon, a god, a human, or an animal, the eye emanates particles of energy or rays, which, when an Evil Eye, strike and harm or destroy all upon which the hostile glance falls. This constituted the *extramission theory of vision* which, of all ocular theories, was predominant in the ancient world.

(3) The eye was thought *linked to, and a channel of, dispositions arising in the heart*. The eye was deemed a window to, and reflection of, the human mind and soul.

(4) An Evil Eye *communicated a hostile attitude* and *conveyed malevolent dispositions* issuing from the heart. It projected them outward through the eye as particles of energy which were directed against resented objects and victims. An Evil Eye was harmful and destructive as well as active; it was a medium of ocular agression.

(5) Among *the malicious dispositions conveyed* by the mechanism of an Evil Eye were miserliness and greed, but in the Greco-Roman world predominantly envy. *Envy* was thought activated by beholding, and being dismayed at, the success of others which was thought to have come at the cost of the envier's own wellbeing (the zero-sum reckoning of the "limited good" notion). The act of envying is regularly combined with, and follows, an act of looking, glimpsing, catching sight of another's good fortune. An envious Evil Eye could be aroused by the sight of another's beauty, success, good fortune, victory, or happiness. It could also be provoked by the utterance of admiration and praise, boasting of personal qualities, or by sight of another's conspicuous consumption. The connection of the Evil Eye and envy was deemed so close that often the terms "Evil Eye" and "envy" were used interchangeably or the less dangerous term "envy" (*phthonos, invidia*) was substituted for the more noxious term "Evil Eye" (*baskanos, fascinus*).

(6) An Evil Eye (*ophthalmos ponêros/oculus malus*) was *connected with an evil tongue* (*mala lingua*); malicious looking worked in tandem with malicious speaking. Linguistically, the standard Greek verb *baskainô* ("injure with an Evil Eye") can denote harmful *looking* as well as malicious *speaking*

(compare also the Indo-Germanic linkage of *baskô* ["speak"] and *phaskô* ["say," "assert"]).

(7) An Evil Eye, in some instances, was considered *an inherited trait* of specific tribes of people such as the Telchines, Thebians, Triballi and Illyrians, of ethnic groups such as the Egyptians, or of women with double pupils.

(8) An Evil Eye could be activated *unintentionally or intentionally*. (8a) Those who inherited an Evil Eye could cast it *unintentionally* as could others such as fathers against their own children or lovers against their beloved. (8b) An Evil Eye could also be activated *deliberately*, as when Medea with her Evil Eye destroyed the monster Talos.

(9) *Suspected or accused wielders* of the Evil Eye (a.k.a "fascinators") included gods, demons such as the Evil Eye demon (*baskanos daimôn*), animals, and humans with distinctive physical features: ocular impairment (blindness, a dimmed eye, a wandering eye = oblique eye, strabismus/ crossed eyes); one-eyed figures (monsters such as the Cyclops), unusual ocular features such as double pupils, knit eyebrows; ill or physically deformed persons (such as Aesop or humpbacks or dwarfs) or widowers and widows—all with cause to be envious of others. Strangers among one's own people and aliens from outside the social group were also feared as fascinators.

(10) *Victims and targets* of the Evil Eye (and envy) included everything that was prized, valued, and honored, but especially children, cattle, crops, personal health and items essential to survival and well-being. Youth, persons of beauty, victorious athletes, conquering generals, or winning contestants were all potential victims of the Evil Eye. Even possessors of an Evil Eye were thought capable of Evil-Eyeing themselves.

(11) The Eye Eye was deemed to be a *major cause* of misfortune, illness, loss, and death.

(12) The Evil Eye was considered a *phenomenon of nature* whose operation and toxic effect could be described in rational terms based on observation and experience.

(13) *Defense* against the Evil Eye was thought possible by a broad variety of apotropaic stratagems and devices that served to distract, divert or repel its deadly power. This arsenal included acts of avoidance as well as the use of powerful words (incantations, formulas spoken and written, obscene verses) actions (spitting, sticking out the tongue, manual gestures [*mano fica, mano cornuta, mano pantea, digitus infamis*]), and an array of amulets involving powerful herbs, stones, gems, horns and other animal parts, objects of adornment (necklaces, bracelets, rings, bells, veils etc.), masks, grotesques, mosaics, the colors blue and red, and designs of figures deemed

to be powerful and functioning on the principle of "like influences alike" (*similia similibus*). These images include representations of the eye and eye-like objects, Eyes of Horus (*wedjat*), Evil Eyes under attack, as well as images of deities (Serapis, Bes, Fascinus, Nemesis, Cunina, Priapus), of mythical figures (Medusa/Gorgo, Medea, Megaera, Polyphemus/Cyclops. Narcissus), and of the male and female genitals (which were associated with the eye and deemed symbols of power, fecundity, and life).

When one takes into account all the extant ancient evidence, one is struck how much of it—by far the majority of sources—concerns ways and means of warding off the Evil Eye's noxious power. Suspicion of the ubiquity of the Evil Eye's presence prompted perpetual fear and constant preoccupation with defense. Worry over its malignant effects continued from birth until death. Precautions taken with infants were matched by those taken at the tomb. Nothing was considered safe. Family, particularly children, property, especially cattle but also prized possessions, the residence itself, even one's honor and prestige—all had to be secured constantly against the potential ravages of the Evil Eye. For this purpose a veritable stockpile of charms and amulets, words and gestures were thrown into the fray.

(14) *Rituals and cures* were practiced for remedying injury caused by the Evil Eye, though the ancient sources on this point are limited.

Clarence Maloney's list[2] of seven features commonly found in descriptions of the belief in the twelve world regions from past to present[3] is remarkably similar to the fourteen points listed here and illustrates the stability of this belief complex over time and across continents.[4]

(15) Belief in, and fear of, the Evil Eye constrained personal and social behavior. It supported and promoted (a) an ethic of moderation and avoidance of excess; (b) a wariness about standing out and showing off and making others look bad or inferior by looking good yourself; (c) a social levelling effect or at minimum a pretense at levelling since actual equality never was established or even desired; (d) adherence to prevailing group norms and standards of conduct; and behavior consistent with group values such as generosity, hospitality, group solidarity and wellbeing. It discouraged divisive envy along with unguarded expression of admiration and praise. Evil Eye accusations, like accusations of witchcraft, were employed to demean, discredit, denounce and destroy one's enemies or rivals. This

2. Maloney 1976:vii–viii.

3. Roberts 1976.

4. For a list of fifteen features associated in antiquity with the Evil Eye and its aversion, most of them similar to features indicated here, see Ogden 2002:224.

activity in turn reinforced group identity, group values and norms, and marked group boundaries.

How Evil Eye belief and practice spread in the Circum-Mediterranean and Near Eastern regions cannot be described with certainty. It represents an amalgam of regional traditions (Mesopotamian, Phoencian, Egyptian, Greek, Etruscan, and Roman) that developed and merged over centuries of economic and cultural contact, colonization and military conquest, eventually covering an expanse of territory from Spain to India and Europe and the British Isles to Africa. Celtic migrations also played a role in this process of dissemination. The Celts (*Galli, Galatai*), major bearers of Evil Eye belief and practice, migrated eastward from Gaul and settled for centuries in Asia Minor (300 BCE) in Galatia, the area named after them. Eventually they turned westward and populated areas of Spain (Galicia), England, Ireland and Scotland, where Celtic and Evil Eye tradition remain strong to this day.[5] The region of Asia Minor settled by the Celts, Galatia, was the scene of a confrontation between an early follower of Jesus, Paul of Tarsus, and opponents at Galatia, both of whom coupled theological dispute with Evil Eye accusation, as we shall see in Volume 3, chap. 2.

This spread of the belief was marked by a striking continuity and consistency in the features constituting the Evil Eye belief complex and aspects of its practice in the Greek and Hellenistic world from Homer and Hesiod to Roman late antiquity. The biblical communities were part of this cultural continuity, embracing Evil Eye belief and practice while also emphasizing some distinctively biblical features. The biblical communities of Israel and the early Church shared the physical and social environments of these ancient cultures where Evil Eye belief flourished, as well as the thought world, the "mentalité," language, and customs expressive of, and supportive of, Evil Eye belief and practice. Thus the evidence we have examined in Volumes 1 and 2 provides the basic context and matrix for detecting and understanding references to the Evil Eye as they appear on the pages of the Old and New Testaments, the focus of Volume 3.

5. Mackenzie 1895; MacLagan 1902; Henderson 1911; MacICulloch 1911; Davidson 1949, 1950; Crenshaw 1996; Synder 2001.

BIBLIOGRAPHY

1. ANCIENT PRIMARY SOURCES

1. A. Greek and Roman Sources

Adespota [fragments of unknown authors]

———. *Comicorum Atticorum Fragmenta*. Edited by Theodor Kock. 3 vols. Leipzig: Teubner, 1880–1888.

———. *Comicorum Graecorum Fragmenta*.1.1. Edited by G. Kaibel. Berlin: Weidmann, 1899.

Aelian, De natura animalium. On Animals. 3 vols. Translated by A. F. Scholfield. LCL. Cambridge: Harvard University Press, 1958–59.

Aelian, Varia Historia. Historical Miscellany. Translated by Nigel G. Wilson. LCL. Cambridge: Harvard University Press, 1997.

Aeschylus. "The Plays of Aeschylus." Translated by G. M. Cookson, *Great Books of the Western World*. Vol. 5, 1–91. Chicago: Encyclopaedia Britannica, 1952.

Aesop. *Aesopica: A Series of Texts Relating to Aesop or Ascribed to Him or Closely Connected with the Literary Tradition that Bears His Name, Collected and Critically Edited, in part Translated from Oriental Languages, with a Commentary and Historical Essay*. Edited by Ben Edwin Perry. Urbana: University of Illinois Press, 1952. [Includes *Vita Aesopi*, G recension and *Vita Aesopi*, W recension.]

———. *Aesop's Fables*. Translated by Robert Dodsley. Chicago: Rand McNally, 1897.

———. *Corpus Fabularum Aesophicarum*. Vol. 1. Edited by A. Hausrath. Leipzig: Teubner, 1970.

Agathon. Fragments in *Tragicorum graecorum fragmenta*. Edited by August Nauck. Leipzig: Teubner 1887.

Alciphron, Aelian, and Philostratus. *The Letters of Alciphron, Aelian, and Philostratus*. Translated by A. R. Benner and F. H. Fobes. LCL. Cambridge: Harvard University Press, 1949.

Alexander (Pseudo-) of Aphrodisias. *Problemata Physica*. In *Physici et Medici Graeci minores*. Edited by I. L. Ideler. 2 vols. Berlin: Reimer, 1841–1842. Vol. 1 (1841):3–80. Reprinted, Amsterdam 1963.

Antisthenes. *Fragmenta*. Edited by A. G. Winckelmann. Zürich: Meyer & Zeller, 1842.

Anthologia Graeca (=*Anthologia Palatina*/*Palatine Anthology*). Edited by F. Jacobs. 13 vols. Leipzig: Dyck, 1794–1803; revised as 3 vols., 1813–1817. See below, *Anthologia Palatina*.

Anthologia Graeca epigrammatum Palatina cum Planudea. Edited by H. Stadtmueller. 3 vols. Leipzig: Teubner, 1894–1906.

Anthologia Palatina. *Palatine Anthology* =*Anthologia Graeca*. The full *Palatine Anthology* was published by F. Jacobs as the *Anthologia graeca sive poetarum graecorum lusus*.13 vols. Leipzig: Dyck, 1794–1803; revised as 3 vols., 1813–1817.

Anthologia Palatina. Edited by P. Waltz et al. Anthologie grecque. 12 vols. CUFr. Paris: Les Belles Lettres, 1928–1994.

Apollodorus. *The Library*. 2 vols. Translated by J. G. Frazer. LCL. Cambridge: Harvard University Press, 1921.

Apollonius of Rhodes. *Argonautica*. Translated by R. C. Seaton. LCL. New York: Putnam, 1912. Cambridge: Harvard University Press, 1912.

Aristophanes. *The Fragments of Attic Comedy*. Edited by J. M. Edmonds. Leiden: Brill, 1957–1961.

Aristophanes. *The Plays of Aristophanes*. Translated by Benjamin Bickley Rogers. London: Bell, 1910.

Aristophanes. *Poetae comici Graeci*. Edited by R. Kassell and C. Austin. III.2. *Aristophanes: Testimonia et fragmenta*. Berlin: de Gruyter, 1984.

Aristotle in 23 Volumes. Translated by H. Rackham et al. Cambridge: Harvard University Press, 1934.

Aristotle. *The Works of Aristotle*. 12 vols. Edited by W. D. Ross and J. A. Smith; translated by W. D. Ross et al. Oxford: Clarendon, 1927–1952.

———. *Aristotelis opera omnia. Graece et latine*. Edited by Ulco Cats Bussemaker, Friedrich Dübner, and Emil Heitz. 5 vols. Paris: A. Firmin Didot, 1854–1874. Vol. 4 edited by U. C. Bussemaker (1857) includes an Appendix containing Aristotle (Pseudo-), *Problemata inedita* (3 books).

———. *Fragments: Aristotelis qui ferebantur libroroum fragmenta*. Edited by Valentinus Rose. Leipzig: Teubner, 1886; reprinted, Stuttgart, 1967.

———. *Historia Animalium*. Edited and translated by D. M Balme. 3 vols. Prepared for Publication by Allan Gotthelf. LCL. Cambridge: Harvard University Press, 1991.

———. *Nicomachean Ethics*. Translated by H. Rackham. Rev. ed. LCL. Cambridge: Harvard University Press, 1934.

———. *On Rhetoric: A Theory of Civic Discourse*. Newly translated, with Introduction, Notes, and Appendices, by George A. Kennedy. New York: Oxford University Press, 1991.

———. *Politics*. Translated by H. Rackham. LCL. Cambridge: Harvard University Press, 1967.

———. *Problemata*. Translated by E. S. Foster. Vol. 7 in *The Works of Aristotle*. 12 vols. Edited by W. D. Ross and J. A. Smith. Translated by W. D. Ross et al. Oxford: Clarendon, 1927.

———. *Rhetoric*. Translated by John H. Freese. LCL. New York: Putnam, 1926.

Aristotle (Pseudo-). *Oeconomica and Magna Moralia*. Translated by G. C. Armstrong. LCL. Cambridge: Harvard University Press, 1947.

———. *Problemata (physica)*. In *The Works of Aristotle*. 12 vols. Edited by W. D. Ross and J. A. Smith; translated by W. D. Ross et al. Vol. 7, translated by E. S. Foster. Oxford: Oxford University Press, 1927.

———. *Problemata inedita*. In *Aristotelis opera omnia. Graece et latine*. Edited by Ulco
   Cats Bussemaker, Friedrich Dübner, and Emil Heitz. 5 vols. Paris: Didot, 1854–
   1874. Vol. 4 edited by U. C. Bussemaker (1857) Appendix.
Athenaeus. *The Deipnosophists*. 7 vols. Edited and translated by C. B. Gulick. LCL.
   Cambridge: Harvard University Press, 1927–41.
Aulus Gellius. *Attic Nights*. 3 vols. Translated by J. C. Rolfe. LCL 195. London:
   Heinemann; New York: Putnam, 1927. Cambridge: Harvard University Press,
   1927. cf. Gellius
Audollent, Augustus, ed. *Defixionum tabellae*. Paris: Fontemoing, 1894, 1904.
Bagnall, Roger S., ed. *The Florida Ostraka: Documents from the Roman Army in Upper
   Egypt*. Greek, Roman, and Byzantine Monographs 7. Durham: Duke University,
   1976.
Bagnall, Roger S. et al., eds. *Ostraka in Amsterdam Collections (O. Amster.)*. Studia
   Amstelodamensia ad epigraphicam, ius antiquum et papyrologicam pertinentia 9.
   Zutphen: Terra, 1976. Nos. 1–108.
Bernand, André. *Sorciers grecs*. Paris: Fayard, 1991.
Die Bremer Papyri. Edited by U. Wilcken. Berlin: Verlag der Akademie der Wissenschaft,
   in Kommission bei Walter de Gruyter, 1936.
Callimachus of Cyrene. *Callimachus: Aetia, Iambi, Lyric Poems, Hecale, Minor Epic
   and Elegiac Poems, and Other Fragments* Edited by Thomas Gelzer. Translated by
   C. A. Trypanes. Cambridge: Harvard Universisty Press, 1975.
———. *Aetia, Iambi, Lyric Poems, Hecale, Minor Epic and Elegiac Poems, and Other
   Fragments*. Edited and translated by C.A. Trypanis. *Hero and Leander / Musaeus*.
   Edited by Thomas Gelzer, translated by Cedric Whitman. LCL. Cambridge:
   Harvard University Press, 1975.
———. *Callimachus: Hymns and Epigrams, Lycophron and Aratus*. Edited and
   translated by A. W. Mair and G. R. Mair. LCL. Cambridge: Harvard University
   Press, 1921.
———. *Callimachus 1. Fragmenta*. Edited by Rudolf Pfeiffer. Oxford: Oxford University
   Press, 1986.
Callisthenes (Pseudo-). *Alexander Romance*. In *Scriptores rerum Alexandri Magni*,
   edited by C. W. Müller, an appendix in *Arrian. Arriani Anabasis et Indica*. . . .
   Reliqua Arriani et scriptorum de rebus Alexandri Magni fragmenta collegit (Pseudo-
   Callisthenes) Edited by F. Dübner and C. Müller. Paris: Didot, 1846.
Carmina Latina Epigraphica. Edited by F. Bücheler and E. Lommatzsch. Leipzig:
   Teubner, 1930.
Carmina Priapea. Edited by C. Goldberg. Heidelberg: Winter, 1992.
Carmina Priapea: Gedichte an den Gartengott. Translated by B. Kytzler. Zurich: Artemis,
   1978.
Catalogus Codicum Astrologorum Graecorum. Edited by F. Cumont et al. 12 vols.
   Brussels: Lamartin, 1898–1953.
Catullus, Gaius Valerius. *Poems (Carmina)*. Translated by F. W. Cornish. LCL.
   Cambridge: Harvard University Press, 1913.
Catullus: The Poems. Translated by A. S. Kline, 2001. Online: http://www.
   poetryintranslation.com/PITBR/Latin/Catullus.htm.
Charisius. *Ars Grammatica in five books. Flavii Sosipatri Charisii Artis Grammaticae.
   Libri V*. Edited by Karl Barwick. Lepizig, 1925; 2nd ed. revised by F. Kühnert.

Bibliotheca Scriptorum Graecorum et Romanorum Teubneriana. Leipzig: Teubner, 1964. CGL 1,1–296.

Chariton: [Chaereas and] Callirhoe. Translated by G. P. Goold. LCL Cambridge: Harvard University Press, 1995.

Cicero, Marcus Tullius. *The Academic Questions: Treatise de Finibus and Tusculum Disputations of M. T. Cicero.* Translated by C. D. Yonge. London: Bell & Daldy, 1872.

———. *Brutus, Orator.* Translated by G. L. Hendrickson and H. M. Hubbell. LCL, Volume V of *Cicero* in 29 vols. Cambridge: Harvard University Press, 1939.

———. *Letters to Atticus 1–89.* Translated by D. R. Shackleton Bailey. LCL, Vol. 22 of *Cicero* in 29 vols. Cambridge: Harvard University Press, 1999.

———. *On the Orator (De Oratore). Books I-II.* Translated by E. W. Sutton and H. Rackman. LCL, Volume III of *Cicero* in 29 vols. Cambridge: Harvard University Press, 1942. Revised, 1948.

———. *On the Orator (De Oratore). Book III. On Fate (De Fato). Stoic Paradoxes (Paradoxa Stoicorum). On the Divisions of Oratory (De Partitione Oratoria).* Translated by H. Rackham. LCL, Vol. 4 of *Cicero* in 29 vols. Cambridge: Harvard University Press, 1942.

———. *On the Republic (De Re Publica). On the Laws (De Legibus).* Translated by C. W. Keyes. LCL, Vol. 16 of *Cicero* in 29 vols. Cambridge: Harvard University Press, 1928.

———. *Orationes de lege agraria contra Rullum,* in *The Orations of Marcus Tullius Cicero.* Translated by C. D. Yonge. London. Henry G. Bohn, 1856.

———. *Tusculan Disputations.* Translated by J. E. King. LCL, Vol. 18 of *Cicero* in 29 vols. Cambridge: Harvard University Press, 1927, 1945.

———. *The Verrine Orations I: Against Caecilius. Against Verres,* Part 1; Part 2, Books 1–2. Translated by L. H. G. Greenwood. LCL, Vol VII of *Cicero* in 29 vols. Cambridge: Harvard University Press, 1928.

Claudian. Vol. I. [*Against Rufinus* and other works]. Translated by M. Platnauer. LCL. Cambridge: Harvard University Press, 1928. 1922.

Comicorum Atticorum poetarum. Vol. 3. Edited by T. Kock. Leipzig: Teubner, 1888. (a.k.a *Comica adespota*).

Corpus Priapeorum/Carmina Priapea. See below, *The Priapus Poems.*

Corrina of Tanagra. In *Poetae melici Graeci.* Edited by D. L. Page. Oxford: Clarendon, 1962; reprinted 1967.

Curtius Rufus. *Historiae Alexandri Magni Macedonis: libri qui supersunt.* Edited by Edmund Hedicke. Bibliotheca Scriptorum Graecorum et Romanorum Teubneriana. Leipzig: Teubner, 1908.

Cyranides. *Die Kyraniden.* Edited by D. Kaimikis. Meisenheim: Hain, 1976.

Democritus of Abdara. *Fragmenta.* Edited by Diels and Kranz, *FVS,* vol. 2. 1960.

Demosthenes. 7 vols. Translated by J. H. Vince, C. A. Vince, et al. LCL. Cambridge: Harvard University Press, 1930–1949.

Demosthenes. *Orations. Against Meidias (Oration 21).* Translated by Douglas M. MacDowell. Oxford: Oxford University Press, 1990.

Diels and Kranz; see *Die Fragmente der Vorsokratiker.*

Dio Cassius. *Roman History.* 9 vols. Translated by E. Cary. LCL. Cambridge: Harvard University Press, 1914–1927.

Dio Chrysostom. *Orations*. 5 vols. Translated by J. W. Cohoon and H. L. Crosby. LCL. Cambridge: Harvard University Press, 1932–1951.

Diodorus Siculus. *Library of History*. 12 vols. Translated by C. H. Oldfather et al. LCL. Cambridge: Harvard University Press, 1933–1967.

Diogenes Laertius. *Lives and Opinions of Eminent Philosophers*. 2 vols. Translated by R. D. Hicks. LCL. Cambridge: Harvard University Press, 1925.

———. *The Lives and Opinions of Eminent Philosophers*. Translated by C. D. Yonge. London: Bell, 1895.

———. *Lives and Opinions of Eminent Philosophers*. 2 vols. Translated by R. D. Hicks. LCL. Cambridge: Harvard University Press. Vol. 1 (1938/1925); Vol. 2 (1931/1925).

———. *Vitae philosophorum* .Edited by H. S. Long. 2 vols. Oxford: Clarendon, 1964.

Dioscorides, Pedanus. *De Materia Medica: Being an Herbal with Many Other Medicinal Materials*. Translated by Tess Anne Osbaldeston. Ibidis Press: Johannesburg, 2000.

Empedocles, Fragments, Diels-Kranz, *FVS*, vol. 2.

Epicharmus, Fragment 285 (ed. Kaibel, *Epigrammata Graeca* = Stobaeus 3.38.21).

Epictetus. *Discourses* and *Encheiridion*. 2 vols. Translated by W. A. Oldfather. LCL. Cambridge: Harvard University Press, 1966 (1925).

———. *Epicteti Dissertationes ab Arriani digestae*. Edited by H. Schenkl. Bibliotheca Teubneriana. Stuttgart: Teubner, 1965 (1916).

Epicurus. *Epicurea*. Edited by Hermann Usener. Cambridge: Cambridge University Press, 1887.

Epicurus. *The Extant Fragments*. Edited by Cyril Bailey. Oxford: Clarendon, 1926.

Euphorion, Fragment. In *Collectanea Alexandrina*. Edited by J. U. Powell. Oxford: Clarendon, 1925.

Euripides. *Cyclops. Alcestis. Medea*. Translated by David Kovacs. LCL. Cambridge: Harvard University Press, 1994.

———. *Suppliant Women. Electra. Heracles.* Translated by David Kovacs. LCL. Cambridge: Harvard University Press, 1998

———. *Trojan Women. Iphigenia among the Taurians. Ion*. Translated by David Kovacs. LCL. Cambridge: Harvard University Press, 1999.

———. *Helen, Phoenician Women, Orestes*. Translated by David Kovacs, LCL. Cambridge: Harvard University Press, 2002.

———. *Bacchae, Iphigenia in Aulis, Rhesus*. Edited and translated by David Kovacs. LCL. Cambridge: Harvard University Press, 2002.

The Flinders Petrie Papyri. 3 vols. Edited by J. Mahaffy and J. Smyly. Dublin, 1891–1905.

Foerster, R., ed. *Scriptores Physiognomonici Graeci et Latini*. 2 vols. Leipzig: Teubner, 1893.

Die Fragmente der griechischen Historiker. Edited by Felix Jacoby. Berlin: Weidmann, 1923–.

Die Fragmente der Vorsokratiker. Edited by Hermann Diels and W. Kranz. 3 vols. 6th ed. Berlin: Weidmann, 1960 (1903).

Fronto, Marcus Cornelius. *The Correspondence of Marcus Cornelius Fronto with Marcus Aurelius Antoninus, Lucius Verus, Antoninus Pius, and Various Friends*. 2 vols. Translated by By C. R. Haines. LCL. Cambridge: Harvard University Press, 1919–1920.

Galen, Claudius, of Pergamon. *Opera Omnia*. Edited by C. G. Kühn. Leipzig: Knobloch, 1821–1833.

Gellius, Aulus. *Attic Nights*. Volume I, Books 1–5. Translated by J. C. Rolfe. LCL. Cambridge: Harvard University Press, 1927.

Grattius. *Cynegetica. Gratti Cynegeticon quae supersunt*. Edited by P.J. Enk. Zutphaniae: Thieme, 1918.

Betz, Hans Dieter, ed. *The Greek Magical Papyri in Translation, including the Demotic Spells*. Chicago: University of Chicago Press, 1986.

Haelst, Joseph van. *Catalogue des papyrus littéraires juifs et chrétiens.* Université de Paris IV. Série Papyrologie 1. Paris: Publications de la Sorbonne, 1976.

Heliodorus. *An Ethiopian Romance*. Translated with an introduction by Moses Hadas. Ann Arbor: University of Michigan Press, 1957.

———. *Ethiopian Story*. Translated by W. R. M. Lamb. Everyman's Library 276. London: Dent, 1961.

———. *Héliodore: Les Éthiopiques. Téagène et Chariclé*. Edited by R. M. Rattenbury and T. W. Lumb. Translated by J. Maillon. 3 vols. Paris: Les Belles Lettres, 1935–43; reprinted, 1960.

Herodas. *Mimiambi. Herodas, Mimiambi*. Edited with Introduction, Commentary, and Appendices by I. C. Cunningham. Oxford: Clarendon, 1987.

Herodianus. *Ab exessu divi Marci libri VIII/ Regnum post Marcum*. Edited by Carlo M. Lucarini. Bibliotheca Teubneriana. Leipzig: Saur, 2005.

Herodotus. *The Histories*. Translated by A. D. Godley. Cambridge, MA. Harvard University Press. 1920.

———. *The History/Historie*s (9 books). Translated by George Rawlinson. Great Books of the Western World. Vol. 6. Chicago: Encyclopaedia Britannica, 1952.

Hesiod, the Homeric Hymns, Fragments of the Epic Cycle, Homerica [including *Works and Days, Theogony*]. Translated by H. G. Evelyn-White. LCL. Cambridge: Harvard University Press, 1914; revised, 1936.

Hippias of Elis. Fragment B 16 (ed. Diels-Kranz, *FVS* =. Stobaeus, *Anth*. 3.38.32)

Hippocarates. *The Hippocratic Treatises "On Generation," "On the Nature of the Child," "Diseases IV."* Translated by Iain M. Lonie. Berlin: de Gruyter, 1981.

———. *Hippocratis quae feruntur epistulae ad codicum fidem recensitae*. Edited by W. Putzger.Wurzeni: Teubner, 1914.

———. "The Sacred Disease." In *Hippocrates*. Vol. 2, 127–84. Translated by W. H. S. Jones. LCL. Cambridge: Harvard Univrsity Press, 1923.

Homer. *The Iliad*. 1990. Translated by Robert Fagles. New York: Penguin.

———. *The Odyssey*. 1963. Translated by Roberts Fitzgerald. Garden City, NY: Anchor.

Horace. *Odes and Epodes*. 2002. Edited and translated by Niall Rudd. LCL. Cambridge: Harvard University Press, 2002.

———. *Satires, Epistles, and Ars Poetica*. Translated by H. Rushton Fairclough. LCL. Cambridge: Harvard University Press, 1926.

Iamblichus. *On the Mysteries of The Egyptians, Chaldeans and Syrians.* Translated by Thomas Taylor. 2nd ed.London: Bertram Dobell & Reeves and Turner, 1895.

Incantamenta magica Graeca-Latina. Edited by R. Heim. Jahrbücher für classische Philologie, Suppl. 10. Leipzig. 1892.

Isocrates in Three Volumes. Translated by George Norlin and LaRue Van Hook. LCL. Cambridge: Harvard University Press, 1929.

Josephus. 10 vols. Translated by H. St. J. Thackery et al. LCL. Cambridge: Harvard University Press, 1926–1965.

———. *Jewish Antiquities*. Translated by H. St. J. Thackery, Ralph Marcus, Allen Wikgren and L. H. Feldman., LCL, vols. 4-10 of 10 vols. Cambridge: Harvard University Press, 1930-1965.

———. *The Jewish War*. Translated by H. St. J. Thackery, LCL, vols. 2-3 of 10 vols. Cambridge: Harvard University Press, 1927.

———. *The Life; Against Apion*. Translated by H. St. J. Thackery, LCL, vol. 1 of 10 vols. Cambridge: Harvard University Press, 1926.

Juvenal. *Satires. Juvenal and Persius*. Translated by G. C. Ramsey. LCL. Cambridge: Harvard University Press. 1918.

Juvenal and Persius. Edited and translated by Susanna Morton Braund. LCL. Cambridge: Harvard University Press. 2004.

Juvenal. *The Sixteen Satires*. Translated by Peter Green. Baltimore: Penguin, 1974.

Kaibel, Georg, ed. 1878. *Epigrammata Graeca ex lapidibus conlecta*. Berlin: Reimer, 1878; reprinted 1965.

Lactantius. *L. Caeli Firmiani Lactanti, Opera Omnia: Accedunt Carmina eius quae feruntur et L. Caecilii qui inscriptus est De mortibus persecutorum liber*. Edited by Samuel Brandt and Georg Laubmann. CSEL 19 and 27. Vienna: Tempsky, 1890-97.

———. *L. Caelius Firmianus Lactantius. Divinarum institutionum libri septem*. Fasc. 1: Libri I et II. Edited by Eberhard Heck and Antonie Wlosok. Bibliotheca Teubneriana, Munich/Leipzig: Saur, 2005.

———. *De Opificio Dei*. In *The Minor Works*. Translated by Sr. Mary Francis McDonald, O. P. *The Fathers of the Church, vol. 54*. Washington, DC: Catholic University of America Press, 2010.

Libanius. *Autobiography and Selected Letters*. 2 Vols. Translated by A. F. Norman. LCL. Cambridge: Harvard University Press, 1993.

———. *Libanii Opera*. Edited by R. Förster, Leipzig: Teubner, 1903-27.

———. *Selected Orations, Volume I. Julianic Orations*. Edited and translated by by A. F. Norman. LCL. Cambridge: Harvard University Press, 1969.

———. *Selected Orations, Volume II. Orations 2, 19-23, 30, 33, 45, 47-50*. Edited and translated by by A. F. Norman. LCL. Cambridge: Harvard University Press, 1977.

Livy. *History of Rome* (45 books). 14 vols. Translated by B. O. Foster et al. LCL. Cambridge: Harvard University Press, 1919-1959.

Lucan. *Civil War (Bellum Civile)/Pharsalia* (10 books). Translated by Edward Ridley. London: Longmans Green, 1896.

Lucian of Samosata. *Lucian*. 8 vols. Translated by A. M. Harmon, K. Kilburh and M. D. Macleod. LCL. Cambridge: Harvard University Press, 1913-1967.

Lucretius. *On the Nature of Things.* Translated by W. H. Rouse; revised by M. F. Smith. LCL. Cambridge: Harvard University Press, 1992, reprint with revisions of the 1924 edition.

———. *De rerum natura*. 3 vols. Edited by Cyril Bailey. Oxford: Clarendon, 1947.

Lysias. II. *Funeral Oration;* VI. *Against Andocides*. Translated by W. R. M. Lamb. LCL. Cambridge: Harvard University Press, 1930.

Macrobius. *Saturnalia*. Volume I: Books 1-2. Edited and translated by Robert A. Kaster. LCL. Cambridge: Harvard University Press, 2011.

Manetho (Pseudo-). *Apotelesmatica. Manetho*. Translated by W. G. Waddell, LCL. Cambridge: Harvard University Press, 1940.

Marcellus Empiricus. *De Medicamentiis Liber*. Edited by George Helmreich. Leipzig: Teubner, 1889.

Martial. *Epigrams*. Translated by Walter C. Kerr. LCL. London: Cambridge: Harvard University Press, 1961 (1919)

Maximus of Tyre. *Philosophumena*. Edited by Hermann Hobein. Leipzig: Teubner, 1910.

Melampus. *Peri palmôn mantikê*. *Melampus. Scriptor de divinatione [Melamp.] peri elaiôn tou sômatos mantikê pros Ptolemaion*. Edited by J. G. F. Franz, Scriptores Physiognomiae Veteres. Altenburg 1780. Diels, Hermann, ed. "Beiträge zur Zuckungsliteratur des Okzidents und Orients." Aus den Abhandlungen der Königl. Preuß. Akademie der Wissenschaften vom Jahre 1907. Berlin, 1908.

Menander. *Menandrea ex papyris et membranis vetustissimis*. Edited by Alfred Körte. Leipzig: Teubner, 1912.

———. *The Principle Fragments*. Translated by F. G. Allinson. LCL. Cambridge: Harvard University Press. 1921.

———. *Menander. The Plays and the Fragments*. Translated with Notes by Maurice Balme. Introduction by Peter Brown. Oxford: Oxford University Press, 2001.

———. *The Sentences of the Syriac Menander: Introduction, Text and Translation, and Commentary by* David Gregory Monaco. Piscataway, NJ. : Gorgias Press, 2012.

New Documents Illustrating Early Christianity. Edited by G. H. Horsley, S. Llewelyn et al. North Ryde, New South Wales: The Ancient History Research Centre, Macquarie University, 1981–.

Nonius Marcellus. *De Conpendiosa Doctrina* (20 books). Edited by Wallace M. Lindsay. Lepizig: Teubner, 1903.

Nonnus of Panopolis. *Nonnus, Dionysiaca* (48 Books). 3 vols. Translated by W H D. Rouse. LCL Cambridge: Harvard University Press, 1940.

Orphei Lithica. In *Orphica*. Edited by E. Abel. Leipzig: G. Freytag, 1885; reprinted, Hildesheim, 1971.

Ovid. *The Art of Love [Ars Amatoria] and Other Poems*. Vol 2 of *Ovid* in 6 vols. Edited and translated by J. H. Mozley, revised by G. P. Goold. LCL. Cambridge: Harvard University Press, 1929. 2nd ed. 1979.

———. *Fasti*. Vol. 5 of *Ovid* in 6 vols. Translated by Sir James G. Frazer, revised by G. P. Goold. LCL. Cambridge: Harvard University Press, 1989.

———. *Heroides Amores*. Vol. 1 of *Ovid* in 6 vols. Translated by Grant Showerman. Revised by G. P. Goold. LCL. Cambridge: Harvard University Press, 1986.

———. *Metamorphoses* (15 Books). 2 vols. Vols. 3–4 of *Ovid* in 6 vols. Translated by Frank Justus Miller, revised by G. P. Goold. LCL. Cambridge: Harvard University Press, 1994 (1951).

———. *Metamorphoses*. Translated by Charles Martin. Norton Critical Edition. New York: W. W. Norton & Co., 2004.

The Oxyrhynchus Papyri. Edited by B. P. Grenfell and A. S. Hunt et al. 72 vols. London: Egypt Exploration Society, 1898–1972.

Palladius. *On Agriculture (Opus agriculturae/De re rustica)*. Palladius. *Opus agriculturae*. Edited by J. C. Schmidt. Leipzig: Teubner, 1898.

Palladius: Opus Agriculturae, De Veterinaria Medicina, De Insitione. Edited by Robert H. Rodgers. Leipzig: Teubner, 1975.

Palladius: The Work of Farming. Translated by John Fitch. Devon, UK: Prospect, 2013.

Papyri Graece Magicae. Die griechischen Zauberpapyri. Edited by. K. Preisendanz (vol. 1, 1928; vol. 2. 1931. 2. rev. ed. by A. Henrichs (1973–1974). Vol. 3 with index, edited by K. Preisendanz, with E. Diehl and S. Eitrem (1941). Stuttgart: Teubner, 1973–1974. ET: *Greek Magical Papyri.* Edited by Hans Dieter Betz.

Papiri greci e latini. 1912. Pubblicazioni della Società italiana per la ricerca dei papyri greci e latini in Egítto. Florence: Arini.

Papyri Osloenses. Edited by S. Eitrem and L. Amundsen. 3 vols. Oslo: Dybwad, 1925–36. (P. Oslo)

Pausanias. *Description of Greece.* Edited and translated by W. H. S. Jones and H. A. Ormerod. 4 Vols. Cambridge: Harvard University Press, 1918.

Persius. *Satires. Juvenal and Persius.* Translated by G. C. Ramsey. LCL. Cambridge: Harvard University Press. 1918.

———. *Juvenal and Persius.* Edited and translated by Susanna Morton Braund. LCL. Cambridge: Harvard University Press. 2004.

Petronius. *Satyricon. Petronius.* Translated by Michael Heseltine. LCL. Cambridge: Harvard University Press, 1956; revised version, 1969.

Pherecrates, Fragment. In *Poetae Comici Graeci.* Vol. 7. Edited by R. von Kassel and C. Austin. Berlin: de Gruyter, 1983–2001.

Philo. 12 vols. Translated by F. H. Colson, G. H. Whitaker and Ralph Marcus. LCL. Cambridge: Harvard University Press, 1929–1962.

———. *Opera quae supersunt.* 7 vols. Edited by L. Cohn and P. Wendland. Berlin: de Gruyter, 1896–1930.

Philostratus the Elder of Lemnos, Philostratus the Younger. *Elder Philostratus, Younger Philostratus, Callistratus.* Translated by Arthur Fairbanks. LCL. Cambridge:, Harvard University Press, 1931. (*Imagines* vol 1 by Philostratus the Elder; *Imagines* vol 2 by Philostratus the Younger).

Philostratus of Athens. *Apollonius of Tyana.* Translated by Christopher P. Jones. 3 vols. LCL. Cambridge: Harvard University Press, 2005–6.

———. *Philostratus: The Life of Apollonius of Tyana.* 2 vols. Translated by F. C. Conybeare. LCL. Cambridge: Harvard University Press, 1912, 1948.

Phylarchus, Fragment. In FGrHist 81F 79a, ed. F. Jacoby.

Phrynichus, *Praeparatio sophistica.* Edited by I de Borries, Leipzig: Teubner, 1911.

Physici et medici Graeci minores. 2 vols. Edited by I. L.Ideler. Berlin: Reimer, 1841–1842. Vol. 1 (1841): 3–80. Reprinted, Amsterdam 1963.

Pindar. *Nemean Odes, Isthmian Odes, Fragments.* Translated by William H. Race. LCL. Cambridge: Harvard University Press, 1997.

———. *Olympian Odes, Pythian Odes.* Translated by William H. Race. LCL. Cambridge: Harvard University Press, 1997.

———. *Pindari Carmina Cum Fragmentis, Editio Altera.* Edited by C. W. Bowra. Oxford University Press, 1947.

Plato. 12 vols. Edited by P. Shorey. Translated by H. N. Fowler et al. LCL. Cambridge: Harvard University Press. 1969.

———. *Platonis Opera.* 5 vols. Edited by J. Burnett. Scriptorum Classicorum Bibliotheca Oxoniensis. Oxford: Clarendon, 1900.

Plautus. 4 vols. Edited and translated by Wolfgang de Melo. LCL. Cambridge: Harvard University Press, 2011–2012.

———. Vol. I: *Amphitryon; The Comedy of Asses (Asinaria); The Pot of Gold; The Two Bacchises; The Captives (Captivi).* 2011.

———. Vol. II: *Casina; The Casket Comedy; Curculio; Epidicus; The Two Menaechmuses.* 2011.

———. Vol. III: *The Merchant; The Braggart Soldier (Miles); The Ghost; The Persian.* 2011.

———. Vol. IV: *The Little Carthaginian; Pseudolus; The Rope (Rudens).* 2012.

———. *Stichus, Three-dollar Day, Truculentus, The Tale of a Traveling-bag, Fragments.* Translated by Wolfgang De Melo. LCL. Cambridge:Harvard University Press, 2013.

Pliny the Elder. *Pliny, Natural History.* 10 vols. Translated by H. Rackham et al. LCL. Cambridge: Harvard University Press, 1938–1963.

Pliny the Younger. *Letters and Panegyricus.* 2 vols. Translated by Betty Radice. LCL. Cambridge: Harvard University Press, 1969.

Plutarch. *Moralia.* 16 vols. Translated by F. C. Babbitt et al. LCL. Cambridge: Harvard University Press, 1976.

———. *The Parallel Lives.* 11 vols. Translated by Bernadotte Perrin. LCL. New York: Macmillan, 1914–1926.

Poetae Comici Graeci. 8 vols. Edited by R. von Kassel and C. Austin. Berlin: de Gruyter, 1983–2001.

Polemon. *Physiognomonica.* In *Scriptores physiognomici graecis et latini.* 2 vols. Edited by R. Foerster. Leipzig: Teubner, 1893–1894.

Pollux, Julius. *Onomasticon. Pollucis Onomasticon.*3 vols. Edited by E. Bethe. Leipzig: Teubner, 1900–1937; reprinted, Stuttgart 1967.

Polybius. *Histories.* 6 vols. Translated by W. R. Paton. LCL. Cambridge: Harvard University Press, 1922.

Pomponius. *Atellanae fabulae. Atellane Fabulae (Le attelane).* Edited by Paul Frassinetti. Poetarum Latinorum Reliquiae, Aetas rei publicae 6.1. Rome: Ateneo, 1967.

———. *De Fabulis Atellanis.* Edited by Eduard Munk, Leipzig, 1840

Porphyry of Tyre. *The Life of Pythagoras.* In *The Pythagorean Sourcebook and Library: An Anthology of Ancient Writings Which Relate to Pythagoras and Pythagorean Philosophy.* Compiled and translated by Kenneth Sylvan Guthrie. Edited by David R. Fiedler. Newburyport, MA: Red Wheel Weiser Conari/Phanes, 1987.

Priapus. *Carmina Priapea.* Edited by C. Goldberg. Heidelberg: Winter, 1992.

———. *Carmina Priapea. Gedichte an den Gartengott.* Translated by B. Kytzler. Zurich: Artemis, 1978.

The Priapus Poems. Edited by Richard W. Hooper. Urbana: University of Illinois Press, 1999.

Priesigke, Friedrich et al., eds. *Sammelbuch griechischer Urkunden aus Aegypten.* Continued by F. Bilabel, E. Kiessling, and H.-A. Rupprecht. 26 vols. and in progress. Strassburg: Trübner, 1915–.

Pseudo-Lucian. *Affairs of the Heart.* Translated by M. D. Macleod. LCL. Cambridge: Harvard University Press. 1967.

Ptolemy. *Optics. Ptolemy's Theory of Visual Perception. An English Translation of the Optics with Introduction and Commentary.* By A. Mark Smith. Transactions of the American Philosophical Society 86.2. Philadelphia: The American Philosophical Society. 1996.

Pythagoras, Fragment. In *Fragmenta Astrologica.* Edited by K. O. Zuretti. Codices Hispanienses. Catalogus codicum astrologicorum Graecorum 11.2. Brussels: Lamertin, 1934.

Quintillian. *Institutio oratoria.* 4 vols. Translated by H. E. Butler. LCL. Cambridge: Harvard University Press. 1922.

———. *Institutio oratoria. The Orator's Education.* 4 vols. Edited and translated by Donald A. Russell. LCL. Cambridge: Harvard University Press. 2002.

Rhetorica ad Herennium. Translated by Harry Caplan. LCL. Cambrige, MA: Harvard University Press, 1954).

Sallust. *The War with Catiline, The War with Jugurtha.* Translated by J. C. Rolfe, revised by John T. Ramsey. LCL. Cambridge: Harvard University Press, 1965.

Sandy, Gerald N. *Heliodorus.* Boston: Twayne, 1982.

Scriptores physiognomonici Graeci et Latini. 2 vols. Edited by Richard Foerster. Leipzig 1893; reprinted. Stuttgart 1994.

Select Papyri .Vol. 1. *Private Documents.* Edited and translated by A. S. Hunt and C. C. Edgar. LCL. Cambridge: Harvard University Press, 1932.

Select Papyri. Vol. 2. *Non-Literary Papyri; Public Documents* Edited and translated by A. S. Hunt and C. C. Edgar. LCL. Cambridge: Harvard University Press, 1934.

Seneca. *Epistulae Morales. Epistles.* 3 vols. Translated by R. M. Gummere. LCL. Cambridge: Harvard University Press. 1917–1925.

———. *L. Annaei Senecae Opera quae supersunt.* 3 vols. Edited by F. Haase. Bibliotheca Teubneriania. Leipzig: Teubner, 1894–95.

Sophocles. *Ajax. Electra. Oedipus Tyrannus.* Edited and translated by Hugh Lloyd-Jones. Vol. 1. LCL. Cambridge: Harvard University Press, 1994.

———. *Antigone. The Women of Trachis. Philoctetes. Oedipus at Colonus.* Edited and translated by Hugh Lloyd-Jones. Vol. 2. LCL. Cambridge: Harvard University Press, 1994.

Stobaeus, Johannes. *Ioannis Stobaei Anthologium* [Eclogues, Books 1–2; Florilegium, Books 3–4]. 3 vols. and appendix. Edited by Curtius Wachsmuth and Otto Hense. Berlin: Weidmann, 1894–1923.

Stoicorum Veterum Fragmenta. Edited by J. von Arnim. 3 vols; vol. 4 (indexes by M. Adler). Leipzig: Teubner, 1903–1924; reprinted. Stuttgart 1978.

Suetonius. *The Lives of the Caesars.* Translated by J. C. Rolfe. 2 vols. LCL. New York: Putnam, 1920.

Supplementum epigraphicum Graecum. Leiden, 1923–1971. Amsterdam, 1979.

Supplementum Magicum I–II. Edited by Robert W. Daniel, and Franco Maltomini. 2 vols. Abhandlungen der rheinisch-westfälischen Akademie der Wissenschaften, Sonderreihe Papyrologica Coloniensia XVI, 1–2. Opladen: Westdeutscher Verlag, 1990–1992.

Symmachus. *Q. Aurelii Symmachi quae supersunt.* Edited by Otto Seeck. Monumenta Germaniae Historica 6. Berlin, 1883; reprinted Munich, 2001. The Epistles/Letters are also published in the Patrologia Latina, Suppl. Vol. 13.

Tacitus. *The Annals.* Translated by J. Jackson. 3 vols. LCL. Cambridge: Harvard University Press; London: William Heinemann, 1931, 1937.

———. *The Histories.* Translated by C. H. Moore. 2 vols. LCL. Cambridge: Harvard University Press, 1925, 1931.

Theocritus. *The Idylls of Theocritus.* Translated by R. J. Cholmeley. London: Bell, 1901.

Theophrastus. *Characters. Herodas, Cercidas and the Greek Choliambic Poets.* Edited and translated by J. M. Edmonds and A. D. Knox. LCL. Cambridge: Harvard University Press, 1915.

————. *Enquiry into Plants and Minor Works on Odours and Weather Signs.* Translated by Arthur Hort. New York: Putnam, 1916.

————. *De Sensu et sensilibus. Theophrastus and the Greek Physiological Psychology before Aristotle.* Translated by George M. Stratton. London: Allen & Unwin, 1917.

Thesaurus Linguae Graece Online. University of California, Irvine, CA. Online: http://www.tlg.uci.edu/.

Thesaurus Linguae Latinae. 11 vols. Leipzig: Teubner, 1900–1999; Saur, 2000–2006; Berlin: de Gruyter, 2007–.

Three Greek Romances [Longus, Xenophon of Ephesus, Dio Chrysostom]. Edited and translated by Moses Hadas. Indianapolis: Bobbs-Merrill, 1964.

Thucydides. *History of the Peloponnesian War.* 4 vols. Translated by C. F. Smith. LCL. Cambridge: Harvard University Press, 1919.

Tibullus, Albius. *Albii Tibulli Elegiarum libri duo. Accedunt Pseudotibulliana.* Edited by Emil Baehrens. Leipzig: Teubner, 1878.

Tragicorum Graecorum Fragmenta. Edited by August Nauck. 2nd ed. Leipzig: Teubner, 1889 (1887).

Tragicorum Graecorum Fragmenta. 5 vols. Edited by Bruno Snell. Göttingen: Vandenhoeck & Ruprecht, 1971.

Trismegistos (an interdisciplinary portal of papyrological and epigraphical resources). http://www.trismegistos.org/index.html

Varro. *On the Latin Language.* 2 vols. Translated by Roland G. Kent. LCL. Cambridge: Harvard University Press, 1938.

————. *Cato and Varro, De Re Rustica.* Translated by W. D. Hooper and H. B. Ash. LCL. Cambridge: Harvard University Press, 1967.

Vegetius. *P. Vegeti Renati: Digestorum artis mulomedicinae Libri.* Edited by Ernest Lommatzsch. Leipzig: Teubner, 1903.

Vettius Valens. *Vettii Valentis. Anthologiarum libri,* edited by W. Kroll, Berlin: Weidmann, 1908; reprint 1973.

Virgil. *Eclogues, Georgics, Aeneid.* Translated by H. R. Fairclough. LCL. Cambridge: Harvard University Press. 1916.

————. *Opera.* Edited by R. A. B. Mynors. Rev. ed. Oxford: Clarendon, 1954.

Xenophon. Translated by C. L. Brownson, O. J. Todd et al. 7 vols. LCL. Cambridge: Harvard University Press, 1914–1940.

1.B. Old Testament

Septuaginta. 1935. 2 vols. Edited by A. Rahlfs. Stuttgart: Württembergische Bibelanstalt.

1.C. New Testament

Novum Testamentum Graece. 1993. 27th ed. revised. Edited by Eberhard Nestle et al. Stuttgart: Deutsche Bibelgesellschaft.

1. D. Early Christian Writings

Acts of Paul and Thecla.
———. In *Acta Apostolorum Apocrypha.* Edited by R. A. Lipsius and M. Bonnet. 2 vols. in 3 parts. Vol. 1 (1891); vol. 2.1 (1898); vol. 2.2 (1903). Leipzig: H. Mendelsohn, 1891–1903; reprinted, Darmstadt: Wissenschaftliche Buchgesellschaft, 1959. Vol. 1:235–272.
———. Acts of Paul and Thecla. "*The Acts of Paul.*" By W. Schneemelcher. In *New Testament Apocrypha.* 2 vols. Edited by Edgar Hennecke, and Wilhelm Schneemelcher. Translated by R. McL Wilson. Philadelphia: Westminster Press, 1965. Vol. 2:322–390, esp. 353–364.
Acts of Thomas
———. In *Acta Apostolorum Apocrypha.* Edited by R. A. Lipsius and M. Bonnet. Vol. 2.2. Leipzig: H. Mendelsohn, 1903; reprinted, Darmstadt: Wissenschaftliche Buchgesellschaft, 1959. Pp. 99–291.
———. "The Acts of Thomas." By G. Bornkamm. In *New Testament Apocrypha.* 2 vols. Edited by Edgar Hennecke, and Wilhelm Schneemelcher. Translated by R. McL Wilson. Philadelphia: Westminster Press, 1965. Vol. 2: 425–531.
Arnobius of Sicca. *Adversus Nationes.* Edited by Concetto Marchesi. Turin: Paravia et sociorum, 1953.
Augustine, Aurelius, of Hippo.
Augustine. In *Patrologia Latina*, vols. 31–47.
Augustine. De civitate Dei. 2 vols. Edited by Bernard Dombart and Alphonse Kalb. *Corpus christianorum* series latina, 47–48. Turnhout: Brepols, 1955.
———. *Concerning the City of God against the Pagans.* Translated by Henry Bettenson. New York: Penguin, 1972.
———. *Confessions.* Translated by R. S. Pine-Coffin. New York: Penguin, 1961.
———. *A Select Library of the Nicene and Post-Nicene Fathers of the Christian Church.* Vol. 3. *St. Augustine on the Holy Trinity, Doctrinal Treatises, Moral Treatises.* Edited by Philip Schaff. Buffalo: Christian Literature Co., 1887.
Basil of Caesarea. "Homily 11, Concerning Envy/*Peri phthonou.*" PG 31. 372–386. In *Saint Basil. Ascetical Works*, 463–74. Translated by M. Monica Wagner. The Fathers of the Church. A New Translation. New York: Fathers of the Church, 1950.
Basil: Letters and Select Works. In *Nicene and Post-Nicene Fathers of the Christian Church.* 2nd series. Vol. 8. Edited by Philip Schaff and 1895. Reprinted, Grand Rapids: Eerdmans, 1968.
Clement of Rome. *1 Clement.* In *The Apostolic Fathers.* Translated and edited by K. Lake. 2 vols. Cambridge: Harvard University Press, 1952.
Clement of Alexandria. *Clemens Alexandrinus.* Edited by Ludwig Früchtel. Berlin: Akademie-Verlag, 1970.
———. *Titi Flaui Clementis Alexandrini opera omnia.* 4 vols. Edited by Reinhold Koltz. Leipzig: Schwickerti, 1831,
Cyprian. *De zelo et livore/On Envy and Rancor.* In *S. Thasci Caecili Cypriani Opera Omnia.* Edited by G. Hartel, *Corpus Scriptorum Ecclesiasticorum Latinorum* CSEL3.1. Vienna, 1868. Pp. 417–432. PL 4. 637–652A.
Eusebius. *Life of Constantine.* Edited and translated by Averil Cameron and Stuart Hall. Oxford: Clarendon, 1999.

Gregory of Nyssa. *The Catechetical Oration.* Edited by J. H. Srawley. Cambridge Patristic Texts. Cambridge: Cambridge University Press, 1903.

———. *The Life of Moses.* Translation, introduction, and notes by Abraham J. Malherbe and Everett Ferguson. New York: Paulist, 1978,

———. *De Virginitate; De Beatitudinibus.* Edited and translated by F. Oehler. Vol. 4 of *Bibliothek der Kirchenväter.* Leipzig, 1859.

———. *Discours catéchétique (Oratio catechetica magna).* Edited by M. Ekkehard Muhlenberg. Translated by M. Raymond Winling. SC 453. Paris: Cerf/Paillart, 2000. PG 45. 11–105.

———. *La Vie de Moïse ou Traité de la perfection en matière de vertu.* Translated by Jean Daniélou. SC 1. Paris: Cerf, 1942.

Isidore of Seville. *Origines/Ethymologiae. The Etymologies of Isidore of Seville.* Translated by Stephen A. Barney, W. J. Lewis, J. A Beach, and Oliver Berghof. Cambridge: Cambridge University Press, 2006.

John Chrysostom. *Homiliae in primam epistulam ad Corinthios 12* (on 1 Cor. 4:10). PG 61.105–106.

Justininus. *Iustinii Historiae Philippicae.* Edited by Frederick Dübner. Leipzig: Teubner, 1831.

Lactantius. *L. Caeli Firmiani Lactanti Opera Omnia: Accedunt Carmina Eius Quae Feruntur Et L. Caecilii Qui Inscriptus Est De Mortibus Persecutorum Liber.* Edited by Samuel Brandt and Georg Laubmann. CSEL 19 and 27. Vienna: Tempsky, 1890, 1893.

Lactantius. *L. Caelius Firmianus Lactantius: Divinarum institutionum libri septem.* Fasc. 1: Libri I et II. Edited by Eberhard Heck and Antonie Wlosok. Bibliotheca Teubneriana. Leipzig: Saur, 2005.

———. *The Divine Institutes, Books I–VII.* Translated by Mary F. McDonald. Washington, DC: Catholic University of America Press, 1964.

———. *De Opificio Dei.* In *The Minor Works.* Translated by Mary F. McDonald. *The Fathers of the Church,* vol. 54. Washington, DC: Catholic University of America Press, 2010.

Nicene and Post-Nicene Fathers. First Series, Vol. 12. *Saint Chrysostom, Homilies on First and Second Corinthians.* Translated by Talbot W. Chambers. Edited by Philip Schaff. Buffalo, NY: Christian Literature, 1889.

Patrologia Graeca. Patrologiae Cursus Completus, Series Graeca. Edited by J. P. Migne. 161 vols. Paris: Garnier, 1857–1866.

Patrologia Latina. Patrologiae Cursus Completus, Series Latina. Edited by J. P. Migne. 221 vols. Paris: Garnier, 1844–1880.

Paulus Silentarius. *Ecphrasis of Hagia Sophia: Three Political Voices from the Age of Justinian: Agapetus Advice to the Emperor; Dialogue on Political Science; Paul the Silentiary Description of Hagia Sophia.* Translated by P. N. Bell. Liverpool: Liverpool University Press, 2009.

Tertullian of Carthage. *Ad martyras, Ad Scapulam, De fuga in persecutione, De monogamia, De virginibus velandis, De pallio.* Edited by V. Bulhart. CSEL 76. Vienna, 1957.

———. *De praescriptione haereticorum, De cultu feminarum, Ad uxorem, De exhortatione castitatis, De corona, De carne Christi, Adversus Iudaeos.* Edited by E. Kroymann. CSEL 70. Vienna, 1942.

———. *De spectaculis, De idololatria, Ad nationes, De testimonio animae, Scorpiace, De oratione, De baptismo, De ieiunio, De anima, De pudicitia.* Edited by A. Reifferscheid and G. Wissowa. CSEL 20. Vienna, 1890.

———. *De virginibus velandis.* Translated and edited by V. Bulhardt. CSEL 76. Vienna, 1957.

Vulgate. *Biblia Sacra: Iuxta Vulgatam versionem.* 2 vols. Edited by R. Weber, 2 vols. Stuttgart: Württembergische Bibelanstalt, 1969.

1.E. Medieval Writings

Dante Alighieri. *The Divine Comedy of Dante Alighieri. Inferno. A Verse Translation* by Allen Mandelbaum. 3 vols. (*I. Inferno, II. Purgatorio, III. Paradiso*). New York: Bantam Classic, 1982.

Thomas Aquinas. *The Summa Theologica of St. Thomas Aquinas.* 5 vols.Translated by the Fathers of the English Dominican Province. Westminister, MD: Christian Classics, 1981.

Roger Bacon. *Opus maius* (1267) *The 'Opus Maius' of Roger Bacon.* Edited by John Henry Bridges. London: Williams & Norgate, 1900.

Marsilio Ficino. *De fascino. In Opera omnia.* Basel: Henricpetri, 1576.

2. SECONDARY LITERATURE

Abt, Adam. 1908. *Die Apologie des Apuleius von Madaura und die antike Zauberei.* Giessen: Töpelmann.

Adams, J. N. 1982. *The Latin Sexual Vocabulary.* Baltimore: Johns Hopkins University Press.

Alvar Nuño, Antón. 2006–2008. "Falsas consideraciones en los estudios sobre el mal de ojo en el mundo clásico." *Antigüedad, Religiones y Sociedades, ARYS* 7:101–114.

———. 2009–2010. "Nocturnae aves: su simbolismo religioso y function mágica en el mundo romano. Nocturnae aves: their religious symbolism and magical function in the roman world." *Antigüedad, Religiones y Sociedades, ARYS* 8:187–202.

———. 2012a. *Envidia y fascinación: el mal de ojo en el occidente romano.* ARYS Supplement 3. Huelva: Universidad de Huelva, 2012. Online: http://www.uhu.es/ publicaciones/ojs/store/numeroscompletos/arys/anejoIII.pdf

———. 2012b. "Ocular Pathologies and the Evil Eye in the Early Roman Principate." *Numen* 59 (2012) 295–321.

Amulet collection. Cabinet des médailles et antiques. Bibliothèque nationale, Paris, 1964. (526 items). Includes the amulet collections of Armand Delatte (up to 193 items), Wilhelm Froehner (1925), Gustave Schlumberger (1929), and Adrien Blanchet (1945).

Andres, F. 1918. "Daimon." PW Suppl. 3 (1918) 296–322.

Antioch: The Lost Ancient City. 2000. Catalogue (with essays) of an exhibit at the Worcester Art Museum, Worcester, MA. Online: 10/8/2000 http//www. worcesterart.org.

Arneth, J. 1850. *Gold- und Silber-Monumente des K. K. Münz- und Antiken Cabinetts in Wien.* Vienna: Braumüller.

Artelt, Walter. 1934. *Die Quellen der mittelalterlichen Dialogdarstellungen*. Berlin: Ebering.

Ausführliches Lexikon der griechischen und römischen Mythologie. Edited by W. H. Roscher. Vol. 1, part 2. Leipzig: Teubner, 1886–1890.

Avalos, Hector et al., eds. 2007. *This Abled Body: Rethinking Disabilities in Biblical Studies*. Semeia Studies 55. Atlanta: Scholars, 2007.

Bailliot, Magali. 2010. *Magie et sortilèges dans l'Antiquité romaine: archéologie des rituels et des images*. Paris: Hermann.

Balch, David L., ed. 1991. *Social History of the Matthean Community: Cross-Disciplinary Approaches*. Minneapolis: Fortress.

———. 2008. *Roman Domestic Art and Early House Churches*. WUNT 228. Tübingen: Mohr Siebeck.

Baldassare, I., and G. Pugliese Carratelli, eds. 1990–2003. *Pompei pitture e mosaici*. 10 vols. Rome: Istituto della Enciclopedia Italiana.

Baldes. Richard W. 1975. "Democritus on Visual Perception: Two Theories or One?" *Phronesis* 20/2 (1975) 93–105.

Bartelink, G. M. 1973. "*Phylaktêrion- phylacterium*." In *Mélanges Christine Mohrmann. Nouveau recueil, offert par ses anciens élèves*, edited by J. Ysebaert et al., 25–60. Utrecht: Spectrum.

Barton, Carlin. 1993. *The Sorrows of the Ancient Romans: The Gladiator and the Monster*. Princeton: Princeton University Press.

———. 2002. "Being in the Eyes. Shame and Sight in Ancient Rome." In *The Roman Gaze. Vision, Power, and the Body*, edited by David Fredrick, 216–35. Baltimore: Johns Hopkins University Press.

Bartsch, Shadi. 2006. "The Penetrating Gaze." In *The Mirror of the Self. Sexuality, Self-Knowledge, and the Gaze in the Early Roman Empire*, 138–52. Chicago: University of Chicago Press.

Bayardi, Ottavio Antonio and Pasquale Carcani, eds. 1757–1779. *Le pitture antiche d'Ercolano e contorni incise con qualche spiegazione*. 5 vols. Edited by Accademia ercolanese di archeologia. Naples: Regia Stamperia.

Bean, G. E. 1960. "Notes and Inscriptions from Pisidia." *Anatolian Studies* 10:43–82.

Beare, John I. 1996. *Greek Theories of Elementary Cognition from Alcaeon to Aristotle*. Oxford: Oxford University Press.

Becker, Jakob. 1861. *Die Heddernheimer Votivhand: eine römische Bronze aus der Römer-Büchner'schen Sammlung*, with plate. Frankfurt: Kruthoffer.

Bergen, Fanny D. 1890. "Some Saliva Charms." *Journal of American Folklore* 79:51–59.

Bernand, André. 1991. "L'envie." In *Sorciers grecs*, 85–105. Paris: Fayard.

Bernert, E. E. 1950. "Phthonos." In PW 20:961–64.

Bernidaki-Aldous, Eleftheria. 1988. "The Power of the Evil Eye in the Blind: *Oedipus Tyrannus* 1306 and *Oedipus at Colonus* 149–56." In *Text and Presentation. The University of Florida Department of Classics. Comparative Drama Conference Papers*, Vol. 8, edited by Karelisa Hartigan, 39–48. New York: University Press of America.

Beschaouch, A. 1968. "Echec à l'envieux, d'apres une inscription metrique sur mosaique decouverte dans les thermes a Sullecthum en Tunisie." *Rendiconti dei Lincei* 23: 59–68.

Besig, Hans. 1937. *Gorgo und Gorgoneion in der archaischen griechischen Kunst*. Berlin: Markert.

Bianchi Bandinelli, R., E. V. Caffarelli, and G. Caputo. 1964. *Leptis Magna*. Milan: Mondadori.

Bidez, Joseph, and Franz Cumont. 1938. *Les Mages hellénises: Zoroastre, Ostanès et Hystaspe d'après la tradition grecque*. 2 vols. Paris: Les Belles Lettres.

Bienkowski, P. "Malocchio." 1893. In *Eranos Vindobonensis*, 285–303. Vienna: Holder, 1893.

Blanchet, Adrien. 1945. Amulet collection. Cabinet des médailles et antiques. Paris: Bibliothèque Nationale.

Böcher, Otto. 1981. "Dämonen." In *TRE* 8:270–74.

Bonneau, Danielle. 1982. "L'apotropaïque 'Abáskantos' en Égypte." *Revue de l'historie des religions* 99:23–36.

Bonner, Campbell. 1950. *Studies in Magical Amulets Chiefly Graeco-Egyptian*. Ann Arbor: University of Michigan Press.

Bowen, Donna Lee and Evelyn A. Early, eds. 1993. *Everyday Life in the Muslim Middle East*. Indiana Series in Arab and Islamic Studies. Bloomington: Indiana University Press.

Bradley, Keith. 2005. "The Roman Child in Sickness and Health." *The Roman Family in the Empire: Rome, Italy, and Beyond*, edited by Michele George, 67–92. Oxford University Press.

Bragantini, Irene and Sampaolo, Valeria, eds. 2009. *La Pittura Pompeiana*. Photography by Luigi Spina. Catalogue of the Museo Archeologico Nazionale di Napoli. Verona: Mondadori Electa.

Bremmer, Jan, and Hermann Roodenburg, eds. 1991. *A Cultural History of Gesture*. Ithaca: Cornell University Press.

Brenk, Frederick E. 1986. "In the Light of the Moon: Demonology in the Early Imperial Period." In *ANRW* 16.3:2068–145.

———. 1998. "Caesar and the Evil Eye or What Do You Do with *kai sy, teknon*." In *Qui Miscuit Utile Dulci*. Paul Lachlan MacKendrick FS, edited by Gareth Schmeling and Jon D. Mikalson, 31–49. Wauconda, IL: Bolchazy-Carducci.

———. 1999a. "Caesar and the Evil Eye or What Do You Do with *kai sy, teknon*." In Brenk, *Clothed in Purple Light. Studies in Virgil and in Latin Literature, including Aspects of Philosophy, Religion, Magic, Judaism, and the the New Testament Background*, 197–210. Stuttgart: Steiner. =Brenk 1998.

———. 1999b. "The *KAI SY* Stele in the Fitzwilliam Museum, Cambridge." *ZPE* 126:169–74.

Brillante, C. 1993. "L'invidia dei Telchini e l'origine delle arti." *Aufidus* 19:7–42.

Bruneau, P. 1964. "Apotropaia déliens. La massue d'Héraclès." *BCH* 88:159–68.

———. 1987. *La mosaïque antique. Lectures en Sorbonne*. Paris: Presses de l'Université de Paris-Sorbonne.

Bryen, Ari Z., and Andrzej Wypustek. 2009. "Gemmelus' Evil Eyes (P. Mich. VI 423–424)." *GRBS* 49:535–55.

Budge, Ernest Alfred Wallis. 1978/1930 *Amulets and Superstitions*. 1930. Reprinted, New York: Dover.

Bulman, Patricia. 1995. *Phthonos in Pindar*. Classical Studies 35. Berkeley: University of California Press.

Burkert, Walter. 1977. "Air-Imprints or Eidola: Democritus' Aetiology of Vision." *Illinois Classical Studies* 2:97–109.

———. 1992. *The Orientalizing Revolution: NearEastern Influence on Greek Culture in the Early Archaic Age.* Cambridge: Harvard University Press.

Buschor, Ernst. 1958. *Medusa Rondanini.* Stuttgart: Kohlhammer.

Buchheit, V. 1960. "Feigensymbolik im antiken Epigramm." *Rheinisches Museum* 103: 200–229.

Bulman, A. P. 1989. "Phthonos in Pindar." PhD diss., University of California, Berkeley.

Cagnat, R. 1900. "Bas-Relief funéraire d'Aumale (Algérie)." In *Strena Helbigiana: Sexagenario obtvlervnt amici. A.D. IIII. non. Febr. a MDCCCLXXXXVIII*, edited by Wolfgang Helbig, 38–40. Leipzig: Teubner, 1900.

Cagnat, R., and V. Chapot. 1916–1920. *Manuel d'archéologie romaine.* 2 vols. Paris: Picard.

Camera Cascudo, Luis da. 1949. "Gorgoneion." In *Homenaje a Don Luis de Hoyos Sainz.* Vol. 1:67–77. Madrid: Graficas Valera.

Carcani, Pasquale, ed. 1767–1771. *De' bronzi di Ercolano e contorni.* 2 vols. Naples: Regia stamperia, Vol. 1: 1767; Vol. 2: 1771.

Carratelli, Giovanni Puglisese. 1990–2003. *Pompei: pitture e mosaici.* Rome: Istituto della enciclopedia italiana.

Cassib, Lionel. 1971. *Ships and Seamanship in the Ancient World.* Princeton: Princeton University Press.

Caylus, Anne-Claude and Philippe de Tubières. 1752–1764. *Recueil d'antiquités égyptiennes, étrusques, grecques et romaines.* 6 vols. Paris: Desaint & Saillant. Vol. 6, 1764.

Cerulli Irelli, Giuseppina, ed. 1973. *Katalog der Wandmalerien: Pompeji, Ausstellungs-katalog.* 2nd ed. Essen.

———, ed. 1990. *Pompejanische Wandmalerei.* Stuttgart: Belser.

Chabot, J. B. 1922. *Choix d'inscriptions de Palmyre.* Paris: Imprimerie nationale.

Chambers Dictionary of Etymology. 2001. Edited by Robert K. Barnhart. Edinburgh: Harrap. (1988).

Chantraine, P. 1968–1980. *Dictionnaire étymologique de la langue grecque: histoire de mots.* 4 vols. Paris: Klincsieck.

———. 1968. "*Baskanos.*" In *Dictionnaire étymologique de la langue grecque: histoire des mots.* Part 1:167.

———. 1980. "*Phthonos.*" *Dictionnaire étymologique de la langue grecque.* Part 4/2:1202.

Charles Picard, Gilbert, 1954. *Les Religions de l'Afrique Antique.* Paris: Plon.

———. 1957. *Les trophees romains.* Bibliotheque des Ecoles Françaises d'Athenes et de Rome 187. Paris: de Boccard.

Cimok, Fatih, ed. 1996. *Antioch Mosaics.* Istanbul: Yayinlari.

———. 2000. *Antioch Mosaics: A Corpus.* Istanbul: Yayinlari.

Cintas, Paul. 1946. *Amulettes Puniques.* Institut des Hautes Etudes de Tunis. Tunis: Publications de l'institut des Hautes Études Tunis.

Clarke, John R. 1991. *The Houses of Roman Italy 100 B.C.—A.D. 250. Ritual, Space, and Decoration.* Berkeley: University of California Press.

———. 2002. "Look Who's Laughing at Sex: Men and Women Viewers in the Apo-dyterium of the Suburban Baths at Pompeii." In *The Roman Gaze: Vision, Power and the Body*, edited by David Frederick, 149–79. Baltimore: Johns Hopkins University Press.

———. 2003. "The Opposite of Sex: How to Keep Away the Evil Eye." In John R. Clarke, *Roman Sex 100 BC to 250 A.D*, 94–113. New York: Abrams.

————. 2007. *Looking at Laughter: Humor, Power, and Transgression in Roman Visual Culture, 100 B.C.—A.D. 250.* Berkeley: University of California Press.

Clerc, J.-B. 1995. *Homines Magici: etude sur la sorcellerie et la magie dans la société romaine impériale.* Bern: Lang.

Collart, Paul and Pierre Ducrey. 1975. *Philippes I. Les reliefs rupestres.* Bulletin de Correspondance Hellénique. Supplement II. Athens: Ecoles Française d' Athènes/ Boccard.

Le Collezioni del Museo Nazionale di Napoli. 1989. A Catalogue edited by Anna Gramiccia and Francesca Pagnotta. Archivio Fotografico Pedicini. Rome: De Luca Edizioni d'Arte.

Cookson, G. M., trans. 1952. "The Plays of Aeschylus." *Great Books of the Western World.* Vol. 5. Chicago: Encyclopaedia Britannica.

Cooley, Alison E., and M. G. L. Cooley. 2004. *Pompeii: A Sourcebook.* London: Routledge.

Condit, Ira J. 1947. *The Fig.* Waltham, MA: Cronica Botanica.

Corbeill. Anthony. 2004. *Nature Embodied. Gesture in Ancient Rome.* Princeton: Princeton University Press.

Cosminsky, Sheila. 1976. "The Evil Eye in a Quiché Community." In *The Evil Eye,* edited by C. Maloney, 163–74. New York: Columbia University Press.

Coss, Richard G. 1974 [1992]. "Reflections on the Evil Eye." In *The Evil Eye: A Casebook,* edited by A. Dundes, 181–91. 2nd exp. ed. Madison: University of Wisconsin Press, 1992 (1981). Reprinted from *Human Behavior* 3 (1974) 16–21.

Cousland, J. R. C. 2005. "The Much Suffering Eye in Antioch's House of the Evil Eye: Is It Mithraic?" *Religious Studies and Theology* 24:61–74.

Crawford, O. G. S. 1957. *The Eye Goddess.* 1957. Reprinted, Oak Park, IL: Delphi, 1991.

Crombie, J. E. 1892. "The Saliva Superstition." In *The International Folklore Congress 1891: Papers and Transactions,* edited by Joseph and Alfred Nutt, 249–58. London: Nutt.

Crooke, W. 1913. "Simulated Change of Sex to Baffle the Evil Eye." *Folk-Lore* 24:385.

————. 1920. "Saliva." In *HERE* 11:100–104.

Croon, J. H. 1955. "The Mask of the Underworld Daemon: Some Remarks on the Perseus-Gorgon Story." *JHS* 75:9–16.

Crummy, N. 1983. *Colchester Archaeological Report 2: The Roman Small Finds from Excavations in Colchester 1971–79.* Colchester: Colchester Archaeological Trust.

Danker, Frederick W. 1982. *Benefactor: Epigraphic Study of a Graeco-Roman and New Testament Semantic Field.* St. Louis: Clayton.

Daremberg, Charles, and Edmond Saglio, eds. 1877–1919. *Dictionnaire des antiquités grecques et romaines.* 10 vols. (5 double vols.). Paris: Hachette. Reprinted, Graz, 1963.

Dasen, Veronica. 1993. *Dwarfs in Ancient Egypt and Greece.* Oxford: Oxford University Press.

Davidson, William L. 1923. "Envy and Emulation." In *HERE* 5:322–23.

DeForest, Mary. 1993. "Clytemnestra's Breast and the Evil Eye." In *Woman's Power, Man's Game: Essays on Classical Antiquity in Honor of Joy K. King,* edited by M. Deforest, 129–48. Wauconda, IL: Bolchazy-Carducci.

Deismann, Adolf. 1923. *Licht vom Osten.* 4th rev. ed. Tübingen: Mohr Siebeck.

————. 1927. *Light from the Ancient East.* 4th ed. Translated by Lionel R. M. Strachen. London: Hodder& Stoughton.

Delatte, Armand. Amulet collection. Cabinet des médailles et antiques, Bibliothèque nationale, Paris. [193 items]

———. 1961. *Herbarius: Recherches sur le ceremonial usité chez les anciens pour la cuilette des simples et des plantes magiques.* 3rd ed. Brussels: Palais des Académies.

Delatte, A., and P. Derchain. 1964. *Les intailles magiques gréco-égyptiennes.* Cabinet de médailles et antiques, Bibliothèque nationale, Paris: Bibliothèque nationale. (526 items)

Del Hoyo, Javier, and Ana María Vázquez Hoys. 1996. "Clasificación funciona y forma de amuletos fálleos en Híspania." In *Espacio, Tiempo y Forma*, 441–66. Revista de la Facultad de Geografia e Historia, Serie II, Historia Antigua, 9.

Delling, Gerhard. 1964. "*baskainô.*" In *TDNT* 1:594–95.

Déonna, Waldemar.1938. *Le mobilier délien.* Exploration archéologique de Délos 18. Paris: de Boccard.

———. 1957. "L'âme pupilline et quelques monuments figure." *L'Antiquité Classique* 26:59–90.

———. 1965. *Le Symbolisme de l'Oeil.* Travaux et Mémoires des anciens Membres étrangers de l'Ecole et de divers Savants, Fasc. 15, Ecole française d'Athènes. Paris: de Boccard.

Deschler-Erb, Eckhard. 2007. "Altes und Neues zum 'Badener Scheusal.'" *Badener Neujahrsblätter* 83:197–206.

Deubner, Ludwig August. 1910. "Charms and Amulets (Greek)." In *HERE* 3:433–39.

———. 1934. "Die Tracht des römischen Triumphators." *Hermes* 69:316–23.

Devereux, Georges. 1983. *Baubo, la vulve mythiques.* Paris: Godefroy.

Dickie, Matthew W. 1983. "*Invidia infelix*: Vergil, Georgics 3.31–39." *Illinois Classical Studies* 8/1, edited by J. K. Newman, 65–79. Chicago: University of Illinois Press.

———. 1987. "*Lo phthonos* degli dèi nella letteratura Greca del quinto secolo avanti Cristo." *Atene e Roma* n.r. 32:113–25

———. 1990. "Talos Bewitched: Magic, atomic theory and paradoxography in Apollonius' *Argonautica* 4.1638–88." *Papers of the Leeds International Latin Seminar* 6:267–96.

———. 1991. "Heliodorus and Plutarch on the Evil Eye." *Classical Philology* 86:17–29.

———. 1993a. "*Baskania, probaskania, prosbaskania.*" *Glotta* 71: 174–77.

———. 1993b. "Dioscorus and the Impotence of Envy." *Bulletin of the American Society of Papyrologists* 30:63–66.

———. 1995. "A Joke in Old Comedy: Aristophanes Fragment 607 *PCG.*" *Classical Philology* 90:181–95.

———. 1999. Review of Thomas Rakoczy, *Böser Blick* (1996). *Classical Review* 49:363–64.

———. 2001. *Magic and Magicians in the Greco-Roman World.* New York: Routledge.

Dictionnaire d'archéologie chrétienne et de liturgie. 1907–1953. Edited by F. Cabrol and H. Leclercq. 15 vols. Paris: Letouzey et Ané.

*Dictionnaire étymologique de la langue latine.*1985. Edited by A. Ernout et al. 4th ed. Paris: Klincksieck.

Dionisopoulos-Mass, Regina. 1976. "The Evil Eye and Bewitchment in a Peasant Village." In *The Evil Eye*, edited by C. Maloney, 46–62. New York: Columbia University Press.

Dobschütz, Ernst von. 1910. "Charms and Amulets (Christian)." In *HERE* 3:413–430.

Dölger, Franz Joseph. 1922. *ICHTHYS: Der heilige Fisch in den antiken Religionen und im Christentum*. 5 vols. Münster: Aschendorff, 1922–1943. Vol. 1 (1922; 2nd ed, 1928); vol. 2 (1922); vol. 3 (1922); vol. 4 (1927); vol. 5 (1943).

————. 1932. "Eine Knabenbulla mit Christus-Monogramm auf einer Bronze des Prov.-Museums zu Trier." *Antike und Christentum* 3:253–56 and Plate 13.

Dörrie, Heinrich. 1981. "Gnade. A. I." In *RAC* 11:315–33.

Dolansky, Fanny. "Coming of Age in Rome: The History and Social Signicance of Assuming the Toga Virilis." M.A. thesis, University of Victoria, Canada, 1999.

Downey, Glanville. 1963. *Ancient Antioch*. Princeton: Princeton University Press.

Drexler, W. 1899. "Alte Beschwörungsformeln." *Philologus* 58:594–616.

Dubuisson, M. 1980. "Toi aussi, mon fils!" *Latomus* 39:881–90.

Ducati, Pericle. 1937. *Le pitture dell tombe delle Leonesse e dei vasi dipinto*. Rome: Istituto Poligrafico dello Stato.

Dunbabin, Katherine M. D. 1989. "*Baiarum Grata Voluptas*: Pleasure and Dangers of the Baths." *Papers of the British School at Rome* 57:33–46.

————. 1991. "*Inbide calco te . . .* Trampling upon the Envious." In *Tesserae: Festschrift für Joseph Engemann*, 26–35 and Plates 4 and 5. JAC Ergänzungsband 18. Münster: Aschendorff, 1991.

————. 1999. *Mosaics of the Greek and Roman World*. Cambridge: Cambridge University Press.

Dunbabin, Katherine M. D., and M. W. Dickie. 1983. "*Invidia rumpantur pectora*: The Iconography of *Phthonos/Invidia* in Graeco-Roman Art." *JAC* 26:7–37 & Plates 1–8.

Ebeling, Erich. 1949. "Beschwörungen gegen den Feind und den bösen Blick aus dem Zweistromlande." *Archiv Orientalni* 17:172–211.

Ebeling, Erich et al., eds. 1938. *Reallexikon der Assyriologie und Vorderasiatischen Archäologie*. Berlin: de Gruyter.

Echtermeyer, T. 1835. *Proben aus einer Abhandlung über Namen und symbolische Bedeutung der Finger bei den Griechen und Römern*. Halle: Buchdruckerei des Waisenhauses.

Eckstein, F., and J. H. Waszink.1950. "Amulett." In *RAC* 1:397–411.

Eisen, Gustavus. 1916. "The Characteristics of Eye Beads from the Earliest Times to the Present." *American Journal of Archeology* 20:1–27.

Eitrem, Samson E. 1953. "The Pindaric Phthonos." In *Studies Presented to David Moore Robinson on His Seventieth Birthday*, edited by George E. Mylonas and D. Raymond, 2:531–36. 2 vols. St. Louis: Washington University.

————. 1991. "Dreams and Divination in Magical Ritual." In *Magika Hiera: Ancient Greek Magic and Religion*, edited by Christopher A. Faraone, and Dirk Obbink, 175–87. Oxford: Oxford University Press.

Eckstein, F. and J. H. Waszink. 1950. "Amulett." In *RAC* 1:397–411.

Elbogen, I. 1916. "Saliva." In *HERE* 11:100–104.

Elder, G. 1996. *The Body: An Encyclopedia of Archetypal Symbolism*. Boston: Shambhala.

Elliott, John H. 1988. "The Fear of the Leer: The Evil Eye From the Bible to Li'l Abner." *Forum* 4/4:42–71.

————. 1990. "Paul, Galatians, and the Evil Eye." *Currents in Theology and Mission* 17: 262–73.

————. 1991. "The Evil Eye in the First Testament: The Ecology and Culture of a Pervasive Belief." In *The Bible and the Politics of Exegesis: Essays in Honor of*

Norman K. Gottwald on His Sixty-Fifth Birthday, edited by David Jobling et al., 147–59. Cleveland: Pilgrim.

———. 1992. "Matthew 20:1–15: A Parable of Invidious Comparison and Evil Eye Accusation." *Biblical Theology Bulletin* 22: 52–65.

———. 1993. *What is Social-Scientific Criticism?* Guides to Biblical Scholarship, New Testament Series. Minneapolis: Fortress, 1993. [On Evil Eye, 67–69, and Evil Eye model].

———. 1994. "The Evil Eye and the Sermon on the Mount. Contours of a Pervasive Belief in Social Scientific Perspective." *Biblical Interpretation* 2:51–84.

———. 2004. "Look it Up: It's in BDAG." In *Biblical Greek Language and Lexicography. Essays in Honor of Frederick W. Danker*, edited by Bernard A. Taylor et al., 48–52. Grand Rapids: Eerdmans.

———. 2005a "Jesus, Mark, and the Evil Eye." *Lutheran Theological Journal* (Festschrift in honour of Victor C. Pfitzner) 39/2–3: 157–68.

———. 2005b. "Lecture socioscientifique. Illustration par l'accusation du Mauvais Oeil en Galatie." In *Guide des nouvelles lectures de la Bible*, edited by André Lacocque, 141–67. Translation by Jean-Pierre Prévost. Paris: Bayard.

———. 2005c. "Deuteronomy—Shameful Encroachment on Shameful Parts. Deuteronomy 25:11–12 and Biblical Euphemism." In *Ancient Israel: The Old Testament in Its Social Context*, edited by Philip F. Esler, 161–76, 330–32. Minneapolis: Fortress.

———. 2005d. "Deuteronomy 25:11–12 LXX: No Tweaking the Twins. More on a Biblical Euphemism and Its Translation." In *Kontexte der Schrift*. Vol. 2. *Kultur, Politik, Religion, Sprache—Text. Für Wolfgang Stegemann zum 60. Geburtstag*, edited by Christian Strecker, 323–42. Stuttgart: Kohlhammer.

———. 2007a. "Envy and the Evil Eye: More on Mark 7:22 and Mark's 'Anatomy of Envy.'" In *In Other Words: Essays on Social Science Methods and the New Testament in Honor of Jerome H. Neyrey*, edited by Anselm Hagedorn et al., 87–105. Social World of Biblical Antiquity 2/1. Sheffield: Sheffield Phoenix.

———. 2007b. "Envy, Jealousy and Zeal in the Bible: Sorting Out the Social Differences and Theological Implications—No Envy for YHWH." In *To Break Every Yoke: Essays in Honor of Marvin C. Chaney*, edited by Robert Coote and Norman K. Gottwald, 344–63. Social World of Biblical Antiquity 2/3. Sheffield: Sheffield Phoenix.

———. 2008. "God—Zealous or Jealous but never Envious: The Theological Consequences of Linguistic and Social Distinctions." In *The Social Sciences and Biblical Translation*, edited by Dietmar Neufeld, 79–96. Symposium Series 41. Atlanta: Society of Biblical Literature.

———. 2011. "Social-scientific Criticism: Perspective, Process, Payoff: Evil Eye Accusation at Galatia as Illustration of the Method." *Hervormde teologies studies* 67/1: 114–23.

———. 2015. *Beware the Evil Eye. The Evil Eye in the Bible and the Ancient World. Volume 1. Introduction, Mesopotamia, and Egypt*. Cascade Books. Eugene, OR: Wipf and Stock.

———. 2015. "Jesus, Paulus und der Böse Blick: Was die modernen Bibelversionen und Kommentare uns nicht sagen." In *Alte Texte in neuen Kontexten: Wo steht die sozialwissenschaftliche Bibelexegese?*, edited by Wolfgang Stegemann and Richard E. De Maris, 85–104. Stuttgart: Kohlhammer.

———. 2016a. "'Envy." By Jerome H. Neyrey, John H. Elliott, and Zeba Crook. In *The Ancient Mediterranean Social World: A Sourcebook*, edited by Zeba Crook. Grand Rapids: Eerdmans. **[AQ]**

———. 2016b. "Evil Eye." In *The Ancient Mediterranean Social World: A Sourcebook*, edited by Zeba Crook. Grand Rapids: Eerdmans.

Elworthy, Frederick Thomas. 1895/1958. *The Evil Eye: An Account of This Ancient and Widespread Superstition*. London: Murray, 1895. Reprinted with an Introduction by Louis S. Barron, New York: Julian, 1958.

———. 1900. *Horns of Honor and Other Studies in the By-Ways of Archaeology*. London: Murray.

———. 1903. "Solution of the Gorgon Myth." 1903. *Folk-Lore* 14:212–42 and two plates.

Enciclopedia dell' Arte Medievale (1991). 12 vols. Libreria arcobaleno. Rome: Istituto della Enciclopedia Italiana.

Encyclopaedia of Religion and Ethics. 1908–1927. 13 vols. Edited by James Hasting et al. Edinburgh: T. & T. Clark. 4th edition reprinted.

Engemann, Josef. 1969. "Fisch." In *RAC* 7:959–1097.

———. 1975. "Zur Verbreitung magischer Übelabwehr in der nichtchristlichen und Christlichen Spätantike." In *JAC* 18:22–48 (+ 14 figures & Plates 8–16).

———. 1980. "Der 'Corna' Gestus—Ein antiker und frühchristlicher Abwehr- und Spottgestus?" *Pietas: Festschrift für Bernhard Kötting*, edited by Ernst Dassmann and K. Suso, 483–98. JAC Ergänzungsband 8. Münster: Aschendorff.

———. 1981. "Glyptik." In *RAC* 11:270–313.

Engemann, J., S. H. Fuglesang, G. Vikan, and M. Bernardini. 1991. *"Amuleto."Enciclopedia dell' Arte Medievale* (1991). [Introduction: Engemann; West: Engemann; North: Fuglesang; Byzantine:Vikan; Islam: Bernardini] Online: www.trecanni

Espérandieu, E. 1913. "Tintinnabulum (*kôdôn*)." In Daremberg-Saglio 5:341–44.

*Etymologisches Wörterbuch der deutschen Sprache.*1963. Edited by Friedrich Kluge. 19th ed. Revised byWalter Mitzka. Berlin: de Gruyter.

Etymologisches Wörterbuch des Griechischen. 1966. Edited by Johann Baptist Hofmann. Munich: Oldenbourg.

Evans, William N. 1975. "The Eye of Jealousy and Envy." *Psychoanalytic Review* 62:481–92.

Faraone, C. A. 1987. "Hephaestus the Magician and Near Eastern Parallels for Alicinous' Watchdogs." *GRBS* 28:257–80.

———. 1991 "The Agonistic Context of Early Greek Binding Spells." In *Magika Hiera: Ancient Greek Magic and Religion,* edited by Christopher A. Faraone and Dirk Obbink, 3–32. Oxford: Oxford University Press.

———. 2013. "The Amuletic Design of the Mithraic Bull-Wounding Scene." *Journal of Roman Studies* 103:96–116.

"Fascino etc." *Thesaurus Linguae Latinae* 6,1 (1912–1926) cols. 299–301. Leipzig: Teubner.

Fehling, Detlev.1988. "Phallische Demonstration." In *Sexualität und Erotik in der Antike*, edited by Andrea Karsten Siemes, 282–323. Wege der Forschung 605. Darmstadt: Wissenschaftliche Buchgesellschaft. Reprint of *Ethnologische Überlegungen auf dem Gebiet der Altertumskunde*. Munich. 1974. Pp. 7–38.

Fernàndez de la Mora, Gonzalo. 1987. *Egalitarian Envy: The Political Foundations of Social Justice*. Translated by Antonia T. de Nicholàs. New York: Paragon.

Ficker, Johannes. 1896. "Amulett." PW 1:467–76.

Foster, George M. 1965. "Peasant Society and the Image of Limited Good." *American Anthropologist* 67:293–315.

———. 1972. "The Anatomy of Envy." *Current Anthropology* 13:165–202.

Foucher, Louis. 1957. "Motifs prophylactiques sur des mosaiques récemment découvertes à Sousse." Actes du 79e Congrès national des sociétés savantes, Alger 1954, 163-86. Paris. Presses universitaires de France.

———. 1960. *Inventaire des Mosaïques: Sousse.* Feuille No. 57 de l'Atlas Archéologique. Tunis: Institut national d'archéologie et arts.

Fowler, R. L. 1995. "Greek Magic, Greek Religion." *Illinois Classical Studies* 20:1–22.

Frankfurter, David. 2006. "Fetus Magic and Sorcery Fears in Roman Egypt." *GRBS* 46:37–62.

Fracastorius, Hieronymus. 1555. *De Sympathia et Antipathia Rerum.* In *Opera Omnia.* Venice: Juntas.

Frachtenberg, Leo. 1918. "Allusions to Witchcraft and Other Primitive Beliefs in Zoroastrian Literature." In *The Dastur Hoshang Memorial Volume.* Bombay: Fort Printing Press.

Frazer, James George. 1906–1915. *The Golden Bough: A Study in Magic and Religion.* 12 vols. (Third enlarged edition of *The Golden Bough: A Study in Comparative Religion.* 2 vols. London: Macmillan, 1890). London: Macmillan.

———. 1967. *The Gorgon's Head and Other Literary Pieces.* Reprinted, Freeport: Books for Libraries Press.

Frazer, James G., and Theodor H. Gaster, eds. 1959. *The New Golden Bough.* New York: New Amerian Library.

Frederick, David. 2002. *The Roman Gaze: Vision, Power and the Body.* Baltimore: Johns Hopkins University Press.

Freire-Marreco, Barbara.1910. "Charms and Amulets." In *HERE* 3:392–98.

Freitag, Barbara. 2004. *Sheela-Na-Gigs: Unraveling an Enigma.* New York: Routledge.

Friedländer, L. 1928. *Roman Life and Manners under the Early Empire.* 4 vols. Translated by L. Magnus et al. London: Routledge.

Friedman, David M. 2001. *A Mind of Its Own. A Cultural History of the Penis.* New York: Free Press, 2001; New York: Penguin, 2003.

Fritz, Karl von 1926. *Quellenuntersuchungen zu Leben und Philosophie des Diogenes von Sinope.* Philologus, Supplementband 18.2. Leipzig: Dieterich.

Froehner, Wilhelm. 1925. Amulet collection. *Cat. Inscr. Gr. Froehner.* Cabinet des medailles et antiques. Bibliothèque Nationale, Paris. 1925.

Furtwängler, A. 1886–1890. "Die Gorgonen in der Kunst." *Ausführliches Lexikon der griechischen und römischen Mythologie,* edited by W. H. Roscher. Vol. 1, part 2: 1701–28. Leipzig: Teubner.

Gager, John G. 1990. "Curse and Competition in the Ancient Circus." In *Of Scribes and Scrolls: Studies on the Hebrew Bible, Intertestamental Judaism, and Christian Origins, Presented to John Strugnell on the Occasion of His Sixtieth Birthday,* edited by Harold W. Attridge, et al., 215-28. College Theology Society Resources in Religion 5. Lanham, NY: University Press of America.

———. 1992. *Curse Tablets and Binding Spells from the Ancient World.* Oxford: Oxford University Press.

Garber, M., and N. Vickers, eds. 2003.*The Medusa Reader.* New York: Routledge.

Garcia Lopez, J. and C. Morales Otal. 1984. "Envidia humana y envidia divina en los epinicios di Pindaro." *Athlon, Satura grammatical in honorem F. R. Adrados*, edited by Alberto Bernabé et al. Vol. 2:315–22. Madrid: Gredos.

Garland, Robert. 1995. *The Eye of the Beholder: Deformity and Disability in the Graeco-Roman World*. Ithaca, NY: Cornell University Press.

Gaster, Moses. 1910. "Charms and Amulets (Jewish)." In *HERE* 3:451–55.

Gaster, Theodor H. 1969. *Myth, Legend and Custom in the Old Testament*, New York: Harper & Row.

Geffcken, J. 1930. "*Baskanos daimôn.*" In *Charisteria: Alois Rzach zum achzigsten Geburtstag dargebracht*, 36–40. Reichenberg: Stiepel.

Geisau, Hans von. 1979a. "Gorgo." In *Der Kleine Pauly* 2:852–53.

———. 1979b. "Gorgoneion." In *Der Kleine Pauly* 2:853.

Germer-Duran, J. 1906. "Amulette contre le mauvais oeil." *Échos d'Orient* 9:129–30.

Gershman, Boris. 2011a. "The Two Sides of Envy." Brown University, October 2011. 45 pages. Online: http://mpra.ub.uni-muenchen.de/34168/ MPRA Paper No. 34168, posted 17. October 2011 16:42 UTC.

———. 2011b. "From Fear to Competition: Envy in the Process of Development." Working Paper, Brown University.

Gerstinger, H. 1954. "Bulla." In *RAC* 2:800–801.

Giangrande, Giuseppe. 1967 "Hellenistic Anagrams." *Classical Review* 17:17–24.

———. 1969. "Interpretationen hellenistischer Dichter." *Hermes* 96: 440–54.

Gilmore, David D., editor. 1987a. *Aggression and Community: Paradoxes and Andalusian Culture*. New Haven: Yale University Press.

———. 1987b. *Honor and Shame and the Unity of the Mediterranean*. Special Publication of the American Anthropological Association 22. Washington, DC: American Anthropological Association.

Glenn, Justin. 1978 "The Polyphemus Myth: Its Origin and Interpretation." *Greece & Rome* 25:141–55.

Glotz, Gustav.1896. "Gorgones." Daremberg-Saglio 2.2 (1896): 1615–29 [including figures 3632–3645].

González-Wippler, Migene. 2001. *The Complete Book of Amulets and Talismans*. St. Paul, MN: Llewellyn Publishers.

Gordon, Richard. 2002. "Magical amulets the British Museum." *Journal of Roman Archaeology* 15: 666–70. [Review of S. Michel, et al, eds. *Die Magischen Gemmen im Britischen Museum*. 2001].

Gouldner, Alvin W. 1965. *Enter Plato: Classical Greece and the Origins of Social Theory*. New York: Basic Books.

———. 1969. *The Hellenic World. A Sociological Analysis*. New York: Harper & Row. [Part I of *Enter Plato: Classical Greece and the Origins of Social Theory*. New York: Basic Books, 1965].

Graf, Fritz. 1991. "Gestures and conventions: the Gesture of Roman actors and orators." In *A Cultural History of Gesture*, edited by Jan Bremmer and Hermann Roodenburg, 36–58. Ithaca, NY: Cornell University Press.

———. 1997a. *Magic in the Ancient World*. Translated by Franklin Philip. Revealing Antiquity 10. Cambridge: Harvard University Press. [ET of *Gottesnähe und Schadenzauber, Die Magie in der griechisch-römischen Antike*. Munich: Beck, 1996]

———. 1997b "How to Cope with a Difficult Life: A View of Ancient Magic." In *Envisioning Magic: A Princeton Seminar and Symposium*, edited by Peter Schäfer and Hans G. Kippenberg, 93–114. Studies in the History of Religions 75. Leiden: Brill.

———. 2002."Theories of Magic in Antiquity." In *Magic and Ritual in the Ancient World*, edited by Paul Mirecki and Marvin Meyer, 93–104. Religions in the Graeco-Roman World 141. Leiden: Brill.

Gramiccia, Anna, and Francesca Pagnotta, eds. 1989. *Le Collezioni del Museo Nazionale di Napoli*. Archivio Fotografico Pedicini. Rome: De Luca Edizioni d'Arte.

Grant, Michael. 1975. *Erotic Art in Pompeii: The Secret Collections of the National Museum of Naples*. Photographs by Antonia Mulas. London: Octopus.

Grant, Michael. 1982. *Eros in Pompeii. The Secret Rooms of the National Museum of Naples*. Photographs by Antonia Mulas. New York: Bonanza.

Great Books of the Western World. 1952. Edited by Robert Maynard Hutchins. 54 vols. Chicago: Encyclopaedia Britannica.

Greek Lexicon of the Roman and Byzantine Periods. 1887. 2 vols. Edited by E. A. Sophocles. New York: Scribner.

Greenfield, Amy Butler. 2006. *A Perfect Red: Empire, Espionage and the Quest for the Color of Desire*. New York: Harper Perennial.

Greenfield, Richard P. 2006. "Evil Eye." In *Encyclopedia of Ancient Greece*, edited by Nigel Guy Wilson, 284–85. New York: Routledge.

Griechisches Etymologisches Wörterbuch. Edited by Hjalmar Frisk. 3 vols. Heidelberg: Winter, 1960–73.

Griffiths, J. Gwynn. 1960. *The Conflict of Horus and Seth*. Liverpool: Liverpool University Press.

Gross, Charles G. 1999. "The Fire That Comes from the Eyes." *Neuroscientist* 5:58–64. Online: https://www.princeton.edu/~cggross/neuroscientist_5_99_fire.pdf.

Gross, K. 1969. "Finger." In *RAC* 7:909–46.

Günther, R. T. 1905. "The Cimaruta: Its Structure and Development." *Folk-Lore* 16:132–61.

Hahm, David E. 1975. "Early Hellenistic Theories of Vision and the Perception of Color." In *Studies in Perceptioned*, edited by P. K. Machamer and R. G. Turnbill, 60–95. Colombus: Ohio State University Press.

Hall, Edith. 1989. *Inventing the Barbarian*. Oxford: Oxford University Press.

Handwörterbuch des deutschen Aberglaubens. 1927–1942. 10 vols. Edited by H. Bächtold-Stäubli and E. Hoffmann-Krayer. Berlin: de Gruyter. Reprinted, 1987.

Hansen, Abby. 1981. "Coral in Children's Portraits: A Charm against the Evil Eye." *Antiques* 120:1424–31

Hansmann, Lieselotte and Lenz Kriss-Rettenbeck. 1966. *Amulett und Talisman. Erscheinungsform und Geschichte*. Munich: Callwey.

Hanson, M. L. 1987. "Eye Terms in Greek Tragedy." PhD dissertation, University of North Carolina, Chapel Hill.

Harrison, Jane. 1955. *Prolegomena to the Study of Greek Religion*. New York: Meridian. (1903).

Hartland, Edwin Sidney. 1894–96. *The Legend of Perseus*. 3 vols. London: Nutt.

Heim, Richard. 1892. *Incantamenta magica Graeca Latina*. Leipzig: Teubner.

Hauschild, Thomas. 1979. *Der Böse Blick: Ideengeschichtliche und Sozialpsychologische Untersuchungen*. Beiträge zur Ethnomedizin, Ethnobotanik und Ethnozoologie

VII. Hamburg: Arbeitskreis Ethnomedizin. 2nd ed. Berlin: Mensch und Leben, 1982.

Helck, Hans Wolfgang. 1979. "Horus." In *Der Kleine Pauly* 2:1231–33.

Hellenica, Recueil d'épigraphie, de numismatique et d'antiquités grecques. 13 vols. 1940–1965.

Hellmann, Marie-Christine. 2006. "La collection Froehner au Cabinet des médailles de Paris." *Les Dossiers d'archéologie* 312:30–37.

Hermann, A. and M. Cagiano di Azevedo.1969. "Farbe." In *RAC* 7:358–447.

Herter, Hans. 1927 "De Mutino Titino." *Rheinisches Museum für Philologie* 76:418–432.

———. 1932. *De Priapo.* Religionsgeschichtliche Versuche und Vorarbeiten. 23. Giessen: Töpelmann. 1932.

———. 1934."Telchinen." In PW 5. A.1: 197–224.

———. 1935. "Nemesis." In PW 16.2:2338–80.

———. 1938. "Phallos." In PW 19.2:1681–748.

———. 1950. "Böse Dämonen im frühgriechischen Volksglauben." *Rheinisches Jahrbuch für Volkskunde* 1:112–43.

———. 1972. "Phallos." In *Der Kleine Pauly* 4:701–6.

———. 1978. "Genitalien." In *RAC* 10:1–52.

———. 1986. "Haus I. A. Nicht christlich. I. Griechisch-römisch." In *RAC* 13:770–85.

Herzog-Hauser, Gertrud. 1937. "*Tintinnabulum.*" In PW 6A:1406–10.

Hess, Robert and Elfriede Paschinger. 1986. *Das etruskische Italien.* 6th rev. ed. Cologne: DuMont.

Higgins, R. A. 1961. *Greek and Roman Jewelry.* London: Methuen.

Hildburgh, Walter Leo. 1906. "Notes on Spanish Amulets." *Folk-Lore* 17:454–71.

———. 1908. "Notes on Some Contemporary Portuguese Amulets." *Folk-Lore* 19:213–24.

———. 1913. "Further Notes on Spanish Amulets." *Folklore* 24:63–74.

———. 1942. "Lunar Crescents as Amulets in Spain." *Man* 42:73–83 + plate.

———. 1944. "Indeterminability and Confusion as Apotropaic Elements in Italy and Spain." *Folk-Lore* 55:133–49.

———. 1946, 1947. "Apotropaism in Greek Vase Paintings." *Folk-Lore* 57:154–78; 58:208–25.

———. 1951a. "Psychology Underlying the Employment of Amulets in Europe." *Folk-Lore* 62:231–51.

———. 1951b. "Some Spanish Amulets Connected with Lactation." *Folk-Lore* 62:430–48.

Hill, Jude. 2007. "The Story of the Amulet. Locating the Enchantment of Collections." *Journal of Material Culture* 12/1:65–87.

Hinterberger, Martin. 2013. *Phthonos: Missgunst, Neid und Eifersucht in der Byzantinischen Literatur.* Serta Graeca series 29. Wiesbaden: Ludwig Reichert.

Holland, Jennifer S. 2013. "The Bite That Heals." *National Geographic* 223/2:64–83.

Hornblower, G. D. 1941. "Cowrie and Evil-Eye." *Man* 41: item 81.

Hornell, James. 1923. "Survivals of the Use of Oculi in Modern Boats." *Journal of the Royal Anthropological Institute* 53:289–321.

———. 1924. "The Evil Eye and Related Beliefs in Trinidad." *Folk-Lore* 35:270–75.

———. 1938. "Boat Oculi Survivals: Additional Records." *Journal of the Royal Anthropological Institute* 68: 339–48.

Hornum, Michael B. 1993. *Nemesis, the Roman State and the Games.* Religons in the Greco-Roman World 117. Leiden: Brill.

Horst, Robert Balz. 2000. "Neid." In *TRE* 24:246–54.

Howe, T. P. 1954. "The Origin and Function of the Gorgon-Head." *AJA* 58:209–21.

Hunt, A. S., and C. C. Edgar, eds. 1932. *Select Papyri.* Vol. 1. *Non-Literary Papyri, Private Affairs.* LCL. Cambridge: Harvard University Press.

———, eds. 1934. *Select Papyri.* Vol. 2. *Non-Literary Papyri; Public Documents.* LCL. Cambridge: Harvard University Press.

Inscriptions grecques et latines de Syrie. 1929–70. Edited by L. Jalabert and R. Monterde. Paris: Geuthner.

Inscriptions grecques et latines de Syrie. 1970. Edited by W. H. Waddington. 4. ed. Paris: Bretschneider.

Interpreter's Dictionary of the Bible. 1962. 4 vols. Edited by George Arthur Buttrick. New York: Abingdon.

Interpreter's Dictionary of the Bible, Supplementay Volume. 1976. Edited by Keith Crim et al., 1976. Nashville: Abingdon.

Jahn, Otto. 1855. *Über den Aberglauben des bösen Blickes bei den Alten.* Berichte der Sächsischen Gesellschaft der Wissenschaften zu Leipzig. Philologisch-Historische Classe, 28–110 & 5 Plates. Leipzig: Hirzel.

Jeffreys, M. O. W. 1942. "Cowry, Vulva, Eye." *Man* 42:120.

———. 1943. "Cowry and Vulva Again." *Man* 43:144.

Jonas, Wayne B., ed. 2005. *Mosby's Dictionary of Complementary and Alternative Medicine.* St. Louis: Elsevier.

Jones, William. 1877. *Finger-Ring Lore, Historical, Legendary, Anecdotal.* London: Chatto & Windus.

Johns, Catherine. 1982. *Sex or Symbol. Erotic Images of Greece and Rome.* Austin: University of Texas Press.

Johnston, Sarah Iles. 1995. "Defining the Dreadful: Remarks on the Greek Child-Killing Demon." In *Ancient Magic and Ritual Power,* edited by Marvin Meyer and Paul Mirecki, 361–87. Religion in the Graeco-Roman World 129. Leiden: Brill.

Johnstone, Paul. 1980. *The Sea-craft of Prehistory.* Prepared for publication by Sean McGrail. London: Routledge & Kegan Paul.

Judge, Edwin A. 1993. *Ancient Beginning of the Modern World. Documents Illustrating the Final Lecture 13 July 1993.* In *Ancient History in a Modern University.*Vol. 2, *Early Christianity, Late Antiquity and Beyond,* edited by T. W. Hillard et al. Ancient History Documentary Research Centre, Macquarie University. Grand Rapids: Eerdmans.

Kaimakis, D., ed. 1976. *Die Kyraniden.* Meisenheim am Glan: Hain.

Kallipolitis, K. 1958. "Céphalonie." In *BCH* 82: 727–32 and figs. 1–3.

Kaster, Robert A. 2003. "Invidia, nemesis, phthonos, and the Roman Emotional Economy." In *Envy, Spite, and Jealousy: The Rivalrous Emotions in Ancient Greece,* edited by Douglas Konstan and Keith Rutter, 253–76. Edinburgh Leventis Studies 2. Edinburgh: University of Edinburgh Press.

———. 2005 "Invidia is One Thing, Invidia Quite Another." In *Emotion, Restraint, and Community in Ancient Rome,* 84–103, 180–87. Oxford: Oxford University Press.

Kelley, Nicole. 2007. "Deformity and Disability in Greece and Rome." In *This Abled Body: Rethinking Disabilities in Biblical Studies,* edited by Hector Avalos et al., 31–46. Semeia Studies 55. Atlanta: Society of Biblical Literature.

Kennedy, A. R. S. 1910. "Charms and Amulets (Hebrew)." In *HERE* 3:439–41.

Kenner, Hedwig. 1957. "Porrecti tres digiti." In *Antidoron: Michaeli Abramić septuagenario oblatum a collegis et amicis*, edited by Duje Rendić-Miočević et al., 177–83. Split; Arheološki Muzei.

Keuls, Eva C. 1985.*The Reign of the Phallus: Sexual Politics in Ancient Athens*. New York: Harper & Row.

el-Khachab, Abd el-Mohsen. 1956. "*Les hammams du Kôm Trougah*." *Annales du Service des Antiquités de l'Égypte* 54:117–39.

King, Charles William. 1885. *Handbook of Engraved Gems*. London: Bell, 1885.

Kirchhoff, H. 1977. "The Woman's Posture during Childbirth, from Prehistoric Times to the Present." *Organorama* 14:14–19.

Klein, Melanie. 1957. *Envy and Gratitude: A Study of Unconscious Sources*. New York: Basic Books.

———. 1975. *Envy and Gratitude, and Other Works, 1946–1963*. International Psycho-Analytical Library 104. London: Hogarth.

Kleine Pauly, Der. Lexikon der Antike in fünf Bänden. Edited by Konrat Ziegler et al. 5 vols. Munich: Deutscher Taschenbuch, 1979.

Kline, Anthony S. 2000. Translation of Ovid, *Metamorphoses*. Online: http://ovid.lib.virginia.edu/trans/Ovhome.htm.

Knight, Richard Payne, and Thomas Wright. 1865. *A discourse on the worship of Priapus, and its connection with the mystic theology of the ancients by Richard Payne Knight* [1786]. *To which is added an essay* [by Thomas Wright] *on the worship of the generative powers during the Middle Ages of western Europe.*). Published by John Camden Hotten, privately printed, 1865. Electronic edition. Leeds, UK: Celephais Press, 2003. Reprinted Secaucus, NJ: University Books, 1974. Reprinted as Knight, Richard Payne and Thomas Wright, *Sexual Symbolism. A History of Phallic Worship*. Julian Press 1957. Online: www.sacred-texts.com/sex/dwp/index.htm

Knuf, Astrid, and Joachim Knuf. 1984. *Amulette und Talismane. Symbole des magischen Alltags*. Cologne: DuMont.

Koerper, Henry C. and Nancy Whitney-Desautels.1999. "A Cowry Shell Artifact from Bolsa Chica: An Example of Prehistoric Exchange." *PCAS Quarterly* 35/2–3: 81–95

Konstan, David. 2003. "*Nemesis* and *Phthonos*." In *Gestures: Essays in Ancient History, Literature and Philosophy Presented to Alan J. Boegehold*, edited by G. W. Bakewell and J. P. Sickinger. 74–87. Oxford: Oxbow.

———. 2006. *The Emotions of the Ancient Greeks: Studies in Aristotle and Classical Literature*. Toronto: University of Toronto Press.

Konstan, David, and Keith Rutter, eds. 2003. *Envy, Spite and Jealousy: The Rivalrous Emotions in Ancient Greece*. Edinburgh Leventis Studies 2. Edinburgh: Edinburgh University Press.

Kotansky, Roy. 1991. "Incantations and Prayers for Salvation on Inscribed Greek Amulets." In *Magika Hiera: Ancient Greek Magic and Religion*, edited by Christopher A. Faraone and Dirk Obbink, 107–37. New York: Oxford University Press.

———. 1994. *Greek Magical Amulets. I. The Inscribed Gold, Silver, Copper, and Bronze Lamellae. Part One. Published Texts of Known Provenance*. Papyrologica Coloniensia 22/1. Opladen: Westdeutscher.

———. 1995. "Greek Exorcistic Amulets." In *Ancient Magic and Ritual Power,* edited by Marvin Meyer and Paul Mirecki, 243–77. Religions in the Graeco-Roman World 129. Leiden: Brill, 1995.

———. 2002. "An Early Christian Gold Lamella for Headache." In *Magic and Ritual in the Ancient World,* edited by Paul Mirecki and Marvin Meyer, 37–46. Religions in the Graeco-Roman World 141. Leiden, Brill, 2002. Cf. PGM XVIIIa.1–4.

Krauskopf, I. and S.-C. Dahlinger. 1988. "Gorgo, Gorgones." In *LIMC* 4:285–330.

Kropatschek, G. 1907. *"De Amuletorum apud antiquos usu capita duo."* Dissertation (Philologie), University of Greifswald, 1907.

Kuhnert, Friedmar. 1909. "Fascinum." In PW 6/2:2009–14.

Kunisch, N. 1990. "Die Augen der Augenschalen."*Antike Kunst* 33:20–27.

Laarss, R. H. 1919. *Das Geheimnis der Amulette und Talismane.* Leipzig: Talis.

Labatut, E. 1877. "Amuletum." Daremberg-Saglio 1.1 (1877): 252–58 and figs. 300–314.

Lafaye, G. 1896. "Fascinum, fascinus (*baskania*), fascination." Daremberg-Saglio 2.2:983–87.

Lamb, Trevor, and Janine Bouriau, eds. 1995. *Colour: Art and Science.* Cambridge: Cambridge University Press.

Lanczkowski, G. 1962. "Speichel." In *RGG*³ 6:229–30.

Langdon, Stephen. 1913. *Babylonian Liturgies: Sumerian Texts from the Early Period and from the Library of Ashurbanipal.* Paris: Geuthner.

Le Blant, E. 1898. "750 inscriptions de pierres gravées." In *Memoires de l' Academie des Inscriptions et Belles Lettres* 36, Paris.

Leclercq, Henri. 1907. "Amulettes." In *DACL* 1.2: 1784–860; cols. 1843–47 on "Le mauvais oeil."

———.1910. "Bulla." In *DACL* 2.1: 1331–34.

———. 1933. "Méduse." In *DACL* 11.1:195–199.

———. 1934. "Oeil." In *DACL* 12.2: 1936–1943, cols. 1936–1941 on "Le mauvais oeil."

Leite de Vasconcellos, J. 1925. *A Figa: Estudio de Ethnografia Comparativa.* Porto: Araujo & Sobrinho.

Lesky, Albin. 1969. "Abwehr und Verachtung in der Gebärdensprache." *AnzWien* 106: 149–57.

Lesky, E., and J. H. Waszink. 1965. "Epilepsie." In *RAC* 5:819–31.

Lethbridge, T. C. 1941. "The Meaning of the Cowrie: Fiji, Egypt and Saxon England." *Man* 41:48.

Leven, Karl-Heinz. 1995. "Die 'unheilige' Krankheit—Epilepsia, Mondsucht und Besessenheit in Byzanz." *Würzburger Medizinhistorische Mitteilungen* 13:17–57.

Levi, Doro. 1941. "The Evil Eye and the Lucky Hunchback." In *Antioch-on-the-Orontes. III. The Excavations 1937–1939,* edited by Richard Stillwell, 3: 220–32. Publications of the Committee for the Excavation of Antioch and Its Vicinity. 5 vols. Princeton: Princeton University Press, 1934–72.

———. 1947. *Antioch Mosaic Pavements.* 2 Vols. Princeton: Princeton University Press.

Levy, Israel. *The Hebrew Text of the Book of Ecclesiasticus.* Semitic Studies Series 3. Leiden: Brill, 1969.

Lewis, Charlton T., and Charles Short, eds. 1955. *A Latin Dictionary.* Oxford: Clarendon.

Lewis, Napthali. 1983. *Life in Egypt under Roman Rule.* Oxford: Oxford University Press.

Lexicon Iconographicum Mythologiae Classicae. 15 vols. Zürich: Artemis, 1981–1999.

Licht, Hans. 1932/1971. *Sexual Life in Ancient Greece.* London: Abbey Library.

Liddell, Henry George and Robert Scott. *A Greek–English Lexicon.* 9th edition revised and augmented by H. S. Jones with the assistance of R. McKenzie. Oxford: Clarendon, 1940. *A Supplement,* edited by E.A. Barber et al. 1968. Revised supplement, edited by P. Glare and A. Thompson, 1996.

Lindberg, D. C. 1976. *Theories of Vison from Al-Kindi to Kepler.* Chicago: University of Chicago.

Lindsay, Jack. 1968. *The Ancient World.* New York: Putnam.

Lovatt, Helen. 2013. *The Epic Gaze: Vision, Gender, and Narrative in Ancient Epic.* Cambridge: Cambridge University Press.

Luck, Georg. 1985. *Arcana Mundi: Magic and the Occult in the Greek and Roman Worlds. A Collection of Ancient Texts Translated, Annotated and Introduced by George Luck.* Baltimore: Johns Hopkins University Press.

MacCulloch, J. A. 1913. "Hand." In *HERE* 6:492–99.

Mack, R. 2002. "Facing Down Medusa (An Aetiology of the Gaze)." *Art History* 25:571–604.

Malina, Bruce J. 1979. "Limited Good and the Social World of Early Christianity." *BTB* 8:162–76.

———. 2001. *The New Testament World. Insights from Cultural Anthropology.* 3rd ed. Louisville: Westminster John Knox.

Malina, Bruce J., and Jerome H. Neyrey. 1996. *Portraits of Paul: An Archaeology of Ancient Personality.* Louisville: Westminster John Knox.

"Malus oculus." 1896. *Harper's Dictionary of Classical Literature and Antiquities,* edited by Harry Thurston Peck. New York: American Book Co.

Marcadé, Jean. 1961. *Roma Amor.* Geneva: Nagel, 1961.

Marganne, M. H. 1978. "Le système chromatique dans le corps aristotélicien." *Les Études Classiques* 46:185–203.

Marques-Riviere, J. 1938. *Amulettes, talismans et pentacles dans des traditions orientales et occidentales.* Paris: Payot.

Marquardt, Joachim. 1886/1975. *Das Privatleben der Römer.* 2 vols. 2nd ed. edited by A. Mau. Leipzig: Hirzel, 1886. Reprinted, Darmstadt: Wissenschaftliche Buchgesellschaft.

Marshall, F. H. 1907. *Catalogue of the finger rings Greek, Etruscan, and Roman in the Department of Antiquities, British Museum.* London: Trustees of the British Museum.

———. 1911. *Catalogue of the Jewellery. Greek, Etruscan, and Roman in the Department of Antiquities, British Museum.* London: Trustees of the British Museum.

Mastrocinque, Attilio, ed. 2003. *Sylloge Gemmarvm Gnosticarvm.* Parts 1 and 2. Ministero per i beni e le attività culturali. Bollettino di numismatica. Monografia 8.2.I. Rome: Istituto Poligrafico e Zecca dello Stato. Libreria dello Stato, http://www.numismaticadellostato.it

Matantseva, Tatiana. 1994. "Les amulettes byzantines contre le mauvais oeil de Cabinet des médailles." *JAC* 37:110–121

Mau, A. "Bulla." 1897. In *PW* 3.1:1048–51.

McCartney, Eugene S. 1924. "Boasting as a Provocation of the Divine Powers." *The Classical Journal* 19:382–83.

———. 1992 [1943]. "Praise and Dispraise in Folklore." *Papers of the Michigan Academy of Science, Arts and Letters* 28 (1943): 257–93. Reprinted in *The Evil Eye: A*

Casebook, edited by A. Dundes, 9–38. 2nd expanded ed. Madison: University of Wisconsin Press, 1992.

McDaniel, Walton Brooks. 1918. "The Pupula Duplex and Other Tokens of an 'Evil Eye' in the Light of Ophthalmology." *Classical Philology* 13:335–46. Reprinted in *Perspectives in Biology and Medicine* 15/1 (1971) 72–79.

Meek, C. K. 1940. "The Meaning of the Cowrie-Shell in Nigeria." *Man* 40:62–63.

———. 1941. "The Meaning of the Cowrie: The Evil Eye in Nigeria." *Man* 1940:47–48.

Meerloo, Joost Abraham Maurits. 1971. *Intuition and the Evil Eye: The Natural History of a Superstition.* Wassenaar (Netherlands): Servire.

Megow, Wolf-Rüdiger. 1997. "Priapos." *Lexicon Iconographicum Mythologiae Classicae.* Vol. 8/1:1028–44; 8/2 (Supplement), Plates 680–94, figs. 6–181B.

Meilach, Dona Z. 1981. *Ethnic Jewelry.* New York: Crown.

Meillier, Claude. 1979. *Callimaque et son temps.* Lille: l'Université de Lille.

Meisen, Karl. 1950. "Der böse Blick und anderer Schadenzauber in Glaube und Brauch der alten Völker und in frühchristlicher Zeit." *Rheinisches Jahrbuch für Volkskunde* 1:144–77.

———. 1952. "Der böse Blick, das böse Wort und der Schadenzauber durch Berührung im Mittelalter und in der neueren Zeit." *Rheinisches Jahrbuch für Volkskunde* 3: 169–225.

Merlin, Alfred. 1915. *Inventaire des mosaiques de la Gaule et de l'Afrique.* Vol. 2. *Afrique Proconsulaire (Tunisie) supplement.* Paris: Ernest Leroux.

———. 1940. "Amulettes contre l'invidia provenant de Tunisie." *Revue des Études Anciennes* 42: 486–493.

———. ed. 1915. *Afrique proconsulaire (Tunisie).* Vol. 2. Supplement of *Inventaire des mosaïques de la Gaule et de l'Afrique. Afrique proconsulaire (Tunisie),* edited by Paul Gauckler and A. Merlin. Paris: Ernest Leroux, 1909–1915.

Metropolitian Museum of Art. *Heilbrunn Timeline of Art History.* http://www.metmuseum.org/toah/hi/te_index.asp?i=20.

Meyer, Marvin, and Paul Mirecki, eds. 1995. *Ancient Magic and Ritual Power.* Religions in the Graeco-Roman World 129. Leiden: Brill.

Michaelis, A. 1885. "Sarapis standing on a Xanthian Marble in the British Museum." *Journal of Hellenic Studies* 6:287–318.

Michel, Simone, Hilde Zazoff, Peter Zazaoff, eds. 2001. *Die Magischen Gemmen im Britischen Museum.* 2 vols. London: British Museum Press.

Millingen, James. 1818. "Some Observations on an Antique Bas-Relief on which the Evil Eye, or 'Fascinum,' Is Represented." *Archaeologia* 19: 70–74.

Milobenski, Ernst. 1964. *Der Neid in der Griechischen Philosophie.* Klassisch-Philologische Studien, 29. Wiesbaden: Harrassowitz.

Mirecki, Paul, and Marvin Meyer, eds. 2002. *Magic and Ritual in the Ancient World.* Religions in the Graeco-Roman World 141. Leiden, Brill, 2002.

Le monde du sorcier. Égypte, Babylone, Hittites, Israël, Islam, Asie centrale, Inde, Nepal, Cambodge, Viet-nam, Japon. 1966. Edited by Serge Sauneron et al. Sources orientales, 7. Paris: Seuil.

Moreau, A. 1976/77. "L'oeil malefique dans l'oeuvre d'Eschyle." *Revue des études anciennes* 78/79: 50–64.

Morrison, John S. 1980. *The Ship. Long Ships and Round Ships: Warfare and Trade in the Mediterranean, 300 BC—500 AD.* London: H. M. S. O.

Morrison, John S., and John F. Coates. 1996. *Greek and Roman Oared Warships.* Oxford: Oxbow.

Morrison, John S., and R. T. Williams. *Greek Oared Ships, 900–322 B.C.* Cambridge: Cambridge University Press.

Moser, Claudia. 2006. "Naked Power: The Phallus as an Apotropaic Symbol in the Images and Texts of Roman Italy." Final Project Paper, April 2006, University of Pennsylvania, Undergraduate Humanities Forum 2005–6: 2005–2006 Penn Humanities Forum on Word & Image, Undergraduate Mellon Research Fellows. Online: http://humanities.sas.upenn.edu/05-06/mellon_uhf.shtml This paper is posted at ScholarlyCommons. http://repository.upenn.edu/uhf_2006/11

Mountfield, David. 1982. *Greek and Roman Erotica.* New York: Crescent.

Mourad, Yusef. 1939. *La physiognomie arabe et le Kitab al-Firasa de Fakr al-Din al-Razi.* Collection des Écrits Médico-psychologiques Arabes. I. Paris: Geuthner.

Müller, C. D. G. 1974. "Von Teufel, Mittagsdämon und Amuletten." *JAC* 17:91–102.

———. 1976. "Geister (Dämonen). C. IV. Volksglaube." In *RAC* 9:762–97.

Mugler, Charles. 1964. *Dictionnaire historique de la terminologie optique des Grecs.* Paris: Klincksieck.

Murray, Margaret A. "The Meaning of the Cowrie" (and other related articles on the cowrie) *Man* (Oct 1939): item 165; *Man* (Jan 1940), item 20; *Man* 40: item 188; *Man* 40: item 209; *Man* 42: item 94.

Muth, R. 1954. *Träger der Lebenskraft, Ausscheidungen des Organismus im Volksglauben der Antike.* Vienna: Rohrer.

Nash, E. 1968. *Pictorial Dictionary of Ancient Rome.* 2 vols. London: Thames & Hudson.

Neveron, O. V. 1978. "Gemmes, baques et amulettes magiques du sud de l'URSS." In *Hommages à Maarten J. Vermaseren*, edited by M. B. De Boer and T. A. Edridge, 2:833–48. EPRO 68. Leiden: Brill.

Nicholson, Frank W. 1897, "The Saliva Superstition in Classical Literature." *Harvard Studies in Classical Philology* 8:23–40.

Nicholson, Mervyn. 1999. *Male Envy: The Logic of Malice in Literature and Culture.* Lanham, MD: Lexington.

Niederer, A. 1989."Beschämung, Lob, und Schadenfreude. Hand- und Fingergebärden mit bestimmter Bedeutung." *Schweizer Archiv für Volkskunde* 85:201–17.

Nikolaou, Theodorus. 1969. *Der Neid bei Johannes Chrysostomus unter Berücksichtigung der griechischen Philosophie.* Abhandlungen zur Philologie und Pädagogik 56. Bonn: Bouvier.

Nilsson, Martin P. 1940/1961. *Greek Folk Religion.* New York: Harper.

Norris, Frederick W. 1991. "Artifacts from Antioch." In *Social History of the Matthean Community: Cross-Disciplinary Approaches*, edited by David L. Balch, 249–58. Minneapolis: Fortress.

Notitiae degli scavi di antichita (1889):398–400; (1890):79, 113.

Nowak, H. 1960. *Zur Entwicklungsgeschichte des Begriffes daimôn. Eine Untersuchung epigraphischer Zeugnisse vom 5. Jh. V. Chr. bis zum 5. Jh. n. Chr.* Doctoral Dissertation, Bonn University. 1960.

Nowak, Troy Joseph. 2006. "Archaeological Evidence for Ship eyes: An Analysis of Their Form and Function." M.A. Thesis, Texas A &M University.

Nusser, Karl-Heinz. 2000. "Neid." In *Theologisches Realenzyklopädie.* Part 2. 24:246–54. Berlin: de Gruyter.

O'Brien, D. 1970. "The Effect of a Simile: Empedocles' Theories of Seeing and Breathing." *Journal of Hellenic Studies* 90:140–79.

The Oxford Classical Dictionary. Edited by S. Hornblower and A. Spawforth. 3rd ed. Oxford: Oxford University Press, 2003.

Odelstierna, Ingrid. 1949. *Invidia, Invidiosus, and Invidiam Facere: A Semantic Investigation.* Uppsala Universitets Årsskrift 10. Leipzig: Harrassowitz.

Önnerfors, A. 1988. "Zaubersprüche in Texten der römischen und frühmittelalterlichen Medizin." In *Études de medecine romaine,* edited by G. Sabbah, 113–56. St. Étienne: Centre Jean Palerne.

Ogden, Daniel. 2002. "The Evil Eye." In Ogden, *Magic, Witchcraft, and Ghosts in the Greek and Roman Worlds. A Sourcebook,* 222–26, §§192–196. New York: Oxford University Press.

Olck, F. 1909. "Feige." In PW 6: 2100–151.

Opelt, I. 1966. "Eule." In *RAC* 6: 890–906.

Opperwall, Nola J., and Robert J. Wyatt. 1982. "Jealousy." In *ISBE* 2:971–73.

Orrells, D. 2005. "A History of the Critical Theories and Approaches Regarding the Phallus in Antiquity: the Greeks and Modern Masculinity." PhD thesis, University of Cambridge.

Orphei Lithika (Lithica by Pseudo-Orpheus). Edited by E. Abel. Berlin: Calvary, 1881.

The Oxyrhynchus Papyri. Edited by B. P. Grenfell and A. S. Hunt et al. 72 vols. London: Egypt Exploration Society, 1898–1972.

Park, David. 1998. *The Fire within the Eye: A Historical Essay on the Nature and Meaning of Light.* Princeton: Princeton University Press.

Parnell, Suzanne Sheldon and Lea T. Olsan. 1991. "The Index of Charms: Purpose, Design, and Implementation." *Literary and Linguistic Computing* 6:59–63.

Parrott, W. Gerrod. 1991. "The Emotional Experiences of Envy and Jealousy." In *The Psychology of Jealousy and Envy,* edited by Peter Salovey, 3–30. New York: Guilford Press.

Parrott, W. Gerrod and Richard H. Smith. 1993. "Distinguishing the Experiences of Envy and Jealousy." *Journal of Personality and Social Psychology* 64:906–20.

Parsons, Peter. 2007. *City of the Sharp-nosed Fish: Greek Lives in Roman Egypt.* London: Weidenfeld & Nicholson.

Pastoureau, Michel. 2001. *Blue: the History of a Color.* Translated by Markus I. Cruse. Princeton: Princeton University Press.

Patterson, Stephen J. 2011. "The Oxyrhynchus Papyri. The Remarkable Discovery You've Probably Never Heard of." *Biblical Archaeological Review* 37/2:60–68.

Perdrizet, Paul. 1900. "Melanges Epigraphiques." *Bulletin de Correspondance Hellénique* 24:285–323

———. 1903. "Sphragis Solomonis." *Revue des études grecques* 16:42–61.

———. 1922. *Negotium perambulans in tenebris.* Publications de la Faculté des Lettres de l'Université de Strasbourg 6, 5–38. Strasbourg: Istra.

Peterson, Erik. 1926. *Eis Theos: Epigraphische, formgeschichte und religionsgeschichtliche Untersuchungen.* Göttingen: Vandenhoeck & Ruprecht.

Petrie, W. M. Flinders. 1914. *Amulets.* London: Constable. Reprinted, Warminster, 1975.

Pfister, F. 1927. "Amulett." In *HDA* 1:374–84.

Phillips III, Charles Robert. 1986. "The Sociology of Religious Knowledge in the Roman Empire to A.D. 284." In *ANRW* 2.16.3:2677–773.

————. 1991. "Nullum Crimen sine Lege. Socioreligious Sanctions on Magic." In *Magika Hiera: Ancient Greek Magic and Religion*, edited by Christopher A. Faraone and Dirk Obbink, 260–76. New York: Oxford University Press.

Phinney, Edward, Jr. 1971. "Perseus' Battle with the Gorgons." Transactions and Proceedings of the American Philological Association 102:445–63.

Picqué, M. C. 1898. "Communication." *Revue belge de numismatique* 54:372–74.

Pilch, John J., and Bruce J. Malina, eds. 1998. *Handbook of Biblical Social Values*. 2nd expanded ed. Peabody, MA: Hendrickson, 1998:— "Envy (and Evil Eye)" (59–63)— "Limited Good" (122–27).

Preisendanz, Karl et al., eds., *PGM*. See above, *Papyri Graecae Magicae*.

Prévot, A. 1935. "Verbes Grecs relatifs à la vision et noms de 'eoils." *Revue de Philologie* 9:233–79.

Purshouse, Luke. 2004. "Jealousy in relation to envy." *Erkenntnis* 60/2:179–204.

Rakoczy, Thomas. 1996. *Böser Blick, Macht des Auges und Neid der Götter. Eine Untersuchung zur Kraft des Blickes in der griechischen Literatur*. Classica Monacensia 13. Tübingen: Narr.

Raiga, Eugène. 1932. *L'Envie*. Paris: Alcan.

Ranulf, Svend. 1933–34. *The Jealousy of the Gods and Criminal Law at Athens: A Contribution to the Sociology of Moral Indignation*. 2 vols. London: Norgate.

Ratschow, C. H. 1957. "Amulett und Talisman." In *RGG3* 1:345–47.

Real-encyclopädie der classischen Altertumswissenschaft. Edited by A. F. Pauly, vols. 1–6 (1839–1852). New Edition begun by G. Wissowa (1890) et al. 70+ vols. Stuttgart: Metzler, 1890–1980.

Reallexikon für Antike und Christentum. 25+ vols. Edited by Theodore Klauser et al. Stuttgart: A. Hiersemann, 1950.

Reichmann, V. 1969. "Feige I." In *RAC* 7: 640–82.

Reitzenstein, Richard. 1904. *Poimandres. Studien zur griechisch-ägyptischen und frühchristlichen Literatur*. Leipzig: Teubner.

Die Religion in Geschichte und Gegenwart. 3rd edition. 6 vols. and index. Edited by Kurt Galling, et al. Tübingen: Mohr Siebeck, 1957–65.

Rettenbeck, Lenz. 1955. *Feige. Wort—Gebärde—Amulett: Ein Volkskundlicher Beitrag zur Amulettforschung*. Munich: Filser.

Revue archéologique. Paris. 1844–.

Revue belge de numismatique, 1844–.

Revue des études Byzantines. Paris, 1943–2005 (continuation of *Échos d'Orient* [Paris, 1897–1942])

Revue des études grècques. 1887–.

Revue Égyptologique. 16 vols. Paris, 1880–1920.

Rheinisches Museum für Philologie, 1827–.

Ribichini, Sergio. 1999. "Nel mondo dei miti. Lo sguardo che ucccide." *Archeo* 15/1:102–4.

Riess, E. "Amulett." 1894. PW 1,2:1984–1989.

Robert, Louis. 1944. "Hellenica." *Revue de philologie, de literature et d'histoire anciennes* 18:41–42.

————.1951. "Bulletin épigraphique." *REG* 64:119–216.

————. 1981. "Amulettes Grecques." *Journal des Savants* 1:3–44.

Roberts, John M. 1976. "Belief in the Evil Eye in World Perspective." In *The Evil Eye*, edited by C. Maloney, 223–78. New York: Columbia University Press.

Rodkinson, Michael Levi. 1893. *History of Amulets, Charms, and Talismans: A Historical Investigation into Their Nature and Origin.* New York: New Talmud Publishing.

Röhrich, Lutz. 1960. "Gebärdensprache und Sprachgebärde." In *Humaniora: Essays in Literature, Folklore, Bibliography: Honoring Archer Taylor on His Seventieth Birthday*, edited by Wayland D. Hand and Gustave O. Arlt, 121–49. Locust Valley, NY: Augustin.

Röhrich, Lutz. 1962. "Zaubersprüche." *RGG*³ 6:1873–75.

Röhrich, Lutz. 1967. *Gebärde—Metapher—Parodie: Studien zur Sprache und Volksdichtung.* Düsseldorf: Schwann.

Roheim, Géza. 1940. "The Gorgon." *American Imago* 1:61–63.

Roodenburg, Herman. 1991. "The 'Hand of Friendship': Shaking Hands and Other Gestures in the Dutch Republic." In *A Cultural History of Gesture*, edited by Jan Bremmer and Herman Roodenburg, 152–89. Ithaca, NY: Cornell University Press.

Roscher, W. H. 1879. *Die Gorgonen und Verwandetes.* Leipzig: Teubner.

Rose, H. J. 1959. *Religion in Greece and Rome.* New York: Harper.

Rostovtzeff, M. I. 1957. *The Social and Economic History of the Roman Empire.* 2 vols. 2nd ed. Revised by P. M. Fraser. Oxford: Clarendon.

Rougé, Jean.1981. *Ships and Fleets of the Ancient Mediterranean.* Translated by Susan Frazer. Middletown, CT: Wesleyan University Press.

Rudolph, Kelli. 2011. "Democritus' Perspectival Theory of Vision." *JHS* 131:67–83.

Russell, James. 1980. "Julius Caesar's Last Words." In *Vindex Humanitatis: Essays in Honour of John Huntly Bishop*, edited by Bruce Marshall, 123–28. Armidale, NSW: University of New England.

Sáenz Preciado, J. Carlos, and María D. Lasuén Alegre. 2004. "El amuleto fálico de oro de Bilbilis (Calatayud-Zaragoza)." *Saldvie: Estudios de prehistoria y arqueología* 4:221–28.

Saglio, E. 1896. "Bulla." In Daremberg-Saglio 1.1:754–55.

Salovey, Peter, ed. 1981. *The Psychology of Jealousy and Envy.* New York: Guilford.

Salovey, Peter, and J. Rodin, 1989. "Envy and Jealousy in Close Relationships." *Review of Personality and Social Psychology* 10:221–46.

———. 1998. "Coping with Envy and Jealousy." *Journal of Social and Clinical Psychology* 50: 7, 15–33.

Salovey, Peter, and Alexander J. Rothman. 1991. "Envy and Jealousy: Self and Society." In *The Psychology of Jealousy and Envy*, edited by Peter Salovey, 271–86. New York: Guilford Press.

Sanders, Ed. 2014. *Envy and Jealousy in Classical Athens: A Socio-Psychological Approach.* Emotions of the Past. Oxford: Oxford University Press.

Sartori, P. 1899. "Die Totenmünze." *Archiv für Religionswissenschaft* 2:205–25

Sauneron, Serge. 1966. "Le monde du magicien égyptien." In *Le monde du sorcier: Égypte, Babylone, Hittites, Israël, Islam, Asie centrale, Inde, Nepal, Cambodge, Vietnam, Japon*, edited by Serge Sauneron et al., 27–65. Sources orientales, 7. Paris: Seuil.

Scarborough, John. 1991. "The Pharmacology of Sacred Plants, Herbs, and Roots." In *Magika Hiera: Ancient Greek Magic and Religion*, edited by Christopher A. Faraone and Dirk Obbink, 138–74. Oxford: Oxford University Press.

Schaaf, Ingo. 2014. "Der 'böse Blick' und die Überwindung der Talos." In *Magie und Ritual bei Apollonios Rhodios: Studien zur ihrer Form und Funktion in den Argo-*

nautika, 311–29. Religionsgeschichtliche Versuche und Vorarbeiten 63. Berlin: de Gruyter.

Schaupp, Manfred. 1962. "Invidia: Eine Begriffsuntersuchung." Diss., University of Freiburg.

Schmidt, Bernhard. 1913. "Der böse Blick und ähnlicher Zauber im neugreichischen Volksglauben." *Neue Jahrbücher für das klassische Altertums Geschichte und Deutsche Literatur* 31:574–613.

Shiaele, M. 2010. "Ovid's Invidia and the literary tradition." *Rosetta* 8/5:127–38.

Schienerl, Peter W. 1984. "Der Ursprung und die Entwicklung von Amutlettbehältnissen in der antiken Welt." *Antike Welt* 15:45–54.

Schlesier, R. 1991. "Mythenwahrheit versus Aberglaube: Otto Jahn und der böse Blick." In *Otto Jahn: Ein Geisteswissenschaftler zwischen Klassizismus und Historismus*, edited by W. Calder III, H. Cancik, and B. Kytzler, 234–67. Stuttgart: Teubner.

Schlumberger, Gustave Leon. 1892. "Ámulettes byzantins anciennes destinés à combattre les maléfices et maladies." *Revue des études grecques* 5:73–93.

———. 1929. Amulet collection. Cabinet des médailles et antiques. Bibliothèque Nationale du France, Paris.

Schnippel, Emil. 1929. "Dill als Mittel gegen den bösen Blick." *Zeitschrift für Volkskunde* 39:194–95.

Schober, Arnold. 1923. *Die römischen Grabsteine von Noricum und Pannonien*. Vienna: Hölzel.

Schoeck, Helmut. 1955/1992. "The Evil Eye: Forms and Dynamics of a Universal Superstition." *Emory University Quarterly* 11:153–61. Reprinted in *The Evil Eye: A Casebook*, edited by A. Dundes, 192–200. 2nd expanded ed. Madison: University of Wisconsin Press, 1992.

———. 1970/1987. *Envy: A Theory of Social Behaviour*. New York: Harcourt, Brace & World, 1970. Reprinted, Indianapolis: Liberty, 1987. ET of *Der Neid: Eine Theorie der Gesellschaft*. Freiburg: Alber, 1966.

Schrire, Theodore. 1966/1982. *Hebrew Magic Amulets: Their Decipherment and Interpretation*. New York: Behrman, 1982. Reprint of *Hebrew Amulets*. London: Routledge & Kegan Paul.

Schuler, Alfred. 1869. *Über Herodots Vorstellung vom Neide der Götter*. Offenburg: Reiff.

Seara, E. Rey. 2002. "El estudio de los amuletos romanos: el caso de Galicia." *Semata. Ciencias Sociais e Humanidades* 14:151–64. https://dspace.usc.es/. . ./1/pg_153–166_semata14.pdf.

Selare, R. 1939. "A Collection of Saliva Superstitions." *Folk-Lore* 50:349–66.

Seligmann, Siegfried. 1910/1985. *Der Böse Blick und Verwandtes: Ein Beitrag zur Geschichte des Aberglaubens aller Zeiten und Völker*. 2 vols. Berlin: Barsdorf, 1910. Reprinted Hildesheim: Olms (2 vols. in one).

———. 1922/1980. *Die Zauberkraft des Auges und das Berufen: Ein Kapitel aus der Geschichte des Aberglaubens*. Hamburg: Friederichsen, 1922. Reprinted, Den Haag: Couvreur.

———. 1926. *Sammlung Seligmann im Hamburgischen Museum für Völkerkunde, Eurasientabteilungen*. Hamburg.

———. 1927. *Die magischen Heil- und Schutzmittel aus der unbelebten Natur, mit besonderer Berücksichtigung der Mittel gegen den Bösen Blick. Eine Geschichte des Amulett-wesens*. Stuttgart: Strecker & Schroeder, 1927. Reprinted, 3 vols. Edited by Jürgen Zwernemann. Berlin: Reimer, 1996–.

Seyrig, Henri. 1934. "Invidiae medici." *Berytus* 1:5–9.

Silver, M., and J. Sabini, J. 1978a. "The Perception of Envy." *Social Psychology* 41:105–17.

———. 1978b. "The Social Construction of Envy." *Journal for the Theory of Social Behavior* 8:313–31.

Sittl, K. 1890/1970. *Die Gebärden der Griechen und Römer.* Leipzig: Teubner. Reprinted 1970.

Six, Jan. 1885. *de Gorgone* [*Specimen literarium inaugurale.* Diss., University of Amsterdam. Amsterdam: Kröber-Bakels.

Slane, K. W., and M. W. Dickie. 1993. "A Knidian Phallic Vase from Corinth." *Hesperia* 62:483–505, and two plates.

Skemer, Don C. *Binding Words: Textual Amulets in the Middle Ages.* University Park: Pennsylvania State University Press, 2006.

Smith, Kirby Flower. 1902. "Pupula Duplex: A Comment on Ovid, Amores I, 8,15." In *Studies in Honor of Basil L. Gildersleeve*, 287–300. Baltimore: Johns Hopkins University Press.

Soderlund, O. and H. 2013. "The Evil Eye in Cultural and Church History." Online: http://aslansplace.com/wp-content/uploads/2013/07/The_Evil_Eye_In_Cultural_and_Church_History-Soderlund.pdf

Spiteris, Tony. 1969. *Greek and Etruscan Painting.* Translated by Janett Sondheimer. New York: Funk & Wagnells.

Spoer, A. M. 1926. "Correspondence." *Folk-Lore* 37:304. [Response to W. Crooke, "Simulated Change of Sex to Baffle the Evil Eye," *Folk-Lore* 24 (1913) 385].

Stein, Howard F. 1974 [1976, 1992]. "Envy and the Evil Eye Among Slovak-Americans: An Essay in the Psychological Ontology of Belief and Ritual." *Ethos* 2:15–46. Reprinted with minor sylistic changes in *The Evil Eye*, edited by Clarence Maloney, 193–222. New York: Columbia University Press, 1976. Also reprinted in *The Evil Eye: A Casebook,* edited by Alan Dundes, 223–56. 2nd expanded ed. Madison: University of Wisconsin Press, 1992.

Steinlein, W. 1944. "*Phthonos* und verwandte Begriffe in der älteren griechischen Literatur." Diss., University of Erlangen.

Stern, Ephraim. 2002. "Gorgon Evcavated at Dor." *Biblical Archaeological Review* 28/6:50–57.

Stevens, E. B. 1948. "Envy and Pity in Greek Philosophy." *American Journal of Philology* 69:171–89.

Story, William Wetmore. 1877. *Castle St. Angelo and the Evil Eye Being Additional Chapters to "Roba di Roma".* London: Chapman & Hall, 1877.

Stuart Jones, *A Catalogue of the Ancient Sculptures Preserved in the Municipal Collections of Rome: The sculptures of the Palazzo dei Conservatori.* 2 vols. Oxford: Claredon.

Stumpf, Albrecht.1964. "*zêlos* etc." In *TDNT* 2:877–88.

Sumner, William Graham. 1960 [1906]. "Uncleanness and the Evil Eye." In *Folkways: A Study of the Sociological Importances of Usages, Manners, Customs, Mores and Morals*, 428–38. New York: New American Library.

Taussig, Michael, 1993. *Mimesis and Alterity: A Particular History of the Senses.* New York: Routledge.

Taylor, Rabun. 2008. "The Mirroring Shield of Perseus."In *The Moral Mirror of Roman Art,* edited by R. Taylor, 169–96. New York: Cambridge University Press.

————. "The Reflexive Evil Eye: Was Medusa a Victim of Her Own Gaze?" In *The Moral Mirror of Roman Art*, edited by R. Taylor, 182–88 and appendix: "Medusa and the Evil Eye," 203–5. New York: Cambridge University Press.

Tempkin, Owsei. 1971. *The Falling Sickness: A History of Epilepsy from the Greeks to the Beginnings of Modern Neurology*. 2nd ed. Baltimore: Johns Hopkins University Press.

Theological Dictionary of the New Testament. 10 vols. Edited by Gerhard Kittel and Gerhard Friedrich. Translated by Geoffrey W. Bromiley. Grand Rapids: Eerdmans, 1964–76.

Theologische Realenzyklopädie. 36 vols. Edited by Gerhard Müller, Horst Balz, Gerhard Krause et al. Berlin:de Gruyter, 1976–2004.

Thesaurus Graecae Linguae. Edited by Henri Estienne. Reprinted, Graz: Akademische Druck-und Verlagsanstalt, 1954.

Thesaurus Linguae Graecae: Canon of Greek Authors and Works. Edited by Luci Berkowitz and Karl A. Squitier. Oxford: Oxford University Press. 1986.

Thesaurus Linguae Graece: A Digital Library of Greek Literature. Special Research Project of the University of California, Irvine, CA. 1972-.

Teiltelbaum, Joel M. 1976. "The Leer and the Loom—Social Controls on Handloom Weavers." In *The Evil Eye*, edited by C. Maloney, 63–75. New York: Columbia University Press.

Thomsen, Marie-Louise. 1992. "The Evil Eye in Mesopotamia." *Journal of Near Eastern Studies* 51:19–32.

Tölken, E. H. 1835. *Erklärendes Verzeichniss der antiken vertieft geschnittenen Steine der königlich Preussischen Gemmensammlung*. Berlin: Königlichen Akademie der Wissenschaften.

Torr, Cecil. 1896. "Navis (Naus)." In Daremberg-Saglio 4/1:24–40.

Trentin, Lisa. 2009. What's in a Hump? Re-examining the Hunchback in the Villa Albani-Torlonia." *Cambridge Classical Journal* 55:130–56.

————. 2011. "Deformity in the Roman Imperial Court." *Greece & Rome* 58:195–208.

Trumpf-Lyritzaki, Maria. 1981. "Glocke." In *RAC* 11:164–96.

Tupet, Anne-Mari. 1986. "Rites magiques dans l'Antiquite romaine." In *ANRW* 2.16.3:2591–675 (on the Evil Eye, 2606–10).

Tylor, Edward Burnett. 1890. "Notes on the Modern Survival of Ancient Amulets against the Evil Eye." *Journal of the Royal Anthropological Institute* 19:54–56.

————. 1891. "Exhibition of Charms and Amulets." In *Papers and Transactions of the International Folklore Congress 1891*, 387–93. London: Nutt.

Ulanov, Ann, and Barry Ulanov. 1983. *Cinderella and Her Sisters: The Envied and the Envying*. Philadelphia: Westminster.

Unnik, W. C. van. 1971. *APHTHONOS METADIDÔMI*. Brussels: Paleis der Academien.

————. 1972. "Der Neid in den Paradiesgeschichte nach einigen gnostischen Texten." In *Essays on the Nag-Hammadi Texts in Honor of Alexander Böhlig*, edited by Martin Krause, 129–32. Nag-Hammadi Studies 3. Leiden: Brill.

————. 1973. "De *aphthonia* van God in de oudchristelijke literatuur." *Mededelingen der koninlijke Nederlandse Akademi van Wetenschappen, Afd. Letterkunde* n r. 36/2:17–55; reprinted separately, *De aphthonia van God in de Oudchristelijke Literatuur*. Amsterdam: Noord-Hollandsche Uitgevers Maatschapij, 1973.

Usener, H. 1873. "Vergessenes.V." *Rheinisches Museum für Philologie* n.f. 28:407–9.

Vanggaard, Thorkil. 1972. *Phallos: A Symbol and Its History in the Male World.* New York: International Universities Press.

Vasconcellos, J. Leite de. 1925. *A Figa: Estudo de etnografia comparativa, precedido de algumas palavras a respeito do "sobrenatural" na medicina popular portuguesa.* Porto: Araujo & Sobrinho.

Veikou, Christina. 1998. *Kakó matí: Hē koinōnikē kataskeuē tēs optikēs epikoinōnias.* Athens: Hellēnika Grammata, 1998.

Vergara Caffarelli, E., and G. Caputo. 1966. *The Buried City: Excavations at Leptis Magna.* London: Weidenfeld & Nicholson.

Vernant, Jean-Pierre. 1985. *La mort dans les yeux. Figures de l'autre en Grèce ancienne.* Paris: Hachette.

———. 1988. *Myth and Society in Ancient Greece.* New York: Zone.

Versnel, H. S. 1970. *Triumphus: An Inquiry into the Origin, Development and the Meaning of the Roman Triumph.* Leiden: Brill.

———. 2002. "The Poetics of the Magical Charm. An Essay on the Power of Words." In *Magic and Ritual in the Ancient World,* edited by Paul Mirecki and Marvin Meyer, 105–58. Religions in the Graeco-Roman World 141. Leiden: Brill.

Veyne, Paul, ed. 1987. *A History of Private Life.* Vol. 1, *From Pagan Rome to Byzantium.* Cambridge, MA: Belknap.

Villiers, Elizabeth.1927. *Amulette und Talismane und andere geheime Dinge: Eine volkstümliche Zusammenstellung von Glücksbringern, Sagen, Legenden und Aberglauben aus alter und neuer Zeit.* Revised and expanded by Anton Maximilian Pachinger. Berlin: Drei Masken, 1927.

Wace, Alan J. B. 1904–05. "Grotesques and the Evil Eye." *Annual of the British School at Athens* 10:103–14.

Wageman, Maryse. 1987. *Amulet and Alphabet: Magical Amulets in the First Book of Cyranides.* Amsterdam: Gieben.

Wagner, M. L. 1937. "Phallus, Horn und Fisch." *Romanica Helvetica* 4:79–130.

Wainwright, G. A. 1961. "The Earliest Use of the Mano Cornuta." *Folklore* 72:492–95.

Walcot, Peter. 1978. *Envy and the Greeks: A Study of Human Behaviour.* Warminster, England: Aris & Phillips, 1978. (Ch. 7: "The Evil Eye," 77–90).

Wallace, R. E. *An Introduction to Wall Inscriptions from Pompeii and Herculaneum: Introduction. Inscriptions with Notes. Historical Commentary. Vocabulary.* Wauconda, IL: Bolchazy-Carducci, 2005.

Walton, E. M. 1970. "Envy in Greek Literature to the End of the Fifth Century B.C." PhD diss., Baltimore: Johns Hopkins University. Baltimore.

Walz, Christian. 1852. *De Nemesi Graecorum.* Tübingen: Fues.

Weber, Wilhelm. 1914. *Die ägyptisch-griechishen Terrakotten.* Berlin: Curtius.

Weidlich, Theodor. 1894. *Die Sympathie in der antiken Litteratur.* Stuttgart: Liebich.

White, Gregory L., and Paul E. Mullen. 1989. *Jealousy: Theory, Research, and Clinical Strategies.* New York: Guilford.

Wieland, H. 1986. "Zu praefiscini." *Museum Helveticum* 43:183–86.

Wifstrand, Erik. 1946. "Invidia: Ein semasiologische Beitrag." *Eranos* 44:355–69.

Wilk, Stephen R. 2000. *Medusa: Solving the Mystery of the Gorgon.* Oxford: Oxford University Press.

Wilken, U. 1900–1901. "Amulette." *Archiv für Papyrusforschung* 1:419–36.

Wilpert, Paul, and Sibylla Zenker. 1950. "Auge." In *RAC* 1:957–69.

Wilson, Lilian M. 1920 "Contributions of Greek Art to the Medusa Myth." *American Journal of Archeology* 24:232–40.

Winter, F. 1903. *Die Antiken Terrakotten: Die Typen der figürlichen Terrakotten.* 2 vols. Berlin: Spemann.

Wolters, Paul. 1909. "Ein Apotropaion aus Baden im Aargau." *Bonner Jahrbücher* 118:257–74.

Wünsch, R. 1910. "Charms and Amulets (Roman)." In *HERE* 3:461–65.

———. 1911. "Amuletum." *Glotta* 2:219–30.

Yatromanalakis, Y. 1988. "Baskanos, Love and the Evil-Eye in Heliodorus' Aethiopica." In *The Greek Novel A.D. 1–1985,* edited by R. Beaton, 194–204. London: Croom Helm.

Youtie, Herbert C. 1979. "Critical Trifles. VIII." In *ZPE* 36:73–76.

Zarzalejos, M. J. Aurrecoechea et al. 1988. "Amuletos fálicos romanos inéditos de las provincias de Madrid y Toledo." *Cuadernos de Prehistoria y Arqueología de la Universidad Autónoma de Madrid* 15:301–18.

Zazoff, Peter. 1983. *Die Antiken Gemmen.* Handbuch der Archäologie. Munich: Beck.

INDEX

INSCRIPTIONS, PAPYRI, EPIGRAPHA, OSTRACA

EARLY CHRISTIAN WRITINGS

MEDIEVAL, RENAISSANCE WRITERS & WRITINGS